NOSWORTHY

838 HIDDEN HILLS DR
BELLEVUE, NE
68005

ALSO BY HUGH THOMAS

Rivers of Gold: The Rise of the Spanish Empire

The Spanish Civil War

The Suez Affair

John Strachey

Cuba: The Pursuit of Freedom

World History

Armed Truce: The Beginnings of the Cold War

Conquest: Montezuma, Cortés, and the Fall of Old Mexico

The Slave Trade: The Story of the Atlantic Slave Trade, 1440–1870

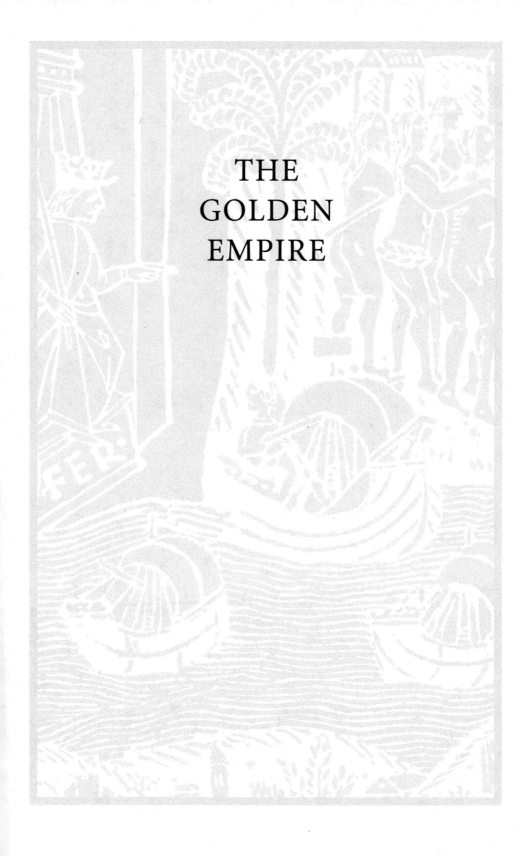

THE
GOLDEN
EMPIRE

THE GOLDEN EMPIRE

Spain, Charles V, and the Creation of America

Hugh Thomas

RANDOM HOUSE

NEW YORK

Published in the United States by Random House, an imprint of The Random
House Publishing Group, a division of Random House, Inc., New York.

Random House and colophon are registered trademarks of Random House, Inc.

Originally published in 2010 in the United Kingdom by Allen Lane,
an imprint of Penguin Books, as *The Golden Age: The Spanish Empire of Charles V.*

Library of Congress Cataloging-in-Publication Data
Thomas, Hugh.
The golden empire : Spain, Charles V, and the creation of America / Hugh Thomas.
p. cm.
Includes bibliographical references and index.
ISBN 978-1-4000-6125-9
eBook ISBN 978-1-58836-904-8
1. Latin America—History—16th century. 2. Latin America—Discovery and
exploration—Spanish. 3. Latin America—Civilization—Spanish influences. 4. Spain—
History—Charles I, 1516–1556. 5. Charles V, Holy Roman Emperor, 1500–1558.
6. Spain—Colonies—America—Administration—History—16th century. I. Title.
F1411.T46 2011
980'.01—dc22   2010035313

Printed in the United States of America on acid-free paper

www.atrandom.com

2 4 6 8 9 7 5 3 1

First U.S. Edition

To Vanessa

A constant inspiration

Contents

Book II

PERU

Book III

COUNTER REFORMATION, COUNTER RENAISSANCE

Book IV

THE INDIAN SOUL

ENVOI

Preface

This book, though I hope it will be seen as complete in itself, is the second in a series of volumes I am writing about the Spanish empire. The first volume was *Rivers of Gold,* published in 2003. I am now at work on a third volume, which takes the extraordinary story to 1580, when Spain ceased to expand her responsibilities. King Philip II decided in that year not to try to conquer China.

I have several acknowledgments: first to Stuart Proffitt and his colleagues at Penguin in London. Stuart showed himself a publisher from whose friendship I gained as much as I did from his expertise and judgment. Also I am grateful to David Ebershoff and his staff at Random House in New York. They were patient, meticulous, and a pleasure to work with. Dana Isaacson of Random House made many helpful suggestions. I am grateful, too, for his work on the text, to Martin Davies, an excellent and learned editor. I am also thankful to Ana Bustelo of Planeta for much help, especially collecting the illustrations, and I am also most grateful to the Museo de Santa Cruz in Toledo. My editorial thanks also go to my agent, my imaginative friend Andrew Wylie, and his remarkable assistants. Teresa Velasco typed and retyped the manuscript with care and accuracy. I owe her and Cecilia Calamante a great deal for their hard work on my behalf.

To sum up one's indebtedness to other writers is difficult. But I should be singularly ungrateful were I not to put on record how much I owe to Manuel Fernández Álvarez, whose work on the sixteenth century is an example to us all; and to the conquest of Peru's great historian John Hemming, whose research and writings have placed all students of the matter under a lasting obligation. He also corrected the proofs and saved me from many mistakes. The extent of my debt to the writings of this close friend of mine is by no means covered by the references in the text. My wife, Vanessa, also read the proofs with attention. I am also grateful to James Lockhart for his remarkable study *The Men of Cajamarca* (Austin, Tex., 1972), and his earlier work *Spanish Peru* (Madison, Wisc., 1968). Like everyone who has worked on Peru in the sixteenth century, I have been much assisted by the work of the late Guillermo Lohmann, whom I used to see at eight o'clock in the morning on the steps of the Archivo de Indias waiting for entrance to the *salón de lectores* in the old building of Herrera in Seville. He was always at his table before me. Other works that were of great value to me included Marcel Bataillon's *Erasme et l'Espagne* and José Martínez Millán's *La corte de Carlos V.* Sir John Elliott kindly corrected some howlers.

Like others who have written of the conquest of Peru, I have depended greatly on the numerous contemporary accounts which I have been able to study, such as those written by Garcilaso de la Vega, Pedro de Cieza de León, Hernando Pizarro, Francisco de Jerez, Pedro Sancho de Hoz, Fray Tomás de Berlanga, Alonso Enríquez de Guzmán, Miguel de Estete, Gonzalo Fernández de Oviedo, Cristóbal de Mena, and Agustín de Zárate. But I have missed the great number of *informaciones de servicios y méritos* that characterized the contemporary history of New Spain/Mexico.

A WORD ABOUT NOMENCLATURE

Carlos I and Carlos V are rendered "Charles" as a matter of course.

In *Rivers of Gold,* I elected to speak of Ferdinand, king of Aragon, as "Fernando." I do the same here. But once the infante Fernando, Charles V's brother, becomes established in Austria, I call him (the archduke) Ferdinand.

"Moctezuma" is rendered "Montezuma," the English translation of the name. I have found it so spelled by Spaniards several times in the sixteenth century.

On the other hand, I have rendered the Aztecs by their more accurate designation, "Mexica." I have normally rendered the capital, Mexico City, by the Spanish usage, "Mexico."

A NOTE ON CURRENCY

The usual item of currency was the maravedí, a piece of copper worth ⅟₉₆ of a gold mark, which in its turn was equivalent to 230,045 grams. A ducado (ducat) was worth 375 maravedís, 1 real was 34 maravedís, 1 peso was 450 maravedís, and 1 castellano was equivalent to 485 maravedís. A cruzado was an old coin, sometimes gold, sometimes silver, and occasionally copper, each of different value. An escudo was worth 40 reales, and a cuento had an indeterminate value.

HUGH THOMAS, MAY 5, 2010

Illustrations

Maps

Prologue

❧❧❧

A TALE OF TWO CITIES:
NEW SPAIN AND OLD

I

Cortés and the Rebuilding of Mexico-Tenochtitlan, 1521–1524

> I assure your Caesarian majesty that these people are so turbulent
> that at any novelty or opportunity for sedition, they rebel.
>
> CORTÉS TO CHARLES V, *Fourth letter*

Hernán Cortés's life was triumphant in a way that has rarely been known by any captain of men. Cortés, who looked on himself as Charles's agent, had both discovered and conquered a great indigenous empire: a regime marked by a sophisticated culture allied to barbarism.[1] In 1522, he was the commander of a small successful Spanish army of about two thousand men, with the assistance of numerous indigenous allies, who relished the chance of rebellion and revenge against their old suzerains, the Aztecs (the Mexica). He was surrounded by a praetorian guard of about five hundred horsemen and four thousand foot, all the latter being Indians.[2] He had no title to any command, but all the same, in the ruins of the old Mexican capital he had all the power. The new world was an echo of the old: Cortés was a great European commander who had conquered indigenous people. He had given the territory the name New Spain, no less, which would remain its designation for three hundred years.

His chief captains (such as the Alvarado brothers, Gonzalo de Sandoval, and Andrés de Tapia) were his political subordinates as well as his military deputies. One or two of these commanders had good connections in Spain: For example, Jerónimo Ruiz de la Mota was the first cousin of the emperor Charles's preceptor, the bishop of Palencia, and Bernardino Vázquez de

Tapia was the nephew of a member of the Council of Castile, Pedro (Vázquez) de Oropesa. Several of Cortés's best-connected commanders had returned to Spain to spread news of what he had done: Francisco de Montejo, of Salamanca, for example, and Alonso Hernández Portocarrero, a cousin of the Count of Medellín and a nephew of Judge de las Gradas in Seville; as well as Diego de Ordaz of León, who had returned to Spain the previous year, in search of preferments of his own.

Cortés knew that what he had done was astonishing; and he had begun to conduct himself self-consciously in the shadow of Alexander the Great, Caesar, or even the Argonauts. The defeated Mexica had been humbled, many had been killed, and several members of the late emperor Montezuma's family had accepted the Spaniards as their new rulers: These included Montezuma's son, Don Pedro Montezuma, who must be supposed to have been his heir, and his daughter, Doña Isabel or Techuipo. There was also Cihuacoatl (Tlacotzin), the majordomo of the old government, who was now working for Cortés in the ruined city of Tenochtitlan. The other defeated rulers of old Mexico—such as the monarch of Tlacopan and Tacuba, Tetlepanqueltzatzin, along with his colleague, the monarch of Texcoco, Ixtlilxochitl, and above all the tragic Cuauhtémoc, Montezuma's successor as the ruler of Tenochtitlan—were prisoners of Cortés. In the immediate aftermath of the Spanish victory, Cuauhtémoc had been tortured by the royal treasurer, Julián de Alderete, of Tordesillas, to cause him to reveal the whereabouts of hidden gold and other treasure. Cortés had accepted that, for he badly needed something to offer his victorious but restless fellow conquistadors. But he does not seem to have initiated the cruelty.

Cortés was the despot of the new territory that he had conquered. A great many people had died in the fighting leading to this despotism, mostly Mexican natives, but also perhaps one thousand Spaniards. That had not been Cortés's intention. He had thought that he could overwhelm the empire of the Mexica by kidnapping its ruler. Charles the Emperor would rule New Spain through Montezuma. This scheme had been thwarted in 1520 by Pánfilo de Narváez, Cortés's Segovia-born rival, in the first pitched battle between Spaniards in the Americas. Fighting began between Indians and Spaniards because of Pedro de Alvarado's fatal preemptive strike, as the twenty-first century would have put the matter (he

anticipated an Indian mutiny). Cortés had wanted control, power, authority, not bloodshed or massacre.

In early 1522, Cortés was still awaiting a reaction from the emperor
Charles to the news of his astonishing victory, details of which he had sent
by letter the previous year—a manuscript letter, of course, like everything
from the Indies.[3] The delay was not surprising, since though the surrender
of Tenochtitlan had been on August 13, 1521, a report of that event did not
reach Spain till March 1522. Charles was still in the Low Countries and
would not return to Spain till the summer of that year. Cortés had planned
that his report would be accompanied not only by Alonso de Ávila; his secretary, Juan de Ribera; and the chief of his bodyguard, Quiñones, but by a
substantial treasure seized from the Mexica: 50,000 pesos in gold, of which
the Crown would receive 9,000 pesos, many large pearls, much jade, several
obsidian mirrors framed in gold, and even three jaguars. There were also
many presents of plumage in the form of turquoise mosaics, cloaks, cotton
cloths, painted maps, ornamental shields, and elaborately constructed parrots and crickets of gold and silver. These were all to go to friends of Cortés,
to influential Spanish officials, to noblemen and sacred places, to monasteries and churches.

Many conquistadors would take the opportunity to send back to Spain
gold to their relations. Most promising of presents in the long run perhaps
was a rubber ball, such as used by the Indians in their strange but elaborate
wall game. This would constitute one of the Americas' most notable gifts to
the Old World.

Alas, much of this treasure was seized by French adventurers led by the
piratical Jean Florin, acting on behalf of his master, Jean Ango, between the
Azores and Spain, and the expedition home suffered other setbacks.[4] But a
brief letter from Cortés describing the final conquest of the Mexica did at
last arrive in Spain in March 1522.[5]

Before Cortés's detailed account in this, his "third letter," reached the
court, however, in November 1522, Charles the King and Emperor had
made several critical decisions. After meeting with those members of the
Council of Castile who had come to deal with matters relating to the Indies, Cortés was, on October 11, 1522—that is, a month before his report
arrived—named *adelantado* (commander in chief with proconsular responsibilities), *repartidor* (distributor) of Indians, and also governor and

captain-general of New Spain. That seemed to represent a political triumph for Cortés, since it formally released him from any subservience to his old master, the governor of Cuba, Diego Velázquez. It was also a victory since it accepted Cortés's grand name for the new land: "New Spain," a designation that indicated the supranational character of this new monarchy of Castile. It seemed, too, to give Cortés complete command: governor and captain-general were substantial titles.[6]

The territory covered by his appointment was, however, vague: No one knew where Cortés's dominions began and ended.[7] But it was assumed that at the least he would control the allies who had helped him so much in his conquest; not just the lords of the valley of Mexico who had been liberated from the yoke of the Mexica but also the Totonaca and the Tlaxcalteca and most of the five hundred other tribes established in the mainland of old Mexico.

A decree issued four days later instructed Cortés about the proper treatment of the Indians and talked of grants of government money to finance representatives (*procuradores*) of New Spain in Castile.[8] This decree had the advantage of accepting Cortés's judgment of the coming of Narváez to New Spain in 1520: "The journey of Pánfilo de Narváez and his fleet was the reason for the rebellion and temporary loss of the great city of Mexico-Tenochtitlan."[9] Charles also wrote to Cortés speaking warmly of his achievements.[10] The latter could no longer complain about a lack of appreciation at home, though these decrees, and the Emperor's letter, did not reach New Spain till September 1523, partly because of the curiously dilatory conduct of the messengers, Cortés's cousins Rodrigo de Paz and Francisco de las Casas. They took an unconscionably long time to set off and decided to travel via Cuba, where they took the bad news of the success of "Cortesillo," as Cortés once had been known in Cuba, to the governor, Diego Velázquez. He was distressed.

The emperor Charles accompanied his praise for Cortés and his acceptance of him as his governor in New Spain with the nomination of four officials whose task would be to assist Cortés in administration of the new provinces. These were a new treasurer, Alonso de Estrada; a *factor*, or general administrator of the new empire, Gonzalo de Salazar; an inspector of administration, Pedro Almíndez de Chirino; and an accountant, Rodrigo de Albornoz.

These men were important. Estrada had been in Flanders, admiral at Málaga and then *corregidor* (representative of the central government) in Cáceres. He was a permanent councillor in his native city, Ciudad Real. He would boast that he was an illegitimate son of the late King Fernando, and perhaps he was. Salazar was a Granadino but his family was originally from Burgos. He had been an attendant in the royal household and went to New Spain with quite a retinue. Almíndez de Chirino came from Úbeda and was seen as the agent of the principal royal secretary, Francisco de los Cobos, the powerful if unimaginative official who dominated that city politically and socially. The fourth official, Rodrigo de Albornoz, was probably from Lugo in Galicia, and seems to have also held a minor position in the court of Spain. He was asked by the Italian courtier Peter Martyr to send home reports by cipher about Cortés's activities. Martyr once talked of Cortés's craftiness, his avarice, and his "partially revealed tyranny."[11]

The nomination of these four courtly men to New Spain certainly showed that the Crown was taking the conquests of Cortés seriously. Yet they were obviously intended to control that conqueror and prevent him from undue assertion of his own authority. But these new councillors, like Paz and Las Casas before them, took a long time to reach the new country. Long before they arrived, Cortés had embarked on his greatest work of art and Spain's greatest achievement in the Americas in the sixteenth century: the rebuilding of the city of Tenochtitlan, the capital of the Mexica, which had been severely damaged during the fighting there between May and August 1521. (The Spaniards referred to this city as Temixtlan till 1524, when it gradually became known as Mexico.)

Cortés had been recommended by some of his friends and fellow conquistadors to rebuild the capital of New Spain in a place removed from the lake of Tenochtitlan, say at Tacuba or Coyoacán. They had argued that the old capital was exposed to the dangers of flooding, as had occurred on a large scale in 1502. Since the environs were swampy, there would always be difficulties of water supply. The critics argued that Coyoacán would be a more suitable site for a capital, as Cortés had surely appreciated since he had established his residence there after 1521 on the southern shores of the lake in a large, cool, spacious mansion built for him immediately after his victory in 1521.[12] But in January 1522, Cortés went ahead with his plan to rebuild on the old site despite these criticisms.

Some enemies of Cortés thought that their leader must be trying to arrange defenses in order to resist any attempt to detach him from power. He decided to rebuild where he did, however, because of the legendary nature of the site of Tenochtitlan. He did not want to leave the place a monument to past glory. The Indians wanted to rebuild, too, and a good workforce for the purpose was easily assembled.

The essential part in the reconstruction was played by a "geometrician" named Alonso García Bravo, who had been born in Rivera, on the road between Málaga and Ronda, in Andalusia, and had educated himself in matters of town planning even before he left Castile in 1513 with Pedrarias. García Bravo reached New Spain with the expedition of Francisco de Garay and subsequently joined Cortés's army. He took part in several battles as a conquistador, but then went to Villa Rica, Veracruz. He remained there during the siege of Tenochtitlan, having been asked to design its planned fortress.[13]

The success of the building at Veracruz led Cortés to ask him to direct the reconstruction of Tenochtitlan.[14] He went up to the capital in the summer of 1522 and studied the ground with Cortés himself. The city had been fought over fiercely. There had been much destruction, since Cortés had felt the need to destroy lines of two-story buildings to prevent the Indians dropping rocks on his men from above. Sometimes the Spaniards had used artillery in these endeavors. But the overall destruction had probably been more modest than has often been supposed. The causeways, the main streets, and the remains of many buildings were all evident even if the two main shrines of ancient Mexico, in the heart of Tenochtitlan and in Tlatelolco, had been damaged.

García Bravo's first commission was to build a fortress with two towers, at the eastern end of the city, beyond the ruins of the old Templo Mayor. This was a maritime station (*atarazanas*), where Cortés could keep his thirteen brigantines, built under the direction of the clever but embittered Sevillano Martín López, which had played such an important part in ensuring the Spanish victory over the Mexica. Again, Cortés's enemies later argued, unjustifiably, the construction of these towers was an act directed against the royal power. These buildings were built under the supervision of Cihuacoatl (Tlacotzin), the high priest of the Mexica and now a rather improbable collaborator with the victors. One tower was high and had lodgings within it.

In planning the main reconstruction of the capital, García Bravo proposed to accept the basic structure of the old Mexican city with its causeways and canals leading to a walled center, which in the past had been a sacred precinct, with the great pyramid and its sanctuaries. From all sides one saw the huge bulk of the great pyramid. The sacred precinct was approached by three causeways: to the north, the west, and the south. To the east, there was no communication with the mainland. The causeway to the north was aesthetically planned, since the direct way—via Tepeyac, now the site of the shrine to the Virgin of Guadalupe—would have been a parallel road a little to the east. To the south, beyond the walls of the city, there was a large marketplace where Indian buyers and sellers were busy within days of the conquest, on August 13, 1521.

Around this open space there were the palaces of the old noblemen. Within the walls, the streets in the past had often been of water, in Venetian style. In the center, those highways were straight, though there were twisted ways beyond the grand heart of the city. To the north of the sacred precinct, outside the walls, the city of Tlatelolco had its own large market and the remains of its pyramid. Perhaps Santa Fe, the artificial city built outside Granada by Fernando and Isabel in 1491, was an inspiration for the new city of Cortés and García Bravo, even though it was smaller.[15]

The great temples of Tenochtitlan and Tlatelolco were in ruins; many others survived. Sixteen years later, in 1537, the bishops of Mexico, Guatemala, and Oaxaca wrote to Charles the Emperor in Spain to say that many Indians were still using their old temples for prayer and worship, though not for sacrifice, which had come to an abrupt end in 1521. Cortés permitted the old worship to continue, though he would encourage proselytization by, first, the Franciscans, and then the Dominicans. The bishops asked the King for his agreement for the destruction of those buildings and the burning of any idols within them, and an agreement that the stones of the old temples be used for making new churches. The King, or the Council of the Indies, wrote back the next year that indeed these buildings should be destroyed "without scandal" and the idols burned. The stone of the old temples should certainly be used for building churches.[16]

Cortés decided to preserve the two main palaces of Montezuma as government buildings, one as the national palace where he, the viceroys, and later, the presidents of independent Mexico would live and have their offices; the other, which Cortés had used as his headquarters in the heady months in the city from November 1519 to July 1520, would eventually become the national pawnshop. In addition, he and García Bravo made an important decision: In the heart of the city there would be a Spanish quarter, where the conquistadors and *pobladores* (the name usually given to later arrivals) would be allotted plots on which to build or reconstruct substantial houses. This was according to the so-called *traza,* a word meaning "plan." Between 1524 and 1526, in consequence, the town council of Mexico-Tenochtitlan allocated 234 *solares* (plots), as well as 201 orchards or gardens in the city.

Outside the *traza,* the old Indian quarters would be maintained without change even though their names would receive a Christian prefix: The districts would henceforth be San Juan Moyotlan, Santa María Cuepopan, San Sebastián Atzacualco, and San Pablo Zoquipan. Each of these districts would have a church—an *iglesia de visita,* as the expression was—under the direction of Franciscans, who from 1522 had their headquarters in a large straw-roofed building a block away from the causeway to Tacuba, the future monastery of San Francisco. Each of these Indian quarters was governed, much as had occurred in the past, by a local elder referred to by the conquerors as a "señor." Meantime, Tlatelolco would be left to its own devices, as a separate town, under a new name, Santiago.

The district within the *traza* began to be rebuilt in the summer of 1522. García Bravo tried to ensure that water would be piped to all houses, that all houses would be built according to a pattern, and that all big roads would be fifteen *varas* wide.[17] The patterns of old canals would be approximately followed, though some canals would be re-dug, while others would be filled in.

García Bravo was assisted in these arrangements by a well-born conquistador, Bernardino Vázquez de Tapia, a man of some complexity. Born in Torralba, near Oropesa, Vázquez de Tapia was the nephew of Francisco Álvarez, abbot of Toro and *inquisidor* of Castile. His father, as we have seen, had been on the Council of Castile (Consejo Real de Castilla).

The Franciscan monk Motolinía thought that four hundred thousand Mexica were working in the city in 1524 under the direction of the high priest Tlacotzin, who had by then assumed the name of Juan Velázquez before his Mexican designation. More people, Motolinía asserted, worked there "than those who had worked on the building of the temple of Jerusalem."[18] They included many from the nearby town of Chalco, in the valley, who were specialists in building and plastering and whose ancestors had probably worked on the original construction of the great city. Several secondary architects came to work under García Bravo, such as Juan Rodríguez, whose task was to adapt Montezuma's palace to serve Cortés. Prominent Mexica such as Montezuma's son, Don Pedro Montezuma, helped the Spaniards to recruit the workers. Motolinía recalled the latter singing and chanting, a normal procedure in the old days during such building projects, "all day and all night (*los cantos y las voces apenas cesaban ni de noche ni de día*)."[19] The historian of imperial architecture George Kubler pointed out that however distressed the Indians might have been at their defeat, they were delighted, and probably won over, by the new mechanisms brought to New Spain by the conquerors—mostly the consequence of the wheel, such as pulleys, carts, and wheelbarrows, but also mules and nails, chisels, and iron hammers. To have a beast of burden also constituted a wonderful revolution in technology. But the nail seemed almost as important, while the pulley had a special fascination.[20] These were the stupendous contributions Spain made to the technology of the New World.

By the summer of 1523, a new city was taking shape. The place needed, for political reasons, to be grand and imposing, for it had to reflect the power required by both conquerors and conquered. Tenochtitlan had not been a mere collection of mud huts, it had been a great city of a European size—a capital of a kind that Spain itself did not yet have. Throughout the year, the surroundings of the city were alive with workers carrying cut stone and large tree trunks. The striking arches in the great square were beginning to be admired, for the European arch, which the ancient Mexica had never known, was soon seen everywhere in the capital.

By early 1524, one could see the beginnings of monasteries and churches, too, chapels crowned with cupolas, as well as private houses with battlements and buttresses, nail-studded doors, and grilled windows. A temporary cathedral was under way. After a time the trees of orchards could be seen rising over the vast walls of new monasteries. A gibbet and pillory, reminders of civilization in one sense, were not forgotten.

Cortés was accused by his critics of having been interested primarily in building palaces for his followers. But by 1526, thirty-seven churches were also being erected.[21] One of Cortés's secretaries, Juan de Ribera—a rather unreliable Extremeño, probably from Badajoz and possibly a cousin, who had come first to New Spain as a notary with Pánfilo de Narváez—would give an account to Peter Martyr of the great effort in New Spain of the master conquistador: "He is striving at this moment to restore the ruins of the great lake city damaged in the war: the aqueducts have been revived, the destroyed bridges and many ruined houses have been rebuilt and, little by little, the city is taking on its former appearance." Ribera added that the old commercial life had also recovered: Markets and fairs were to be seen again, boats came and went as "actively as before," and "the multitude of traders" seemed to be "as great as during the time of Montezuma."[22] In addition, two hospitals had been built, one specifically for lepers—San Lazarus, near Tlaxpana—and one for all other diseases except madness and syphilis.[23]

Soon after the great business of the restoration of Tenochtitlan had begun, Cortés wrote his third letter to Emperor Charles about the conquest. In this Cortés not only made the comment that he was distressed that his previous letters had received no answer but explained that, in the circumstances, he had been "almost forced (*casi forzado*)" to grant *encomiendas* to his fellow conquistadors because of his need to do something for those who had helped to achieve the great victory over the Mexica. He could not, unfortunately, offer them gold or pearls enough with which to retire to Spain! He had discussed the matter with his captains, including, we assume, such beneficiaries of his decisions as the Alvarados, Tapia, and Sandoval. He commented: "I entreat Your Majesty to approve."[24]

Encomienda was a medieval term. It indicated not a grant of land but a grant by the governor, or captain-general, of the labor and tribute of a certain number of natives (*naturales*) living in a specific place. There were precedents in the reconquest of Spain from the Muslims, and the scheme had been used in the Spanish dominions of the Caribbean. Several of Cortés's men had had such in Cuba or La Española, now the island of Hispaniola, including the modern Haiti and Dominican Republic. The grant of an *encomienda* satisfied the desire of conquistadors for lordships. It did not indicate territory but in some circumstances led to it.

The *encomienda* would have a controversial history throughout the sixteenth century, since the Crown soon wanted to argue that the grant only applied to one generation. The *encomenderos* wanted it for several generations if not indefinitely.

The first *encomendero* in New Spain appeared in April 1522: a relatively unknown conquistador, Gonzalo de Cerezo, who, though he had gone to New Spain with Narváez, had become a page of Cortés. He received the *encomienda* of the important town of Cholula, probably because he had helped to carry wood from Tlaxcala to Texcoco to make López's brigantines. Later, he made a fortune in commerce, and played a significant part in the early life of the colony.[25] Other early *encomenderos* were the golden-haired leader Pedro de Alvarado, who obtained the *encomienda* of Xochimilco; Francisco de Montejo, then in Spain, who was granted the silversmiths' rich town of Azcapotzalco; and Alonso de Ávila, who accompanied Cortés's letter of May 22 to Spain and was captured by the French on the high seas, and who had received Cuautitlan, Zumpango, and Xaltocan. Cortés allowed himself Coyoacán, the builders' town of Chalco, Ecatepec, and Otumba, the scene of the great battle of 1520.

An essential activity in these early days was a Spanish attempt to implicate numerous leaders of old Mexico in their plans. Thus Cortés gave the ancient city of Tula to Pedro, son of Montezuma. Tacuba, with 1,240 houses and several hundred *naturales,* went to Isabel (Techuipo), Montezuma's daughter and an ex-mistress of Cortés.[26] It was understood that the surviving monarchies and leaders in society would be accepted as such by the conquerors, provided that they not direct themselves against the Christian religion.[27] This rule would be observed for many years in the empire. The indigenous lords would have to accept the absolute prohibition of polygamy and of human sacrifice. *Encomenderos* would have the right to the labor of the people in the place concerned, and to receive appropriate produce. In return, the *encomendero* would concern himself with the religious life of the people in his district. He would not live there, but in a plot (*solar*) in Mexico-Tenochtitlan allocated to him within García Bravo's *traza.* Here was the link between the urban and agricultural arrangements in New Spain that reflected what had been done in the Caribbean colonies—La Española, Cuba, Puerto Rico, and Jamaica—and in Pedrarias's domain in Darien and Panama. These plans would be copied elsewhere in the Spanish empire in South America.

In 1522, Cortés sent back to Spain a map of Tenochtitlan, which was published in the Latin editions of his second and third *cartas de relación* to Charles V. It had, some modern authors point out, both fantastical and realistic features. This Latin production was completed in Nuremberg, the capital of German printing at that time. It was "a capricious representation of the Aztec capital" in the style of the so-called islands in the *Isolario*, by Benedetto Bordone (Vitto), in which there were illustrations of the most famous islands in the world. Bordone completed at least four editions after one in Venice in 1528, and in one there was a plan of Mexico-Tenochtitlan deriving from Cortés's map.[28] We were approaching the era of good maps, after all.

2

Valladolid, 1522

If a war threatens, popes must use all their efforts either to secure a settlement without bloodshed or, if the tempest in human affairs makes that impossible, to urge that the war is fought with less cruelty and does not last long.

ERASMUS, *Enchiridion*

Charles of Ghent, Karl von Habsburg, King of Spain and Emperor in Germany, duke of many European lands, and lord of many more beyond the ocean, reached his temporary, many-towered capital of Valladolid, in northwest Spain, at the end of August 1522, a year after Cortés's triumph in Mexico. Already a much-traveled monarch, though still only twenty-two years old, he had come from the Low Countries with two thousand people and more than one thousand horses. This entourage had seemed too large for the English when, along the way, Charles had visited his uncle by marriage, Henry VIII. Half had, therefore, been left in Calais. Henry signed his letters to Charles "*votre père, frère, et cousin et bel oncle Henry.*"[1] This itinerant court included chambermaids, butlers, grooms, and tapestry cleaners, as well as soldiers and clerks, courtiers, and counts.

In those still chivalrous days, kings traveled with tapestries. So in the court of Charles V, the keeper of tapestries, Gilleson de Warenghien, was particularly important. His family had been in the royal Burgundian service for several generations. When Charles's aunt Margaret arrived in Spain in 1497 to marry the Infante Juan, she was met at the port of Santander on the north coast by 120 mules laden with plate and tapestries.[2]

The Emperor and his friends entered Valladolid over a big bridge across the river Pisuerga—deep, rapid, and clayey—just where a smaller torrent, the Esqueva, joins it. Charles then crossed the Paseo de las Moreras (Mulberry Walk), before passing the substantial new palace of the multititled ducal family the Benaventes, on the edge of what had been, till a generation before, the Jewish quarter. Charles had stayed with the Benaventes on his previous visit to the city, in 1517. Now, in 1522, he went to live in the rambling mansion of the Enríquez, his Spanish cousins. (Charles's great-grandmother had been an Enríquez, a semi-royal noblewoman who had been the mother of King Fernando the Catholic; Charles, however, was the last king of Spain to have had commoners as near cousins.) The Enríquez dwelling was in the center of Valladolid, in the Calle de las Angustias.[3] The remainder of the court lodged in rented houses, mostly to the east of the town.

There is a fine picture of Valladolid in the sixteenth century in the collection of drawings by the Flemish artist Anton van den Wyngaerde. Wyngaerde, who came from Antwerp, worked, when young, in the Netherlands; in middle life in England and Italy; and later in Spain, where he became an official artist to King Philip II. He sketched most of the towns of Castile—so carefully that in 1572, he retired to Madrid with his hands crippled. His drawings form a fine topographical guide.[4]

Valladolid was a place of churches, convents, and private palaces, some of which had become public buildings, such as the supreme court (*audiencia*) and the royal chancellery. The *audiencia* was established in the palace of the Vivero family, built by the chief accountant to King Juan II, Alonso Pérez de Vivero, who had been murdered in 1453, a violent time in Spanish history almost forgotten by the 1520s. Pérez de Vivero's son, Juan, had had the same task in the household of Enrique IV. The family were converted Jews, conversos, like most high officials of the Trastámara dynasty. They served the Crown well, and Juan de Vivero had enabled King Fernando to meet Queen Isabel in his palace, and then to marry there, in the Sala Rica. That palace became the seat of the *audiencia* in 1479.

There must have been several hundred *señorial* houses in Valladolid in the early sixteenth century. These were stone buildings often in whitewashed Mudejar style, but it was easy to see that the Renaissance, which took so long to reach Spain, had come to Valladolid. Windows there seemed larger than they were elsewhere; doors were carefully placed in the centers of façades. Italian-style medallions depicting individuals could sometimes be seen above the main entrances. Patios were bigger than in other cities, as were the façades. At first sight, the palace of the Benaventes looked like a medieval fortress, but on examination, the courtyard there had an air of the Renaissance, with acanthus leaves at the tops of pillars, cameos recalling old family members, and a plateresque frieze. Soon there would also be a Renaissance garden there, organized by the count-duke, who had been one of the regents of the country during the recent time of troubles.

Other noblemen were building in Valladolid, as it was becoming evident that the town was, for the time being at least, the capital of the newly united kingdom of Spain. Thus the marquesses of Astorga, Villafranca, Denia, Viana, Villasantes, Poza, and Villaverde—*marquess* being a title much more used in Spain than in England[5]—sponsored imposing edifices, with their coats of arms over their main doors; so did the counts of Miranda and Ribadavia. These dwellings were mostly in the west of the town, and since they were new or even still being finished, they had an invigorating effect on the citizenry. The owners did not live continuously in them, but they provided both curiosity and employment for many of the forty thousand or so inhabitants of the city, a figure that made the town the largest in Castile. The noble houses also had often to lodge the Court; and if some courtiers, such as the chancellor Gattinara, Juan de Vergara, the enlightened secretary to Alonso de Fonseca, archbishop of Toledo, or the royal secretary Alfonso de Valdés might have been a pleasure to have as guests, others would have been merely demanding.

Even more striking to the eye than the palaces were about thirty convents or monasteries—half for women, half for men—as well as a *beaterio*, or guesthouse, for Dominicans and later, an oratory for the fathers of San Felipe Neri.[6] A foreign traveler would have been impressed to have found so many large buildings in the hands of religious professionals. Of these, the biggest was the Jeronymite foundation established in the mid-fifteenth century and now surrounded by gardens. When Charles had been in residence before, in 1517, some of its monks had preached against the Flemings who seemed to surround the monarch.[7] Almost as large was the Franciscan monastery, built in the late thirteenth century, in the Plaza del Mercado near the Plaza Mayor. The garden of that building occupied all the nearby land.[8] Then there was the rambling monastery of the Dominicans, with its magnificent church of San Pablo, in the center of the town.

San Pablo had been begun in the thirteenth century and much expanded by María de Molina, the astute widow of King Sancho IV of Castile. (She died in Valladolid in 1321.) The façade of that palace had been rebuilt by the theologian Cardinal Torquemada[9] in the 1460s, and the church was added to by Fray Alonso de Burgos, using two famous brother-architects from Germany, Juan and Simon of Cologne. Burgos, like Torquemada a converso, was a coarse, immoral but clever Dominican who had been for a time confessor to Queen Isabel. He became bishop of Cuenca and then of the rich dioceses of Palencia, in which Valladolid lay. His sermons were a pleasure to hear. Perhaps it was because he had lived for years in a cell cultivating solitude that he later spoke well.

It was in the church of San Pablo in 1517 that the nobility of Spain had sworn homage to Charles of Ghent, led by the Count of Oropesa carrying a sword of justice.[10] Three archbishops, seven bishops, eight dukes, five marquesses, twenty-one counts, two viscounts, five *comendadors,* and seven archivists of military orders had mounted the three steps before the altar to subject themselves to the King. That homage had been a religious as much as a political ceremony, and was concluded by the oath Charles himself swore on a cross and the Bible. The Te Deum was then sung. It was an occasion for celebration, and many noblemen who did not swear homage came simply to observe.

Other important churches in Valladolid included Santa Clara, founded by a friend of that saint herself in 1247, though the new buildings were of the 1490s; and Santa María la Antigua, with its beautiful pillars and square Romanesque tower.

We should remember, too, Santa María de las Huelgas,[11] a convent for Cistercian nuns, built to the east outside the town, on the site of the palace of María de Molina, who had left it to them. The beautiful Church of Santiago, recently built by the merchant Luis de la Serna, would soon be adorned by a marvelous picture by Pedro Berruguete, *The Adoration of the Kings,* on the reredos. Berruguete was the best Spanish painter of those days, and the emperor Charles made him notary of the chancellery in Valladolid, a sinecure that gave him leisure to paint. Charles's aunt Margaret of Austria would surely have approved of the arrangement since it gave her patronage a point. Berruguete had been in Rome when the famous Greek marble sculpture of Laocoön had been discovered in 1506 on the Esquiline Hill, the greatest archaeological discovery of the Renaissance and a sight that excited him all his life. He had been born in Paredes de Nava, forty miles to the north of Valladolid, a little town with which another Spanish Renaissance master was associated, the great poet Jorge Manrique, whose father was count of the place.[12]

The Benedictine monastery had been a royal palace and had been given to the monks by King Juan I at the end of the fourteenth century; and the church had been commissioned by Alfonso de Valdivieso, bishop of León. A small chapel had been added by Inés de Guzmán, the widow of the resilient chief accountant, Alonso Pérez de Vivero. The stalls in the main church were well carved by Andrés de Nájera, an illegitimate offspring of the great noble family of that surname. ("We do not descend from kings but kings descend from us" was a famous boast of the dukes of Nájera.) The educational church known as the Colegiata was expanded on the insistence of its abbot Juan and a town councillor of another great family, Nuño de Monroy, though the plans were incomplete. The Church of San Andrés was famous for being the burial place of those executed by the state—Álvaro de Luna, the long-lived first minister of King Juan II during the previous century, among them.

Valladolid had its secular life like any modern city. Printing had begun there in 1476, the first press being that at Nuestra Señora del Prado, which started by publishing bulls of indulgence. But a Frenchman, Jean de Boncour—many of Spain's first printers were foreigners—set up a private printing house, and in the first twenty years of the sixteenth century, many belles lettres were published, including romances such as the delightful Valencian work *Tirant lo Blanc,* in its first Spanish translation (from Valencian). At that time, only Seville, Salamanca, and possibly Toledo surpassed Valladolid as a printing town. The court could thus have much to read if it needed it. Even Boccaccio would be printed there in 1524.

For members of the court with less intellectual tastes, Valladolid had other charms. The Count-Duke of Benavente had an elephant. The women, thought the Venetian ambassador in the 1520s, Andrea Navagero, were beautiful even if, as the Flemish courtier Laurent Vital commented, they were heavily painted.[13] There were, in these happy days before the Reformation, many fiestas: "*Tout est pretexte à fêtes.*"[14] There was much dancing in summer along the banks of the river Pisuerga and many special celebrations for Christmas, Holy Week—especially Holy Thursday, when the procession leaving the Church of Magdalena was spectacular—and Corpus Christi, not to speak of the night of San Juan in July, the day of the Assumption in August, and the Nativity of the Virgin Mary in September. On Good Friday, two brotherhoods (*cofradías*) would set out, that of Our Lady at the Foot of the Cross, and that of the Prayer in the Garden of Olives. The second of these processions had in the early sixteenth century more than two thousand pilgrims (*nazarenos*) and several beautiful floats, including a model of the Last Supper and a Saint Veronica. All these splendid religious occasions were excuses for music and dancing, as well as for bullfights.[15] Plays were often performed, especially brief sketches of everyday life known as *sainetes.*

The university was already an ancient foundation. Established in 1346, it was dominated by the Church, though by 1522 it was full of humanists. Law, medicine, theology, and arts could all be studied there. New chairs were being regularly founded. It was then, with its one thousand students, the third-biggest university of Spain, following Salamanca and Alcalá.[16] The best modern student of the city, the French historian Bennassar, tells us that no other city in Castile had in the sixteenthth century such a strong intellectual spirit. No doubt there were, as in most Spanish institutions of learning of that time, two ways of looking at the classical authors: There were those who, like the Sicilian Lucio Marineo, Peter Martyr, and the Geraldini brothers, thought of the beauty of the poetry; and those who, like Nebrija, Diego de Muros, and Diego Ramírez de Villaescusa, prized poetry for the truth it expressed.[17]

When one mentions intellectual matters in 1522, it is a short step to talk of Erasmus. That humane Dutch scholar had declined to come himself to Spain. But his ideas had arrived and infested every place of learning and theological institute. Erasmus himself was still optimistic about the evolution of both European society and religion; he had recently written, "I could almost wish to be reborn in a few years because I see a golden age dawning." He pointed out that all the Princes in Europe were in agreement and were leaning toward peace. "I cannot but feel," he went on, "that there will be a new revival and in part a new unfolding of law-abiding behaviour and Christian society, but with a cleansed and genuine literature. We owe it to their pious minds that we observe the awakening and arising of glorious minds."[18]

Alas, the optimism was premature. All the same, the works of Erasmus enjoyed extraordinary popularity in Spain. No other country had a comparable experience: "At the Emperor's court, in the towns, in the churches, in the convents, even in the inns and on the high roads, everyone has the *Enchiridion* [Handbook of a Christian Soldier] of Erasmus in Spanish. It had been read till then by a minority of Latinists; and even those did not always understand everything. But now it is read in Spanish by people of every kind."[19]

Erasmus had come to see the need to consider the problems of the Christianization of the new realms in the Americas. In a note of a conversation added to *L'Ichtyophagi* in 1526, he reflected on the smallness of the territory controlled by Christians. His spokesman asks: "Have you not seen all those southern banks and the multitude of islands marked by Christian symbols?" "Yes," replies Erasmus's character Lanio, "and I have learned that from there one can bring back plunder. But I didn't hear that Christianity had been introduced."[20]

While Erasmus was optimistic, many simpler Christians also could believe that a new, tolerant, and intellectually rewarding Catholicism was imminent. Scores of cultivated citizens of Castile also spent their hours of leisure reading one or other of the famous novels of chivalry with which Spain was awash in those years. *Amadís de Gaula* was still the favorite, and it was followed by sequels—*Las sergas de Esplandián* and *Lisuarte de Grecia*—and a new series, *Palmerín de Oliva,* and the historian Oviedo's strange novel *Don Claribalte.*

With respect to dress, Flemish courtiers were surprised at the heavy chains of gold in Valladolid, and the bright colors of the clothes. Men showed a taste for luxury as much as women did, for they wore silk, brocade, velvet damask, and taffeta. Women, too, wore damask skirts and jackets. Feminine dress in the 1520s was marked by a taste for narrow shoulders and a narrow waist, with large extensions onto the floor. Not surprisingly, there was an army of tailors in Valladolid: In 1560, there would be one tailor per two hundred inhabitants, not to speak of the many hosiers, braid-makers, shoemakers, and jewelers. The most important jewelers of Valladolid were the Arfe family from Germany. Enrique de Arfe and his son Juan not only designed beautiful objects to wear but also refined the art of making gold and silver vessels for religious purposes.

As will be easily imagined in a town with an expensive if itinerant court, a large army of both black and Moorish slaves was to be found in Valladolid, as well as a colony of "new Christians" of both Muslim and Jewish descent. The section of the city called Santa María just east of the Calle Santiago was the *morería,* the Moors' ghetto, and there was a substantial number of builders there working on noblemen's new palaces, many of whom were Muslims. Nowhere in Castile did the poor get better treatment than they did in Valladolid, no doubt because there was so much work and because there were so many charitable foundations.[21] Sometimes there were accusations of Muslim secret propaganda, including the suggestion that a prophet had emerged in the community.[22]

And the empire in America? There were two buildings in Valladolid that would remind the friars, the noblemen, and even the King that it existed. First, at the side of the great church of San Pablo stood the college of San Gregorio. It had been begun in the late 1480s, with Enrique de Egas, Juan de Guas, and Gil Siloé contributing to the design, while Philippe Vigarny made the tomb there of Bishop Alonso de Burgos, the refounder of San Pablo. Egas was a Brussels architect who had built the *hostal* in Santiago de Compostela, as well as reconstructed the cathedral at Toledo; Vigarny was a Burgundian. The first inspiration for the college was Diego Deza, Columbus's friend from Zamora who afterwards became archbishop of Seville and *grand inquisidor.* Vigarny was the most interesting of these men. Coming to Burgos in his late twenties, in 1498, he is considered by historians of art as "one of the three foreign masters who taught the Spaniards perfect architecture and sculpture."[23] He created a chapel in the cathedral of Granada, where his "delicate chisel" sculpted the tombs of King Fernando and Queen Isabel.[24] By 1520, he already had an effective partnership with Pedro Berruguete. Probably it was these two who inspired the medallions in the Italian style on San Gregorio's, which so impressed the Flemish courtiers who accompanied King Philip the Handsome and Queen Juana when they heard Mass there in 1501.

But what drew the attention of the court to the New World, to the soldiers, explorers, and adventurers known increasingly as conquistadors, to the Renaissance man of empire, and to the modern "Americanist" was the façade of this college. It depicts hairy natives with clubs in their hands, such as those Columbus, that adopted Vallisoletano, said he had found in the Caribbean. These were referred to as *maceros* (wild mace-bearers). The primitiveness of the scene was compensated for by a family tree of the royal family and also one of Alonso de Burgos, as well as a depiction of that bishop kneeling before San Gregorio.

In this college, the Dominicans gave seven years' instruction in philosophy, logic, theology, and study of the Bible. Among those who studied at the college were later famous theologians who would insist that the Indians in the New World had souls, such as Fray Francisco de Vitoria and Fray Domingo de Soto; civil servants who administered the new empire, such as Fray García de Loaisa, who would become the long-serving President of Charles's Council of the Indies; and the first bishop of Lima, Fray Vicente de Valverde. Also among the old boys of this college would be Fray Bartolomé de Carranza, the archbishop of Toledo who was so unfortunate in his intellectual trajectory.[25]

The College of Santa Cruz nearby was as elegant a foundation as that of San Gregorio, but its style was dramatically Renaissance, as one would expect from a building provided by the "Third Monarch of Spain," Pedro González de Mendoza, archbishop of Toledo till his death in 1494. But here we see no sign that the cardinal wished his students to recall the achievements of his protégé, Columbus, which he had himself so furthered. It is González de Mendoza whom we should recall as we consider Charles V's other realm, that in New Spain, since relations of the cardinal, Mendoza upon Mendoza, would play as large a part in bringing Spanish order there as they did in bringing the Renaissance to the mother country.[26]

There was one more connection with the New World in Charles's court in 1522. Among those who came to Valladolid with the Emperor was Jean Glapion, his French confessor-counselor. He had been born in La Ferté–Bernard in the province of Maine, and he had spent many years in the Franciscan monastery in Bruges. He was enlightened and austere, lighthearted and pious, a dependent of Charles's aunt, the many-sided Archduchess Margaret at Bruges. When he became Charles's confessor, he sought to persuade him to leave the handling of the ideas of Luther to Erasmus, to whom he was devoted. Glapion accompanied the Emperor in his meetings with the main committees that governed the realms. But then in 1520, Glapion and a colleague in the Franciscan fraternity, Fray Francisco de los Ángeles, hearing of Cortés's discoveries, volunteered to go to New Spain to convert Indians. Pope Leo X, in his bull of April 1521, *Alias Felicis*, had approved. But Fray Francisco was named general of the Franciscan order and Glapion became a counselor of the Emperor as well as his confessor. Whether he would have continued to think of going to New Spain— as Mexico was then being called on the initiative of Cortés—is impossible to know. Glapion had an important role in the formation of imperial decisions from 1520 to 1522, including the nomination of officials. Alas, that fascinating Franciscan died in September 1522, leaving his place to a more conventional confessor-counselor, García de Loaisa.[27] Had Glapion lived, the history of Spain, Europe, and the Catholic Church would have been more tolerant, more open to new ideas, and, indeed, more Erasmian.

Valladolid was in 1522 already a great metropolis. Places like it would soon be under construction throughout the Americas. There would soon be, in the New World, the same confusion of palaces and churches, monasteries and markets, squares, and streets, often with the same names as those in Valladolid. Spain carried to the Indies the urban tradition of Rome and the Mediterranean. It remains.

3

Charles, King and Emperor

History is "a great mistress," a leader "even among our great
teachers," and our surest guide to an honest and virtuous life.
ERASMUS, QUOTED IN QUENTIN SKINNER, *The Foundations
of Modern Political Thought*, VOL. 1

The emperor Charles had been named after his great-grandfather Charles
the Rash (*le Téméraire*), the last Duke of Burgundy, a Christian name
familiar in France but almost unknown then in Spain.[1] He was born in
1500, on February 25, then the day of Saint Matthew, the evangelist who
played a part in his life: Charles often sought protection in that saint's
memory.[2] His birthplace, Ghent, had once been the capital of the medieval
counts of Flanders and the center of a cloth industry as well as of the
Burgundian principality. As Charles of Ghent, the Emperor had learned to
behave in his childhood and youth as a Burgundian nobleman. Burgundy
was in those days a complex international organization: It was the premier
French duchy, with a German monarch and a Flemish heart. Flemish was
Charles's first language.

Charles was an international man but among his thirty-two immediate
ancestors, there was only one German, a Habsburg, alongside a great
gallery of Castilians, Aragonese, and Portuguese. He even had an English
forebear, in John of Gaunt (Ghent), Duke of Lancaster, "time-honoured
Lancaster" in Shakespeare's *Henry IV*. Still, multinational though he
seemed, Charles's childhood had been Flemish. His Spanish mother,
Joanna the Mad (Juana la Loca), lived a long way away in Tordesillas,
Castile; his father, Philip von Habsburg, the Fair, died suddenly in 1506.

But Charles had in his father's clever sister, Margaret, an effective substitute for a mother. Regent of the Low Countries—in effect queen—she was twice widowed, having married the infante Juan, the son and heir of the monarchs of Spain, and then the Duke of Savoy, whose memory, along with her own, she would preserve in the exquisite church of Brou, near Bourg-en-Bresse.[3] She had a palace in Malines (Mechlin), which boasted the first Renaissance façade in the Netherlands, a building where the transition from late medieval Gothic to the Renaissance can be most clearly seen, for the styles stand in relation to each other in almost perfect symbolical balance.

In the shadow of the large cathedral of Saint Rombout, Margaret maintained an elegant court surrounded by poets, musicians, and painters. She collected pictures and unusual, beautiful, and exotic objects. She painted, wrote poems, and played chess and backgammon, and her library was famous as one of the first great collections of books after the recent invention of printing. Her librarian was a poet. She knew that in courts there had to be painters, and hers included the excellent Bernard van Orley from Brussels and the magnificent Albrecht Dürer from Nuremberg, not to speak of the prince of tapestry-makers, Pieter van Aelst, from Enghien. Margaret was confirmed by her nephew, Charles, in her semi-regal place, and she signed herself to him as "your very humble aunt." Her influence over Charles was profound. While she was suspicious of France, she also taught her nephew, above all, that a court could be a salon.[4]

Charles was subject to at least two other influences. First was the tutor whom Margaret had found for him, Adrian of Utrecht, dean of Saint Peter's in Louvain, a member of the order of the Brethren of the Common Life, a pious, ascetic society founded in the northern Low Countries at Deventer at the end of the fourteenth century. Proto-humanists, perhaps they might be described as. Adrian was the son of a ship's carpenter and could tell Charles how ordinary people lived. From Adrian, "Charles acquired the popular easy-going and simple ways which made him so beloved by his Flemish subjects."[5] The Brethren of the Common Life was one of those new Catholic bodies determined to simplify the Church's life, which, had they enjoyed greater success, might have rendered the Reformation unnecessary. The order had a cult of indigence, a deprivation of which Adrian sought to remind his famous pupil.[6] Some of the most remarkable men of the time were brethren—such as Mercator, the inventor of mapping,[7] and Thomas à Kempis, who was close to the order with his *Imitation of Christ.*

Adrian had, however, found himself able to accept worldly appointments. From being a mere doctor of theology at the University of Louvain, he became its chancellor. From being tutor to Charles, he became, first, the Flemish ambassador to Castile and then Regent there, in Charles's absence, after May 1520. Though he was unable to control the revolution that followed in that year,[8] something extraordinary then occurred. For in January 1522, the cardinals in Rome unexpectedly named him pope. The Florentine historian Francesco Guicciardini, who lived at the time, recalled that Adrian had been proposed "without anyone having any inclination to elect him but just to waste the morning. But then came several votes in his favour, the Cardinal of San Sisto began to speak in support of him in an almost perpetual oration, whereupon several cardinals began to move to his cause." Others followed, "more by impulse than by deliberation, with the result that, that same morning, he was elected pope by a unanimous vote, those who chose him not being able to give any reason why, amidst so many travails for the church, they should elect a foreigner from a 'barbarous country' who had not won any favour either because of his achievements in the past or from conversations, which he might have had with cardinals, who scarcely knew his name, and who had never been in Italy."[9] Adrian himself wrote to a friend that he "would have preferred to be a canon of Utrecht than become Pope."[10]

Elected in January, Adrian took a long time to reach Rome. Indeed, he only arrived at the end of August, and a plague began immediately: a bad omen, it was understandably thought. Adrian was mocked in the Vatican because he liked beer more than wine and because he refused to commission Cellini, the great Tuscan jeweler and sculptor, to do anything. He caused consternation by refusing to countenance nepotism. A large placard was placed on the door of the Vatican announcing "This palace to let." Another poster denounced the cardinals who had elected Adrian as "robbers, betrayers of Christ's blood" and asked, "Do you not feel sorrow to have surrendered the Vatican to German fury?" "This pope of ours knows no one," wrote a courtier, Girolamo Negri, "the whole world is in despair."[11] Adrian was called the *munidor* of the pope's election, the beadle. The cardinals had voted for him because they thought that they would do well to have a tutor of the new emperor in the Vatican. But Charles had not tried to back him. Indeed, he seems to have preferred the English cardinal Wolsey.

Adrian was a politically stupid choice. He saw the classical antiquity that surrounded him in Rome as the debris of paganism. He would have preferred a simple, small house to a palace. He had other concerns: One of his first decrees was to forbid the wearing of beards in the Vatican.[12] True, he celebrated Mass daily and spoke Latin well, if without polish. But he was inexpert in politics. Ludwig von Pastor, the historian of the popes, wrote that "Adrian's single-hearted anxiety to live exclusively for duty was to Italians of that age like an apparition from another world, beyond the grasp of their comprehension."[13]

A third influence on the emperor Charles in his early years was Guillaume de Croÿ, Sieur de Chièvres. Coming from a powerful Flemish family that had served all the great dukes of Burgundy in the preceding century, he became Charles's "governor and grand chamberlain" in 1509. His influence was a contrast to that of Adrian, but it was considerable, for he stood for the Burgundian tradition even more than did the archduchess Margaret. "The truth is," Charles told the archbishop of Capua, "as long as he lived, Monsieur de Chièvres governed me."[14] He slept in Charles's bedroom and had his eyes on him all day. Charles told a Venetian ambassador to Spain, Gasparo Contarini—a writer and a future cardinal—that he had early learned the value of Chièvres and "for a long time subordinated his will to his."[15] Chièvres was artful but observant, a hard master. When asked by the French ambassador, Genlis, why he made Charles work so hard when only fifteen years old, he replied: "Cousin, I am the defender and guardian of his youth. I do not want him to be incapable because he has not understood affairs nor been trained to work."[16] Trained to work! Can there be anything more important to gain from an education?

Chièvres was interested in promoting his family interests. All the same, it was he who gave Charles the chivalrous education that meant so much to him, and who told him about the use of arms, about riding, and about such heroic writings as that of the elaborate courtier Olivier de la Marche. La Marche, an official from Franche-Comté, had been captain of the guard to the still much regretted Charles the Rash. He wrote notes about the etiquette and ceremonial of the court, giving pride of place to the Order of the Fleece. He also composed an allegorical poem about Charles the Rash in 1482, *Le chevalier délibéré* (The Resolute Knight). He also wrote memoirs, which were much read in the early sixteenth century.

La Marche was the author of a book describing codes of behavior in different countries of Europe, which was read by Charles's maternal grandfather, the emperor Maximilian, and probably was also studied by Maximilian's well-educated daughter Margaret. La Marche, who seems to have seen life as one long challenge with recurrent dangers, recalled the memory of Charles the Rash as important in the young emperor Charles's makeup—for "no one," wrote the Dutch historian Huizinga, "had been so consciously inspired by models of the past or manifested such a desire to rival them" as that duke.[17] The same could have been said of Charles the emperor. Like his ancestor, Charles was also proud of the famous order of the Golden Fleece, which gave him a sense of the importance of valor, loyalty, piety, and even simplicity.

In Valladolid in 1522, Charles still seemed the lanky, gangly, curiously featured youth with the ever open mouth, painted often by his aunt Margaret's favorite portraitist, Bernard van Orley. He had a pronounced Habsburg jaw.[18] He was thin. The Venetian Contarini describes him "as of a middle height neither tall nor short, more pale than rubicund, a fine leg, good arms, his nose rather sharp but small, restless eyes with a serious look neither cruel nor severe."[19] He was certainly not yet the wise man we see in the masterpieces of Titian—the standing figure with the dog, the seated monarch wearing the Golden Fleece, much less the armored knight at the battle of Mühlberg. But then Charles remained contradictory in his physique, as he did in other things.

When he was a young man, his negative qualities seemed to dominate him. His confessor Glapion told Contarini that Charles remembered too much the injuries that people gave him; he was not able to forget easily.[20] Talking seemed to bore him, and it seemed to be something he could not do without difficulty.[21] Alonso de Santa Cruz said of him that he was "a friend of solitude and a critic of laughter."[22] One ambassador thought that it looked as if his eyes had been pasted on to a too long face. To one courtier, de Longhi, his temperament seemed in the 1520s a mixture of passivity and impatience. Charles impressed his contemporaries with what Ramón Carande, the Spanish historian of the early twentieth century, would describe as "his extraordinary psychological penetration."[23]

He had begun to impress people. His magisterial biographer, the German Karl Brandi, thought that he became eventually "imperial in word and deed, in look and gesture . . . Even those who have long been in attendance on him were astonished not only at his youthfulness, but at his energy, severity and dignity."[24]

He began to seem, when on the throne, to courtiers and civil servants, to be magnanimous, liberal, generous. If still apparently unhealthy, and slow in his movements as in his speech, even ugly in person, Charles had something powerful about him, the weight of a leader. He never moved among men with natural ease, but his personality was beginning to reflect his high sense of honor and his sureness of purpose. As his brief volume of memoirs suggests, he had already become earnest and questioning. Some of this was evident at Valladolid in 1522.[25]

Charles was a Burgundian nobleman thanks to Chièvres. Adrian of Utrecht made him pious. His aunt Margaret gave him a sense of politics and of art, as well as a concept of public service, which all the Habsburgs had. This combination of influences gave him, as Karl Brandi put it, "serious principles and a desire to confirm them; a courtly bearing; the ideal of knightly honour and that of fighting for the Christian faith in the style of the code of the Golden Fleece." Burgundy also made him conscious of the political benefit of a rigorous court ceremonial. Thus he seemed extremely dignified when, on his first visit to England in 1513, he was considered a possible bridegroom for King Henry's sister Mary, the widow of King Louis XII of France. Already he had by 1522 an appetite for stylish dressing; he seemed "*muy rico y galán.*" He was a good sportsman, and his grandfather, Maximilian the emperor, had said that "he was glad that he was making such progress as a huntsman for, were it not so, it might have been supposed that the boy was a bastard, not his grandson."[26] From early in life, he expected to be buried at the beautiful charterhouse of Champnol, outside Dijon, the site of the tombs of his ducal Burgundian ancestors designed by Nicholas Sluter. He hoped always to be able to win back from France that part of Burgundy; he would tell Philip, his son, "never to forget our duchy of Burgundy which is our ancient heritage."[27]

Charles, like all members of his family, liked music. He delighted in hearing his aunt Margaret's violin and tambourine players, as well as her fifes and choristers. At the archduchess Margaret's court he learned the clavichord and loved to hear good music in his chapel.[28] A childhood friend, Charles de Lannoy, from a family as distinguished as the Croÿs—his grandfather, Hugues de Lannoy, had been a founding member of the Order of the Golden Fleece—remarked that to like music was effeminate. Charles challenged him and chose lances and heavy horses for the duel. The exchange was dramatic. Though Charles won in the end, his horse fell and he always bore the marks of his injuries. Lannoy continued as Charles's chamberlain (*caballerizo mayor*) and, in March 1522, became Viceroy of Naples.[29]

Though intellectually well prepared, in his youth Charles always associated with young aristocrats such as Lannoy; John Frederick of Saxony, the elector palatine with whom Charles's sister was so unwise as to have fallen in love; Frederick von Fürstenberg; and Max Sforza, all of whom became his pages and all of whom considered it more important to be able to splinter a lance without losing one's seat on a horse than to construe a Latin sentence. They would all play an important part in Charles's life, though John of Saxony would have a tragic role in consequence of Charles's politics.

Though Charles had many kingdoms, he spoke only French and Flemish fluently. He began to learn Spanish in 1517, but in 1525 the clever Polish ambassador to Spain, Dantiscus, wrote that he still found that language difficult and seemed to have no German. (Poland had something like a family pact then with the Habsburgs.) He never learned Latin well, despite the lessons of Adrian of Utrecht and despite his later often-repeated belief that it was essential that his son, Philip, should know it. It was said that if someone addressed him in Latin, and he did not understand what was said, he would reply, "This man takes me for Fernando," a reference to his grandfather, the King of Aragon. But if he did realize what had been said, he would say, "This man is without letters, he speaks a really bad Latin."[30] In the end his Spanish improved. But his German was never good. His French was always good, and he could understand Italian.

Charles lacked in his childhood any connection with his Spanish inheritance. Courtiers such as Juan Manuel, intriguing and malicious, and friendly churchmen, such as Alonso de Fonseca, archbishop of Santiago, and Ruiz de la Mota, bishop of Palencia, had limited influence in comparison with the Archduchess, Croÿ, and Adrian of Utrecht. Santa Cruz thought that Charles found it difficult to have confidence in Spaniards.[31]

But Erasmus presented him in 1516 with his *Education of a Christian*

Prince, while Antonio de Guevara's *The Dial of Princes*, published in 1529, became, according to Méric Casaubon, the most widely read book of the entire sixteenth century in Europe. For Charles, historical knowledge became "the nurse of practical wisdom."

Those who have the best understanding of the past may be said to have "the best title to act as advisers to Princes."[32] Guillaume Budè, the French philosopher, thought that reading history led to an understanding of the present and future as well as of the past.

In respect of his politics, it has been said that it is hard to see whether Charles was more a monarch of the Middle Ages or one of modern times. He twice would challenge the King of France to a single combat whose outcome would have settled all their differences. Charles did not warm to nationalism, nor even patriotism, but loyalty to the Habsburg family was a different matter. He disliked the idea of having a fixed capital: "Kings do not need residences," he once told his son, Philip, when the two had passed an uncomfortable night at the royal pavilion at El Pardo.[33] In these ways, Charles seemed still a medieval monarch. But all the same he knew, from the advice of his chancellor Mercurino Arborio de Gattinara, of the benefits of an organized civil service, and his rearrangements of his governmental committees would have reflected well on a post-Renaissance Prince.

The public servants who worked for Charles at that time included many Flemings or Burgundians, as was indeed Gattinara, a Savoyard from near Stresa, in Piedmont, who had first been with Charles's aunt, Margaret, as a legal adviser. Gattinara, chancellor from 1522, was the most influential of all these officials. He was clever if persnickety, being fond of disputing the finer points of the uses of the subjunctive. But he combined such detail with broad vision. He also gloried in talking of Charles's imperial role in powerful, frequent memoranda; and his advice touched many lesser things, such as recommending Charles to have his hair cut short, and to grow a beard such as that worn by Hadrian.[34]

The emperor Charles and his chancellor Gattinara were not on the kind of warm terms that a great emperor and his most important public servant should be. Charles evidently wearied of Gattinara's continual grandiloquence. Early in 1523, in Valladolid, Gattinara wrote to his master that he thought that Charles was in danger of following the path of his grandfather Maximilian who, despite his many gifts, was called "the bad gardener" because he would never harvest his fruit in the right season. A proper budget of income and spending should be made. The *cortes* (parliament) in Spain should seek a new source of revenue. He, Gattinara, would draft speeches for Charles whenever necessary. But he wanted Charles to adopt a "forward policy" in Italy: "I implore you, in the name of God, that, neither in council nor elsewhere, neither in jest nor in earnest, do you make it known before your going to Italy that you intend to take personal possession of Milan. Do not hand over the citadel to the Spaniards, do not take away the town secretly from the Duke. Such things must not be spoken of, be it ever so secretly, since walls have ears and servants tongues . . ." And, if Charles continued to go on as if daily expecting God to work miracles for him, then he, Gattinara, would beg to be excused from further involvement in matters of finance or war. Otherwise he would like to remain in the royal service till the day that Charles was crowned in Italy. Then indeed he would be able to say "*Nunc Dimittis, servum tuum domine.*"[35]

In April 1523, still in Valladolid, Gattinara wrote to Charles about his own position, wanting to have his powers either reaffirmed or withdrawn. He had noticed that the chancellors of England and France were paid four times what he was. He complained that he sometimes had to wait two hours for an audience with Charles, while the Emperor saw people whom Gattinara considered nonentities. The chancellorship, he feared, was being reduced to a tavern sign.[36] In another note at much the same time, Gattinara told Charles: "If your Majesty were to add to all your gifts the wisdom of Solomon, you would not be able to do everything yourself." God had even advised Moses to seek assistants. Nor should Charles embark on anything unless he could be sure of carrying it through. The ordinary costs of government should be distinguished from extraordinary costs, such as war. Gattinara, nothing if not a Lombard, believed that he who controlled northern Italy had the key to world power. The Emperor's coronation there would put the seal on his achievements. A Roman diplomat wrote: "Let the Emperor rule Italy and he will rule the world."[37] Meantime the love of all his subjects should be for Charles an "impregnable fortress," as Seneca had put it. Their friendship should be cultivated, their complaints heeded. Charles should arrange that, if unpopular actions were needed, others would take responsibility. The Emperor should not have to perform trivialities.

Then Gattinara touched on policy in the Indies. He asked whether the

Emperor believed that the natives should be converted to Christianity. Counselor Gérard de la Plaine (Señor La Roche), a Burgundian much used by Charles for diplomatic missions, had said that the Indians had been treated not as men but as beasts.[38] That should surely not be permitted. Charles was responsive to that kind of suggestion. Had he not listened to, and largely sided with, Bartolomé de las Casas in 1518, had he not himself suggested that the Indians sent home by Cortés in 1519 should be given warm clothes cut by the best tailors in Seville?

In July 1523, Charles held a *cortes* at Valladolid. As usual, representatives (*procuradors*) were present from half the cities of Castile. In a long speech written for him by Gattinara, Charles admitted mistakes but blamed them on his youth. He cited Caesar, Trajan, and even Titus, who all believed, so he said, that the pursuit of peace was the greatest of foreign policies. Gattinara also spoke, declaring the divine origin of the royal power. God, after all, had the heart of kings in his hand. Gattinara did not explicitly mention the Indies. But he did speak of the need to continue the conquest of Africa.[39] The *cortes* were impressed and voted for the grant of ducats for which Charles had asked, though the quantity was smaller than on any other occasion in Charles's reign.[40]

In politics, Charles was as much a mixture as he was in blood. At one moment he seemed liberal, humane, tolerant. At other moments he seemed to bridle at the slightest criticism. His consideration of the defeated rebels after the war of *comuneros* in 1522 was a model of toleration for any age: Fewer than a hundred died in Castile, and some of those died of disease in prison.[41] The high point of this second stay of Charles in Valladolid was a ceremony outside the church of San Francisco on All Saints' Day, 1522, when he proclaimed a general pardon for all who had been engaged in that conflict—except for twelve "*exceptuados*" to whom Charles retained an aversion. Considering that the rebels had mounted, for whatever reason, a serious attack on the authority of the Crown and had even offered power to the King's poor, nervous mother, Juana, such clemency was remarkable.

In the 1520s, Charles was convinced, above all by his chancellor Gattinara, that he had a superhuman position in Christian society. Gattinara had hailed Charles in 1519 as the "greatest Emperor since the division of the empire in 843." He was assured, and came himself to think, that God had chosen him to be the supreme universal monarch. Charles believed that he was the second sword of the Christian Commonwealth, with the Vicar of Christ, the pope, the first. He knew "the confessional nature of his Crown."[42] The empire implied an inalienable mission, one over other kings, and a right to demand their support for his declared crusade against Muslims—either the Sultan's army in Hungary or the fleet of Barbarossa at sea. He was told by Gattinara that the climax of the universal monarchy was at hand. The chancellor said that he hoped that Charles would lead the entire world back to a "single shepherd," presumably as in Roman days.[43] The rest of the world would be conquered or fall into a subservient place.[44] Gattinara's powerful dreams were intoxicating. They sometimes convinced Charles, but often they were rejected by him.

The idea that Charles had a grand place in what Pope Julius II had called "the World's Game" was widespread. Cortés in 1520 would urge that Charles should think of himself as a "new Emperor" of New Spain, no less than of Germany.[45] He would go further in 1524 by referring to Charles as "Your Majesty to whom the whole world is subject."[46] In the 1530s, a bishop of the remote see of Badajoz would pray that the Christian Princes "would all join with Your Sacred Majesty as monarch and Lord of the world in order to exterminate and persecute the pagans and infidels."[47] Thus even in Mexico/New Spain, a conquistador of no great importance, Juan de Ortega, from Hernán Cortés's hometown of Medellín, in testimony on behalf of his leader in 1534 spoke of the emperor Charles as "his Majesty the Lord of the world."[48] Earlier, at the time of his election as Emperor in 1519, Charles's friends had argued that his greatness, resting on such mighty foundations as the Crown of Spain and the empire, might mean that, having achieved the imperial Crown, he could make all Italy and a great part of Christendom into "a single monarchy."[49]

Charles's attitude to the Church was ambiguous. He saw himself first and foremost as the first protector of Christianity. Thus he was always a devoted, even a rigid, Catholic. He heard Mass daily, sometimes twice.[50] But he was not very interested in dogmatic matters and often quarreled with popes—even when, as in 1522, that dignitary was an old friend of his own. He would even urge war against popes, as he did against the second Medici pope, Clement VII, in 1527. In his early days, he had quite radical views about Church reform. He read with apparent pleasure such destructive dialogues on the papacy as those of Alfonso de Valdés, a brillant new secretary from Cuenca.

Valdés was a public servant of quality. He was in 1522 still merely a notary in Gattinara's office, but he would soon become controller-general of the entire secretariat. He had been a protégé of Peter Martyr and had a quasi-religious enthusiasm for Erasmus. His dialogue *Mercury and Charon,* written at the end of the 1520s, relates how the first-named thought that the fact that all Christendom seemed to be at war was the consequence of the machinations of the Emperor's enemies. But Mercury's reflections were constantly interrupted by the arrival of souls ferried across the river Styx by Charon. These souls were mostly ignorant, not evil, and were astonished to find themselves on the way to damnation after a life of nothing worse than conventionality. Perhaps Valdés was influenced in choosing his theme by the great painting of Charon crossing the Styx done by the Flemish master Joachim Patinir a few years before?[51] It was a rare example of a classical theme at the service of Christianity.

Valdés wrote, as an Erasmian, not against the principles of Christianity but against the Church and the Curia. He looked on himself as the proselytizing councillor[52] of the monarch, the *Erasmista* who sought to convert his master into an enlightened despot. Rebellion against bad Kings was always necessary. About this time, Charles obtained a great concession from the papacy, in the bull *Eximiae devotionis affectus* of 1523, which gave him and his successors, as kings of Spain, the right of presentation and patronage of all archbishops and bishops of Spain and its empire.[53]

Charles always had a tolerant side: Even in his last will, written at a time when pain and exhaustion caused him to seem unbending, he would suggest that inquisitors should be given canonries and so would not have to live off goods confiscated from accused persons.[54] He often seemed an Erasmian inclined to compromise with the Reformation: In theology, he was even prepared to yield on the matter of the articles of the faith, the doctrine of justification, the use of the chalice for the laity, even the idea of marriage for priests.[55] But he never wanted it to seem that he had been advised to these things by people such as Valdés. He always thought that the popes were mistaken not to interest themselves in the internal reform of the Church, which his preceptors in Flanders had taught him was necessary and which most German princes, including most Catholics, wished to see.

As for the Church in Spain, Charles would soon appreciate the "tremendous efficacy" of the power of the Inquisition at the service of the Church and the Crown. Charles came to realize the benefit of a tribunal that sought to guarantee the unity of the Christian faith, thus making possible the secular utopia of the universal Christian empire. But in 1522 that was not so; he was unenthusiastic about the Inquisition and remembered that his father, Philip, had toyed with the idea of the abolition of the institution and had actually requested Pope Leo X to finish with it. Then Charles seems to have thought that the Inquisition could be put to good use.[56]

A new inquisitor general, Alonso Manrique de Lara, was following Charles's ideas in these actions despite the opposition of his new confessor, the Dominican García de Loaisa. In his last years, however, Charles regretted having given a free pass to Luther at Worms in 1520 and would murmur in Spanish "*Muerto el perro, muerta la rabia.*" ("If you kill the dog, you finish with the rabies too.")[57] He allowed García de Loaisa and other conventional prelates to push Manrique de Lara to one side, persuading him to devote all his time to his archbishopric of Seville and leave the business of the Inquisition to the council to manage.[58]

Already in 1522 people talked constantly to Charles of his need to marry. An heir was necessary. It seems possible, however, that he had a mistress in Spain in the surprising shape of Germaine de Foix, the pretty young widow of his grandfather Fernando the Catholic. Had not that grandfather requested in his will that Charles should concern himself with her? The conclusion that there was at the least an *amitié amoureuse* between the two was argued by Melchor Fernández Álvarez, while Lorenzo Vital recalled that the Emperor had a little wooden bridge made from his lodgings to hers, which enabled him to visit her secretly.[59]

In 1522, after Charles had left Flanders, a girl whom Charles had casually seduced in the Netherlands, Joanna van der Gheest, daughter of a tapestry-maker of Oudenaarde, gave birth to a baby girl, who was recognized by Charles as his daughter. This was the future Margaret of Parma who, having been looked after and educated by her namesake the Archduchess, would thirty years later become Regent in Brussels.

Two other girls were apparently born to Charles at this time: first, Juana de Austria, daughter of one of the ladies attached to Henry of Nassau, who would be brought up in the convent of Augustinians in Madrigal de las Altas Torres; and second, Taeda, an Italian daughter of Ursolina della

Penna, "the beauty of Perugia" who reached the imperial court of Brussels in 1522. Juana remained a nun in Madrigal; Taeda lived in Rome, being still alive in 1562.[60] There is also a possibility that Isabel, daughter of Germaine de Foix, King Fernando's widow, was the child of the Emperor. She was still living in 1536.[61]

Charles was a remarkable figure. None of his predecessors had his ambitions. His grandfather Maximilian was a Renaissance prince and reveled in his Burgundian antecedents. But he was no intellectual statesman; rather, he was a German politician. Charles was a multinational king served by Burgundians such as Gattinara. He was the dominant statesman of his time and took his grandeur for granted. The New World seemed something that he deserved and needed. But he was not surprised by it. New Spain appeared a natural development.

4

Christianity and the New World

The people owe you much but you owe them everything. Even if your ears have to hear the proud titles of "invincible," "inviolable," and "majesty" . . . do not acknowledge them, but refer them all to the Church to whom alone they belong.

ERASMUS, *Enchiridion*

In his third letter to the emperor Charles, which reached Spain in November 1522, Cortés requested that more churchmen be sent to New Spain. At that time, there were still only four there: two secular priests, Fray Juan Díaz, of Seville, who had been on Cortés's expedition throughout; Fray Juan Godínez; and two friars, Fray Pedro Melgarejo de Urrea, a Franciscan, also from Seville, and Fray Bartolomé de Olmedo, a Mercedarian from a town near Valladolid. A little later, Fray Diego de Altamirano, a Franciscan and a cousin of Cortés's, and Fray Juan de las Varillas, another Mercedarian, from his name also a distant cousin of Cortés's, arrived in New Spain. They had, as they knew, multiple responsibilities.

Cortés's letter requesting further clerical help was supplemented by a letter signed by him, Fray Melgarejo, and Alderete, the treasurer. After speaking of the good services that Cortés and all the conquistadors had performed, the writers continued: "We beseech His Majesty to send us bishops and clerics from every order that are of good life and sound doctrine that they might aid us to establish more firmly Our Holy Catholic Faith in these parts." The writers went on to request the King to grant the government of New Spain to Cortés, for he was "such a good and loyal servant of the Crown." The letter ended on a wise note: "We beg the king also not to send us lawyers because by coming to this land they would put it in turmoil." Such direct language was characteristic of the time. The writers of this letter also hoped that Bishop Fonseca would not "meddle" anymore in Cortés's affairs and that Governor Velázquez in Cuba would be arrested and sent back to Spain.[1]

Christianity had, of course, been engaged in the conquest of the Indies from the beginning. The cross was the symbol of conquest as well as of conversion. Columbus had had priests on his second voyage;[2] priests accompanied most of the conquistadors in the West Indies; and there were two bishops in Santo Domingo by 1512, a third in Puerto Rico, and another bishop, Fray Juan de Quevedo, was appointed to Panama in 1513. Quevedo had taken a good suite of priests and canons. His remarkable argument with Las Casas about the treatment of natives, in the presence of King Charles, has been amply described.[3] So have the controversies in Santo Domingo following the marvelous sermon of Fray Antonio de Montesinos. The conquistadors were in some ways the reincarnation of those Spaniards who recovered Spain itself from the Moors; but they also saw themselves winning new lands for Christianity against the natural allies of the sixteenth-century Muslims.[4] The pope's decision to grant rights in Africa and the Indian Ocean in the fifteenth century to Portugal and to allocate to Spain a new zone of influence in the Indies had given the frame to all the conquests. In a bull of July 1508, Pope Julius II gave King Fernando the right to present to all bishoprics and other ecclesiastical benefices.

In 1517, Cardinal Cisneros, Regent of Spain, received a letter from Las Casas suggesting that the Inquisition be sent to the Indies.[5] Cisneros agreed. The pope made concessions. First, Alonso Manso, bishop of Puerto Rico, was named *inquisidor general* of the Indies. The bishop had been *sacristán mayor* at the court of the Infante Juan in the 1490s and had ever since been a protégé of Archbishop Deza. Then, as we have seen, the bull *Alias Felicis* of April 25, 1521, gave a license to two Franciscans to go to New Spain: Fray Francisco de los Ángeles (Quiñones), a brother of the Count of Luna in Seville, and Fray Jean Glapion of Flanders, the Emperor's confessor. But they did not carry through the assignment, for the former became general of his order, and the brilliant Glapion died in Valladolid before he could arrange his voyage.

In 1523, three other Franciscans went to Mexico-Tenochtitlan. These were Johannes Dekkus (Tecto), Johann van der Auwern (Juan de Ayora), and Pedro de Gante.[6] The first named had once been a subsidiary confessor to the Emperor, as well as a professor of theology in Paris. He had taken the place of Fray Jean Glapion at Bruges. The second claimed to have Scottish forebears and was even said to be an illegitimate son of King James III of Scotland.

Fray Pedro de Gante was born about 1490 in Iguen, Budarda, a part of Ghent near the abbey of Saint Pieter. He never mentioned the names of his parents but was perhaps the illegitimate son of the emperor Maximilian. After all, he would write to the emperor Charles in 1546: "Your Majesty and I know how close we are and how the same blood runs in our veins." Fray Alonso de Escalona, provincial of the Franciscans, would tell King Philip of Spain in 1572, after Fray Pedro's death, that Pedro had been "a very close relation of your most Christian father, thanks to which we had been able to receive many and large grants."[7] The way that letter is phrased rather suggests that Fray Pedro was a brother of Charles. But we know for certain of two illegitimate sons of Maximilian, both bishops in their maturity.[8]

Pedro de Gante studied at the University of Louvain, then became a lay brother at the Franciscan monastery of Ghent, where he spent several years. He left there in 1522 with the Emperor, his supposed brother or nephew, and the next year embarked in May for New Spain, where he and his two comrades arrived on August 13, 1523, the second anniversary of the conquest of Mexico-Tenochtitlan. Perhaps his decision to go to the New World was influenced by the failure of Glapion to do so. He passed three years in Texcoco, where he founded the school of San Francisco behind the chapel of San José. Here he developed workshops for blacksmiths, tailors, carpenters, cobblers, masons, painters, designers, and candlestick-makers. This vocational work was of great importance for the Mexica.

Pedro remained in New Spain all his life and taught thousands of Mexicans how to read, sew, and write. He deliberately fostered the fusion of Spanish and Indian ways. Thus if he was to observe an Indian ceremony, he would compose a Christian song for it. He drew new patterns for Indian cloaks in a Christian dance: "In this way, the Indians first came to show obedience to the Church." Considered beautiful to look at by his innumerable friends, Habsburg or not, Pedro was a majestic figure, worthy of his alleged ancestry. He remained a lay brother and never accepted ordination, and so never had a grand position. All the same, the second archbishop of Mexico, the Dominican Fray Alonso de Montúfar, would say, "Pedro de Gante is archbishop of Mexico, not me."[9]

Several officials of the Inquisition were soon named for the New World. In 1523, the first auto-de-fé was celebrated in the Indies: Alfonso de Escalante was condemned in Santo Domingo. Escalante had been the notary of Santiago de Cuba. He had also been a witness in Diego Velázquez's inquiry of 1519 into the conduct of Francisco de Montejo. All the same, he was burned as a practicing Jew.[10] His execution was preceded by the usual vile torments that marked the Inquisition at this stage of its development.

That same year, Pope Adrian VI conferred special privileges on the Franciscans in the New World. They would be able to elect their own superior every three years who would have all of the powers of a bishop except those of ordination. The consequence was the departure for New Spain of twelve further Franciscans early in 1524.

These fine men reached Santo Domingo in February, Cuba in March, and Veracruz on May 13 of that year, and began to walk barefoot up to Mexico-Tenochtitlan. They were not just ordinary Franciscans but men from the province of San Gabriel in Extremadura, members of a reformed section of the order that sought to reflect in their lives the poverty of the Evangelists or of the first centuries A.D. They were radical friars, all of them of good birth, whose principles caused them to clash with ordinary settlers. This millenarian sect had been founded by Juan de Guadalupe in the new monastery of San Francisco in Granada in 1493. Soon there were six new such monasteries, five in Extremadura and one in Portugal.

These new Franciscans were led to New Spain by Fray Martín de Valencia, from Valencia de Don Juan. He was fifty years of age when he reached New Spain and, though one of the most pious of men, did not have the ability to learn a new language. He strove to compensate for that by praying in public places so that, by imitating him, the Indians might come to God, because, he said, "the natives are very prone to do what they see others doing." They were, that is, excellent mimics. All the same, he is said to have beaten Indians in order to hasten their learning when he thought it was too slow. Not long before his death, he thought that he ought to sail across the Pacific to seek "men of great capacity in China."[11]

Once while preaching in Spain of the conversion of infidels, he experienced a vision about a great multitude being converted. Exclaiming three times "Praised be Jesus Christ," he was assumed by his brother Franciscans to have lost his senses and was locked up till he exclaimed that his vision was leading him to a mission of conversion.[12]

The other Franciscans included Fray Luis de Fuensalida, who, from his name, must also have come from Old Castile. He had a most humane view of the task ahead of him. He knew that Christianity was a creed for all the world and those who refused to accept that fact were men who had never taken the trouble to learn any Indian language (a thrust, perhaps, at Fray Martín) and had never preached to them nor confessed them. He praised the Indians' fear of God and seems to have considered that their piety exceeded in many respects that of Spaniards.[13] In order to catch the imagination of the Indians, whose souls he desired to capture, he would one day write a play in Nahuatl, in the form of a dialogue between the archangel Gabriel and the Virgin Mary. The archangel was depicted presenting the Virgin with letters from patriarchs in limbo asking her to receive her ambassadors. He was the first Spanish cleric to be able to preach in Nahuatl and was offered the bishopric of Michoacán, which, however, he declined.[14]

Fuensalida was the second-in-command of this remarkable expedition. He was a friend of Cortés and supported his cause in his *residencia* (judicial inquiry), defending him against the accusations of, for example, the Dominican Fray Tomás de Ortiz, who, like most members of his order, was an opponent of the captain-general.[15]

Of the other friars, the most interesting was Fray Toribio de Paredes, who was born in Benavente and took that place as his name before assuming the name Motolinía, which signified "poor man" in Nahuatl—he apparently heard himself being so referred to. He was a clever, passionate, and noble individual, who expressed his admiration for old Mexico's grandeur but his repulsion for its religion. His walk made a great impression on him: "Some of the villages [in New Spain]," he said, "are on the tops of mountains, others are on the floors of valleys, so religious people are obliged to climb up into the clouds and at times they must descend into the abyss. Since the country is rough, and because the humidity causes it to be covered in mud in many places, there are slippery places where it is easy to fall."[16] Motolinía wrote extensively of his experiences, and both his *Memoriales* and his *Historia* remain of great value in depicting whatever he was an eyewitness to.[17]

The other Franciscans included the aged Francisco de Soto, the austere Fray Martín de la Coruña, the able Fray Juan Suárez, who became the first guardian of the monastery of Huejotzingo, Fray Antonio de Ciudad Rodrigo, Fray García de Cisneros, who was the inspiration for the imaginative college of Tlatelolco, the jurist Fray Francisco Jiménez, and two lay brothers, Fray Andrés de Córdoba and Fray Juan de Palos. These were great men who took the lead to ensure that New Spain became a fine province of Christianity.

The twelve walked up barefoot to Mexico-Tenochtitlan. Cortés, however, had roads swept for them, and huts were built whenever they wanted to sleep. The journey was disagreeable because the weather was hot and they were always crossing ravines or streams, while mosquitoes and snakes did not relax their attacks. These Franciscans went first to Tlaxcala and then, in mid-June, were received in Mexico-Tenochtitlan by Cortés on his knees, a gesture that much impressed the old Mexican rulers, such as Cuauhtémoc, who saw it. When they arrived, the twelve naturally attached themselves to the three other Franciscans who were already in the capital.

Soon after they arrived, the Franciscans held a general meeting. Probably all fifteen Franciscans then in New Spain attended. They agreed to build four monasteries—in Mexico, Texcoco, Tlaxcala, and Huejotzingo—for which they would obtain the necessary financial support from the captain-general. Each would have four friars, and each would dominate both teaching and converting over a large territory.[18] These friars had already engaged in formal conversations with Mexican priests, hoping to convert them. The latter had answered: "Is it not enough that we have lost? That our way of living has been lost? That we have been annihilated? Do with us as you please. That is what we answer, all that we reply to your words, O our Lords!"[19]

The only texts available describing how this early instruction was carried out are the sermons preached by the twelve Franciscans and some conversations reported by Fray Bernardino de Sahagún in his Florentine codex. The catechism proper is missing but the preliminary discourses are interesting. The friars said to the Mexican priests:

Do not believe that we are gods. Fear not, we are men, as you are. We are merely the messengers of a great lord called the Holy Father who is the spiritual head of the world and who is filled with pain and sadness by the state of your souls. Yours are souls which He has charged us to seek out and to save. We desire nothing better and, for that reason, we bring you the book of the Holy Scripture which contains the word of the only true God, the Lord of Heaven whom you have never known. That is why we are here. We do not seek gold nor silver nor precious stones. We seek only your health.

You, on the other hand, say that you have a god whose worship has been taught you by your ancestors and your Kings: Is that not so? You have a multitude of gods, each with his own function. And you yourself recognize that those gods have deceived you. You insult them when you are unhappy, calling them whores and fools. And what they demand of you, in sacrifice, is your blood, your heart. The images [of those sacrifices] are loathsome. On the other hand, the true and universal God our Lord Creator and dispenser of being and of life . . . has a character different from your gods. He does not deceive. He does not lie. He hates no one. He despises no one. . . . He is the essence of love, compassion and mercy . . . Being God, He has no beginning and no end, for He is eternal. He created heaven and earth, and hell. He created for us all the men in the world and also all the devils whom you hold to be gods.

The Mexican priests replied by saying that it seemed unjust to call on them to abandon ceremonies and rites that their ancestors had praised and held to be good. They were not yet learned enough to discuss the propositions of the Franciscans. But they wanted to call together their priests and discuss the matter. They did so. But these priests "were greatly troubled and felt sad and fearful and did not answer." Next day, they returned and the leaders said that they were very surprised to hear the Franciscans say that their gods were not gods, for their ancestors had always thought them so, had worshipped them as such, and had taught their descendants to honor them with sacrifices and ceremonies. It could be a folly to set aside ancient laws, which had been introduced by the first inhabitants of these places. The priests thought that it would be impossible to persuade the older men to abandon their old customs. They thought that "if the people were told that their gods were not gods, there would be a popular uprising. They repeated that it was difficult enough to have to admit defeat and they would prefer to die rather than have to give up their gods."[20]

In 1525, Tzintla, the indigenous monarch in Tzintsuntzan, begged Fray Martín de Valencia to send him some friars. He did so, under Fray Martín de la Coruña, though Tzintla must have been shocked at Fray Martín's insistence on destroying his temples and his idols.

This was a harsh time. Christian opinion was divided. Several friars were optimistic about the possibilities of conversion, generous, and patient, such as Pedro de Gante and Motolinía. Others, like the first Dominican to come to New Spain, Fray Tomás de Ortiz, had opposing views. Fray Tomás testified to the Council of the Indies: "The Indians are incapable of learning . . . They exercise none of the humane arts or industries . . . The older they are, the worse they behave. About the age of ten or twelve, they seem to have the elements of civilisation but, later, they become like brute beasts . . . God has never created a race more full of vice . . . The Indians are more stupid than asses."[21] What seems evident, however, is that all the main orders—the Augustinians as well as the Dominicans and Franciscans—were allies of the Crown in their frequent clashes with *encomenderos*.[22]

In 1525, Peter Martyr wrote: "To tell the truth we hardly know what decision to make. Should the Indians be declared free and we without any right to exact labour of them, without their work being paid? Competent people are divided on this point and we hesitate. It is chiefly the Dominican order who, by their writings, drive us to an adverse decision. They argue that it would be better, and would offer better security for both the bodily and spiritual good of the Indians, to assign them permanently and by hereditary title to certain masters . . . It may be shown by many examples that we should not consent to give them their liberty [for] these barbarians have plotted the destruction of Christians wherever they could."[23]

The frame of all these Christian activities was, of course, ultimately provided by Rome. Unusual things were occurring there at that time. Thus Pope Adrian VI, the last non-Italian pope till John Paul II, reached the Vatican only on August 29, 1522. His first consistory caused astonishment when it expressed the hope that the Christian Princes could unite against the Ottoman Turks. Then he turned to the Curia. He spoke as if he thought that in all the palaces of the cardinals, iniquity reigned. He urged those cardinals to be content with an annual income of 6,000 ducats and generally rebuked the way of living of the Roman court.[24]

Alas, in December, the Ottomans captured the fortress of the knights of Saint John at Rhodes. The grand master was forced to surrender. Where would the Turks stop? The question seemed urgent. All the same, the states of Germany were reluctant to help. Adrian exclaimed, "I should have died happy if I had united the Christian Princes to withstand our enemy." He added, "Woe to Princes who do not employ the sovereignty conferred on them by God in promoting his glory, and defending the people of His election, but abuse it in internecine strife."[25] Adrian continued in that style. For example, in January 1523, he was denouncing Luther and his extraordinary posture in Germany: "We cannot even think of anything so incredible that so great, so pious a nation should allow an apostate from the Catholic faith which for years he has preached, to seduce it from the way pointed out by the Saviour and his Apostles and sealed by the blood of so many martyrs."[26]

The swift reform of the Church was not to be: Adrian succumbed to a harsh illness in September 1523. On this occasion, the cardinals made no mistake about their choice of his successor. Thirty-five cardinals quickly assembled in the Sistine Chapel, the French ones arriving in riding clothes. Who would be the next successor to Saint Peter? Giulio de' Medici, a son of Lorenzo de' Medici, was the favorite, as he had been three years before. The conclave continued for several weeks. On November 19, Cardinal Medici was indeed elected, as Clement VII. The Duke of Sessa, the son-in-law of the Gran Capitán, who was now imperial ambassador in Rome, commented a shade optimistically: "The Pope is entirely your Majesty's creature. So great is your Majesty's power that you can change stones into obedient children."[27]

Neither Adrian nor Clement had a serious concern for the New World. They had to approve the nomination of bishops and Franciscan and other missions there. But they did not see yet the vast opportunities opening up there for Spain, for Europe, and for Christendom. Their nominations to sees had, of course, political consequences, as Charles the Emperor knew better than anyone.

5

Charles at Valladolid, 1522–1523

Here people believe that His Majesty wants to reform his council
and his household.

MARTÍN DE SALINAS TO FRANCISCO DE SALAMANCA, TREASURER
OF THE ARCHDUKE FERDINAND, VALLADOLID, SEPTEMBER 7, 1522

Charles the Emperor was in Valladolid from September 1522 to August
1523, an unusual quiescence for a monarch used to travel, who grew up in
a world of journeys in which his predecessors, Isabel and Fernando, had
lived all their reigns. Charles spent most of this time in the rambling
Enríquez palace, though twice, in September 1522 and in April 1523, he
went down to Tordesillas to see his mother, the doomed Juana, in the
convent of Santa Clara. Once or twice, too, he went for a retreat from the
world to the celebrated monastery of the Bernardines (Cistercians) at
Valbuena del Duero, a day's ride to the east.

Charles had set about reforming the administration of his realm, first
reordering the number of officials attached to the Council of State, which
was principally concerned with foreign affairs. That council in 1522 depended on an inner caucus headed by Gattinara, who was the motor of
most of the changes.[1] Other members were Charles's gallant friend Henry
of Nassau, who was great chamberlain in the Low Countries. Though lighthearted and charming personally, he was also responsible for introducing
the rigid formalities of Burgundian ceremony into the Spanish court. Nassau had commanded the imperial army in 1521 and then accompanied
Charles in 1522 to Spain, where he served as President of the new Spanish
finance council. Despite becoming enormously fat, he married a Spanish

heiress, Mencía de Mendoza, Marquess de Cenete, one of the two sisters about whom the governor of Cuba, Diego Velázquez, would joke with his friends in Santiago de Cuba by saying he would one day wed. The ceremony was a royal occasion in Burgos in June 1524. Mencía was very well connected as well as very rich and had a famous salon in the Low Countries in the 1530s, encouraging Flemish painters and writers. The historian Oviedo spoke of her warmly as "very cultivated, knowledgeable and gracious, an echo of the marquess her father whom no knight in Spain of the time could equal in good manners and benign disposition."[2]

Charles consulted two other Burgundians frequently: Charles de Poupet, Lord of Chaulx, and Gérard de la Plaine, Lord of La Roche. Poupet had been born in Burgundy's golden age, in 1460. He had served Philip the Handsome in Spain but most of his life was spent in Flanders. He was back in Spain to negotiate with Cardinal Cisneros, the Regent, and then Adrian VI, when he had just been named pope. Poupet had already seen the positive qualities of the great Cortés.[3] He had been for a time a preceptor, as well as a member of the secret council of Charles.

The Lord of La Roche, Gérard de la Plaine, who had been in Germany to confirm Charles in his imperial title, had been in England as ambassador and would soon join Henry of Nassau on the Castilian finance committee.[4] He was a grandson of Margaret of Austria's great friend Laurent de Gorrevod—who had been the lucky contractor of the African slave trade to the Spanish Indies in 1518—and was also a member of the Council of State.

The two Spanish members of the inner circle of Charles in early 1522 were Bishop Ruiz de la Mota, a native of Burgos of converso origin, and Juan Manuel. Ruiz de la Mota had been chaplain and preacher to Queen Isabel and then in Flanders to the emperor Maximilian. He had been a tutor of sorts to the emperor Charles, too. Back in Spain, he had at a meeting of the *cortes* in Santiago coined the phrase "the new world of gold" to describe New Spain. Named bishop of the then rich diocese of Palencia, Ruiz de la Mota had little opportunity to enjoy being on the supreme council of the empire, for he caught a fever in England on his way back to Spain and died in September 1522. Some alleged that he was poisoned. That was a setback for the interests of the Indies, for Ruiz de la Mota had a first cousin who was with Cortés at Tenochtitlan.[5]

Juan Manuel had much property in Spain, including the fortress of

Segovia. He was son of a counselor of the same name who had worked for Kings Juan II and Enrique IV of Castile. He was a bastard member of the royal family. His first important post had been as ambassador of the Catholic Kings in 1495 to Philip the Handsome in Flanders, who married Juana la Loca. He worked to prevent the growth of French influence on the Habsburgs. He accompanied Philip to Spain in 1506 and was the architect of that Prince's triumph there. Then he remained in Flanders throughout the childhood of Charles. Juan Manuel played his cards so successfully that he became the first Spaniard to be given the Order of the Fleece. His patience in Flanders was rewarded: From 1520, he was imperial ambassador in Rome, where he helped to ensure the papacy of Adrian of Utrecht, with whom he was, however, on bad terms. Charles the Emperor asked Juan Manuel to return to Spain; he did so in February 1523 and began to serve his old masters on the Council of Finance. The chronicler Jerónimo Zurita wrote of him that he was both "valiant and astute and, although small of stature, full of imagination and a great wit, very discreet and a great courtier, of a resolution and sharpness so alive."[6]

The Council of State, which affected all Charles's kingdoms in the 1520s, had upon it in 1519 six Flemings or Burgundians—Gattinara, Gorrevod, Plaine, Lannoy, Henry of Nassau, and Poupet—or seven if one adds to the list the confessor-counselor Glapion. There were just two Castilians, Ruiz de la Mota and Juan Manuel. It is easy to understand that this large number of "bureaucrats from Brussels" must have seemed an imposition in Spain. Even the secretary was a Saxon: Jan Hannart, who had worked for Maximilian as well as for Charles. In 1524, he was accused of corruption and replaced by a clever Burgundian, Jean Alemán, sieur de Bouclans, who assumed the role in 1521 of controller-general of the realm of Aragon, which gave him responsibility for Naples.[7] Charming and intelligent, dispatching much work with alacrity, Alemán made himself indispensable to both Gattinara and to Charles in 1522, when the former was away many months in Calais. Alemán and Gattinara had both served their time at the *parlement* of Dôle, the former as a mere clerk, the latter as President. They both emerged from Franche-Comté, which gave so many great public servants to the Habsburg family. By 1526, Alemán seems to have become already more a rival of Gattinara than a protégé.

This group of men, with the two secretaries, met every other Monday and was Charles's best source of advice. He would also see the members on other occasions, including privately.

Castile itself was at that time governed by a series of councils, of which the Council of Castile (Consejo Real de Castilla) was the most important.[8] It met every Friday, as it had done in the time of King Fernando. Whereas the Flemings dominated the Council of State, which concerned itself with foreign policy, the Council of Castile was concerned with the detailed administration of Castile. It constituted the real government of the country—a cabinet, as it would be termed in a later age. The President in 1522 was the bishop of Granada, Antonio de Rojas. He came from an important Castilian family that had members in Cuba and later in Peru. Antonio de Rojas had been preceptor of the Emperor's brother, the infante Fernando, whom his grandfather and namesake, the King of Aragon, had seemed to favor as his heir. In 1522, he was prominent among those seeking, in Gattinara's shadow, to improve the effectiveness of the government. He earned superlative attention in a report made by the reliable Extremeño Galíndez de Carvajal, who wrote in 1522 that Rojas was a faithful public servant, with clean hands and a zeal for doing justice. Sometimes Rojas was impatient and indignant, but Galíndez himself commented, "I believe one could not find a better man for the work which he has."[9]

From 1523 or so, there were seven other councils: that of war, which met every alternate Wednesday except when the country was actually in conflict; the Council of the Inquisition; of the military orders; of the *Contaduría Mayor* (finance); and that of Aragon. There was a council for raising money as well as spending it. The latter, the Council of Finance, was new. Most of these bodies had in the 1520s some Flemish membership: For example, the president of the Council of Finance was Henry of Nassau. (The Finance Office was for raising; the accountant's office was for spending.) Finally, there was the Council of the Indies. This committee had previously comprised a group of councillors of the Council of Castile managed by Rodríguez de Fonseca, the omni-competent bishop of Burgos, but it was now more formally independent. The date when this body began to have a separate function is not quite clear, but by 1520, something close to such an institution was in existence.[10] All the same, it never lost its close relation to the Council of Castile.

The first president of the Council of the Indies was not Rodríguez de

Fonseca, who for so long had been the Crown's "Minister for the Indies without the name,"[11] but the general of the Dominicans, Fray García de Loaisa, who had succeeded Jean Glapion as confessor of the Emperor. He was also bishop of Burgo de Osma, a bleak town with a fine cathedral whose splendid grille had been recently paid for by the cardinal archbishop of Toledo, Alonso de Fonseca.

The other members of the Council of the Indies were: Peter Martyr de Anglería, the Italian humanist who in the 1490s had educated so many members of the Castilian nobility and had always had a consuming inter- est in the Indies, being, on his own insistence, the Vatican's chief informant on the subject in Spain; Luis Cabeza de Vaca, bishop of the Canary Islands; and Gonzalo Maldonado, bishop of Ciudad Real. Dr. Diego Beltrán was the only full-time councillor. It was these men, with Francisco de los Cobos as secretary, who took the critical decisions in respect of Spain's American empire. They named the governors—later the Viceroys—approved new expeditions (*entradas*), and decided on the salaries of judges. They ap- pointed minor officials, listened to complaints, and heard appeals. They gave themselves sinecures and benefits in the New World, though no mem- ber of the council had any firsthand idea of what the Indies were really like. Francisco de los Cobos was chief "founder" of the Indies, an office that brought him a helpful salary. Equally concerned with foundries, Gattinara, the imperial chancellor, collaborated with enthusiasm from the begin- ning.[12]

Of these men, the President was of course the most important. García de Loaisa is elusive, and there is no biography of him.[13] Gattinara, who was not a good judge of men, had apparently suggested him for his office.[14] García de Loaisa came from Talavera de la Reina, where his father, Pedro, had been a councillor; and he had studied in Salamanca, where he became *corregidor.* His mother was a Mendoza, though it does not seem that she derived from the main branch of that great family. García de Loaisa entered the Dominican order early in his life. He became prior of Saint Thomas in Ávila, with the exquisite if simple church in which there had been already for ten years the delicate white marble sepulchre of Charles's uncle, the in- fante Juan, the only son of Fernando and Isabel. This beautiful tomb was the masterpiece of the Florentine Domenico Fancelli. The first *inquisidor general,* Torquemada, is also buried there (he founded the monastery). García de Loaisa was general of the order by 1518.[15] His subsequent success seems to have derived from his ability to win over rebel *comuneros* in 1521–22.[16] He was offered the archbishopric of Granada and refused it, presumably because it was too complicated a post. He settled, improbably, for Burgo de Osma, which was then a rich diocese. But he was the chief preacher at court from 1523.

A tranquil, discreet, and far from adventurous man, García de Loaisa had reprimanded his colleague, Fray Pedro de Córdoba, for allowing the famous sermons of Montesinos in Santo Domingo. For the presidency of the Council of the Indies, he would be paid 200,000 maravedís a year. He had been for a time also *inquisidor general,* when he aspired to reduce the Inquisition to its medieval size.[17] He lived at court, and the meetings of the Council of the Indies would be in his lodging there. Of course, García de Loaisa's work as the Emperor's confessor enabled him to be well-informed. The splendid Dr. Pastor wrote of him that, though he was a great ecclesiastic and a man of "high moral character, being full of energy and loyalty to the Emperor," he was "wanting in the qualities of statesmanship." He showed "a lack of consideration and a rigid hardness . . . which gave general offence." He had no tact. He would show his vehement nature even to the pope. That was in the future. In 1524, he seemed an honest man, a contrast with his predecessor, Rodríguez de Fonseca. Still, he was a churchman, selected at a time when bishops were thought to be the right men to rule empires.

García de Loaisa was firm to the point of intolerance about Protestantism. He was in no way an Erasmian and so found himself in opposition to such shining lights of the age as the humane archbishop Alonso de Manrique de Lara, who succeeded him as inquisitor in 1523, and Alfonso de Valdés, the Erasmian secretary to Gattinara. He was nevertheless brave in relation to his master, the Emperor. Thus he wrote to Charles deploring the fact that he, the Emperor, "had lowered himself to try to persuade heretics that they take account of their errors . . . And if they just want to be clogs, Your Majesty closes his eyes because you don't have force at your disposal to punish them."[18] He later reflected about the Reformation: "Force alone suppressed the revolt against the King [the war of *comuneros*]. Force alone will suppress the revolt against God."[19] He once urged Charles "to raise himself from the deep pits of sin to embark on a new book of conscience."

The bishop continued harshly: "You should rest assured that God gives no one a kingdom without laying on him an even greater duty than on ordinary men to love Him and to obey his commands. . . . In your person indolence is perpetually at war with fame. I pray that God's grace will be with you in government and that you will be able to overcome your natural enemies, good living and waste of time."[20]

Charles later wrote of García de Loaisa, perhaps appropriately in view of these last comments: "He would do better to go back to his clerical duties rather than live at court. If his health were not so bad, he would have been outstanding in politics. He has always advised me very well. But his feeble health and his inability to get on with the cardinal of Toledo [Tavera, for many years president of the Council of Castile] are two great drawbacks."[21] Yet García de Loaisa had two children by the saintly María de la Torre.[22]

Though García de Loaisa had never been to the Indies, he was not quite isolated from the reality of imperial life, since his first cousin, Fray Francisco García de Loaisa, knight of San Juan and till recently ambassador to the Ottoman Empire, was even in 1522 preparing to lead an expedition to the Straits of Magellan and then the Moluccas. His purpose was to seize the Moluccas for Spain from Portugal. The pope had decreed, and the two governments had agreed, in 1494, that the world to the west of the line of the Treaty of Tordesillas should be given to Spain, and that to the east to Portugal. But there had been no discussion of where the west was to begin in the world of the Far East. Spain now believed that the west was theirs, the Far East included. Francisco García de Loaisa wanted to prove the point, and an expedition set off from Corunna on July 24, 1525, with seven ships, one of which was commanded by the immortal Elcano, who three years before had returned in command of Magellan's *Victoria*. The journey did not prosper. But at least it gave the President some personal knowledge of some of the affairs over which he was to preside.[23] Meantime, some discussions were held in Valladolid about the dividing line with Portugal. Peter Martyr reported them with his customary competence.[24]

The other members of this first Council of the Indies are less important. Luis Cabeza de Vaca, from Jaén, had been, while in the Netherlands, the emperor Charles's instructor in reading and writing Spanish, as well as in the history of Spain. An Andalusian and related to the resolute explorer

Álvar Núñez Cabeza de Vaca, he returned to Spain with Charles in 1517. He seems always to have been trusted by the Emperor, but apart from later hearing of the life of the Indies from his cousin Álvar, he had no direct personal connection with it. But his grandfather Pedro de Vera had been the conqueror of Grand Canary. Thus it was appropriate that he should be named bishop of the Canaries in 1523. He was one of the few Spanish bishops to live in his diocese.

Another member of the Council of the Indies was Gonzalo Maldonado, of Ciudad Rodrigo, a protégé of Alonso de Fonseca, who secured his nomination as bishop of his native town in 1525. He was used by Charles the Emperor in several unexpected missions, for example, being sent from Parma in 1529 to seek a variety of special financial support from Genoese bankers. Such a role was not then inconsistent with that of a provincial bishop.[25]

The last member of this first Council of the Indies was Peter Martyr, the humanist from Lake Maggiore. He had been called after Saint Peter the Martyr, who had been canonized after his murder in a place somewhere between Como and Milan in 1252 and had been the object of a cult in fifteenth-century Lombardy. Peter Martyr descended from the ancient counts of Anglería, but his branch of the family was unsuccessful. Count Giovanni Borromeo, a rich man from Milan, paid for his education. In the late 1470s, Martyr went to Rome and worked for several cardinals before he became secretary to Francesco Negro, governor of Rome. He became friendly with Cardinal Ascanio Sforza, the richest cardinal after Borgia. He was then taken up as a brilliant young intellectual by Iñigo López de Mendoza, son of the great Marquess of Santillana, who had come to Rome as Spanish ambassador. Martyr went back to Spain with López de Mendoza.

In 1487, he gave some lectures in classical literature at Salamanca, and new friends begged him to remain. He agreed, and Cardinal Sforza asked him to send regular letters about what was going on in Spain. He did so, writing to the pope as well as to Sforza. Peter Martyr's letters, which talked very interestingly of Columbus and other adventurers in the New World, were eagerly awaited in Rome, their arrival constituting a literary event of the first magnitude. The King of Naples would request a copy from Cardinal Sforza, and Pope Leo X would have them read out at dinner. Martyr wrote in Latin, which he treated as a living language, though he sometimes used Italian or Spanish words, thereby incurring the mockery of his audience.[26] He seems at some point to have lost the ear of López de Mendoza, his first Spanish patron, who began to think Peter Martyr verbose. But he continued to lecture with success at Salamanca,[27] and he taught classics to young scions of the nobility in Spain: A list of his pupils was a who's who of the up-and-coming.[28] Martyr became chaplain of the royal household and then ambassador to the Ottoman sultan, who sympathized with the Muslims expelled from Granada and threatened to treat similarly the Christians in the Levant, not to speak of the Franciscans of Palestine. Martyr seems tactfully to have persuaded the sultan of the benefit of good relations with Spain.

Given that success, it was not surprising that the royal secretary, Miguel Pérez de Almazán—a converso from Aragon who became secretary for international affairs to Isabel and Fernando, and was a favorite of the latter—should ask Peter Martyr to seek to promote similar good relations between King Fernando and King Philip. After the death of Fernando, however, Martyr wrote hostilely to Rome of the austere Cardinal Cisneros.[29] He was later, under the emperor Charles, as hostile to the Flemings as any Spaniard, though he admired Gattinara. He was among the first men in Spain to realize the importance of Cortés's conquests. Later, Peter Martyr acted as interpreter to Adrian of Utrecht—from Latin into Spanish—when he was the Regent in Spain. Perhaps he hoped for a reward from Adrian when he became pope. But Adrian did not give presents.

From 1523, Peter Martyr enjoyed the benefits of the archpriestship of Ocaña, one of Queen Isabel's favorite towns, about forty miles south of Madrid. (An archpriest is a senior secular priest.) He spoke of Jamaica as if he had been married to it: "My spouse," he called it. "I am united to that charming nymph," he commented, adding, "Nowhere in the world is there such an enjoyable climate."[30] One supposes that he had talked to those who had been there.

Martyr had endless curiosity. He would ask people with experience of the Indies to dine with him. "I have often invited this young Vespucci [Amerigo's nephew] to my table," he wrote, "not only because he has real talent but because he has taken notes of all that he has observed during his journey." "Cabot frequents my house," he recorded, "and I have sometimes had him to my table."[31] He was referring to Sebastian Cabot, who had become *piloto mayor* (chief pilot) in 1518, in succession to Díaz de Solís. Martyr's fellow Italian, for years a professor at Salamanca, Marineo Siculo, said that, when he dined with Martyr, he observed the beautiful chairs with much enthusiasm, for they were of a "perfection and unequalled art." He had gold and silver in abundance, and also manuscripts and other books all piled up with some negligence.[32]

Francisco de los Cobos was the secretary to the Council of the Indies from its beginning. Just as interested in his own financial prosperity as the late bishop Rodríguez de Fonseca had been, he had little real interest in the New World, over whose fate he was such a powerful influence.[33] He was the essential cabinet secretary to Charles V—meticulous, dry, competent, interested in women, unimaginative. He was born in 1490, and his father was Diego de los Cobos Tovilla, who fought in the last battles of the war against Granada. Oviedo, in his *Quinquagenas,* wrote that the family originally did not have a penny.

García de Loaisa wrote to the Emperor, "[Cobos] knows how to compensate for your carelessness in dealing with people, . . . He serves you with the highest loyalty and he is extraordinarily prudent, he does not waste your time saying clever things, as others do, and he never gossips about his master and he is the best-liked man we know."[34]

A modern historian wisely wrote that Cobos was "intelligent and resourceful, an indefatigable worker, an expert diplomat, charming to talk to, with some pretensions to be a humanist, a good writer (of letters), but, at the same time, hard, vengeful, and above all greedy for gain."[35] In Cobos's own time, López de Gómara recalled that he was "fat, good-looking, merry and gay and so pleasant in conversation." He did think, though, that Cobos "was diligent & secretive . . . he was very fond of playing the card game *primera* and of conversation with women." He never seems to have read anything: he never mentioned Erasmus in his letters, in which there is no discussion of any of the great issues of the day.

For Las Casas, he was "good-looking and well-built." That great friar added that he was "soft in speech and voice."[36] Bernardo Navagero, the second Venetian ambassador of that surname, thought: "Cobos is very affable and very skillful. The greatest difficulty is getting to see him but, once you are in his office, his manner is so engaging that everyone goes away completely satisfied."[37]

Cobos had gained his entrée to the court through Diego Vela Alide, the husband of his aunt, Mayor de los Cobos: Vela Alide was the accountant and secretary to Queen Isabel. From the beginning, Cobos's rise was steady. By 1503, he was named a royal notary at Perpignan. He became chief accountant (*contador mayor*) of Granada in 1508. That year he became a councillor of Úbeda, which remained his headquarters in Andalusia.

Cobos was in Brussels for most of the time of Cisneros's regency. Oviedo thought that it was Ugo de Urriés, Charles's secretary for Aragonese affairs, who introduced him to the all-important Chièvres, with whom he worked.[38] He became formally a secretary to the King on January 1, 1517, receiving 278,000 maravedís as salary, a sum greater than that of other secretaries. Charles wrote to Cisneros saying that he had appointed Cobos "to take and keep a record of our income and finances and what is paid out and consigned to our treasurers and other persons, that all is done in conformity with what you have established and discussed." Cobos took responsibility for the Indies after Charles's return to Spain in September 1517, in truth succeeding Lope de Conchillos.

Las Casas describes him as "surpassing all the others [among the Spanish secretaries] because M. de Chièvres [Croÿ] became fonder of him than of any of the others, since in truth he was more gifted than them, and he was very attractive in face and figure . . . He was also soft of voice and speech and so he was likeable. He was likewise greatly helped by the information & experience he had in all the years of the kingdom."[39]

By September 1519, Cobos became a Knight of Santiago; by November of that important year—important in New Spain, that is—he was named founder and inspector of Yucatán. In May 1522, this appointment was extended to cover Cuba, Culiacán, and San Juan de Ulloa (New Spain). Meantime, in late 1521 Cobos was named commander of León in the Order of Santiago, in succession to Gutierre Gómez de Fuensalida, who, however, would retain the income from that office for his lifetime. That was a useful sinecure with money attached. Cobos also made a good marriage with María de Mendoza y Pimentel, daughter of Juan Hurtado de Mendoza, count of Rivadavia, in October 1522, soon after Charles's return. She brought a dowry of 4 million maravedís. A million of this came from the town of Hornillos, near Valladolid, next to the rich Jeronymite monastery of La Mejorada. María was a relation of the Count-Duke of

Benavente, of Velasco the constable, and of Enríquez the admiral of Castile.[40]

By 1522, Cobos had begun to have serious responsibilities in the Indies though he never went near them. He had a license to sell African slaves in 1524, which he leased. It was Cobos, founder, to whom the emperor Charles V gave Cortés's famous silver phoenix; sadly, he had it melted down. In 1527, he was named by the King to be founder for the entire coast of the Gulf of Mexico from Florida to Pánuco and from Darien to the Gulf of Venezuela. In November 1527, Charles gave Cobos and the questionable Dr. Beltrán the right to export another two hundred slaves each to the New World and, the next month, they agreed with Pedro de Alvarado to export six hundred Indian slaves to work the mines in Guatemala, each to pay for a third of the slaves at 10 pesos a head and share in the profits.

Member of the Council of Castile in 1529, commander of León in succession to Fernando de Toledo, and from then on, with Granvelle (Nicholas Perronet de Granvelle, Keeper of the Seals), Cobos was soon the Emperor's chief adviser. He had an accumulated annual income of 6,688,200 maravedís, a very large sum for that date: Judges in the supreme court in Mexico (the *audiencia*) were at that time paid only 150,000 maravedís a year.[41] He was building a family of assistants to whom he was as loyal as they were to him: for example, Alonso de Idiáquez, a mediocre individual whom Cobos trusted; his nephew, Juan Vázquez de Molina; Juan de Samano, longtime co-secretary of the Council of the Indies; and Francisco de Eraso, an aristocrat whom the Duke of Alba called "cousin." To them, Cobos was *el patrón* who dominated the administration. The most interesting of these men was Samano, who in 1524 had been named chief notary of the government of New Spain. Because of Cobos's frequent absences, he was in fact the real secretary of the Council of the Indies for more than thirty years (1524–58). But Samano was uninspired. How strange that that should have been so when the most original empire in the world was being created!

Cobos was soon also the controlling figure in the new Council of the Treasury, which had been founded in 1523. From then on, he was busy outmaneuvering the chancellor, Gattinara.

His money enabled him to begin to commission great buildings, for example, the chapel of San Salvador at Úbeda, designed by Andrés de Van-

delvira, the gifted pupil of Siloé and the future architect of the cathedral at
Jaén.

He owed his success to his decisive personality, his charm, and his indefatigable industry. Many years later, Charles wrote of him to Prince Philip:
"I hold Cobos to be loyal. Up till now he has had little passion in his life. I
think that his wife bores him and that explains why he has begun to have
many affairs [such as that with the pretty countess of Novellara in Man-
tua] . . . He has experience of all my affairs and is very well informed about
them . . . He is growing older and is now easier to manage . . . The danger
with him is his ambitious wife. Do not give him more influence than I have
sanctioned in my instructions . . . above all, do not yield to any temptation
he may throw in your path. He is an old libertine and he may try and
arouse the same tastes in you. Cobos is a very rich man, for he draws a great
deal from bullion in the Indies, as also from his slate mines and other
sources . . . Do not let [those appointments] become hereditary in his family. When I die, it would be a good moment to recover those rights for the
Crown. He has great gifts for the management of finance. Circumstances,
not he, nor I, are to blame for the deplorable condition of our revenues."

Another essential adviser of Emperor Charles in those years was Cardinal Juan Tavera, archbishop of Toledo and for many years President of the
Council of Castile. He was born in Toro in 1472, and his father, Arias Pardo,
was a Gallego. He was named a canon of Seville in 1505 and in November
of that year became a member of the general council of the Inquisition. In
1507, Tavera was President of the town council of Seville, and he sustained
his uncle Deza in his local disputes. He was the protégé par excellence of
Deza, who helped him. Bishop of Burgo de Osma till 1523, member of the
royal Council of Castile already with Fernando the Catholic, in 1524 he was
named archbishop of Santiago, where he remained for ten years. A man
learned in law, Tavera was rarely in Santiago but lived mostly at court. That
did not prevent him giving benefices and other prizes to his relations,
which infuriated the local clergy of Santiago. Clever, if taciturn and narrow
in his approach, he opposed most of Charles's universal policies. He became a cardinal in 1531. He was the chief of the *Africanistas* in the councils
of Charles, hoping for conquests in Africa rather than in the Indies. After
Manrique de Lara fell from favor in 1529, Tavera took most of the decisions
in respect of the Inquisition, whose chief or general he would eventually
become.[42]

Tavera was an efficient adminstrator. When later he became chief inquisitor he cut the number of informants (*familiares*), demanded regular
hours of work for the employees, concerned himself with the need to ensure good food for the prisoners, and limited investigations of purity of
blood to the children and grandchildren of suspects.[43]

Dr. Diego Beltrán, the one permanent official on the Council of the Indies and also a councillor from 1523, is a more shadowy figure. He was
probably of converso origin.[44] He belonged to the Fernandine party at
court in 1506, and his first mission seems to have been to act as judge in respect of an enquiry into the conduct of the *corregidor* of Granada in 1506.
Earlier, in 1504, he began to work in the Casa de la Contratación, the essential institution of Spanish commerce in the New World. Beltrán moved
to Brussels, along with other ambitious civil servants, and then went back
to Castile to prepare for the coming of Charles, in whose Council of Castile
he figured as early as 1517. He was in Spain during the dark days of the war
of the *comuneros*, between 1519 and 1522, but he was considered a dangerous individual who was said to have sold state secrets to the count of Benavente. Beltrán was even supposed to have lent money to the *comuneros*.[45]
But all the same, Peter Martyr evidently thought highly of him, asking, "In
the Spanish world, who is there more exquisite?"[46] In March 1523, he became the first salaried member of the Council of the Indies. He was, it
turned out, a great gambler, for which reason he needed much money. Dr.
Lorenzo Galíndez de Carvajal, an older and much more austere courtier,
wrote of him harshly: "He is certainly cultivated [*tiene buenas letras*] and
he is sharp. Yet his defects are so many that, even publicly, one could say
that there is not enough paper to write them down." He added, "Neither in
his birth nor in his way of living, nor in his habits, nor in his faithfulness to
the secrecy of the Council, is he worthy to be a counsellor of a great lord,
much less that of a great King and Emperor."[47] In fact, Beltrán was already
corrupt, for twenty years later, when his career was being investigated, he
confessed to having had financial dealings with Cortés. Cortés at one point
before 1522 had needed assistance in the council and perhaps Beltrán
helped to achieve it, for payment, which the conqueror of Mexico was usually ready to make.[48]

Other constant advisers in the shadow of Charles's court was a group of
bankers known as the four evangelists. These were Juan de Fonseca and
Antonio de Rojas, both archbishops, and Juan de Vozmediano and Alonso

Gutiérrez, both bankers of verve. Alonso Gutiérrez was from Madrid and was treasurer of that city, though he was also apparently a councillor, a *veinticuatro,* of Seville, where he had lived since 1510. He was a converso.[49] He was a *regidor* of Toledo and treasurer of the Casa de Moneda as of the Hermandad, in which capacity he resolved the question of the payment to the knights whose horses were taken by Columbus in La Española in 1493. He was one of those who received the national taxes. He had many minor financial activities, such as being the accountant of the orders of Santiago and Calatrava.[50] He became controller of the income of the order of Calatrava in 1516, and from 1519 to 1522 he was accountant of all the feudal grants. Later he was the link between the court and the Fuggers. He assisted López de Recalde in 1518, selling the license—to old associates of both of them—that he had bought from Gorrevod, to carry four thousand slaves to the New World.[51] He seems to have made money by cheaply buying up possessions confiscated from the *comuneros* after their defeat. In 1523, Gattinara wanted him as treasurer in the new *Consejo de Hacienda,* but he was outmaneuvered, by Cobos probably. He appears to have been chief accountant in 1523. In 1530, Charles described him in a letter to the Empress as being "*muy servydo*";[52] and Charles wrote to him, also in 1530, thanking him for his efforts to find money to send to him. He had a contract with Juan de Vozmediano, the treasurer, and Enciso, which was apparently treated hostilely by Archbishop Tavera.

In 1531, the Inquisition became interested in him.[53] But he remained chief accountant of the order of Calatrava till his death in 1539. He received from that order 350,000 maravedís, of which 1,500 were in cereals, half in wheat, half in barley. The precise influence of Gutiérrez is impossible to judge. But he was always at court, always ready to advance money, and always becoming richer.

One should not conclude that Charles gave up all his time to work and study. His brother Fernando's representative at court, Martín de Salinas, wrote to his treasurer Salamanca in March 1523 that the news at court was that to give entertainment the Emperor devoted a lot of time to playing canes and to jousting; and Cortés in New Spain knew well that rulers danced as well as issued ordinances.[54]

6

Cortés in Power, 1521–1524

Those who have written about your kingdoms in Peru, as well as
the conquest, as writers, they don't write what they saw but what
they heard said.

PEDRO PIZARRO

Meanwhile, in New Spain Cortés ruled from August 1521 until October
1524. He acted as an absolute monarch and an active one. Thus, in early
1522, he sent the oldest member of his expedition, his fellow Medellinés
Rodrigo Rangel, to Veracruz to bring back Pánfilo de Narváez. Narváez,
still a prisoner from his expedition to New Spain in 1520, had talked to
Cristóbal de Tapia, the agent of the friars of La Española and of Bishop
Rodríguez de Fonseca, and assured him that Cortés had not reached the
end of his luck. So he said he should return to Castile and tell the court
what was going on in New Spain. Then Narváez went up to Tenochtitlan.
Cortés received him in Coyoacán well, and Narváez was generous in his
reaction: "The least of the things which you and your valiant soldiers
accomplished in New Spain was defeating me." He added, "Your Excellency
and your soldiers deserve the greatest favours from His Majesty."[1]

Cortés reported to Charles that in his time in Mexico-Tenochtitlan, and
in addition to the several expeditions of discovery and conquest he had inspired, he had found a gunsmith among his followers. This was Francisco
de Mesa of Mairena, Seville, who worked with Rodrigo Martínez, who had
directed Narváez's artillery. He was asked by Cortés to work for him as
early as September 1521, only three weeks after the final victory. They
found copper and tin at Taxco, about eighty miles southwest of Mexico-

Tenochtitlan, and later, iron. At that time, Cortés had thirty-five bronze cannons, seventy-five lombards, and other small guns, many of which had been sent to him since the conquest. For ammunition, he had saltpeter and sulfur, most obtained so remarkably by Francisco de Montaño, an imaginative conquistador from Ciudad Rodrigo who had entered the volcano of Popocatépetl in search of it.[2]

Within a few months of his victory over the Mexica, Cortés was already inspiring other journeys of discovery and conquest. He did this before the news of his triumph had reached Spain and long before the Council of the Indies had pronounced on what it wanted to see in the new empire of New Spain.

First of all, Cortés dispatched his most successful commander, his fellow Medellinés Gonzalo de Sandoval, to Tuxtepec, halfway between Veracruz and Oaxaca, and then to Coatzacoalcos, on the Caribbean coast. Sandoval was a good soldier and a fine horseman whose mount, Motilla, was the best horse in Cortés's army. Still in his teens at the beginning of the campaign against the Mexica in 1519, Sandoval rose to be a superior commander, since Cortés knew that he would always do well what he was asked to do. He was not impetuous and unpredictable, as was Pedro de Alvarado, with all his gifts. Sandoval now had to fight an indigenous monarch with some bowmen at his disposal before he was able to set up a Spanish settlement some twelve miles south of the mouth of the river Coatzacoalcos. This he named Espíritu Santo, after a settlement in Cuba where he had lived.

It seems that this region was populated by Indians who worshipped stone and clay idols for which they had special sanctuaries (*casas diputadas a manera de hermita*). The word *Coatzacoalco* means "the sanctuary of the serpent."[3] The territory was well provided with maize, beans, sweet potatoes, and pumpkins, as well as many tropical fruits, game, and fish.[4] Sandoval divided this newly conquered land between several followers of Cortés: Francisco de Lugo, the Genoese Luis Marín of Sanlúcar, Pedro de Briones, and the chronicler Bernal Díaz del Castillo. These men came from very different parts of Spain: Lugo was an illegitimate son of Alfonso de Lugo, lord of Fuencastín, in northwest Castile, and a distant relation of Diego Velázquez of Cuba; Briones, a native of Salamanca, was one of the few conquistadors in Mexico to have fought in Italy. He had been, Bernal Díaz wrote, sharply, "a good soldier in Italy according to his own account."[5]

Luis Marín's father had been born Francesco Marini, in Genoa, being one of the many bankers from that city to establish themselves in Andalusia at that time, especially in Sanlúcar de Barrameda. Luis Marín had become a close friend of Sandoval during the campaign against the Mexica. A brother of his had been killed. There was also Díaz del Castillo, who would become the great chronicler of the conquest, being a native of Medina del Campo, home of the author of *Amadís de Gaula,* Montalvo, whom Díaz must have known as a child.[6] He had probably been on two expeditions to New Spain before that of Cortés, those of Hernández de Córdoba and of Grijalva.[7] Espíritu Santo, a small place, became a base for the subsequent penetration of Guatemala and Yucatán.[8] Díaz subsequently married a Spanish lady named Teresa Becerra; they settled in Guatemala after Alvarado's conquest of it, and there he planted oranges and wrote his legendary work.[9] The Spaniards who settled there were pleased with the salt, pepper, cotton fabrics, sandals, jade, gold, amber, and large green quetzal feathers that were all to be found in this region.[10]

These conquistadors did not have an easy time. They would approach several pueblos where they assumed that there would be friendly Indians and propose peace—of course on their terms, an offer of vassaldom of the emperor Charles being invariably included. Often they were attacked. Díaz del Castillo was wounded in the throat. Luis Marín returned to Mexico-Tenochtitlan to ask help from Cortés, who sent him back to Coatzacoalcos with thirty soldiers, led by Alonso de Grado from Alcántara, one of the most interesting of Cortés's critics at the earliest stage of his campaign. Bernal Díaz, his companion in 1522, said of him that he was well informed, with good conversation and a fine presence, but "more of a troublemaker than a fighter."[11] He was an *encomendero* in Buenaventura, La Española. Despite his reputation, and despite his constant quarrels with, and punishments by, Cortés, the latter allocated him Techuipo (Isabel), daughter of Montezuma, as a wife.

Having assured himself of the subservience of Coatzacoalcos, Sandoval and his friends set out in the spring of 1523 to conquer what is now the state of Chiapas. They then had twenty-seven horsemen, fifteen crossbowmen, eight musketeers, and a black gunner with a cannon. They led seventy foot soldiers and rather more than that number of native Mexicans, principally from Tlaxcala. There was a good deal of sporadic fighting against

the Chiapenec Indians, who were armed with fire-hardened javelins and
bows and arrows, as well as long lances with cutting edges. These Indians
had good cotton armor, plumes and swords (*macanas*), slings for stones,
and also lassos for catching horses. These natives sometimes used burning
pitch against their enemies as well as rosin,[12] and blood and water mixed
with ashes. There was a battle at Ixtapa (Estapa), twelve miles from San
Cristóbal, which became the capital of Chiapas. The Indians killed two
Spanish soldiers and four horses, and wounded Luis Marín, who fell in a
marsh—these were victories of bows and arrows.

In the end, the Indians were defeated and the Spaniards slept in triumph on the battlefield, eating cherries which they found nearby. Some
Xaltepec Indians, who were enemies of the Chiapanecs, assisted the Spanish with guides over the fast-flowing River Chiapas. That help enabled
Grado and Marín to besiege the town of Chiapas itself. They summoned
the chiefs there and asked them to give tribute to the emperor Charles,
which they did. They found three jails with wooden railings full of prisoners with collars round their necks. The Spaniards freed them and then went
on to conquer Chamula, whose siege was more difficult. Díaz del Castillo
entered first and was accordingly allocated the town by Cortés (he already
had Teapa as an *encomienda*).[13] As frequently occurred in those days, the
defeat of the Indians was followed by a dispute between the Spaniards; arguments between Marín, Grado, and Godoy, the notary, led to the dispatch
of the complicated Grado as a prisoner to Mexico-Tenochtitlan under
armed guard. Godoy and Díaz del Castillo then quarreled as to whether the
prisoners should be branded as slaves.

In the summer of 1522, Cortés also dispatched his lieutenant Cristóbal
de Olid to Michoacán.[14] This kingdom had withstood the Mexica in the
past, most famously in 1478–80. It was a small empire—or is that a contradiction in terms?—of about twenty cities roughly coterminous with the
modern state of Michoacán. The people called themselves the Purépecha,
but the Spaniards knew them as the Tarascans. They were the only people
of the region to possess advanced metallurgical techniques such as gold-
plating, casting, soldering, and cold hammering, which enabled them to
produce remarkable copper masks, copper bells shaped as turtles and fish,
lip plugs of laminated turquoise, and above all, copper weapons. With
these they had decimated the Mexica in the 1470s; the Mexica had died "as

if they were flies which fell into the water."[15] Cortés had earlier received an embassy from the Tarascans led by Tashovo, the brother of the *cazonci*, the ruler there.

Olid—from Baeza, in Andalusia—had an excessively turbulent temperament but was a magnificent fighter, Bernal Díaz considering him a veritable Hector—classical comparisons were frequent at that time—in hand-to-hand combat. He had allowed himself to be courted for a time in 1521 by Cortés's enemy Cristóbal de Tapia, and Cortés had reprimanded him. He had a beautiful wife, Felipa de Arauz, who joined him in New Spain in 1522. He went up to Michoacán with 130 foot, twenty horse, and twenty crossbowmen. He had with him Cortés's great friend Andrés de Tapia and his cavalry commander, Cristóbal Martín de Gamboa, who had fought with Ovando in La Española, where he had a good *encomienda*.[16]

When Tzintla, the *cazonci*, heard that a detachment of Spaniards was making its way toward his principality, he very sensibly fled from his capital city of Tzintzuntan. He had previously good relations with two Castilians, Antonio Caicedo and Francisco de Montaño, the last of whom was the hero of Cortés's singular recovery of sulfur from the volcano of Popocatépetl.[17] But the *cazonci* realized that two Spaniards were different from the 150 or so who rode up so nonchalantly with Olid. The latter, finding Tzintzuntan empty of authority, had no hesitation in sacking the *cazonci*'s palace and destroying his idols, even though he had been well received by Tashovo, the *cazonci*'s brother, and by an Indian leader, "Pedro" Curiánguari. When the sacking was done, the *cazonci* bravely returned, to say that he was astonished that the Spaniards were so interested in gold. Why did they not prefer jade, as the Tarascans did? Olid had the *cazonci* sent to Tenochtitlan with three hundred loads of gold, and there the former leader was fêted. He became, for a few years, a willing collaborator of Spain, alongside Tashovo and Curiánguari.

This conquest concluded, Olid moved west to the Pacific coast, leaving Juan Rodríguez de Villafuerte, a Medellinés and friend of Cortés, in his place. Olid joined Sandoval, and after avenging a minor defeat suffered by Juan de Ávalos and Juan Álvarez Chico at Zacatula on the Pacific, he and Sandoval established a shipyard at what soon became known as the Villa de la Concepción de Zacatula. Blacksmiths, marine carpenters, and sailors were dispatched from Veracruz with anchors, rigging, and sails, these being carried across the center of old Mexico by 1,600 bearers recruited by the *ca-zonci*. Within months, brigantines and caravels were being built. Cortés would report to the emperor Charles that his plans for a fleet on the Southern Sea were more ambitious than anything else he was working on in the Indies. His schemes would surely make Charles "lord of more kingdoms and realms than up till now we have in our nations heard of."[18] Perhaps that would entail a new claim to China.

For the moment, however, Cortés contented himself with prizes nearer at hand. Thus Miguel Díaz de Aux—an experienced settler of Santo Domingo, son of the enterprising conquistador who had discovered a famous "nugget of gold" with Francisco de Garay—went with Rodrigo de Castañeda, by this time a good interpreter, to conquer Taxco, where they knew that iron could be found. Then, on February 5, 1524, Cortés sent the elderly Rodrigo Rangel and Francisco de Orozco, a conquistador from Cobos's city of Úbeda, southward to Oaxaca to fight the Zapotecs and the Mixtecs, with their long flint-headed lances. They took 150 foot and four pieces of artillery.

Oaxaca was characterized by tropical coastlands, the humid region of the Papaloapan River, a large temperate valley, and high mountains with a colder climate. The two peoples in this territory were the Zapotecs, centered on the wonderful ancient site of Monte Albán, and the Mixtecs, associated with Mitla. The Zapotecs were admirable architects; the Mixtecs were better known for their production of beautiful smaller objects such as turquoise mosaics, jade and gold jewelry, polychrome pottery, and carvings in hard stone. The Mixtecs were known, too, for their pictographic books, which the admirable Ignacio Bernal thought the "most important feature of Mixtec culture."[19] But there was an extraordinary palace of many courts at Mitla, and something similar at Yagul.

The conquistadors from Spain would soon have become aware of many characteristic elements of local culture in Oaxaca—for example, funerary paintings, a style of writing that became associated with figures known as *danzantes,* fine ceramics (Monte Albán "grayware," cream ware, and the coarser brown and yellow ware), much lapidary work, copper work, and gold work. There was interesting jade work. Of these crafts, the extraordinarily skilled work of the people of Oaxaca as goldsmiths stands out. From them, the Mexica seem to have learned the art of working metals. The

Franciscan Sahagún later attributed the invention of metallurgy to the Toltecs.[20] But that legendary origin should not displace the real achievements in Oaxaca, whose metallurgical tradition came there from Panama and Costa Rica[21] or possibly Peru.[22] We know about the quality of Zapotec and Mixtec gold work—and, to a lesser extent, silver work—from the opening in the 1930s of the famous Tomb 7 in Monte Albán. But Spaniards of the sixteenth century had much broader knowledge of it because of the abundance of such objects known in the old royal treasury of Mexico, which were often melted down to be sent back to Spain. But there were enough pieces sent back in an original form to dazzle men in Europe as sophisticated as Albrecht Dürer.

Oaxaca perhaps held about 1,500,000 people in 1519. They were established in some twenty or so towns that paid tribute to the central city, which was ruled by a monarch—or a local chief (cacique)—who was independent of, but allied to, the Mexica. Mitla would seem to have been, anomalously, ruled by a priest, whose subjects were accustomed to pay to Tenochtitlan tributes of gold dust, gold disks, cotton mantles, turkeys, rabbits, honey, and slaves.

This society had had in the past no draught animals, nor did they have the wheel. The only form of conveyance was that of men and women. War was continuous, the wooden sheathed *macana* (sword) being in perpetual use. The main conflicts were those against the Mexica. The purpose of the latter was to capture slaves and, by winning a victory, gather tribute. The religion of the region was comparable to that in Mexico-Tenochtitlan, but human sacrifice was on a smaller scale. All religious ceremonies were elaborate and marked by the usual marriage between music, dancing, and the consumption of pulque. The main crops were maize, chile, sweet potatoes, and squash; turkey, bees, and dogs were bred; and many other animals were used for food. A native tobacco was used for medicinal purposes.

Ancient Oaxaca had a sophisticated society in which a trained priesthood educated the public into an ancestor cult, a culture of sacrifice, ceremony, and a respect for the calendar. The society was built on the idea of a settled agriculture supplemented by hunting and fishing. The local priests and nobility led their people into traditional ways.

Led by the elderly Rodrigo Rangel, the venture of Cortés to absorb this society was completely successful. At that time, Cortés himself had gone down to Veracruz to inspect the old sites of the towns on the coast. He wanted a good port on the Gulf of Mexico. In the end, he found one a few miles from the first place where he had landed in 1519, to which he ordered the town of Medellín to move. This became La Antigua, on the river Canoas. This move was rendered easier by the fact that the Mixtecs were still in a state of conflict with their neighbors, the Zapotecs, the Mixes, and indeed, the Mexica. Rangel died shortly after his success, of syphilis.

Meantime, on Midsummer Day, June 24, 1523, Francisco de Garay— the governor of Jamaica, veteran of Santo Domingo, where he had arrived in Columbus's second expedition in 1493—mounted a fleet of twelve ships with nearly 150 horse and 850 Castilians, as well as some Jamaican Indians, to go to Pánuco on the Bay of Mexico. Garay had in his army two hundred musketeers and three hundred crossbowmen and stocked his ships with merchandise, taking care before he left to receive the permission of the *audiencia* of Santo Domingo to mount an expedition in an area already conquered by Cortés. According to Díaz del Castillo, he was inspired to act by a series of conversations with Cortés's brilliantly intelligent pilot, Antonio de Alaminos.[23] He, too, had been fascinated by the idea of establishing a settlement in the region for many years. Garay had known Cortés in La Española. So it was not surprising that the conqueror of the Mexica should write to Garay encouraging him to come, saying that if he encountered difficulties with the Huastec Indians, he, Cortés, would help him. Garay thought that Cortés's offer was treacherous and continued with his plans, which he did not explain to anyone.

Garay reached the Río de Palmas to the north of the Río de Pánuco. He founded a city, which he bombastically named Vitoria Garayana. Councillors and magistrates were appointed from among several aristocrats with Garay's troops, and then Garay set off by land to Pánuco, while the old hand in that territory, Juan de Grijalva, directed the fleet along the coast. The land journey was a terrible one for men used to the relative comforts of Jamaica. The march was long, the heat overpowering, the mosquitoes relentless, the forest trackless, the suffering appalling. There were desertions. Men walked desperately away from the expedition into the jungle to seek relief, never to be seen again. Morale collapsed. Garay sent his lieutenant, Gonzalo de Ocampo, to San Esteban del Puerto, where Cortés's representative Pedro de Vallejo, a survivor of Narváez's expedition, greeted him.

Ocampo was experienced in the Indies and even had a brother, Diego, an equally experienced conquistador who had fought in both La Española and Cuba before going to New Spain with Cortés. Vallejo sent a messenger to Cortés requesting instructions, while telling Garay that he could not possibly feed so many newcomers. So Garay established himself at nearby Tlacolula, where he unwisely told the Indians that he had come to punish Cortés for having harmed them. This ill-judged comment led to an affray between a number of Garay's men and Vallejo's, in which the latter, more experienced in the land and more accustomed to the climate, though less numerous, emerged triumphant. Numbers, however, were on Garay's side. Surely they would eventually win any pitched battle against Cortés's men.

But Cortés was favored still by fortune, as Narváez had predicted would be the case, for some time yet. That was September 1523. That month Rodrigo de Paz and Francisco de las Casas, his cousins, at last reached New Spain with the news that the Emperor had named him captain-general and governor, the letter of appointment being accompanied by an instruction to Garay not to settle in Pánuco, but if he wanted to stay in New Spain, to go down to Espíritu Santo or, better, beyond it. Cortés immediately sent to inform Garay of these orders and dispatched Diego de Ocampo and Pedro de Alvarado with a notary from Tordesillas, Francisco de Orduña, to enforce the decree.[24]

Garay's men were still melting away through desertion and he, at that time still in his Vitoria Garayana, was ailing. His ships were seized by Vallejo, his artillery by Alvarado. In these circumstances, Garay had no alternative but to accept to go up to Mexico-Tenochtitlan, Coyoacán, as Cortés's guest. It was a humiliating conclusion to his great adventure. Cortés and Garay embraced and exchanged reminiscences of old days together fifteen or more years before in Santo Domingo. But to no avail: After dining with Cortés on Christmas Day 1523 in the house of Alonso de Villanueva, a friend of Garay as of Cortés, Garay died of a stomach complaint. Going into Garay's room, Alfonso Lucas, one of Garay's friends, and probably a Sevillano, heard the governor of Jamaica at midnight shouting, "Without doubt I am mortal." He was.[25]

Within a few months, however, Cortés had himself to repair to Pánuco, for the Huastecs were priding themselves on what they believed to be their skill in expelling Garay and wreaking vengeance on his followers. The

Huastecs, who were Maya-speaking, were enemies of the Mexica, but their way of life was luxurious, since, in their tropical land, they had plenty of food and there was a cult of pulque, which made them strong drinkers. They had also created much three-dimensional sculpture and were serious players of the famous ball game of the region. They were highly licentious.

Cortés swiftly established Spanish control in Pánuco and then, to his and his companions' shocked horror, found the faces displayed in the town of several who had in 1523 come to the region with Francisco Garay. These had been flayed and cured as if their skins had been glove leather. This unpleasing discovery concentrated the minds of all the conquistadors.[26]

Thereafter, Cortés established Vallejo as his commander in the region in the new settlement of San Esteban del Puerto, which soon had over a hundred settlers of whom twenty-seven were horsemen and thirty-six were musketeers or crossbowmen. Juan de Burgos, a merchant of that city, who would become an enemy of Cortés, maliciously suggested that Cortés had ordered the Huastecs to kill as many as possible of Garay's men, but the accusation contains no truth.

Afterwards the Crown sent a letter of complaint to the *audiencia* in Santo Domingo because of their permission to Garay to embark upon an expedition in an area already conquered by Cortés.[27]

At much the same time, Cortés sent his most turbulent lieutenant, Cristóbal de Olid, to Honduras to found a settlement there. He had returned from both Michoacán and Zacatula and was pestering Cortés for a new employment. Cortés believed that there was much wealth in the region concerned; and he told the emperor Charles that "many pilots believe that there is a strait between that bay and the other sea [the South Sea] and this is the thing which I most desire to discover because of the great service which I am certain Your Caesarian majesty will receive thereby."[28] Cortés had also heard that the nets used for fishing in those parts were a mixture of gold and copper, so he assumed that they were rich. A new settlement under Cortés's direction would also presumably be a way of restructuring the territory of Pedrarias in Central America.

So Olid set off from Tenochtitlan on January 11, 1524, with six ships, with good guns and five hundred men, of whom a hundred were crossbowmen. Cortés assumed that Olid and Alvarado would meet if no strait divided them, for the latter had already begun a land journey to Guatemala.[29]

Two clerics accompanied Olid. They were to root out sodomy and human sacrifice "in a friendly manner." All houses where Indians were being fattened for human sacrifice were to be broken open and the prisoners freed. Crosses were to be established everywhere.

Cortés sent Olid to Honduras via Havana. There, Cortés hoped, he would pick up Alonso de Contreras, from Ordaz, Toledo. He was one of those who had accompanied Cortés to New Spain in 1519, with horses, pigs, cassava (roots), and bacon. But Olid called on his old master, Diego Velázquez, who was then on his deathbed. Despite his condition, Velázquez encouraged Olid's rebellious instincts.

Some other Spaniards from Cuba accompanied Olid to Central America. There Olid immediately set himself up in opposition to Cortés. His settlement of May 3, 1524, was at Naco on the river Chamelecón, in Higueras, thirty miles south of Puerto de Caballos on the Bay of Honduras.[30]

When he heard of this unilateral declaration, Cortés's first reaction was fury: Peter Martyr—in old, not New, Spain—said that "his neck swelled" at such bad news.[31] Díaz del Castillo, who was with Cortés at the time, however, wrote that he became very thoughtful, but since he was at bottom high-spirited, he did not permit such matters to get the better of him.[32] Cortés dispatched a loyal force, under his cousin Francisco de las Casas, against Olid, with five ships and one hundred soldiers.[33] They reached Honduras in good time and sought to land. Olid tried to prevent that. There was a short sea battle between Las Casas and Olid. The latter must have felt surrounded by enemies, since he had some days before sent two companies of men down the Río Pechin to try to stop, or even seize, Gil González Dávila, an eternal adventurer who was the elder brother of Cortés's Alonso de Ávila and who was making his way northward from Panama.[34]

So Olid offered a truce to Cortés's cousin Las Casas, who agreed to stay for a time aboard his ship. But alas for hopes of a peaceful solution! A storm pushed Las Casas onto the shore, in which torment he lost thirty men and all his arms. He was now a refugee with Olid, and he soon found himself joined in his confinement by Gil González Dávila and Juan Núñez de Mercado, an ex-page of Cortés, who were seized as they struggled northward.

Olid was delighted by these unexpected events and wrote, very pleased, to Diego Velázquez in Cuba to say how he had outmaneuvered everyone

(Velázquez died before he could read the letter). He also sent one of his captains, Pedro de Briones, to establish his supremacy in some nearby settlements. But Briones was not to be trusted, for he planned to rejoin Cortés in Mexico. At that point, Las Casas and González Dávila decided to kill Olid, which was easy enough because, though more prisoners than refugees, they had not been chained. They found some scriveners' knives, and then, while González Dávila was talking to Olid, Las Casas seized the latter by the beard and cut his throat. González Dávila added some thrusts of his own. But Olid was strong, and broke away to hide in a thicket. Las Casas proclaimed: "To me, those for the king and Cortés against the tyrant Olid!" No one supported the latter, who was soon betrayed.

A charge of rebellion was swiftly and almost formally brought against Olid in an arbitrary trial. Las Casas demanded a sentence of death for rebellion, and Olid, one of the great men of the conquest of Mexico, was accordingly beheaded forthwith in the square of Naco. The victors soon founded a city there, which they named Trujillo, for Las Casas was from that city in Extremadura. Both he and González Dávila then began to prepare to return to Mexico.

These events, so advantageous for Cortés, occurred in September 1524. But, not knowing of them, Cortés decided on an expedition of his own. His aim was to punish Olid. This was a controversial decision and one which he must have later bitterly regretted. Why he thought it necessary is a mystery. Why at least did he not wait till he had heard the result of Las Casas's expedition? He was advised against leaving Mexico-Tenochtitlan by all his friends there. He did not listen. Perhaps he was bored by problems of administration and coveted a return to campaigning.

In any event, and for whatever psychological reason, the great conqueror of Mexico set off for Honduras-Higueras by land on October 12, 1524, a month after Olid had been done to death. He left Alonso de Estrada and Rodrigo de Albornoz, the royal treasurer and the accountant, as lieutenant-governors to act in his stead while he was away. The chief magistrate would be Alonso de Zuazo, an experienced lawyer who had just completed the *juicio de residencia* of Diego Velázquez in Cuba. Two other royal officials—Gonzalo de Salazar and Pedro Almíndez Chirino—accompanied Cortés, as did the unfortunate Cuauhtémoc, last of the Mexican rulers, and his colleagues Tetepanquetzal and Cohuanacoch, the leaders, or ex-monarchs, respectively, of Tacuba and Texcoco. Others in his train were the resilient interpreter Marina, the reliable Sandoval, the complex Alonso de Grado, the fortunate Juan Jaramillo, the Genoese Luis Marín, Pedro de Ircio, and Bernal Díaz, all of whom had accompanied him in 1519.

Cortés took with him also a large personal staff, which included a majordomo, two maîtres d'hôtel, a steward, a shoemaker, a butler, a doctor, a waiter, two pages, eight footmen, and five musicians. His followers included, so he himself reported, nearly a hundred horse and thirty foot, with perhaps three thousand Indian followers.[35] Cortés's cousin Rodrigo de Paz would remain behind as majordomo of his property in Mexico, Cuernavaca, and on Coyoacán.

Soon after he had abandoned the heartland of old Mexico, Salazar and Pedro Almíndez Chirino left the expedition to return to Mexico. The bad relations between Estrada and Albornoz had been reported to Cortés, who assumed that the return of these two other officials, whom he believed loyal, would make everything easier in the great city whose rebuilding he had begun so well.

After Espíritu Santo and Coatzacoalcos, Cortés found himself in new country. The expedition passed through the center of the Yucatán Peninsula; bypassed Copilco, where there was much cacao and good fishing; and stopped briefly at Anaxuxuca, Chilapao, Tepetitán, Zagoatan, Istapan ("a very large town on the banks of a beautiful river, a suitable place for Spaniards to settle"), and Teuticacar ("a most beautiful town with two very fine temples," in one of which pretty virgins were regularly sacrificed). Cortés had many bridges built of brushwood, sometimes of timber. Occasionally they had to cross marshes by bridges, including one built by Indians from Tenochtitlan; they experienced "much distress through hunger," many curious conversations with Indians in canoes, while sermons were given by Cortés via Marina on the virtues of Christianity. Indian chiefs, such as Apasolan, became Christians and burned their idols. Sometimes Mass was celebrated accompanied by the music of sackbuts and flageolets. Cortés received many gifts of gold and girls, honey and beads, fallow deer and iguana. There were jungles, which the expedition had to cross on their knees, and there were flat pasture lands. They encountered high inland seas over one hundred miles in diameter, and met nights of torrential rain amid plagues of mosquitoes. There were "fearful northern gales"; there were days when the expedition was carried onward only by powerful currents in vast rivers; and there was the unmasking of an alleged plot of Cuauhtémoc, Co-huanacoch of Texcoco, and Tetepanquetzal of Tacuba, and their subsequent execution by hanging at Izancanac on Ash Wednesday, February 28, 1525. (Two senior Mexica—Cihuacoatl, or "Juan Velázquez," and Moyel-chuitzin, or "Tapia"—seem to have betrayed their colleagues' conversations about possible rebellion.)[36] Guanacalin, Prince of Texcoco, and Tacitetle, his equivalent in Tacuba, were left frightened but uncharged.

Cortés met merchants of the Mexican commercial centers of Xicalango and Los Terminos selling cacao, cotton materials, dyes, torches, beads made from shells, sometimes gold mixed with copper. The expeditionaries ate dried maize, cacao, beans, pepper, salt, and many hens and pheasant, as well as dogs bred for food. Sometimes they traveled by raft, each one of which carried about seventy bushels of dried maize and quantities of beans, peppers, and cacao, as well as ten men.

Eventually, after many privations, the expedition reached Nito, at the corner of Yucatán and Honduras, and there they encountered some eighty Spaniards, including twenty women who, unarmed and without horses, seemed to be dying of hunger. They had been left behind by Gil González Dávila, who had returned to Panama. Cortés's own expedition was short of food, and perhaps all might have starved to death had it not been for the unexpected arrival of a ship from Santo Domingo with thirteen horses, seventy pigs, twelve casks of salted meat, and some thirty loaves of bread "of the kind used in the islands"—that is, presumably cassava bread. Cortés began to build a caravel and a brigantine that would reestablish his relations with those outposts. Of course, he found out about the fighting between Olid, Las Casas, and González Dávila, as well as the death of the first of these. He complained fiercely about the trade in Indian slaves, which continued on a large, ever-growing scale in the bay islands off Honduras in those days, and he explained how he had freed those slaves previously seized by Rodrigo de Merlo of Cuba.[37] Cortés was now presenting himself as the friend of the Indians.

In the meantime, many strange, disturbing, quite unexpected things were going on in Mexico-Tenochtitlan. At first, Cortés's absence seemed not to matter. Thus on January 1, 1525, a meeting of the town council of the city was held in the house of Licenciado Alonso de Zuazo, Cortés's friend. There were present Gonzalo de Salazar, the majordomo, and Pedro Almíndez Chirino, the inspector, sent back to Mexico to maintain order while Cortés, the governor-general and *adelantado,* was on his journey. Also present were Gonzalo de Ocampo, Garay's majordomo who had become mayor in Mexico; Cortés's cousin Rodrigo de Paz, the chief magistrate, who had brought the good news of his governor-generalship; and Bernardino Vázquez de Tapia, the well-born conquistador from Talavera de la Reina, who had been with Cortés throughout the campaign of the conquest and who had not yet revealed himself the bitter critic of the great conquistador that he would soon become. These Spanish conquerors then elected for the following year two mayors, four town councillors, and a public spokesman.

There was thus nothing untoward in the names of the new members.[38] They seemed much as they had been in the past, and they duly distributed 211 *solares* in 1525, of which 114 were urban but 97 were orchards. Several shares were granted for the establishment of mills, and one was given to a woman, Isabel Rodríguez, wife of Miguel Rodríguez de Guadalupe, who had cured the wounds of "*los enfermos de la conquista.*" [39] But more was afoot.

During the course of 1525, the temporary rulers of New Spain, especially Pedro Almíndez Chirino and Gonzalo de Salazar, convinced themselves that since they had had no news from or of Cortés, he must be dead. On August 22, the town council formally decided to that effect. On December 15, Rodrigo de Albornoz wrote to the Council of the Indies a hostile letter about Cortés, whom he accused of being "consumed by avarice" and "a tyrant." [40] When Rodrigo de Paz, Cortés's cousin, protested against the new self-assumed authority—Salazar and Pedro Almíndez—he was peremptorily imprisoned in the new fortress of the Atarazanas. He was asked the whereabouts of Cortés's treasure. He denied that it existed. He was tortured and soon killed. It was an extraordinary development, heightened by the seizure by Salazar and Pedro Almíndez of much of Cortés's property. Something like a reign of terror was instigated. Juana de Mansilla, wife of a conquistador who was with Cortés in Honduras, sustained the view that Cortés and her husband were still alive. She also refused to remarry. She was condemned to ride through the city on a donkey with a rope round her neck and to be whipped. Others of Cortés's friends took refuge in the monastery of San Francisco. Judge Zuazo escaped to Cuba. The legitimacy of the new empire seemed to be on the verge of collapse.

Then on January 28, 1526, Martín de Dorantes, one of Cortés's grooms, who came from Béjar, reached Mexico with his master's order displacing Chirino and Salazar. He talked in the monastery of San Francisco to Jorge de Alvarado and Andrés de Tapia. After a struggle, Cortés's party regained control. Then in a few months, the city council received a letter from Cortés himself in which he explained that he had arrived at San Juan Chalchicuyecan, Veracruz. The council read this on May 31, the day of Corpus Christi, with the council preparing to leave the new makeshift cathedral in procession. This missive led the council to revoke the grants of *solares* in the city and *huertas* outside it that had been made by Salazar and Pedro Almíndez Chirino.[41]

Cortés returned on June 19 to the city he had conquered and had then rebuilt. He had been away for more than a year and a half. In a letter to the emperor Charles he described how the population welcomed him as if he "had been their father."[42] Presumably he meant the Indians as well as the Spaniards in the place. The treasurer Estrada and the inspector Rodrigo de Albornoz rode out in fine array to meet him, though Albornoz had written so critically of Cortés the previous year; the majordomo Salazar and the inspector Pedro Almíndez Chirino, hid in their houses. Cortés went first to the monastery of San Francisco, where he was effusively greeted by all his friends who had taken refuge there. There he was told by old associates, such as Francisco de Ávila, his friend since Cuba, of what had happened in his absence. Almost his first move was to rescind his grant of the *encomienda* of Tacuba to Pedro Almíndez Chirino and to give it formally to Isabel Montezuma on the occasion of her new marriage, to Alonso de Grado.[43] His next action was to arrest Salazar and Chirino and hold them both in a wooden cage.

Cortés had not been back more than two weeks when a new crisis arose personally for him. This was the arrival at Veracruz of Luis Ponce de León as judge of *residencia*. This was a normal procedure for retiring administrators. This official was a distant relation of the great Sevillano family with his name. He was young, with a high reputation for integrity. Named judge for Cortés in November 1525, he set off for New Spain in February of the next year in a fleet of twenty-two ships. According to Peter Martyr, he was told that if he should find Cortés alive, "he should overwhelm him with flattery and seek to inspire him with truly loyal sentiments."[44] He waited impatiently for two months in Santo Domingo for a ship to take him on to New Spain. When he arrived at Veracruz, he heard that Cortés had been there only a few days before. That was both unexpected and unwelcome.

Ponce de León went up to Mexico-Tenochtitlan in haste. He was offered a banquet on the way, at Iztapalapa. There he was offered presents, which he refused, and blancmange, which he ate. He and Cortés then met in the monastery of San Francisco in Mexico in the presence of Estrada, Albornoz, and most of the council of the city. A *residencia* of Cortés was proclaimed on July 4. This meant in theory that all executive power passed to the judge. Cortés, a stickler for correct conduct, and with his own legal training in his mind, prepared for the transfer of authority and handed to Ponce the *vara* (staff) of office. But Ponce was already ill, allegedly because of eating the blancmange at Iztapalapa. He must have been the first man to die of such a thing. For he and several of his traveling companions did succumb on July 20, and there were some who accused Cortés of poisoning them. The Dominican Fray Tomás Ortiz was the first to spread this rumor, though he only arrived in New Spain on July 2, with twelve colleagues. There is no evidence for the story.

Before he died, Ponce had placed his authority in the hands of an elderly lawyer, Marcos de Aguilar, who had accompanied him. He passed him the staff of office. Aguilar, a native of Écija, a fine Roman city between Seville and Córdoba, had gone out to the Indies in 1509. He had become chief magistrate in Santo Domingo and always supported the Columbus family, for which imprudent loyalty he was briefly imprisoned in 1515. He continued in office but was then expelled on the royal request for being a *persona escandalosa*. What could that have signified? Homosexuality? Hardly, for he had an illegitimate son, Cristóbal, by an indigenous girl.[45] To live with an indigenous girl was not a scandal since almost everyone had at least one such liaison. Drink? Not a scandal at that time!

In any event, Aguilar assumed the title of *justicia mayor* in New Spain and for nine months exercised authority, though he knew nothing of the place and was so badly crippled that he had to be fed.[46] Cortés conducted himself arrogantly but correctly. Aguilar for his part began the business of arranging Cortés's *residencia,* the assembly of witnesses, the preparation of questionnaires and of counter-questionnaires, and the hiring of notaries, who it was hoped would write down with ease and grace all that was said by retired warriors. The process continued for years.

Among those who would be a witness was Jerónimo de Aguilar, a cousin of the licenciado and an essential ally of Cortés, since in 1519–21, he had interpreted Spanish into Maya for the conquistadors, leaving the process of translation of Maya into Nahuatl to the Indian Marina.

But then once again death intervened. In March 1527, Licenciado Marcos de Aguilar followed his legal leader into his grave. This was the fourth swift death encountered by Cortés, his wife's, Garay's, and Ponce's being the previous ones; the accusations that he was in some way concerned were even more numerous.[47]

Aguilar had named the treasurer Estrada as his successor, *justicia mayor*. But Cortés's captain, the resolute Gonzalo de Sandoval, was called on by the town council to assist him, and that captain moved into the *justicia mayor*'s suite for a few months, till Estrada received a notice from Spain that he alone was to rule New Spain. But Sandoval was not to take the *residencia* of Cortés, which was delayed endlessly.

Despite that concession, Cortés began to see that he was being sidelined in the arrangements to manage his own conquests. He seems never physically to have recovered from the privations of his journey to Honduras.

In these months people from all parts of Spain arrived in the New World, in particular New Spain. "Foreigners" were permitted to come between 1526 and 1538, which meant that all inhabitants of Aragon were allowed to venture there. Jews, Moors, Gypsies, and heretics were in theory forbidden, but it was in these years fairly easy to evade the regulations, and we find many new Christians entering the New World. Perhaps one thousand to two thousand immigrants would come every year, more men than women, of course.[48]

Book I

❦

VALLADOLID AND ROME

7

Charles V: From Valladolid to the Fall of Rome, 1527

> The year 1527 was full of atrocities and events unheard of for many centuries: falls of governments, wickedness of Princes, most frightful sacks of cities, great famines, a most terrible plague almost everywhere.
>
> GUICCIARDINI

Between 1523 and 1529, Charles the Emperor, Charles of Ghent, was above all Charles the King—of Aragon, of course, as well as of Castile and its substantial entanglements overseas. He had, remarkably, been in Valladolid a year, from July 1522 to August 25, 1523, when he set off for Navarre and then Aragon, specifically Monzón, in the mountains between Barbastro and Lérida, where the Segre joins the Cinca, and where kings of Aragon customarily held their local parliaments. Thereafter he was in Catalonia, Andalusia, Seville, and Granada. By 1524, his travels seemed to combine to make him King of Spain, indeed.

Like every bachelor monarch in those days—and later days, too—he was being every day advised on his need for marriage. He seems to have settled by this time on the merits of his first cousin, the Infanta Isabel, daughter of King Manuel of Portugal by a Spanish princess, María, who was herself daughter of Fernando and Isabel. The English princess Mary, who had been talked of as a candidate, was too young, being only nine years old in 1525, and Charles had been persuaded that his marriage could not wait. He adopted a rather worldly view of such a wedding: "My marriage," he wrote in a private notebook—he was the first monarch to confide thus—"will be a good reason to demand a great sum from the Spanish kingdoms." He knew that the Portuguese princess was rich. He reflected that he could make the princess of Portugal, once she was Queen and Empress, his Regent whenever he left Spain: "In that way I ought to be able to set out for Italy with the greatest splendour and honour this very autumn."[1]

He had his personal difficulties, above all with his mother. In January 1525, Fadrique Enríquez, the admiral of Castile, his cousin, wrote to him to say that he had visited Queen Juana and that she had complained to him of her ill-treatment by the Marquess de Denia, who was both his and her close relation.[2] This dry and callous Marquess, Bernardino Sandoval y Rojas, was governor of Tordesillas and therefore warder-in-chief of Juana la Loca. Dealing with him that time, Juana had been lucid. But "in the rest of her conversation, she wandered."[3]

Charles was also short of money. The Polish ambassador, Dantiscus, thought in February 1525 that he had never seen the court "so poor" as it was then. "Money is procured by unprecedented methods and all is sent to the army in Italy. The Emperor is suffering from an extreme penury," he added in his diary after he received the Order of the Golden Fleece for his own monarch, the cultivated Sigismund I of Poland (conversation between Charles and Dantiscus was in German and Italian). Dantiscus himself was suffering from poverty, though in receipt of an income from Poland. With only 60 ducats a month, he could not live as an ambassador needed to: He could afford only six or seven horses and ten servants.[4]

Yet happier times were coming. Peter Martyr, in what turned out to be his last letter to Rome,[5] spoke of two vessels arriving at Seville from New Spain, commanded by Lope de Samaniego, who would later play a part in the administration of the overseas empire, with two tigers on board, and a culverin made of silver sent by Cortés before he left Mexico-Tenochtitlan the previous October.[6] Dantiscus reported good news about the Indies, such as the "discoveries of new islands," which he did not name but which he said were "abundant in gold, spices and perfumes" (*aromas*) adding that in just one day, seventy thousand men and women in New Spain had received the sacrament. He said that since there had been a severe drought, the Spaniards had persuaded the Indians in that land to form a procession preceded by a cross, whereupon it began to rain and the indigenous people saved their crops. "These Indians were more human than those who had been previously discovered [in the Caribbean] and the journey to their islands was shorter than the way of the Portuguese."[7]

On March 10, even more remarkable news reached the emperor Charles: that his army in Italy, in pursuit of triumphs in Naples, led by the brilliant Francisco de Ávalos, who had become Marquess of Pescara, had defeated the French at Pavia. The King of France, the unscrupulous charmer Francis I, had even been captured.

The Viceroy of Naples, Lannoy, received King Francis's sword in person. But the victory was particularly the work of Ávalos, one of the most admirable gentlemen-warriors of the age. Captain-General of the light cavalry of Spain in 1512 when still young, he had been captured and wounded by the French at Ravenna that same year. He was known "for his strong frame," and for "his fine large eyes which though usually soft and mild" in expression "shot fire" when he was roused. In 1524, he had skillfully covered the Spanish retreat from France and had given back to France the body of the valiant Bayard before the battle of Pavia.[8] Connected indirectly by blood ties to Cortés, he inherited an Italian title, but he spoke only Spanish.[9] In 1509, he had married in sumptuous style the beautiful poetess Vittoria Colonna, who would later be the great friend of Michelangelo and who forgave Ávalos his many absences and infidelities. He was a Renaissance man, for his life was full of extraordinary feats, his attitude to noble ardor and desire for glory being awoken by his heady reading of Romantic novels. The playwright Torres Naharro, a very Italianate Spaniard, dedicated his *Propalladia* to him in 1517.[10] Vittoria Colonna wrote him poems: *"Que fece il mio bel sole a noi ritorno/De regie spoglie carco e ricche prede . . . ."* The last chapter of Machiavelli's *The Prince* suggests that many Italians agreed with Ávalos's idea of patriotism. His wounds at Pavia distressed him and left him bitter at the lack of recognition by the Emperor. But Isabella, Duchess of Milan, wrote, "I would that I were a man, signor, if for nothing else than to receive wounds in the face as you have done, in order to see if they would become me as well as they do you."[11] But his last months were tarnished by the suspicion that he was toying with the idea of backing Italian nationhood, through the machinations of the gifted patriot Girolamo Morone.[12] He died of his wounds in December.

The Emperor remained in Spain, and with the King of France in his control, he seemed to have the world at his feet. Charles's dignified brother, Ferdinand, wrote enthusiastically, "Your Majesty is now monarch of the whole world."[13] What a tempting phrase!

But the strategic problems seemed as serious as ever: What was to be done with Francis I? How was Charles now to handle his ally Henry VIII of England, who, he was coming to realize, was self-obsessed? Gattinara thought that his Emperor should now claim the whole of his Burgundian inheritance. "Burgundy, no more, no less." Perhaps, too, he should demand Provence for the constable of Bourbon. A general council of the Church should surely be called, and the Emperor should organize it, for Pope Clement could only organize excuses.

But nothing happened. It was apparently Francis who, at last in the castle of Pizzighettone, between Cremona and Piacenza, persuaded Viceroy Lannoy that it would be best if he were sent to see Charles in Spain. There, the Council of Castile was divided. Gattinara wanted territorial acquisitions, solutions hostile to France, and most of the other Flemings took that view. So did the Duke of Alba. But Lannoy and Ávalos, the actual victors in battle, advised a conciliatory treaty, as did the Emperor's confessor, García de Loaisa.[14] At a Mass held to give thanks for the victory, a Dominican gave a sermon asking for a common front against the infidel. He preached "universal concord."[15] The humanist philosopher Vives, then at Oxford, urged tolerance, for it was a wonderful chance "to do good, to gain merit before God and glory before men."[16]

The indecision of Charles after Pavia was due first to the confusion in the imperial chancellery headed by Gattinara, who, though a fine intellect and an able official, was also always suspecting plots against him. For example, in July 1525 at Toledo, the Venetian ambassador, Gasparo Contarini, was reporting that Gattinara had complained to the Emperor that others were usurping his authority. Charles asked Gattinara to put his complaint in writing. He did so in a fierce denunciation of secretarial corruption that seems to have included not only the by-now-irreplaceable Cobos but also his own protégé, Lalemand, who was beginning to displace Gattinara himself. At another meeting in Toledo with Gattinara, on July 9, Charles explained that the chancellorship in Spain was different from what Gattinara imagined it. The chancellor was the supreme adviser to the King, not the head of the civil service. Gattinara immediately asked leave to retire from the court. Charles agreed to this sad request, then repented of his agreement and sent Laurent de Gorrevod to make things up. Gorrevod called on Gattinara, while the president of the Council of the Indies, García de Loaisa, asked Gattinara to dine with the King.

Charles greeted his longtime adviser with affection and declared how much he loved him. Then they settled down to dine extensively on beef and beer, as was then the Emperor's custom. It now seemed that Gattinara had been upset by the destruction caused by imperial troops to his own territory in Piedmont. He had written to Charles: "The abuses which your troops commit are so abominable that the Turks and infidels would not do them and, instead of naming you 'liberator of Italy,' people will be able to say that you have introduced the greatest tyranny that ever was."[17] No doubt Charles was aware of these scandals, but he did not like to hear them from his chancellor, of whose tirades—and even of whose exhortations— he was wearying.

Soon afterwards, Francis I arrived as a prisoner in Madrid. Charles did not hasten to see him. Only when Charles heard that the captive king was seriously ill did he visit him, and then only briefly.[18] After a month, Margaret, duchess of Alençon, a sister of Francis, a cultivated, beautiful Renaissance princess, arrived in Madrid to open negotiations on Francis's behalf. She was a poet, playwright, and Neoplatonist, as well as a reformer in so far as the Church was concerned, and that side of her is well expressed in her play *Le miroir de l´âme pécheresse.* She later married the King of Navarre, Henri d'Albret, and was the grandmother of Henri of Navarre. Charles received her with courtesy, and negotiations followed in Toledo.

The second reason for Charles's lack of attention to Francis and the treaty of peace to be made with him was that he had decided, as he told his brother, Fernando, in June 1525, to marry his cousin the infanta Isabel of Portugal. A marriage with a Portuguese princess would help to cement the good relations that Castilian monarchs had coveted with Portugal since the days of Isabel.[19]

A courtier, Alonso Enríquez de Guzmán—eccentric and indiscreet, but modern minded and articulate—had gone to Lisbon to tell the King of Portugal of Charles's victory. On his return, Charles told him: "Don Alonso, you have performed this service well. Now tell me of the people whom you met in Lisbon." He replied, "Sire, I saw a fat monarch, rather short, with a very small beard, youthful and not very discreet [King John III the Pious, who had been King since 1521].... I saw the Queen, his wife who seemed very well prepared and on the spot, honourable and wise [Charles's sister]. Then I saw an Infanta very self-possessed [*bien ansi*] and more [*más*], and more, if one can say so, who seemed to look like you, sir." This was the Emperor's cousin and future wife, whom he came to love deeply. She was beautiful, as we can see from Titian's portrait of her.

On October 24, wedding arrangements were agreed between Charles and the Infanta, the titles of Charles including that of "monarch of the isles of the Canaries and of the Indies, the isles of the mainland and the Ocean Sea."[20] The Infanta would bring a handsome dowry: 900,000 *doblas de oro castellanas*.[21]

The negotiations with Francis I over peace and those with the Portuguese Infanta over marriage overlapped. Thus on December 19, Viceroy Lannoy produced a list of fifty articles upon which the King of France would have to agree with Charles. The most important one was that Francis would accompany Charles in a crusade. The King of France would be released when his two elder but still small sons, Henry and Charles, were exchanged as hostages for him. France would renounce all claims to Milan, Naples, and Genoa, and abandon her overlordship of Flanders and Artois. Francis also assented, in somewhat distant terms, to the cession of Burgundy to Charles.

There was drama in the King's room in Toledo. Charles agreed to let his sister Leonor (Eleanor), the widow of King Manuel of Portugal, marry Francis. It seemed a moment of promise even if Gattinara the chancellor did not agree and did not countersign the treaty.

The Emperor and King remained, and then celebrated at the Alcázar in Toledo. They were joined by the ex-queen, Germaine de Foix, and the Marquess of Brandenburg, whom she would soon marry; Mencia de Mendoza, the Marquess de Cenete, the rich wife of the count of Nassau and the granddaughter of the great cardinal Rodríguez de Mendoza, Columbus's patron;[22] and, above all, Leonor, the future queen of France and Charles's sister, whom Dantiscus thought had lost her looks since he had last seen her at Brussels.[23] He wondered whether, having lost her looks, she had not lost her purpose. Immediately afterwards, Leonor and Francis went north to Burgos, where he remained to await the arrival of the future hostages, his sons by his first marriage.

Charles, on the other hand, went with the court south to Seville, where on March 10, 1526, he found the infanta Isabel already waiting. To his relief, he found that she spoke excellent Spanish, which he, too, had come to speak adequately by then. They were formally betrothed by Cardinal Jacopo Salviati, the papal legate to Spain, and married in the Alcázar almost immediately afterwards.[24] There was a ball, opened by Charles's favorite Fleming—La Chaulx, Charles de Poupet—who had much to do with the negotiation of the marriage.[25]

The lovely Alcázar had been redecorated beforehand with Genoese motifs, an appropriate embellishment for a place that owed so much to that Ligurian city. The court remained in Seville for about two months. Dantiscus reported to King Sigismund that the wedding was not allowed to cost much because it was Lent. Also, the court was in mourning for Charles's other sister, the Queen of Denmark. No ambassador seems to have been invited.

In June, the imperial and Spanish court left Seville for Granada, a city that had by then been ruled by Castilians for thirty years. Here they remained till December, and here the court did welcome ambassadors.

The stay was evidently a prolonged honeymoon for Charles and his young bride, Isabel (she had been born in 1503): Their heir, Philip, was conceived in September.[26]

But the court now received much bad news. First, no sooner had King Francis I become free than he forged a new and entirely unexpected alliance at Cognac with Pope Clement VII, which became known as the Papal League.[27] The papal legate, Salviati, left Granada in haste. Francesco María Sforza, in Milan, and the rulers of Florence and Venice, Duke Alessandro and the doge, gave support to Charles. The Emperor was astonished at what he saw as Pope Clement's perfidy. Yet Clement now wrote to Charles denouncing him for disturbing the peace. A reply was drafted by Charles's new secretary, the brilliant Alfonso de Valdés, secretary for Latin correspondence, who was the son of an old Christian who had committed the mistake, or had the good taste, to marry a *conversa*.[28] A convinced Erasmian, Valdés sought to influence his master Charles to that end through the drafts of his speeches and his writings—as modern speechwriters often do also. Valdés had an idea of empire that would have made Charles a reformer precisely by becoming an Erasmian. In his dialogue *Ánima*, he wrote: "The first thing I did was to give everyone to understand that I had such influence with the King that I could do anything that I wanted to with him and that he could do nothing without me."[29] He was a natural ally of Alonso Manrique de Lara, the *inquisidor general* who thought that he had royal support to use the Holy Office for humane purposes.

Charles was present in Granada at the lodgings of Gattinara on September 17, 1526, when the letter for Clement was handed to the new nuncio. This papal representative was amply competent to judge the weight of such documents, for he was none other than the Mantuan writer Baldassare Castiglione, who had earlier been ambassador to Leo X in Rome on behalf of the Duke of Urbino. In 1519, he had also been the Gonzagas' representative in Rome, before going to Spain in 1524. He became naturalized there and was soon named bishop of Ávila. He really did not want to send such a sharp communication as was suggested, but Charles insisted. Castiglione was in 1526 at work on his study *The Courtier*, and it would be published in Venice in 1528. It would be a great success for many generations. Charles said: "My Lord Nuncio, after you accept that paper for His Holiness, in which I report several unjust accusations, I take occasion to express myself yet more fully by word of mouth and I can but hope that, hereafter, the Pope will resume towards me the attitude of a good father towards a devoted son."[30] The Emperor added that he wanted to see peace not only in Italy but in the whole world, for only by those means could the Turks be defeated. But if the pope acted not as a father but as an enemy, not as a shepherd but as a wolf, Charles would have to appeal to a general council of the Church.

The nuncio reluctantly agreed to pass on this comment to his master in Rome.

Castiglione's conversations with the emperor Charles continued at Granada. Charles admired him. On August 17, Castiglione reported that a French representative had, in the presence of himself and the Venetian ambassador, Gasparo Contarini, explained how the new Papal League had been founded. The Emperor was angry and said to the Frenchman, "Had your King kept his word, we should have been spared this. He has cheated me, he has acted neither as a King nor a nobleman. I demand that, if he cannot keep his word, the most Christian King should again become my prisoner. It would be better for us to fight out this quarrel hand to hand, rather than to shed much Christian blood." This challenge to a hand-to-hand conflict was a typically chivalrous Caroline gesture. At that time, it still seemed to many good advisers that Spaniards counted for nothing in the formulation of the policy of Charles V; policy was the work of a narrow group of Flemish counselors.[31]

Gattinara said that perhaps those who put their trust in France to the neglect of Italy now had something to answer for. In order to gain support from the German princes, including his brother, Ferdinand, Charles offered a general pardon to all who had defied him at Worms. On August 20, a brief reply came from Pope Clement. Charles seemed not to be angry, Castiglione noticed with pleasure. Gattinara prepared another reply, in twenty-two pages, which Valdés, with the pride of the official speechwriter, claimed that he himself had drafted. This was *Pro divo Carolo . . . Apologetici libri duo*. Gattinara presented it to the Council of Castile in the house in Granada of the Centuriôns, the family of Genoese merchants. It seemed in the circumstances excessively Erasmian, for it tried to destroy the political pretensions of the papacy and to reduce the pope's role to a pastoral mission.[32]

Then, however, news of a further disaster broke: The sunny world of Granada in the days of the royal honeymoon was transformed in September by terrible news from Hungary. On August 29, the sultan Suleiman in Hungary had smashed the Christian kingdom there at Mohács. King Louis (Charles's brother-in-law), two archbishops, five bishops, and many noblemen were killed. New, accurate Turkish artillery played a large part in the defeat. The blow was utterly unexpected; the young king of Hungary had unwillingly taken part. A week later, Suleiman was in Buda. Where could the Turkish army be halted? At Vienna? King Louis's widow, Charles's third sister, Mary, was distraught. She did what she could to ensure that her brother, Ferdinand, who had married her sister-in-law, Anne of Hungary, Louis's sister, should succeed her dead husband. There was for once a powerful Christian reaction: Nobles, prelates, cities—all the institutions of the realm were ready for a supreme effort. "Once more," says a modern historian, "Castile showed her European and Christian vocation."[33]

All the same, the reply of Gattinara to Pope Clement was dispatched.

The document denounced Clement for disloyalty and justified Charles in his treatment of Reggio, Modena, and Milan. The language was often sarcastic, for it commented that it was scarcely credible that any Vicar of Christ should acquire any worldly possessions at the cost of a drop of human blood—was that not a contradiction of the teaching of the Gospel?[34]

In the event, the archduke Ferdinand was finally elected king of Bohemia, but most of what was left of Hungary was physically seized by a Transylvanian nobleman, John Zápolya, with whom, and with whose heirs, the Habsburgs would maintain an intermittent civil war for two generations.

Generally delighted by their long stay in Granada, the King, Queen, and court left that city on December 5 and made for Úbeda, where they for a time lodged in a new, and grand, house of the secretary Cobos. It was here that Charles signed a contract with Francisco de Montejo that allowed him to conquer and colonize Yucatán. This represented a cancellation of an older grant of Yucatán to Laurent de Gorrevod in 1519. On December 7, an edict was issued in Granada, to which the Inquisition established at Jaén had been transferred. The edict set out to eliminate many marks of local culture and identity—Arabic, local dress and costume, jewelry, and baths.

A week later, Charles also signed an agreement with another veteran of New Spain, that experienced conquistador Pánfilo de Narváez, to "discover, penetrate and populate" the territory from the river of the Palma [near Pánuco] to the cape at the southern point of Florida—the entire coastline of modern Texas, Louisiana, Mississippi, and Florida.[35] Narváez needed a new mission, and here was one to which he seemed suited.

Next day, on December 12, the bishop of Badajoz spoke of Charles as "monarch and lord of the whole world with the aim of persecuting and exterminating the pagans and the unfaithful."[36] In Andalusia, no one flinched at the use of *exterminating*. Before leaving Granada, the Emperor had accepted that the people of Granada should abandon Moorish dress slowly. They would have six years to wear out the clothes they had already. Charles named Gaspar de Ávalos and Antonio de Guevara to act as inspectors to check against the continuation of Moorish customs.[37] These men were successful in resisting such interventions as those of Jerónimo Poda and the count of Ribagorza, who had been deputed by the Aragonese Mudejars to try to preserve their old status.[38] Now these dignitaries as well as some Granadinos presented pleas on behalf of the old guard. Some had fought well for the royalists in the wars of the *comuneros.*

The court made its way from Úbeda to Valladolid, stopping on the way at Madrid, the small city in the center of Spain that Cardinal Cisneros had made his temporary capital. There Charles and Isabel remained, until they went to the nearby monastery of El Abrojo for Holy Week.

The morale in Italy of the imperial army that had beaten King Francis at Pavia was now low. Payment to the soldiers was scandalously behind. The chivalrous Ávalos had died of his wounds. A *cortes* was held at Valladolid, where the nobles explained that if the King were to take part personally in a war against "the Turk," their lives were at his disposal; but they refused to be taxed to provide money for a campaign. The prelates, too, said that they had no money to give, and the *procuradores* representing the towns of Castile, said that the country was too poor for any such extravagance. The mendicant orders said that their mission was to pray for victory. The Jeronymites did say that they would sell their silver chalices if it became evident that it was the Christians who had really made peace first. The Benedictines also offered 12,000 doubloons, while the military orders offered one-fifth of their pensions.

Charles was considering the implications of these disappointments when yet more bad news came, this time from Italy. The previous autumn, the private army of the Colonna family had entered Rome. The pope had fled to his Castel Sant'Angelo on the Tiber. It was reported that the old papal palace in the Vatican had been stripped. Even the wardrobe and the bedroom of the pope had been ransacked.[39] Given this encouragement, Charles's unpaid imperial army took the hint. In May 1527, it, too, entered Rome, the constable of Bourbon as commander giving an order for an assault. The chaos was remarkable. No one was safe. Bourbon himself was killed, perhaps by a shot from Cellini's firearm, which was an arquebus; the Prince of Orange was wounded; and the Sistine Chapel, as yet without Michelangelo's attention, became a stable for horses. The abbot of Nájera said that nothing comparable had been seen since the destruction of Jerusalem.[40] Most movable objects, such as the gold cross of Constantine, the golden rose presented to Pope Martin V, and the tiara of the reforming Pope Nicholas V, disappeared. Perhaps four thousand were killed. The li-

brary in the Vatican was only saved by the intervention of the Prince of Orange on his sickbed. The courtier Castiglione saw the death of Bourbon as
a sign of divine fury against Charles's army.[41]

Charles the Emperor, learning of the event in mid-June, said that he had
not wanted this denouement, and we cannot doubt that he opposed the
cruelties practiced by his army. All the same, the pope in the Castel Sant'-
Angelo was now his prisoner, just as Francis I had been. Charles wrote to
Bourbon before he knew of his death that what he wanted most was "a
good peace" and he hoped that the pope would come to Spain to help to
achieve it.[42] Gattinara remained in touch, and his gifted secretary Alfonso
de Valdés wrote in his dialogue *Lactancio y un arcediacono,* rather remarkably, that Rome got no more than it deserved.[43]

Charles then gave himself up to the pleasure of celebrating at Valladolid
the birth of his heir, the infante Philip, in the house of Bernardino Pimentel, of the great family of the Count-Duke of Benavente, just opposite
the church of San Pablo. The Emperor had with him for the first time the
beautiful set of tapestries made in honor of his coronation in Aachen in
1520, "The Honors," they were called. They depicted all the necessary qualities of a prince.[44]

In June, Francisco de Montejo, that most experienced conquistador
who would have benefited from all those virtues himself, left Sanlúcar with
his expedition of four ships and 250 men for Yucatán;[45] and Pánfilo de
Narváez left for Florida with his six hundred men in three ships.[46]

Intellectual Spain settled down the same month to discuss the importance of the works of Erasmus, under the benign chairmanship of the remarkable grand inquisitor Alonso de Manrique de Lara, the liberal
churchman to whom Erasmus had dedicated his *Enchiridion militis cris-
tiani.* Manrique de Lara, a cousin of the Duke of Nájera, was a half brother
of the great poet Jorge Manrique ("Our lives are rivers which flow into the
sea"). The new inquisitor knew much. He had become a friend of Charles
during his childhood in the Netherlands and had presided over the Mass in
the cathedral of Saint-Gudule proclaiming Charles King of Spain in 1516.[47]
Earlier, Manrique de Lara had been bishop of Badajoz, where he spent
much of his time converting Muslims, many of whom took the name of
Manrique. He had been a strong *felipista*—a supporter of the late King
Philip—and later was imprisoned by that monarch, but he was also a cor-

respondent of Cisneros, who made him bishop of Córdoba. Manrique de Lara was with Charles at his coronation at Aachen and was named archibishop of Seville as well as chief inquisitor by him in 1524. A modern historian calls him *"un hombre ilustre, cortesano, erasmista y abierto."*[48] Such adjectives are not easy to apply to later chiefs of the Holy Office.

The Spanish translation of Erasmus's *Enchiridion,* which issued from the press of Miguel de Eguía, printer of Alcalá, now had a popular success without precedent in the history of printing up to that time. The translator was a famous preacher, Alonso Fernández de Madrid, canon of Palencia and archdeacon of Alcor.

Manrique made the effort to try to convert the Holy Office into an agent for the diffusion of Erasmian ideas, a most remarkable epoch in the history of that institution. Perhaps Bartolomé de las Casas had similar hopes for the Holy Office when in 1517 he urged Cisneros to support its establishment in the New World.

All the great names in the Spanish Church were at the discussions of Erasmus's ideas in Seville: Antonio de Guevara, author of *The Golden Book of Marcus Aurelius,* which he was still pretending that he had discovered in the library of Cosimo de' Medici in Florence; Francisco de Vitoria, the great jurist then still at San Esteban, the Dominican monastery in Salamanca; Siliceo, young but already known as a hard-line anti-Semite. They heard the chief inquisitor give a powerful defense of his Flemish friend Erasmus. This was the second such discussion, for there had been something similar, on a lesser scale, in March. The Council of the Inquisition firmly maintained their support for Erasmus. The Augustinian Fray Dionisio Vázquez, looked upon as the greatest of preachers at that time and renowned in Italy as much as in Spain, even made an elegy about the great Fleming.[49] After all, even the pope had praised the Renaissance humanist.

But danger lay ahead for all friends of the great Rotterdam thinker. After the transfer of the *chancellería* to Granada in 1505, the Spanish bureaucracy took a harsh line in most matters. When the Inquisition that had been established at Jaén was also transferred there, this line was all the more emphasized.

8

Four Brothers in a Conquest: The Alvarados and Guatemala

> I again fitted out Alvarado and dispatched him from this city
> [Mexico] on the sixth of December 1523. He took with him
> 120 horsemen with spare mounts, a total of 160 horse, together
> with 300 footsoldiers, 130 of whom were crossbowmen and arque-
> busiers.
>
> CORTÉS TO CHARLES V, *Fourth letter*

These heady theological uncertainties in Seville seemed far away from the practical politics of New Spain. For another remarkable expedition mounted by Cortés was led by the brilliant, brutal, unpredictable, fascinating, and brave Pedro de Alvarado, an Extremeño from Badajoz, to the Tehuantepec peninsula and subsequently to Guatemala. Far away Guatemala may seem, yet the Spaniards were conquistadors from Extremadura. In November 1522, Alvarado had obtained a large *encomienda* in watery Xochimilco, just to the south of Mexico-Tenochtitlan, and then one in Tututepec in Tlaxcala.[1] He had been used by Cortés since the conquest of Mexico-Tenochtitlan in August 1521, in a variety of ways: in Veracruz, in relation to Cristóbal de Tapia, the King's representative (or the bishop of Burgos's), sent improbably in December 1521 to seize command from Cortés; then in Pánuco in 1523 to deal with Francisco de Garay. But this complex and usually successful Extremeño now wanted a theater of conquest for himself.

In December 1523, Cortés gave Alvarado the mission to go to Gua-temala to see if indeed, as he had been told, there were there "many rich

and splendid lands inhabited by new and different races."[2] Presumably
Cortés had also been informed that the region was fertile, that it produced
both cotton and cacao, and that it had once contained the wild forebears of
such plants as maize, tomato, avocado, and sweet potato. Cortés was always
anxious to give his close friends a chance to fulfill themselves. With Alvarado in particular, he was always generous, for he had known him since
their childhood together in Extremadura and throughout the conquest of
Mexico. Alvarado's reckless valor (with his own life, as well as those of others) and insolent pride impressed Cortés, who was prudent, cautious, cultivated, and patient: it was the charm of opposites. Alvarado, sometimes
known as Tonatiuh (Son of the Sun) or sometimes just El Sol (Sun), to the
native Indians because of his fair hair, height, good looks, and blue eyes,
was the most popular of the many brave men whom Cortés had in his
army.[3] Bernal Díaz wrote that Cortés had asked Alvarado "to try and bring
the people [of Guatemala] to peace [with Spain] without waging war and
to preach matters concerning our holy faith by means of the interpreters
which he took with him."[4] He took the opportunity to say that Alvarado
was "very well made and active, of good features and bearing, and both in
appearance and speech so pleasing that he seemed always smiling."[5] He was
an excellent horseman, liked rich clothes, always had round his neck a
small gold chain on which hung a jewel, and he wore also a ring with a
good diamond. Díaz del Castillo's criticism was that he talked too much
and sometimes cheated at *totoloque*.[6] Others would complain that he was
insensitive to the feelings of Indians, whom he treated as beneath con-
tempt.[7] Several of his soldiers in this journey to Guatemala later testified to
his brutality.

Alvarado set off. The distance was, of course, considerable. Even now to
travel by land from Mexico to Guatemala is a challenge. Aldous Huxley
wrote of the journey from Oaxaca to Chiapas with awe. But he did not
travel by foot or on a horse, as Alvarado did, seeing for himself the long line
of the Pacific coast.

Alvarado took with him about 330 men, of whom 120 were horse, the
rest infantrymen. He had four pieces of artillery, which he arranged to be
pulled by Indians,[8] and he had a strong force of crossbowmen and musketeers. It was a family expedition from the beginning. With him rode his
brothers—Jorge, Gonzalo, and Gómez—all of whom had accompanied

Cortés on his dramatic journeys, as well as two nephews, Diego and Hernando de Alvarado, and his future son-in-law, Francisco de la Cueva. He had a chaplain in the shape of Fray Bartolomé de Olmedo, the Mercedarian who had been with Cortés: He was responsible for 2,500 conversions before the end of 1524, when he died.[9] All these friends and relations worshipped Pedro de Alvarado. In addition, Alvarado had with him a substantial number of "natives" from central Mexico—perhaps six thousand or seven thousand men, according to Antonio de Luna, in an inquiry of 1570—including, it would seem, both Mexica and people from Tlaxcala, the Spaniards' chief allies. There seem also to have been a prudent number of black African slaves.[10]

Alvarado took a month to reach Soconusco, a territory well known for its chocolate and, then as now, for its beautiful, large women. Jorge de Alvarado was allocated that place as an *encomienda* by his brother, Pedro (Cortés himself had had it for a year or two).[11] It had been fully conquered by the Mexica only in the early years of the century, in the days of Montezuma, but it had been sending semiannual tribute to the Mexica in Tenochtitlan for forty years before that.[12] It was known for its supply of beautiful green feathers from the quetzal bird. Probably the plumage in the famous headdress in Vienna derived from birds from here.

The Alvarados were now on the verge of entering present-day Guatemala. At that time, three dominant peoples lived there: the Quichés, the Cakchiquels, and the Tzutúhil. All were close in social structure to the Mexica, and their priests said that they and their leaders originally came from Tollan and Teotihuacan. Beyond were a warlike tribe called the Mam. Archaelogists argue that there had been three waves of invasion from the north. These northern invaders had brought with them the idea of cremation rather than burial, they used caves (in which they deposited deities) for worship, they had a cult of war, they had good metallurgical traditions, they had experimented with a bicephalous system of government in the style of Rome or Sparta, they had sunken ball courts with vertical walls, they preferred *tortillas* to *tamales,* and they had regular commercial relations with Tenochtitlan. They fought with grenades of pottery sometimes filled with fire, sometimes with wasps or hornets: they decapitated prisoners; and they had bark on which to write painted genealogical trees. Their people wore cotton clothing: the women sarongs, the men loincloths. They had above all brought down from old Mexico the god of rain, Tlaloc, and

some of his companions in the pantheon of Mexican deities such as Xipe
Totec, the terrifying flayed fertility god, and Xolotl, the evening star who
was Quetzalcoatl's half brother. Their calendar contained, as did that of
Tenochtitlan, a sacred cycle of fifty-two years. They did not celebrate
human sacrifice on anything like the scale that was practiced in the sixteenth century by the Mexica, which makes one see that the legends suggesting that the practice had much increased in the last generations before
the arrival of the Spaniards were probably right. Famous opponents were
the only ones to be routinely killed.[13]

Though the Quiché and the Cakchiquels were plainly related, they had
fought one another for years over possession of cacao and cotton fields.
That was what marked them. Had the Spaniards not come, the region
would probably have been eventually conquered by the Mexica.[14] The land,
Alvarado reported to his leader, Cortés, was so thickly populated that
"there are more people than Your Excellency has governed till now."[15] Like
all comments at that time on populations, or the size of armies, that was an
exaggeration. But archaeologists have found pyramidical mounds of old
Guatemala in which there were fifteen million shards, perhaps from about
half a million vessels, suggesting that the mounds must have been built in
the early Christian era by ten to twelve thousand laborers.

The country included the Cuchumatan highlands, the most sensational
nonvolcanic region of Central America. The name may signify "that which
has come together with great force," but it can also mean, in Nahuatl, "place
of the parrot hunters." There are also the jungle lowlands of Petén and a
chain of active and geologically young volcanic peaks, which can be seen
from the sea and which inspired Disraeli's famous comment about the
aging Whig cabinet of 1868.[16]

Guatemala was also the land of *Popol Vuh,* a poem composed in the
fourth century A.D. about the creation of the world. By 1500 it probably
had as many versions as there are dialects of Maya, but the one that has survived is that of one of the leading clans of the Quiché. The book that contained it was traditionally said to have been obtained as a result of a
journey to the Atlantic or Caribbean coast and would be consulted by the
lords of Quiché when they sat in council. The Quiché referred to the volume as "The light which came from near the sea." Other names for it were
"Our place in the shadows" or "The dawn of Life."

The existence of this remarkable poem along with high-class pottery, elaborate ball courts, and dance platforms for the performance of religious and historical music dramas, as well as the Annals of the Cakchiquel,[17] made Guatemala one of the most sophisticated countries the Spaniards set out to conquer. Repetitive, contradictory, and often incomprehensible to the modern reader, *Popol Vuh* has about it an unquestionable profundity, which makes it a landmark of indigenous literature.

Once beyond Soconusco in January 1524, Alvarado sent messages to the lords of Guatemala asking them not to impede his progress but to submit themselves to him as the representative of Charles the Emperor. If they resisted, he declared, he would make war on them. He understandably received no reply. Such communications were relatively easy, since Nahuatl was understood in many Quiché and Cakchiquel towns. So Alvarado's mercenaries from Tlaxacala or Tenochtitlan could talk together easily and secure supplies at least of maize made into *tortillas,* or into drink (*atole*), or even boiled in a leaf (*tamale*), as today.

Alvarado moved on, passing Zapotitlán, the land of the sapodilla plum. Afterwards, the journey became more difficult since they were obliged to continue along the coastal plain, the *llanura costera,* between the sparsely populated Sierra Madre de Chiapas, which rises to about 4,000 feet at its border with Oaxaca and to 10,000 feet on the southeast frontier into Guatemala and the Pacific Ocean. The mosquitoes never left the Spaniards, who suffered thereby more than if they had met ferocious enemies. These, too, they encountered, though on a small scale. On February 19, they struck inland and up the hillside. This was the first time that any European had seen, much less visited, these Pacific-facing hills.

The pueblos of the mountains were small clusters of twenty-four to thirty-six mud-walled houses with palm-leaf roofs. The only certain item in these houses was a tripodal stone for grinding corn—a rounded or rectangular slab of hard igneous rock whose grinding surface would have been worn in the center. The villages were usually undefended, there were no avenues or fine plazas, nor, indeed, any kind of urban planning. What they did have, though, was much superb monochrome or bichrome pottery made into bowls, pots, and incense burners with three legs, as well as figurines and whistles.

Popol Vuh seemed to have forecast the Spaniards' arrival: "And it is not clear how they crossed the sea, They crossed over as if there had been no

sea. Where the waters were divided, they crossed over." The Quiché people
were, therefore, on a war footing. They fell on Alvarado's indigenous mercenaries with pleasure. Their temporary success was set back by Alvarado's
horsemen. But the Quiché had heard of the menace of the horsemen and
recovered to attack the Spaniards from above, in a valley under the volcano
Santa María, approximately where there is now the city of Quezaltenango
(Xela in Maya). The attack was eventually held and pressed back, the
Quiché leader Tecún Umán being killed, perhaps by Alvarado himself. The
Maya insisted that Tecún Umán immediately became a god, in the shape of
an eagle with quetzal plumes.[18] The legendary ability of many Quiché to
become animals impressed even Alvarado.

After the battle, the Spaniards rested several days, only to receive yet another attack by another Quiché army, numbering, so Alvarado grandly put
it, twelve thousand. This was also defeated by a clever Spanish combination
of artillery and cavalry. After this, the Quiché agreed to seek peace and invited Alvarado to negotiate with them at Utatlán, their main city, a characteristic hilltop fortress town, known for the legend of the so-called
"marvellous Kings," Gucumatz, who died in 1425, and Quicab, who died in
1475.[19] Those mythical individuals have reminded some learned archaeologists of the great god Quetzalcoatl in Mexico (Ehecatl, in Guatemala)
and there were in Guatemala certainly the circular temples with which that
deity had been associated in Tenochtitlan. There were ceremonial plazas
and buildings that served as tombs, painted temples, and good avenues
alongside pyramids as in Teotihuacán. The fine pottery from here included
many figurines. The Spaniards duly went there in March, by then knowing
of the tribal hatreds between the Quichés and the Cakchiquels, with the
last-named of whom Alvarado had just made an alliance and who were
said to have provided him with four thousand men.

Alvarado found the city closed. Rightly afraid of being trapped with his
horses and all his followers if he went inside, he camped outside the walls.
There he received a visit from two lords who emerged from inside Utatlán.
The discussions went badly, and Alvarado imprisoned them. This infuriated the other Quiché leaders, who ordered an attack. Alvarado responded
by putting the city to the torch and, in the fire, amid sporadic fighting, the
leaders whom he had captured were burned.[20]

Alvarado was later accused of inhumanity in this instance: A number of

Spanish witnesses were asked in interminable later lawsuits in Spain if they knew that when "the said Pedro de Alvarado was the captain . . . at Utlatan [sic] and at Guatimala [sic] . . . certain lords came in peace and said Pedro de Alvarado seized them and burned them for no good reason other than that he wanted to know if they had any gold."[21] The accusations never ended, but Alvarado was never charged.

In April 1524, Alvarado turned on the Cakchiquel who, from their capital at Quahtematlan, had observed with pleasure the defeat of their Quiché enemies. All the same, they were fearful of the Spaniards with their guns, their horses, and not least, their terrifying war dogs. They urged Alvarado to take his army against the people of Atitlán, another town of the Cakchiquels, who had already shown their hostility to Spaniards by killing four messengers who had come to propose a pact. So on April 17, 1524, Alvarado led a detachment of sixty horse, 150 foot, and a large unit of Cakchiquels toward Atitlán. After a skirmish with Tzutu Indians by a lakeside, they reached their destination with ease. But the city was deserted, for the people were justifiably terrified. Alvarado did, however, find some Indians and sent them to tell their lords that he would make peace with them if they returned and declared themselves vassals of the King of Spain. The lords soon accepted these conditions, but whether they understood what they had undertaken is doubtful. The word *vassal* is not easily comprehended.

In May, Alvarado embarked on a new journey to the south of Guatemala to Panatcat (Escuintla), where some of Alvarado's indigenous allies, especially some who had come with him from Texcoco, were caught off their guard and slaughtered. Alvarado punished the town by burning it. He continued onward, passing through Atepac, Tacuilulá, Taxisco, Moquisalco, and Nancintla, and across the river now known as the Río Paz, into what is now El Salvador. Everywhere the meeting between the Spaniards and the *naturales* was similar: The former were received in peace; the *naturales* then abandoned the town and fled to the hills, where they planned a resistance. The only serious battle was at Achiutla, the gateway to El Salvador, where about six thousand fighters launched a serious attack and killed many of Alvarado's indigenous allies. No Spaniards died, but some were wounded, including Alvarado himself. An arrow went through his leg and left him for a time crippled, one leg seeming for a long while shorter than the other. Alvarado's life was for several months at risk because of infection.

Alvarado eventually continued into El Salvador, putting up with further attacks at Tlacusqualco and halting at Cuzcatlán, the most important of these towns, where the Spaniards would shortly found a settlement that they named San Salvador. One of Alvarado's soldiers, Román Lópes, would testify later that, on the way to this city, the population of all the towns en route "came out in peace and Alvarado then burned them and made slaves of the people and branded them." Pedro González de Nájera, who had come to New Spain with Narváez, said the same: "This witness was with Pedro de Alvarado and was present when those concerned were burned because they desired to burn them."²² The lords in this last place offered food, fruit, cloaks—and obedience. But they then fled to the hillside as usual. After two and a half weeks, the Spaniards moved on to Ixmide, which they reached on July 21, and where soon, because of the date, they decided to found Santiago de los Caballeros de Guatemala (the day of Saint James, Santiago, is July 25). It would become the main city of the colony, though it suffered several changes of site (one can still see the narrow causeway that Alvarado and his men used to storm the old city). Alvarado gave this new city several municipal councillors or *alcaldes ordinarios* (Diego de Rojas from Seville and a son of Leonora de Alvarado, Baltasar de Mendoza) while his brother Gonzalo became the *alguacil mayor* (chief constable). Thus the ways of Spain were once again transferred to a new site in an unknown country.

Here, eight months after leaving Mexico, Alvarado and his men rested. All his surviving indigenous troops except the loyal people of Tlaxcala made their way homeward. But "Tonatiuh" himself imposed on his Cakchiquel allies a tribute in gold, which he said that they had to pay even though they were helping him so substantially. The lords of the Cakchiquels refused and recommended all their people to abandon the cities and take refuge in the hills. The friendship between Alvarado and these people was thus broken.

But once again old hatreds were the best allies of the invaders. The Quichés and the people of Atitlán were happy to fight against their Cakchiquel enemies, even under new circumstances. The Cakchiquels had, however, learned new tactics from their months of alliance with the

Spaniards, whom they forced to return to Quetzaltenango. Diego de Alvarado, nephew of Pedro, took two years reducing Cuzcatlán, while Gonzalo, his uncle, conquered the territory of the Mam between Chiapas and the Quiché. Gonzalo de Alvarado was named by his brother to conduct this campaign after it became evident that an abortive plan to burn the Spaniards at Atitlán in 1524 had been suggested to the Quiché leader, Chugna Huincelet, by the Mam, Caibil Balam. Chugna was killed, but his son Sequechul wanted to avenge him. Sequechul offered to guide Gonzalo to "the great and rich territory" of the Mam, which boasted what he explained was an abundant treasure.

For a year or so the initiative for further conquests lay with Gonzalo de Alvarado, not Pedro, who took many months to recover from the wound in his leg. Gonzalo had been in the Indies since 1510 and had been with Cortés throughout the great campaigns of conquest. He was devoted to his famous family and had even married into it since his wife, Bernardina, was his niece, being the daughter of Jorge de Alvarado (who himself had married Luisa de Estrada).

In July 1525, Gonzalo de Alvarado left Tecpán-Guatemala for the country of the Mam with forty horse, about eighty infantry, and two thousand or so Mexica and Quiché Indians, who acted either as porters or warriors in the early stages of the battles. He was delayed by the onset of rains. They went first to Totonicapán, on the edge of the Mam land, then to what they named the Río Hondo, "the deep river," and seized the town of Mazatenango, which they re-christened San Lorenzo. Marching beyond that pueblo toward Huehuetenango, they met a Mam army from Malacatán. But Gonzalo de Alvarado charged it with his horsemen, and the Mam leader Cani Acab was killed by the Spanish commander himself with his lance. As so often after the death of a leader, the native resistance collapsed, and Gonzalo occupied Malacatán, whose inhabitants swiftly accepted to become vassals of the King of Spain.

The next Mam town to be occupied was Huehuetenango, where fine birds such as the quetzal, parrot, and cotinga could be found, with feathers for headdresses and cloaks, and whose inhabitants fled first to the fortress town of Zaculeu with ravines on three sides. This had been an important center of Mam culture for one thousand years. It had been captured by the Quichés in the early fifteenth century. But recently it had asserted what seemed to have been independence.

Gonzalo de Alvarado demanded its peaceful surrender: "Let it be known [to Caibil Balam] that our coming is beneficial to his people because we bring news of the true God and of the Christian religion sent by the Pope, the Vicar of Jesus, as of the Emperor King of Spain so that you may become Christians peacefully of your own free will. But if you should refuse our offer of peace, the death and destruction which will follow will be your own responsibility."[23] Gonzalo gave his opponents three days in which to consider his offer. No answer came. Instead, a Mam army came from the north to relieve Zaculeu. Gonzalo left his deputy, Antonio de Salazar, to continue the siege (Salazar had been with Narváez in New Spain and had subsequently been in most of Cortés's battles round the lake of Tenochtitlan).[24] He turned on the relief force, though by now his men were hungry, without much hope of food until Zaculeu was taken. The Spanish mercenaries were as usual held by the Indians, who were forced into defeat by the horsemen. Gonzalo returned to Zaculeu with starvation threatening. His surviving Indian auxiliaries were forced to eat dead horses. But then Juan de León Cardona, whom Pedro de Alvarado had made captain of the conquered Quiché territory, sent a substantial shipment of food. Zaculeu surrendered in September 1525, and Gonzalo assumed the command of all the western Cuchumatans.

By then, Pedro de Alvarado had recovered adequately from his wound to be able to contemplate a new expedition of his own, this time into Chiapas, seeking to meet his old commander and comrade Cortés, who was then en route for Higueras to punish the willful Cristóbal de Olid. Chiapas, it will be recalled, had some years before been conquered by Sandoval. Alvarado wanted Cortés's support for his claim formally to become governor of Guatemala. But the dense jungles, the colossal rivers, and the wonderful mountains made any thought of meeting Cortés impracticable.

Alvarado returned to Guatemala, where he found that several of his settlements, such as San Salvador, had been destroyed. All the same, he had become attached to Guatemala and its people, even though he had treated them so harshly. Perhaps the landscape counted for him, improbable though it may seem. Relentless men have soft sides. The range of altitude, climate, and vegetation along the Pacific coast is astonishing. Perhaps he liked the cypresses, the high fertile valleys, the temperate climate, the volcanic stone for grinding maize and sharp knives, the availability of lime for mortar. The narrow coastal plain is very well watered. There was obsidian for weapons and iron pyrites with which to make looking glasses. There was a little gold in the streams, as well as copper, and also abundant fresh fish, and shellfish at the coast. There was bark for making paper, silk and cotton for quilted armor, tobacco, pumpkins for music, bees for honey. Some Spaniards were impressed by the diversity of gods in Guatemala, as by the ritual invoked on all occasions of celebration and by the speed with which Catholic saints were identified with local gods. Certainly this was a territory much richer than Alvarado's hometown of Badajoz in Extremadura.

Hearing that Francisco de Montejo, a comrade of his in the early days of the campaign in New Spain, had been granted the governorship of Yucatán, Alvarado determined to return to Mexico-Tenochtitlan and then to Spain to obtain a similar nomination for himself in Guatemala. He had by then taken "such a fancy to this land of Guatemala and its people that he decided to stay there and colonise. So he laid the foundation for Santiago de Guatemala and prepared a cathedral."[25] He also established *encomiendas* and a town council for his new city, from whose members he went through the motions of requesting permission, as acting governor, to leave for Spain. His brother Jorge then became acting governor from August 1526.

Though the conquest of Guatemala was far from complete, Alvarado had made his mark there, and as Tonatiuh, Son of the Sun, he would be remembered in his absence. The Quiché lords would perhaps echo the prayer of the lords in *Popol Vuh*: "Heart of Sky, heart of earth, give me strength, give me the courage, in my heart, in my head, for you are my mountain and my plain."[26]

9

Charles and His Empire

I counted from a mosque [in Cholula] four hundred and more towers in the city and all of them are mosques.

CORTÉS FROM CHOLULA TO CHARLES V, *Third letter,* 1522

Some modern historians have fallen into the trap of thinking that the emperor Charles paid little attention to his transatlantic possessions.[1] These suppositions are not borne out, even considering his activities in Valladolid in 1522. For example, we hear that, early in that year, he prolonged for another four years the lucrative monopoly of Laurent de Gorrevod, the Savoyard governor of the Bresse, and protégé-friend of the archduchess Margaret of Austria, on the sale of black African slaves in the Empire. From November 1523, this arrangement was annulled, and the import of slaves was permitted to the Indies along new lines: 1,400 were permitted a year in Santo Domingo, seven hundred in Cuba, six hundred in Mexico, five hundred in San Juan and Castilla de Oro, and three hundred to Jamaica (Santiago). Gorrevod was compensated by receiving the duty (*almojarifazgo*) on the 1,400 slaves destined for Santo Domingo.

That demanding but blunt and simple tax was always changing. In 1524, it was introduced on all goods entering New Spain, and 50,000 pesos were raised by it in the next seven years.[2] Then, as we have seen, in October 1522, only three months after his return to Spain for his second stay, Charles sent there those four important officials to "assist" Cortés in the government of Mexico; and there was also the reception of the world travelers Elcano and Pigafetta when they came back from the journey they had made, at Charles's cost, round the world on the initiative of the dead Magellan.[3] First as an emergency, from 1523 onward the Crown seized all precious metals sent home from the Indies. Then as a matter of course all such private gold was automatically turned into *juros,* which resulted in periodic payments of a fixed rate of interest.[4]

It is true that in the 1520s the Spanish income from the Indies was modest. The total amounted in 1520 to 1525 to a mere 134,000 pesos; the Crown's share was 35,000. In comparison, between 1516 and 1520, these figures were 993,000, with the Crown's share 260,000.[5] Between 1526 and 1530, the income was more than a million pesos, of which the Crown's share was 272,000. Very soon, events in Peru would transform this situation for the better.

In 1526, Charles was persuaded to grant the government of Yucatán and Cozumel, which had often been visited by Spaniards but not yet conquered, to Francisco de Montejo, the hidalgo from Salamanca who had represented Cortés in Spain in the early days of his great adventure.[6] Montejo had been a friend of Diego Velázquez, the governor of Cuba, before Cortés's expedition had begun, but had become one of Cortés's allies in consequence of his achievements. Montejo's character was not grasping. He wanted glory more than gold. Now he was requesting a theater of operations for himself.

The same year, it became normal that those who undertook to grow sugar in the Indies could obtain a government loan, as Juan Mosquera did in February 1523 in Cuba. Mosquera was a notary (*escribano*) as well as an *encomendero* in Santo Domingo, where he was once "visitor," that is, an occasional inspector, and where he had the luxury of a stone house. He was said to have been "a man of very low manners, very passionate and the enemy of good men."[7] Mosquera's laudable aim, however, was to achieve free trade for the settlers in Cuba with other islands in the Caribbean.[8]

Another imperial concession of this time was to Licenciado Lucás Vázquez de Ayllón, an old hand in the Indies. Born in Toledo, he was the son of a certain councillor of that city, Juan de Ayllón, known as "the Good." He had gone out to the Caribbean in 1504, in Ovando's day, and to begin with dedicated himself to agriculture and to mining, becoming *alcalde mayor* (chief magistrate), in Concepción, in Santo Domingo. Perhaps he was a converso.[9] He made money on a property at Chicora, where he owned several hundred Indians.[10] In 1505, he appears as a university graduate in support of the intelligent judge Alonso de Maldonado. Back in Spain for a year or two, he returned to Santo Domingo in 1509 to take the *residencia* of Ovando. In 1512, he was rather improbably (given his past) named judge in the first supreme court (*audiencia*) of the Indies.

This appointment did not prevent him from continuing to deal in indigenous slaves from the Lesser Antilles, many of whom were destined for the icy-cold pearl fisheries of Cubagua, off Santa Margarita. Mosquera was moreover a financial backer of Juan Bono's expedition for slaves to Trinidad in 1516, and he also had for a time a monopoly on selling slaves from the Lucayos (the Bahamas or "useless islands").[11] His headquarters was Puerto Plata on the north coast of La Española. There he had by 1522 a half share in a new sugar mill. Thinking perhaps of the labor needed in that enterprise, he commented that it was "far better that these Indians became slave men than free beasts."[12] Difficult though it may be for a later age to face such a dilemma, the consideration was almost a normal one in the sixteenth century.

Vázquez de Ayllón was the leading figure in the destruction of the free population of the Bahamas, as well as a leading colonist of Santo Domingo, where he married Juana, daughter of Esteban de Pasamonte, treasurer of the island after the death of his uncle Miguel.

This Vázquez had been sent by the court of Santo Domingo, of which he remained a member, to Cuba to detain Narváez's fleet against Cortés in 1520. But he was confronted by Narváez and, after a stay in New Spain as unfortunate as it was brief, he returned in a long sea journey to Santo Domingo.[13] Going back to Castile, he was an influential witness testifying against Diego Velázquez in favor of Cortés. He became a Knight of Santiago. Now he pursued his new adventure in Florida, which he was told was ruled by a giant ("*señoreado de un hombre de estatura de gigante*"). He went back again to Santo Domingo and spent his fortune on the Florida expedition, which he would not embark upon till 1526.[14]

The early decisions of the Council of the Indies included: a license to allow merchants from ports other than Seville to trade with the Indies without registering in the Casa de la Contratación (the board in Seville that managed relations with the New World);[15] a contract for Santa Marta on the north coast of South America for Rodrigo de Bastidas, Cortés's backer, an adventurous converso merchant of Triana; a permission to all subjects of the Spanish world to go to the New World without distinction as to whence they derived;[16] and a ban on future conquistadors seizing people from the West Indies or the mainland except for those who might be needed as interpreters. This last was a benign idea, which was not carried through. A similar fate had befallen one of the most liberal orders to emerge from the Council of the Indies before it had formally taken shape on March 8, 1523, when it was decreed that henceforth no war should be made against the Indians nor should any harm or damage come to them.[17] This was an early manifestation in Spain of the ideas of Fray Bartolomé de las Casas, who at this time was still in his Dominican monastery in Santo Domingo studying for his subsequent campaigns.

In July 1523, Charles gave a coat of arms to Tenochtitlan, or Mexico, as it was by then increasingly known. The grant was a great accolade, for no such concession had previously been made in the Caribbean. The device was characteristic: a shield colored blue like water to recall the great lake on which the city had been built, and a gilded castle in the center of it connected to the mainland by three causeways or stone bridges. A lion was guarding each of these bridges, and its arms lay on the castle as a memory of the victory the Christians had gained. The border of the design consisted of ten ears of green prickly pears (*nopals*) with thistles.[18]

The year 1523 significantly saw the publication in Toledo of what became a popular novel, *Clarín de Landanís,* by Jerónimo López, as well as *Raimundo of Greece* by Francisco Bernal in Salamanca. The latter treated of a powerful king of Egypt named Cleopatro; a wise lady, Piromancia, who lived in Alexandria; and a duke, Pirineo, who lived in India. The kings of Scotland and Norway make fleeting appearances.[19] All the signs are that this work, too, became popular and that it inspired, as well as amused, the court and, the conquistadors.

The Council of the Indies was certainly active by April 1526,[20] when it announced that, being in Seville for the wedding of the King-Emperor, it was asked to investigate the activities of the Casa de la Contratación, which continued to be based in that city. There had been many rumors of corruption. The council asked the chief magistrates of nearby maritime towns (Sanlúcar, Palos, Moguer, Puerto de Santa María, Niebla) and the *corregidores* of Cádiz and Jerez de la Frontera to proclaim this visit by town crier.

The council began by taking statements from witnesses, and it undertook to make a report within thirty days. All the chief pilots were consulted. But the council took longer in their work than they had promised. In November 1527, they said that, having finished the accounts of the Casa itself, they would examine those of the officials and the treasure fleets' accountants. In the end, they found one official guilty of corrupt practice: Juan López de Recalde. All the same, they did find much evidence of incompetence. For example, the administration of the goods of people who had died in the Indies had been spectacularly badly managed.

López de Recalde's condemnation was a blow to the Casa de la Contratación. He had been a power in Seville since the institution had been founded and had been accountant of it since 1505. It had been he who, in 1518, had initially bought Gorrevod's grant of a monopoly on slaves for the Spanish empire, though he had resold it immediately. He had been the chief assistant to Rodríguez de Fonseca in organizing the King's fleet to Germany in 1520.[21] He had been the great friend in Andalusia of numerous successful Basque merchants.[22] He had married Lorenza de Idiáquez, a sister of Alonso de Idiáquez, who was Cobos's majordomo and who would play a considerable part in bureaucratic policies in the next twenty years. López's denunciation by Juan de Aranda (who had organized Magellan's expedition and milked the participants) marked the end of the power of the old Fonsequistas in the Casa.

For the moment, the only consequence of this investigation was the building in August of a chapel in the Casa de la Contratación, where prayers for the souls of the dead explorers could be offered beneath the Flemish painter Alejo Fernández's beautiful picture *The Virgin of the Mariners.*[23]

In November 1526, the Council of the Indies met in Granada in the Alhambra. Charles, unusually, was presiding. There were present the three bishops who played the determining role on the council (García de Loaisa, Maldonado, and Cabeza de Vaca), together with Cobos, Dr. Beltrán, Juan de Samano, and Cortés's distant relation, Dr. Ladislao Galíndez de Carvajal, who was a member of the Royal Council and who had much curiosity about the Indies. There was also Urbina, secretary to the chancellor in the absence of his master, Gattinara himself.[24]

The council took what seems to read now as a remarkably humane decision. Talking of "the disorganised greed of some of our subjects who go to our Indies" and of "the bad treatment which they show to the Indians native to those islands and on the mainland," not to speak of the "great and excessive labour which they provide for them in mines to find gold" and "in the pearl fisheries and in other farming," the conquistadors were accused of "making the Indians excessively and immoderately tired, not giving them enough to wear or to eat, treating them cruelly and with the reverse of love, much worse than if they were slaves." That had been the cause of the death of "a great number of the said Indians on such a scale that many of the islands and part of the mainland remain barren and without any population."

In addition, there were so many Indians who fled from the mines that "it was a great hindrance to the enterprise of trying to arrange the conversion of the said Indians to our Catholic faith" . . . "Too many captains, moved by the same greed, forgetting the service of our Lord God, went to kill many of those Indians in the discoveries and conquests and also seized their goods without the said Indians giving any cause for such a thing."

As for the *Requerimiento,* "when the captains of the King discovered or conquered a new territory, they were obliged to proclaim immediately to its Indian inhabitants that they had been sent to teach good customs" to "dissuade them from such vices as eating human flesh and to instruct them in the holy faith and preach it to them for their salvation." A list of wrongs done to the natives followed. Every leader licensed by the Crown to carry out an expedition was to take with him a copy of the so-called *Requeri-miento* and have it read by interpreters as many times as might be necessary. Every expedition henceforth also had to be accompanied by two churchmen, priests or friars, approved by the Council of the Indies. These men were to instruct the Indians in religious matters, to protect them from the rapacity and cruelty of (some) Spaniards, and ensure that the conquest was justly carried out. War was only to be waged after the ecclesiastics had given their consent in writing; and any such conflict had to be fought according to the methods permitted by law, the holy faith, and the Christian religion. In addition, no one could make a slave out of any Indian under pain of losing all his goods.[25]

This remarkable declaration remained the formal rule for the conduct of Spaniards in the New World for two generations. It was written into all capitulations and grants of opportunities from that day on, including, for example, the grant already mentioned to Francisco de Montejo in respect of Yucatán on December 6 of that year. That did not mean, however, a complete end to trading in Indian slaves. Thus on November 15, 1526, Charles the Emperor agreed to allow Juan de Ampiés to take Indians from the "useless isles" off Venezuela—Curaçao and Cubagua, for example.[26] The same day he gave full permission for any subject of his from anywhere in Europe to go to the New World.[27] This was a special benefit to Germans who wished to share in the banquet of the Indies.

These new decrees did not pass without challenge. The Cuban settlers, for example, thought that Indians might be made to wash for gold in rivers but not in mines. Even that led to complaints: Rodrigo Durán, a settler of Santiago de Cuba, said that, if the royal order even as modified were carried out, many colonists would leave the island. The settlers in Cuba described mining as easy work and insisted that "their" Indians preferred it to clearing land. Also, the Spaniards argued, workers were well fed at the mines on cassava bread and pork every day, whereas Indians in *encomiendas* had meat or fish only once a week. Ruin would surely follow any attempt to put these laws into effect.[28]

Rome continued to play a decisive part in the administrative history of the Indies. Thus in October 1523, the Flemish Erasmian Bishop Juan de Ubite, a Dominican in Cuba, was permitted to move his cathedral from the eastern extremity of Baracoa to "the most powerful place on the island— namely, Santiago."[29] (The King gave half his share of tithes in Santiago toward the completion of the cathedral.) Then in 1524, the new Pope Clement created a new patriarchate of the West Indies: the first to fill that role would be Antonio de Rojas Manrique, bishop of Palencia, then one of the richest Spanish dioceses (Valladolid was part of it).[30] This was a time when the Rojas family seemed to be filling every empty benefice, secular or ecclesiastical, in Spain. Bishop Antonio, after all, had been president of the Council of Castile for several years.[31]

Diego Colón, son of the immortal Christopher, had meantime returned to his governorship in Santo Domingo in 1520. He found the intrigues in that colony even worse than those in Seville. The chief intriguer remained the royal treasurer, the converso from Aragón, Miguel de Pasamonte, who had dominated the colony since his arrival there in 1508.[32] Despite Pasamonte's evident disposition to conspire, Díaz del Castillo wrote well of him: "personally worthy, of great good sense (*cordura*), honest to a fault, chaste all his life."[33]

After three years of revived proconsular life in Santo Domingo, Diego Colón and his wife, María Toledo y Rojas, niece of the Duke of Alba—they had all the pretensions of royalty—returned to Spain in October 1523, and two months later Charles, or rather the Council of the Indies, finally brought to an end the regime of the Columbus family in the New World. The title of Admiral of the Ocean Sea was suspended. All that the Columbuses retained was their dukedom of Veragua, a territory allegedly close to Panama. But though the regime of the Columbuses was at an end, María Toledo y Rojas retained her financial interests in the Caribbean. Having been a prominent dealer in Indian slaves, she became so in Africans. For the moment, she also retained her husband's income from the New World. Why the commerce in Africans was permitted and that in Indians discouraged is one of the mysteries of those days.

These events required a new governor of Santo Domingo. The government was for a time in the hands of a president of the court, and the choice of the Council of the Indies fell on Dr. Sebastián Ramírez de Fuenleal, a reliable public servant from a tiny village south of Cuenca, Villaescusa de Haro, who had been a judge in the Alpujarra Mountains during the Muslim rebellion there in 1500. Then he became an inquisitor in Seville.[34] Despite that role, which must have tried him, Ramírez de Fuenleal showed himself a humane proconsul. At that time, many liberal churchmen still sought to enter the Holy Office in order to humanize it. "There is no doubt," Ramírez once declared, "that the natives have sufficient capacity to receive the faith and that they greatly love it." He also thought that "they had sufficient capacity to carry on all mechanical and industrial arts."[35]

But Ramírez took a long time to reach Santo Domingo. Indeed, he only arrived in December 1528. In the meantime, Pasamonte had enjoyed, as he had so often before, de facto authority. He used this interregnum to allow many of his friends to trade in Indian slaves.

The leaders of these entrepreneurs were by now Juan (Martínez) de Ampiés and Jacome de Castellón. The former was an Aragonese friend of Pasamonte who had been the factor of Santo Domingo in 1511. Ampiés had given evidence of a rather harsh character to the legal enquiry mounted by the Jeronymites in 1517, agreeing that Indians were "lazy, luxurious, gluttonous and with a disinclination to have any affections if left in liberty."[36] Despite that, in 1524, he sent an armada to bring eight hundred Indian slaves to Santo Domingo from islands off Venezuela, and in 1525 he sent another expedition to the same region.

All these slaving expeditions derived from the use of captives in war or from kidnapping. There was none of the negotiation that by then characterized the purchase or exchange of African slaves. Ampiés spent eight months making friends with people in Curaçao and Aruba. He soon convinced himself that only he could establish good relations with the South American Indians. He had a plan to take some of the chiefs of Indians in what became Venezuela to Santo Domingo, educate and convert them, and then send them back to their old homes as Spanish agents. Ampiés would put up some of these doomed leaders in his own house in Santo Domingo. In order to protect his own interest on the South American coast, he also built a fortress on the island of Cubagua and named it, optimistically, Nueva Cádiz, which soon became a center of the pearl trade.

Cubagua, a small barren island off Santa Margarita, had been identified as a possible pearl fishery as early as 1502 by Rodrigo de Bastidas, the converso businessman who made a fortune in Santo Domingo. Within a few years, several Spanish adventurers had established pearl beds around the island, which was already mercilessly overfished. Spaniards did not know then that pearl fishing should be confined to the months of February, March, and April. They did realize, though, that the pearls were of good quality, if inferior to those of the East. The Blanca Rosada dominated.[37] Las Casas recalls what hard work fishing for pearls was. It meant diving deep in cold water, a task that even the strongest Indians performed under duress.

The other entrepreneur of importance was Jacome de Castellón, the natural son of a merchant of Genoa, Bernardo Castiglione, and a Spanish girl in Seville, Inés Suárez. At the time of his birth, the commerce of Seville and southwest Andalusia had been dominated by Genoese, and the early activities of trade in the West Indies were similarly marked. Jacome's elder brother, Tomás, had, to begin with, represented the family in La Española, but he had then gone to Puerto Rico, where he built the first sugar mill on the island and exploited the salt beds at San Juan. A cousin, Marcos Castellón, had an olive farm near Seville.

Jacome went out to the Indies for the first time in 1510, being then

eighteen. He became a partner of another Hispano-Genoese, Jerónimo
Grimaldi, with Diego Caballero. They together kidnapped Indian slaves
from the Bahamas or from the mainland. By 1522, he was captain of a
flotilla of his own, which went regularly to Cumána on the mainland just
beyond Cubagua, where, like Ampiés, he built a fortress and where he became chief magistrate (*alcalde mayor*) and received a salary in consequence. All the same, he continued to live in Santo Domingo. When he
received a coat of arms in 1527, it depicted a fortress with four Indian
heads bordering it.[38] By the 1530s, Jacome de Castellón, like his brother
Tomás in Puerto Rico, would have a sugar mill, "La Española," near Azua de
Compostela.[39]

The seizing, branding, and carriage of Indians as slaves from the Bahamas and northern South America seemed the major activity for Spanish
entrepreneurs in the 1520s. But Ampiés and Castellón were unable to carry
on after 1526, since the Crown allocated the geographer Fernández de Enciso most of the zone and then began to favor the German Welsers, to
whom the emperor Charles owed money.

Diego Caballero, however, received a contract in 1525 for the discovery,
development, and settlement of the coast of Maracaibo, from Cabo de la
Vela to Cabo de San Roman. It was thought that Lake Maracaibo might indeed lead to, or even constitute, the great strait to the Pacific, or Southern
Sea, of which so much had been said. That was one reason for the interest
of the Welsers from Augsburg.

Pedrarias, Panama, and Peru;
Guzmán in New Spain

The good soil discovered is the most abundant and possible to populate with Christians that you have ever seen . . . it has very fine gold.

FRANCISCO PIZARRO, ON GALLO ISLAND, TO PEDRO DE LOS RÍOS,
GOVERNOR OF PANAMA, JUNE 2, 1527

Pedrarias Dávila (Pedro Arias Ávila) was still the controlling genius in Spain's dominions in Panama and Nicaragua, though he was now well over seventy years of age. He had survived every challenge to his authority. He had outlived his benefactors, including King Fernando, as well as his enemies, such as Núñez de Balboa. It was said that he had made a pact with the devil to enable him to live so long. The judge of his *residencia,* Juan Ruiz de Alarcón, persuaded the aged governor to agree that he had discovered the Southern Sea at his own cost and founded there the city of Panama and so gained the credit for it.[1] No friend of Núñez de Balboa would have agreed with such a claim, but Balboa had now been forgotten: Indeed, in the many questions of Pedrarias's *residencia* questionnaire, the name of Balboa did not figure. Perhaps because Pedrarias had arranged a new distribution of ten thousand Indians to the Spaniards there, he was judged favorably: eighty-three *encomenderos* benefited.

The most recent distribution of Indians, it is true, particularly favored Pedrarias himself, since he would have the services of five hundred of them. Among the less well favored were resourceful men such as Diego de

Almagro, probably from the town of that name in New Castile, who received a new allocation of twenty Indians, just off Panama, in addition to the eighty that he already had on Susy; and the priest Hernando de Luque, a Sevillano from Morón de la Frontera, in the sierra near Seville, who received seventy Indians; and the illiterate giant Francisco Pizarro, from Trujillo in Extremadura, who also gained 150 Indians, on the island of Taboga, some fifteen miles off Panama. Of these last dependants of Pedrarias we shall soon hear more.[2]

The new allocation caused intense resentment, and a new lieutenant-governor of Panama, Licenciado Hernando de Celaya, who had already been named by the Council of the Indies in succession to Pedrarias as governor, reduced the old adventurer's share of Indians to 378. The sudden death of Celaya followed. His friends were not slow to draw a malign conclusion about Pedrarias's responsibility.

Soon Gil González Dávila, the royal accountant in Santo Domingo, came to Panama. Like so many officials in the Indies in the early days, he came to royal notice first through having been employed in the household of the much regretted Infante Juan. He then became a *contino* (courtier) of the royal household, a favorite of the courtly, corrupt, but competent bishop Rodríguez de Fonseca, and he had gone to La Española in 1509 with Diego Colón. He was one of those who, with Pasamonte, promoted the idea of taking Indians as slaves from the Bahamas. Elder brother to Alonso de Ávila, that successful captain of Cortés, he went first to Darien with Pedrarias. After several journeys back and forth to Spain, he reached Panama in 1522 to propose a journey to the West to explore the land, a companion being Peralonso Niño, a shipowner of the Columbine family of seamen of Moguer. The two went to Spain and gained a license to explore three thousand miles of the coast of the Southern Sea. That permit ordered Pedrarias to give them the ships that Balboa had had built near Panama. Pedrarias was reluctant to comply, royal decree or no, until he was offered a good financial share in the expedition.[3]

At much the same time, the governor gave permission to a companion of his, Pascual de Andagoya, to make a journey to the south. Andagoya was a Basque from a town of that name in Álava, the son of a hidalgo, Joan Ibáñez de Arza.[4] He went to the Indies in 1514 as a *criado* of Pedrarias, who indeed, in the will that he made before leaving Spain, left him a horse and

6,000 maravedís. Andagoya eventually established himself happily in Panama, becoming in 1521 a town councillor, and married a señorita Tovar, who had been in the train of Isabel de Bobadilla, the famous wife of Pedrarias. He once wrote: "Being already rich, I requested permission of the Governor Pedrarias to explore the coast beyond the bay of Saint Miguel"—that is, toward Peru, then known as Birú, of which he had heard rumors of wealth. It seemed that there might be another rich empire there, even comparable to that of New Spain.

Andagoya therefore set off and, after clashing with the Chocama, encountered a subordinate of the ruler, the Inca, from Birú. When an accident upset the canoe in which he was traveling, he swallowed a lot of water and narrowly escaped drowning. He returned to Panama to recover. It was three years before he could ride again. It is not clear what had happened to him, but obviously he was struck by a serious setback that removed him from the list of those who might first exploit Peru. He naturally told Pedrarias what he had seen. That governor in reply thought that he should himself act immediately to prevent anyone else becoming interested. He asked another friend, Juan Basurto, to prepare an expedition, but Basurto died. The field was again opened up to others.

Some indication of who these others might be was already evident in 1524. For, in May of that year, Pedrarias himself joined with three successful and rich *encomenderos* of Panama to explore Birú: Francisco Pizarro, Diego de Almagro, and Fray Hernando de Luque.

Pizarro, from Trujillo in Extremadura, was a distant cousin of Hernán Cortés, whose grandmother Leonor had been a Pizarro.[5] Almagro was probably from the town in New Castile that bore his own name, Almagro, while Luque was a Sevillano who may have been a converso. These three had a half share of the planned expedition between them in three ships, the other half being in the hands of Pedrarias. Pizarro had a reputation for leadership, endurance in difficult circumstances, and physical strength; he was also easy and popular with his men. The fact that he was illiterate seemed less important. It was suggested that he had in his youth looked after swine, which, considering the importance of those animals in the economy of Extremadura, would not have been improbable.[6] Almagro was also illiterate. But Luque could read and write, and indeed preach. He was one of the eleven churchmen who had accompanied Fray Juan de Quevedo, the first bishop of Darien (*Betica Aurea*), to the New World. The Peruvian historian Busto considered that Luque had an unusual gift for business.[7]

These men prepared their expedition carefully in 1524, and in November Pizarro set off in two small ships with less than two hundred men, from Panama down the Pacific coast, leaving Almagro to find reinforcements. It did not seem a very promising enterprise; they had with them only four horses, one fighting dog, no muzzle-loaded firearms nor crossbows, and no artillery.[8]

Actually, Spain had already made a mark on Peru. Even though no Spaniard had yet been there, in 1524 smallpox had been carried there from Castile.

In the meantime, in January 1523, Gil González Dávila and Andrés Niño, convinced that wealth lay to the north, not the south, had set off north toward Guatemala from the Isle of Pearls off Panama with four small vessels. Like all early explorers in this region, they hoped to light upon a strait to the Pacific. They sailed north and, in the next eighteen months, discovered several new Indian kingdoms. But no strait appeared. At the end of this time, their ships were so damaged by worms that they had to continue by land.

They thereupon went into the interior about three hundred miles farther up the Central American coast with a hundred men, and Gil González Dávila received presents worth over 100,000 pesos. This was land adjacent to Alvarado's Guatemala, with the same customs, gods, costumes, and language. More than thirty-two thousand natives received baptism voluntarily, wrote Peter Martyr, as usual exaggerating. Gil González reported that, in this part of Central America, all the carpenters' tools were made of gold, but he, too, must have been mistaken, confusing gold for copper. They passed through land where the rivers were alluvial, and wound up their journey at a place they named San Vicente at the foot of the Volcán de Chichontepec in the valley of the Joboa. A little farther on, Gil González came upon a local Mayan lord named Nicoiano (Nicoya), whom he persuaded to accept baptism and who, in consequence, gave him six gold figures of gods each over a foot high. Nicoiano spoke of another lord named Nicaragua who lived about 150 miles to the west, and Gil González continued there, persuading him to become a Christian, along with nine thousand of his people. Nicaragua gave the Spaniards 15,000 pesos in the form of gold necklaces. Gil González presented him in return with a silk jacket, a linen shirt, and a red hat.

A long conversation followed during which Nicaragua said that the total destruction of the human race would soon come, brought on by man's many crimes and unnatural lusts. This lord asked all kinds of interesting questions of Gil González Dávila, which that conquistador must have found surprising: What was the cause of heat and of cold? Were dancing and drinking acceptable? Did men have souls? Gil González delivered a good sermon describing the benefits of Christianity and the evils of human sacrifice. He was made aware that these Indians were terrified of the Spaniards' beards.

Gil González and his comrades were also astounded at the high level of culture of these Indians. They were in particular impressed by their large palaces, and considered that their ceremonial centers with "an urban disposition" would have given them little to envy in the world of Spain.[9] Still, every so often, to recall their essential "barbarism," they would sacrifice girls to the nearby volcanoes.

Gil González moved on to Lake Nicaragua, which was supposed to be the site of the entrance to the strait so long sought. They named it the Sweet Lake (El Mar Dulce). Niño, meantime, was still exploring the coast by sea. He reached the Gulf of Choluteca in what is now Honduras, to whose sea outlet he politely gave the name of Fonseca after the bishop of Burgos, which it retains.[10]

Both conquistadors then returned to Panama, claiming to have baptized eighty-two thousand Indians. They also had brought with them 112,000 pesos of gold. Pedrarias predictably claimed a fifth of that for himself, but González returned to Santo Domingo with his treasure without bidding him, nor indeed anyone, goodbye. He sought reinforcements there and dispatched Andrés de Cereceda to Spain with presents for Bishop Fonseca and a request that he, Gil González Dávila, should receive a governorship in Nicaragua independent of Pedrarias.

But the latter was not prepared to abandon anything. Pedrarias wrote letters of protest to the Crown via his son and via Gaspar de Espinosa, a *licenciado* (graduate lawyer), and a bachelor of arts, who had been chief magistrate under Pedrarias.

Pedrarias immediately dispatched Francisco Hernández de Córdoba to Nicaragua and Costa Rica to take possession of that region.[11] That conquistador had come out to the Indies in 1517. Perhaps he was a distant relation of El Gran Capitán, who shared his name.

Hernández de Córdoba set off by ship in the course of 1524. He and his men made for the Costa Rican coast to the south of Nicaragua and landed at Urutina, on the Gulf of Nicoya, near where a year earlier González Dávila had rested his expedition. He founded several towns: Bruselas (Brussels), for example, near Puente Arenas; Granada on Lake Nicaragua, near the Indian colony of Jalteba; Segovia; and León la Vieja, which would soon become the capital of the new settlement. Among the first thirty Spanish settlers there were men with brilliant futures in Peru such as Sebastián de Benalcázar and Hernando de Soto, who became chief magistrate of this new city. There was complete uncertainty among these isolated Spaniards in respect of their northern frontier: Whom would they have to defeat in order to establish their "independent" regime? Olid? González Dávila? Alvarado? Cortés himself? Or perhaps Pedro Moreno, the prosecutor of Santo Domingo, who, acting for the supreme court of that city, had been sent to Central America to find out where these and other conquistadors actually were.

Hernández de Córdoba heard that González Dávila was planning a return expedition to those same Central American lands. He had, in fact, already come back with his friend Andrés Niño to Honduras and settled at Puerto de Caballos, hoping to prove to the Indians that Spaniards did not die. When they landed, they quickly came into contact with Hernández de Córdoba, and the two little Spanish armies fought two pitched battles. Eight Spaniards and thirty horses died.

Hernández de Córdoba pressed the new municipalities of the places he had founded to recognize him as their governor. His usurpation of authority was not universally accepted, in particular not by Hernando de Soto, a brilliant horseman from Jerez de los Caballeros in Extremadura, the same city that had given birth to Balboa, who had married Pedrarias's daughter, Isabel, and in consequence looked on Hernández de Córdoba's actions as destructive. Hernández de Córdoba imprisoned Soto, but a friend, Francisco de Compañón, freed him, and the two rode back to complain to Pedrarias, who mounted an expedition to seize Lake Nicaragua. To that generation of conquistadors, the lake seemed a "paradise of God," in the words of Las Casas, who relished not only the beautiful dark water but the rich black soil and the long row of volcanoes near the sea.[12]

In these years, a number of powerful persons were trying to assert themselves in too small a space in Central America. But they were soon to find a way to prosperity and advancement, if not happiness. Pedrarias, aged but brutal to both his fellow countrymen and the Indians, remained, apparently, impossible to remove.

The politics of Central America in the late 1520s is the central element in the preparations for the conquest of Peru. Most of the characters in that drama emerge from what happened in Panama or in Darien, in particular the dynamic figure of Francisco Pizarro.

In 1528 Pedrarias was, however, still the dominant authority in the territory, as he had been for fourteen years. He was now governor of Nicaragua, taking up his new office there on Holy Saturday, 1528, finding anarchy.[13] Diego López de Salcedo had illegally seized power as governor of Honduras, with no permission from the Council of the Indies. López de Salcedo was a nephew of the great governor of La Española, Fray Nicolás de Ovando, with whom he had first come to the Indies in 1502. There was a rebellion of Indian leaders.

López de Salcedo eventually surrendered to Pedrarias and, after some months in the new fortress of León, was sent home to Spain. His lieutenant was Gabriel de Rojas, a member of the famous family of Cuéllar in Castile (Gabriel was a brother of Manuel de Rojas, then governor of Cuba, both being cousins of Diego Velázquez, whose palace in Cuéllar was next to their own). Pedrarias continued to be reproached even by his own men, such as his chief magistrate Castañeda. But it made no difference to his conduct. He was defended by Martín de Estete, whose brutality toward Indians was without parallel.

At that time, the traffic in slaves still seemed the only way to make any money in Central America. Among those active in the commerce were Hernando de Soto and Juan Ponce, who collaborated with the mayor Castañeda; "their" Indians were sold not only in Panama but in the Caribbean. Ponce's galleon *San Jerónimo* habitually carried 450 *piezas* (fully grown slaves); Soto and Ponce's *La Concepción* could carry 385.

Soto and Ponce were also already showing interest in Birú. But Pedrarias, having been persuaded to sell his own interests in Pizarro's dramatic project there for 1,000 pesos, was reluctant that anyone under his command should engage in it. If Soto and Ponce went to Peru, he argued, Nicaragua would lose her best men.

Francisco Pizarro's friend the pilot Bartolomé Ruiz de Estrada arrived at Soto's farm, La Posesión, in the *Santiago* looking precisely for new projects for Birú. Pedrarias prohibited all contact with them. But Ruiz himself met Soto and Ponce and almost certainly undertook to provide ships in return for a major role in what Pizarro was planning. Soto also agreed to supply thirty or forty men, mostly debtors, and perhaps three hundred slaves. Then, in August 1526, Pedrarias gave permission to Ponce to ship slaves for the estancia at La Posesión in the *San Jerónimo*. But Soto had to agree to stay on in León. On October 15, Ponce left La Posesión in the *San Jerónimo* carrying 402 slaves, with the royal factor Alonso Pérez on board. But once in Panama, he seized the opportunity to discuss with Pizarro's friends his and Soto's hope to participate in the promising Peruvian adventure.

We recall how in 1522 Pascual de Andagoya had sailed two hundred miles south of Panama in the Pacific Ocean (the Southern Sea) and ascended the Río San Juan; we have observed how Francisco Pizarro, Diego de Almagro, and Fray Hernando de Luque bought Andagoya's ships and secured the financial support of Licenciado Gaspar de Espinosa, the second most important man in Castilla del Oro after Pedrarias. In 1524, Pizarro himself sailed south along the Pacific coast from Panama with eighty men and four horses to reach Puerto de Ayuno, where his comrade Almagro lost an eye in a skirmish with Indians at Pueblo Quemado.

In March 1526, Pizarro set off on a second voyage south with fewer than two hundred men and a few horses in two small ships captained by his friend, the pilot Bartolomé Ruiz de Estrada. Crossing the equator for the first time in the Southern Sea, they came in touch with Peruvian civilization—though they were still far to the north of where modern Ecuador gives way to Peru. They encountered a balsa raft traveling northward and fitted with sails of cotton, which was preparing to trade Peruvian artifacts: silver and gold, cotton and woolen cloaks, and other clothing in many colors, not to speak of tiny weights with which to measure gold. Eleven of the men on that raft leaped into the ocean to avoid capture, but three were held by the Spaniards, to be trained as interpreters. The conquest of Mexico had taught Spaniards that a good interpreter is more valuable than one thousand soldiers. The sight of sails inspired the Europeans, for neither the Mexica nor the Maya had enjoyed such a benefit.

In June 1527, Pizarro caused his men, now reduced to eighty, to turn back north to take shelter back on Gallo Island, a barren spot, off Panama near Perequeté. Thence he sent Almagro to Panama for supplies, and Bartolomé Ruiz carried a letter to the new governor, Ríos, in Castilla del Oro, insisting that his encounter with the balsa raft showed that Birú was full of riches: "Very fine gold," he reported.[14] In August 1527, other letters were sent by Pizarro's men about their hunger, their despair, and their physical determination to survive. Some of them said that they were being detained on the expedition against their will.[15] Governor Ríos gave permission for those of the expedition to leave if they wished. Many did so in boats sent by the governor under the command of Juan Tafur, who brought a message from Governor Ríos's wife, Catalina Saavedra. She wanted to buy cotton cloth from Peru.

Pizarro held a meeting of his followers on the beach. He told the eighty or so Spaniards who were still with him that they were all free to leave. But he appealed to them to stay with him. He recalled the riches of the raft. He drew a line with his sword in the sand, and proposed that those who preferred the glory and the gold of an adventure in Peru to the misery and obscurity of Panama should cross the line. Only thirteen did so. The rest had heard too many promises of wealth and glory.[16]

The thirteen became famous. There were among them five Andalusians, two Castilians, three Extremeños, a Cretan, a Basque, and one whose origins are unclear.[17] Pizarro sent his remaining boat back to Panama under the inspector Carbayuelo to bring back Almagro.

On Gallo Island, Pizarro and his thirteen followers did what they could to survive. They made a canoe out of a ceiba tree and went fishing daily, catching excellent fish. Then they killed animals called *guadaquinajes*, which were bigger than hare and gave good flesh to eat. There was little other food but "mosquitoes enough to make war against the Turks." After a month or so, some of Pizarro's men thought openly that "death would be the end of our sufferings."

Back in Panama, Almagro and Luque are said by the chronicler Cieza to have allowed many tears to fall when they read the sad letters brought back from Gallo Island—though those two hardened conquistadors did not often weep. It was said that Pizarro had personally sent back a couplet, which ran:

Oh my lord governor look well and take pains
For there goes the knife and the butcher remains.

Ruiz eventually set off back to Gallo Island and found Pizarro in despair. Ruiz suggested that all return to Panama in six months' time. Pizarro agreed but suggested that first they should together sail to the south and see what the coast of Peru was like. Ruiz agreed to do this, leaving behind the most debilitated of the Spaniards.

In the next few months, Pizarro and Ruiz made their way to Tumbes, a town on the coast where they were well received, and then to the island of Santa Clara and the Río Santa to the south of the modern Trujillo, just north of Chimbote. The Andalusian Alonso de Molina here gave a cacique two pigs, a cock, and two Spanish chickens, and the Cretan Pedro de Candía gave an exhibition of shooting with an arquebus. Antonio de Carrión, a Castilian, then took possession of the land in the name of the King of Castile. The unimpressed Indians gave many presents: llamas, pottery, fine cloths, metals, and also some more boys to be trained to act as interpreters.

Pizarro's expedition in this year may have reached as far as the mouth of the river Chincha, well to the south of the modern capital of Lima. There were several such stops on the way back, for example at Tumbes, where Alonso de Molina was left behind to learn Quechua. Pedro de Halcón, from Seville, fell in love there and also asked to be allowed to remain. A sailor of Ruiz's named Cunés decided to remain for a similar reason at Pinta. The rest returned to Panama, where they were well received by the governor, Ríos.

The story of "the thirteen of Gallo Island" kept Panama agog for a long time with tales of llamas, gold, cotton cloaks, and other wonderful textiles. For a while, Pizarro was silent. Then he, too, talked with his old friends Almagro, Luque, and Espinosa. It was agreed that an expedition should be mounted to establish settlements in Peru. Nothing was said of conquest. But it was understood that if the people of Peru were to refuse the King's command, transmitted by the immortal Requirement, they would be made dependent—of course, in the most humane way possible. Pizarro would be

governor, Almagro proconsul (*adelantado*), Luque bishop, and the pilot
Ruiz would be *alguacil*. But Luque thought it essential to send a representative to Castile to receive the Crown's formal approval. He thought that
Diego del Corral, an experienced Castilian from Hoz de Ovejar, in the
province of Burgos, would be the best man to do this. Almagro thought the
right man was Pizarro himself. Luque was doubtful, since he considered
Pizarro "a consummate warrior but one with little culture and little informed of the subtleties of rhetoric." He was popular, and Oviedo wrote of
him that he was "a good person with a good temperament if slow and de-
liberate in conversation."[18] In the end, Pizarro went to Spain, accompanied
by Diego del Corral and Pedro de Candía, the Cretan artilleryman.

Pizarro in 1528 was in his fifties, and very experienced in the Indies,
where he had arrived in 1502 with Ovando. He was tall, lean, and strong.
Like Ovando and, indeed, Cortés and Núñez de Balboa, he was an Extremeño, being the illegitimate son of a well-known soldier and aristocrat,
Gonzalo Pizarro, who had fought in Navarre as well as in Italy. Pizarro's
mother, Francisca González, had apparently been a servant girl who had
worked in the convent of San Francisco in Trujillo, for Sister Beatriz
Pizarro de Hinojosa, a distinguished member of the family. Francisco may
also have been in Italy with his father in the 1490s, but in his early days in
Santo Domingo, he was just one more impoverished soldier, though impressed by Ovando.[19] When he received a coat of arms in 1537, it was recalled that he had served in Italy.[20] He reached Darien before Pedrarias
went there and worked under Núñez de Balboa, though it was he who arrested the latter in 1519. He also was second-in-command to other leaders.
He showed himself incomparably tough, a good leader, and one loved by
those who served with him. He could neither read nor write, and his horsemanship was modest since he had not been brought up to live with horses.
The gossip and memoirist Alonso Enríquez de Guzmán, however, said that
he was "a good companion without any vanity or pomposity."[21] Garcilaso,
the half-Peruvian chronicler who wrote so well, said of him that he was
"kindly and gentle by nature and never said a hard word of anyone."[22] He
once saved an Indian servant from death by leaping into a river, exposing
himself to great danger. When reproached for taking such a risk, he replied
that his interlocutor obviously did not know what it was to be fond of a servant. He practically never altered the style of the clothes he had worn in his

youth: a black cassock with a skirt down to the ankle, with white deerskin shoes and a white hat, his sword and dagger worn in an old-fashioned way, though he would later often wear a fur coat that Cortés sent him from Mexico. He often wore napkins round his neck since he spent much of his life in time of peace playing bowls or some ball game such as ninepins and "they served to keep the sweat from his face."[23]

Despite all these good qualities, like most conquistadors he was quite prepared to be cruel to enemies and to kill Indians in a ruthless manner in order to achieve a psychological advantage, thereby compensating for his inferiority in numbers.[24]

His friend and eventual rival Almagro was of a different character, though he, too, was illegitimate and illiterate. He was a few years younger than Pizarro and so, in 1528, must have been in his late forties. He seems to have been born in Bolaños de Calatrava on the road from Manzanares to Ciudad Real. Probably he was the illegitimate son of a Gallego hidalgo, Juan de Montenegro, by Elvira Gutiérrez, a servant girl in Almagro. Elvira perhaps had Moorish blood, a fact that later exposed Almagro to fierce insults. He lived for a time with his mother's cruel brother, Hernán Gutiérrez, and fled to find his mother married to a shopkeeper named Celinos in Ciudad Real. Almagro then went to Toledo, where he served Licenciado Luis González de Polanco, one of the court magistrates (*alcaldes de corte*) of the Catholic Kings and a long-lived counselor of the Crown in Castile. Almagro had a violent fight with another boy; in consequence, he fled to Seville, where in 1513 he joined the expedition of Pedrarias in the humblest of fashions, as a page, and he was then involved in many of the *entradas* in Central America, becoming an intimate friend of Pizarro about 1515.[25]

Almagro had different qualities from Pizarro. He was apparently "so excellent a woodsman that he could follow an Indian through the thickest forests merely by following his tracks and, although that Indian might have a league's advantage, Almagro would catch up." He was always swearing, and when angry, he treated those who were with him very badly, even if they were gentlemen. But his soldiers loved him for "his liberal disposition." Enríquez de Guzmán thought him "generous, frank and liberal, affectionate, merciful, correct and just-minded, very fearful of God and the King." He also forgave debts as if he were a Prince, not a soldier. To look at, Cieza says, he was "a man of short stature with ugly features but of great courage and endurance."[26]

Almagro never got closer to the court than Toledo in his teens. For that reason, he played a lesser part than did Pizarro in the manufacture of the myth of the empire. It is uncertain whether the Emperor knew his name except as one who challenged and disputed royal authority. Yet he played an essential role in imperial politics in his lifetime.

The two conquistadors were linked in those days of exploration by their joint membership of a so-called "companía," a society made up of a firm or a group of men, each of whom was in charge of his own equipment and weapons and received in return a previously stipulated share of the spoils. This was a change from the idea of a *compaña*, a type of organization based on an Italian model whereby a group of men such as the Columbus family hired the services of salaried men.

It seemed for a time likely that Pizarro and Almagro had a third partner, the cleric Hernando de Luque. That now seems improbable. But the first two were linked in their companía, which went by the name of the Compañía del Levante. Pedrarias the governor seems to have taken an interest, and some money was probably provided by the rich settler Gaspar de Espinosa, a financier from Medina de Rioseco, who had much experience in Panama, and who acted through his son Juan, who was for a time Almagro's secretary.[27]

Charles the Emperor received news regularly from Cortés in New Spain, from Santo Domingo, from Governor Rojas in Cuba, from Pedrarias in Panama, and from the north coast of South America. As for New Spain, the *cabildo* (town council) in Mexico-Tenochtitlan was continuing to allocate town and country properties, and that *cabildo* remained a mixture of new men and experienced conquistadors who had been through all the battles of Cortés.

Twelve Dominicans had arrived in New Spain in July 1526, led by an enemy of Cortés, Fray Tomás de Ortiz, to add their presence to the well-established Franciscans. Ortiz was also, it seems, an enemy of Indians. He and three other friars became ill and returned to Spain as fast as they could. This left Fray Domingo de Betanzos, a Gallego, with a deacon, Fray Vicente de las Casas, as the spokesmen for the Dominican order.[28]

After living modestly in lodgings for a while, the Dominicans moved in 1529 to a monastery being built specially for them at Tepetlaostoc, just outside Tenochtitlan, where Miguel Díaz de Aux, a survivor of the days of the conquest, received an *encomienda* in 1527. To begin with, their impact would be less than that of the Franciscans because they were not interested in founding schools and were unenthusiastic about the idea of teaching Latin to the natives.[29]

All the same, the latter's interest was increasingly secured: In October 1526, there is record of an indigenous marriage along Christian lines when "Don Hernando," brother of "señor" Cacama of Texcoco, and seven companions were married to Indians. Several well-known conquistadors (Alonso de Ávila, Pedro Sánchez Farfán) were present, with gifts and, "the jewel most appreciated," much wine. After the Mass in the monastery, there was a banquet and a ball attended by two thousand people.[30] This wedding was, however, less imposing than that of Techuipo, favorite daughter of Montezuma, who married Pedro Gallego de Andrade, her previous Spanish husband, Alonso de Grado, having died. She most surprisingly had a daughter, Leonor, by Cortés, some months after this marriage.[31] Pedro Gallego was from Seville; he was a poet and later had an inn on the road to Veracruz. He also had the *encomienda* of Iscuincuitlapilco and a daughter, Juana Andrade.

When Nuño de Guzmán arrived at San Esteban del Puerto in Pánuco in May 1527 to take up a new appointment, some sixty or seventy Spaniards lived there, in thatched houses surrounding a brick church also with a thatched roof, and a pomegranate-colored council house. Guzmán summoned the Spaniards and read out his instructions in the church. Guzmán dismissed most of the town council immediately and replaced them with new men who had come with him. Guzmán told the caciques that he was in Pánuco as representative of the King of Castile, who was his own supreme mentor, though there was always God in Heaven. If one lived a Christian life on Earth, one would one day live in His presence in Heaven. If not, one would go to an inferno of eternal fire and burn forever. To ensure that they went to Heaven, the Indians would have to build a large church in Pánuco and go to it regularly to beg forgiveness. In their souls, these caciques had to bear complete obedience to the King of Castile and to Guzmán in his name. They were to fulfill their duties to their new Spanish masters but not more. If their master asked more, he was to be reported to Guzmán, who would punish him.[32]

Seeing that their new commander was going to be demanding, and would cost them something, several *encomenderos,* such as Cortés's friend and fellow Medellinés Antonio de Mendoza, who had been lieutenant governor in Pánuco, left Pánuco–San Sebastián, taking their sheep and slaves with them. It was Mendoza who had returned to Castile with Diego de Ordaz on Cortés's behalf in 1521, carrying the third letter of the great commander to the Emperor, written in October 1520.[33] One *encomendero* who did not leave now was Diego Villapadierna of Matlactonatico, who told the Indians to avoid giving any presents to Guzmán since, he said, Cortés would soon come there to sweep him away. But it was Villapadierna who suffered, since he was soon tried for conspiring with Cortés to make him King of New Spain, an idea that was far from the captain-general's imagination. He was sentenced to the pillory, a fine of 50 pesos, and the loss of his *encomienda*.

Similar punishments were met by others who challenged the new authority. For example, Guzmán had three of his compatriots hanged from an avocado tree for allegedly mistreating Indians when they had in fact merely tried to prevent Guzmán from presenting his commission in Mexico-Tenochtitlan. Guzmán also approved a slave trade in Mexican Indians (Huastecs, principally) from Pánuco to the West Indian islands, the business being organized in 1527 by one of the new governor's intimates, Sancho de Caniego, who had come to New Spain with him. Guzmán set the prices: No one, for example, could pay more than fifteen slaves for a horse. Slaves were not to be traded for items such as wine or cloth, only for livestock. Caniego was cruel: On the slightest provocation, he would beat an Indian to death.[34]

Nor were Spaniards much better off: Caniego put the former comandante of San Sebastián del Puerto in irons and kicked him to death.[35] Still, Guzmán tried also to be positive about "his" Indians. In August 1527, he decided that no Indian women were to be seized by the Spaniards (and several Spaniards were hanged in consequence), that no Spaniard was to seize agricultural produce from Indians, that vagrants were to be given permanent homes, and that Spaniards should limit the number of their bearers. None of them were to be made to carry more than an *arroba* (twenty-five pounds) of weight as well as his food. Nor were Spaniards to keep swine or livestock within half a league (say, a mile and a half) of an indigenous settlement's fields. Blasphemy was roundly condemned. Thus Guzmán has to be judged at two levels: He was a characteristic man of his time; with a black side and a benign one. He also invited Fray Gregorio de Santa María, a Carmelite who had landed in Pánuco on his way to Tenochtitlan, to remain in his territory, and Santa María did so for a time.[36]

Guzmán abandoned Pánuco at the end of 1527, when he accepted an invitation to preside over the new supreme court of New Spain (*audiencia*).[37] The evidence is that this appointment was made to ensure that the Crown had a representative tough enough if necessary to oppose Cortés, whose motives in New Spain had been made to seem so suspect by his many enemies at court at home. Bishop García de Loaisa, President of the Council of the Indies, was responsible. There were to be four judges of first instance who had been named in Spain.[38]

The supreme court was supposed to hear civil as well as criminal cases. Among the cases the court heard very early on was the strange case of the young Tlaxcalteca Cristóbal, who was killed by his father, Acxotecatl, for trying to convert him to Christianity.[39] A parallel case was that of Hernando Alonso, a blacksmith whom the Dominicans found guilty of such Jewish practices as forbidding his wife to go to church during her menstrual periods and carrying out a baptism according to Jewish rites. Alonso was found guilty and was later burned in Mexico-Tenochtitlan, the first conquistador to meet this fate.[40]

When Guzmán went up to Tenochtitlan, he was succeeded in Pánuco by Licenciado Pedro de Mondragón, a judge who must have had some good feelings since he refused a pardon for a Spaniard who had violated an Indian girl aged eight, though he felt guilty the rest of his life because he thought that he had been too harsh.[41]

In Cuernavaca in another part of New Spain, Cortés began to realize that despite his stupendous services and his remarkable letters about his achievements (his fifth letter to Charles V was written in September 1526), he would never overcome his difficulties with his rivals unless he had overt royal support. In April 1528, the emperor Charles had ordered him to come home, and he was advised to comply by supporters of his, such as the Duke of Béjar, who had befriended the Cortés family. Guzmán had behaved unacceptably in Pánuco. Estrada, now the supreme authority in Mexico, was distinctly unfriendly, though he had been explicitly told that he could not be the judge of *residencia* against Cortés; and Estrada's assistant, Juan de Burgos, an experienced trader who had sailed a *nao* full of supplies to Cortés in New Spain from the Canary Islands in 1521, was equally hostile.

So in early 1528, Cortés decided to go home for the first time since his journey to Santo Domingo in 1506, more than twenty years before. He left almost immediately, leaving power over his property in New Spain to his cousin Licenciado Juan Altamirano, to Pedro González Gallego, and to Diego de Ocampo. He took with him Gonzalo de Sandoval and Andrés de Tapia, a large collection of treasure and works of art, plants and minerals, and numerous Indians, headed by a son of Montezuma (Don Pedro Montezuma) as well as a son of Maxixcastin, "Don Lorenzo," of Tlaxcala. There also came eight Indians who could play elaborate ball games with their feet.[42] He arrived at Palos, Columbus's port in 1492, in May 1528. There, at the monastery of La Rábida, Sandoval fell ill. He was too weak to prevent the theft of his gold and died soon afterwards.[43]

The news to reach Spain in 1528 from Panama was that Pedrarias had punished the rebellion, as he put it, of Hernández de Córdoba by having him executed. González Dávila had died. This last information led Isabel de Bobadilla to secure the renomination of her husband as governor and captain-general of Nicaragua (in July 1526).[44]

Florida, meantime, remained an unsuccessful venture for the Spaniards. Váquez de Ayllón set out from Puerto Principe in Santo Domingo in mid-July 1526; it was the first expedition that he led in person. He had three good ships—his flagship *La Bretona,* the *Santa Catalina,* and the *Chorruca*—as well as a brigantine, which carried five hundred men and about eighty horses. His comrades included Fray Antonio de Cervantes, Fray Pedro de Estrada, and Fray Antonio de Montesinos, a cousin of the great preacher of that name. He reached a river, which he called the Jordan, where *La Bretona* ran aground, though other vessels navigated it successfully. They decided, however, that it was a bad place for a colony and instead went far north, to a river that seems to be in what is now New Jersey. There Ayllón died, and all his plans came to an end.[45] His expedition limped back to Santo Domingo.

There were other journeys in these years: For example, Sebastian Cabot's voyage from Corunna to the river Plate and then the Paraguay River. He was, it will be remembered, *piloto mayor* for the Casa de la Contratación. He was in search of the mysterious great white chief of the region (El Gran Cacique Blanco). There he came upon Diego García, who had come on a similar journey from Seville. They could not agree on whose rights were at stake but continued together all the same. They left behind a small garrison at Espíritu Santo, the site of the future Buenos Aires. Sailing up the Paraguay and the Pilcomayo, they were severely attacked, and so returned to find all the Spaniards whom they had left at Espíritu Santo dead and the garrison destroyed. Upon returning together to Spain, they embarked on a lawsuit against each other, which, like so many at that time, never ended.

Cabot was one of the half-dozen great men of the new generation of conquering explorers. But great man though he was, his standing never approached that of the conqueror of New Spain nor that of the Extremeño Pizarro, who knew that his mission lay in Peru.

II

Giants of Their Time:
Charles, Cortés, Pizarro

Though your goodness rouses great hopes in me, I shall never cease
to fear until you have bid farewell to this most unjust and
dangerous world and have withdrawn to a monastery as to a safe
harbour.

ERASMUS, *De Contemptu Mundi*

In 1528, the three greatest men of the age were in Spain: Charles, King and
Emperor, and his two most important subjects, Hernán Cortés, conqueror
of New Spain/Mexico, and Francisco Pizarro, the future conqueror of Peru.
Charles that year was still at war with King Francis I of France and had sent
Balthasar Merklin, vice-chancellor of the empire, to urge the German
princes to arm against that country. Heralds from England as well as
France had appeared in Burgos with a declaration of a war for "the safety
and soul of Christendom." Charles had replied with a challenge to a duel
with King Francis I, whom he accused of failing to meet the code of honor
that they both accepted. Francis I accepted the challenge, and demanded
time and place for the duel. Afterwards, rational counselors on both sides
dissuaded their monarchs from a such a personal test.

At the same time, Charles was preparing to visit Italy, where he hoped
to be crowned by the pope, perhaps in Bologna. That meant a preparation
also of his empress, Isabel, for her work as regent. Charles sent her advice
on her bearing, as well as on affairs of state. She was to have a meeting of
the Council of the Realm every Friday. He issued a general authority for the

Queen. He explained to her how the President of the Royal Council was now Don Juan Pardo de Tavera, the archbishop of Santiago (he received the cardinalate in 1531), and he explained something of Tavera's cautious, correct, and cultivated personality. Tavera was an enemy of the exuberantly liberal Erasmian Alonso de Manrique de Lara, the general of the order. Tavera is now remembered for his magnificent hospital at the gates of Toledo. Technically the hospital of San Juan Bautista, it was also known as the "hospital outside the walls" (*hospital de Afuera*). It is the great building of the Toledan Renaissance, designated as a hospital for all ailments, perhaps as a copy or at least a successor to the great hospital of Santa Cruz in Valladolid. Like Santa Cruz, Tavera's hospital began as a mortuary as well as a clinic. It was begun in 1540; the first architect was Alonso de Covarrubias, and then Hernán Gonzalez de Lara. Afterwards there was the exquisite Nicolas de Vergara, who was working on the towers of the hospital in the 1570s.

In April 1528, the court was in Madrid. In May, the infante Philip was recognized in the church of the monastery of San Jerónimo in Madrid as heir to the throne. In September, Charles addressed both the Royal Council of Castile and the Council of the Realm. He told their members that he intended to go to Italy to be crowned Emperor by the pope. He would also seek to persuade the pope to call a general council of the Church so as to give a formal answer to Luther.[1] Charles did not ask the councils for their permission to go to Italy. He merely told them that he was going. Gattinara later explained that there were many who tried to prevent Charles's departure. They hated the idea of important decisions being made by the unknown Empress Isabel, who would be regent. The grand duchess Margaret of Burgundy, like the Empress, was also urging Charles not to go to Italy.[2] She believed that all his efforts and money should be spent on defending Europe against the Turks.

But the plan to be crowned had its idealistic side. Erasmian schemes for the future of the Church were constantly heard. Could not the Church show itself tolerant as well as generous? A speech that Charles delivered in Madrid announced a great rendezvous with the pope in Bologna. Charles imagined that he was going to Italy for a spiritual renovation as well as a coronation.

Only a little before Cortés's return to Spain in May 1528, his erstwhile lieutenant, Pedro de Alvarado, received from the Crown the title of governor and *adelantado* of Guatemala at 562,500 maravedís a year, and was named to the Order of Santiago. It was an honor that he had in his youth pretended to have received in his father's stead. As a preparation for his new appointment in Guatemala, Alvarado married a cousin of the Duke of Alburquerque, Beatriz de la Cueva. The conquistador had earlier married an elder sister of hers, Francisca, who had died.

The court at that time was at the mercy of contrasting reports about Cortés. On the one hand, Alvarado and Fray Diego de Altamirano spoke in favor of him, but Estrada and Albornoz, as well as the Dominican Fray Tomás de Ortiz, were hostile. In the circumstances, Charles thought that the best he could do was to appoint a cousin of his to go to New Spain with three hundred armed men ready to cut off Cortés's head and those of his friends if Cortés turned out to be guilty of the high crimes of which the Dominicans had accused him (the murder of his wife and of other associates).

Cortés's return to Spain in 1528 was, all the same, full of contradiction. It was difficult to know how to treat him. Columbus, too, had returned with a train of treasure, having discovered a new world, but since Cortés had done something just as remarkable, the question was should he be given a title, a pension, a European command?

Landing in Palos with an escort of fifty persons, Cortés went first to the Franciscan monastery of La Rábida, Columbus's favorite retreat nearby. At La Rábida, Cortés is sometimes said to have met his distant cousin Francisco Pizarro. But that meeting could not have been in May 1528 since Pizarro was then still in Panama. If such a thing happened at all, it must have been later, in Toledo.

Cortés traveled from La Rábida to Seville, where he stayed with the Duke of Medina Sidonia in his palace in the west of the city.[3] The Duke gave him good horses with which to continue his journey to the court in Toledo. The conqueror of the Mexica went on, perhaps stopping to salute his mother at Medellín and then remaining for some days at the Jeronymite monastery of Guadalupe, where he is said to have flirted with Francisca de Mendoza, sister of Cobos's wife. But with the support of his now dead father, Cortés had already been formally engaged to Juana Ramírez de Arellano, niece of the Duke of Béjar, a marriage that would ensure his entry into the aristocracy, as it would ensure the further enrichment of a great

Castilian family, the Zúñiga. Everywhere Cortés offered presents: not least to the Mendoza sisters and also to the monastery of Guadalupe, giving the latter a golden replica of that scorpion such as had once bitten him in Pátzcuaro, the body being covered by emeralds, pearls, and mosaics.[4]

Cortés was presented to the Emperor at Toledo by his prospective father-in-law, the Duke of Béjar, by Fadrique Enríquez, the admiral of Castile, and by Cobos. Cortés talked of his conquests, his travels, his Indians, his jaguars, and his privations. But Charles had little time to spare: He was preoccupied by his disputes with the King of France, and by his first serious attack of gout. Cobos was charged to inspect Cortés's treasures. But when Cortés, still in lodgings in Toledo, seemed to be on the verge of a serious illness (brought on, said Bernal Díaz, by the revival of heavy Spanish dinners), the Emperor, "very accompanied by the nobility," went to visit him, a great honor.[5]

Charles put three questions to Cortés: What demands did he make for grants? What kind of policy did he support for dealing with the indigenous populations? How could the royal income be increased from New Spain?[6]

In reply, Cortés wanted his concession of twenty-five thousand Indians to be confirmed by the cession to him of twenty places in New Spain, which he listed;[7] he said that Spain should aim at the "conservation and perpetuation of the natives through good treatment by pastors of the Church." To increase the royal income, the land conquered should be divided among the Spaniards as if it had been Castile. Cortés suggested that taxes should be paid when land was bought or sold, and that the main cities of New Spain should be reserved for the Crown. The royal reaction to these responses was that Cortés seemed to be demanding large grants, and the few people in Castile who knew something of the geography of New Spain were naturally astonished—especially when they realized that some of the places concerned (Texcoco, Tehuantepec, and all seaports) had been assumed to be royal holdings. The matter of what power Cortés would have over his vassals was also at issue: Would it be only be a matter of civil justice, or of criminal jurisdiction, too?

The conqueror of the Mexica remained on and off at court between May 1528 and March 1530. His first public appearance was at Mass in Toledo—presumably in the cathedral, where he arrived late, and sat himself down next to Henry of Nassau, in the Emperor's stall. That was considered an act of arrogance, when it was in fact the scarcely less pardonable one of ignorance.[8]

Thereafter, Cortés traveled with the court, along with his following, to Monzón, to Saragossa, back to Toledo. After several months, in July 1529, in Barcelona, the Emperor named him Marquess of the Valley of Oaxaca and confirmed him as Captain-General of New Spain as well as of the Southern Sea.[9] These titles were curious since Oaxaca was among the most doubtful of Cortés's conquests, and oceans usually were guided by an admiral, not a captain-general. All the same, though Cortés soon lost political control of Oaxaca, he was henceforth always referred to as Marquess of the Valley. It was lost on no one that he was not again named governor of New Spain, a title he had received in 1522. Charles spoke of this in a letter to him in April 1529, saying that, of course, he knew that Cortés could perform that gubernatorial role, but "it was not convenient" (*pero no conviene*).[10] Cortés did receive some other and unexpected benefits: for example, the supreme court of New Spain was ordered to respect his property. They would pay the costs of an expedition to the Moluccas, while various other debts would be forgotten.

During this prolonged stay in Spain, Cortés also sent an associate, Juan de Rada (sometimes, Herrada), to the Vatican with rich presents of stones and golden jewels as well as two foot-jugglers. Pope Clement was delighted and made Rada a count palatine; and he issued a bull legitimizing three of Cortés's bastard children.[11] Another bull conceded to Cortés the trusteeship of the Hospital of Nazareno Jesús.

Cortés's stay in Spain was concluded by his long-prepared marriage to Juana Ramírez de Arellano at the Duke of Béjar's castle in April 1529. Cortés gave his new wife a present of five emeralds that, it was said, were worth 100,000 ducats. One emerald was made into a rose; another a hunting horn; one a fish with eyes of gold; one a bell, with a pearl as the clapper; and the last a cup with a golden stem and the legend "*Inter natos mulierum non durrexit.*"[12] A group of Genoese who saw these emeralds in La Rábida offered 40,000 ducats for just one of them. It is said that the Empress heard of the present and implied that she would like it herself. Cortés told her that he had already given it to Juana, who held on to it. The only one of Cortés's fellow conquistadors from Mexico present at the wedding in Béjar seems to have been Diego de Ordaz, who wrote of it in a letter to his nephew Francisco Verdugo in New Spain.[13]

It is characteristic of the sixteenth century that though monarchs were often painted, and sometimes, as with Charles V, by great painters, lesser men were usually ignored by them. But Cortés was depicted at least twice by a German painter from Strasbourg, Christoph Weiditz. Weiditz came to Spain in the train of the accomplished Polish ambassador Dantiscus. His career was a happy recollection of a time when rich Poles could afford poor German artists in their entourage. His first portrait of Cortés was a sketch in pencil and watercolor standing next to his coat of arms. Weiditz must have painted this about 1528. It is a light work and surely does not capture the real Cortés. It gives him a blond beard, which clashes with accounts by chroniclers (for example, Bernal Díaz) who reported that his beard was black (*prieto*). Weiditz became a friend of Cortés and also did a medallion of him, of which there are several copies. It is a somber depiction, more mature and serious than the painting. There seems to have been a third work by Weiditz, for Dantiscus writes of it in a letter to his friend the Polish chancellor Szydlowiecki, in Cracow.[14] Afterwards, a portrait was painted by the Hispanized Fleming Pedro Campaña (Pieter de Kempeneer) for the Italian art lover Paolo Giovio. This was painted about 1546 but has vanished. Various copies were, however, made.[15]

From all these portraits, we see Cortés as a shrewd, thoughtful, serene, calculating individual of power and authority: a suitable representation of a Renaissance general who was also a proconsul.[16]

In the weeks before he left Toledo for Italy on May 8, 1529, Charles also saw Francisco Pizarro, who had reached Spain in January 1529 from Nombre de Dios. Between there and Spain, he had stopped in Santo Domingo. Then he arrived at Sanlúcar de Barrameda and thence went up to Seville, where he was rudely received by the geographer Martín Fernández de Enciso, who claimed that he owed him money from the time long ago that they were together in La Antigua.[17] Pizarro and his comrades were soon behind bars. But the Council of the Indies released them on payment of a fine from the money they had brought with them.

Among Pizarro's companions, it will be recalled, was first, Licenciado Diego del Corral, a veteran of the early days of Darien. An enemy of Balboa, if much liked by Pizarro, he seemed a good person to argue Pizarro's case for him. He was by 1528 rich and had an Indian mistress, by whom he had had many children. Pizarro's second companion in Spain was Pedro de Candía, a giant Cretan who had been an artilleryman in the Spanish army since 1510. Greeks were often used in that capacity in those days. He had served in Asia Minor, in Italy, and in Spain itself. He had gone to the New World in 1526 in the train of the new governor of Panama, Pedro de los Ríos. By that time, he had a Spanish wife, who lived in Villalpando, Zamora, a town between Benavente and Valladolid. His accounts of his adventures in Peru were heard in Spain with astonishment by an amazed audience.

Pizarro spent about a year in Spain after January 1529. He presented himself and his companions at court in Toledo, where he arrived with several Indians, llamas, and many cases full of interesting objects from Peru, including the all-important gold.

The Council of the Indies had since 1523 been formally headed by the conventional Bishop García de Loaisa, but since he was also royal confessor, the Emperor took him with him to Rome, where he lingered some years without activity, as holy men can easily do in the Vatican, so that the president de facto was the Count of Osorno, García Fernández Manrique, a rather hard civil servant who would remain in place till 1542. He was distantly related to the royal family through an Enríquez grandmother.[18] Osorno was a balanced man in public life but foolish in private.[19] He was the first secular aristocrat to exert an influence on American matters. The Emperor eventually found him too bureaucratic. But for the moment, the substitution of a count for a cardinal seemed a relief.[20] He was a close friend of Cardinal Pardo de Tavera, which then meant a great deal in Spanish administrative politics.

The other councillors of the Indies who talked to Pizarro were Gonzalo Maldonado, bishop of Ciudad Rodrigo; Luis Cabeza de Vaca, bishop of the Canary Islands; and Licenciado Juan Suárez de Carvajal, previously a justice of the supreme court of Valladolid, and once married to a niece of President García de Loaisa. More recently he had been bishop of the distant diocese of Lugo in Galicia.

Also present was Pedro Manuel, the son of Juan Manuel, the longtime courtier and feline ambassador, supporter of both Philip and Charles in

Flanders, who had been concerned with the Moluccas; and Gaspar Montoya, of Miranda de Ebro, author of a shrill defense of Catherine of Aragon against Henry VIII. He had worked with Pardo de Tavera. Another member of the council was now Rodrigo de Castro, who had been judge of the chancellery of Granada. He was another protégé of Pardo de Tavera, who, though formally President at the Council of Castile, would be seen to have been indirectly in control of the Council of the Indies, too, as if that were still dependant and not a separate institution.

Pizarro told his interlocutors all that he had seen in South America. He wanted the council's approval of his grand project for the conquest of Peru. The Council listened and were impressed by hearing of the tall Extremeño's hardships. They consulted Charles and, in July, Pizarro was granted the governance and other formal support that he wanted in the new, if still unknown, land. Pizarro was awarded the name of *adelantado mayor* of Peru, which was to be named New Castile, as well as the captaincy-general and governorship of whatever land he should conquer. It was the Empress Regent Isabel who finally gave the license.

In this contract (*capitulación*) of July 26, 1529, Pizarro was to be allowed to "continue the said discovery and conquest and settlement of the province of Peru up to 200 leagues [600 miles] along that coast."[21] This limitation would later give rise to controversy and even civil war among Spaniards. Second, there was a passage about the captaincy-general and governorship of Peru with a lifetime salary of 725,000 maravedís a year— an income well above what Pedrarias had received (that had been 366,000 maravedís) for the same office, and there had been no inflation to speak of. That salary would be gained in the land to be conquered, and Pizarro would have to pay from it a chief magistrate (*alcalde mayor*), ten shield bearers, thirty foot soldiers, one doctor, and an apothecary. He would also have to pay for the journey of the friars whom he would take with him.

There were some other nominations: Pizarro, recalled the chronicler Cieza, "secured the most and best for himself without remembering how much his partner [Diego de Almagro] had suffered and deserved."[22] So Pizarro forgot about the *adelantamiento* that Almagro had expected. Almagro would become lieutenant-governor of the fortress of Tumbes, a town visited by him and Pizarro on their earlier journey; and Luque the priest, who had also contributed to the financing of the future expedition, was to be bishop of it and protector of the Indians in that province. Actually, at this time Tumbes was desolate. There had been fighting between it and nearby Puna, which the latter city had won.

All those who had been with Pizarro on Gallo Island, "the thirteen of fame," were to be named hidalgos; if they were that already, they would be named knights of the Golden Spur. That brought Pizarro's expedition fully into line with new chivalrous romances such as *Amadís de Grecia,* newly published in Cuenca in January 1530 by Cristóbal Francés.[23]

Pizarro's contract was signed by the Empress Regent (*yo la reina*).[24] Though Pizarro had had brought to Spain some Indians from the periphery of the Inca empire, as well as one or two animals, it was still surprising that the Crown interested itself in a modest way in the financing of the adventure.[25]

Other nominations for the journey to Peru included Bartolomé Ruiz de Estrada, the able pilot who would become *piloto mayor del mar del sur* and town councillor of Tumbes at a salary of 75,000 maravedís a year. A native of Moguer, next to Palos, he had already worked for Pizarro and Almagro for several years. Candía, Pizarro's Cretan companion in Spain, was named chief of artillery of the expedition, at 60,000 maravedís a year. He, too, would become a councillor of the phantom city of Tumbes.

Gold from Peru would carry a tax of 10 percent for six years, 20 percent later. Other taxes (*almojarifazgo, alcabala*) were delayed. Pizarro would have six months in which to prepare his expedition, and he could take 150 men from Spain itself and another one hundred from the Americas. Pizarro was prohibited from taking with him new Christians (converted Jews or Muslims), Gypsies, foreigners, and lawyers.

Pizarro went "home" to Trujillo and recruited four of his brothers. There seem to be no records of that visit, though a priest, Fray Pedro Martinez Calero, recalls meeting him then.[26] The outstanding recruit was Pizarro's brother Hernando, whom, Oviedo wrote, was the only legitimate one, and legitimate in his pride.[27] He was only twenty-five. Trujillo at that time had about two thousand citizens with full rights. Of these about seventy were hidalgos while 213 of the population belonged to the town nobility.

Others also recruited at this time included a Franciscan, Fray Vicente de Valverde; Pedro Barrantes, a distant cousin; and Francisco de Ávalos, of the great family of the Marquess of Pescara; and Juan Pizarro de Orellana, who was also a distant cousin.[28] He surely visited bankers in Seville such as the Illescas brothers or Francisco García or Diego Martínez.[29] Perhaps he saw one or two of the famous Genoese who were to be found in Seville—men such as Andrés Lomelín, Cristóbal Centurión, Juan Jacob Spinola, and Jerónimo and Gregorio Cataño, not to mention Florentines such as Jacob Boti.

Then Pizarro went down to Sanlúcar de Barrameda, Seville's port, and bought four ships on which he would leave for the New World, with 185 men in all.[30] Six of these passengers were Dominican friars. On the way, Pizarro at Seville was awarded the much prized Order of Santiago as a knight. They then traveled via the Canaries as usual, stopping at La Gomera, and at Santa Marta on the north coast of South America. The governor there, García de Lerma, promoted the fancy that Peru was full of serpents, lizards, and wild dogs. This news dissuaded some weak hearts from continuing. The rest went on to Nombre de Dios, where the news of Pizarro's success in Spain had preceded him and where Diego de Almagro and Bartolomé Ruiz, the pilot, as well as the priest Luque, awaited the returning Pizarro with fury at what seemed the neglect of their interests.

This was incidentally a promising moment in the history of the Spanish empire, for in January, the Council of the Indies had opened up commerce in the New World to eight new ports—Corunna, Bayona de Galicia, Avilés, Laredo, Bilbao, San Sebastián, Málaga, and Cartagena—a great step forward, even though to ensure taxes were paid, all ships had to return to Seville.[31]

In 1528, Isabel, the Empress Regent, was beginning to exert an influence. Serene and pale-cheeked, she had been brought up by her mother's confessor, Fray García de Padilla, and by Fray Hernando Nieto. These were men who had introduced into Portugal the austere interpretation of religion known as the *Observancia*. Another influence in the same direction was Guiomar de Melo, later her chief attendant. Her chief secretary was the count of Miranda, another Zúñiga, the elder brother of Prince Philip's tutor. Though she was Regent in Charles's absences, "Her Majesty is pained by the Emperor's departure, for fear that he will stay longer than he says, and she is right, for her life is very dreary when he is not here."[32] The Empress took the partings from her husband very hard but consoled herself "with the consideration that the absence of her husband whom she so dearly loved, was for the service of God, for the benefit of Christendom and for the faith." She did in 1529 have a well-prepared council of regency in the shape of Miranda, Tavera, and the ultra-experienced Juan Manuel. Her household was much smaller than the large enterprise associated with the Burgundians.

When Charles arrived by sea in Genoa, via Monaco and Savona (which town the French had once planned to make an alternative outpost for their control of Liguria), the city had arranged for him to be greeted with cries from two hundred small boats of "Carlo, Carlo, *Imperio, Imperio,* Cesare, Cesare," and he landed by a long specially built pier hung with tapestries and cloth of gold. A great ball appeared with an eagle on top, which showered scent, and a boy symbolizing justice handed the Emperor the keys of the city. This entry had been made possible for Charles by the opening in 1527 of this commercial city to him by Admiral Andrea Doria, who had changed sides from France to the empire. Charles had even sailed across the northern Mediterranean in one of Doria's boats. (He had left Barcelona in great style, too: as his armada left harbor, the crew on the flagship called out his motto "*Plus ultra, plus ultra,*" and the cry was echoed on the other galleys.[33]) Charles was then greeted by three cardinals sent by the pope, by the Duke of Ferrara, and by Alessandro de' Medici, last of the main line of that great family (even if he was illegitimate).[34]

Charles's success in Italy seemed even more striking since his dear aunt Margaret and Louise de Savoie, the mother of Francis I, signed in August the so-called "peace of ladies," which was largely favorable to Charles. It was a confirmation of the Peace of Madrid of 1526, save that the recovery of Burgundy was omitted. Francis recognized Charles as sovereign in Flanders and Artois, and renounced all his old claims to Milan, Genoa, and Naples. The young French Princes who had been hostages in Madrid were released on the payment of a large ransom. The Emperor's sister Leonor was confirmed as Queen of France.

The Emperor went on to Bologna, where in November he at last met Pope Clement. Here, too, Charles had a great welcome: There were inscriptions everywhere: "*Ave Caesar, Imperator invite.*" Every statue in Bologna was garlanded; there were triumphal arches and portraits of Caesar, Augustus, and Trajan. These imperial allusions did not, however, seem to embrace the territories that had been won in the New World. New Spain was not considered. For weeks, Charles and Clement were in discussion in public.[35]

Spain was implicated in Bologna for two reasons: First, it was the seat of the famous college of San Clemente founded in the fourteenth century for Spanish students by Cardinal Gil Álvarez de Albornoz, the College of the Spaniards; and secondly because Santo Domingo himself had died there and was buried there.

On Saint Peter's Day, February 22, Charles received the iron crown of Lombardy, and two days later, the imperial coronation was held on Saint Matthew's Day, Charles's birthday, in San Petronio in Bologna, the largest church in the city, with its light, then as now, superior to that in the Duomo in Florence. It was begun in 1390 in emulation of other large churches in Gothic style. It is the most highly developed creation in Gothic church architecture in Italy. Charles's presence is still recalled in the small chapel of San Abbondio which, however, was reconstructed in 1865. We know nothing of the impression made on Charles by the other twenty-one chapels, of which one or two—the Chapel of the Magi, for example—contained fine pictures. Perhaps Gattinara showed these to Charles; certainly, at least the great door of the Basilica decorated by the Sienese sculptor Jacopo della Quercia. Of the German princes, only the elector palatine of the Rhine was present. He carried the orb of empire, the Marquess of Montferrat the golden scepter, the Duke of Urbino the sword of state, and the Duke of Savoy the kingly crown. These were great Italian noblemen.

The Spanish delegation was also large and distinguished. It included the poet Garcilaso de la Vega and his great friend the young Duke of Alba.

Charles's head was anointed with oil by Cardinal Farnese, the most senior of the cardinals and Clement's eventual successor. The pope officiated. For the last time in history, the two highest dignitaries of Christendom were present together in their robes. The historian, collector, and papal favorite Paolo Giovio stood in a doorway and, in a resonant voice, proclaimed, "*Rex invictissime hodie vocaris ad coronam Constantinopolis.*" Charles smiled and waved aside the aspiration to the recovery of the East.[36] The people of Bologna cried "*Imperio, imperio.*" The Spanish contingent called out "Spain, Spain." Gattinara, now a cardinal, felt his work as chancellor had been finally sanctioned the moment the imperial crown of

Charlemagne was placed on Charles's head.[37] He died shortly after, and with him vanished the supreme proponent of the idea of Charles as universal monarch. In his baggage, Gattinara left a map of the world. He had no successor.[38]

Six months later, at the beginning of December, the governess of the Netherlands, Charles's cultivated, intelligent, and competent aunt the archduchess Margaret also died in her princely palace at Malines, age fifty. Her death was an accident deriving from a poisoned foot caused by broken glass in her embroidered slipper. Her career was one more reminder that the sixteenth century had as many women in great places as the twentieth. FORTUNE INFORTUNE FORT UNE was her mysterious motto, which is everywhere reproduced on the tombs, walls, woodwork, and stained glass of the church at Brou, which she had built near Bourg-en-Bresse. Her successor in Flanders would be Charles's sister Mary, the erstwhile Queen of Hungary.

Margaret's library alone would have entitled her to a grand place in international society. Only the collections of Cardinal Albert of Brandenburg, of Fernando Colón, and of the elector Frederick the Wise of Saxony competed. In the library there were pictures as well as books.

Margaret had planned her sepulchre at Brou for twenty years. There already rested the remains of her second husband, Philibert of Savoy. There was the tomb of her long-dead mother-in-law, Margaret of Bourbon. The three tombs were the work of the splendid German-born sculptor Conrad Meit. Her feet lay on a stone greyhound. There, too, would be in future the coffin of Laurent de Gorrevod, governor of Bresse, the first to enjoy a large monopoly to carry black slaves to the New World, a grant that he sold and whose proceeds presumably helped to finish this exquisite church. Gattinara advised her in the construction.[39]

Margaret had been Charles's best adviser, as her letters to him make clear. It was a tragedy for him and his causes that she died so relatively young and was not present for the brilliant conquests made in his later days.[40]

The Germans at the Banquet:
The Welsers

No rural household numbers less than forty men and women, besides which two slaves attached to the soil.

SIR THOMAS MORE, *Utopia*

An unexpected manifestation of the early days of the Spanish empire was the involvement in it of the German banking family the Welsers, of Augsburg. One optimistic genealogist claimed that their surname derived from Justinian's great general Belisarius. However that claim might turn out to be, the Welsers traded many luxurious and expensive items such as silk, cloves, hemp, cinnamon, and saffron. Through a marriage with the Vöhlin von Memmingen family, they acquired Spanish interests, especially in the Canary Islands. They had representatives in Madeira by 1490; in India by 1505. Unlike their rivals the Fuggers, who were strong Catholics, the Welsers were neutral in the religious quarrels of the sixteenth century. Some were even Protestants. The Fondaco dei Tedeschi on the Grand Canal in Venice was their headquarters in that city, while in Amsterdam they could be found at the the Golden Rose.

In 1519, the future emperor Charles borrowed nearly 150,000 ducats from the Welsers to help him bribe the seven imperial electors to vote for him (less than half what the Fuggers made available but still a large sum).[1] Apparently, the Welsers saw Cortés's Mexican gold in Brussels when it was exhibited in 1520 and were impressed. They also bought 480 quintals of cloves that had been brought back to Spain by Elcano in 1522 from the

Philippines, and in 1524 they established a branch factory in Seville specially dedicated to trade with the Americas. Their factor there was the most
powerful German merchant in Spain at that time, Lázaro Nuremberger,
who arrived in Seville in 1520. He married a daughter of the famous
printer Cromberger.[2] In June 1526, the Welsers set up a similar institution
selling pearls from Cubagua in Santo Domingo. The factors were two merchants, Jorge Ehinger and Ambrosio Alfinger, from the city of Ulm. Jorge
was the brother of several distinguished merchants by then established in
Constance, above all of Heinrich, who signed the letters lending money to
Charles in 1519. Ambrosio Alfinger came from a family that had been
prominent in the guild of tailors in Ulm. He had invested heavily in the
voyage of 1526 of Cabot to the river Plate, and his father had made a fortune through the cloth trade.

The emperor Charles was usually short of money. He asked the Welsers
in 1526 for a new loan. They agreed, the collateral to be "the island of
Venezuela." In 1528, they arranged a contract to manage the settlements in
that place, and they also secured the succession to Gorrevod's grant of the
import of African slaves into the Spanish empire.[3] They had been led to assume that the large Lake Maracaibo would conduct them to the magic
strait leading in its turn to the Southern Sea about which there was such
fascinated speculation for so long. Subsequent loans were made by the
Welsers to the Crown in Burgos on November 22, December 20, and
December 30, 1527. More loans of the same kind were made in early 1528
by the merchants of Burgos.[4]

The acceptance of these Germans as a power in the Indies was brought
closer in early 1528 when the King and the Council of the Indies signed a
capitulación that gave Jorge Ehinger and Jerónimo (Hyeronimus) Seiler the
responsibility for sending an armada to assist to maintain order in Santa
Marta, the new settlement near the mouth of the great river Magdalena in
what is now Colombia. Seiler was one further powerful German to become
engaged in the Indies. A native of the lovely city of Saint Gallen in Switzer-
land, he was ennobled by Charles V in 1525 and had succeeded Nuremberger as the chief factor of the Welsers in Seville in 1528.

The contract of 1528 obliged the Welsers to send an expedition with
three hundred men to Santa Marta within a year and to build three
fortresses there at their own expense. They were to take with them fifty

German "master miners" who would supervise the exploitation of gold in Santo Domingo and find new veins of that metal. The Welsers had experience of this kind of contract since they had married into a silver-mining family in the late fifteenth century.

Santa Marta was a perplexing town in the expanding radius of Spanish interests. It had been discovered as a useful place for trade by Rodrigo de Bastidas, that son of a converso merchant in the Triana, across the river from Seville. Bastidas was a man experienced in voyages and in the Caribbean. He seems to have first gone to the New World in 1500. Then captain on the *nao Santa María de Gracia,* he explored the Gulf of Uraba and the Río Hacha and was probably the first conquistador to bring back pearls from the Americas. After 1504, he was resident in Santo Domingo, and he assisted Cortés in February 1521 with reinforcements in three vessels. Among those who traveled thus to New Spain were the Franciscan Fray Melgarejo and the royal treasurer, Julian de Alderete. Already rich by 1510, he abandoned the sea and became a merchant in Santo Domingo. Old but still full of enterprise, he persuaded the Crown to make him the first governor of Santa Marta in 1524. He ruled there autocratically and was overthrown by his own followers in 1526. Bastidas was sent back to Santo Domingo but died on the journey, the rumor being that his end was hastened by his sometime subordinates. Then Santa Marta lived a year or two without an effective ruler (though Bastidas's deputy, Palomares, assumed that he was in control). Finally, the Council of the Indies appointed a businessman, a man similar to Bastidas, García de Lerma, as governor.

Before he was surprisingly named governor, Lerma had been a page in the household of Diego Colón in 1510. His own economic activity began with his interest in a gold mine in Puerto Rico. Oviedo summed up his character: "He is short of money but not of words."[5] He went to Flanders on Diego Colón's behalf in 1516 and there became a courtier and a friend of Charles, who later always treated him well. He intrigued successfully to obtain a monopoly of the pearls of Cubagua and, in succession to Francisco de Vallejo, became inspector (*veedor*) of the north coast of South America, where he concerned himself in trading brazilwood. In Santa Marta as governor, Lerma seems to have acquired an immediate name as a hard taskmaster.

The Welser business in Santo Domingo was asked to organize the dis-

patch of slaves to the New World, and it did so, but Licenciado Serrano, a
rising lawyer in the Welsers' factory, wrote, "The Germans bring in very
black blacks, so much so that, despite the great necessity that we have for
them, no one buys."[6] (Later, "very black" Africans rather than paler ones
enjoyed a vogue among slave buyers.) There was evidently a profitable collaboration between Governor Lerma and Ehinger, the Welser factor:
Ehinger estimated the value that he had to make to help Lerma maintain
order at 6,000 ducats. Lerma used his influence at court to preserve
Ehinger's monopoly on slaves.[7]

These arrangements did not work very well for the employers of slaves:
In 1524, Alonso de Parada, a friend of Diego Velázquez, the governor of
Cuba, who in 1528 became a judge in the *audiencia* in New Spain, proposed a contract whereby the King of Portugal would provide slaves to the
King of Spain in a good cousinly exchange.[8] Actually Charles gave another
small grant to take slaves to the New World to his secretary for American
affairs, Francisco de los Cobos: two hundred black slaves exempt from all
taxes. Of course, no one expected that that license would be taken advantage of by Cobos in person; sure enough, he sold it to Seiler and Ehinger in
Santo Domingo and also gave a share to three Genoese: Leonardo Catano,
Batista Justiniani, and Pedro Benito de Basiniano. In February 1528,
Ehinger and Seiler received a license to introduce four thousand slaves in
the next four years, a third of them to be women.[9] This was in effect a continuation of the old grant to Gorrevod.

The Welsers profited. The new grant of Venezuela to them was based on
a sketch map by the veteran geographer Fernández de Enciso, who had received a contract for the governorship of Tierra Firme—that is, Venezuela.
The contract was worked out by Ehinger, Seiler, Gessler (a new employee of
the Welsers in Seville), and also Bartolomé Welser and his associates in
Augsburg, who controlled several large warehouses in Andalusia. The contract not only gave the Welsers the right to trade in "metals, herbs and
spices" between the Indies and Spain but allowed them to arrange their
commerce directly between the Indies and Flanders—something never
granted before and, indeed, refused to the city of Santo Domingo the previous year.[10]

The agreement with the Welsers did not mention their name but spoke
of the factors in Santo Domingo, Alfinger and Ehinger. They were, as usual

in these circumstances, to be governor and captain-general for life; they would also be in perpetuity the captains (*alcaides*) of the two fortresses that they would build. The task of these men would be to found two Spanish pueblos with three hundred citizens each and introduce the miners.[11] The Germans would be free of taxes for six years; they could introduce cows as they wanted and take with them a hundred pine trees from Tenerife to plant. The governor could enslave all Indians who were shown to be rebels but no one else.

All the enterprising Spanish merchants of Santo Domingo who had already been extensively trading with the north coast of South America were distressed by this arrangement. For the 1,500 miles of coast of South America from Urabá to the mouth of the Orinoco was depopulated because so many Indians had fled into the interior to escape enslavement. There were in 1528 only two settlements, Santa Marta and Coro, as well as one improvised fortress at Cumaná.[12]

The experienced Juan (Martínez) de Ampiés had been permitted by the supreme court in Santo Domingo to go to Coro, which clearly needed an injection of life. His journey was delayed by a shipwreck in Saona, an island off La Española first visited by Columbus, and by a request from the supreme court in Santo Domingo to reinforce the fleet because of a recent French attack on San Germán in Puerto Rico. (It had ruined San Germán's short-lived prosperity.) Ampiés fell on the French fleet by surprise and killed thirty of their sailors in what must have been the first European Caribbean sea battle. Then he went on with fifty men to Coro via Higüey in Puerto Rico and Curaçao just off the coast of Venezuela. His aim was to prevent the Welsers from establishing themselves on the Colombian–Venezuelan coast. He hoped that they (whose representatives in Santo Domingo he knew) would content themselves with the coast to Santa Marta, while he, Ampiés, would hold on to the longer shore near Coro. Ampiés succeeded in persuading an ally of the past, the chief Manaure, to receive him with affection. Manaure even became a Christian.

Alfinger set off by sea from Santo Domingo for Coro with fifty men of his own in January 1529 and arrived on February 4. All seemed desolate. Ampiés was living in a stone house, which he had built for himself, on the island of Curaçao, and Lerma was in Santo Domingo, too, awaiting his own journey to Santa Marta, some of his men being among Alfinger's troops.

Alfinger was horrified at the misery of Coro. His putative capital consisted of a few incomplete and dull buildings on the edge of a dusty plain. This was not what he had expected when his contract had been negotiated. The fact that Ampiés had abandoned his pretensions was little consolation—he had proclaimed himself *justicia mayor* and was now claiming to have founded Coro only in order to export brazilwood. It was Alfinger who without enthusiasm now laid out the town in Spanish metrical style with grants of sites (*solares*) to appropriate settlers. Alfinger found that Ampiés had left nothing behind him and was even stirring up the Indians against him. He seized him when he returned and put him on a ship bound for Santo Domingo, with orders not to return to Coro under any circumstances. In this, Alfinger was eventually supported by the Council of the Indies, whose members declared that they would condemn anyone new going to Venezuela if he did not have the permission of the German governor.

Among those who had reached Santo Domingo with the miners was a remarkable man who would make his mark on the history of South America. This was Nicolás Federmann, like Alfinger originally from Ulm. Federmann had been born about 1505, so in 1529 would have been in his mid-twenties. In Ulm, his father, Claus, had a property with a mill next to the church. Federmann had been educated at the famous Fondaco dei Tedeschi in Venice, which was assuming educational significance. After that, he began to work for the Welsers. They sent him to Seville. Thence he went to Santo Domingo, where it was supposed that he could help Alfinger, who was still away, now supposed lost, on an expedition to Maracaibo.

Federmann reached Santo Domingo in December 1529, and went posthaste to Coro. He summed up the situation quickly and returned to Santo Domingo to seek supplies. He persuaded another employee of the Welsers, Sebastián Rentz, also of Ulm, to help him. He was assisted as well as hindered by the arrival of three ships direct from Spain under the command of Juan Seissenhofer (Juan Alemán to the Spaniards).

Once he had settled in Coro, Alfinger began preparing an expedition to Maracaibo, the entrance to which lagoon he had seen on his first journey to Venezuela. In August 1529, he captained 180 men out of the 300 whom he had brought from Santo Domingo. He found sweet water and concluded, in consequence of some primitive calculations, that the lagoon must be about six hundred miles in circumference. He was convinced that this led to an even bigger sheet of water, which in turn would open onto the Southern Sea. He and his friends ascended a mountain, which seemed to be called Coromixy and which marked the entry to a province where the men had beards and the houses were stone. It seemed that the Southern Sea was only fifteen miles away. Hugo de Vascuna, one of Alfinger's captains, reported that there was a valley there called Unyasi, where there were large "sheep"—the llamas found in the land of Birú.

Alfinger crossed the mountains of Jideharas, south of Coro, to find the east side of the lagoon, founding the settlement of Maracaibo on September 8. He also founded a less long-lasting settlement, which he named Ulma after his own faraway city in Germany. But he did not find a way to the Southern Sea.

Alfinger returned to Coro after losing a hundred men, mostly to Indian attacks, for the Indians on that coast were by then strongly opposed to Spain, having lost so many of their number as slaves, in a trade that also interested Alfinger. Coro soon began to compete as a slaving port for that trade with Cubagua. Of course, Alfinger and his German fellow controllers needed Spanish lieutenants for this undertaking. In December 1529, we hear for the first time of the name Venezuela being applied to the entire territory of the settlement, and Alfinger was being spoken of as its governor.[13]

Further confusion was sown in the mind of Alfinger. Diego de Ordáz, Cortés's companion and a veteran of the campaign in Mexico in 1519–20, persuaded the Council of the Indies to let him explore and exploit the eastern end of Venezuela precisely as far as what he called the Río Marañón, though it would seem better now to call it the Orinoco. Ordáz was to be allowed to take two hundred fifty men and would receive the habit of the Order of Santiago.[14]

There were other more domestic disputes for Alfinger to try and settle. For example, the prices in the colony seemed far too high—above all for wine, but also for soap and for horses. Further, neither Alfinger nor his colleagues in Santo Domingo had been able to fulfill the demand for slaves to work there, neither Indians nor blacks. The bishop of Santo Domingo would write shortly to the emperor Charles (1530) that the very survival not just of his island but also of Puerto Rico and of Cuba depended on the provision of African slaves. He suggested that all these colonies should be able to import them without licenses.[15]

There was much support for this demand. In 1529, Ehinger sought and obtained a new contract for the carriage of slaves to the New World. He was helped by a temporary alliance that he made in Medina del Campo, that great market city of Castile, with Rodrigo de Dueñas, whose large Castilian fortune was based on the import of cinnamon.[16]

Other agitation in favor of an extension of the slave traffic continued. For example, in 1527, Alfonso Núñez, a merchant of Seville, on behalf of a Portuguese, Alonso de Torres, undertook to sell to Luis Fernández de Alfaro, a backer of Cortés, ex–ship captain, and surely from his name a converso, one hundred black slaves, of which four-fifths were to be men. These would be procured in the Cape Verde Islands, the Portuguese slave mart off Africa, and sold in Santo Domingo.[17] Two years later, Fernández de Alfaro himself went to buy slaves in the Cape Verde Islands. He had by then arranged a contract of his own to supply another hundred black slaves to Santo Domingo.[18] There were lesser merchants who undertook the same kind of service to Puerto Rico.[19] The first merchant of Seville implicated in the African trade on a large scale was, however, Juan de la Barrera, who, returning in 1530 from the Indies already wealthy, soon became one of the richest of traders with establishments for the sale of slaves and other items in Cartagena, Honduras, Cuba, and New Spain. He would regularly make the Seville–Cape Verde–Veracruz journey in one of his own boats.[20]

These procedures, and this route, marked an innovation. Until now, black slaves of African origin had usually been taken to the Americas from Europe, having probably been born in Portugal or Spain. But now slave ships began to sail direct from Africa to the New World, following the precedent of *Nuestra Señora de Begoña.* Belonging to a Genoese merchant, Polo de Espiñola of Málaga, the vessel left São Tomé, off what is now Nigeria, in 1530. Aboard were three hundred slaves bound direct for Santo Domingo.[21]

Clearly, too, many of the slaves taken from Spain or Portugal to the Spanish empire now came from Africa, as was testified by the belief that all the difficulties encountered in disciplining them derived from Muslim *wolofes,* a term used to describe a Muslim tribe in West Africa—an anxiety which led to a ban in 1526 on the import of such slaves. The Germans who had secured the contract for carrying slaves from Seville entered negotiations with the Casa da Mina in Lisbon. They reached an understanding that these slaves would be sent from São Tomé, in the Gulf of Guinea. In

1530, King João III of Portugal gave permission to ships' captains to export slaves regularly from both the Cape Verde Islands and from São Tomé.[22] He does not seem to have hesitated a moment before agreeing to this, any more than King Fernando the Catholic had hesitated in 1510 about arranging for slaves to be sent to Santo Domingo. If these monarchs gave the matter any thought at all, they would have supposed that a slave in Christian hands would be much better off than a free African in Africa.

The first boat to travel from Guinea direct to the Caribbean was the *San Antonio,* whose captain, Martim Afonso de Sousa, took 201 slaves, branded G for Guinea, from São Tomé in November 1532, a consignment that he delivered to the royal factor in San Juan de Puerto Rico, Juan País.[23] This was the forerunner of three hundred years of such traffic. In 1533, nearly 500 slaves were taken direct from São Tomé to the Spanish Indies and, in 1534, about 650 were sent, even though at that time the royal factor at São Tomé was sending more than 500 slaves a year to the Portuguese castle of Elmina and 200 or 300 a year to Lisbon.[24] In 1530 and 1532, rules were written against the shipment of *ladinos,* as slaves directly shipped from Spain were called, because they, too, were supposed to be potentially irresponsible.

A decree from the King in 1526 had repealed the slaving provision in the more tolerant code of Alfonso el Sabio, the *Siete Partidas* in the thirteenth century, which provided that a slave who married would become free: Already the complexities of black slaves marrying free Indians had begun to preoccupy agile state lawyers.[25]

Thereafter, nevertheless, black slaves, tied to their masters or no, would play a decisive part in most European ventures in the Americas.

Thus, when in 1527 Pánfilo de Narváez, veteran survivor of Cortés's expedition, set off for the conquest of Florida, he had his expected crew of men with names such as Cuéllar, Alanís, and Enríquez. But there were also several black slaves, their names forgotten but their work essential.

13

Narváez and Cabeza de Vaca

Who will count the gold which entered Spain from this quarter?

PEDRO DE CIEZA DE LEÓN

Bent on founding a new settlement in Florida, Pánfilo de Narváez, with his Segovian upbringing, his deep voice, and his long experience of fighting in the Indies, set off from Sanlúcar de Barrameda with six hundred men in five ships on June 17, 1527. On board were five Franciscans, headed by Fray Juan Suárez, the commissary of the expedition. Other important participants were Alfonso Alonso Enríquez, the accountant; Antonio Alonso de Solís, the factor; and Álvar Núñez Cabeza de Vaca, the treasurer. There was, too, as often in those days, a Greek sailor: This one was named Doroteo Teodoro. There was a captain, Valenzuela, a relation of Narváez's wife, María de Valenzuela. It was thus a typical expedition of the late 1520s.[1] A Spaniard named Esquivel, another named Velázquez de Cúellar, and an Alanís as notary completed the crew.

Of these men, Cabeza de Vaca would make history on this voyage. His extraordinary surname means literally "head of a cow." It derives from the legend that King Sancho of Navarre gave the name to an ancestor, the shepherd Martín Alhaja, who marked a path for the Christian armies at the battle of Las Navas de Tolosa in 1212. Álvar Núñez Cabeza de Vaca was brought up in Jerez de la Frontera by his uncle, Pedro de Vera, and Beatriz Figueroa, his aunt. He became a chamberlain in the household of the Duke of Medina Sidonia, who sent him to Valladolid with urgent messages during the war of the *comuneros,* fighting also in Seville for the royal forces. Then he was in Italy with the imperial army. He married María de Marmolejo before he joined Narváez. He was a cousin of the Cabeza de Vaca who was bishop of the Canary Islands and on the Council of the Indies.

After stopping in the Canaries as was de rigueur in those days, the expedition of Narváez reached La Española by mid-August. There Narváez tried unsuccessfully to recruit more men. Instead of gaining new adherents, indeed, he lost 140, who preferred the local scene, being "influenced by the offers and promises made to them by the people of the islands."[2] Florida, after the journeys of Ponce de León and Vázquez de Ayllón (about which people in Santo Domingo were informed), did not now seem so inviting, and more attractive rumors of a rich new country to the south of Panama were already beginning to be current.[3] With the remainder of his followers, Narváez set off for Cuba, where they remained for the winter of 1527 to 1528.[4] Narváez had been in Cuba most of the time between 1511 and 1520, so he had many friends there to draw upon. He had a son in Cuba, too, Diego Narváez, as well as his wife, María de Valenzuela, who managed his estates. One of his friends was Vasco de Porcallo de Figueroa, now of Trinidad, where he had a large *encomienda,* which he treated as an estate rather than as a grant of individuals. He had been in New Spain in Narváez's expedition of 1520 and had a bad name for mistreating Indians. Rather surprisingly, he went with Cortés to Spain in 1527.[5] He offered to supply Narváez.

Narváez set off for Trinidad but in the event waited at Cabo de Santa Cruz. Cabeza de Vaca went back to Trinidad with a captain named Pantoja to obtain the supplies. They encountered a fierce storm, and Cabeza de Vaca went alone to see Porcallo. A hurricane almost destroyed the place while he was there. The houses and the church were blown down, and Cabeza de Vaca said that he had to link arms with several others to avoid being blown away. Narváez then assembled his fleet outside Jagua, a town in Cuba he had himself established in 1511.

In February 1528, Narváez, Cabeza de Vaca, and the rest of the expedition set off for Florida with the experienced Diego Muriel as their chief pilot. Muriel had already been to the west coast of Florida and had also been with Narváez on his disastrous expedition to New Spain in 1520.[6] He left behind in Havana one of his captains, Álvaro de la Cerda, with forty men and twelve horse. Another storm caught them off Havana, and they were near Florida rather sooner than they had expected or desired. They found themselves in a bay, which seems to have been Moore Haven, on Thursday, April 12. Narváez landed there on Good Friday, and the following day he raised the flag of Castile and took possession of the land in the name of the distant Emperor. He was then proclaimed governor of Florida by his men and Cabeza de Vaca, as treasurer, and Alonso de Solís, as *veedor*, presented their credentials to him. After that, forty-two thin horses were landed, being in a very poor way after such a bad journey. Alonso Enríquez exchanged some Spanish goods for venison from local Indians who had first made threatening gestures and then left, leaving a large hut, which could have sheltered three hundred.

Narváez immediately wanted to investigate the interior, and he set off with Cabeza de Vaca and forty men, with six of the healthier horses. They found what seems to have been the bay of Tampa, where they spent the night. They then returned to the fleet, and Narváez sent a brigantine back to Havana to seek more provisions from Álvaro de la Cerda. He also seized four Indians, whom he asked to lead him to where maize was grown. They took him to such a place, though the sought-after cereal was far from ripe. They found there some cases belonging to traders from Castile, with their bodies inside, each covered with painted deerskin. There was also some gold and some feathered objects, which looked as if they had originated in New Spain, home of feather mosaics. The Indians explained that these objects came from Apalachee, where there was everything that the Spaniards might want. Enríquez burned these reminders of previous Spanish defeats to avoid demoralization.

The Castilians, meantime, disputed the right course: Cabeza de Vaca thought that they should re-embark and seek a better harbor, but Fray Juan Suárez thought quite differently, explaining that Cortés's fief of Pánuco was only about thirty miles away to the west. Narváez agreed. He suggested that Cabeza de Vaca should stay with the ships while he went ahead. Cabeza refused, saying that he preferred to risk his life than lose his honor. A Captain Carvalho stayed behind with the ships. But Pánuco was in fact more than one thousand miles away.

The expedition set off, meeting a river, which they crossed with difficulty. They made rafts for the supplies, and some Spaniards swam. Two hundred Indians were waiting on the other side. The Spaniards captured some of them and were then led to their settlement, where the explorers at last found ripe maize. Cabeza said that they should now seek the sea again, but Narváez refused to commit his men to such a journey. Cabeza went ahead on his own but found only a river with oyster shells, which cut explorers' feet through their boots. In the event, it was an expedition led by Valenzuela that found the sea in a small bay.

The expeditionaries continued their journey, which was generally westward in direction, though it was by now quite unclear where they were going. They occasionally met and made friends, as they supposed, with Indian chiefs such as a certain Dulchanchellin, who was attended by men playing reed flutes, and with him they exchanged beads and hawks' bells for deerskins. The aim was to find a good place for a settlement, but one did not appear. Occasionally they obtained maize, sometimes a Spaniard (as Velázquez de Cuéllar) was drowned, sometimes horses were killed. Occasionally, there were golden moments, as when "we saw that we had arrived at a place where they told us that there was an abundance of food and also gold [so that] it seemed that a large part of our weariness and hunger had been lifted from us." The abundance included pumpkins and beans. They encountered such interesting animals as rabbit, hare, bear, geese, hawks such as sparrow hawks, heron, partridge, and teal ducks. While up to their necks in a lake, which they could not cross in any other way, they were attacked by "tall, naked, handsome, lean, strong and agile Indians" with powerful bows, which they managed "so surely that they never miss anything." Narváez sent Cabeza de Vaca with about sixty men again to seek the sea. He found it at the Bay of the Cross (or Mobile Bay). The whole expedition set off for there, but the journey was long and there were many who were sick (perhaps a third of the total). Cabeza de Vaca noted that "most of the horsemen began to steal away in the hope that they could find some recourse for themselves by abandoning the governor and the invalids." But "those who were hidalgos could not bring themselves to do this without telling the governor and we, the officials [the inspector, the treasurer, the accountant], reproached them and they agreed to stay." Then Narváez asked each man separately his advice "about this evil land and how to get out of it."

At the sea, they built boats, but that meant making nails, saws, axes, and other tools out of stirrups, spurs, and crossbows. They made rigging from the tails of horses, sails from shirts, oars from juniper wood. Doroteo

Teodoro made pitch from pine trees. They tanned the hides of dead horses to obtain pails for water. The building of boats began on August 4, and by September 20 they had five of them, each twenty-two cubits long.[7] On September 22, they ate the last of the horses and embarked, with Narváez on the first ship with forty-nine men and the auditor Enríquez. Forty-eight men sailed with Andrés de Dorantes, forty-eight with captains Téllez and Peñalosa, and forty-nine with Cabeza de Vaca. They set off, with no one on board having any knowledge of navigation, for none of these conquistadors were sailors. The boats were loaded so high they were scarcely a hand's breadth above the water.

After seven days, they landed at an island, which seems to have been in the delta of the Mississippi. They sailed on in a westerly direction and ran short of water as well as of food (the horses' hides rotted) and reached an island without sweet water. They began to drink seawater, five men becoming almost insane as a result. At last they reached an Indian port where there were canoes, freshwater, and cooked fish, all of which the Indians offered Narváez, apparently because they admired his sable coat. But at midnight the Indians attacked, Narváez was injured, and the Greek Doroteo Teodoro deserted. It was observed that the Indian canoes seemed to be cutting off the Spaniards from the open sea, so the flotilla of five boats set sail again. Cabeza de Vaca was swept out into the Gulf of Mexico, but he managed to return and saw again three of the boats, including Narváez's. Cabeza de Vaca caught up with him, but as the governor's boat carried "the strongest and healthiest people among us there was no way whereby the others could follow him." Cabeza was able to ask Narváez for a line so that he would not be left behind and also to ask for orders. Narváez said that "this was no time to give orders to others, each of us must do what seems best to save his life and that was what he intended to do." So saying, he drew away with his boat. No one ever saw him again. It became known that he remained on board his ship, on which there was no food, and in the course of the evening, the ship was blown out to sea without anyone seeing him go, "and no one learning more of him" ("*Nunca más supieron de el*").[8]

It was a tragic end to the life of a resolute adventurer whose ambitions were boundless even if his capacity was limited. He was good-hearted, optimistic, and resourceful but also ruthless and foolish.

For a time, Cabeza de Vaca sailed alongside the boat of Téllez and

Peñalosa, but on the fifth day of sailing, a storm separated them. "Next day all the [forty-nine] men in my boat were lying heaped upon one another so near death that few were conscious. Not five men were able to stand. When night fell, only the mate and I were capable of sailing the boat and, at night-fall, the mate told me to take over for he thought that he would die that night. . . . At midnight I went to see if he was dead but he was better."

At daybreak, this boat was flung on to the shore, and nearly all the ship's company revived. They found themselves with freshwater on an island, which they called Malhado, island of ill fortune. There, Indians gave them food, for which the Spaniards offered more hawks' bells and beads. They decided to set off again, but waves overwhelmed the boat, Fray Juan Suárez drowned, and the rest of the expedition were flung naked on to the shore. It was now November 1528. Indians emerged from a village and offered to take the survivors into their houses. There was a general disposition to accept such kindness, but the few of Cabeza's conquistadors who had been in New Spain (Alanís, Dorantes) refused because they thought the concession was certain to lead to their being sacrificed. The Indians had built a hut for their unexpected guests, with beds of reed mats inside it. The Indians danced and made revelry, though, wrote Cabeza, "for us there was neither pleasure nor revelry nor sleep for we were waiting to know when they were going to sacrifice us."

These Indians had their nipples pierced and reeds were driven two and a half inches through them. Their lower lips were also cut open. Their staple food was the swamp potato, but in the summer, they also ate fish.

Matters began to improve when Cabeza's men discovered that another of Narváez's five ships had docked nearby—that of Dorantes, whose crews, remarkably, were still clothed. The two groups pooled such resources as they had. Cabeza and Dorantes decided to try to spend the winter on this island. They despatched a boat under Álvaro Fernández with three other strong men to try to reach help in Havana. They set off, but must have been wrecked on the way. Very cold weather came upon the survivors. Five Christians who had had to camp on the beach ate one another's bodies. By then, only fifteen from the two boat crews were alive. A stomach complaint then hit the Indians, who were tempted to kill the remaining Spaniards, but they abandoned the idea when they considered that if the Spaniards were so strong, they would surely have saved more of their own people.

The Indians tried to make the Spaniards into medicine men. Cabeza was unenthusiastic, but his fellow castaways felt that they had to accept. They established their authenticity by arranging to blow on the part of the body where there seemed to be pain and then make the sign of the cross. They recited a Paternoster and an Ave Maria. This sometimes worked.

Cabeza de Vaca soon went to the mainland, where he lived for a month eating blackberries. He became ill, and the other survivors of the expedition visited him. Then he returned to Malhado, where the Indian chiefs prescribed hard labor for him and the other survivors. His first work was to seek swamp potatoes under water. He eventually became a trader, procuring sea snails, shells, fruit, hides, flints for arrowheads, dried reeds, glue, and tassels of deer hair. But since these Indians were constantly at war with their neighbors, commerce was limited. In these circumstances, Cabeza became famous among the Indians of the Mississippi delta. He remained there almost six years.

14

Ordaz on the Orinoco;
Heredia at Cartagena

> Those who do military service for the world pant, sweat, and endure
> the tumult of battle for many years. And for what perishable and
> worthless concerns, and with such uncertain hope!
>
> ERASMUS, *Enchiridion*

Several of the captains who had accompanied Cortés in his years of
struggle against the Mexica wished to have the opportunity of achieving
something similar themselves. These were in particular Pedro de Alvarado,
who, as has been seen, was carving out for himself a principality in
Guatemala; Francisco de Montejo in Yucatán; Pánfilo de Narváez, the
tragic Segoviano who as we have seen would die off the Mississippi; and
Diego de Ordaz, who embarked on a great adventure on the river Orinoco.

Diego de Ordaz had been born in Castroverde de Campos, a small town
in northwestern Castile near Medina de Rioseco, surrounded by flat, fertile
land and fed by the river Valderaduey. Castroverde is a remote place, and it
is at first sight astonishing that so determined a conquistador should have
come from it. Ordaz was, however, a blood relation of other conquistadors
who had accompanied Cortés, such as Cristóbal Flores from Valencia de
Don Juan, a friend of Cortés who was punished by him for blaspheming.
Ordaz was an uncle, too, of Francisco Verdugo, one of the many men of
Cuéllar to take part in Diego Velázquez's enterprises and who had left
Spain with Ordaz in 1510. It seems likely that Ordaz had been present at
the disastrous battle of Turbaco, in what is now Colombia, where the

Spaniards were defeated and where the veteran explorer Juan de la Cosa had been killed.

Diego de Ordaz and his brother Pedro also took part in the conquest of Cuba: Diego became majordomo to the governor, Diego Velázquez. He became well known for leaving behind his brother Pedro in a swamp in the south of the island, but Pedro survived to be able to volunteer to join Pánfilo de Narváez in his expedition to New Spain in 1520.

Ordaz had joined Cortés's expedition in 1519. Velázquez thought of him as one of "his" men on the journey He was asked to keep an eye on Cortés on Velázquez's behalf. Ordaz was a captain of one of Cortés's ten ships in 1519, and Cortés sent him to obtain supplies from Jamaica. Later, Ordaz tried to kidnap Cortés by asking him to dine on board his ship at Havana, but Cortés wisely refused the invitation. Ordaz's brigantine in Yucatán went in search of the lost Andalusian Jerónimo de Aguilar. He seems to have plotted against Cortés in Veracruz, and he was arrested, condemned to death, and then pardoned. (As captain-general, Cortés had the right to make such condemnations.)[1] Ordaz had no doubts about Cortés's lack of morals: "The Marquess has no more conscience than a dog," he wrote to his nephew Verdugo.[2]

Ordaz's next exploit was to climb the volcano Popocatépetl, and he was able from that height to observe and, later, describe the beautiful site of Mexico-Tenochtitlan on its lake.[3] It was the first European ascent of a mountain in the Americas. The Spaniards, therefore, knew which route to take to the Mexicas' capital. Understandably, Ordaz took a volcano as his coat of arms. He lost a finger in the fighting "on the bridges" in 1520. That same year, Cortés, who now trusted him, sent him back to Spain to support his cause at court. Ordaz was not much missed in the last battles around Tenochtitlan, for he was no horseman and he stuttered in speech.[4] But he was one of the conquistadors who interested himself in the achievements of the Indians, and later, in Spain, he requested his nephew Francisco Verdugo to send him some feather mosaics, which the Mexica arranged so artistically.[5] He was also a good letter-writer, as his letters to Verdugo show.

In 1524, we find Ordaz branched out into new activities of his own. He was the owner of two-thirds of the ship *Santa María de la Victoria,* which sailed with merchandise for the Americas from Santo Domingo. But like all the successful captains in New Spain, he had his *encomiendas*: Teutla, Huejotzingo, Caplan, Chiautla. In 1529, the Crown also gave him the peninsula of Tepetlacingo, on the lake of Mexico.[6] Then he went back to old Spain and was the only conquistador from New Spain present at Córtés's second wedding, in 1529 in Béjar.

This was the background of the Castilian who, in May 1530, obtained a contract to "discover, conquer and populate" the towns that were to be found between the Río Marañón [that is, the Orinoco] and the Cape de la Vela ("of the Sail") in what is now western Venezuela, on the west side of the peninsula of Guajira.[7]

Ordaz was able to organize a new expedition of five hundred men.[8] He also had thirty horse. His captains were the famous and persistent Gil González Dávila, as *alcalde mayor,* Jerónimo Dortal as treasurer, and Juan Cortejo as captain-general, while Alonso Herrera was *maestre de campo.* Of these men, the first named had by then been active, as we have seen, in innumerable ways in the Indies over twenty years. Alonso Herrera, who came from Jerez de la Frontera, had been in Mexico in the last stages of the conquest. He had then been sent by Cortés to suppress a rebellion of the Zapotecs in Oaxaca in 1526: "He was a practical man experienced in military matters with a singular capacity to attract young soldiers." Thus it was that he persuaded one hundred men to go with them. This included three brothers named Silva. They sold all they had in order to go with Ordaz, whom they joined late, in the Gulf of Paria, in the galleon of a Portuguese merchant, which they had stolen—or rather, persuaded the daughter of the merchant to make over to them without payment.

Most of the money for this expedition was found by two Italian bankers established in Seville, Cristóbal Franquesín and Alejandro Geraldini.

There was a clear ambiguity between Ordaz's license and that already assigned to Welser's men, the Germans Micer Enrique Eyniger and Jerónimo Seiler. It was also feared in Spain that Ordaz might touch the land of the most serene King of Portugal, "our brother"—that is, the territory that became Brazil. In the other direction, Ordaz would control the entire coast of Venezuela. How did that square with the existing concessions to the Germans? In this territory, Ordaz would become governor and captain-general for life and receive a salary of 725,000 maravedís a year. Out of this, he would, as the custom then was, have to pay a chief magistrate, thirty infantrymen, 110 squires, a physician, and an apothecary. Ordaz would be able to grant such *encomiendas* as he thought fit and would receive twenty-five mares from the Crown, which he would pick up in Jamaica. He would also receive 300,000 maravedís for artillery and munitions. He would have the right to carry with him fifty black slaves, of whom a third would be women.

The obscurity in the license of Ordaz was mitigated by the fact that Ordaz himself had no intention of interfering with the Germans on the northern coast of South America. Instead, he wanted to explore the great Río Orinoco/Marañón, which he believed led to a land with extensive supplies of gold.[9]

Ordaz's fleet sailed from Sanlúcar on October 20, 1531. He had two large *naos* and a smaller ship, which he called a *carabelón*. He had been maintaining his expedition at his own cost already for two months.

They stopped at Tenerife, where he picked up another hundred men, about forty horses, and some mares.[10] Then, after a storm that dispersed the ships, they reached the Cape Verde Islands on December 26. They sailed easily across the Atlantic to make landfall in the Americas sixty miles east of the Río Orinoco. Perhaps that was just inside the territory now known as Guiana. No European before had seen this wild, green landscape. Ordaz sent out a *chalupa*, a small launch, with thirteen men on board. But three days later, it returned, having been unable to land because of the mud. They then found some islands, which they named San Sebastián, and from there sailed up the river for eight days, "but all the land which appeared was flooded." They could find nothing to suggest that there was any settlement in the neighborhood. On one of these islands, they left a wooden cross to help to guide those who would follow them.

This is how Ordaz's account appears in a later investigation in Santo Domingo. But some chroniclers talk of a wreck of the two caravels that formed part of the flotilla and how everyone aboard them took to small boats as best they could and left their colleagues to—in some cases—a terrible fate. It was sometimes said of those who disappeared at this stage that they had sailed on upriver and discovered a magical golden land, El Dorado, but the only certain thing is that nothing more was heard of them. A small group indeed set off in two little boats to look for Ordaz and his flagship, but they in turn found themselves swept northward into the Gulf of Paria. One of the boats was lost there with all hands.

Ordaz, meantime, had indeed gone north to where he knew there was water. He found himself in the Gulf of Paria and, after another forty days, on the island of Trinidad (so christened by Columbus on his third voyage). He had only one barrel (*pipa*) of water left. They waited four days there to gather more water and grass for the horses. Then they reached land in the gulf, presumably to the west of the channel already known to Spanish captains as the Dragon's Mouth. There they were approached by Indians in two canoes. Ordaz gave them some good shirts of that staple Holland cloth, which had played such a part in relations between Spaniards and Indians.[11] He also gave them some Venetian glass beads, which had played a similar part in those relations.

These people talked a great deal: Ordaz and his friends considered that a good sign. But here the expedition came into contact with Antonio Sedeño, an aggressive ex-notary like Cortés and a man who had made a fortune selling Carib—that is, allegedly man-eating yellow-skinned Indians of the Leeward Islands—slaves. In 1530, he had been named governor of Trinidad, though the island had not yet been conquered. He had gone to the mainland, where he had started to build a fortress. This caused him to seem as much a threat to Ordaz as Ordaz was to him. A lieutenant of Sedeño tried to seize Ordaz, but Jerónimo Dortal got the better of him, and on June 14, 1531, Ordaz established the pueblo of San Miguel de Paria.

Ordaz sought then to establish the different responsibilities in the zone of the Orinoco: Sedeño in Trinidad, the Germans in Venezuela, and even the pearl fisherman Pedro Ortiz de Matienzo in Cubagua. But his Spanish rivals were unyielding. It was hard to reach any agreement about land in a continent where the distances were enormous, knowledge modest, and hatreds intense.

Advised of the real route of the great Río Orinoco, Ordaz began to sail up the delta of that river on June 23 in his splendid galleon. What a sight it must have been! He had still over 350 men with him, though some of them derived from Sedeño and Ortiz de Matienzo.

He sent Alonso Herrera ahead. He found the Indians on the first large settlement on the bank, probably Uyapari, unfriendly (*fuera de amistad y concordia*). Most of the people in these pueblos were warlike bowmen and fighters (*flecheros y guerreros y muy belicosos*). Ordaz soon caught up with Herrera and proceeded to scrutinize (*tantear*) other pueblos. In one of these, which he and his friends named Tuy, after the pretty Portuguese–Spanish border town, they learned that on the other side of the mountains there was a large province called Guiana. Ordaz sent there one of Sedeño's men, Juan González, who returned with the bad news that the way was difficult for horses, the land being sharp underfoot and sterile.

Ordaz now decided to continue up the Orinoco on land, leaving at Uyapari twenty-five sick men under the command of Gil González Dávila. But after several weeks' march and having traveled about six hundred miles to what is now Puerto Ayacucho, an astonishing distance, it became impossible to go any farther. The jungle was too intense, the heat unbearable, the mosquitoes triumphant, the diseases merciless. Carib Indians attacked regularly. Ordaz withdrew to the confluence of the Orinoco and the Meta. Some Caribs persuaded the gullible Spaniards that there was gold high up the Meta. Ordaz and his men went some way up that great tributary by boat. But rapids and currents prevented them going very far. Ordaz decided to return to Paria, a rough spot which seemed to him by then a memory of tranquillity. His idea was to reenter the zone of the Meta with its golden promise later overland via Cumána. But there were further difficulties. Gil González Dávila, veteran of so many odd encounters in the Indies, was halted and imprisoned by Ortiz de Matienzo. Ordaz eventually found himself in Cubagua with a mere thirty men. Ortiz de Matienzo captured him, too, and dispatched him under guard to Santo Domingo. The judge there released him. Ordaz tried to recruit new men for his journey back to the Orinoco. He was refused permission to do so, thus he determined to return to Spain with the same intent. He set off but died on July 22, 1532, halfway across the Atlantic. According to Fray Pedro de Aguado, a historian of Venezuela, he had been poisoned by Ortiz de Matienzo.[12] He was yet another of Cortés's contemporaries to die in suspicious circumstances.

In 1532, another contract was made by the Crown for the conquest and settlement of a part of the territory that had been left with the German Welsers—namely, the land between Darien or the Gulf of Urabá and the mouth of the wonderful river Magdalena. The arrangement was made by the only Madrileño among any of the leading conquistadors, Pedro (Fernández) de Heredia.[13]

Heredia was a small-time businessman who left for the New World to escape his creditors. His first visit to the Indies was financed by his wife, Constanza Franco, who had inherited a fortune from her first husband. On that first voyage, Heredia went to Santo Domingo and founded a sugar mill and plantation at Azua de Compostela, where Cortés had served as a notary in his youth, on land that he inherited from a cousin.[14] There he and his brother, Alonso, busied themselves in the Indian slave trade from the north of South America, indeed from the territory close to Cartagena, where he would receive his contract in 1532. Heredia went to Santa Marta, where he was for a time lieutenant-governor to Pedro de Valdillo, who himself took over from Álvarez Palomino in 1528. He must have seen then that no one was taking any notice of the zone between Darien and the Magdalena. Then he returned to Spain, where he pursued his plan of gaining his grant of Cartagena, which he obtained in August 1532.[15]

In September 1532, only a month afterwards, Heredia left Sanlúcar with a single galleon, a caravel, a small boat (*fusta,* or light rowing boat), and 115 men. Again, his wife, Constanza, seems to have been the principal backer. They sailed via the Canaries (La Gomera), then to Puerto Rico (the island of Mona), then to Santo Domingo, where Heredia enrolled more men, including some left over from Ordaz's unhappy expedition to the Orinoco. At Azua, where Heredia had had his plantation, they secured a new caravel. They went on to Santa Marta, where the commander looked for interpreters who spoke the language of the natives in Cartagena. Finally, early in 1533, probably on January 14, Heredia and his expedition disembarked on the Colombian coast in the bay of Cartagena.[16]

Soon after their landing, Heredia was joined by his brother, Alonso, who sailed in with reinforcements from Guatemala, where he had been with Pedro de Alvarado. Together, the brothers mounted expeditions from Cartagena southward into the territory of the Cenú people, and toward Urabá. Some further Spanish settlements were founded in unpromising circumstances: San Sebastián de Buenavista in the Gulf of Urabá, for example, Villa Rica de Madrid in Cenú territory, and Santa Cruz de Mompox, some way up the Magdalena. Their remarkable colonial architecture can still be appreciated by the adventurous traveler.

Cartagena was difficult to turn into a successful colony, largely because the supply of food was bad. The land nearby was marked by marsh and swamp. Sugar plantations and mills were founded, but for the time being, Heredia granted no *encomiendas.* This territory, which lay between two rivers, was soon to seem no more than a bridge to Peru. The governor of Santa Marta, at that time still García de Lerma, the businessman converted into proconsul, believed that Cartagena should be a dependency of his own city. Thwarted in that, he placed as many obstacles as possible in Heredia's way, even seeking to avoid his training interpreters in his city to assist him.[17] The Spanish settlers in Santa Marta were always raiding Cartagena for Indians, whom they could sell in "the islands," that is, the West Indies. On the other hand, the people in Cartagena considered the charm of their city that it was close to the provinces of the Cenú, who could be used as a workforce. All the same, they were soon using black African slaves for all the hard, or dirty, work.[18]

Almost before Cartagena had time to settle down, Juan de Padilla, a judge in Santo Domingo, came to carry out the *residencia* of Heredia. A second and third such enquiry were commissioned. Heredia was accused of neglecting the defense of Cartagena, of dividing the land nearby into *encomiendas* that favored his own friends, of defrauding the royal treasury, and of forgetting the need to maintain public morality.[19] All these accusations seemed unfair, premature, and inappropriate, and it transpired that the *residencia* had been introduced because Heredia was a mere commoner without the pretensions of a Montejo, the aristocratic Alvarado, or even Pedrarias.

Heredia later had great difficulties with his wife, who claimed that his adventures in the Indies had left her with no money. He eventually returned to Europe, but only in 1554; his fleet was wrecked off Zahara in January 1555, and he and more than one hundred others drowned. By that time, Cartagena de las Indias was a much-valued port in an empire that seemed to command two oceans, the Ocean Sea (the Atlantic) and the Southern Sea (the Pacific).

15

Cortés and the *Audiencia* in New Spain

> You know, don't you, that to the right hand of the Indias there is an
> island called California which is populated by black women?
> *Las Sergas de Esplandián*, Garci Rodríguez de Montalvo

Cortés returned in July 1530 from old to New Spain with no illusions. In his absence, there had been a political upheaval. Guzmán, the President of the *audiencia,* arrived in the capital of New Spain in December 1528; and there had appeared, too, the saintly, austere, intellectually determined, strong-minded, and unbending first bishop of the Mexicans, Juan de Zumárraga, a Basque Erasmian of originality and strength of character. He was of the great generation of liberal Spanish bishops, such as the inquisitor Alonso Manrique de Lara, and Alonso Fonseca, archbishop of Toledo. Zumárraga had met the Emperor in the Jeronymite monastery of El Abrojo, and Charles had asked him to eliminate the witches of Navarre—a task that he was said to have carried out to perfection. Nominated to Mexico in consequence of this triumph, Zumárraga proclaimed himself one who believed that the Indians were rational beings whose souls could be saved.[1] He was a Utopian as well as an Erasmian.[2]

Zumárraga at once entered upon quarrels in Tenochtitlan with the supreme court, whose members, he thought, were neglecting their duties, spending their time "promenading in public gardens." But Zumárraga was in a weak position since he had left Spain hastily, before his confirmation in office, so that it was easy enough to argue that he was just a "religious"

Charles V, age about twenty-two, with the Golden Fleece around his neck
(Master of the Magdalen Legend)

Mercurino Gattinara, chancellor to Charles V,
who dreamed of world power for his master

Gonzalo Pérez, Charles V's chief
secretary in the 1540s

Francisco de los Cobos:
reliable, covetous, patient

Granvelle, chancellor to Charles V
in all but name, who, like many
servants of the Habsburgs, came
from Franche-Comté

The empress Isabel of
Portugal, named regent
of Spain by Charles V
during his many
absences (Titian)

The archduchess Margaret of Austria, the
governess of the Netherlands as well as of
Charles V (School of Bernard van Orley)

Clement VII, the second Medici pope, whom Charles ruined at Rome in 1527 *(Sebastian del Piombo)*

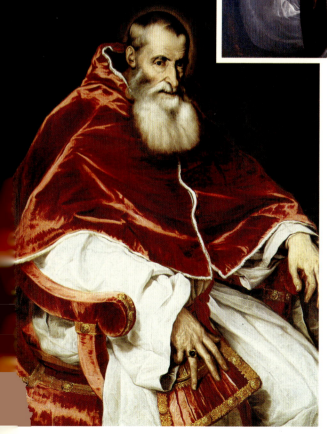

Paul III, Alessandro Farnese, who, though preoccupied with his family, also concerned himself with American Indians *(Titian)*

Quiroga, Bishop of Pátzcuaro, tried to apply More's principles in *Utopia* to New Spain.

The Erasmian Zumárraga, first bishop and then first archbishop of Mexico, was Mexico's first prince of the church.

AVE MARIA GRATIA PLENA

Antonius D Mendoça. 1° noua Hispanie Pro
Rex et dux Generalis ~ Año. 1535.

Antonio de Mendoza, first viceroy of New Spain, a great
aristocrat who organized an empire

Spanish galleon full of passengers. Galleons carried gold, silver, passengers, and crews across the Atlantic throughout the sixteenth century.

The lombard was an early type of artillery that terrified natives all over the Americas.

man like so many others. Zumárraga presented his authority as "Protector of the Indians"; the court agreed to give him all necessary powers but argued that he had delegated his authority. The judges also insisted that Indian complaints were their business and that Zumárraga's task was just to teach the catechism. They threatened the new bishop with exile, and the leading Indians, seeing how things were going, fled from their protector. Zumárraga denounced the judges in a sermon and threatened to report them to the emperor Charles.[3]

There then came the curious affair of Huejotzingo, a town on the eastern slopes of the volcano Iztaccíhuatl, some six miles from both Tlaxcala and Cholula. Cortés had taken the place as an *encomienda* in 1524. In 1528, the Indians there complained that, in addition to their tribute to him, they were being forced to pay dues to the court, including to the Crown's representative, García del Pilar, an experienced conquistador who had accompanied Cortés throughout the campaign leading to the conquest. He had the reputation of being the first Spaniard to learn Nahuatl. Zumárraga, apprised of the problem, asked the court for a schedule of the tributes. Guzmán said that the court was not answerable to him and told Zumárraga that if he persisted in his troublemaking he would have him hanged, as Charles had hanged Bishop Acuña of Zamora after the war of the *comuneros*. Guzmán sent a magistrate to arrest the complaining Indians of Huejotzingo. Zumárraga warned the Indians in time, and they took refuge in the new Franciscan convent in their town. Fray Motolinía was the guardian of the convent, and soon Fray Jerónimo de Mendieta would be writing his books in his cell there.

Zumárraga set out for Huejotzingo, being followed by the magistrate, who proceeded to arrest the Indians and take them to Mexico. Zumárraga remained in Huejotzingo, where a town meeting was held. This called on a Franciscan, Fray Antonio Ortiz, to go to Mexico to insist that the court respect justice. He preached thus at a pontifical Mass chanted by another Erasmian, Fray Julián Garcés, the Dominican bishop of Tlaxcala. Guzmán tried to silence Ortiz, and an *alguacil* on his orders expelled him from the pulpit. Next day, Garcés's vicar-general announced that all those who had been involved would be excommunicated—that is, both Guzmán and the constable. Guzmán ordered the vicar-general exiled and dispatched another magistrate to escort him to Veracruz. The vicar-general went to the church of San Francisco in Tenochtitlan, where Cortés's friends used to forgather, and which Guzmán now had surrounded. Zumárraga returned to the capital and persuaded the two junior members of the *audiencia* (Delgadillo and Ortiz de Matienzo) to go to Huejotzingo to perform a penance and recite a Miserere.[4] They went and withdrew a document that they had previously issued denouncing the Franciscans. But Guzmán sought his revenge by giving orders to hold up all the bishop's letters to Spain. That seems certain to have become normal practice.[5] One letter, though, reached its due destination. This letter to the emperor Charles recalled how many in Mexico had looked forward with pleasure to the coming of the new supreme court. It would surely be a breath of fresh air and a legal respite after the rough rule of Estrada. But the supreme court had seemed well-disposed to nobody. Helped by the interpreter García del Pilar, Guzmán was robbing the land.

Zumárraga also reported that Pánuco had become a slave emporium, for many slaves were kidnapped there, and thence shipped to the West Indies.

Guzmán, probably aware that he would soon be relieved of his responsibilities as President of the court, cleverly turned his attention to the conquest of the northwest. He had remarked that only fifty miles from the capital, the Chichimeca (a wild Indian people) were still in control. To mount an expedition against them, many horses were seized from private individuals, 10,000 pesos were taken from the treasury, and four hundred men were dragooned to take part. Juan de Cervantes was designated lieutenant of the captain-general in Pánuco and ordered to drive north from there at the same time as Guzmán drove northwest. He hoped that they would together fulfill a "grand design" of an empire running from sea to sea, north of New Spain. Guzmán asked the Crown to approve his title as governor of "Greater Spain."

The Crown refused to concede that, but agreed that the new territory might be called New Galicia, a territory to which Guzmán was indeed named governor in February 1531. But his larger ambition failed because the distances were too great. Guzmán did, however, conquer what became the future states in Mexico of Jalisco and Sonora, founding Compostela and Guadalajara in the first, San Miguel and Chametla in the second.

While these negotiations continued, the Council of the Indies in Valladolid was coming to terms with the fact that it had made a mistake in re-

lation to the government of New Spain.[6] It took the unusual step of meeting in November 1529 in conjunction with the councils of Castile and of
the treasury. Archbishop Pardo de Tavera, the president of the Council of
Castile, presided. The letters of Zumárraga, a man known to be of a just
spirit, had distressed all who had read them. The councillors studied an *información* critical of Guzmán, and also a response that Guzmán treated as
a rebuttal.[7] The council decided to change the composition of the court
there and then. In the long run, they thought, there should be a viceroy but,
in the interim, a new court would serve. Both Gattinara and Pardo de
Tavera, as well as García de Loaisa, took it upon themselves to suggest possible presidents, but the matter was difficult to decide. Though he would
not be receiving a large salary, a man of great integrity was essential. A further discussion was held on December 10, 1529, when the count of Osorno
and some members of the Council of the Treasury agreed that the new
president of the court in New Spain should be a prudent, strong man of
good birth with, if possible, a fortune in Castile. Such a person was hard to
find.[8]

The Empress, who was present, suggested a clever young Gallego, Vasco
de Quiroga, whose father had been governor of the Priory of San Juan in
Castile. Tavera was his father's friend and had always been helpful to the
Quiroga family. In 1525, he had been judge of the *residencia* of a *corregidor*
in Orán, Alfonso Páez de Ribera. At court, Quiroga later became friendly
with Bernal Díaz de Luco, the secretary to Pardo de Tavera, and it was with
him that Quiroga discussed a controversial passage in Antonio de Guevara's play *El Villano en el Danubio.* Perhaps it was this Bernal Díaz, as well
as the Empress, who suggested Quiroga as a judge.

Another nomination was Antonio de Mendoza, the son of Fernando the
Catholic's favorite public servant, the Count of Tendilla, a notably liberal
governor of Granada. Eminently a gentleman and not an intellectual, Mendoza had been a victorious commander, if on a small scale, in the war of the
comuneros and then an emissary in Hungary. Apparently when chamberlain
to the Empress Regent in Saragossa in 1529, he had told her that he would
like to go to New Spain in some capacity.[9]

Things were still going politically from bad to worse in Mexico itself.
Perhaps to distract attention from his other failings and setbacks, in late
1529, Guzmán led a large and well-equipped force up to Michoacán. He
was accompanied by the old monarch of the realm there, the *cazonci*, who

had been a compliant dependant on Spain since 1523. In February 1530, Guzmán had the *cazonci* tried, tortured, and then executed for organizing an attack on the Spaniards near the beautiful Lake Chapala.

The surviving judges (*oidors*), Diego Delgadillo and Juan Ortiz de Matienzo, were conducting themselves almost equally badly in the city of Mexico itself. Two conquistadors, García de Llerena and Fray Cristóbal de Angulo, had been imprisoned by an episcopal court in the Franciscan convent. Both had offended the judges, who had the two men arrested and tortured in the common jail. Zumárraga and the superiors of both the Franciscan and Dominican orders, along with numerous friars, made their way in procession to that building to demand their release. Zumárraga lost his temper and Delgadillo's guards chased away the procession. Zumárraga threatened to suspend all religious services in the city unless the prisoners were released in three hours. The judges then ordered Angulo to be hanged and quartered, and Llerena to have a foot cut off and be whipped one hundred strokes. Services were indeed suspended, and the Franciscans left their convent for Texcoco. The horrifying sentences seem to have been carried out. Negotiations began between Fray Garcés, the bishop of Tlaxcala, and the Dominicans acting for the judges. Services were revived for Easter 1530, but suspended once more on Low Sunday. The judges, who had not begged for absolution, remained under their excommunication.[10]

But they were now to be removed. On July 12, a new court for New Spain was at last chosen. The President would be Bishop Ramírez de Fuenleal, at that time President of the *audiencia* in Santo Domingo, a responsible and hard-headed civil servant who showed that he could work effectively with Zumárraga. There were also Juan de Salmerón, who had been a judge in relation to Pedrarias in 1522, and Alonso Maldonado, who had married a daughter of Francisco de Montejo, whose interests in Yucatán and elsewhere he supported. He was a great gambler and games player. There was, too, Francisco de Ceynos, who had once been prosecutor in Spain for the Council of the Indies. These men assumed office on January 12, 1531. Their arrival marked a fundamental change from the anarchic rule of the cruel Guzmán, who, however, managed to remain for a time as governor of his vast realm of New Galicia (Jalisco, Zacatecas, Aguascalientes, and part of San Luis Potosí).

The first action of the new court was to remove the restriction that the

old one had put on the movements of Cortés. He had in 1531 been forbidden even to approach the city that he had fought, destroyed, and rebuilt.
He had brought his mother, Catalina, and his new wife, Juana, to see the
sights, but they had only been able to observe it from afar: a fitting commentary on how the world has often treated the memory of its greatest
men. Another initiative by the court was to seek to collect all the sons of
Spaniards by Indian women to give them a Spanish education.[11] This *audiencia* was asked by the Council of the Indies gradually to eradicate the *encomienda,* an instruction that clearly contradicted an order of October
1529 by the first supreme court to allow *encomiendas* in perpetuity. But we
must not expect consistency as yet in Spanish imperial administration. The
encomienda was confirmed as a system of labor and of landholding in
1535.[12]

16

Montejo in Yucatán

Hernando Pizarro gave his word that . . . good soldiers are not to
be judged by their horses but by the valour of their persons.
Whoever showed himself brave would be rewarded in conformity
with his service; for not to possess horses was a matter of fortune
and no disparagement of persons.

Cited by Sir John Elliott, Empires of the Atlantic World

Francisco de Montejo was an accomplished conquistador from Old Castile
with experience in Cuba, Panama, and New Spain. He knew something of
the two oceans already in Spanish control, and he had helped in the
conquest of Panama as well as of New Spain. On December 8, 1526, he
obtained a contract from the Emperor, while he and the court were still in
Granada, for the conquest and settlement of Yucatán, and of Cozumel, a
delectable island surrounded by the deep blue water of the Caribbean Sea,
off the Mexican mainland, where both Grijalva and Cortés had stopped
before embarking on their serious adventures in New Spain. Montejo was
given the titles of *adelantado,* governor, and captain-general, designations
intended to continue for two generations. He would have a salary of
150,000 maravedís as governor and another 100,000 as captain-general.

Up to that point, there was nothing unusual in the contract. Other
terms in it, however, were unexpected. Thus the conquistadors would be
asked to found two pueblos, inhabited by a hundred men each, both with
fortresses, in "the most convenient and most necessary places." Montejo
would have to finance his own army but would not have to pay any taxes.
He and his heirs were granted "in perpetuity" 4 percent of all income gen-

erated in Yucatán, and only one-tenth would have to be paid to the Crown for three years after the conquest. Then the figure would fall to one-ninth and slowly thereafter to one-fifth. Each conqueror would receive two *caballerías*[1] of land and two *solares* in the towns. Montejo would be able to name town councillors for his towns, as captains of these expeditions usually could, and it was assumed that they would be chosen from among his closest followers. A bishop would be named for Yucatán within five years, and from then on, a tithe would be gathered to support the clergy and to build churches. Montejo was entitled to enslave Indians if they refused to accept the benefits of Spanish rule. Neither Jews nor Muslims, nor indeed criminals, were to be allowed to go to Yucatán. Finally, a few humane articles were written in November 1526 into Montejo's contract, which was signed by the Emperor and all the court bureaucracy of the Indies—Cobos, as well as by the three bishops who then participated in the Council of the Indies (of Osma, of Ciudad Rodrigo, and of the Canaries), that is, García de Loaisa, Maldonado, and Cabeza de Vaca.[2]

Montejo was of a good family established in Salamanca. He was born sometime between 1473 and 1484 and so was of the same generation as his onetime commander Cortés. He was a man of medium height, with a cheerful countenance, a good horseman, and of an openhanded nature. He usually spent more than his income, as the censorious Bernal Díaz del Castillo put it.[3] Montejo went to live in Seville in the early 1500s, where he seduced Ana de León (daughter of Licenciado Pedro de León, who was probably a converso), by whom he had a son who took his name and who later became famous as Francisco de Montejo, "*el Mozo*" (the Boy).[4]

Montejo the father went to the Indies in 1514 with Pedrarias, who sent him ahead to recruit volunteers in Santo Domingo.[5] Disappointed by what he found in Darien and Panama, Montejo went to Cuba, where a personal friendship with Diego Velázquez enabled him to establish a large farm near what is now the pretty port of Mariel. There he met Hernández de Córdoba returning from New Spain/Mexico looking very "badly treated." Montejo himself went to New Spain in Grijalva's expedition and was a captain of one of his *naos*. Then, like Ordaz, he went as one of Diego Velázquez's friends in Cortés's expedition in 1519, but he seems to have been easily persuaded by Cortés to work with him—at a salary of 2,000 pesos, said Bernal Díaz.[6] He started late in 1518 from Santiago in his own ship and caught up with Cortés at Havana, where he sold the latter five hundred rashers of bacon.[7] He went across to Cozumel, an island that he said, in the *residencia* of Cortés, he had visited "many times"—a claim which, by 1530, may have been true. At Veracruz, Cortés sent him north to look for a good harbor at a time when he himself was carrying out his coup de main against the friends of Velázquez. When Montejo returned, he was rewarded for his lack of complaint by being named first magistrate of Veracruz. He then returned to "the kingdoms of Castile," as he put it, on Cortés's behalf, being accompanied by another hidalgo, a cousin of the count of Medellín, Alonso Hernández Portocarrero.

On the way, Montejo stopped off at his Cuban property at Mariel, where he committed what a modern historian calls "an unpardonable indiscretion": Montejo could not resist showing his old friend and neighbor Juan de Rojas the breathtaking treasures that he was taking back to Spain— "an infinite amount of gold, so much so that there was no ballast in the ship except for gold," as a servant on Montejo's property put it, grossly exaggerating.[8]

Montejo's crossing of the Atlantic back to Spain in 1520 was interesting since the great pilot Antonio de Alaminos took a route between Florida and the Bahamas along the line of the Gulf Stream (the usual route was still through the Windward Islands). Governor Velázquez later criticized that route as being dangerous, but it became normal within a short time. Indeed, Alaminos pioneered it.

Leaving Cuba on August 26, the conquistadors stopped again at Terceira in the Azores Islands, which must have been well-known to Alaminos, and were in Spain by November. Then Montejo and Hernández Portocarrero embarked on a long struggle at court to establish the respectability of Cortés, whose enemies—above all, Diego Velázquez—were active, powerful, and unforgiving.

After the Crown found in favor of Cortés, thanks largely to Montejo and partly to Cortés's father, Montejo was named *alcaide*, or commander, of Villa Rica de la Veracruz.[9] He returned to New Spain in 1524 but went back once more to Castile quite soon with 60,000 pesos of gold,[10] having obtained from Cortés the valuable *encomiendas* of Azcapotzalco, Matlactlan, and perhaps Chila, worth 1,500 pesos a year. Montejo was at that time the *procurador* (official representative), of New Spain in Castile. There he sought his contract for Yucatán, in which pursuit he was supported by Pán-filo de Narváez and some others of his point of view. Having talked to Jerónimo de Aguilar, the interpreter, who had spent some years in Yucatán as a prisoner, Montejo had been led to believe that the territory in his con-tract was rich. Having obtained Charles's permission in December 1526, he was able to set off from Sanlúcar in June 1527, with 250 followers.[11]

This group included one important veteran of the wars in New Spain, Alonso de Ávila, who must have remembered Cozumel from his time there with both Grijalva and Cortés. Ávila had had recently an even more com-plicated life than Montejo since he gained both the respect and the distrust of Cortés, but returning to Castile in 1522 in one of Cortés's famous treas-ure fleets, he had been seized off the Azores by the French. He spent three years as a prisoner in France, and then he spent "all which I had in my pat-rimony" as a ransom.[12] He had been a protégé of Bishop Rodríguez de Fonseca, and for that reason Cortés had distrusted him. Ávila was famous but penniless, so it is understandable that he should seize the chance of re-covering his fortune under Montejo.[13] Montejo secured four good ships, on which he loaded cannon, some small arms, horses, meat, flour, biscuits, wine, oil—enough food for a year.

Montejo was drawn to Yucatán less, it would seem, by the precious met-als and jewels that he expected to find (though there were admirable jade objects there)[14] than by the realization that Yucatán could be made a good agricultural-pastoral province. Commerce and industry could be devel-oped. Even in the sixteenth century, the Maya were skillful makers of tex-tiles. They had time and wealth enough for the production of good textiles and ornaments, as shown by their special preoccupation with headdresses.

Montejo was thus a man of vision and wisdom as well as of ambition. His attitudes toward the Indians were comparatively humanitarian. He must have known before he sought, and obtained, his contract that Yu-catán was, as Bishop Landa would put it later, "a very flat land with no mountains for which reason it cannot be seen from ships till they are close inshore."[15]

On his way to Yucatán, Montejo, as was customary, stopped at Santo Domingo to obtain more horses and soldiers, but he did not then seek an interpreter, though he should have known of the special value of such peo-ple from his own experience with Cortés. But he did add to his expedition in La Española Gonzalo Nieto, whom he made chief lieutenant (*alférez mayor*). Nieto had been at the *comuneros'* battle against the Crown at Villalar in 1521, he had served against France, and he had been in New Spain with Luis Ponce and with Ayllón in Florida.

The fleet then continued along the southern coast of Montejo's old home, Cuba, and made for Cozumel, just as Grijalva and Cortés had done. Montejo paid attention to the cacique there, Naum Pat, who over the previous ten years had become quite used to Spaniards.

Montejo and his little army crossed to the mainland. Gonzalo Nieto raised a standard and shouted the word *Spain* three times, adding, "In the name of God, I take possession of this land for God and the King of Castile."[16] That must be approximately where there is now to be found the delightful Playa del Carmen. There Montejo established a settlement, which, after his own birthplace, Salamanca, he named Salamanca de Xelhá, the last part of the name commemorating the previous Mayan settlement. The historian Oviedo drily commented that this was in a palm grove "near a swamp in the worst place of all the province." Oviedo continued, "In that bad place, the ships were unloaded and a large house swiftly constructed to act as a residence for Governor Montejo."[17] Several Spaniards then set about learning Maya, among them Montejo himself and Fray Rodríguez de Caraveo, who recognized that his work of conversion would be far easier if he knew the language of his proposed flock. Pedro de Añasco of Seville turned out to be the best short-term interpreter.

After only a matter of weeks, difficulties arose. Although he had been assured that he had enough food for a year, Montejo's supplies were soon used up, and Indian substitutes seemed inadequate, despite the assistance of the local cacique of Zama. It seems that Montejo's men disliked tortillas and anything made from maize. The conquerors even began to be short of clothes. Montejo sent a ship up to Veracruz to buy more of them, but the master of the ship died there and his ship sailed off to Cuba instead of back to Yucatán.[18] Montejo began to seize food from the Indians, an act which, of course, damaged relations. In an effort to avoid any attempt at desertion, Montejo did what Cortés had done: He destroyed his boats. The Catalan Juan Ote Durán plotted to leave with the seamen on the *San Jerónimo*.

Early in 1528, Montejo set out on a journey to find a better port than Salamanca de Xelhá. Though Montejo was different from most of his contemporaries because of his preoccupation with agriculture, his technique was much the same. He would march toward an Indian pueblo, out of which the natives would be inspired to emerge in a friendly fashion carrying presents of maize, turkey, and beans. The Spaniards would be astonished at the large number of idols that they observed everywhere, on the streets and temple steps, as well as in the shrines and temples themselves. Most were made of clay. Fray Diego Landa, later the first bishop of Yucatán, would comment, "There is not an animal or insect of which they did not make a statue."[19] Montejo would then receive the Indians as vassals. Indians who did not receive the Spaniards in peace would surround them close to their pueblos on the road and would quickly build half-moon palisades and prepare an ambush. Naum Pat of Cozumel was helpful to Montejo, however, and offered to test out the ground ahead of the Spaniards on several occasions. This enabled the latter to ensure his safe arrival at Mochí, a place of one hundred "good houses" with temples and shrines of stone. They there received chickens, tortillas, and *fisol,* a drink of fermented maize and honey. This town, like many others in Yucatán, had four ceremonial entrances at the cardinal points. But it was not, inside, laid out in regular streets. In the center of the town there was a raised temple in a plaza, surrounded by the houses of the rich—not unlike cities of Spain.

Then Montejo continued to Belma, perhaps the "Gran Cairo" that he and Ávila would have recalled from their previous visit ten years before with Cortés. The caciques there were friendly; they summoned their neighbors and looked at the horses. Montejo obliged with an impressive horse show, at which the natives were more afraid than impressed.[20] Here the Spaniards were given jewel-encrusted necklaces of gold, which cheered them greatly. Montejo did not, however, accept what was offered him since he did not wish to give the impression that he had come just for gifts.[21]

Montejo was still looking for a place where he could establish a settlement as his capital. After Salamanca de Xelhá, he was impressed by Conil, a large commercial town in northeast Yucatán, with ample supplies of freshwater from springs close to the sea, a good port, and a generally friendly population—and perhaps as many as five hundred houses.[22] Here a man of great strength in the suite of the Indian lord of Chicaca seized a cutlass from a black boy belonging to Montejo and tried to kill the commander, who defended himself with his own sword till his men came "and the disturbance was quietened."[23]

They moved west via Cachí, with its large square, and entered Sinsimato, in the land of the warlike Chikinchel, pervaded with a sweet scent of the resin copal. Then they reached Chuaca, the main city of the cacique of the Chikinchel, with its many ponds and artificial watercourses, with some buildings of carved stone and thatched roofs. The temples and other shrines were characterized by their fine workmanship. This territory had been ancient Mayan land in the past, so it is understandable that the level of craftsmanship should have been high.

The cacique received Montejo in friendly fashion, and the latter therefore abandoned his customary caution. But next morning, he and his army found the town abandoned and they themselves surrounded by "bowmen who aimed well [*buenos punteros*]," as Oviedo put it.[24] Battle was engaged at first light. The Indians had weapons much like those Montejo was used to in New Spain—wooden bows and arrows with slender shafts and very hard stone heads. They had also the same *macanas* (swords) as the Mexica, with sharp stones set in wooden frames. They painted their faces to make themselves look more frightening in war.

Montejo showed much personal courage as he and his men ensured that, with their superior weapons and their horses, they checked and then pressed back the Maya. Then they moved on to Ake, a rival town to Chuaca but nevertheless ready for war: The lords there told those of Ake that the Spaniards were coming to steal their wives.[25] When Montejo arrived, the people of Ake first abandoned their city and then prepared an assault on it.

The Spaniards entered Ake and made ready to defend themselves. They were attacked next day by what seems to have been a large force, but they fought well, killed many Maya, and lost no men themselves. At dusk, Montejo received the submission of the lords of Ake without any retribution. He and his men then continued their journey to Loché, where they encountered a cacique who kept a curtain of thin cloth between himself and the Spaniards when he talked to them. Montejo moved on along the coast toward Campeche. On the way, he divided his men into two sections, one group being asked to cut across the peninsula back to Chetumal, making their way through cacao and copal groves, till they reached the salt pans near the eastern coast.

To the explorers' surprise, they encountered no golden city in the interior of Yucatán. There was neither gold nor silver nor emeralds. Nor, indeed, did there seem to be markets. There were in the northern towns fine cloths, which were sold in Campeche itself, said to boast two thousand homes, and in Champoton to its south, where the first Spanish expedition in 1517 had been defeated and their commander, Hernández de Córdoba, fatally injured.[26] Cortés's legendary interpreter Marina had originally come from Champoton. Montejo found that all these settlements had a deep *cenote* (natural well), which descended to the water table below. There was no other water supply and no rivers; many of the disputes and wars between these Mayan villages, even wars between provinces, were about water or access to remote cenotes. Most cenotes were close to the houses of lords.[27] Maize was, as in New Spain and Guatemala, the principal food and indeed provided the main alcoholic drink. The Indians ate turkey, duck, and even little dogs. The temples in the places were usually of stone, but the houses, including the houses of the lords, were always of wattle, twigs, reeds, branches, and adobe. Many such settlements were remote: "Only birds could visit them freely," recalled Fray Lorenzo de Bienvenida, one of the first eight Franciscans who later came to Yucatán.[28]

Inga Clendinnen has described the geographical background: "Scattered through the forest were the villages or towns, each sustained by cleared patches . . . where the Indians grew their maize and other basic crops. But without local knowledge of the vague tracery of paths webbing the forest it was easy to pass them by. . . . There were no vantage points in that flat land from which distances gained could be measured [or] future objectives identified. What small elevations there were revealed only the grey forest stretching to the rim of the horizon."[29]

In these months, Montejo learned something of the structure of Mayan society. It naturally had much in common with Alvarado's Guatemala. He may, however, not have appreciated the extent to which Mayan society, torn apart by wars, had declined absolutely in quality since the golden days. For example, the rich or upper class could still read and write, but neither letters nor important contracts were written down. Much Mayan science and learning had been forgotten.[30]

Among the lords there was something similar to primogeniture. Montejo gathered that sometimes caciques were subservient to a principal lord. Montejo also found that the entire peninsula of Yucatán talked the same Maya language but that there were many variations of dialect and vocabulary (Chontal, Yucatec Maya, Chol, and Chorti competed). Bishop Landa much later (in the 1560s) discovered that the lords of Yucatán, like the Spaniards, were interested in the ancestry of their families. Those who shared a patronymic regarded themselves as members of the same family and so avoided intermarriage, as if they were Christians limited by the rules of consanguinity. Bishop Landa, a curiously ambivalent witness, because his deep interest was balanced by his fanatical intolerance of "heresy," would comment: "Before the Spaniards . . . the natives had lived together in towns in a politic fashion and they had kept the land very clean and free from weeds and [in the towns] had planted good trees. In the middle of the towns, there were temples with beautiful squares and, around the temples, were the houses of lords and priests."[31]

There were in most of these towns professionals: potters, carpenters, sorcerer-surgeons, bead manufacturers, and, above all, merchants who would exchange, in Tabasco or even on the river Ulúa near Veracruz, salt, cloaks, and slaves for cacao and stone beads. Slaves were an important commodity and a stimulus here, as in the Old World, too, to wars. The Maya would count their beads and other things in their usual eccentric style—by fives up to twenty, by twenties up to one hundred, by hundreds up to four thousand, and by four hundreds up to eight thousand. They would usually do their counting on the floor.[32]

Harvesting was an activity common to the place concerned, but hunting was done in packs of men about fifty in number. They sowed, Landa commented, in many places so that, if one sowing failed, another harvest could replace it. Such social activities had communal consequences, making for economic collaboration in all spheres. Most Maya lived in multi-generational groups of a father and his sons, married and unmarried, and it was a group of related males who usually made up the people who went to work in the milpa, their system of crop rotation. Each person was expected to master the basic skills necessary for collective life. The Spaniards found that the Maya had the principle of recalling the names of both parents in the names of children: thus the son of Chel and Chan would be called Na Chan Chel. The Spaniards had a comparable tradition.

The invaders found, too, that the Maya admired a special type of facial beauty where the hair was brushed back to extend the curve of the nose in a single straight line. To enhance this elongated line, newborn babies often had their heads bound between two boards while they were still soft. The

Maya also considered that to be cross-eyed was beautiful, and this devia-
tion was encouraged by mothers, who hung from the foreheads of children
a little black patch that was contrived to reach down between their eyebrows. Whenever the child raised his eyes, this patch moved in front of
him, the process assisting the cross-eyed deformity to grow. Another family habit was to burn the faces of children with hot cloths to prevent the
growth of beards and other bodily hair. Men used mirrors made of obsidian, though women did not. Clothing for both sexes was a strip of cloth the
size of a hand, which was wound round the waist several times.

Houses in Yucatán had roofs of straw or palm leaves. The former were
sloped steeply to carry off the rainwater. The Indians would build walls in
the middle of their simple houses to divide them into two, and they would
usually sleep in the back part. In front, the roof would be low, for protection against both heat and rain—and also human enemies.

The Maya seem to have considered that the Spaniards were uncouth
warriors with their codpieces and their breastplates in quilted cotton, in
imitation of Mexican armor. They seemed a new version of the Itzá, a
group of soldiers who, led by Kukulcán, the feathered serpent (Quetzalcoatl among the Mexica), came down from central Mexico in the tenth
century to establish themselves at the well of Chichén.

The Maya, like the Mexica, were addicts of sacrifice, but on a smaller
scale. Thus they made sacrifices of their own blood, sometimes cutting
pieces from the outer part of their ears. They also sometimes made a hole
in the penis and passed thread through it. Women might draw the hearts
out of animals and offer them whole to their gods. Sometimes the Maya
might sacrifice individuals by shooting them with arrows, "turning the
place in his chest above his heart into a hedgehog of arrows." They might
give the heart of a captive a blow with a stone knife, make a deep incision,
and then, as happened in Mexico-Tenochtitlan, plunge in a hand to draw
out the heart, which would be given to the priest, who would anoint the
face of an idol with the fresh blood. Then they would throw the body down
the steps of the temple. Priests would pick up the outraged body and flay it
thoroughly, except for the hands and feet. Then the priest might strip
naked and cover himself with that skin while others danced before him. It
was the ruthless ghoulishness of this kind of scene that caused the
Spaniards to harden their hearts and assure themselves that they were right

to insist on bringing Christianity to the New World. Montejo and Alonso de Ávila had had experience of this kind of behavior over ten years since 1518, but newcomers from Castile were shocked. All the same, the number of human sacrifices—as in Guatemala—was far less than in New Spain/ Mexico.

From Champoton and Campeche, Montejo, with his sixty remaining men, his vanguard, cut across about 150 miles of the peninsula to rejoin his first settlement and those whom he had left behind at Salamanca de Xelhá. It is not at all clear whether or not he passed by such ancient sites as Uxmal, Chichén Itzá, Cobá, or Tulum. He would now have seen how the peninsula was a vast plain with thin soil, most of which was covered by dry scrub forest, with no large rivers but many cenotes. The land was sparsely populated, but the Indians may have numbered three hundred thousand in 1520.[33]

After some weeks of reconsideration and stocktaking, Montejo decided to set off for the south of his peninsula, making for the Bay of Ascension, which had been so named by his own old captain, Grijalva, in 1518 (it had been Ascension Day). They made for the town of Chetumal. This was a combined land-and-sea operation: Montejo went by boat, Alonso de Ávila by land, while Alonso de Luján remained behind at New Salamanca. He was to build a ship and follow.

The plan was for all three sections of Montejo's expedition to meet at or near Chetumal, one of the richest Mayan towns on the west of the bay. It was a town characterized by the cultivation of bees, in large apiaries. Much maize and cacao also were grown there. And there Montejo came across an unexpected stranger: Gonzalo Guerrero.

Guerrero, a Spaniard from the little town of Niebla, on the Río Tinto, about twenty miles upriver from Palos, had accompanied Diego Colón to the Indies in 1509. He seems to have been literate. Bored with life in Santo Domingo, he set off with Diego de Nicuesa for the South American mainland. He was shipwrecked. Saved from being fattened and eaten, he and Jerónimo de Aguilar, who later became Cortés's interpreter, settled down in Yucatán. Guerrero found a Mayan girl, by whom he had several children. He was a slave, but all the same, he became a military adviser to Na Chan Can, the cacique in Chetumal. Fray Diego Landa thought that he taught the Indians "how to fight, showing them how to build fortresses and bastions."[34] Guerrero was said to have advised the Maya to attack Hernández de Córdoba in 1517. In 1519, he had refused to return to Spanish life, as Jerónimo de Aguilar did, saying to him, "Brother Aguilar, I am married and have three children, the Indians treat me as a chief and as a captain in war. You go [back] and God be with you but I already have my face tattooed and my ears pierced. What would the Spaniards say if they saw me in this guise? And look how handsome those boys of mine are! For God's sake give me those green beads which you brought and I will give them to my sons and I shall tell them that my brothers have given them to me." Guerrero's Maya companion said to Aguilar, "Be off with you and don't give us any more trouble."[35]

That had been in 1519. Eight years later, in 1527, Guerrero received a letter from Montejo. It read: "Gonzalo, my special friend and brother! I count it as your great good fortune that I have arrived and I have learned of you through the bearer of this letter. I remind you that you are a Christian created by the blood of Christ our Redeemer to whom you should give infinite thanks. You have a great opportunity to serve God and the Emperor in the pacification and baptism of these people and, more than that, to leave your sins behind you with the grace of God and so benefit and honour yourself. I shall be your good friend in this and you will be treated very well. Thus I beseech you not to let the devil influence you to decline what I ask, so that he will not possess himself of you forever. On behalf of His Majesty, I promise to do very well by you and fully to comply with what I have said. On my part and as a gentleman [*como hombre hidalgo*], I give you my word and pledge my faith to make my promises to you without any reservation whatever . . . and I shall make you one of my principal men, and one of the most dearly loved and select of these parts. Consequently, I beg you to come to this ship or the coast without delay to do what I have suggested and help me carry out this work of conversion by giving me your wisest advice and opinions."[36]

Guerrero, however, could not be persuaded to rejoin his compatriots. He wrote on the back of this letter: "Señor, I kiss your lordship's hand. As I am a slave, I have no freedom. I have a wife and children, even though I remember God. You, my lord, and the Spaniards will find in me a very good friend."[37]

But in truth, Guerrero remained an enemy. Thus he seems to have ensured that news passed to Alonso de Ávila, who was coming down the coast with reinforcements, included the story that Montejo had died; and news went to Montejo that Ávila was dead.

Montejo sailed down to Honduras where he briefly put in to the Río Ulúa, an eminently navigable river in that territory. Perhaps he went there out of curiosity. He then sailed north again to Salamanca de Xelhá, to find it deserted, so he assumed that Luján, Ávila, and their men were lost. But farther north still, at Cozumel, he received the news that they were alive. Montejo crossed to the mainland for a new meeting with those old comrades.

In the summer of 1528, he went back even farther than Cozumel: He returned to New Spain, to seek reinforcements, in his ship *La Gavarra*. He still had his valuable *encomiendas* near Mexico-Tenochtitlan, and he thought that he would be able to borrow a substantial sum of money on their security and so persuade about another hundred new soldiers to accompany him, including his own half-converso son, Francisco Montejo, El Mozo, who had been brought up at court in Spain and who had accompanied Cortés to Honduras-Higueras in 1524. He also bought another ship, which he loaded with supplies, but it sank in a storm in the harbor of Veracruz. Undaunted, he bought yet one more vessel. He next made an arrangement with a rich shipowner, Juan de Lerma, perhaps related to García de Lerma, the pearl king of Cubagua, who agreed to make his ships available for trade in Yucatán, perhaps in return for eventual trading privileges there, though no document proves it. Lerma later became treasurer of Yucatán and also inspector of Higueras and Honduras.

The supreme court, headed by the odious Nuño de Guzmán, arrived in New Spain while Montejo was in Tenochtitlan. But Guzmán conjured up no enmity with such a well-born conquistador. The court ordered Montejo to return to Yucatán from the west: Proximity to New Spain would be a help. He went back via Tabasco and Acalán. Guzmán agreed to help Montejo and made him chief magistrate of the first-named place.[38]

Before returning, Montejo wrote (on April 20, 1529) to the emperor Charles the first of many reports about Yucatán: "All the towns have an orchard for fruit, but are a little rough for our horses. I found many signs of gold [*hallé mucha nueva de oro*]." The great difficulty was that there was no port. "And, for that reason," he wrote, "I wonder whether I could not be given the river Grijalva as part of my grant." So he changed his mind and said that he would found a few towns in the west, perhaps one precisely on the Grijalva, another in the mountains, and a third at Acalán. Then he would send ships to "the islands" (the West Indies) for more men, horses, and livestock.[39]

In April 1529, Montejo set off for Tabasco with his son, El Mozo, as his second-in-command and Gonzalo Nieto as his general factotum, being formally chief magistrate of Tabasco. Montejo "El Padre" went by land with twenty-five men, among them Baltasar Gallegos, who had been sent back to New Spain by the settlers of Santa María de la Victoria on the Grijalva, a colony that had been founded in 1519 on the suggestion of Cortés but whose existence had been threatened by Indians and which took a long time to attract residents.[40] Montejo arrived at this Santa María in time to prevent its complete disintegration. He sent for Alonso de Ávila's men in Salamanca de Xelhá, where they had been busy capturing Indians, probably to enable Montejo's backer, Juan de Lerma, to sell them in the West Indies. These troops, if that is what they were, sailed back around the head of the peninsula to meet Montejo at Guayataca, west of Xicalango.

Montejo was really hoping to make Xicalango, on the Laguna de Términos, his forward base for the conquest of Yucatán. The Indians seemed complaisant. Leaving there his son, Montejo turned west and soon overcame the populous districts of Tabasco along the river Copulco. Then, with Ávila again his second-in-command, he moved up the river Grijalva into the mountains with about a hundred men, his horses being carried upstream on rafts. He reached Teapa, at the foot of the mountains of Chiapas. There were what Blas González, one of his captains, called "excessive tribulations."[41] But Montejo himself later described how, "at a cost of much effort" both for himself and all the soldiers, he conquered and pacified "all the provinces of the Río Grijalva." Some thirty Spaniards were killed, a high figure for those days. But Montejo carried through the institution of the *encomienda* successfully, a remarkable achievement in the circumstances.

Montejo had planned to return to Santa María de la Victoria and then go on to establish a settlement at Acalán. But he learned that another Spanish force under Juan Enríquez de Guzmán, one of Alvarado's captains in Guatemala, was coming up northward from Chiapas, hoping to conquer the border areas. The two met and reached a rough agreement as to where

Alvarado's domain of Guatemala should stop and where that of Montejo
begin. Enríquez de Guzmán suggested that Montejo should make his way
to Acalán via Alvarado's new city, San Cristóbal de las Casas. Montejo
agreed, but sent Ávila to perform this journey. He himself, ill, returned to
Santa María de la Victoria.

Ávila had a long and weary march through the mountains, first to San
Cristóbal, then to Acalán. It was the rainy season, and the suffering of the
Spaniards in these jungles was considerable. On the river Usumacinta,
Ávila placed his horses in canoes attached to one another, the forelegs in
one canoe, the hind legs in another. They then went down a cascade between cliffs of such a height that "to those who were there, it would not
have seemed worse to voyage in the shadows of Mount Athos."[42] They later
came across both a lagoon and the remains of a bridge built by Cortés on
his way to Higueras. But it was too much in decay for Ávila and his men to
benefit from it. They still had to use canoes that some friendly natives of
Tenosique provided them. They then went on toward Acalán, which had
been an important trading port for the Indians in the days of Montezuma
and before. Ávila sent a message to the ruler of this town saying that he
hoped to be welcomed since he intended no injury. But the natives did not
believe him since Cortés, when passing there a year or two before, had said
the same but had carried off the cacique and six hundred bearers who were
never seen again.[43] So they fled. Ávila reported Acalán to be a city of about
a thousand people, with good buildings of stone and white stucco, with
thatched roofs. It was on a river, which the Spaniards had already christened the Candelaria and which flowed into the lagoon of Términos. After
a day or two, the cacique returned with a train of about four hundred
people—so Ávila reported—and swore fealty to the Emperor. He brought
presents of birds and supplies. All the same, Ávila seized and chained him,
for he feared treachery, since his own force was so small. He must have been
influenced by the precedent of Cortés in relation to Montezuma.[44]

Shortly thereafter, the rest of the population of Acalán returned and
began to serve the Spaniards with relative enthusiasm. Ávila soon freed the
cacique and his followers, and in the tradition of Montejo, soon began to
allocate *encomiendas.* He gave Acalán the name of Salamanca de Acalán, to
recall Montejo's birthplace.

Despite its excellent communications, Acalán was, however, not to be the capital city of the new Yucatán that Montejo wanted to establish. There was no gold, the population was small, the supplies of food were poor. Ávila became interested in another town, Maztalán, a little to the east, where the Spaniards remained for a few weeks before they began to think of Champoton, the town whose people had defeated Hernández de Córdoba in 1517.

Champoton, like Acalán, was a town of many stone houses with thatched roofs. It was on the sea, and from it many canoes set out daily to fish. Just offshore, there was an island filled with idols, where the fishermen went to pray and to make offerings. The people were the Cuohes, of whom a large detachment went to greet Ávila on his arrival. Montejo had previously sent messengers there, and the Spaniards found that a special district had already been prepared for them—a square, houses with stables and, in the square, enough food to last a month. Every day the Spaniards could eat turkey and ample maize, with good fish. The cacique said that he wanted to become a Christian. So his island was abandoned and his idols thrown into the sea.[45]

Montejo, meantime, was having difficulty confirming his control of the passage from New Spain to Yucatán. A previous chief magistrate of Santa María, Baltasar de Osorio, had succeeded in persuading the *audiencia* in Mexico-Tenochtitlan to restore his own control of Acalán, going back on the decision to give it over to the Montejos. Osorio even managed to seize part of Montejo's property in Tabasco, and he persecuted Montejo's followers. Though Montejo succeeded in securing the reversal of some of these judicial decisions, he was obliged to delay his new plans for the conquest of Yucatán. When finally he felt able to set out again, he reached only as far as Xicalango. He and his expedition were in poor morale, men deserting from his side and Montejo himself believing that Ávila was lost. Fortunately, his mercantile backer, Lerma, came to the rescue by sending several ships full of men, supplies, horses, and clothing bought in Cuba.[46]

Learning that Ávila was still alive in Champoton, Montejo repaired there himself in the early days of 1531. On his way, he completed his organization of the port of Xicalango: Ávila and Montejo then agreed to establish their real base not at Champoton, with its bad memories of defeat in 1518, but at Campeche, some forty miles north. The people there could support a Spanish settlement, and there were well-populated places nearby, capable of being the center of *encomiendas*. Campeche might also turn out to be a most useful port. So Montejo went ahead and optimistically read the Requirement to a number of local lords. He explained that all Christians worshipped God in Heaven, asked the lords to permit his clergy to preach the Gospel, and told them to recognize himself as the representative of the emperor Charles. A number of local lords accepted these views, or pretended to. Then Montejo proclaimed the foundation of a new Spanish city, which predictably he called Salamanca de Campeche.

Here Montejo set about making plans for the conquest of the rest of the peninsula, which was still largely unknown to the Spanish explorers. So he then sent Ávila back across the center of the peninsula to Chetumal with fifty men, who included Alonso de Luján and Francisco Velázquez, a mining specialist. Montejo's nephew, a third Francisco Montejo, son of one of his brothers, was of this party. They went from Campeche to Maní, where the Xui Maya made themselves friendly, continuing on to Cochuah, Chablé, and then Bacalar, where the treacherous Guerrero had influence. Ávila requested the lords in Chablé to go to Chetumal to explain that he wanted peace, but the messengers returned with the reply that "the people there were not interested in peace but desired war, and would give us chicken in the form of lances, and maize in the form of arrows."[47]

All the same, when they arrived at Lake Bacalar, Ávila and his men obtained canoes to go across to Chetumal. That town was now deserted. Ávila determined to establish a new settlement, which he named Villa Real. He was planning this when the news came that the Maya, assisted if not led by Guerrero, were about to attack. Ávila struck first and destroyed an Indian encampment. He took sixty prisoners and suffered no losses, although the cacique and Guerrero, if he had indeed been there, escaped. The Spaniards did find gold and turquoise masks at this place, and Ávila sent those prizes back to Montejo with six Spaniards, who were, however, all killed en route, at Hoya.

Ávila returned to Bacalar. He became aware that a general "rebellion" was being mounted by the lords of a place named Macanahaul. Chablé also came out in revolt, but Ávila cleverly surprised his enemies by attacking the town from the rear. He then returned to Villa Real at Chetumal, but everywhere there were rumors of rebellion. It became evident that any idea of alliance with the Indians of Chablé would fail since the project was "false and with evil intent."[48]

Ávila met another conflict at Cochuah, where the town was destroyed by a hurricane and where, after its capture, he found the wells filled in with earth and stones. One well twelve feet deep was dug out, and two Indian boys were let down into it by straps made from horses' harnesses, to bring up water. Ávila then decided to return to his Villa Real—a difficult journey through swamp and maquis, and also with frequent attacks by Maya. Oviedo reported, however, that one of the sentinels had a vision of Santiago, accompanied by six or seven knights with a divine scent. A sighting of Santiago was, of course, a good sign—even if it was one traditionally balanced by the appearance of the Moorish knight Alfatami on a green horse. All the same, by the time they reached Villa Real, Ávila's force was reduced to forty men, of whom ten were maimed in the arm or in the leg, being able to call on only four horses.[49]

Alonso de Ávila sent a message to Montejo to tell him that, though in a poor condition, he and his men had survived. The messenger, a captured cacique, was to return in a month to report whether all was or was not well with the *adelantado*. Yet after that month, there was no message. It transpired that neither the cacique nor his son had taken the message. On the contrary, he and his friends plotted an attack to destroy Ávila once and for all. What should the Spaniards do? They had no food, and they had seen no brigantine on the coast that might help. They assumed that Montejo believed them dead.[50] Could they evacuate Villa Real? If so, how?

In the end, Ávila decided to go to Honduras, by canoe. They encountered a furious sea: "such a manner of coast as had never been seen before," commented Oviedo, exaggeratedly.[51] They met several merchantmen in large boats but, though they sometimes seized them, they could not rely on such piracy as a source of food. After seven months of escapes and privations, Ávila reached Puerto de Caballos, on the Bay of Honduras. That seemed a good place for a settlement since it was fertile and well peopled. The Spaniards were also impressed by the river Ulúa, which boasted groves of cacao on both its banks. Here, though, a storm destroyed their canoes. So they went on to the town of Trujillo by land, where they were well received by Andrés de Cereceda, the acting governor of Higueras, and his treasurer, Juan Ruano. Ruano had been an enemy of Cortés, who looked on him as responsible for Olid's treachery.[52] After some painstaking negotiations, they set sail on a merchant ship that had come from Cuba and set off for home or, rather, for Campeche.[53]

Montejo had passed the long months of waiting to hear of Ávila's accomplishments in almost continual fighting. First with forty-five soldiers, including nine horsemen, he was attacked by a large force led by Nachi Cocom. These sought first and foremost to seize Montejo himself. A great number of Indians penetrated his camp; some seized his horse and its reins; some caught him by the arms. He would probably have been captured had he not been protected by Blas González, who "set upon them and killed many."[54] Thus, as another Spanish combatant, Pedro Álvarez, would put the matter, "the victory of our Holy Faith was gained."[55]

In the middle of the year 1532, Montejo embarked on a new campaign in the east and northeast of Yucatán. His persistence seemed as remarkable as his patience. He appointed his son to lead it. El Mozo brought a galleon to carry his men from Tabasco, the invaluable Lerma organized supplies, and he set off with two hundred men, leaving a number to guard Campeche with his father in control. El Mozo's aim was to establish Spanish control wherever possible without fighting. He was to make allies whenever he could. In this respect, he landed in the *cacicazgo* of Ceh Pech, whose support he received and who urged him to go on to Chichén Itzá, an ancient temple that to the Maya was hallowed ground. The remains of the place could be made into excellent fortresses. Ávila named it Ciudad Real, after the city of Castile in which he had been born. But that did not prevent the caciques from giving a haughty negative answer to the reading of the Requirement: "We already have Kings, oh noble lords! Foreign warriors, we are the Itza!"[56]

These Indians were from the proud tribe of Cupul, headed by Nacon Cupul, who was determined to expel, if not destroy, the Spaniards. At a parley with , Nacon tried to kill him there and then. El Mozo saved himself with difficulty, and Nacon was himself soon killed. But the Cupul then refused absolutely to deliver any supplies to Montejo el Mozo. The Spaniards seized them. This worsened relations, and the Cupul, though leaderless, mounted a new attack, killing ten or twelve of El Mozo's men, as well as ten horses and all the Indian slaves who were serving the Spaniards. El Mozo, with his large force of 150 to 170 men, held them off, but a much bigger attack was to follow, after a siege. El Mozo made an onslaught, but though he killed many, he could not break through the Indians' cordon. He determined to escape in darkness, as Cortés had done in Mexico-Tenochtitlan.

He was more successful than Cortés, for the Spaniards successfully gave the Indian besiegers the slip. They then turned successfully on the Maya vanguard who pursued them. They completed their escape thanks to an Indian ally, An Kin Chef.

Ávila managed to return to Campeche, traveling by sea in a Cuba-based merchant ship. He and the Montejos together sought to reestablish their Ciudad Real at Dzibilkan, on the coast. They were there when the intoxicating news came of the discovery of Peru: "Because of this news, and the slight reward which they had had in . . . this country [Yucatán], the citizens made off against my will."[57] It was not surprising that the depleted army of Montejo could not maintain itself. Again they evacuated an advanced settlement and returned to Campeche.

Montejo now penned a gloomy dispatch to the King: "There is [in Yucatán] not a single river, though there are lakes. The entire land is covered by thick bush and is so stony that there is not a single foot of soil. No gold has been discovered nor is there anything else from which advantage can be gained. The people are the most abandoned and treacherous in all the lands discovered until this time, being people who never yet killed a Christian except by foul means . . . in them I have failed to find the truth touching anything. With the news from Peru, the soldiers will not remain here any longer."[58]

It seemed in 1534 that seven years of continuous conflict in Yucatán were thus ending in failure. The Spaniards had a base in Campeche, little more. Their efforts to establish Spanish power on the eastern seaboard of the peninsula had failed. Montejo el Padre had now only thirty men at his disposal, not enough of a force to conquer such a large country full of high-spirited and alert natives. He had made the mistake of dividing his men too often and did not seem to realize that Indians often gave their verbal loyalty to Spain only as a temporary expedient.

Just as Montejo recalled from New Spain, in Yucatán there were many governments, not just one. The defeat of one cacique left his neighbors untouched. Also, the Mayan weapons were superior to those of the Mexica. They had strong bows, more straight than curved; their obsidian or flint-tipped arrows could inflict serious wounds; their lances and darts, their swords of hard wood with razor sharp flakes of obsidian, could cause much suffering. The arrows, made from reeds growing in lagoons, were often five palms long. The bowstrings were made successfully from local hemp. They also had little copper hatchets, which could be used both as weapons and for working wood.[59] As for defense, their shields were made of reeds lined with deerskin and were carefully woven. They also wore jackets of quilted cotton. A few lords even had wooden helmets. Priests and sometimes others went to war in animal skins.[60] Finally, Indian tactics had been intelligent. Soon realizing that their vast superiority in numbers could not make much of an impact on the Spaniards, they would defend their towns in these "harsh, stony and dry lands" (as the Mérida Council spoke of the region in 1561), and then destroy them, fleeing into the forests or the unconquered South.

17

To Pass the Sandbar

Now that we have passed your sandbar, be pleased to have us return
and pass over it again with a good and safe voyage.

Prayer to Our Lady of Barrameda

The most complex machine of its time, as a modern historian has
described the sixteenth-century *nao*,[1] was a fortified warehouse that had to
be loaded and unloaded as well as steered across the ocean. These ships
were also, as Dr. Samuel Johnson put it two hundred and more years later,
very like a jail, with all, even grandees, living in conditions that on land
would be considered intolerable.[2]

In the reign of the emperor Charles—between 1516 and 1555—some
2,500 ships left Spain for the Indies, an average of about 60 a year; 1,750 returned. That meant that 750 were lost; a few of them were destroyed in battle.[3] The ships that crossed the Atlantic in 1504 numbered 35; in 1550,
more than 200.[4]

The small size of these vessels is what captures our attention first and
foremost. The Genoese and Venetians might have carracks of more than
one thousand tons; some of them were always in Portuguese or Spanish
waters in those days. But Columbus's three ships, we recall, were sixty, seventy, and one hundred tons each. The great "Admiral of the Ocean Sea"
thought a boat as big as seventy tons too large for coastal exploration. Nor
could anything over two hundred tons have sailed easily up, or down, the
often shallow and risky fifty miles of the river Guadalquivir that led to and
from the port of Seville (8 percent of losses of these fleets were on the
river!).

At first, ships might take on their cargoes in ports other than Seville, but even so, they were required, before they crossed the Atlantic, to go up the Guadalquivir and register with the officials of the usually bureaucratic Casa de la Contratación. Larger vessels, even in the first half of the sixteenth century, were unable to ascend the Guadalquivir without unloading their cargo eight leagues (twenty-four miles) below or south of the city. This procedure was supervised by an official known as the "visitor," who would inspect vessels before departure as well as before arrival. After a while, this individual was appointed directly by officers of the Casa. That body decided that that it should have a permanent resident at Cádiz since that port was becoming the effective nerve, the jugular vein, *juzgado*, of the trade to the Indies.

Captains might choose eccentric ports from which to sail, but the rule was they had to return to the Guadalquivir. The government relied on the payment of customs and other taxes, and it also required that gold and silver be paid to them in a regular fashion. Even so, ships sometimes returned to other ports, such as Málaga or Vigo, or even Lisbon. Almost all stopped, on their way out to the Indies, in the Canaries, a convenient watering and victualing station for ships on their way west or east, with tolerant attitudes by the Spanish authorities toward English and other foreign merchants.

In 1502, Ovando's ships in his great fleet were all between 30 and 90 tons. Díaz de Solís's three ships in 1508 were 90, 60, and 35 tons, respectively. Pedrarias's ships in 1514 averaged 80 tons. Magellan's expedition of 1519 left with no ship over 120 tons and the *Victoria,* the voyage's surviving vessel, was 75 tons.[5] The average tonnage of ships in these years was just under 100 tons. Between 1521 and 1550, it rose to an average of between 100 and 150.

Afterwards, ships increased in weight, but rarely in the sixteenth century did a ship exceed 200 tons, even though in 1509 there was an *ordenanza* that established a minimum of 80 tons.[6]

Such vessels might carry sixty passengers and twelve crew, and also perhaps eighteen mares and twelve calves. If adapted for military use, there would be four great cannon, two at each end of the ship, and perhaps a dozen smaller cannon (falconets, culverins) would be each side on a second deck.

A ship of one hundred tons would probably be fifty feet long, fifteen feet wide, and seven feet deep in the hold from keel to the lowest planked deck. Most ships had a single deck, though sometimes there were awnings (*toldos*) or bridges (hence a "bridge") connecting with what was known as "the chimney," sometimes as "the castle." They could be much larger. For example, the great merchants Portinari in Holland constructed a boat 120 feet long and 36 wide.[7]

At first, most of these oceangoing ships were known as caravels (*carabelas* was a word used in Spanish coastal waters since the early fifteenth century). The word *nao* was used interchangeably. Caravels were rarely mentioned after 1530. The Portuguese usually gave them triangular or lateen sails. The Spaniards preferred square or round sails on the main masts.

The galleon was much bigger than the caravel and eventually became the typical Atlantic ship. It was first mentioned in a list of ships registered in 1525. A galleon might measure up to five hundred tons and would have a crew of fifty or sixty, and perhaps a company of 120 or 150 soldiers.

There were many other smaller ships. For example, the *burcho,* a large launch powered by rowers, was much used in the fifteenth century off Africa. A smaller vessel, also a launch, was the *falúa,* with two masts. There was, too, the brigantine, a small boat suitable for traveling on rivers or with sail. Sometimes it was covered, sometimes it was open, like a pinnace. Most expeditions of importance had one or two of these accompanying the larger craft. We also find *filibotes, pataches, fragatas,* and *urcas,* useful little ships comparable to the English pinnaces.

All these vessels would dock in Seville in the strangely rough port known as the Arenal, a sandbank between the river and the cathedral that was the center of trade, provisioning, and stocking up. The Arenal was dominated by the Golden Tower, the Torre de Oro: an Arab defense bastion, on which there was, in the sixteenth century, a crane, which had been constructed to help in the unloading of stone for the building of the nearby cathedral and which was afterwards used for landing merchandise. Because of the primitive nature of the port, the rest of the lower river, almost as far as Sanlúcar, fifty miles down at the mouth of the river—constituted an informal shipyard.

If between sixty and seventy tons,[8] these ships cost perhaps 500 ducats or about 3,000 maravedís a ton. On top of the cost of the vessel, the crew of, say, ten sailors and eight cabin boys, as well as apprentices and pages, were probably paid an average of 1,000 maravedís each. The total cost of a ship of this kind about to set off on an expedition, therefore, might be 180,000 maravedís.

The social standing of a man who went to the sea was set at whatever level he joined his ship. All the same, an experienced mariner who had been a page or an apprentice could look forward to a professional life as a sailor, his credentials being confirmed by a document attesting to his expertise.

Shippers or captains gained something, too, from passengers, who played a decisive part in financing most outward voyages. The average number of passengers per caravel in the first half of the sixteenth century was perhaps twenty. For example, in November 1514, the passengers on board a ship owned by Andrés Niño paid 8 ducats (3,000 maravedís) to go to Santo Domingo;[9] while Cortés paid 11 ducats for the same journey in 1506.[10]

No ship carried much in the way of furniture. The captain's cabin would have a few chairs, but there would be no others. The chests of the sailors did, however, serve as seats as well as trunks, and even sometimes as beds. They were customarily fastened down on the deck by ropes.

These vessels usually had short lives, perhaps only four years. The difficulty was the *broma*, a small sea worm, which seemed especially aggressive in tropical waters. To guard against it, there could be caulking, which meant covering the vessel with resin. The masters on Pedrarias's fleet of 1514 were the pioneers of a leaden covering. The actual inventor of the process was a certain Antonio Hernández. But lead was expensive, it often wore out, and it was heavy.[11]

Pilots had to have a license from the *piloto mayor*, which meant an apprenticeship under that official's direction. A pilot had to be Spanish by birth or by naturalization, have six months in the profession, spend six months on a course of cosmography, and have a precise knowledge of the route. Every ship had to have two pilots. All would probably have read Fernández de Enciso's geography, and later, Pedro de Medina's *Arte de Navegar*.

The average journey from Cádiz to Veracruz in New Spain was 90 days, a minimum of 55, with a maximum of 160. The return journey was longer, averaging 128 days, a minimum of 70 and a maximum of 298 days.[12]

Most of the ships' expeditions were collaborative financial enterprises, the shipowners having to provide incentives for men to enroll. Thus large parts of the ship were reserved for *quintaladas* (the space in quintals in which the officers and crew could ship goods to the New World). The captain could perhaps ship ninety quintals, the boatswain thirteen, sailors a mere three and a half.

The great shipowners were financiers such as Cristóbal de Haro of Burgos, who already thought in the 1520s that it would be better to give sailors an income in cash rather than a space for merchandise on the ships.[13] Many of these mercantile families were conversos.[14]

Masters of ships were often part owners of them, and they would arrange to be paid two and a half times what was received by a sailor. A master could also ship a certain amount of merchandise free. He would travel in a good cabin, where he would have a silver dinner service and probably be waited on by African slaves. He would hire the crew and be responsible for the safe delivery of the cargo.[15]

An admiral or major commander, such as Hernando de Soto, might travel with an escort of twelve "gentlemen of honor."

As a rule there would always be a mate or boatswain (*contramaestre*), who, with his short thick cable, the *rebenque*—for beating lazy apprentices—would control the ship if the captain was a soldier without maritime experience. After a time, there would usually be a notary, a carpenter, a caulker, a cook-steward, and as many seamen as necessary—the maximum being forty for a large galleon (but seventy on naval vessels).

The level of literacy was modest on ships. Even captains and generals would scarcely know more than how to sign their names. Most masters would have done so, though perhaps 17 percent could not do even that. Twenty-five percent of pilots could not either. A minority of officials, such as boatswains and stewards, could do so, but only 21 percent of sailors.[16] All the same, those who were literate read a great deal.

Wages and salaries were usually partly paid before a journey. Sometimes these advances, up to 20 percent of the expected income, were paid months before departure. Sailors might be paid as little as 100 to 300 pesos for a year's voyage. Little enough, it might be said, for a journey in an immensely complicated craft with its hundreds of pulleys, its cables, its rigging, often sailed in conditions of great danger and overcrowding. Sailors on royal naval vessels were paid less than others (1,500 maravedís, or 4 ducats a month).

Men of the sea usually received less than skilled laborers on land. But many who went to Seville in the sixteenth century in the hope of finding work in the city had to fall back on going to sea. They might be compensated by the fact that a sailor could hope to rise in the ranks and become a ship's officer.

Many increased their wages by stealing from stores: Carpenters would steal wood, boatswains rope, stewards provisions. Admirals would carry illegal passengers and contraband.

In his splendid history, Pablo Pérez-Mallaína has several excellent paragraphs devoted to his idea that wages paid to the Renaissance sailor made him less well off than his medieval equivalent, who would customarily have had an interest in the enterprise of the ship.[17]

Passengers both then and before slept on bags, which were often just sacks filled with straw. Hammocks, though used by Indians, were as rare as beds. Rich passengers might establish little private rooms under the awnings, formed by panels nailed together by the ship's carpenter. Many hulls were transformed into a labyrinth of little cabins in consequence.

The latrines of ships were usually set up on a wooden grating jutting out at the prow over the sea. Officers would have their own latrines, "gardens," as they were called, on the poop deck. The smells were normally overpowering. Dirty clothes remained dirty for most of the journey.

Storms were appalling experiences and might necessitate many sailors spending hours pumping water from the ship to prevent it from sinking. If pumping did not work, every weight would be thrown into the sea. Sometimes masts would be cut down to prevent them breaking open the ship. Waves of colossal size could strike a terrifying blow on the keel, opening up the hull to floods of water. Divers would have to be ready with tarred canvas "palettes," or lead ones, to patch the outside of ships below the level of water. Fires were also a cause of shipwrecks.

Many sailors were citizens of Triana, a town across the river from Seville in the shadow of an Arab castle, which had begun to be used as a prison by the Inquisition. In 1561, a census suggested that out of thirty-four pilots, thirty-one lived in Triana.[18]

Seville was still a growing city, by far the largest port of the south of

Spain, rising in population from forty thousand in 1500 to double that by 1550. Many of the new citizens were from Old Castile or Extremadura. Other ports nearby were tiny in comparison and until 1529 were not permitted to engage in transatlantic trade.

The international aspect of this Atlantic traffic should be remembered. A surprisingly large number of new citizens of Seville were foreigners. Italians—principally Genoese but also some Florentines—had dominated the commerce of Portugal from the fourteenth century. The first discoveries in the Canary Islands were, as emphasized in *Rivers of Gold,* brought about with Genoese capital. Many of the first sugar mills and other investments had Genoese support or were initiated thus. The Genoese knew all about money, insurance, investments, loans, and mortgages. Bankers and merchants from Genoa disguised themselves as Spaniards: The Marini became the Marín, the Centurioni the Centurión.

In addition, many sailors on the ships were not Spanish. Fifteen percent of those who sailed with Pedrarias were born abroad. At least ninety out of the 265 on Magellan's voyage were foreigners, mostly from Portugal or Italy. Greeks, Frenchmen, and Flemings usually managed a representative or two on a big expedition. Portuguese sailors often pretended to be Spaniards. That was easy enough if they claimed that they were Gallegos, as the languages of Galicia and Portugal are close. An Italian could pose as a Catalan. All the same, the Spanish control of this vast enterprise cannot be ignored. Before the seventeenth century, Spain and Portugal were the only colonial powers to speak of, and Portugal's imperial greatness was displayed mostly in the East.

During most of the reign of Charles V, ships bound for and coming from the Indies sailed independently. Would-be permanent emigrants would have to make a detailed application to the Casa de la Contratación as well as pay for their food and fare.

The first French corsair was apparently a pirate of 1506.[19] The increasing danger at sea from France caused some to argue as early as the 1530s that commercial vessels should sail in fleets. In 1543, this Spanish fleet was also accompanied by ships of war for protection.[20] In 1564, after further French intrusions, these anxieties would mature into a regular organization whereby two escorted merchant fleets a year would head for New Spain. Both fleets would normally stop after about a week, or a little more, for supplies and water, or recovery from seasickness, in the Canaries. The fleets would then sail direct for the West Indies. The ships for New Spain would usually travel via Puerto Rico to San Juan de Ulúa, opposite Veracruz; those for the admirable harbor of Cartagena would not as a rule make a stop. San Juan de Ulúa was inhospitable but convenient, and both merchandise and crews would be shipped from there to the mainland by barge.

On return journeys, both the northern and the southern fleets would sail home via Havana, the best harbor in all the Americas. Both would wait there for a naval escort. The return across the Atlantic would usually be via the Azores, still Portuguese, whence it would be usual to expect another month's voyage home to Castile. Welcomed home they might then well be, but many seamen would be sent off to the special maritime hospital of Buena Aire in Triana.

Regular voyages across the Pacific incidentally began in the 1560s and on most occasions were a fearful experience. One had to take into account the battles with the French or other pirates, which consisted of boarding or defending against boarding by the enemy. Cannon would be fired and all manner of objects would be thrown: flaming arrows (*alacranes*); gunpowder, tar, and oil mixtures (*alquitranes*); and pieces of iron with four sharp points (*abrojos*).

By 1550, the main items of trade with the Indies were: first, agricultural— wine, olive oil, eau-de-vie; then horticultural products such as vinegar, olives, raisins, almonds, spices, wax; then clothes; metal objects such as iron, agricultural machinery, nails and nail-making equipment; leather, soap, glass, medicines, even works of art. Then there was mercury, a Spanish state monopoly but much used for securing good silver. In the sixteenth century, textiles constituted over 60 percent of all exports to the Americas. Many came from Rouen or Angers. Then there were paper, rosaries, pens, and strings for violins. Slaves were considered as an item of commerce second to none.[21]

But there were also cochineal, indigo, and brazilwood. Colorings and dyes seem to have constituted about half the exports of the time, these being the American products most easily sold. At the end of the sixteenth century, leather, tobacco, ginger, and pearls were regularly being shipped back from the Indies.

The ships on both the Atlantic and the Pacific would be stocked with sacks of biscuit, salt, and firewood; barrels of wine and of water; flagons of oil and vinegar; huge packs of salt meat, salt fish, and beans or rice; dozens of cheeses. The staple elements in the diet of a sailor would be biscuit, water, and wine. The usual daily diet on a transatlantic ship would probably have been a pound and a half (690 grams) of biscuit, and a liter both of water and of wine, 150 grams of a mixture (*menestra*) of horsebeans and chickpeas, and 150 grams of salt fish—probably *tollo* (dogfish), *pargo* (red snapper), or cod. Some days the *menestra* would be replaced by 46 grams of mixed rice and oil, and 230 or even 460 grams of salt pork. Small rations of cheese might sometimes be distributed, particularly when storms or possible battles made it unwise to light the stove.[22]

Masters would expect grander menus: white rather than black biscuit, roast chicken, dried fruit, good wine. Fresh fish would be frequently found in the sea, and most sailors would have a fishhook and a line. The caloric content of their diet, about four thousand calories a day, was adequate for the efforts demanded.[23]

Most sailors slept on the deck in sacks or on mattresses filled with straw, or in unexpected places. Some would bring small pillows with them. The fact that a third of the crew would at any one time likely be on some kind of guard duty created space. Masters and captains often had good beds, a mark of their superior status. They also would have copper chamber pots.

Most seamen wore loose-fitting clothes—trousers known as *zaragüelles* or *greguescos,* and capes or jackets called *capotes de mar* or *chaquetillas,* such as those sketched by the painter Christoph Weiditz. Most such clothes were blue. Most travelers would carry knives in their belts.

Though scarcely a man of much maritime experience, Fray Antonio de Guevara tells us that at sea there were three diversions: gaming, talking, and reading. The first included gambling at dice or card games, but it also included chess. The third included the reading of many books, some religious, such as the *Libro de la oración y la meditación* of Fray Luis de Granada, the most-read book in Spain in the sixteenth century; some technical works; some chivalrous, such as *Amadís de Gaula* and its successors. There were also seductions of boys (by sailors) and the few women traveling—female servants or perhaps widows. Homosexuality naturally played its part.

Commerce with the Indies was every year increasingly dominated by regulations. To begin with, on April 10, 1495, a decree was proclaimed giving all Spanish subjects the right to establish, exploit, or carry out commerce in the New World under prescribed conditions.

On May 6, 1497, another decree stated that participation in commerce was to be under the direction of the Crown. A few years later, on September 6, 1501, another decree prohibited foreigners from going to the Indies.

All the same, at this time any ship that kept to the rules had the liberty to travel freely and whenever convenient.

A decree of October 12, 1504, spoke of the need for commerce to be directed by Isabel from her realms. On December 10, 1508, Spanish merchants were able to register their merchandise at the Canary Islands. The following year, it was laid down that all ships whose captains wanted to would be able to load their merchandise at Cádiz.

In 1510, the ordinances for the Casa de la Contratación instructed that body not to allow foreigners to go to the Indies and not to allow ships to go to the Indies without a permit, which should insist on three inspections. A *vistador* (visitor) would take a look before any permissions were granted. Then there would be a look at the loaded ship, in Seville. Finally, there would be a general search at Sanlúcar seeking to ensure that the vessel was not overloaded and therefore dangerous.

From the beginning, all merchants who wanted to send goods to the Indies had to pay taxes known as *almojarifes de Indias* and obtain a license from the Casa de la Contratación. Similar permits were needed in the Indies for both the outward-bound and the inward-bound journeys. All goods—above all, gold, but also brazilwood—had to be registered, any smuggler being required to pay four times the value of the amount siezed. The property of anyone dying in the Americas would be carefully listed and later sold in a regular way. All such regulations were published by Andrés de Carvajal, one of the many of that surname who played a part in the Indies.

In 1513, there was another striking change: the Casa de la Contratación was ordered to send two caravels to Cuba to defend the coast there against French pirates; and in 1521, a little squadron of four or five ships was charged to patrol the waters off Cape Saint Vincent in Portugal. In 1515, there was a protest against the monopoly on trade enjoyed by Seville. In 1518, we hear of a decree forbidding the visitors Diego Rodríguez Comitre and Bartolomeu Diaz from having any financial connection with any vessel engaged in commerce with the Americas. Though like most officials they would buy their offices, they were well paid and expected to be experts in ship care such as careening (beaching a ship to do the maintenance below the water line). They would eventually carry out the prescribed three inspections of all ships, all at Sanlúcar de Barrameda, sometimes checking that all priests had regularized their passage. They were later concerned with loading, and were also concerned by the need to prevent smuggling.[24]

On April 5, 1522, orders were given to the officials of the Casa de la Contratación not to permit a stranger of any sort to travel who had not given proof of identity. Also excluded were non-Catholics, Jews, Moors, and the children, even grandchildren, of those who had publicly worn a San Benito in consequence of the punishments of the Inquisition. On July 14, numerous further ordinances were proclaimed: Thus every ship of one hundred tons was obliged to carry at least fifteen mariners, including a gunner, eight apprentices or cabin boys (*grumetes*), and three pages (*pajes*). There would have to be four large iron guns, provided with three dozen shot each, and twenty-four swivel guns (*pasavolantes* and *espingardas,* six dozen shot for each of them). Two hundredweight of powder and ten crossbows with eight dozen arrows would be provided, along with four dozen short lances, eight long pikes, and twenty shields. Naturally, every soldier carried a sword, usually at his own expense.

On January 15, 1529, a decree at Toledo again reserved all commerce to the people of Castile, but also named nine ports, including some in Galicia as well as Seville, from which ships would be allowed to sail: Corunna, Bayona, Avilés, Laredo, Bilbao, San Sebastián, Cartagena, Málaga, and Cádiz. In September 1534, it was insisted that no ship unless it was new might leave for the Americas without being careened first. The crew as well as the ship had also to be examined by the pilot-major. The upper deck and main cabins had to be kept free of merchandise. Only provisions, artillery, and passengers' chests were permitted above deck. But it turned out that first-rate ships were more rarely sent to the Americas than seemed likely.

Thirty was the maximum number for a ship of thirty tons. Very often, however, the regulations insisting on these limitations were not kept. Bureaucratic rules are meant to be broken and, in the Spanish Empire as in other such undertakings, were frequently only an indication of what the civil servants in Seville hoped might happen. Captains, boatswains, passengers, and sailors exploited the rules as best they could.

In 1537, a royal fleet was sent to the Indies to guarantee the safe dispatch of the treasures of the place. In 1540, there was a reference to the idea that all ships active in the Indies would have to be Spanish.

From August 23, 1543, the annual departure of the fleets was formalized: Only ships of 100 tons or more were allowed to take part, two annual fleets of at least ten ships lifting anchor, one in March and another in September. In 1552, it was decided temporarily to suspend convoys and to arm all ships against possible foes. Ships were now classified in three categories: from 100 to 170 tons; from 170 tons to 220; and 220 tons to 320. Armaments were mostly of brass. Crossbows were being supplemented in these years by the more efficient arquebus.

In 1558, a *cédula* of April 3 abrogated the rule of obligatory return from Puerto Rico and Santo Domingo to Seville. From 1561, ships that were damaged and might not be able to pass the sandbar at Sanlúcar were also allowed to discharge merchandise at Cádiz.[25] Special naval vessels were allocated to the defense of the treasure fleets from now on; they were paid for by a duty on exports.

Colonists to the New World were encouraged by the Crown in numerous ways. For example, those on their way to Santo Domingo or Tierra Firme (Venezuela) were now given maintenance and free passages from the day that they arrived in Seville until they disembarked in "America." They were provided with the land, livestock, plants, and agricultural implements that they needed. For twenty years, they were free of the tax known as *alcabala* and other taxes except tithes to the Church. Land was provided to them on whatever scale they wanted. Doctors and apothecaries would be provided. Special prizes were offered for good husbandry: Thirty thousand maravedís would be given to whoever produced twelve pounds of silk, and there were similar compensations for those who produced comparable quantities of cloves, cinnamon, and olive oil.

Long before that arrangement, however, Spain had become preoccupied by a new territory to the south, namely a land known to the conquistadors of Darien and Panama as "Birú."

Book II

❧❧❧

PERU

18

Birú

It rarely happens that new islands emerge out of the sea. But should
that occur and some new island . . . appear, it should belong to him
who first settles it.

Las Siete Partidas, PARTIDA III, TITLE 28, LAW 29

The land that now became the subject of Spanish attention—even obsession,
particularly in the isthmus of Panama–Darien—was one that seemed at first
sight similar to that which Cortés had conquered in New Spain. Peru and old
Mexico were powerful monarchies that knew nothing of each other. Both
were also relatively recent in power, having accumulated their capacities in
the fifteenth century. Both monarchies had rulers taken from the same royal
family throughout their histories. Both had dominating religions with
priestly castes. The Incas also worshipped the moon as well as the sun. Some
coastal societies in Peru (the Chimú) thought that the moon was more
important than the sun. The Mexica and the Incas included savagery and
high culture in their ceremonials and customs but the violence in Mexico
was never seen in Peru. War and fighting were persistent with them both. In
neither society is there any evidence that anyone had a sense of humor,
whereas the Spaniards were always laughing. Both had settled capital cities—
in Tenochtitlan and in Cuzco—something that at that stage Spain had not.
Both had sophisticated systems of landholding. Both the Mexica and the
Inca were peoples who had succeeded in exerting their dominance over
neighboring tribes to whom they had themselves once been subordinate.
The rise in Peruvian power had been slower than that of the Mexica, but all
the same, the great conquerors of the two dynasties were fifteenth-century
contemporaries. The ruling houses of both Mexico and Peru were large

family autocracies, not unlike the Saudi royal family of today. In neither country did primogeniture play a part. The best man was expected to gain power. The Scots had that kind of arrangement in the tenth century and before, with their Law of Tanistry. In Mexico, a succession was less of a crisis than it was in Peru, because the reigning emperor (*hueytlatoani*) would select his successor soon after his enthronement. All important positions were filled by members of the royal house.

Both the Mexica and the Incas thought that they were in some ways chosen peoples. The Inca rulers, like the Mexica, were in one respect comparable to the English monarchy after Henry VIII: They were at the summit of the national religion, though the "King" was not a high priest. The two monarchies were both absolute ones: The power of the ruler was unquestioned. Both rulers were in constant touch, it was said, with the sun. The popular adulation attached to the monarch was exorbitant, and protest or dissent unthinkable.

Both Peruvians and Mexica made fine cotton clothes, including tunics and cloaks deriving from sophisticated weaving. On occasion, both wore feathers arranged as cloaks or in headdresses. The Incas valued their cloth so highly that they burned it rather than allow it to fall into Spanish hands.[1] Both empires used languages—the Mexica Nahuatl, the Inca Quechua—that seemed to be lingua francas in the territories concerned, though the Incas also had a private language for use within the royal family. Both societies liked alcohol and some drugs: The Peruvians had *chicha,* a mild beer made from maize, while the Mexica had pulque, made from the agave cactus; the Incas enjoyed coca rather than the elaborate range of hallucinogenic drugs available to the Mexica from mushrooms. Both the Mexica and the Peruvians supplemented their staple diet of maize and potatoes (in the Peruvian case[2]) with fish (anchovies, sardines, tuna, sea bass, salmon off the coast of Peru) and birds. The Peruvians also ate dried llama meat and guinea pig. They would organize great hunts for vicuña, guanaco, roe deer, mountain fox, hare, and puma, as the Inca Manco would show to Francisco Pizarro in 1534. Though both societies made elaborate pottery, neither had the benefit of the potter's wheel. Perhaps in the Mexican case that convenience was not far away. Nor had either any means of writing, though the Peruvians used quipus, knots and rows of colored strings that represented mathematical units.[3]

The Spanish conquerors recorded what they observed of the old societies with much attention to detail. The greatest of these writers was the Franciscan Fray Bernardino de Sahagún, in Mexico. By recalling the voices of the Indians themselves to tell of what used to happen, he interpreted the old world that had already passed away. Relations of Montezuma, such as Ixtlilxochitl, also wrote accounts of great interest; and in Peru, Titu Cusi Yupanqui, second son of Manco Inca and an ebullient administrator of his reserves, made a historical record of a similar sort for the Augustinian missionaries.

Even before the arrival of Cortés at Veracruz and of Pizarro at Tumbes, there were similar expressions of anxiety in both Peru and New Spain about the future. Peruvians, for example, were said to have heard prophecies of an ex-king that the empire would be overcome by bearded people who would preach the virtues of a new religion. But this seems to have been a late-sixteenth-century tale. Some news of the fate of Central America under the brutality of Pedrarias may have filtered down to Peru before 1530, just as some information about the Spanish actions in the West Indies reached Mexico before 1519. The Peruvians had also suffered from one or two Western diseases, such as bubonic plague, before 1530, though they were unaware of their provenance. They had a legend that predicted cataclysm: a *pachakuti*, a turning over of time and space, such as, according to a convenient myth, had occurred four times before the 1530s.

Both the Inca and the Mexica used stones in fighting, and both employed slings, which could accurately fling a stone the size of an apple some hundred yards. Both used battle-axes with bronze or stone blades, which were sometimes effective in war, though they were less than efficient against the Spanish steel swords. Some Peruvians had throwing sticks shaped like Mexican *atlatls,* and both societies had bows and arrows. These weapons had been used in the campaigns to create the Inca and Aztec empires. The Spaniards admired at Tumbes the Peruvians' "long arrows, spears and clubs."[4]

There were, of course, differences between these two indigenous societies. The most important one was that ancient Peru had no commercial life, while Mexico enjoyed a lively one: Mexican merchants also played an important part in informing the rulers, the "Emperors," about other places, as if they were secret agents. A related difference was that there was no private landholding in Peru. The peasants farmed elaborate, productive, and even beautiful terraces, but they were held in common. Never was there a more pervasive government than that of the Incas. Personal liberty was practically nonexistent. Blind obedience and unquestioning self-abnegation had forever to be accorded. But if much was demanded of the subject, much was done for him. Marxists have talked of "Inca communism," and they may have been correct thus to designate the Peruvian social structure, in which almost everything was supervised by officials.[5] Aztec society was much less controlled. Montezuma's remark about the necessity of dealing harshly with his people if they were going to be ruled effectively is well known.[6]

Mexico had no domestic animals. Peru, on the contrary, had the guinea pig, the alpaca, and the llama, which the Spaniards thought were large sheep. The Inca used them to carry light loads—up to fifty or sixty pounds, actually—but also to convey their wool and meat. They were the heart of the Inca economy, and herds were carefully bred to ensure that they were always there. Alpaca wool was invaluable. They could last several days without drinking. Otherwise, both communities employed men as runners and porters. Both used wooden rollers to assist the movement of great stones or lumps of masonry, especially the Peruvians.

Another difference was that the Peruvians had sails on their rafts and canoes, which the Mexica and Mesoamerican people, such as the Maya, do not seem to have had. The Peruvians used the sea as a means for trade more than the Mexica did. Yet a high percentage of Andeans (perhaps two-thirds of the population) lived at heights over nine thousand feet.

The Mexica had remarkable artistic achievements to their credit: for example, their painting, poetry, and sculpture, monumental and tiny, relief and in the round. In these matters, the Peruvians were more limited, and no pre-Hispanic poetry is known from Peru.[7] Both societies prized gold and silver jewels, but the Peruvians had more of them. Both had a process for creating metals of quality out of ore. But the Peruvians created more elaborate gold ornaments than the Mexica did.

The Inca built magnificent roads and suspension bridges, far superior to anything then found in ancient Mexico—or, thought the Sevillano chronicler Pedro de Cieza de León, in old Europe.[8] There was an elaborate network of storehouses, which held food, arms, and clothing, on the roads. Along these roads, the state's llama and human porters traveled incessantly.

The Peruvians had devised a decimal system of numbers to enable the accurate gathering of tribute. Inca decimal administrators were, at the time of the coming of the Spaniards, painstakingly taking over the business of collecting tribute from the old chiefs, who had calculated before with more-conventional methods.[9]

The Inca capital of Cuzco was much smaller, less elaborate, and less grand than Tenochtitlan in New Spain–Mexico, but both cities boasted stone or stone-faced houses, as well as streets well washed by streams, with sewers. The main square at Cuzco had something in common with the Zócalo in the center of Tenochtitlan, though it was smaller. In the architectural use of stone, the Inca were, however, superior to the Mexica. The Inca did not have the arch, but they paid much attention to the exactness of the fitting of the joints between the huge stones. These essential elements in construction were maneuvered into place by teams of men using wooden levers.[10] Throughout the age of the Inca, people depended on homemade chipped stone tools for scraping, chopping, cutting, and even drilling.

Based on a straightforward worship of the sun, Inca religion was simpler than that of Mexico. Human sacrifices occurred but on a *much* lesser level than in ancient Mexico—the victims in Peru being usually beautiful boys and girls, often prisoners of war. Still, the death or investiture of a ruler could inspire the sacrifice of hundreds.[11] Local deities survived conquest by the Inca. As in the empire of Montezuma, effigies of the gods of conquered tribes were taken to the capital almost as hostages for their peoples.

In Peru, the dead were not left to rest but played a part. Pedro Pizarro, a cousin of the conquering band of Extremeño brothers, who had been brought up in Toledo, recalls how, when he arrived in Cuzco, the citizens took out the coffins of the dead into the main square and placed them in a row, according to their age. There the citizens sat, ate, and drank *chicha*. They made fires before the dead from dry wood, and in those combustions, they burned what in the past they had given to the dead. In front of the coffins, they placed large pitchers of gold, silver, or pottery, and these they filled with *chicha*. When these were full, they emptied them into a round vessel of stone in the middle of the square.[12]

The priests in Peru, headed by Villac Umu, the high priest, often then produced a small covered bundle, which they assured observers was the sun itself. This was guarded by men with lances decorated with gold, "the arms of the Sun." The precious object was placed on a bench in the plaza and offered feathers or cloaks. Then it was offered food, which was afterward burned. The ashes of the sun's dinner were then thrown into a round stone trough shaped like a teat.

Villac Umu was also the name for the supreme Inca deity. The word actually meant "foam of the sea." Cieza de León, one of the most responsible of Spanish chroniclers, said that he thought that this Villac Umu was a tall white man, large of stature, with a white robe reaching to his feet. He had a belt, his hair was short, he carried something that looked like a breviary, and he wore a crown. The Indians explained that he traveled constantly till he came to the sea, where he spread his cloak, moved on it over the waves, and never appeared again. Atahualpa's nephew pointed out that the Spaniards appeared from the same sea into which the creator god had disappeared. Perhaps it was the same sea where the Mexican god Quetzalcoatl had also vanished.

The sun in old Peru had a palace covered with gold, which was guarded by two hundred women. Devoted to the deity, these ladies were supposed to be chaste, but Pedro Pizarro tells us that they often "involved themselves with the male servants and guardians of the Sun." Nearby was a garden filled with golden representations of maize stalks, trees, fruit, and vegetables.

The kingdom of old Peru was, like Mexico, the heir of many traditions and was made up of the coming together of many small entities. The Chavín culture had dominated central Peru in the time of the classical Greeks. In the north, there had been the Moche, much of whose pottery has survived, depicting as they do most of the facts of life including love and war. In the South, inland on the dry peninsula of Paracas, the Nazca were the most civilized of the Incas' predecessors, being responsible for elaborate, interesting, and sophisticated textiles, much preserved in graves in the deserts there.

About A.D. 100, an empire known as that of Tiahuanaco was established, beginning on the shores of the high inland Lake Titicaca. Other sophisticated urban societies had a brief hour of glory at Wari (or Huari) in the Ayacucho basin and at Tiwanaku, south of Lake Titicaca. There was also Chan Chan, a city of the Chimú renowned for its smiths.

The Incas emerged from the valley of Cuzco about the time of the establishment of Tiahuanaco, though to begin with, the idea that they might soon dominate the whole of Ecuador and Peru, as well as half of Chile, would have seemed as absurd as to suppose at the same time that the Castilians were about to conquer the Americas. Their descendants thought that the Inca had emerged from "the House of Windows" at the "Inn of Dawn."

The Incas gradually progressed up the valley of the river Urabamba, adding tribe after tribe to their roll of dependents, sometimes by arms, sometimes by diplomacy. About A.D. 1200, the third mythical Inca—the ruler was so called—carried the tribe's authority beyond Lake Titicaca, with expeditions to the eastern forests as well as to the Pacific and beyond La Paz to include what is now Bolivia. Nazca and Arequipa came into Inca control in the early fifteenth century, and in the next hundred years, the seventh Inca, who took as an additional name that of the god Viracocha, defeated and absorbed the till then powerful Chanca at the battle of Xaquixaguana, a turning point in the history of the country. Then Pachacuti, "the best all-round genius produced by the native races of America" in the words of the archaeologist Sir Clements Markham, established in the early fifteenth century what seems to have deserved the name of *empire*, comprising much of the coastal plain and an important part of the Andes. Pachacuti's four sons directed large tracts of well-farmed coastal valleys and imposing towns more impressive than anything that the Incas had up till then controlled (hence the kingdom was usually known as "the Four Parts Together," or Tawantinsuyu). It was an entity of about eighty provinces. Pachacuti was the Ch'in emperor of the New World. His son Tupac Yupanqui added much of Ecuador to the Inca empire in the second half of the fifteenth century and conquered half of Chile.

The last independent ruler of Peru was Huayna Capac, who reigned from 1498 till 1527 and who seems to have been inactive, being perhaps ill from syphilis.[13] His power revolved round his skillful use of Quechua.[14] He may have died from smallpox, a disease from the Old World that certainly seems to have killed his eldest son. Huayna's weakness was that he left two sons: Huascar (Tita Cuso Hualpa), his son by his first wife, and Atahualpa, a son by his second wife, a princess of a northern tribe, the Carab Sapri. Huayna apparently considered dividing his large kingdom into two, leav-

ing the northern part to Atahualpa, the southern to Huascar—a sensible
policy, it might seem. But both sons wanted everything. Hence a civil war
ensued, dividing both the Inca family and the honorary Inca nobility,
though, about the time that the Spaniards arrived, Atahualpa had won. The
family of the defeated Huascar had been cruelly killed, with Huascar himself forced to watch. When the Spaniards arrived, Atahualpa was going
south on the main Inca highway on his way to be crowned in Cuzco.

19

Pizarro's Preparations

Yet surely Master More . . . wherever you have private property, and all men measure all things by money, there it is scarcely possible for a state to have justice or prosperity.

SIR THOMAS MORE, *Utopia*, BOOK 1

Pizarro spent a year in Panama preparing his expedition to Peru. He knew little of the politics of the place—far less, say, than a reader of the last chapter.

In the end, he left without Almagro, his nominal partner who—fatally for himself—undertook to follow later. He had organized his endeavors in the Compañía del Levante, with Almagro, Hernando de Luque, and one or two others, such as Gaspar de Espinosa. Pizarro sailed with three ships and about 180 men—no women—and about thirty horses: "as many Spaniards and horses as his ships would hold."[1] The expedition had been financed by Pizarro himself and by Almagro. Hernando de Luque had a minor investment, but he was not a partner on the same level as the other two leaders.[2] Pedro Pizarro said that those participating had to pay their own expenses, including money for their passage.[3] There were other investors, for example the rich *licenciado* Gaspar de Espinosa, a native of Medina de Rioseco, the city of the royal family of Enríquez. The ships seem to have been stocked with food, water, and armaments by their masters. Pizarro was the captain-in-chief. His power was limited by royal officials appointed to ensure that the Crown received a fifth of all income or loot. But Pizarro was able to leave those government officials behind in reserve positions waiting for military success.[4] He was, as it were, the commander of a company such as was often seen in those days.[5]

Pizarro left Panamanian waters on December 25, 1530, without his first ship, which was captained by Cristóbal de Mena, a native of Ciudad Real, like Almagro, of whom he was a close friend. Mena had been an *encomendero* and a councillor in Granada in Nicaragua. Pizarro had paid for horses and several black African slaves for the expedition. His captain and pilot was his friend Bartolomé Ruiz de Estrada, who came from that nursery of good sailors, Moguer, on the Río Tinto. He also had worked for Almagro and had recruited men for the journey. The three boats were jointly owned by Hernando de Soto, Pizarro, and Hernán Ponce de León, but the most important men on the journey were members of the Pizarro family.

Of these, Hernando, then about thirty years of age, was the only legitimate brother, being twenty years younger than Francisco. Oviedo, who knew him, said that Hernando was "a heavy man, but tall of stature with thick lips and tongue, and the tip of his nose was fleshy and red."[6] His cousin, Pedro Pizarro, however, said that he was "a man of good stature, valiant, wise and brave, albeit a heavy man in the saddle."[7] Garcilaso, the chronicler, thought him "rough and ill-tempered."[8] Enríquez de Guzmán said that Hernando was a "bad Christian with no fear of God and less devotion to the King . . . a great and boastful talker."[9] Being legitimate, he inherited a large house in Trujillo and also the nearby village of La Zarza, some miles south of Trujillo, which long had been a Pizarro holding. Hernando had accompanied his father, Gonzalo Pizarro, in the war against France in Navarre and so had experience of courts and royal armies. He was one of two men on the expedition to Peru who had experience of war in Europe. (The other was the giant Cretan artilleryman Pedro de Candía.)[10] Hernando's education had also given him some knowledge of finance, which he would put to good effect during the next few years. He could be witty and was articulate. His letter of 1533 to the *audiencia* in Santo Domingo made him one of the best eyewitnesses of what occurred in Peru in those years.[11] He was his brother Francisco's chief confidant. He disliked Almagro, whom he now met in Panama for the first time and whom he called "the circumcised Moor." The bad relations that developed between Francisco Pizarro and Almagro were worsened by these attitudes of Hernando Pizarro.

The other Pizarro brothers with Francisco were in 1531 still too young to count for much. Yet it was obvious that Juan Pizarro, still in his twenties, was "affable, magnanimous, impetuous—and popular."[12] "The flower of all the Pizarros," Ceiza, the chronicler, called him.[13] He had been brought up by his aunt Estefanía de Vargas, but he lived with the other Pizarros.

Then there was Gonzalo Pizarro, a little younger than Juan, of whom he was a full brother. (Their mother had been María Alonso, probably a maid in the Pizarro house.) He loved hunting and was good at it; he was always graceful, was well proportioned with a striking face, and had a capacity for camaraderie, which enabled him to make friends easily. Garcilaso, the most imaginative, but not the most accurate, chronicler of those days, said of him that "his nature was so noble that he endeared himself to strangers" and that "he was full of nobility and virtue and . . . [so] was beloved and respected by everyone." He was also a fine rider, a good shot with both arquebus and crossbow, and it was said that he was "the best lance who crossed to the new world."[14] Pedro Pizarro said of him that he was valiant with a good countenance and a fine beard but "knew little."[15] Gonzalo's day, however, would come.

In the early stages of Pizarro's expedition, Pedro de Candía from Crete had a strong influence. Physically a giant, he had been in the Spanish army since 1510, as an artilleryman, a position for which the Greeks were then known. He had been one of Pizarro's elite "thirteen" at Gallo Island. Pizarro had always liked him, often asking him to dine with him—an important test. He took Candía with him in 1528 to Spain, where his tales of Peru were too extravagant for comfort and Pizarro had to ask him to be quiet.

The journey to Birú was long and drawn-out. The Spanish expeditionaries sailed south under Bartolomé Ruiz's direction; their first port of call, thirteen days after leaving Panama, was the Bay of San Marcos, at the mouth of the river Esmeraldas. It was in the extreme north of the country which we now know as Ecuador, not Peru. The names had been given to the places by Bartolomé Ruiz, without much reflection, during Pizarro's previous expedition. Men, matériel, and horses were all disembarked.

They had intended to sail to Tumbes, but that seemed impossible because of a strong south wind. After a preliminary look for the emeralds that Bartolomé Ruiz assured his comrades were to be found in substantial quantities, the force then moved southward by land to what is now Atacames, along the coast. There were new difficulties, with mosquitoes and a severe shortage of water. The Spaniards took formal possession of the place following the reading of the Requirement, in the town of Cancebi, whose inhabitants were not enthralled at hearing the incomprehensible if threatening declaration. The expedition by land continued, with Pizarro trying to educate his men in the complexities of a new landscape. The land was barren but intersected by large rivers. These Pizarro and his men crossed by making rafts of wood, rushes, or osiers, built according to the captain's instructions. Pizarro was a real example, for "he often carried the sick over rivers on his back, being experienced in such tasks and he went about them with a patience and a courage that stimulated the others' spirits."[16]

These Spaniards' first obvious act of pillage was at the town of Coaque, which they reached on February 25, 1531. They found a place of about four hundred houses. They were met by very surprised Indians, who had not realized that they were threatened in any way: Pedro Pizarro recalled that the Spaniards attacked suddenly without warning, for "had it been otherwise, they would not have captured the quantity of gold and emeralds which was found there."[17] Pizarro distributed this treasure "in conformity with each man's merits and services." There was, it seems, "a shameful mistake on the part of certain members of the expedition who did not know the value of things . . . Others scorned the emeralds saying that they were glass."[18] They also seized 2,000 pesos of gold and silver, and Pizarro ordered Hernán Ponce de León, with one of his ships and some of his treasure, to return to Panama in order to show what he had found and encourage the people there to volunteer to join him.[19] Bartolomé de Aguilar, one of Pizarro's recruits from Trujillo, also returned. While waiting in Coaque, Pizarro seized the local chief of the town. The prisoner seems to have been treated humanely, with the result that he ordered his people to supply the Spaniards with the food that they wanted. But then the Spaniards "bothered and offended the natives so much that . . . they took to the forests."[20]

The Spaniards remained at Coaque seven months.[21] The news spread about "the arrival of bearded men who came in floating houses."[22] Also a strange disease of growths (*verrugas*) developed. It was either Oroya fever or verruga peruana—probably the latter. The attacks began with pains in the muscles, bones, and joints, and were followed by the growth of large nodules or boils like nuts.[23] No one knew how to treat these things, and many died. Garcilaso says that "at first a wart appeared as large as a black fig. It hung from some kind of stem, produced a great deal of blood and caused pain and nausea. The growths could not be touched and made the appearance of the sufferer most repulsive."[24] Pedro Pizarro suggested that the fault lay with some unusual fish that the Indians gave the Spaniards to eat. But it also could have been the woolen mattresses that the Indians had. If the Spaniards threw themselves down on them, they rose crippled, for if the arm or the leg were to be doubled up during sleep, "it could not be straightened without great difficulty."[25]

At Coaque, Pizarro was joined by reinforcements. But still Almagro did not come. He was apparently continuing to seek "supplies and men." One cannot avoid supposing that he may have been waiting to see how the expedition would turn out. But those who did come now included the royal treasurer, Alonso Riquelme; the official supervisor, García de Salcedo, who came from Zafra; and the royal accountant Antonio Navarro.[26] The whole force set off on October 12 for the South, again by land. They crossed the equator just short of Pasao, where they came on excellent fields of maize and where the chief gave Pizarro girls: Both were welcomed. The expedition soon found itself in Puerto Viejo, on what is now the Bay of Manta.

Here, Cieza tells us, the Spaniards realized for the first time that the great Inca kingdom, their object and their destination, had been torn apart by the civil war between the brothers Huascar and Atahualpa. Spaniards, of course, with their memories of La Cerdas fighting Trastámaras, knew all about such wars. The news of the arrival of the Spaniards also reached the Inca Princes. Atahualpa—who had, to begin with, been his brother's Viceroy for Quito—commented that, since there were so few Spaniards, perhaps they could serve him as superior servants (*yanaconas*). But the rumor soon spread that the Spaniards wanted "to rule over them and take their land."[27]

Moving down this Pacific coast, the Spaniards were provided by the Indians with food and water. They passed strange places and sights. In a city not far from the modern Guayaquil, for example, the chief was a woman, and according to Juan Ruiz de Arce, a conquistador from Alburquerque, the people were all homosexuals.[28] Here a Spaniard named Santiago was killed, and Pizarro caused the chief to punish those responsible. One of these was tied to a pole and allowed to die in that position.

Pizarro was shortly joined by a new Spanish force from Panama led by

Sebastián de Benalcázar. Like Pizarro, Benalcázar was illiterate. He probably came from a place that his surname reflected, even if it was slightly differently spelled: Belalcázar, a village in the Sierra Morena. He was from a
family of muleteers. He probably went out to the Indies in 1505, first to
Santo Domingo in the days of the iron proconsul Ovando. He joined Pedrarias in Panama and served with Gaspar de Espinosa in a brutal expedition to Azuero, in Central America, in 1519.[29] He was present at the
execution of Núñez de Balboa. He became an *encomendero* of Natá,
Panama. By then he had already known Almagro and Pizarro for some
years. Cieza considered that he was "a man of little knowledge, poor origin
and a low intellect." But all the same, he was brave and instinctively clever
in battle, and liberal in his relations with his men; and he had real qualities
of leadership, which were to serve the Spanish cause well, virtues that he
had in common with Pizarro himself. He also realized sooner than other
Spaniards how the Cañari Indians could become Spanish allies against the
Inca.

Benalcázar came to Peru with thirty men: among them, the first *conquistadora* in Peru, his sister, Anastasia. Pizarro's expedition was thus
staffed by adventurers from families that had distinguished themselves in
Spain in the fifteenth century. But none of those with Pizarro had been in
New Spain with Cortés, even if Cortés's memory was green among them.

Pizarro, Benalcázar, and their friends moved on to Santa Elena, where
they suffered a serious shortage of water. Many of the men were disaffected
and wanted to go back to a town that they had left a few days before, Puerto
Viejo. Pizarro refused to allow it, saying that to turn round would look like
a defeat. They continued to the island of Puna, in the Gulf of Guayaquil.
There they remained four months. To begin with, the local chief was benign, but, after a few days, he ordered and persuaded his men to rise and to
try to destroy the visitors. Their attack began with the organization of a
great noise—said to be a preparation for dancing but in fact a mobilization. Some conquistadors were wounded, among them Hernando Pizarro.
The attack quickly ended when the Spaniards took the chief, Tumala, prisoner with several of his lieutenants.[30] Nothing the Indians could do had the
slightest effect on the Spaniards' swords and horses.

In Puna on December 1, 1531, the expedition was enhanced by the arrival of further reinforcements from Panama. This was a force in two ships

of nearly one hundred, led by Hernando de Soto, a hidalgo who had gained much credit for his conduct in Nicaragua and who had helped to finance Pizarro's ships.[31] Soto was considered "dashing,"[32] and he was certainly brave. He was small in build but, said Pedro Pizarro, "dextrous in warfare and affable with soldiers."[33] He probably went first to the Indies in 1513 with Pedrarias, whose daughter Isabel he later married. He explored part of what is now Colombia in 1517. He had a company with Hernán Ponce de León from 1517. In the 1520s he was in much brutal conflict in Central America and gained good *encomiendas* in León. To chart his trajectory among the squabbling conquistadors in that new territory is a hard task, but we know that he and Hernán Ponce de León were busy selling slaves from Nicaragua in the Caribbean and in Panama also. Before they set off, Soto concluded an informal agreement with Pizarro whereby he would receive the lieutenant governorship of "the main Peruvian city"—Cuzco, we assume. Pizarro promised good *encomiendas,* too. Soto's hundred men were financed by himself or by some of those taking part, some of them selling their property in order to be able to participate.

In Puna, for the first time, Pizarro and his friends encountered obvious signs of the Peruvian civil war between the two royal brothers, Huascar and Atahualpa. Thus they found six hundred prisoners from the port of Tumbes. They were in a loose form of confinement. The chief of Tumbes, Tumala, sued for peace and presented the Spaniards with gold and silver presents. He also gave them presents of rafts maliciously devised to disintegrate by allowing the ropes that held the timbers together to unfasten when they had been at sea a few minutes.

Pizarro with his expedition now had nearly four hundred Spaniards and one woman, Benalcázar's sister. They were hated by the local Indians, who could not understand their motivation. Those Indians devised a hunt of deer. While the Spaniards were watching the conclusion, it was supposed, the Indians would fall on them. But by a fatal weakness in Peruvian discretion, one of the Indians told of this scheme to Pizarro's Quechua interpreter, "Felipe," a boy who had been captured in 1527 and trained in Spanish.[34] Pizarro seized sixteen chiefs who had been engaged in the plot. A large body of Indians then tried to attack the Spaniards—3,500 of them, according to Cieza. "They attacked in three directions, with determination and boldness." The Spaniards awaited the charge with horses and shield-bearers well placed. As usual, the Indians made little impact. Many were killed, and they wounded only two Spaniards and three horses. Pizarro requested Tumala to order his men to call off the battle. He refused, saying that wild beasts would not make them accept peace with people who had done them such damage. But for the moment, there was no more fighting, and the Spaniards assembled a great quantity of gold, silver, and cloth, the first two items in sheets, as if ready for use as linings of the interior walls of temples.[35]

The expedition set off by raft and ship from Puna to Tumbes. Pizarro assumed that the people of that port would help him since he had returned six hundred prisoners there. But the Indians under Quillemin organized a conspiracy to kill all the Spaniards there and then. One small raft-borne expedition included a certain Hurtado, who was captured and murdered when he landed, with two boys, both of whose eyes were gouged out and their penises cut off. But the Indians did not have the courage to attack the main body of Spanish expeditionaries. Cieza says that the Indians wanted to leave "without hearing the snorting of the horses."

Pizarro found Tumbes desolated. In the civil war, the place had been laid waste. All the same, the temple of the sun remained there, painted with large pictures, which Miguel de Estete claimed were of a "rich variety of colour."[36] (Estete was from Santo Domingo de la Calzada, a well-known halt on the pilgrim route from France to Santiago. He was a notary and had come to Peru with Benalcázar.) This temple had in 1527 much impressed Alonso de Molina, and his description of the sheets of silver and gold there, confirmed by Candía, was one of the decisive reports that led to Pizarro's expedition in 1531.

Pizarro and his men camped in two fortresses in Tumbes, one of which he commanded himself, the other being controlled by his brother Hernando. An expedition was sent out to "punish" the murder of Hurtado. They found few Indians upon whom to wreak revenge, but the Spaniards pillaged what they could, stealing llamas as well as other treasures. With them, they returned to the camp. But Pizarro's anger remained, and he ordered Soto, his newest captain, to pursue the local Indians where he could.[37] Soto was always adept at finding Indians to kill, and he drove one enemy leader, Quilterosa, into the mountains. At last, the Peruvians agreed to beg pardon for what they had done and to offer peace, realizing that otherwise Pizarro would destroy their settlements. They therefore asked the Spanish commander to have mercy on them in the name of the sun. Pizarro agreed: Drily, he commented that "he needed them to give him guides and to help the Spaniards to carry their baggage."[38]

At some point, in the empty city of Tumbes an Indian came up and said that he had no wish to flee with all the others since it seemed to him that the new arrivals, being "men of war and of much power," were destined to conquer everything. He begged that his house not be sacked. Pizarro told him to put a white cross on his house and instructed his men that no one was to attack a place so marked. This was the Indian who told Pizarro for the first time of Cuzco and its great riches.[39] Pizarro learned, too, at this time of such great centers of Peru as Vilcas, with its stone temple and many open squares, and of Pachacamac, whose magnificent buildings were said to be coated with gold and silver.

The chiefs of Tumbes, having been sought by Soto and his seventy horsemen, then appeared and thanked Pizarro for his patience with them. They had been impressed by the Spaniards' superior qualities when they saw the horsemen ride uphill![40] At a town nearby, which the Spaniards christened San Miguel because it was then Saint Michael's Day (April 10), these chiefs offered a rich booty of gold and silver jewels. Thereafter, the chief Quillemesa (Chilimasa) was *mucho nuestro amigo*. At that time, there was a halfhearted rebellion against Pizarro by Soto, who wanted to go up to conquer the Peruvian sub-capital of Quito. Soto was betrayed by Juan de la Torre, a survivor of the famous "thirteen" of 1527, and thereafter Pizarro made a point of ensuring that Soto was customarily accompanied by his brothers Juan and Gonzalo, who acted as a combination of jailers and bodyguards.[41]

The news that Pizarro heard of the dazzling riches of Peru and its interior caused him to change his strategy. He had intended to proceed to the heart of the country—including Cuzco, for example—by continuing down the coast. But then he heard that Atahualpa was not far off in Cajamarca, a town in the mountains some fifty miles from the sea. Pizarro resolved to seek a meeting with Atahualpa. Pizarro left Tumbes on May 16, 1532, leaving behind about twenty-five sick Spaniards and fifteen others, forty in all, under Captain Antonio Navarro, who had been the accountant of the expedition for the previous year. He also left there two other royal officials,

Alonso Riquelme and García de Salcedo and, as his own representative, his half brother, Francisco Martín de Alcántara, a younger son of his mother, whose devotion to him was lifelong. Pizarro made his first grants in this settlement to these stay-behinds, and he planned squares, public buildings, and some private houses in San Miguel, this first Spanish city of Peru.[42] Four soldiers and two Franciscans also returned from Tumbes to Panama.

Pizarro's army—now of about two hundred men, of whom about half were horsemen—pressed on through fertile lands. Thus Miguel de Estete reported: "The Tallan river is heavily populated with *pueblos* and has a very good fruit-growing sector, of a better kind than Tumbez. There is an abundance of food and native livestock. All the area to the sea was well exploited because it seemed to have a very good port."[43] They continued to cover about four to six leagues (twelve to eighteen miles) every day, passing through Huauillas, Silar (el Tambo de la Sed), Cerro Prieto, Jagay Negro, and the banks of the rivers Chira and Poechos. They saw many unusual people, such as the Tallares, who, according to Pedro Pizarro, dressed in cloaks of cotton with woolen shawls round their heads, which they tied under their beards. The women had lip ornaments, as the Mexican natives had also had. They worshipped the sun and would send it a large supply of dried lizard to eat.[44] They were great drinkers and ate maize. Their priests dressed in white and fasted by abstaining from salt as well as garlic. They cultivated watermelons and other fruit. They tended llamas and were fishermen and shellfish enthusiasts. They danced and made music, the leaders lived in adobe palaces, and they were polygamous as well as patriarchal. Their lords traveled by hammock. Coming originally from the mountains, they now lived on the coast. Their conquest by the Incas in about 1470 had not yet led to their speaking Quechua.[45]

In this zone, the Spaniards noted an Indian who wore the ample cloak of the desert as well as a great shawl on his head and shoulders, and who carried a basket full of wares. He spent the whole day in the Spanish camp seeking to sell his objects, yet at the same time, he was admiring the work of the expedition's blacksmith, the shaving by the expedition's barber, and the horse taming by the skillful Hernán Sánchez Murillo.[46] Hernando Pizarro guessed that this Indian was more than he at first sight seemed. Indeed, he turned out to be Apoo, a spy for Atahualpa, to whom he reported that the Spaniards were not gods. Rather, they were bearded robbers who

came out of the sea and who could probably be both conquered and enslaved.[47] There were only 190 of them.

Atahualpa seems to have thought it best to allow these "robbers"—the
Spaniards—to advance, and then he would seize them and make them
work for him. It was surely for that that the gods had sent the Spaniards.[48]
Apoo made the Spaniards show him their swords, and he pulled the beard
of one, who gave him many blows in return.[49]

Then Pizarro received a messenger from the Inca Huascar, the defeated
Prince of the civil war, who asked for the Spaniards' protection since they
had claimed to have come to Peru to undo injustices. Pizarro rather drily
replied that he was always ready to put such things right.[50]

This was a hard march, even if some presented it as if it were a carnival.
There was much sun, little shade, much sand, and no water except what
was carried. Yet they encountered one vast royal house that had an abundance of freshwater, and both the soldiers and the horses refreshed themselves. They saw, too, a river and a beautiful and cheerful valley through
which the broad highway of the Inca passed, with elegant resting places
and marked by brilliantly contrived swinging bridges.

Pizarro sent the useful Soto and the powerful Benalcázar ahead on
horses to explore. They found ample provisions and gold in many temples.
The Indians attacked them, but Soto's force responded very effectively, the
local people having no answer to Spanish swords.

Through Soto, Atahualpa's captain Ciquinchara sent Pizarro a present
of some duck and two model earthenware fortresses. He also sent *chicha*
and tiles of gold. Ciquinchara stayed with Soto till he returned to Pizarro,
who, in his turn, sent to Atahualpa the typical Spanish present of a good
Holland shirt of fine white linen, two crystal glasses from Venice (only
slightly less typical), some pearls from Panama, and a random collection of
scissors, knives, combs, and mirrors from Spain.[51]

The Spanish expedition was still in the pretty valley of the river Puira
on October 8, 1532; it was at Serrán on October 16, and then passed several
towns at the foot of the sierra on October 19. From there, Pizarro sent an
emissary to Atahualpa. At the same time, he held an open meeting of his
followers at which he declared that his intention was "to carry this barbarous people to their union with Christianity without doing them any
damage."[52] In the mountains, Atahualpa asked his secret agent all kinds of

sensible questions, including whether the Spaniards ate human beings, to receive the correct reply: "I have seen them eat nothing but sheep [llamas], lamb, duck, pigeon, and venison and with these they eat tortillas of maize."[53] As they marched south, Soto was sent inland on a reconnaissance to Cajas on the main Inca road. He took over five hundred women from their "convent" in the main square and allowed his men to rape them (the evidence is that of Diego de Trujillo, an eyewitness).

On November 15, 1532, Pizarro and his men made their way to Atahualpa's city of Cajamarca, through plantations of cotton.

At this time, Atahualpa, with a large army of perhaps forty thousand soldiers, was at some baths about four miles outside Cajamarca, at Kónoj. In a palace with two towers that rose from a courtyard, there was a pool, in which the Inca was taking the waters. There were two pipes, one of cold, one of hot water. The Spaniards could easily identify with such a spa.

20

Cajamarca

The courtier's chief purpose and end to which he is directed must
be to provide the ruler with sound political advice and to ensure
that the public seeks honour and profit.

CASTIGLIONE, *The Courtier*

The Pizarros and their expedition of now 168 men, of whom sixty-two
were horsemen, reached Cajamarca by what the Romans would have
named forced marches. The last part of the road had been harsh:
Hernando Pizarro, every day more important because of his superior
education and his experience in a European army, later said that if the Inca
had taken any trouble "they could have stopped us easily."[1] But Atahualpa
took no such trouble. He had a big army with him. It was the last day of one
of his fasts. He was looking forward to seeing these strange animals, horses,
of which he had heard so much.[2] One report was that when they had to
walk uphill, the Spanish footsoldiers hung on to the horses' tails.

One conquistador, Juan Ruiz de Arce, from Alburquerque in Extremadura, from a family of petty hidalgos that had long fought for the
Christian cause in Castile, said that, from the hillside over which they had
come, the Indian encampment beyond Cajamarca looked like a beautiful
planned city. But, he commented, it would have been a serious psychological mistake to indicate any kind of fear, so they "descended into the valley
and entered the city."[3]

Cajamarca lay in a fertile flat valley with complicated watercourses, a
sun temple, and sacred buildings full of women chosen either for their
birth or their beauty. Their main task seems to have been to make *chicha*
for the Inca.

Pizarro's first action on reaching Cajamarca was to dispatch his brother Hernando with Soto and fifteen horsemen to go to Atahualpa and ask him to come and meet them. They went with one of the native interpreters whom Pizarro had seized on his first visit to Peru and trained in Spain. He was not up to the task and must be considered partly responsible for the tragedy that followed. For the translator rendered Spanish words barbarously, giving some of them the meaning opposite to what was intended. The mistranslations irritated Atahualpa: "What does this fellow mean stammering from one word to another and from one mistake to the next as if he were dumb?" The interpreter also found it difficult after two years' absence to render the speech of the Inca adequately.[4]

The Inca said that he knew that the Spaniards were gods—sons of Viracocha, that is—and messengers from the long-lost god-king Pachacutí, and that their arrival had been foreshadowed by his father, Huayna Capac. So he, Atahualpa, had decreed that no one should take up arms against them. All the same, he wondered why the Spaniards continually spoke of peace while often killing people. For example, he had heard from Marcavilca, the chief of the Poechos on the river Zuracan, how Pizarro had put several chiefs into chains.[5]

Hernando Pizarro replied by saying that his brother Francisco loved Atahualpa. That was why he had gone so far to find him. He wanted Atahualpa to know that if any enemy should appear, he, Francisco Pizarro, would send ten horsemen to destroy them. That should be adequate. Even that turbulent tribe the Chachapoyas would be easily beaten.[6]

At this, Atahualpa asked the Spaniards to drink *chicha* with him. Comforted by this sign that the New World had something at least in common with the old, when the offer was made of a drink, Hernando accepted. Atahualpa also asked his visitors if they would like to stay the night. They refused, saying that they had to return to their friends in Cajamarca. Atahualpa said that the Spaniards could stay in the center of Cajamarca, where there were three large dormitories that might suit them.

Before they left the spa, Hernando performed before the Inca on a small horse that had been trained to rear. Atahualpa was very interested. Like most of Pizarro's horses, this beast was small, Arab stock from Andalusia, hardy and intelligent. The other Hernando, Hernando de Soto, gave the Inca a ring from his finger as a sign of peace. The Spaniards then went back to Cajamarca. Before they left, Atahualpa promised to pay a return visit the following day, with an escort of several thousand men. Pedro Pizarro commented that one or two of Atahualpa's followers who had shown signs of fear were executed "to encourage the others."[7]

On the return of Hernando Pizarro's mission, he and his brother Francisco examined the main square in Cajamarca. Each side was about two hundred yards long. On three sides, there were low buildings, each with twenty gates. The fourth side had a low wall of adobe with a tower and gate in the center. The Spaniards moved into the buildings on the first three sides but left the fourth unattended.[8]

The Spaniards present at Cajamarca have been carefully studied by James Lockhart in an admirable work.[9] Of the hundred or so men whose past is known, about half had been in the Indies for five or more years. All the captains (Pizarro, Soto, Benalcázar) had been there for twenty or more years, while Cristóbal de Mena and García de Salcedo had been there for ten years. Most of those who had been in the Indies for any length of time had, like Francisco Pizarro and Soto, been companions of Pedrarias. None of the men with Pizarro had been with Cortés in New Spain.[10] Practically nobody except Pizarro himself had spent any time in the Caribbean. Most of the rank and file were in their twenties, but the captains were mostly in their thirties. Pizarro was exceptional, since having been born about 1479, he was, as we have seen, in his fifties. Candía said that he was forty.

Of those whose origins we know something, thirty-six came from Extremadura (fourteen from Trujillo), thirty-four came from Andalusia (mostly Seville), seventeen were from Old Castile, and fifteen were from New Castile. Perhaps thirty-six out of the 168 were hidalgos and could read and write. Two had Italian surnames (Piñelo, Cataño) but many men with such names were considered Spanish: The Piñelos had been major entrepreneurs in Seville for two generations. Almost certainly these men were merchants as well as soldiers. There was only one man who certainly had been at a university, the priest Valverde. So, perhaps, had Hernando Pizarro. About three-quarters of this Spanish army were literate: One hundred and eight could sign their names, thirty-three could not. One in ten was a notary. Two may have had Muslim blood.[11] There seems to have been a small unit of perhaps thirty African slaves at Pizarro's orders.

The Spaniards in Cajamarca did not know what their plan for the following day should be. Pedro Pizarro wrote of real doubt among the rank and file: "We took many opinions," he said, "as to what should be done. All were full of fear, because we were so few and so far away from home that we could not be reinforced. All assembled in the governor's [i.e., Pizarro's] quarters to debate what should be done next day. There was [in this discussion] no distinction between great men and unimportant ones, nor between foot soldiers and horsemen. All carried out their sentry duties fully armed. On that night all were gentlemen. The Spaniards had no knowledge whatsoever as to how the Indians would fight."[12] At the same time, Miguel de Estete thought that the "campfires of the Indian army [being so many] were a terrible sight. Most were on the hillside and they seemed like a star-studded sky."[13] There were moments of alarm, even of panic, effectively restrained by Pizarro's comforting self-confidence.

John Hemming suggests that it was agreed among the Spaniards that Governor Pizarro himself should decide on the spur of the moment the course of action to be taken the next day.[14] It seems, though, likely that the brothers Pizarro had in truth already decided what to do. They remembered Cortés's successful seizure of Montezuma. Surely they, too, had decided to act similarly in respect of Atahualpa.

Probably Pizarro wanted Atahualpa to be absolutely at his disposal. He had a dais made for the Inca to sit upon: "He would be asked to sit there in the square of Cajamarca and then order his men to return to their camp."[15]

Pizarro also prepared for a battle. He organized his modest cavalry in two groups, one under his brother Hernando, the other under Soto.[16] Candía was to control the artillery as well as a detachment of trumpeters. Pizarro himself, always a footsoldier, would lead the infantry, with his brother Juan as his deputy. When Atahualpa arrived in the square, Candía was to fire his guns and have trumpets blown. At that signal, the cavalry, bells attached to the bridles of the horses, would ride out of the long building where they were in readiness.

Things did not go according to plan. Atahualpa made no appearance in the morning. Indeed, he did not come to Cajamarca till the late afternoon, the sun sinking. He was accompanied by about five hundred men—so it was said—each carrying small battle axes, slings, and pouches full of stones under their tunics.[17] The Inca himself was carried on a litter with silver ends, and he was adorned with jewels (including emeralds round his neck), with many highly colored parrot feathers, and with some plates of gold and silver. The work of carrying the litter was performed by about eighty nobles—that is the Castilian estimate—surrounded by others in checkered clothing who were busy singing and sweeping away rubbish in front of the Inca, including straw and feathers. These attendants were armed with slings. The lord of Chincha, a prominent courtier, was present, too—also, it seems, on a litter. Pedro Pizarro reflected that it was "a marvel to see how the sun glittered" on the gold and silver of the litter of Atahualpa. The latter had charmingly explained to his court that the Spaniards were ambassadors of God and so it was not necessary to carry offensive arms.

The only Spaniard who came to greet the Inca was Hernando de Aldana, an Extremeño from Valencia de Alcántara, close to the Portuguese frontier, who had already learned a little Quechua. Atahualpa was astounded to find only one man present. But shortly, the Dominican Fray Vicente de Valverde also came out to address him. Apparently this was improvised. He spoke to Atahualpa through an interpreter. One native source explained that Atahualpa was surprised by Valverde's uncouth appearance: Perhaps he had not been able to shave for a time.[18] Valverde gave Atahualpa in effect a rough version of the famous Requirement. This included a short history of Christianity. Valverde insisted that Atahualpa should begin to pay tribute to Emperor Charles V and become his vassal. He should hand over his kingdom to him and repudiate his gods. He also said, "If you obstinately seek to resist, you may rest assured that you and all your Indians will be destroyed by our arms, even as the Pharaoh of old and all his host perished in the Red Sea."[19] That abstruse biblical reference could not have been appreciated by the unfortunate Inca.

There followed a moment of confusion. According to Garcilaso de la Vega, Valverde by mistake dropped his daybook and his cross; but Pedro Pizarro said that Atahualpa had asked to see these objects. The Inca could not open the book, perhaps because it was locked, and so threw it onto the ground. Or did he throw it to his relations? At all events, Atahualpa fumbled, and this gave the Christians what they later considered a good excuse for their extraordinary conduct.[20]

Candía's moment had come. He fired two guns, the trumpets were sounded. The cavalry streamed out of their quarters at a gallop. The infantry followed, their steel swords mercilessly active. Though they were in a vast majority over the foreigners, the Indians had no knowledge of what to do. Most panicked and broke through the adobe wall on the square's fourth side. They fled into the country, but Spanish horsemen followed and caused many further deaths. In the square, hundreds were quickly killed. No Spaniards seem to have died, but the Indians killed were without limit: Garcilaso thought that five thousand Indians died that afternoon. Other Spanish chroniclers made similar estimates: Trujillo thought in terms of eight thousand; Ruiz de Arce, seven thousand; Mena, six to seven thousand; Xerez, two thousand.[21] If we accept the lowest estimate, Xerez's, it still must seem a vast number to be killed by fewer than two hundred Europeans.

Atahualpa was captured by Pizarro himself, having been wounded by Miguel de Estete, the notary from Santo Domingo de la Calzada, who had wanted to kill the Inca with a knife.[22] Almost all the nobility of old Peru were killed, however, and Atahualpa, the Inca, became a frightened prisoner, being held at first in the temple of the sun and then in Pizarro's own lodgings, in one of the palaces in the square.

The explanation of this massacre must be sought in the mood of anxiety and apprehension among the Spaniards, who, even outnumbered, thought that they had to fight in order to live. The Spaniards felt an extreme unease at being surrounded by a large horde of people of a quite different race to themselves. That done, they assumed that violence worked, and that terrible day in the square of Cajamarca was not forgotten. Indeed it would be repeated. The barbarity of the Spaniards was due to their fear, isolation, and uncertainty.

That does not justify their disgraceful behavior, for which the illiterate but charming Francisco Pizarro must take full responsibility. It is true that his achievement was a triumph of European warfare, though the numbers reported to have been killed have an unbelievable implication! Nevertheless, the probability is that even Xerez exaggerated and that casualties did not in reality exceed a thousand.

21

The End of Atahualpa

It is better for a ruler to be feared than loved. Better to rely on
punishment than considerateness.

MACHIAVELLI, Discourses

It must seem improbable that anything new can be said of the imprisonment of Atahualpa, last independent Inca in Peru. Such great historians as
Prescott and Hemming have admirable pages on these matters in their
famous books. Macaulay in an essay of 1840 pushed aside any such pretensions when he made his famous comment that every schoolboy knew
who strangled him.[1] Yet little is clear in history.

Atahualpa was afraid that he would be killed the day following his capture (November 13, 1532). He was led by the interpreter to think that the
Pizarros and their expedition really favored his defeated brother, Huascar,
which would explain to him what had occurred the previous day.
Atahualpa realized that he had been deceived by his agent, Apoo, about the
Spaniards' capacity to fight. Atahualpa told the interpreter Martinillo that
he would give Pizarro a quantity of gold and silver. He had been fully informed by Apoo and others of the Spaniards' preoccupation with gold.
Pizarro came to ask how much he would provide. Extremeños such as
Pizarro liked to have such questions clear. Atahualpa replied that he would
fill the room where they were talking with gold "as high as he could reach
with his hand on the wall."[2] He made "a line on the wall" (*hizo una raya en
la pared*).[3] This room was apparently twenty-two feet long by seventeen
feet wide by eleven and a half feet high. That would mean a gift of three
thousand cubic feet.[4] This present would be procured in two months. An

escribano (notary) wrote everything down.[5] Pizarro seems to have promised Atahualpa his life if this undertaking was fulfilled, but this detail seems
a little unclear, as events were to show.[6] Perhaps that was merely the implication of Pizarro's response.

The Spaniards settled down to wait. Some went with Hernando de Soto
again to see Atahualpa's camp, which they found full of troops behaving as
if nothing had happened. Instructed by the Inca, these troops made the
sign of the Christian cross as a mark of surrender. Soto and his men also
ransacked the Inca's camp at Cajamarca and seized what is said to have
been 80,000 pesos of gold and 7,000 silver marks. They also seized fourteen
emeralds.[7] These thefts were independent of the promises to fill the room
where Atahualpa was. A little later, three Spaniards set off for Cuzco, of
which Pizarro and his friends by now had heard a great deal. These were
Martín Bueno, Pedro Martín de Moguer, and Juan de Zárate. They were
carried in hammocks by Indians on Atahualpa's orders. Atahualpa had established his general Quizquiz also at Cuzco, to ensure the collection of the
ransom—if that is what it was. Publicly he continued to conduct himself as
the leader of the empire, consulting advisers, appointing new officials (necessary after the killings in the square), seeing messengers from the outer
provinces, issuing orders. The mood was much as it had been in New Spain
in November 1519 after the kidnapping of Montezuma, except that at the
equivalent stage, Cortés had killed no one.

The Spaniards reached Cuzco after a journey of two months.[8] They
were lodged in a round-towered palace known as that of Huayna Capac (it
was later replaced by the Jesuit building). They found a great deal of treasure. The Peruvian general Quizquiz had thirty thousand men in the capital. Another general, Chalcuchima, was at Jauja with thirty-five thousand
men. Atahualpa had asked these soldiers to guarantee the safety of the
Spaniards on their journey. He had also ordered that the gold was to be
taken from the temple of the sun in the capital, though nothing that had
anything to do with Huayna Capac was to be touched. The Spaniards who
were there removed seven hundred gold plates from the temple with cross-
bars which they had brought with them. Each plate was about three or four
handsbreadths long; each weighed four and a half pounds.[9] The Spaniards
also seized a sacrificial gold altar weighing 19,000 pesos and a gold foun-
tain weighing 12,000 pesos.[10] Of course, they did not neglect to take pos-

session formally of Cuzco—"the navel of the world," as it was known in Quechua—in the great name of the emperor Charles.

Yet one more expedition was that of Hernando Pizarro to Pachacamac, passing near what would become the city of Lima. He arrived on February 5, 1533. There was a large temple there on top of a stepped pyramid of adobe. He was accompanied by two of Atahualpa's captains, who told the conquistadors of the whereabouts of this temple.[11] Miguel de Estete recalled the shrine in the heart of the temple being a small room of cane wattle characterized by posts decorated with gold and silver leaf. But on top of the pyramid was a rough, small, dirty cavern such as the conquistadors in New Spain had encountered on the summit of the pyramids in Mexico-Tenochtitlan. There was a post in the center of the cavern, on top of which there had been placed the uncouth head of a man. Hernando Pizarro seized a quantity of gold from there, then destroyed the shrine. But he also spent some time looking for further treasure that he believed had been hidden in the vicinity. He apparently had the support of Atahualpa for these actions, since the Inca was angry with the priests and gods of Pachacamac because they had falsely predicted that Huayna Capac would recover from his last illness, that Huascar would defeat Atahualpa, and that Atahualpa himself would be well advised to fight, not to welcome, the Christians.[12]

This journey was of considerable importance, for in the course of it, Hernando Pizarro found sweet potatoes for the first time, saw holes in the ground being made by foot-powered plows, and observed thatched huts and terraces in the valley. Returning, he encountered the Peruvian general Chalcuchima at Jauja. They had several hours of conversation. Hernando explained that Atahualpa himself wanted Chalcuchima to return with him. The general said that if he were to leave Jauja, the place would declare for Huascar. But the next day, Chalcuchima unwisely changed his mind and agreed to go to Cajamarca with Hernando.[13]

These Spaniards also traveled in hammocks carried by Atahualpa's Indians. These Indians at first gave the horses gold to eat, insisting that that was better for them than the iron bits to which they seemed accustomed. They also sometimes shod the horses with silver.[14]

On their way back to Cajamarca with gold, Hernando Pizarro met Huascar Inca, now a prisoner of Atahualpa. Huascar greeted the Spaniards with enthusiasm and told them that if he had been the victor in the civil war, not Atahualpa, he would have filled the room in Cajamarca to its top, not just up to the line that his brother could reach. Soon after that, Atahualpa had his brother Huascar killed, perhaps because, contrary to what he said to Soto, that prince claimed that some of the gold offered to the Spaniards was his. Pizarro by that time believed that Atahualpa was a bastard younger brother of Huascar.[15]

The Spaniards who remained in Cajamarca became impatient. They passed the time gambling, seducing the virgins of the temple, and studying the Inca's personality. They observed his grand habits.[16] Some came to think the Inca "the most educated and capable Indian who had yet been seen in the Indies." He "seemed very anxious to learn our ways," wrote Licenciado Gaspar de Espinosa from Panama. Espinosa continued, "[He] even plays chess rather well [*xuega al ajedrez harto bien*]. By having him in our power, the whole land is calm." But he was also cruel and intolerant.[17]

The Spaniards saw that Atahualpa seemed to be convinced that he was a divine monarch, for he was "in constant touch with the sun, his father. He was guarded by women, he was surrounded by beautiful objects and he and everyone around him wore very fine, soft clothing."[18] Once Atahualpa challenged Pizarro to put up a powerful Spaniard who could wrestle and defeat one of his own giants: Alonso Díaz, a Spanish blacksmith, did so and "strangled the giant [only] with a great effort."[19] Who could say that the chivalrous novels were not being relived? One Spaniard gave Atahualpa a beautiful Venetian glass. Atahualpa admired it and said that surely nobody but kings would use such a thing in Spain. The donor said that not only kings but common people and lords also would use one. Atahualpa deliberately dropped the glass, which, of course, broke.[20]

Though he was a captive, provincial leaders continued to call on Atahualpa. The nobility, the *orejones* (ear men), so called since they wore golden plugs in their ears, maintained their privileges: the right to chew coca; the use of special bridges and roads; fine cloths, good ornaments, and the company of beautiful ladies; and even permission for incest.[21]

The gold for Atahualpa's ransom from Cuzco and Pachacamac began to arrive, usually in large jars capable of carrying two *arrobas* worth, on some days 20,000 pesos, on others 30,000, occasionally even 60,000. Completion depended on the collection of sheets of gold from the temple of the sun at Cuzco. Sometimes the gold came shaped as exquisite or realistic stalks of maize, hibiscus blossoms, palm leaves, trees ripe with fruit, and even life-size deer.

These shipments occurred at a fortunate moment for the expedition, since on April 15, Almagro, the lost ally, at last reached Cajamarca from Panama. He had 150 to 200 men with him, as well as fifty horses. He came angry, impatient, and restless. For he appeared at a time when it was too late for him to share in the spoils. Almagro's new force settled down alongside the Pizarros' experienced one, but they remained two separate undertakings with long-term difficulties between them. These were to fester.

Ten days later, on April 25, Hernando Pizarro returned from Pachacamac, with a large caravan of treasure, bringing with him the tragic figure of the general Chalcuchima, who remained yet another prisoner of Pizarro. He was constantly asked for the whereabouts of his secret supply of gold; he denied that he had any such thing. The general was tortured by Soto, Riquelme, and Almagro, to no avail.[22]

In early May, the melting down and assaying of the gold in Pizarro's hands began. The total value counted in May 1532 was apparently more than one and a half million pesos' worth, far more gold than had ever before been found in the Indies. Francisco Pizarro had decided that all but the King's fifth would go to the 165 or so men of Cajamarca. The cavalry at Cajamarca would be allocated 8,000 pesos each, the infantry 4,000. Furious, Almagro argued that he and Francisco Pizarro should each take half of the whole and that then they should give to each of their followers 1,000 or 2,000 pesos.[23] He got nowhere with these reasonable demands. Hernando Pizarro meantime busied himself with the organization of encomiendas, the details of which he arranged on May 8 with his majordomo.[24] Hernando was always busy with his finances.

In June, Pizarro's division of the treasure followed. First, the hoard was divided into shares of 4,440 gold pesos and 181 silver marks, worth altogether 5,345 golden pesos (at that time a peso of gold was reckoned as being worth 450 maravedís). Indian smiths did the melting down of the priceless gold and silver objects in nine large forges under the direction of a notary from Córdoba, Gonzalo de Pineda, now a close adviser to Francisco Pizarro.

More than eleven tons of precious metals were fed into the forges to produce eventually 13,420 pounds of twenty-two-and-a-half-karat gold and 26,000 pounds of silver. Much of this had been in the form of jewelry whose details are now lost. Two hundred and seventeen shares were carefully divided according to Pizarro's judgment of the contributions of the individuals concerned. The rough idea was that an infantryman would receive one share, a cavalryman two, and captains more still. But, in the end, all was decided by a committee of *repartidores* headed by Francisco and Hernando Pizarro. This committee would include Pineda, the master of the forges; Pedro Díaz, a silversmith who weighed the silver, though he had not been himself in the fighting at Cajamarca; and two other captains, Hernando de Soto and Miguel de Estete, whom we have met as a chronicler. These men ensured that there would be no treasure for Almagro nor for any of his followers.

The apportionment was nothing if not biased. Thus Francisco Pizarro received 13 shares, as well as "the governor's jewel," Atahualpa's golden seat, worth 2 shares. Hernando Pizarro received 7 shares, Juan Pizarro 2½ shares, and his brother Gonzalo the same. All these allocations were enough to make the people concerned very rich. In round terms, a little more than 135 shares went to the 62 horsemen, 81 shares to 103 infantrymen. The Pizarro brothers received 24 shares out of the 217. Almost certainly some of the gold and silver allocations were left out of the calculations.[25] Benalcázar had a small share, but no doubt he received more than was officially registered. Pizarro also divided the Indian chiefs' and their vassals' among his followers who were encamped at Cajamarca and whose lands would soon become *encomiendas*.

Soon after the division of the treasure, Hernando Pizarro left Peru for Spain to tell of the great conquest that had been carried out. He took with him a substantial quantity of gold and silver and 100,000 castellanos for the King, which, his enemies were quick to point out, was less than half the royal fifth. He carried, too, thirty-eight beautiful vessels of gold and forty-eight of silver. He took also fifteen or twenty men with him: Francisco Pizarro prevented more from leaving on the ground that he could not afford their loss. Of those who were left, seven were older men and could not be expected to last long in Peru—though none was as old as Francisco Pizarro. One or two were sent home as possible critics or even enemies.[26] Some who went back with Hernando did so for precisely opposite reasons: They were friends of the Pizarros and could help to propagate their cause.

When Atahualpa heard that Hernando was returning to Spain, his heart sank. The Inca had just seen a large green-and-black comet, which he believed meant that his death was certain. He had been on easy terms with Hernando and believed that nothing would go wrong for him if he were still second-in-command. He had no such confidence in Almagro, nor in the royal treasurer, Alonso Riquelme. But though those men were unhelpful to Atahualpa's cause, his downfall may have been due to the Peruvian interpreter Felipe. By that time, Atahualpa believed that he should be set free because, of course, the great "ransom" had been paid. At the very least, he said, he should be allowed to go to eat and drink with his subjects. But Felipe had apparently fallen in love with one of the Inca's favorite ladies and wanted him out of the way for that reason. She was a certain Cuxirimay, whose name meant "very fair skinned and beautiful." The interpreter now is said to have falsely alleged that the Inca was planning to escape and, with his surviving general in Quito, Rumiñavi, was organizing a new campaign against the Spaniards.

Pizarro is believed to have taken this tale seriously. Sentries were doubled. Pizarro planned to go to Cuzco. But how would the Inca be guarded while the Spanish army was on its way? Could he be left with a guard in Cajamarca? Surely, that would be difficult to arrange. But to take Atahualpa to Cuzco would also have risks. Felipe was incompetent as an interpreter. He did not understand Christianity, and there were few direct translations of the holy words used in connection with it. Yet he was supposed to explain the Gospel to the Inca.

Pizarro sent a small detachment of his followers toward Quito under the command of Soto, with the chronicler Estete and three other conquistadors. The aim of this little expedition was to see if Rumiñavi was really on his way with an army toward Cajamarca.[27]

These adventurers would soon return with the news that there were no signs whatever of Rumiñavi being on the move. But in their absence, the rumors of Atahualpa's "rebellion" grew in intensity. Almagro made no bones about being in favor of killing Atahualpa. Would this not be the easiest way out of the dilemma? But the Inca argued that the Spaniards were behaving foolishly, for there was not an Indian in the country whom they could hope to manage without his assistance. Since he, the Inca, was their prisoner, what did they fear? If the Spaniards were motivated by a desire for more gold (and Almagro, having been left out of the division of April, certainly was), he would give them twice what they had already received. Pedro Pizarro says that Atahualpa saw the governor (that is how Francisco Pizarro was now always designated) weep: He could not give Atahualpa his life, because he could neither be guarded indefinitely nor released.[28]

The Inca submitted to a trial of a sort. Pizarro and Almagro were the judges. Sancho de Cuéllar, presumably a member of that astonishing family of conquistadors from the city of Diego Velázquez, was the notary. Atahualpa was then condemned to death by Pizarro, who, allegedly against his will, commanded that he should be killed by the garrote. After his death, his body was to be burned.[29]

The Spaniards were divided about the wisdom of the sentence. At least fifty expeditionaries were hostile. Some of them had wanted the clever young lawyer Juan de Herrera as Atahualpa's advocate.

Atahualpa heard his sentence with resignation. He was told by the priest Valverde of the inestimable benefits he would encounter in Heaven, and how he would save his soul for eternity if he was to ask to be received as a Christian.

On July 26, 1533, Atahualpa was brought into the center of the same main square of Cajamarca where he had been captured the previous year. Trumpets greeted him, and he was tied to a stake. Valverde briefly instructed him in the articles of the Christian faith. The Inca then formally requested baptism, which was administered to him by Valverde, who named him Francisco.[30] Then he was garroted. Pedro Pizarro explained that Atahualpa had told his wives and other Peruvians that if he was not burned, he would eventually return to them. He left his small sons to be looked after by Pizarro. Afterwards, two of Atahualpa's sisters "went about giving utterance to lamentations accompanied by the beating of drums and by singing and by accounts of their royal husband-brother." They explained to Pedro Pizarro that since the Inca had not been burned, he would return to them. Pedro Pizarro told them that the dead do not return: "They wailed till all the *chicha* was drunk."[31] Almagro's priest, Fray Morales, presided and took off Atahualpa's headband indicating royalty.

Pizarro organized a solemn funeral. The Inca was buried in the newly built church of Cajamarca. But the manner of his death excited an immediate argument. Soto, for example, when he returned from his journey to

Quito, was furious that such an important decision should have been carried out in his absence. He said that he thought the dead emperor should have been sent alive to the emperor Charles. Espinosa, the clever governor in Panama, later wrote that the Inca's guilt should have been established clearly before he was killed. He thought that it would have been better if he had been exiled to another Spanish territory: Panama, for example, where he could have been treated as if he had been a great noble of Castile.[32] Others thought that it would have been easier to convert Peru to Christianity if the Inca had not been killed—if, indeed, his baptism had not been accompanied by the execution. Later, too, the emperor Charles wrote to Pizarro: "We note what you say about the execution of the cacique Atahualpa." Charles accepted that Atahualpa had probably ordered a hostile mobilization. Nevertheless, he wrote: "We have been displeased by the death of Atahualpa since he was a monarch and particularly since it was done in the name of justice."[33]

22

News of Peru

I reached this port of Sanlúcar today, Wednesday, January 14, from New Castile which is the land which Francisco Pizarro conquered on behalf of Your Majesty. I have to inform Your Majesty of what has been done in that country to serve you. I bring for Your Majesty your share, some 100,000 castellanos [of gold] and five million of silver.

HERNANDO PIZARRO

In the winter of 1533 to 1534, the standing of the Spanish empire in the New World had at first seemed low in comparison with Naples, the Netherlands, and Milan. Charles the Emperor and King was, however, in Monzón in December with the *cortes* of Aragon, which always met in that remote valley. The meeting lasted so long that neither King nor court could leave till the last day of the year.

The Council of the Indies told the Emperor that, in La Española, the reinvigorated Fray Bartolomé de las Casas, now an active Dominican, was refusing absolution to *encomenderos* on grounds of their heretical status. He was emerging from several years of retreat in his monastery.

They also informed Charles that Las Casas had persuaded a colonist on his deathbed to leave his goods to the Indians as restitution for past wrongs. In Cuba, there was a rising of black slaves in the region of Bayamo. In New Spain, the supreme court was in control, for a viceroy had not been named. The condition of the new realm was much superior to what it had been under Guzmán, and there was a large Spanish population, but it was difficult to imagine the place's future.

Some aggressive expeditions were still proceeding. For example, in October 1533, Jerónimo Dortal, veteran of Ordaz's journey on the Orinoco, who had up till then been responsible for a small stretch of the coast of Venezuela, filled three ships with men in Spain, and with horses and weapons bought in the Canaries, and set out, aiming to pass by the Gulf of Paria and, first sailing up the Orinoco, reach the extraordinary river Meta. Dortal was convinced that this was the route to the world of gold that he thought of as El Dorado.[1]

Spain was then stirred into a new mood of enthusiasm for the Indies by the unexpected arrival in Seville of the *nao María del Campo,* owned by Soto and Hernán Ponce de León, with Hernando Pizarro on board. On January 9, 1534, Cieza the chronicler, still a boy, saw many pieces of gold and silver being unloaded from that ship on the Arenal, outside the city. Cobos ordered the Casa de la Contratación to impound all the gold and silver. Hernando is said to have brought 153,000 pesos of gold and 5,048 marks of silver for the King alone. Private conquistadors sent back 310,000 pesos. In fact, between the end of 1533 and the middle of 1534, ships arriving in Seville brought nearly 800,000 pesos in gold and nearly 50,000 marks in silver belonging to the Crown or to private persons.[2] Hernando went to Toledo taking samples of his gold and silver jewelry, also some unusual animals such as llamas, and even nuggets of gold. He met the emperor Charles and the court, first at Calatayud. The King and Cobos ordered all the jewels to be melted down. Hernando expostulated. Charles agreed to exhibit the treasure for some weeks but no longer.[3]

Henceforth the magic glint of Peruvian treasure lit the imagination of King, courtiers, and common people. There was a general disposition to believe all that was said of the New World. One historian wrote that if seventy ships had arrived at Laredo with ten thousand Amazons on board, to seek fathers for their children to whom they would give 50 ducats, with the girls being sent back to the New World, the boys to stay in Spain, the tale would have been believed. Meanwhile, the treasure of the Pizarros was looked after by two faithful friends, Martín Alonso and Juan Cortés. In 1534, two new famous chivalric novels, *Lidamor de Escocia,* by Juan de Córdoba, and *Tristan el joven,* by María Luzdivina Cuesta Torre, were published in Castile. It was not easy to distinguish what was said in those books from what was reported by Hernando Pizarro, whose account was, if anything, the more unbelievable. Hernando asked the King many things for his brother, for example (an echo of what had been granted to Cortés), the service of twenty thousand Indians for himself and his descendants in perpetuity, and the title of Marquess, without it being evident of what place exactly he was to be such.[4]

Charles the Emperor was preparing in Barcelona for the conquest of Algiers. This expedition would not have been possible if the monarch had not received so much gold from Peru. For example, twenty-two cartloads of gold arrived in Barcelona from Seville on April 29, and twenty mules came heavily laden on May 22. The Genoese bankers who had advanced credit were also repaid in American gold. The consequence was that the expedition to Algiers was the most impressive ever mounted by the Christian powers in the western Mediterranean.

The Emperor's brother, Ferdinand, the ruler of Austria, always interested in the Indies, was given a silver nugget worth 212 castellanos by Cobos the same year.[5] The penniless courtier Enríquez de Guzmán, who set out from Sanlúcar for the Indies in September 1533, was suddenly supposed to have made for the first time a wise decision.[6]

Those were the years, too, when Mercator was busy sketching his idea of a new printed terrestrial globe—his intention was to "publish a globe or sphere of the whole world on which the recently discovered islands and lands will be added."[7] The cosmographers would be protected from copyists. To fulfill his charter's instruction, Mercator had to make a sphere the likes of which nobody at court would have seen before, a globe of exquisite beauty crammed with the latest geographical data, new coastlines, hundreds of place-names, even stars.

The new enthusiasm for the Peruvian adventure was not confined to the mother country. The news shook the Caribbean, too. Antonio López wrote that Yucatán was emptying because of the news from Peru. Officials in Puerto Rico explained that the news was so extraordinary that even men of fifty who had settled down to their modest *encomiendas,* as if their highest lot was indeed to plant the bergamot, became suddenly restless. In Santa Marta, the governor, García de Lerma, wrote that "the greed of Peru was gripping everyone." Greed was to be found in Spain also. Thus Hernando Pizarro was allowed by the royal officials to take some of the pieces that he had brought for Charles V to see. But the latter soon confirmed the order to smelt down almost everything.[8]

The Council of the Indies proclaimed that no one could leave for Peru unless he was a substantial merchant or a married man ready to take his wife with him.[9] But this rule was of no avail. No one obeyed it.

Among the most restless was Pedro de Alvarado, the second-in-command of Cortés in New Spain, now the governor of Guatemala, who had been told by a friend of his, García Holguín, that the possibilities for enrichment in Peru were limitless. Alvarado was quick to take action and, by January 23, 1534, he had gathered an expedition that he hoped would share in the pleasures of the great Peruvian adventure. He left La Posesión, his estate in Guatemala, with twelve ships, on which he planned to carry five hundred Spaniards from his province, including 119 horsemen and one hundred crossbowmen, to sail down the west coast of Central America to Peru. He was also said to have carried several thousand Indians from Guatemala. His chief pilot was a typical seaman of that day, Juan Fernández, who combined low birth, illiteracy, and intelligence. He had earlier been "captain-master" to the Pizarros on their galleon the *San Cristóbal*.[10]

Alvarado also took Fray Marcos de Niza as his chief chaplain, an intelligent Franciscan who had been born in Nice and who had already interested himself in learning several native languages. He had been in Santo Domingo and Nicaragua before joining Alvarado in Guatemala. This expedition landed in Ecuador in late January 1534.

By then the condition of the old Peruvian kingdom had fundamentally changed. First, the people of Cajamarca had been the witnesses of the coronation of a new Inca, Tupac Huallpa, a younger brother of Huascar and Atahualpa, in that same main square of the town where the latter had died. Under the patronage of Francisco Pizarro and his brothers, the chiefs of the country assembled in white plumes. A great feast followed, accompanied by singing, dancing, and drinking of *chicha* on an epic scale. Francisco Pizarro wore a white silk shirt, the Spanish royal standard was raised, and the Requirement was read out by Fray Valverde.

Then on August 11, Pizarro had led the main body of his followers from Cajamarca on the way to Cuzco. Almagro accompanied him, the force totaling perhaps 350.[11] This included most of Almagro's men. It also included, as a captive, the Inca general Chalcuchima. A few Spaniards were left behind to maintain the royal presence in Cajamarca.

Pizarro's journey was by Cajabamba, Huamachuco, and the valley of Huaylas where, on August 31, they crossed a gorge using one of the Incas' best suspension bridges. Pedro Sancho de Hoz, a notary whom Pizarro had named as his secretary, described how the bridge trembled and how the horses were afraid, as indeed were some of the conquistadors. They waited a little more than a week at this bridge to ensure the passage of the entire expedition and the equipment. They then marched on to Recuay, below Mount Huascarán, and continued, via Jauja and Bombón, on Lake Chinancocha.

Pizarro divided his army. He decided himself to press ahead to Cuzco with seventy-five to a hundred horse and thirty foot, a force that included Almagro, Juan and Gonzalo Pizarro, Soto, and Candía, as well as the well-guarded Chalcuchima; and he left behind the artillery with the infantry, the tents, and such treasure as they had obtained on the journey. The command of this latter reserve force would lie with the royal treasurer, Riquelme.

Pizarro was no horseman, but he survived well enough in this new venture all the same. A local Indian commander killed several of his rivals, Pedro Pizarro reported, by making these leaders put stones on their heads, which were then hit by another stone, so flattening the heads "as if they were *tortillas*."[12] There was a skirmish with Indians, when the Spanish advantage in weapons (swords, steel-tipped lances, armor, horses) as usual told against the Peruvians' superiority in numbers and local knowledge backed by slings with stones, javelins, maces, and stone clubs. Just short of the settlement known as Bombón, Riquelme founded a city, at Jauja, with an initial establishment of eighty citizens from men of his command. He had with him the new Inca, Tupac Huallpa, but that prince died there—poisoned by Chalcuchima, according to the Inca's friends. The inhabitants there were busy hunting down the followers of Atahualpa.[13]

Pizarro's journey was a remarkable one. True, he took the route to Cuzco of his brother Hernando earlier in the year, and some who had been with Hernando accompanied Francisco. They crossed magnificent wild land and came to several fine bridges. Pedro Sancho de Hoz recalled a stop at Parcos at the summit of an extraordinary mountainside. From there Pizarro divided his men yet again, sending the best horsemen ahead under the resourceful Soto. He remained in a new rearguard with Almagro, Pedro Sancho de Hoz, and Miguel de Estete. But the small Spanish force was now strung out over two hundred miles in four groups, scarcely a wise disposition.

Soto had been determined to be the first Spaniard of the new expedition to enter Cuzco. Pedro Pizarro said that he had "the evil intention" of doing this.[14] But to accomplish his aim, he had to cross the canyon of the Apurímac where, at Vilcaconga, he was attacked and nearly destroyed by an Indian army under Quizquiz, who had by then learned much about Spanish tactics. The Spaniards lost five men immediately.[15] They would have been in grave difficulties had it not been for the arrival of reinforcements under Almagro. His trumpeter Alconchel cheered them greatly with his horn as it re-sounded, like that of Roland, across the high valleys. This was the most serious battle that the Spaniards had had to fight since the death of Atahualpa. (Alconchel had been one of Pizarro's recruits in Extremadura, though he came from La Garganta de Béjar, in the Sierra de Gredos.)

Pizarro had been encouraged by the discovery of several slabs of silver at Andahuaylas. "While I was looking for maize," wrote his page, Pedro Pizarro, "I entered by chance a hut where I found these slabs of silver . . . ten in number [with] a length of 20 feet each, a width of one foot and a thickness of three fingers. These had been intended to decorate a house for an idol named Chino."[16] Afterwards, Pizarro joined Almagro and Soto, and the reconstituted Spanish force of 350 moved on to Jaquijahuana (now Anta) about twenty miles from Cuzco. Here on the Apurímac River, the Pizarros were greeted by Manco Capac, the youngest brother of Huascar and Atahualpa.[17] This Prince gave Francisco Pizarro a golden shirt. He gave also a vivid, but surely inaccurate, commentary on the cruelties practiced by Atahualpa. This new friendship enabled Pizarro to enter the city of Cuzco with Manco Capac at his side. He imaginatively told Manco that he had come to Peru for no other purpose "than to free you from the slavery of the men of Quito."

Atahualpa's general Quizquiz remained a threat. When Pizarro saw smoke rising in the distance, he sent horsemen forward to prevent any destruction before he reached the capital. There was a brief skirmish between Quizquiz and Pizarro. The two armies rested at night on two nearby hillsides, but the Indians lost heart, for at dawn, Quizquiz had disappeared. So on November 15, 1533, the Spaniards entered Cuzco without resistance and were well received by such authorities as were there.[18]

Cuzco, wrote Pizarro's page Pedro Pizarro, lay in a hollow between two ravines through which two brooks ran, though one, which passed through the central plaza, had only a very little water. The city "was dominated by a strong fortress with terraces and flat places on top of a hill with two high round towers, surrounded by walls of stone so large that it seemed impossible that human hands could have set them in place . . . They were so well fitted together that the point of a pin could not be inserted into a joint." In this redoubt, ten thousand Indians could be concealed, the place being full of arms, lances, arrows, darts, and clubs, as well as helmets and shields. There were great labyrinths in this building which even Pedro Pizarro, who was there for months, never understood completely.[19] Pizarro's secretary, Sancho de Hoz, thought Cuzco "so grand and beautiful that it would be worthy of being seen even in Spain since it is filled with palaces of lords. No poor people live there . . . the majority of the houses are of stone. The houses are made with great symmetry."[20] Cieza de León recorded: "In all Spain I have seen nothing which can compare with these walls and the laying of their stone."[21]

The journey of the Spaniards, said Murúa, had not been very interesting![22] All the same, they now quartered themselves in old Inca palaces with vast halls, central courtyards, and impressive stone walls. Francisco Pizarro, for example, established himself in the onetime Casana palace of the Inca Huayna Capac, which Garcilaso said was capable of holding three thousand people. Soto took over the palace of Amarucancha, a building of red, white, and multicolored marble, with two towers and a large, beautiful thatched hall. The young Gonzalo Pizarro took the house of the Inca Yupanqui, while Almagro selected the newest Huascar palace. Valverde, the chaplain of the expedition, installed himself in the palace of Suntur Huasi, which eventually became the site of the new Spanish cathedral. All these leaders collected a great deal of treasure in these edifices, this time more silver than gold.[23] Looting and ravaging were on a large scale.[24]

The temple of the sun at Coricancha would eventually become the Dominican convent. But the palaces of Hatun Cancha, Hatun Rumiyoc, and Pucamara became the stables for the Spanish cavalry.

Pizarro proclaimed Cuzco a Spanish city, but he accepted Manco Inca as the ruler of the empire. He encouraged the Inca to found an army to defeat Quizquiz. After a few weeks, he had assembled what was said to have been five thousand men, who, with the troubleshooter of Spain, Hernando de Soto, soon set off to look for Quizquiz. They were actually in the wild country of Condesuyos, on the Apurímac, but the rebellious general seems

to have been depressed by this third failure to defeat the Spaniards and retreated toward Quito, leaving Pizarro in control of Cuzco and its surroundings.[25]

The next manifestation of Spanish power was a denunciation of Chalcuchima by Pizarro, who thought him responsible for the continued rest-
lessness of the Indians. Manco Capac supported this theory: He asserted
that Chalcuchima had told Quizquiz details of Spanish planning for fighting. He had certainly told Quizquiz that the Spaniards were mortal, and
that they were wont to dismount in bad passes and even to hand their
lances to their servants to be carried. At such places, their horses tired.
So, he said, they should be attacked there. Manco Capac handed over
to Pizarro three messengers who, he alleged, had taken this news to Quizquiz. Pizarro denounced Chalcuchima, who denied any such contact. But
Pizarro believed, probably rightly, that he was lying, and Chalcuchima was
accordingly burned to death in the main square of Cuzco. Valverde failed to
persuade him to become a Christian first and so be killed without pain.[26]

An early ceremony in the square at Cuzco was the coronation there of
Manco Capac as Inca, at the end of December 1533. There was the usual
ceremony of a parade of mummies, a feast, and much singing and dancing
over thirty days, and drums were heard throughout the city at night. The
Spaniards were astounded at the drinking by both men and women, that
resulted in two large drains running with urine throughout the day for a
week.[27] This coronation was more traditional and more elaborate than that
of the shortlived Inca Tupac Huallpa at Cajamarca, and it lasted much
longer. Pizarro used the occasion once again by ordering Pedro Sancho de
Hoz to read out the Requirement, the Inca implying that he had understood. Manco Capac drank from a golden cup with Pizarro. He also
brought out all the bodies of his ancestors on litters. Once again, the
Spaniards raised their now-famous standard and greeted it with trumpets.
The Peruvians sang songs, which, among other things, expressed their grat-
itude to the Spaniards for expelling their Atahualpine enemies. Manco
Capac, though he asked for the return of his empire, said that he was entirely happy to let the Spanish priests preach Christianity. Pizarro heard
what Manco Capac said and implored him to wear the traditional scarlet
fringe of the Inca for the ceremony in order to show that he accepted the
new order of things.[28]

This kind of festival was a characteristic of the life of the nobility (*ore-jones*). There were sometimes festivals with fasting, which meant doing without salt, garlic, and *chicha,* not to speak of walks to see the god Guanacaure, an idol of stone, who was worshipped a mile and a half outside the city. Meantime, porters were placed on the main roads outside Cuzco to prevent thefts of gold and silver. Pedro Pizarro described how there were large storehouses for tribute above the city: "all in such vast quantities that is hard to imagine how the natives can ever have paid such tribute on so many items."[29]

Diego de Trujillo, one of Pizarro's most dedicated followers, reported that the priests at the temple of Coricancha reproached him and other Spaniards. "How dare you enter here?" they demanded. Trujillo explained: "Anyone who enters here has to fast for a year beforehand, and must enter barefoot, and bear a load; but we Spaniards paid no attention to what was said and went in."[30]

Pizarro embarked on a division of the spoils of the city of Cuzco. He sought to do this in an orderly manner, as usual reserving a fifth of the treasure for the Crown, which was accumulated in a shed attached to the palace that he had seized, where it was listed by Diego Narváez.

The melting down began on December 15, 1533. Pizarro authorized new gold and silver marks. The value of the treasure seized in Cuzco was even more in aggregate than that which had been gathered for Atahualpa's ransom at Cajamarca. The temple of the sun had lost a great deal of gold for Atahualpa's ransom, but there was still much there. The conquistadors with Pizarro were astonished at other vast storehouses of several generations' collections of cloaks, weapons, feathers, sandals, knives, beans, shields, and cloth. But the golden image of the sun itself that had been in that edifice was lost forever.[31] Still, there was plenty of gold left, and many storehouses were found with fine clothing, coarser clothes, wheat, coca, sunflowers that looked like pure gold, very slender feathers grown on the breasts of small birds ("hardly larger than a cicada," reported Pedro Pizarro), mantles with mother-of-pearl spangles, sandals, copper bars, golden slippers, lobsters and spiders made of gold, and pitchers of both pottery and gold.

The coronation of Manco Capac was the signal for the establishment of large *encomiendas* for the conquistadors in or attached to Cuzco. The

conquistadors of Cajamarca—"first conquerors," as they were known—
occupied all the municipal offices. Sometimes they received huge benefits. In Cuzco, where there were to be over eighty *encomiendas* in a few
years, no one received fewer than five thousand vassals; one received
forty thousand.[32]

These dispositions affected Jauja as well as Cuzco. But the former was
threatened by Quizquiz and his alarmingly itinerant army. So Soto and Almagro went back to save that staging point, as well as the lives of the treasurer Riquelme and his eighty or so men. This relief traveled slowly because
Quizquiz had cut many essential bridges. But before Soto and Almagro arrived, Jauja and Riquelme were relieved by two thousand Huanca Indians
who were hostile to Atahualpa and the men of Quito. Still, one Spaniard
was killed and almost all the others were wounded, Riquelme included.

Other unexpected help was afforded by Gabriel de Rojas, an old hand
in Pedrarias's Nicaragua. Rojas also brought the news, both alarming and
encouraging, to Pizarro's expedition that Pedro de Alvarado, with his large
army, had landed at Puerto Viejo, in what is now Ecuador, and was striking
up toward Quito.[33]

Benalcázar, at San Miguel, was the most disturbed of Pizarro's men at
this news since he was the commander closest to Alvarado. He had his own
plans for the conquest of Quito, which—quite without foundation—was
assumed to be very rich. Benalcázar made his own decision and set out
from San Miguel for Quito with two hundred experienced foot and sixty-
two horse. The Indians were far from quiescent, however, and Atahualpa's
general Rumiñavi headed a powerful army against Benalcázar.[34] Once
again, Indian allies—in this case, Cañari Indians—made a major contribution to the Spanish cause.[35] Benalcázar skillfully forced Rumiñavi to a
pitched battle at Teocajas on May 3, 1534, in open land where his well-led
cavalry could act much as it wished. Rumiñavi had upset what remained of
the Inca upper class by drugging them and then killing their children. He
had women in Quito burned alive for laughing when he described the
Spaniards' codpieces.[36] Oviedo reported that fifty thousand Indians took
part in the many efforts to trick the Spanish horses—traps for horses to fall
into, for example. Despite such attacks, Benalcázar's Spaniards reached
Quito on June 22. He was disappointed since Rumiñavi had already seized
such treasure as there was in the city. He had kidnapped surviving mem-

bers of Atahualpa's family and what was said to have been several thousand other women. He sought to set fire to Quito after he had left it.

Benalcázar conducted himself with his usual ruthlessness. He killed all the women at the village of Quinche, where the men of military age were with Rumiñavi. He was also joined by Almagro, who, though he criticized Benalcázar for leaving San Miguel, was pleased that he had conquered Quito and had done so in his, Almagro's, name, as well as that of Pizarro.

Shortly after, Benalcázar was joined by yet a third conquistador army, that of Alvarado, which had passed through jungle and across mountains with great difficulty, due to a shortage of food and because of the cold in the high Andes. The coastal Indians whom Alvarado had assembled died in great numbers. Alvarado's cruelty to the Indians whom he encountered was legendary, for they "repeatedly tortured Indians in order to be informed of the route."[37]

Alvarado was eventually faced by Almagro. For a time, there was a risk of a battle between the two Spanish armies at Riobamba. But a prolonged discussion convinced Alvarado that he would be unable to prosper, much less emerge as a leading captain, in Peru, which was so much better known by Almagro, the Pizarros, and Benalcázar. Much to the surprise of his fellow Spaniards, Alvarado agreed to sell his ships and artillery to the Pizarros for 100,000 castellanos. He would himself go back to Guatemala, but his men would remain in Peru under the command of Almagro and Pizarro. An agreement to this end was reached on August 26, 1534. The two captains then went to Quito, where with Benalcázar they founded a new Spanish city.

Almagro and Alvarado thereupon left to see Pizarro. On the way, they encountered Quizquiz, the morale of whose army collapsed when he heard that Quito was lost. There was a mutiny, and Quizquiz was killed by one of his own captains. Benalcázar forced Quizquiz's ex-rival Rumiñavi to take up a fortified position near Pillaro. There the Indians soon dispersed after they had exhausted their supply of missiles. Rumiñavi was betrayed to Benalcázar, whose captains captured him. A third Peruvian commander was captured on the mountainside and executed in Quito's main square with Rumiñavi.

Alvarado met Pizarro at Pachacamac. After friendly embraces, Pizarro gave Alvarado the promised 100,000 castellanos for his ships and his guns, and offered places to Alvarado's men in his army. Several of Alvarado's relations remained with Pizarro. These included his brother, Gómez de Alvarado, who had fought all the way through the campaign in New Spain, and García and Alonso, his nephews. Alonso would play a large part in the politics and combats of Peru in the future. Alvarado then returned to Guatemala after confessing a failure of the first magnitude. It was not something to which the "Son of the Sun" was accustomed. "What a disgrace for the Alvarados!" commented his cousin Diego, who had been his camp master.

In Peru, the allocation of gold and silver continued. Many poor conquistadors became newly rich entrepreneurs overnight. Thus, in Cuzco in March 1534, a quantity of silver estimated to be four times what had been distributed in Cajamarca was allocated by Pizarro with the help of Valverde, according to their judgment of each soldier's merits, extra shares being given to those who seemed to deserve it. Those who had remained in Jauja and who had returned with Benalcázar to San Miguel were included. These decisions were generally accepted as fair by the conquistadors: Francisco Pizarro was even recognized as being just by the Spaniards.

Pizarro also went ahead in March 1534 with a ceremony refounding Cuzco as a Spanish city. He divided it among eighty-eight of his soldiers, naming two of them magistrates and eight councillors. Each soldier would have the ample provision of a length of two hundred feet of housing in a street of the city. The founding documents insisted that the Indians should be treated as "brothers" because they were descended from "our first ancestors."[38] Manco Capac was to be recognized as the leader of the Indians. Pizarro went through the motions of building a city wall and a church from existing material taken from unoccupied palaces and warehouses. At the same time, he ordered the Spaniards to stop asking the Indians anymore for gold and silver, for he now believed that, if they were continually refused, they could be tempted to rebel.

Pizarro and Manco Capac set off back to Jauja, on the way to Cajamarca. The former had the idea to found another Spanish city there. He left his brother Juan Pizarro, then twenty-four years of age, as the acting governor in Cuzco. The Indians would have Paullu Inca as their leader in Manco Capac's absence; he was a member of the royal family, who had decided almost immediately that collaboration with the conquerors was not only desirable but essential.

Francisco Pizarro did establish Jauja as a Spanish city on April 25, 1534. He distributed the property among fifty-three Spaniards who had been there a year by the chance of having been left in the place by Pizarro on his first outward journey to Cuzco.

Pizarro went on in August 1534 to the ancient site of Pachacamac to seek the Indian treasure said to have been hidden there. On his way back, he saw Indian porters struggling to carry European supplies up to the con-quistadors in Cuzco. There and then he decided to move the capital to the coast. It was a decision of genius. He discussed the idea in Jauja and se-lected a point named Lima, at the mouth of the river Rímac. To begin with, it was known as Ciudad de los Reyes (City of the Kings), because it was founded soon after Epiphany, January 6, 1535.

At the same time, the governor gave a general license to Spaniards to leave Peru. About sixty conquistadors availed themselves of the opportu-nity to return: They did so as rich men, for some went back with 40,000 pesos, none with less than 20,000.[39] Their return journey was in some cases a triumphal progress, for some stopped in the isthmus or at one or other of the Caribbean islands. With their golden jars and figurines, they dazzled those whom they met, and their stones filled many in those places "with [a desire for] fame and wealth."[40] Admittedly, their money was usually held by the Casa de la Contratación in Seville for a time, and the returning mil-lionaire would be allocated an annuity (*juro*), which would give an income. The negotiation of that might oblige the returning adventurer to spend several months in Seville. He would probably obtain a coat of arms. Then he would return to his old home, where he might live very well. Take the case of Juan Ruiz de Arce in Alburquerque. Twelve squires served him at his table, and he had also pages, lackeys, black slaves, and horses. He had splen-did tableware. When he went hunting, he took many horsemen and gave them dogs, falcons, hawks.[41] Ruiz de Arce reported after meeting the Em-press: "She received us very well, thanking us for the services we had ren-dered, and offering to reward us; and so great was her kindness that anything we wished was given to us and there was not one disappointed man among us. . . . There were twelve of us conquistadors in Madrid and we spent a great deal of money."[42] This was a major change from all other fortunes made in the New World. Few had returned rich from New Spain. Indeed, nearly all of Cortés's followers remained in the country that they had conquered.

Pizarro now considered that his conquest of the Inca empire was complete. He had contrived an excellent friendship with Manco Capac. The surviving Indian noblemen and the conquistadors who had decided to remain in Peru shared a great hunt in honor of Pizarro: Ten thousand Indians took part as beaters or hunt advisers, and eleven thousand animals (vicuña, guanaco, roe deer, fox, puma) were killed.[43]

The Spaniards who had taken part in this extraordinary conquest were amazed at what they had done. They could not imagine how they could still be alive or how they had survived such hardships as they had suffered. How could they have survived such long periods of hunger?

The Inca world was never integrated into the political theory of Europe. The Inca was definitely a monarch, but he was not seen as such by the officials or philosophers of the Old World. The only person to see the Inca in imperial terms seems to have been Charles V, who did make a comparison between monarchs of the Old World and those of the new one. There are, however, no allusions to the emperors of the Mexica or to the Inca in European theoretical discussions of monarchy.

23

The Battle for Cuzco

My sons and brothers! We are going to ask whom we regard as children of our god Viracocha for justice, for they entered our country declaring that their main purpose was to dispense justice all over the world.

GARCILASO DE LA VEGA

The conquest of Peru was complete. But the ambitions of the conquerors had not all, by any means, been resolved. Almagro in particular had to be satisfied. That was one of the matters that Hernando Pizarro tried to settle in Spain. On May 21, 1534, a contract (*capitulacíon*) signed by the Council of the Indies granted Almagro the right to assume the government of two hundred leagues (six hundred miles) of territory to the south of Pizarro's Peru. He would have the titles of governor and *adelantado* of those lands as well as chief magistrate, and he would be captain-general there—not only himself, but his heirs.[1]

This contract, in effect, made Almagro the conquistador of Chile. Chile was believed at that time likely to be as rich as Peru, if not richer. But the geographical boundary of the grant was unclear. How far inland did it stretch? Where exactly did the two hundred leagues begin? The contract spoke of the lands and provinces that were on the coast of the Southern Sea to the south, "those 200 leagues beginning from the limits of the government which had been entrusted to Francisco Pizarro." Hernando Pizarro figured in the contract as the representative of Almagro. This must have seemed inappropriate to anyone who knew them both, since Hernando always spoke critically of Almagro.[2]

There was one particular uncertainty in the contract of Almagro, and that was the place of Cuzco in Spanish official thinking. It was so far to the south that it could be argued, as Almagro would, that it was in his zone. But Pizarro had conquered it. So it surely was his to exploit.

In the meantime, Almagro, who had been a difficult ally in Cuzco, set off for Chile in July 1535. He took with him nearly six hundred Spanish foot, one thousand Indian auxiliaries, and one hundred black slaves.[3] Pizarro gave financial backing, perhaps made possible because he had re-opened the furnaces in Cuzco to enable him to accumulate more gold and silver. Almagro also took with him Paullu Inca, the representative of the Inca collaborators in Cuzco and a high priest of the Peruvians, whom the Spaniards called Villac Umu. The Spaniards included most of those whom Almagro had himself brought to Peru, such as the converso Rodrigo Orgóñez, a fine horseman who had fought in Italy, perhaps even at the battle of Pavia, before coming to the Indies in the 1520s. Soto had offered himself in that place, but Almagro preferred Orgóñez, who was more of a friend. There were also most of the better-known men in Alvarado's expedition who had stayed on in Peru, such as Juan de Saavedra of Seville and Alvarado's brother Gómez, that other conquistador of New Spain.

This army made heavy weather of the long journey to central Chile, but eventually Almagro established himself in the fertile valley of Aconcagua. Thence Almagro sent off several secondary expeditions, such as that of Saavedra, who went to the bay of Valparaíso, where he laid the foundations of a city, and that of Gómez de Alvarado, who went even farther south, to the valley of the Maipo. How wonderful it was for Spain to discover such fertile agricultural land, and so beautiful, too! But these conquistadors had eyes only for precious metals, of which Paullu Inca alone knew the whereabouts.

Some months after he had reached Aconcagua, Almagro was reinforced by Ruy Díaz and Juan Herrada, accompanied by about a hundred Spaniards and a large number of Indian bearers. Díaz had come to Peru with Almagro, and Herrada was a Navarrese who had been with Cortés in Higueras. He had been so much in Cortés's confidence that he had gone on his behalf to Rome in 1529 to present the pope with gifts from the New World.[4] Then he went to Panama and to Peru with Almagro, to whom he became majordomo.

Herrada brought more than just much needed reinforcement. He brought a document, which was the contract (*capitulación*) between the Crown and Almagro about his territory to the south of Pizarro's realm. Almagro and his friends studied this carefully—though since the former could not read, he had to rely on the reading aloud of Ruy Díaz and others. These conquistadors, none of them men favored by Pizarro, were ambitious and wanted much more wealth than they had obtained. They painfully read through the twenty-five paragraphs of the document, which they believed gave Almagro control not just over the happy valleys of Chile, where anyone could see that good wine could be produced, but over Cuzco, too, where gold and silver could be found in such quantity.[5] Almagro's advisers urged Almagro to return to Cuzco "and govern." That is precisely what he decided to do.[6]

Francisco Pizarro passed much of early 1535 planning his new capital, Lima, La Ciudad de los Reyes. The city was beautifully laid out, with a large square in the center surrounded by fine cool houses, but it had a hot, damp climate, which made it more unhealthy than distant Cuzco, about three hundred miles away, where Soto, Pizarro's man of all work, had been dispatched as lieutenant governor. Pizarro himself gave the impression now of being a retired peaceful proconsul concerned with urban planning.[7] He had a well-established household, his mistress, Doña Inés Yupanqui, previously known as Quispe Sisa, a half sister of Atahualpa, having given him in late 1534 a daughter, Francisca. He was, naturally, busy apportioning *encomiendas.*

About one thousand miles to the north, a great church of San Francisco, in Quito, would soon be built as a focal point for northern Peru, in the grounds of the palace of Huayna Capac. It was intended to be what it still is, a magnificent commemoration of a great religion. The architect was Fray Jodoko Ricke, the Peruvian counterpart of Pedro de Gante in New Spain. He was the counterpart in every sense for, like Pedro de Gante, he was also supposed to have Habsburg blood.

San Francisco would be Italianate in style. The exterior staircase was inspired by the palace of Nicholas V in the Vatican. It was one more sign that the Renaissance had reached Spanish America.

The construction of this building would take many years: The main cloister, in a very Andalusian style, was still being built in 1573; the church was only finished in 1575. Its elaborate façade would be the model for many others.[8] The towers were not complete till the eighteenth century. Like many Franciscan foundations, it was to be a place of education as well as prayer—a center of training for artisans as well as one of worship.

That autumn, Bishop Tomás de Berlanga noted these things in a detailed report as to how the Pizarros were coping with their mission.[9] Francisco Pizarro also faced several accusations of corruption and arrogance made by some of his collaborators.

Pizarro was visited by an old ally, Gaspar de Espinosa, who came down to Peru from Panama, age seventy, with his daughter and two hundred men.[10] He tried to act as peacemaker between Pizarro and Almagro.

The absence of Almagro did not bring Cuzco the peace that Pizarro might have expected. That was partly because Manco Capac had been flattered by Almagro, partly because of intrigues within the Inca family. Was Manco Capac really the right man for Peru in this perilous moment? Manco apparently persuaded a resourceful Basque, Martín Cote, to lead a Spanish gang to murder a cousin of his, Atoc-Sopa, who, some thought, had a good claim to Manco's position. Afterwards, Manco Capac hid in Almagro's house. Spanish followers of Pizarro are then supposed to have robbed Manco's own empty palace. Almagro complained, but Pizarro took no action. Cote then joined Almagro. Apparently, Almagro the commander asked him to guard Paullu Inca, who seemed now to be a dangerous element among Almagro's followers.[11]

The first months after Almagro left for Chile were relatively calm. Francisco Pizarro believed that he could safely leave Lima to found another Spanish city, to be called Trujillo, between Piura and Lima, about 250 miles to the north of the latter city.

Hernando de Soto meantime decided to return to Spain to seek a new, independent field of action for himself. He had been disappointed not to have been at least second-in-command on Almagro's journey to Chile, and indeed he would have liked the command itself. He is said to have offered Almagro 200,000 pesos for the post. But, thwarted, he packed up and returned to Seville, leaving behind his beautiful Peruvian mistress, Tocto Chimpu, daughter of Huascar, with her daughter by him, Leonor the mestiza.[12]

In these circumstances, the affairs of Cuzco were ruled by Juan Pizarro and his younger brother Gonzalo. Juan Pizarro had many qualities; Cieza, we remember, called him "the flower of all the Pizarros." Pedro Pizarro, the page, said of him that "he was valiant and very courageous, a good fellow, magnanimous and affable."[13]

Gonzalo Pizarro also began for the first time to make an impact on his fellow Spanish conquerors. The youngest of the Pizarro brothers, he was, as we have said, graceful, handsome, and well proportioned. He could read and write. He had a great capacity for camaraderie and for friendships. Garcilaso said of him, "His nature was so noble that he endeared himself to strangers."[14] But López de Gómara, Cortés's biographer and confessor, who did not know him personally, said that he was rather dull of understanding.[15] He did in these months achieve a new personality, and his magnetism played a major part in events. People were prepared to put all their hopes in him and look on him as their new start.

Late in 1535, Manco Capac began to be more restless under Spanish control. Perhaps things would have been different had he been looked after by men older than the young Pizarro brothers. But these Spaniards subjected him sometimes to mocking rudeness even though they permitted such gatherings as the eight days' festival of the sun—a great ceremony in which all the major figures of the Inca nobility were concerned. Fray Bartolomé de Segovia, an emissary of Alvarado to Pizarro, who was present, described how "they brought out all the effigies from the temples of Cuzco onto a plain just outside it, in the direction of where the sun came up. The richest effigies were put under finely worked feather canopies. When the sun rose, the Inca began to chant, there were offerings of meat which were consumed in a great fire, much *chicha* and coca were offered in sacrifice, llamas were let loose, and Manco broke the earth with a foot plow, so inaugurating the plowing season."[16]

Manco had decided on a radical uprising. He summoned a secret meeting of all Peruvian leaders, among them the chiefs of southern Callao. To them, Manco described the indignities that he had had to suffer. He determined to leave Cuzco immediately. But it was hard to keep a secret in old Peru. Servants (*yanaconas*) were present and informed Juan Pizarro of what was being planned. Manco Capac, it seemed, had already left in a litter. Riding hard, Juan and Gonzalo Pizarro caught up with him at night, and in the morning, they found him hiding in reeds near Lake Muyna.

They took him back to Cuzco in chains. Manco later accused some of the Spaniards of urinating on him, burning his eyelashes, and sleeping with his wives. All the accused men were strong supporters of the Pizarros and had been with the expedition from the beginning—indeed, all had been recruited by the governor in Spain in 1529. Probably they had been drunk when they were at their most offensive.[17]

This behavior, or the rumor of it, had its consequences. The only general of the Inca who remained was Tiso. He went to Riquelme's *encomienda* at Jauja, and to Bombón, and encouraged revolts by promises of advancement.

Hernando Pizarro had now returned to Peru after his journey to Spain. Apart from visiting Trujillo to see his family, he had done little after presenting his treasure, and himself, to the Emperor in 1534. He came back with two ships full of Spanish goods for profitable sale to his friends and his brother's men. He assumed, justifiably, the airs of a great general. In Cuzco, relations between the two peoples improved after his return as *corregidor*. He not only released Manco but showed him every possible kindness, partly because he had been asked to do so by the emperor Charles.[18] But all the same, the conduct of Spaniards toward Indian women continued to cause intense resentment among the male Indians, who saw the most attractive of their girls disappearing into Spanish households.

During Holy Week 1536, Indian resentment came to a head. On Holy Wednesday, Hernando Pizarro gave Manco Capac permission to accompany his best-known priest, Villac Umu, to perform religious ceremonies in the nearby Yucay valley. Manco promised to return with a large golden statue of Huayna Capac. In fact, he had gone for a final meeting to coordinate attacks by his followers against the Spaniards. He made what Murúa described as a "general appeal" to all the provinces of the Inca empire.[19] Perhaps he chose this moment knowing that both Francisco Pizarro and Soto were away.

On Easter Saturday, April 21, 1536, Hernando Pizarro was informed that a major revolt of Indians was now inevitable. He recognized his misjudgment in releasing Manco Capac and dispatched his brother Juan with seventy horsemen to disperse the Indians. Hernando rode out with his usual energy and found himself on top of the Yucay valley looking down on a colossal assembly of Indian warriors. Some chroniclers, Mena among them, speak of one hundred thousand Indians in the encampment.[20] Below, Villac Umu, a real warrior priest, was pressing for an immediate attack. But Manco wanted to wait till all his Indians had gathered. This did not prevent the latter doing whatever they could to murder any Spaniards whom they encountered on their way to or from their *encomiendas*. About thirty such were killed. They included Martín de Moguer, one of the first three Europeans to have seen Cuzco.

At the same time, Villac Umu occupied the fortress of Sacsahuamán overlooking the city and also destroyed Cuzco's irrigation canal. That action flooded the fields near the city as well as denied water to those in the city, including the Spaniards.

Faced with the likelihood of an immediate attack, Hernando prepared his defense as well as he could. He divided his cavalry into three bands of twenty-five men each, one commanded by his brother Gonzalo, one by Hernán Ponce de León, and another by Gabriel de Rojas—an Extremeño, a Sevillano, and a Castilian from Cuéllar. Hernando Pizarro himself, Juan Pizarro (taking the formal rank of *corregidor*), and the treasurer, Riquelme, remained at the center of the defense in the heart of Cuzco. In addition to approximately seventy-five horse, Spain had nearly two hundred foot. All withdrew to the main square of Cuzco, where, "owing to its great size, they could more easily dominate the enemy than in the [smaller side] streets . . . the infantry were in the middle and the cavalry stayed on each side."[21] But this must have seemed a tiny force in comparison with the vast horde of Indians. The infantry were under the direction of Alonso Enríquez de Guzmán, a new arrival from Spain, an experienced soldier though not as experienced as he made himself out to be in his engaging memoir. Thus a regular siege began, the Spaniards numbering a little fewer than two hundred, about half mounted.

The Indians, wrote Pedro Pizarro, held the Spaniards in the main square. The latter "obtained water from the stream which ran through that square and gained maize from the adjacent houses which they cheerfully sacked. Some Indians returned to their Indian masters by day but at night brought food to the Spaniards." The besiegers, however, "began to set fire to all parts of Cuzco, by which they gained many parts of the town [for] we Spaniards could not go out through them. We gathered . . . in the plaza and

in the houses adjoining it such as the Hatun Cancha. Here we were all collected, some [sleeping] in tents . . . To burn down the houses where we
were, [the Peruvians] took stones and threw them into a fire where they became red-hot. They wrapped these up in cotton and threw them by means
of slings into houses which they could not reach . . . Thus they burned our
houses without us knowing before we understood how . . . at other times
they shot flaming arrows at the houses which soon took fire."[22] Another report was even more vivid: "It looked as if a black cloth had been spread
over the ground for half a league round Cuzco . . . At night there were so
many fires that the scene looked like a very serene sky full of stars . . .
[with] much shouting and the din of voices."[23]

An early mounted counterattack was organized by the Castilian Gabriel
de Rojas. Though many Indians were killed, their numbers prevented any
continuing thrust, and several groups of cavalrymen were surrounded, one
such having to leave behind Francisco Mejía, another Extremeño, to be
killed with his horse.

The main Indian attack was on May 6. The Indians moved down the
narrow streets to occupy that part of Cuzco known as Cora Cora, which
overlooked the north corner of the main square, making a withering fire of
hot stones on two places held by the Spaniards: the hall of Subur Huasi, the
onetime palace of the Inca Viracocha and already the main church of the
city; and the Hatun Cancha, where many Spaniards had plots for their
town houses. But the Indians failed to burn the Spaniards' houses despite
their being roofed with straw. This failure they attributed to a decision of
the gods.

Garcilaso reported that the Spaniards were saved on this occasion by
Santiago himself on his usual white horse, but the chronicler Murúa insisted that that knight was the Basque Mancio Sierra de Leguizamón. He
reported, though, that the Virgin Mary did appear on this day in the sky,
dressed in a blue cloak.[24]

Despite this setback, the Indians captured nearly the entire city. The
Spaniards were left with little more than the main square and the houses
around it. The Indians were protecting themselves effectively by the pits
that they devised against the horses. They also used slings to good effect.
There were also *ayllus,* three stones tied to the ends of llamas' tendons,
which entangled horses' legs. Hernando Pizarro was advised by some of

his men to escape in the direction of Arequipa but he held on, partly persuaded that he had a chance of victory by using the Cañari Indians, the
old enemies of the Incas. Their assistance was essential in a night attack
on the wicker palisades behind which the Indians sheltered as they advanced.[25]

Comforted by this limited success, Hernando Pizarro instructed his
brother Juan to lead an attack on the fortress on Sacsahuamán, which, with
its polygonal masonry, dominated the city. Juan Pizarro advanced with
fifty horse, among them his brother Gonzalo, and about a hundred friendly
(Cañari) Indians. They decided to move on a night of full moon, when
they suspected that the Inca and his men would be celebrating. They faced
a fierce onslaught by stones from above as they went forward. Juan Pizarro
was wounded in the head, which made him unable to wear a helmet. He
then led a successful frontal attack. But he died in the effort, being again hit
on the head by a stone. Many were wounded. Hernando led a force scaling
up ladders at night, with Hernán Sánchez of Badajoz becoming the hero of
the battle, since he climbed steadily up a steep ascent. Alonso Enríquez de
Guzmán argued that 1,500 Indians were killed in this onslaught, including
one brave *orejón* who threw himself off the tower rather than surrender.
With fifty Spanish foot and a hundred Cañari Indians, Hernando Pizarro
garrisoned Sacsahuamán.

That commander wanted now to send fifteen cavalrymen to tell his
brother Francisco that the resistance was continuing in Cuzco. But those
horsemen requested that they not be sent since they considered that the
Spanish position could not be sustained without them. Thwarted of that
venture, Hernando decided to strike at Manco Capac's headquarters at Ollantaytambo in a fertile valley some fifty miles away. It had been an Inca
property of importance. It consisted of a series of residential structures and
a temple complex built round a large carved rock. It was surrounded by
terraces. There were canals.[26]

The Spaniards found this place well fortified and the Indians there well
supplied with stones to throw down at them, or to send down by sling.
Manco also had jungle bowmen from the other side of the Andes as allies.
Some Indians had learned by now how to use captured Castilian swords,
shields, even lances, culverins, and arquebuses. It was not that knowledge
that caused Hernando Pizarro to withdraw but the diversion by the Indi-

ans of the river Patacancha to flood the valley.[27] A smaller Spanish contingent, headed by Gonzalo Pizarro, routed another army of Indians, and Pedro Pizarro recalled rounding up two thousand llamas.

Still the fighting in Cuzco continued brutally, and the two sides were surprisingly unyielding. Alonso Enríquez de Guzmán commented: "This was the most dreadful and cruel war . . . Between Christians and Moors, there is usually some fellow feeling and it is in the interests of both sides to spare those whom they take alive, because of the ransom. But in this Indian war there is no such fellow feeling. We give each other the most cruel deaths we can imagine."[28] The Peruvian historian José Antonio Busto informs us that in this fighting about a thousand Spaniards died.[29]

In Lima, Francisco Pizarro learned quickly, through Indians, of the fighting in Cuzco, and he organized several relief expeditions: Thirty men were dispatched under Francisco Mogroviejo de Quiñones, seventy horse under Gonzalo de Tapia, a relation of the Pizarros, and sixty men under Diego Pizarro, another kinsman. He also recalled some of his captains from new expeditions. Pizarro also sent his half brother Francisco Martín de Alcántara to warn the Spanish settlers along the coast of the Indians' campaign. About 1,500 Spaniards altogether were isolated at different points in the vast territory of Ecuador-Peru. But all these cautions took time to be effective. In the meantime, the few Spaniards left in Jauja after the foundation of Lima had mostly been killed by Quizo Yupanqui, a new Peruvian commander. Smaller forces of Spanish fighters met similar ends: Thus the seventy horse under Gonzalo de Tapia were destroyed in a gorge on the upper river Pampas; Diego Pizarro was killed with sixty followers near the river Parcas; sixty horse led by Alonso de Gaeta and Francisco de Godoy y Aldana, an Extremeño from Cáceres, were defeated and nearly all killed. These were extremely difficult times for the Pizarro mission, comparable to the moment when Cortés had been forced in 1520 to withdraw at night in disorder from the Mexicas capital of Tenochtitlan.

Manco Capac wanted his new general Quizo to go on from Cuzco to Lima, not only to kill the Spaniards but to burn all their buildings. Only Francisco Pizarro would be spared, for Manco wanted him as a prisoner, for what disagreeable purpose one can only guess.

But the tide had turned. Quizo took his army to San Cristóbal, a hill overlooking Lima, where he was held by good Spanish cavalry tactics. Some Indians opposed to the Incas, not just the Cañari, fought well for Spain. Quizo inspired a general attack, promising his men that the fourteen or so women inside the city would be given to them—Indians all. But the Spanish cavalry killed that resilient commander, and the mountain Indians who had accompanied him felt ill at ease in the close climate of the coast. In any case, the coastal Indians could not make common cause with their comrades from the mountains. Divisions among the indigenous people were—as usual in the Americas—partly responsible for the natives' defeat.

Further assistance came to the Spaniards in Peru in late 1536 from an unexpected quarter. First Diego de Ayala of Toledo took a letter from Pizarro to Alvarado, of all people, appealing for his help. Hernán Cortés dispatched Rodrigo de Grijalva—probably a son of Grijalva, the second conquistador of New Spain—with a quantity of weapons, to Peru. Gaspar de Espinosa, the persistent governor of Panama, also sent supplies. Cortés himself would have liked to have gone to Peru, and he did what he could to arrange it.[30] The new president of the supreme court in Santo Domingo, Alonso de Fuentemayor, bishop, too, of that city, sent his brother Diego with a hundred cavalry and four hundred foot, following that with two hundred Spanish-speaking black Africans. The governor of Nicaragua sent his brother Pedro de los Ríos, with men, arms, and horses on a big ship. Juan de Berrio sent four shiploads in February 1537.[31] All this help was, however, slow to arrive and slower still to make any impact on events. Nor should we be in any doubt that the willingness of so many from elsewhere in the Americas to assist the Spanish mission in Peru derived from an expectation of gold as well as glory.

More significant perhaps than the promised reinforcements from abroad was the gathering of a new Spanish army led by Alonso de Alvarado, who had come back easily enough from his campaign against the Chachapoyas. Alonso de Alvarado had been among the many Alvarados who had arrived in Peru with his cousin Pedro in 1534 and who remained there when Pedro was bought off. His army probably amounted to 350 men, including one hundred horse and forty crossbowmen. He was challenged by a small Indian force led by Illa Tupac, of whom one hundred were captured. Alvarado had some of them killed, others mutilated. Two

Indian chiefs who hated the Inca were with him throughout, and they relished these cruelties. Gómez de Tordoya of Badajoz brought two hundred men to help him. They moved on slowly to Cuzco.

By the time they arrived, the situation had been transformed: Almagro was about to arrive on his return from Chile.

24

Almagro

Your lordship has let the bull loose. He will attack and kill you
without respect for his word or his oath.

RODRIGO DE ORGOÑO, ON ALMAGRO'S RELEASE OF
HERNANDO PIZARRO, GARCILASO DE LA VEGA

Bitter and resentful at his failure to find precious metals in the south,
Almagro arrived back in the vicinity of Cuzco in March 1537. He had
found "New Toledo" fertile but poor. Potosí, on the way, had not yet been
discovered as the wonderful mountain of silver that it came soon to be
known as. Almagro's failure had been marked by brutalities to Indians,
who in consequence tried to avoid working for him. Gangs of Spanish
horsemen would hunt down these reluctant serfs as if they were game,
kidnapping their wives and children as if they were toys. Any Spaniard who
stood up for Indians was mocked.[1]

All the same, this journey was much assisted, perhaps had even been
made possible, by the presence among the Spaniards of Paullu Inca, Manco
Capac's half brother, who had acted as the expedition's guide and prepared
the ground for reception by local leaders.

The difficulty now was that still no one really knew for certain if Cuzco
was legally in Almagro's jurisdiction or that of Pizarro. It was not easy to
see what the royal decree of May 21, 1534, was trying to say. Perhaps it was
too much to expect the *letrados*—clergymen and noblemen of the Council
of the Indies sitting in Valladolid, who had no experience of Peru—to set
this matter straight.[2]

As he approached Cuzco from the south, Almagro learned that his old comrade Pizarro's Peru was at war with Manco Capac. Almagro was led to think that Manco Capac now had the advantage in the conflict. That was actually the reverse of the facts, even though Hernando Pizarro was short of food.

Almagro began to correspond with Manco. From the safety of his army at Urcos, only eighteen miles from Cuzco, he sent two emissaries to the Inca (Juan Gómez Malanes and Pedro de Oñate, both of whom had been with him from the beginning).[3] Through them, Almagro assured Manco that if Manco would surrender to him, he would punish the Spaniards guilty of abuse toward him. While Oñate was with Manco, an Indian runner came with a note from Hernando Pizarro telling the latter not to trust Almagro—a somewhat bizarre message since Manco and Hernando had been fighting each other for nearly a year. Manco asked Oñate to prove his enmity toward the Pizarros by cutting off the messenger's hand. Oñate obliged by cutting off the fingers.

Another friend of Almagro soon made his appearance. This was Ruy Díaz. Manco asked Díaz: "If I were to give the Christians a great treasure, would the King withdraw all the Christians from the land?" Ruy Díaz asked how much treasure Manco would give. Manco replied by taking a *fanega* of maize, holding up one grain, and saying: "As much as this grain is the quantity of the gold and silver which you have found for the Christians, and what you have not found is as this *fanega* from which I have taken this grain." Ruy Díaz seems to have been defeated by this proposition and merely replied, "Even if you were to give the King all these mountain peaks made in gold and silver, he would not remove from this land the Spaniards who are now in it." Manco answered, "Get you away, Ruy Díaz, and tell Almagro that he may go where he will, for I am bound to die and all my people too, till we have made an end of the Christians."[4] The exchange seems to have led Manco to change his mind about Almagro, and he caused one of his commanders, Paucar, to attack him. He also imprisoned Ruy Díaz, had his beard cut off, and had guavas fired at him, which may have been more disagreeable than it sounds. He did not know how bad the relations were between Almagro and the Pizarros and assumed that, in the end, Almagro's 450 men would be a good reinforcement for Hernando Pizarro's 200.

So he decided to call off his siege of Cuzco, attributing his setback to the gods. Pursued by Spaniards, he withdrew first from Calca, then to the fortress city of Ollantaytambo, and next to the upper Vilcabamba valley, specifically to the forest of Antis Vitcos. He took with him a golden statuette of a small boy, Punchao. Solar rays issued from the figure's head and shoulders, and he had a royal headband, while lions and serpents projected from his body.[5] The fighting was severe in Ollantaytambo, though the Indians held out effectively against Hernando Pizarro.

Paullu Inca sent a message to Manco saying that Almagro seemed in truth ready to help Manco fight the Pizarros. He suggested that they kill Francisco, Hernando, and Gonzalo Pizarro, and "afterwards the surviving Peruvians could live quietly with no one to injure them" [*después vivirian quietos sin que nadie a el le injuriase*]. This apparent treachery to the Spanish cause did not prevent Almagro from sending his lieutenant Orgóñez to capture Manco. Though Orgóñez succeeded in sacking the sun temple at Vitcos, Manco escaped farther into the mountains.

Almagro was approaching Cuzco. He first had to meet the reinforcement army of five hundred men under Alonso de Alvarado, which Almagro succeeded in defeating on the Abancay bridge, even capturing Alvarado himself with several of his captains. Cuzco was then at his feet. Hernando Pizarro sent a messenger to try to bring over Almagro's troops by playing on the ambitions of Juan de Saavedra, who was now his commander. Saavedra refused.[6] Next, Hernando suggested to Almagro that he should set himself up in one part of Cuzco, while he and his brothers would remain in another. But Almagro demanded that Hernando give up all Cuzco to him. A battle between Spaniards seemed inevitable, despite the serene efforts of Diego de Alvarado, a cousin of the great Pedro, "a model of good sense and discretion, an accomplished gentleman in all respects"[7]—and, it must be said, an unusually tolerant figure for a member of his family.

On April 18, 1537, Almagro and his men entered Cuzco by three separate gates, drums and fifes playing. Almagro's men shouted his name when they entered the palace of Pizarro, which they set on fire. They also set fire to the roof of the house of Hernando Pizarro, who was captured with twenty of his men, including his brother Gonzalo. These prisoners were walled up in a round tower at the palace of Huayna Capac, which had only one small window, through which food could be introduced. Almagro told the Pizarros that "they, with their insolence and arrogance, were the chief reasons for the rebellion of Manco."[8] In some way, Almagro had been apprised of the news that the Pizarros would never forgive the death in action of their brother Juan.

Hearing of these events, Francisco Pizarro first sought an accommodation with Almagro. He was always inclined to compromise if he could. Licenciado Gaspar de Espinosa, the experienced ex-governor of Panama, who had come down to Peru the previous year, was asked to act as an intermediary. But unfortunately he died. Almagro set off to face Francisco Pizarro, taking with him Hernando Pizarro as a prisoner. Francisco organized his army of eight hundred with care. Two hundred of his men were horsemen, and the future conqueror of Chile, Pedro de Valdivia, renowned as a brilliant captain, was his chief commander.[9]

Several further efforts were made to arrange a reconciliation between the two sides. Almagro's representatives were, however, not loyal. For example, having been asked to act for Almagro, Fray Francisco de Bobadilla, a Mercedarian, treacherously decided for the Pizarros.[10] A committee was named to establish a line between Pizarro's and Almagro's land. But they could make no progress. Still, Diego de Alvarado skillfully negotiated the release of Hernando Pizarro. (Most realized that he would disturb the situation. It was true.) The two conquistadors met south of Lima, at Mala, but nothing transpired. Francisco Pizarro proposed that Almagro should be given good land at Arequipa and Chencas. But Almagro wanted Cuzco or nothing. He arranged a ceremony whereby Paullu Inca was given the imperial crown as well as the ancient palace of Colcampata in Cuzco.

Everything now seemed to be leading toward the tragedy of a civil war.

The critical battle occurred in April 1538 at Las Salinas (the salt mines), outside Cuzco. It was a site where the road goes uphill, leaving a swamp on one side and a narrow but flat place on the other. The clever if footloose courtier Enríquez de Guzmán, still with Almagro, wrote that, though the encampments of the two armies were close, one was in summer, the other in winter, for Almagro was at Huaytara, in the sierra, while Pizarro was below. In the sierra, it rained or snowed half the year, while on the coast there was no water.

Suffering from a fever, Almagro could not himself fight at Las Salinas. He left his command to Orgóñez, who had with him four infantry captains. He had two cavalry detachments. Hernando Pizarro's cavalry was divided into two also, led by Diego de Rojas and Alvarado on one side, and himself with Gonzalo, his brother, on the other. His infantry was controlled by Diego de Cerbina (pikes) and Castro from Portugal (arquebuses). Thus an Alvarado was to be found on each side, a characteristic feature of those tragic days.

First, Orgóñez ordered a cavalry detachment to attack the Pizarros' pikemen and arquebusiers. But Pizarro's men were by then well established in the swamp, which held up the cavalry of Almagro. They charged all the same. Hernando Pizarro and Pedro de Lerma, one of Almagro's more important commanders, were met with lances, and the first named was wounded. But Almagro's commander was blinded before being killed. Enríquez de Guzmán was wounded when his horse fell into a ravine.

Victory lay eventually with the Pizarros, though about two hundred were killed on each side. These included Fernando de Alvarado. Ruy Díaz and Lerma were killed after the battle, the latter treacherously. Almagro was captured after the battle, too, and imprisoned in one of the round towers where he had previously placed Hernando Pizarro and Gonzalo.[11] Hernando Pizarro thought of sending him to Spain, but he heard that Gonzalo de Mesa, one of his own captains, planned to rescue Almagro on the way to Lima. So, after a perfunctory trial, Hernando sentenced Almagro to death. He appealed against this but without success. On July 8, 1538, Almagro, already over seventy-five, was strangled in his cell, then publicly beheaded in the square of Cuzco and buried in the main church. The only witness of his funeral was his favorite African slave.[12] Almagro's dead body lay for a while naked in the square, and a Pizarrist examined it carefully to see whether he had been, as was rumored, a sodomite. Gonzalo de Mesa, Almagro's would-be rescuer, was also beheaded. These executions were carried out by Alonso de Toro, a *criado* of the Pizarros and a native of Trujíllo, who soon became lieutenant-governor of Cuzco. In 1546, he, too, was murdered, by his father-in-law.[13]

In Peru, the general use of heavy field artillery was now begun. Henceforth, thousands of *encomienda* Indians would be employed carrying big guns round the country. The battle of Las Salinas of April 1538 was the last major battle fought in medieval fashion, with lances and swords playing a decisive part. It was not, however, a chivalrous occasion.

25

Pizarro's Triumph and Tragedy

This doctor is worth a Peru.

LORENZO DA PONTE, *Così fan tutte*

Fray Vicente de Valverde, the Valladolid- and Salamanca-educated Dominican, who was the only churchman to have accompanied Pizarro throughout, had returned to Spain in 1534. He now returned having been named first bishop of Peru. He was escorted by a retinue of fifty soldiers and a hundred arquebusiers and crossbowmen. Valverde had received instructions in Spain as to how to be a model bishop. He was to ensure that *repartimientos* (parcels of land) were moderate, to ask for accounts from the royal officials, to ensure that the payment of the royal fifth was honestly made, and to collect tithes. Here the Crown surely hoped to establish a truly separate authority.[1] In 1539, Valverde sent a long report to the King in which he urged the Crown to defend the Indians against his Spanish friends, whom he described as "so many wolves." Yet the indigenous people, he said (as he had said on other occasions), were very ready "to receive the doctrine of the holy Gospel."[2] The Pizarros had always been friendly with the Dominicans and the Mercedarians.

All the same, it was a complicated moment to write thus, for now that Almagro was dead, Manco Capac was planning a new rebellion. He had as his main commander Illa Tupac, a general who had attacked Pedro de Alvarado in 1537. Their plan was to inspire many small-scale local risings, causing much damage. The decisive moment seems to have been when a people called the Conchucos fell on Trujillo by the sea and carried out many killings or tortures of travelers. Manco himself was pursued by a commander of Pizarro's, Illán Suárez de Carvajal. (His brother, Juan Suárez de Carvajal, was on the Council of the Indies.)[3] But Manco turned successfully on this enemy, twenty-four out of thirty men being soon killed.

Francisco Pizarro took command in new counterattacks. Still, his main interest was to found new settlements. For example, in full campaign, he founded San Juan de la Frontera at Huamanga under Francisco de Cárdenas.[4] Pizarro also went to Charcas and to the famous inland lake Titicaca. He learned there that rebellious Indians were busy trying to destroy a pontoon bridge of boats across the lake to the south. It was there that Pizarro received a request from one of his most brilliant men, Pedro de Valdivia. "The golden captain," as he was known for his good qualities, asked Pizarro for permission to go and explore, and also conquer, the land abandoned by Almagro. "Seeing my determination," Valdivia wrote later to the King, "he graciously opened the door to me."[5] But such grants were not without their cost: At the same moment as giving him carte blanche in Chile, Pizarro withdrew his earlier grant to Valdivia of the valley of Canela and its silver mine.

The Pizarro family were busy establishing their control in the center of Peru, east of the conquered lands. Thus Hernando found and took for himself the mines that the Indians had begun at Porco. Gonzalo occupied the entire valley of Cochabamba.[6] Francisco established himself and his family in equally excellent estates.

Feeling that his conquests had at last been completed, Hernando Pizarro again took leave of his brothers. To Francisco, he declared, "Look, your lordship, now I am going [again] to Spain, and consider that safety lies first in God and then in your lordship's life . . . do not permit those who wish it to gather ten people together within fifty leagues of wherever your lordship may be, for if you let them assemble, they are certain to kill you. If they kill your lordship, I shall be sure to conduct our business badly and no memory of your lordship will remain."[7] With that unexpectedly modest statement, he set off for Spain with the intention of justifying before the Council of the Indies his already much-criticized execution of Almagro. He traveled via New Spain, avoiding Panama since he was afraid of being seized or killed by his enemies there.[8]

Francisco Pizarro had aged during the crisis over the Almagros. The Emperor had named him marquess, as he had named Cortés. But Charles was allowing Pizarro to choose his title, leaving it up to him as to of what territory or city he would be marquess.

Pizarro dispatched his brother Gonzalo, accompanied by their cousin, Pedro the chronicler, and Paullu Inca to seek out Manco in his refuge beyond Vilcabamba. They went as far as horses could go, then continued on foot. With Pedro del Barco temporarily in control of the expedition, the Spaniards were ambushed by Indians, who killed five of them. Gonzalo retreated, and his brother Francisco sent more troops to assist him. Next day, they reached Manco's secret redoubt, while another section of their forces went into the forest nearby without the Indians knowing of it. Gonzalo sought to negotiate, but his emissaries were Huaspar and Inquill, two brothers of Manco's Queen, Cura Ocllo. Here the Indians tried unsuccessfully to experiment with arquebuses.

Manco Capac escaped downstream with three followers. The Spaniards then embarked on persecution. For example, Queen Cura Ocllo herself was captured; she tried to avoid rape by smearing filth over herself. Manco sent a messenger inviting Francisco Pizarro to meet him at Hucay, with three or four followers. Pizarro sent a pony, a black slave, and some other presents. Manco had all these killed. Pizarro's reply was the brutal murder of Cura Ocllo by shooting arrows at her. She made no complaint at the evident pain.[9] Her body was put in a basket in the river Yucay so that it would be found by Manco's people. Pizarro then executed several of his grander prisoners, such as the general Tiso. Among others killed were Villac Umu, the high priest, who had been fighting Pedro de los Ríos in the Condesuyo for at least eight months. These enemies of the Spanish were killed by being burned.

After this, there were no more large-scale Indian rebellions. Alonso de Alvarado returned to the conquest of the Chachapoyas, north of Cajamarca, and his relatively humane treatment of Indians secured him a reasonable reception. He founded the town of Rabantu. But in Huánaco, a new and inexperienced Spanish force under Alonso de Mercadillo was busy terrifying the natives in the hope of finding gold. There were many complaints, causing Pizarro to order his brother Gonzalo to stop there on his way to becoming governor of Quito. Another rebellion that had to be quenched was on the road to Chinchaysuyo, which was the responsibility of Alonso de Orihuela. In July 1539, two *encomenderos* were killed in the

Callejón de Huaylas. Francisco de Chaves, one of Pizarro's most successful but more brutal captains, swept through the valleys of the northern central highlands to carry out fearful reprisals, killing children as well as women.[10]

Franciso Pizarro himself was busy founding two new towns, La Plata and Arequipa. There he and his secretary, the much disliked Antonio Picado, made themselves even more unpopular by cutting back large *repartimientos* that had already been allocated. Picado was also hated because he unjustifiably desired that all should show reverence to him.

In the summer of 1541, several plots against Francisco Pizarro were reported to him. Perhaps a priest betrayed the discretion of the confessional. The news also came that Hernando Pizarro had been indicted in Spain, as a result of complaints by Diego de Alvarado, on account of the execution of Almagro. Diego, either poisoned or worn out by his exertions, died soon after making these allegations, but Hernando was seized and arrested. Though by now immensely rich, he passed the next quarter century as a prisoner, if a privileged prisoner, at first in Madrid, in the Alcázar, then in the Castillo de la Mota, just outside Medina del Campo. He could receive guests, children, mistresses, and food from the town, and he could buy houses and properties (and did so); but this certainly seemed an extraordinary conclusion for the life of a great conquistador who had won so much of South America for the Spanish Crown.[11]

The castle of La Mota is a formidable brick building on the south side of Medina del Campo, which had always been a royal city. Famous for its great annual fairs in the late fifteenth and early sixteenth century, it had been the favorite city of Queen Isabel the Catholic, who died there. She had said that, if she had had three sons, she would have liked one to be king of Castile, another to be archbishop of Toledo, and a third to be a notary in Medina del Campo. La Mota had been the prison of numerous dangerous persons, including for a time Cesare Borgia, the Italian adventurer, who made a daring escape from it in 1506.

Francisco Pizarro continued to walk about Lima, the new city that he had created in Peru, near the sea. The Almagrists continued with their complaints and plots, though it had been his brother Hernando, not Francisco, who had executed the elder Almagro. Manco Capac lived on in secrecy in Vilcabamba. Gonzalo Pizarro led an attempt to destroy that Indian claimant. Pizarro was told by the mayor of Lima, Dr. Velázquez, that "those of Chile"—that is, the friends of Almagro—had determined to attack "the Marquess" (as the governor was now known) at Mass on Sunday, June 26, 1541. These Almagrists seemed in a majority. They sensed Pizarro's alarm. Emerging from the house of Diego de Almagro *hijo,* a mestizo son of Almagro, they shouted ferocious declarations: "Down with the traitor and the tyrant who has killed the judge whom the Emperor has sent to punish him."[12] Actually, no such official had yet arrived. Nor had the young Almagro taken much interest up till then in avenging his father. He was the son of Almagro by a Panamanian Indian girl. Pizarro consulted his friends Francisco de Chaves and Juan Blázquez, the deputy governor. The latter said, "Have no fear, while I have in my hand this staff, none will dare to attack you." The three concocted a plan. Pizarro would pretend that he was ill. So he would not go to Mass. Then, in the afternoon, he would order his cavalry to seize the young Diego Almagro and some of his friends.[13]

When the hour of Mass came, the Almagrists assembled to kill Pizarro on his way to church. When he did not appear, they dispatched a Basque priest to Pizarro's house to see what had happened.[14] Pizarro invited the priest in and asked him to celebrate Mass. He heard Mass with Dr. Velázquez, the mayor; Francisco de Chaves, his deputy; and Francisco Martín de Alcántara, his half brother, who was usually in attendance on him. Hearing a tumult in the square, Pizarro asked his captain, Chaves, to go and see what was going on. Chaves, ill prepared, went outside to ask the crowd's intentions. Forty men appeared at Pizarro's door, including men who had been looked on as "those of Chile." The Indian servants fled. So did Dr. Velázquez. Pizarro had no armor, just a sword and a shield. He, his half brother, and two pages defended the door as best they could, but Martín de Alcántara, Chaves, and the pages were soon killed. Pizarro was left alone. He was surrounded and struck in the throat. He apparently made the sign of the cross with his thumb and index finger, and died kissing the hand that had made the sign.[15] He was about sixty-five.

Juan de Rada (Juan Herrada), the most prominent enemy of Pizarro, inspired the young Almagro to mount a horse and ride round Lima to say that there was no other governor of that city than he. The houses of Pizarro and his staff—including the feared secretary, Antonio Picado, and his half brother—were sacked. Picado was soon apprehended and also killed after horrible tortures. A friend of Pizarro, Juan de Barbarán of Trujillo, and his wife, with some black slaves, were brave enough to haul Pizarro's body to the church, which the dead governor had built, and buried him, with Diego de Almagro's permission. Barbarán also made it his business to look after Pizarro's children and he disposed of many of his possessions. "The Chileans" went into the square and shouted that Diego de Almagro *hijo,* aged twenty-one, was now King of Peru. That mestizo had himself sworn in more modestly as the governor, and named Rada as his captain-general. Various others assumed perilously fragile posts as judges or captains. But there were still "monarchists," and they soon rallied, their captain-general being Pedro Álvarez de Holguín, with Alonso de Alvarado, Garcilaso de la Vega, and Pedro Ansúnez as the main captains. A new civil war was now certain.

Pizarro died rich. He had allocated to himself thirty thousand Indians in his numerous *encomiendas,* and he had about four hundred staff— Spaniards—working for him. In Peru, Pizarro's special interest was his *encomiendas* in the valley of Yucay, which included the Ceja de Selva, where coca was grown. It had been reserved for the personal use of the Inca rulers. Hernando and Gonzalo Pizarro held *encomiendas* in the neighboring valley of Tampu.[16] He also had *encomiendas* at Chuquiago, Puna, Huaylas (very good agricultural land), Chimú, Conchucos, Lima, and Chuquitanas. Pizarro had mines at Porco with a partner, García de Salcedo, who became the companion of his daughter Francisca. He also had a mine at El Collao. Pizarro, when he died, had a large staff of *criados,* a word applied to people performing many subordinate activities but meaning essentially "servants."[17] Most of them were from Extremadura, and the part played in his life by men from Trujillo was always notable. Bishop Berlanga, who was known for introducing the banana to the colony of Santo Domingo, had commented: "It is publicly said that Your Lordship and your brothers and officials have as many Indians as His Majesty and all the other Spanish conquistadors."[18] They could not hold them very easily, however.

26

Vaca de Castro in Peru

Mrs. Pipchin had a way of falling foul of all meek people; and her
friends said who could wonder at it, after the Peruvian mines!

CHARLES DICKENS, *Dombey and Son,* 1846

Peru was much too rich to be left with no governor. So, within months of
the murder of the Marquess, a name was put forward in the Council of the
Indies to take his place. It was not that of Hernando Pizarro, as would have
seemed logical, given his prominence in the conquest: Hernando was in
prison in Medina del Campo. Nor was it the name of Gonzalo Pizarro,
who, as governor in Quito, was in Amazonia seeking cinnamon and was
passed over, though he was Francisco's legal heir. The name suggested as a
temporary governor was Cristóbal Vaca de Castro, a Leonés who had been
a judge at Valladolid.

Cobos and García de Loaisa had earlier recommended Vaca to act as
governor of Peru alongside Pizarro, and though no one had worked out
what that might mean in practice, he was already on his way, to Quito if not
to Lima. The assumption was that, sooner or later, a viceroy would be
named, as had occurred in Mexico, and when that happened, Vaca de Castro would step aside in an honorable fashion.

Vaca asked three men to act for him till he reached Peru. These were a
Dominican, Fray Tomás de San Martín; Jerónimo de Aliaga, an educated
disciple of Pizarro; and Francisco de Barrionuevo. The first was the provincial, or leader, of the Dominican order in Peru and a humane and warm-
hearted individual who would later play a decisive part in the creation of
the National University of San Marcos in Lima. Aliaga, from Segovia, had
been recently inspector of the treasure seized in Cuzco. Finally, Bar-

rionuevo was a remarkable conquistador who had been in Florida with Ponce de León, in Cubagua looking for pearls, and in Santo Domingo charged with defeating the rebellion of the Indians led by Enriquillo. He and his nephew Pedro had built the first stone house on the pearl island, Cubagua. He had also been in Tierra Firme (Venezuela), which he used as a base to become a merchant in Peru. Barrionuevo entered into a commercial agreement with one of the largest entrepreneurs, Antonio de Ribera, a magistrate also, and with him shared the profits of a mine.[1] He owned a good sugar mill in Puerto Plata, on the north coast of Santo Domingo. Concerned in a broad sweep of Spanish imperial adventures, he was rightly called "one of the most fascinating men in the history of America" by the German historian Enrique Otte.[2]

The letter from Vaca de Castro explaining the designation of Fray Tomás, Aliaga, and Barrionuevo was received by the first-named in the new Dominican convent in Lima, a makeshift building at that time but already on the magnificent site that would make the completed building a triumph of colonial architecture.[3] The land had been given to the Dominicans by Francisco Pizarro. The city council of Lima welcomed the arrangements with alacrity but then apparently abandoned the city, for Diego de Almagro *hijo* was suspected of wanting to burn down the whole settlement. When Vaca arrived and began to wear the appropriate robes of an acting governor, many fair-weather friends and allies of the young Almagro deserted him.

Some of "the Chileans," survivors of Almagro's journey to Chile, suggested that they or Almagro should kill the remaining Pizarrists whom they had as prisoners in their power. These included Pedro Pizarro the chronicler. A recently arrived *licenciado*, Rodrigo Niño, advised against such actions, and instead, the people concerned were imprisoned on a boat in the port of Arequipa, under the captaincy of Pedro Gómez. Gómez had, however, his price. The Pizarrists found that it was 500 ducats, with which they bought their freedom.[4]

Vaca de Castro went to Quito, then to Trujillo. Pizarrists and ex-Almagrists both crowded his drawing room. Soon an army sprang up at his disposal. The commander would be Gómez de Tordoya of Badajoz. He had been a friend of the Marquess and had been hunting when he died. When the news came of Pizarro's death, he said: "Now is the time for war, smoke and blood, not for the hunting and pastimes."[5] This was, however, still a time when wars often seemed to be hunting carried on by other means.

Vaca reached Lima, where he named Barrionuevo his chief lieutenant, and Juan Vélez de Guevara, a lawyer from Jerez de la Frontera, became captain of his increasingly important arquebusiers. They awaited the arrival of Almagro *hijo* in trepidation, for his force was large. They need not have worried, since he was still in Cuzco, and his two chief lieutenants, García de Alvarado and Cristóbal Sotelo, had fallen out so badly that the former killed the latter in the main square of the city.

None of these brawling conquistadors had been colleagues of the Pizarros in the great battles of the early days: They were new men with less than five years' experience in the country. García de Alvarado, for example, had come down to Peru with his kinsman Pedro de Alvarado in 1535. Now, to save himself, he decided to kill Almagro *hijo*, his putative commander, and invited him to a banquet. Young Almagro accepted; then, at the last minute, suspecting the worst, declined, saying that he was ill. Alvarado went to taunt Almagro, and persuaded him apparently to change his mind. As they left for Alvarado's lodging, Alvarado said to him, "You are under arrest." Almagro, however, remarked, "But you are not under arrest but dead," and he killed Alvarado there and then.[6] Almagro with his 250 horsemen set off against Vaca de Castro, whose numbers were three times that.

They met in June 1542 at Huamanga, in some fields called Chupas. Before the armies fought, Vaca de Castro, usually prudent, sent two of his men, Diego Mercado and Francisco de Idiáquez, to offer terms. They would include a general pardon. The intrepid Almagro said that he would accept the terms, provided the pardon included all his followers and that he, Diego de Almagro, would be named governor of a new kingdom of "New Toledo"—that is, Chile—as well as being given ownership of its gold mines. Vaca, who knew that many of Almagro's men were unenthusiastic about the idea of a battle, also sent Alonso García to offer terms privately to many captains. Though he was disguised, García was unmasked by Diego, who had him hanged. Diego then prepared for battle. Vaca, proclaiming a list of Almagro's crimes, did the same. It was one more tragic event in the tragic early history of Peru.[7]

Almagro had with him Pedro Suárez, who had fought in Italy. He told

Almagro that he could win any battle now simply by using artillery—which, in his case, may have been so, since his guns were controlled by Pizarro's onetime artillery king, Pedro de Candía, who had made an astonishing series of changes of front in the preceding years.[8] But Candía had by now betrayed yet another leader and aimed his guns high so as deliberately to cause no damage. Almagro realized what was going on and had him executed as a traitor. Pedro Pizarro says that the real battle did not begin till darkness. He adds that the royalist infantry sang a song of victory amid the confusion, and by this the cavalry of Almagro was disheartened.[9]

Pedro Suárez reported that he told the young Almagro, "My Lord, if your Lordship had followed my advice, we should have won a victory today. But you took other counsel and so we shall lose. I do not want myself to be on the losing side so that, since your Lordship won't let me win on my terms, I'll do so on the other." With that, he cantered over to join Vaca de Castro. There were other such actions in this battle. Almagro's arquebuses, however, continued to do much damage, killing several important royalists.

The fighting continued into the night, till Almagro *hijo* admitted defeat and rode back disconsolate into Cuzco, where he was shortly detained by Rodrigo de Salazar, who had once been his deputy, and Antón Ruiz de Guevara, whom he himself had named a magistrate. Next day, Vaca arrived in Cuzco, where he had Almagro *hijo* beheaded in the same place that his father had died. Like his father, he was buried in the Mercedarian church. Some Almagrists, however (Diego Méndez, for example), escaped into the forest, where they were welcomed by Manco Capac.

This victory inaugurated some years of relative serenity in Peru. Vaca de Castro governed with rectitude. He divided those Indians who had no masters among those royal subjects who had no Indians but had done well on his behalf in the war. Vaca's laws were generally received with favor by the Indians, who admitted that they were comparable to those of their Indian monarchs in the past.[10] There were, of course, Spanish complainers, such as Hernando Mogollón, who received no Indians but had done well: Vaca agreed with his self-appraisal and gave him an *encomienda*. Vaca also sent deserving captains to remote places to win new conquests: Vergara to Pacamura; Diego de Rojas, Nicolás de Heredia, and Felipe Gutiérrez to Musu; Vélez de Guzmán to Muyupamba; and Gonzalo de Monroy to help

Valdivia in Chile. But though Vaca at last seemed to have found a peaceful settlement, there were still many tragedies ahead.

For a time, however, the surviving members of the Pizarro family were not engaged in these battles, since the putative leader, Gonzalo, was physically far away from the center of power.

Gonzalo Pizarro and Orellana Seek
Cinnamon and Find the Amazon

You shall understand, Sancho, that Spaniards and those who embark themselves at Cádiz to go to the Indies, one of the greatest
signs they have to know whether they have passed the equinoctial,
is that all men that are on the ship, their lice die on them . . .

MIGUEL DE CERVANTES, *Don Quixote*

In late 1540, Francisco Pizarro had named his younger brother, the
charming and valiant Gonzalo, governor of Quito. He had also given
Gonzalo an *encomienda,* which included the Cañari people, Spain's best
friends among the indigenous population. This gave Gonzalo control of
the north of the old Inca empire. Atahualpa had had his supporters there.
Gonzalo behaved curiously, however, in his new position. He took up his
office formally on December 1, 1540, but immediately devoted himself to
arranging an expedition whose aim was the search for cinnamon on the
eastern side of the great Andes.

He left Quito in February 1541 with nearly two hundred Spaniards, a
large number of Indian porters (though surely not approaching the figure
of four thousand given by chroniclers), many llamas as beasts of burden,
about two hundred pigs to supply bacon on the way, and a large number of
fighting dogs, without which, at that time, no Spanish army could be complete. Gonzalo Pizarro at that time was powerful because of his association
with his brother, the Marquess. His own qualities of leadership also seemed
magnetically attractive. So, as Ortiguera would one day put it, "there fol-

lowed him in that undertaking a large number of the noblest and most prominent people of the realm." Ortiguera added, "It was a great achievement to have been able to bring them together and with them 260 horses," as well as a good number of arquebuses and crossbows, munitions, other implements of war, slaves, and Indians—a "magnificent body of men and one well prepared for any adventure."[1]

They began by going east over the Andes, where Gonzalo reported: "We came to some very rugged and wooded country with great ranges out of which we were obliged to open up roads anew not only for the men but also for the horses." At least a hundred Indians died from cold crossing the Andes. They continued thus, till sixty leagues (180 miles) to the east of Quito, they found themselves in the flatlands of the jungle, at the headwaters of the Napo, in a province that they named Zumaco. The Napo was at this stage a large meandering river, with a big floodplain.[2] There Gonzalo expected to find cinnamon bushes.

Cinnamon was native to Brazil, though it is generally supposed that the quality of the product there is inferior to that found in the Old World, for example in Ceylon. The flavor that we expect from cinnamon derives from a fine aromatic oil made by powdering the bark of the tree, macerating it in seawater and then distilling it. It has then a golden yellow color with a special smell and a very hot taste. It had already by the sixteenth century become much sought after in cookery, and this provided an appropriate motive for an expedition such as Gonzalo Pizarro now mounted.

From Zumaco, Gonzalo and his men went down into the beautiful valley of the river Coca, an abundantly flowing river. They followed the Coca down to where there was a stretch of narrows. Here Gonzalo built a good wooden bridge, over which he could carry his expedition to the north side. There they remained for several weeks.

They were now joined by a smaller force led by another Extremeño, Francisco de Orellana. This conquistador, though his name is from a place in the beautiful valley called Serena, was born, like the Pizarros, in Trujillo. Like them, he was a distant cousin of Hernán Cortés.[3] He was in Nicaragua by 1527 and probably was among the lionhearted men who came down to Peru with Alvarado in the company of Pedro Álvarez de Holguín, another Extremeño friend of the Pizarros. Orellana established himself at Puerto Viejo, and afterwards went as a senior captain to help the Pizarros at Lima and at Cuzco. He became ensign-general of the seven hundred men sent by Hernando Pizarro to Cuzco and lost an eye at Las Salinas. At some point in these undertakings, he gained a rough knowledge of Quechua. Then he was sent by Francisco Pizarro to reestablish the settlement at the port of Guayaquil and La Culata, which had been founded by Benalcázar but then destroyed by Indians. He became a link between the *tierras del sur* and the Ecuadorian plains.

There began to be discussions as to how one could go directly from Quito overland to the Mar del Norte, or the Atlantic. A pioneer in this field had been Gonzalo Díaz de Pineda, who was the first Spaniard (or European) to cross the great range of the Andes.[4] Orellana soon became captain-general and lieutenant-governor in this province—lieutenant, that is, to Francisco Pizarro. In these offices, Orellana emerged as a strong opponent of sexual deviations. Thus he had two compatriots burned for sodomy and their goods confiscated.[5] Gonzalo Pizarro then became his overlord.

Gonzalo Pizarro expected Orellana to assist and accompany him, and indeed the conquistador was anxious to do this, though he first had to go down to Guayaquil, on the Pacific coast. Thus he was too late to accompany Gonzalo in February and only caught up with his commander at the end of March. They met at Quema, about four hundred miles east of Quito. Orellana came with his twenty-three companions almost starving and, as was said at the time, no one had more than a sword and a shield with him. Quema had a savanna about six miles long and about a mile broad, so it was a reasonable place for a rest. Pizarro pressed on, however, seeking a way to food and fertility, while Orellana rested. Before he left, Gonzalo Pizarro brutally interrogated several Indian chiefs about the country ahead. Though some said that there was soon to be found good country, where the population was a large one and the people wore clothes, most said that they knew only of forests usually inundated with water.

On this journey of reconnaissance, Gonzalo Pizarro left his horses behind. He was away seventy days and found a few cinnamon trees. The cinnamon here was not in the bark but in the form of flower buds, a sample of which Gonzalo sent back to the King. A small detachment went ahead farther, to discover on a new river (which turned out to be the Napo) settlements with houses on the bank and, indeed, people wearing clothes. Gonzalo captured some fifteen canoes from these Indians. "In these," Gonzalo recalled, "we went up and down the main river in search of food and there we built [also] a brigantine to protect and to accompany the canoes, because we were compelled to cross over from one side of the river to another and, without this [brigantine], the men of the expedition could not have been kept in condition both from the point of view of food and from the point of view of carrying weapons and munitions for the arquebuses and [whatever was necessary] for the crossbows and iron bars and pickaxes, [not to speak of shoes for horses]. But I was informed by Indian guides that ahead of us lay a great uninhabited region where there was no food whatsoever."[6]

By this time, Orellana had joined Gonzalo Pizarro. Although he had been against building the brigantine, once the decision had been made, he busied himself, as the de facto second-in-command, in finding iron for nails and wood for timber and so on. There was no shortage of wood, nor of lianas for cordage, nor resin, nor indeed metal for nails.

With these canoes and with this brigantine, the *San Pedro*, Gonzalo Pizarro and his men reached the junction of the rivers Coca and Napo. The equipment, the supplies, and the sick were here placed on the brigantine, and Juan de Alcántara (presumably, from his name, an Extremeño) was placed in command. The rest of the expedition struggled with their horses along the banks of the river, though the undergrowth was thick and there were marshes and tributaries flowing into the main river that necessitated bridge building. The adventurers found little food, and by that time, all the pigs of the expedition had been eaten. They continued thus for forty days and covered another 150 miles.

Orellana told Pizarro that he had been able to talk to guides whom he considered reliable (his Quechua was by then reasonable), who had said that the uninhabited region ahead was indeed vast and that there was no food whatever to be had until the point "where one great river [the Amazon] joined up with that down which we were proceeding and that, from that junction, one day's journey up the other river [the Amazon], there was an abundance of maize. And Captain Orellana told me [Pizarro] that, in order to serve His Majesty, and for love of me, he was willing to go in search of that food where the Indians said that it was and that, if I would give him the brigantine *San Pedro* and the canoes manned by sixty men, he would go in search of that food and bring it back."[7]

Gonzalo trusted Orellana, since he had been such a friend of the Pizarro family for so long and they both came from Trujillo. Pizarro agreed, though he specified that Orellana had to be back with him in twelve days. He allowed him fifty-seven men.[8] This was the crucial moment of Orellana's life, the origin of his glory and of the terrible accusations that would be made against him. For Orellana sailed off in the brigantine, with about ten canoes tied to its sides, with the plan of returning with such food as he had procured. But he never came back.

Orellana took with him on the *San Pedro* many heavy objects, such as most of the clothing and bedding of the expedition, the "munitions," spare weapons, and a small quantity of food, but probably not, as was afterwards alleged by Gonzalo Pizarro and his friends, many emeralds and gold. On their second day out, still on the Napo, the *San Pedro* hit a fallen tree in the middle of the river, and much damage was caused. Had they not been close to the shore, the ship would have been destroyed. Orellana and the crew hauled the boat to the side of the river, mended the hole in its side, and then continued their journey. The river had a fast current, so that they found themselves traveling sixty or seventy-five miles a day, the river always increasing in width since so many smaller streams were entering it, especially from the south.

The first three days, they traveled without seeing any settlement. As they had by then long distanced themselves from where they had left Gonzalo, and since they had so little to eat and their route seemed so unclear, Orellana and his leading companions began to talk quite soon of their return and how they would cope with the tremendous current against which they would have to row. Fray Carvajal, the chaplain of the expedition, recorded that it seemed from very early on necessary to have to choose between two evils: One, which the captain and most of his fellow leaders thought the lesser danger, was to continue on and follow the river; the other, which seemed to spell certain death, was to try to return upstream. To go back by land seemed impossible.

They continued onward, with no idea what they would encounter. They did realize that the river would eventually meet the Atlantic, but no one had any knowledge of how far away that meeting would be. Food was now nonexistent, and the Spaniards were reduced to cooking shoes, belts, and other leather clothes, sometimes seasoned by herbs. But no one knew which herbs were edible, and some found themselves poisoned in consequence and at the point of death "because they became like mad men and did not possess sense."[9] They did have, it is true, some maize and wine, but Fray Carvajal was attempting to preserve the latter so that he could celebrate Mass.

In one sense, conditions began to improve, for after New Year's Day, 1542, Orellana's Spaniards began to hear the distant beat of drums. It slowly became evident that they were not far from an Indian pueblo. Then, after several weeks of seeing nothing, they came upon four canoes full of Indians. Orellana sailed the *San Pedro* fast downriver, to find the pueblo of Aparia. This was probably near the watersmeet of the Napo and the Curaray, a black-water river, which is the Napo's largest tributary. There Orellana addressed the assembled elders of the place in Quechua and told them not to be afraid and that he and his friends would do nothing wrong or evil. The chief of the place was pleased at the Spaniards' reception of him and asked whether they needed anything. "Only food," replied Orellana, and in a short time, they were brought a selection of meat, including game and fish of many types. There was also maize, yucca, and sweet potato.

After they had eaten, Orellana called a meeting of his fifty-odd companions. He said that he himself favored going back up the river by boat to rejoin Gonzalo Pizarro, however difficult that might seem. But most of his companions thought that it would be "disastrous for us if we were to go with Your Lordship back up the river."[10] They hoped that Orellana would not put them in a compromising situation where they would be compelled to disobey him and in which they would appear traitors, saying that, on the other hand, they would be ready to follow him on any other route by which their lives might be saved. They concluded by saying that "they had been assured by the seamen who are here, or in the boat, or in the canoes, that we are some 600 miles or more by land from the expeditionary force of governor Gonzalo, all without road or settlement but, on the contrary, with very wild and wooded regions which we have come to know well from experience." Like most Spaniards at that time, those who thought like this committed their views to paper, and they signed a document where one could see the names of the Dominican friar Gaspar de Carvajal; the notary Francisco de Isasaga; and several Enríquezes, Gutiérrezes, and Rodríguezes.

Next day, January 5, 1542, Orellana called the notary Isasaga and declared that, though it was against his wish, the expedition would indeed continue, provided that they waited where they were for a time to see whether Gonzalo Pizarro and his friends would catch up with them. For since they had on board many objects that belonged to the men with Gonzalo, they might otherwise risk being accused of being thieves. This scene before a notary in a spot so remote that there could have been no European for over one thousand miles, on the edge of a colossal river that had never been visited by any European before, expresses an astonishing side of the great Spanish adventure.

Later, there was much argument about this conversation. Some recalled thinking that they could with ease have sailed back up the river, others thought that the currents and the rains would have prevented them going any distance upstream at all. Yet others said that the brigantine could not have gone back, and that left the canoes, which they thought would have been easily overwhelmed. Orellana seems to have become dominated by the desire to see where the rivers on which he had embarked reached the sea. In the meantime, in the name of the King, he took possession of the pueblo they were in and gave the territory the name of Victoria.

Fray Carvajal noted, "We stayed in that *pueblo* longer than we should have done, eating whatever we could find (the Indians had stopped bringing food regularly) in such a way that, thereafter, we went ahead with great speed and we discussed again whether there was some way of finding out what was going on in Gonzalo Pizarro's camp."[11] Orellana agreed to give 6,000 castellanos to any group of his men willing to return to give news to Gonzalo, and he promised them two black slaves also. But he found only three men prepared to do this.

The Spaniards left this Amazonian pueblo on the day of the fiesta of Candelmas, as they remembered—that is, February 2—which commemorates the purification of the Virgin. They rowed their way farther down the Napo, past a point where the turbulence of the waters was intense and where a chief named Irrimorrany visited them, bringing food, including turtles and parrots. The prevalence of mosquitoes was great. On February 11, some hundred miles beyond where the Napo meets the Curaray, Orellana and the *San Pedro* finally came upon the Amazon proper, not far from what is now Iquitos. The place itself is now called Francisco de Orellana.

At the next halt, they received more food in abundance, such as turtle, sea cow, roast monkey, roast cat, and partridge. Orellana gave a sermon to the Indians of the region, which explained how the Spaniards were Christians and vassals of the "Emperor of the Christians and the King of Spain, Charles." The Spanish, Orellana insisted, "were children of the sun."[12] The Indians seemed pleased to hear that interesting claim.

Orellana set about making another boat to substitute for the *San Pedro*, which had much deteriorated. Juan de Alcántara, the Extremeño, and Sebastián Rodríguez, from Galicia, neither of whom had experience of such labors, promised to make the necessary nails, which they did: Two thousand such were ready in twelve days. They also made bellows from boots. A forge was built, timber was cut, cotton was used as oakum to fill in cracks in the wood, resin from trees was used as tar, and the new vessel was ready in about forty days. Diego Mexia, a carpenter, was the director of these operations. He wrote, "[It was] a wonderful thing to see the happiness with which our comrades worked. There was no one amongst us who was accustomed to such work but, all the same, they conducted themselves as if they had been professionals."[13] The Spaniards bore in mind that the Amazonian Indians cut wood only in the last quarter of the moon's cycle, to avoid the rotting that they believed occurred if they cut at other times. Thus it was that Orellana and his expeditionary force spent Lent 1542.

On the Amazon in April, Orellana traveled fast with his two ships. When the river broadened, it was impossible for them to land and sleep. So they again became short of food. Still, on May 6 they succeeded in shooting a vulture with a crossbow, and a large fish was caught the same day. Fray Carvajal wrote, "[From then on,] we endured more hardships and more hunger and passed more uninhabited regions than before because the river led from one forested territory to another and we found no place to sleep nor could any [more] fish be caught, so we were reduced to our customary fare of herbs and occasionally roasted maize."[14] On May 12, they reached the junction of the Tefé with the Amazon, and a great number of canoes full of warriors suddenly appeared. Orellana prepared for battle, but alas, the powder for his arquebuses seemed damp, so he had to rely on crossbows. There followed a confusing conflict. Half the fifty Spaniards found themselves quickly in the water, but Orellana and Alonso de Robles, with the other half of the Spaniards, captured a riverine pueblo. There they seized a good quantity of food, including turtles in corrals, much fish, some dried meats, and biscuit. This they placed on their new brigantine and set off down the river again, the arquebuses now being able to be used since the munitions had become drier. Still the Indians pressed hard, and there were some difficult moments, Orellana himself being nearly killed just before his assailant was himself killed by a Spaniard with an arquebus.

The two Spanish ships soon reached Omagua, which was the first territory where neither Orellana nor any of his friends could communicate with the natives. The language spoken there bore no relation to Quechua. There were other surprises. For example, the Indians of this region were skilled potters, and Fray Carvajal thought the pottery there was "superior to that of Malaga."[15] It is now known as Guarita ware. They also found two giant idols elaborately decorated with feathers. Here was a riverine town about six miles long, whose lord, Paguana, received the Spaniards hospitably. The Indians awaited the Spaniards in their houses as if it were the most normal thing to welcome foreigners, though they had never before met such people as the Castilians. Carvajal wrote that "from this *pueblo* there were many roads running inland, with many llamas, and there seemed a good deal of silver about." The land seemed happy, and the people wore clothes with bright colors. The people evidently ate fruit of all kinds: There were pineapples, pears, cherries, and avocados.[16]

Another riverine town also seemed to continue for miles, with every section of it having its own embarkation point. The houses here were designed for living on the land, but the people had large dwellings in trees, "like magpies' nests," with everything ready for when the river was in flood.[17] Some towns gave the Spaniards "much war." Others supplied them with food. Other peoples fled. Thus it was that Orellana and his men reached the junction of the Amazon proper with what they called the Black River, the Río Negro as it has been known ever since, because its waters were as "black as ink," and for more than sixty miles after joining the Amazon, it preserved its menacing dark color.

After this great union of the two immense rivers, Orellana and his expedition met an extraordinary variety of towns. There was a town with two towers, several with temples to the sun, and one where an Indian explained by signs that the population were "subjects of the Amazons whom they served only with the feathers of parrots, which they used as linings of the roofs of their houses." It turned out that there was here a lady who ruled the whole territory, directing the wars of these women with zest and verve.[18] It was this improbable experience that led Orellana to christen the river that they soon would know so well as the Amazon.

Soon after this, they came to another great confluence, where the Amazon met the river Madeira. In one of the towns here, they captured as a potential interpreter an Indian girl. She told them that inland there were many Christians, among them two white women—left behind, it seemed, in 1531, eleven years before, by Diego de Ordaz. In this territory of the "Amazonas," they were attacked fiercely by bow and arrows, including poisoned arrows such as one that wounded Antonio Carranza and another that killed García de Soria. In this battle, the Spaniards found themselves facing about ten naked women who were white skinned, tall, with big heads.

Fray Diego Carvajal lost an eye in the next town, which was surrounded by a temperate land. The Spaniards thought that this region would be a good one for cattle, wheat, and fruit trees. Orellana asked an Indian who the women were who had attacked his expedition. The Indian replied that there were seventy pueblos inhabited only by women. Orellana asked if these women had children. The reply was: "The lord who lived next door carried the women to his own land, his men impregnated them and returned them to their own residence. If they had a son, he would be killed but, if they had a daughter, she would be well looked after and trained for war."[19] One can only imagine that the Spaniards heard in this conversation what they expected to hear. The historian Oviedo commented that these were not real Amazons, for they had two breasts: A real Amazon did not have a right breast since it would get in the way of the bow.[20]

Soon after that, Orellana and his friends noticed that the river was becoming tidal and realized that they must be approaching the sea. The land was also clear of woods: the high banks and savannas were replaced by lowlands; and soon they were plainly in the estuary of the great river, surrounded by islands instead of mainland. Here one of the brigantines was damaged by a log in the river, and at the same time, the other one was left high and dry on the riverside. They were attacked by Indians in great numbers, but withstood them. They found a beach where they could haul out and repair their vessels. In two weeks, both ships were adequately restored, and new rigging was made out of vines, and sails out of the blankets in which they had been sleeping. But these last days in the Amazon were days of penance, because of the hunger from which they suffered. They did not eat anything save what could be picked up on the edge of the river—a few snails and some tiny crabs. At this stage of the journey, they lacked anchors and used stones instead, but sometimes, the tide picked them up and carried them back in an hour or so to where they had been that morning.

At last they were able to sail out of the mouth of the great river. It was, as they all knew, August 25, Saint Louis's Day, 244 days since they separated from Gonzalo Pizarro. They had lost fourteen men in that time. Fray Carvajal noted: "We rested a day making ropes and, as the rest of the things with which we fitted ourselves out were imitations, and made by men without experience and unaccustomed to such professions, they lasted only a short time. So it was necessary to keep working and fitting ourselves out at random. In this way in one place, a sail was made and in another a rudder, in a third a pump, and in one further instance some rigging. In the case of each of these things, so long as we did not have them, we were in great danger." Carvajal went on to say that he was leaving out a "list of many other things which we lacked such as pilots and sailors and a compass . . . and without them there was no man, however devoid of common sense, that would thus dare to go to sea except ourselves."[21]

They emerged into the Atlantic by sheer chance in a zone that the Treaty of Tordesillas had given to Spain, not to Portugal.

Meantime, Gonzalo Pizarro was at the confluence of the Napo and the Coca, about 1,600 miles away as the crow flies: It took a long time for the truth of what had happened to be realized by Gonzalo Pizarro. He later accused Orellana of treachery. He said that Orellana had "shown the greatest cruelty in which any faithless man could indulge, abandoning Gonzalo Pizarro and the rest in those wildernesses among so many rivers and without food and caught in vast uninhabited regions, also carrying off all the arquebuses and crossbows, the iron materials of the whole expeditionary force. After great hardship, that expeditionary force did arrive at the junction of the rivers Coca and Napo."[22] Gonzalo never considered what might have happened to prevent his friends' return, and since then his view has been widely canvassed. Even the historian Oviedo, who came to know Orellana afterwards, seems to have thought that he should, and could, easily have returned to where Gonzalo Pizarro was waiting.[23] Few appreciated that the force of the currents made a return virtually impossible.

Gonzalo went on in his accusation: "And paying no heed whatever to what he owed to the service of Your Majesty, and to do what was his duty as he had been instructed by myself, instead of bringing back the food, he [Orellana] went on down the river without leaving any arrangements [to inform me] . . . And when my expeditionary force, having gone that far [saw] that there was no relief for them in the way of food . . . they became greatly discouraged, because for many days they had eaten nothing but palm shoots and some fruit which had fallen from trees and which they found on the ground, together with all kinds of noxious wild beasts which they had been able to find since they had eaten in this wild country more than 1,000 dogs and more than 100 horses."

Gonzalo Pizarro led his men down to where the rivers met. Having been told that food was to be had up the river that the Coca joined, he went there. Indeed there was food in abundance. There they rested and all the same ate their remaining eighty horses. Realizing that Orellana and their other friends were gone for good, they returned to the point where the two companies had parted and began a long, dispiriting journey home to Quito.

This was one of the worst journeys in the history of the empire. Lost in forests without paths, in heavy tropical rain, Gonzalo's men floundered slowly west, many barefoot, suffering as much from the thorns and the roots as from the mosquitoes and wild animals, often having to clear the way with their swords. It rained so much that days went by without their being able to see the sun. The Spaniards were always drenched, and such clothes as they had rotted, so that they had no alternative to going naked. All the four thousand or so Indian porters had died, and two-thirds of the Spaniards, also. About eighty Spaniards reached more open land, which they knew to be close to Quito. There, they found game—there were birds—and thus, unshod, they walked into the neighborhood of that city, kissing the earth and eating with such passion that most nearly died of a surfeit. Gonzalo Pizarro said: "At the cost of great suffering and with the loss of everything which we had taken with us, we returned to Quito with only our swords and a staff in hand. To Quito from where we turned back must have been more than 800 miles and a much greater distance by the route by which we returned."[24]

Quito was for emptier than it had been when Gonzalo had left, for half the population had gone to the war against Almagro. All the survivors of Gonzalo's expedition needed new clothes, but tailors were hard to find. Six suits were brought out by the citizenry to greet Gonzalo, but he and his close friends did not wish to wear what could not be worn by everyone in their party. So, half-naked, they went to the cathedral to give thanks for their survival, in scenes of great emotion. Then the bitterness at Orellana's action took shape with a vengeance.

28

Orellana and New Andalusia

The nearer the church the further from God, and all is not gold that
glistreth.

MIGUEL DE CERVANTES, *Don Quixote*

The extraordinary journey of Orellana was, meantime, continuing. Leaving
the Amazon, he and his friends soon found themselves north of the estuary
in the alarming Gulf of Paria. Once in it, like most sixteenth-century
travelers there, they found it very difficult to leave. Fray Carvajal described
how this took seven days, "during all of which time our companions never
dropped the oars from their hands and during all these seven days, we ate
nothing but some fruit resembling plums called *hogos*." Carvajal added,
"Having escaped from this prison, we proceeded for two days along the
coast [of Guiana] at the end of which, without knowing where we were, or
where we were going, nor what was to become of us, we made port in the
island of Cubagua [on September 11, 1542] and then in the city of Nueva
Cádiz, where we found our company and the small brigantine which had
arrived two days before."[1]

Most of the survivors, about forty all told, returned to Peru. In no time,
Fray Gaspar de Carvajal found himself in charge of the Dominican house
in Cuzco—a foundation that had become rich because of the hundred
sacks of coca leaf given to it by Hernando Pizarro. But Orellana and some
of his close associates bought a ship in Trinidad and went first to Santo
Domingo, then to Spain via Portugal. In Santo Domingo, Orellana met the
historian of Spain in the New World, Oviedo, who eventually wrote a good,
clear, and detailed account of the journey down the Amazon.[2]

Orellana returned to Europe, where he was delayed some days in Portugal. He reached Valladolid in May 1543. The secretary of the Council of the Indies, Juan de Samano, wrote to the King's principal secretary, Cobos: "There has arrived from Peru one who came out by going down a river which he navigated for a distance of 1,800 leagues and emerged at the Cape of San Agustín; and because of the particulars which he has brought with him covering his voyage, Your Lordship will not hear him without fatigue. I shall not relate these particulars since he will shortly come himself." In the margin of this letter Cobos made a note: "Would like an account sent to H.M."

The account by Orellana was based on the notes of Fray Carvajal. It was widely read, sometimes with disbelief. People laughed at the idea that there were Amazons. López de Gomera, Cortés's chaplain and biographer, commented that "women can shoot perfectly well with a right breast still there." He added that others besides Orellana had proclaimed this same story about Amazons ever since the Indies had been discovered. There was also anxiety whether the river on which Orellana had traveled was in Portuguese territory according to the Treaty of Tordesillas. Still, the river of Orellana remains known as the Amazon, and the course of the Amazon is actually to the west of the longitude 48° and, therefore, beyond the border of the Spanish zone as declared by the pope at Tordesillas.

Orellana also faced the bitter criticism of Gonzalo Pizarro, who had already reported to the Council that "he ran off with a brigantine and canoes filled with men and property belonging to him and, as a consequence a certain number died of hunger." Orellana, however, wrote a note to the King about the great size and wealth of the country that he had seen and across which he had traveled. He ended by stating that the natives inhabiting the land alongside the Amazon were intelligent and so "will be able to come into a knowledge of our Holy Catholic Faith." Because of that, he beseeched the King "to see fit to give it to me as territory to be held by me as governor in order that I may be able to explore it and colonize it on behalf of Your Majesty."[3]

The Council of the Indies was more cautious in respect of this demand than it would have been a generation before: "It may be a rich country," it conceded, "and one by which Your Majesty might be rendered a service." The Council agreed, however, that "it would be advantageous to the service of Your Majesty that the banks of the river be explored and settled and taken possession of within the shortest time." The Council noted that the Portuguese had built flotillas to go up the Amazon from the coast and that the King of France was also interesting himself in these regions. It was, however, the view of a majority on the Council that the business of exploration and colonization should be entrusted to Orellana. The minority opinion was confined to the untrustworthy Dr. Bernal, who thought that Orellana was inappropriate as a commander since he was poor. Nor did Dr. Bernal believe that Orellana could live up to the instructions that would be given to him. The land would be stirred up, and people would come to hate the Christian religion. Bernal thought that a peacefully inclined captain should be sent to the Amazon without soldiers in attendance but with clergymen "who would try out all the good and most feasible means for bringing the land round both to the service of God and to obedience to Your Majesty."[4]

Another member of the Council of the Indies was now Licenciado Gutierre Velázquez, who had never left Spain. He assumed that any new expedition on the Amazon would begin from Peru—approximately, indeed, from where Orellana had started off. Orellana, he thought, should take 180 men from Spain, of whom seventy would be cavalrymen. They should not take food from the Indians by force but should barter for it.[5]

In the end, in February 1544, Orellana did receive a contract from the Crown "to discover and populate the lands which are called New Andalusia." Who suggested this name is not evident from the surviving papers; presumably it was not Orellana himself.

Prince Regent Philip accepted Orellana's version of what had happened: "Owing to the current, you were all carried down the said river for over 600 miles to a place where you could not turn back." Orellana's new territory would extend many miles from the mouth of the river. There would be a city founded at the mouth and another at some distance inland at a place where he, the royal officials, and the friars thought best. Orellana would be *adelantado,* that coveted title, also governor and captain-general.[6] He would take with him two hundred infantrymen, one hundred horse, and eight friars, as well as material to build brigantines in which to sail up the river. Orellana's salary would be 5,000 ducats a year, to be paid from the profits of the lands conquered and settled, together with a twelfth of the royal revenue, provided it was not more than one million maravedís each year. He would be exempt from taxes, and he would be able to take eight African slaves with him. Orellana was warned: "If some governor or captain shall have explored or colonised some section of the river bank and shall be on it when you arrive, you should not do anything in detriment to his interests . . . even though you may find this to be within your jurisdiction as governor, so that we can avoid those disturbances which have arisen out of such situations in Peru and elsewhere." Orellana was told to keep to the rules that had been agreed with the "most serene King of Portugal" regarding the division of the Indies and also with regard to the Moluccas and the Spice Islands.[7]

There were several minor instructions: No Indians were to be carried on Orellana's boats "unless it be an occasional Indian boy whom the Spaniards . . . may have brought up [to be an interpreter]" and even for that, authorization had to be given by the Viceroy of Peru. Orellana was told that neither he nor any member of his party should take away from the Indians "any married woman nor child nor any woman whatsoever, no gold nor silver nor cotton nor feathers nor precious stones nor any other article unless it be by bartering and by payment." But when the food which the expedition was to take from Spain ran out, they should "be entitled to ask the Indians for some with offers of barter and, in cases where this may fail, then they may appeal to them for the said food with entreaties and kind words and means of persuasion, in such a way that they shall never go so far as to take it by force except after all these means, as well as others which the inspector and the friars together with the captain may advise, shall have been tried out." It was also stipulated that in no way whatsoever was war to be waged against the Indians unless it be to defend themselves, with the restraint that the situation might demand. For His Majesty was sending Orellana and his men "solely to teach and instruct the Indians"— not to fight them, but "to impart to them a knowledge of God and our Holy Catholic Faith and the obedience which they owe to Your Majesty."

Finally, the provisions stated: "No occasion is to be allowed to arise to be an excuse wherewith the Spaniards may hold Indians or maltreat them or prevent them from becoming Christians."[8] These provisions were written after the passage of the famous New Laws of 1542.

From May to November 1544, Orellana was busy in Spain recruiting men for his expedition. Thus he found that there was in Seville a shortage of sailors who wanted to take part. So Orellana thought that he would do well to take Portuguese sailors "because they are experienced in small, well-fitted-out vessels." Nor was there any Castilian who knew the region of the Amazon at all. Orellana told the Emperor that he wanted to be able to take as many Portuguese pilots as he desired. Then guns could not be found unless the Emperor provided them. In September 1544, we find a letter from Prince Philip (the regent) writing from Valladolid to Orellana saying that, through Fray Pablo de Torres, he had become informed of the preparations for the great journey and of the excellent prospects that there were. As to Torres, because he was so experienced and so good, "it would be wise to get advice from him in whatever you undertake." The Prince added, "Be warned against taking any Portuguese because it is believed that they would be a source of trouble."

When, a few weeks later, Fray Torres reported that Orellana seemed to be running out of money, the Prince wrote to the friar, "There is no possibility of our helping out with any money at all. I am telling, too, the *Casa de la Contratación* not to allow on this expedition anyone of whom you disapprove. But it is perfectly all right to take stallions as well as mares." He was in agreement that arms should be neither given nor sold to the Indians. But general Spanish opinion was that there was advantage in the Spaniards giving attention to the teaching of the Indians to be artisans. At the end of October, we read of Orellana writing to the King to say that his stepfather, Cosme de Chaves of Trujillo, was helping with the expedition to the extent of 1,600 ducats and that Genoese merchants were going to assist with another 2,500, thanks to the dealings of Vicente del Monte. This letter received a sharp answer: Directed to Orellana, "Governor of the province of New Andalusia," the Prince said, "[I have] learned that Orellana was entering into a contract for aid from various merchants . . . we do not consider that to be true because we don't think that you could do such a thing." The Prince added, "You must not go against what Fray Pablo says."[9]

At the end of November 1544, Orellana explained something else: "In order the better to perpetuate myself, I have become married."[10] This was to Ana de Ayala, who agreed to travel with him to New Andalusia, along with "a few sisters-in-law." This seems to have made Orellana unpopular. But not as much as his nomination of a Genoese camp master did.

By now, the preparations for the voyage back to the Amazon were almost complete, but relations on board and in the dockyard in Seville continued poorly. Cristóbal de Maldonado, the chief constable on board and in effect in control of discipline, was on bad terms with Orellana, whom he knew well, having been with him on the Amazon. Orellana hired as pilot a good sailor from Cádiz, Francisco Sánchez, who, however, did not know the coast of Brazil. A Portuguese who did know that territory was also hired, but it took time to secure approval for his participation.

Fray Pablo de Torres reported ill of these preparations. He wrote that when he arrived in Seville, he found the whole expedition to New Andalusia in a "very disorganized and even desperate condition." One of the ships was damaged, so that it had to be replaced by another, smaller one. To those who complained, Orellana said that he planned to take on the horses that he needed in the Canary or the Cape Verde Islands and that he already had all the materials necessary to build small boats *in situ*. Seville was outraged at the fact that not only were many of the sailors Portuguese but also some of them were even English, German, or Flemish. The master of the flagship (the *capitana*) came from Dubrovnik! Torres was unable to examine the expedition's accounts, which were kept secret by Orellana and his Genoese friends. Orellana seemed to have managed everything so badly that "no organiser of an expedition would have let him go from [there] to Naples," much less to the Amazon. Fray Torres wrote, "I do not wish to relate the infinite errors . . . which have been perpetrated in connection with the enterprise. The man who has completely ruined things has been [Vicente] del Monte, who has made himself rich out of the money of the Genoese through deals, and the *adelantado* [Orellana] has been putting up with all this. How could the fleet be well fitted out if to his own wife, who is excessively poor, they have given jewels, silks and embroideries and if the Genoese have handed over the 3,000 ducats in small change; and if the *Adelantado* and Del Monte had money in their pockets while the rest of the expedition is perishing from hunger and thirst." It seems to have been the incompetence of Orellana that most shocked Fray Pablo, who wrote to the prince regent Philip, "I assure Your Highness that he is not carrying enough water to reach the Canaries nor jars in which to secure any if it takes them fifteen days to get there . . . and also the deck of the ship on which the *adelantado* is sailing is full of women [*llena de mujeres*]."[11]

All the same, on May 11, 1545, the voyage finally began, with four ships and 400 fighting men on board. The journey was slow since Orellana chose to stop three months in Tenerife and then two months in Portugal's Cape Verde Islands. In the latter, ninety-eight members of his expedition died; fifty remained there because they were too weak to continue. Orellana also left behind one of his ships because he needed some of its equipment to repair the other vessels.

At last, in November he set off on the relatively short voyage from the Cape Verde Islands across to Brazil. But bad luck still attended him. A ship with seventy-seven men on board, as well as eleven horses, foundered and was lost. Despite the long stay in the Cape Verde Islands, water became short.

Finally, Orellana reached one of the mouths of the Amazon. He started upstream, despite requests for a rest. All the dogs and horses were eaten. Another fifty men died. One of the two caravels was wrecked; those on board took refuge on an island where the natives were unusually friendly. In the next three months, they built a new brigantine. Orellana, his wife, and Fray Pablo set off on this vessel looking for the main river Amazon, leaving Diego Muñoz and thirty or so men behind on the friendly island. These thirty eventually built their own boat using some of the timber and nails from the one that had foundered. In this craft, they went upriver in search of Orellana, but there was no sign of him. They returned to the sea; then six of them ran away because they believed that the territory was promising for agriculture. Four others absconded because they feared going on upstream in a small boat. The rest continued, though marooned one night in a mangrove swamp and driven mad by mosquitoes. Led by Francisco de Guzmán, they found a cultivated zone with cassava and maize as well as sweet potatoes, yams, duck, chickens, and also a turkey. Thus fortified, they had the energy to sail back up the South American coast, through the Gulf of Paria, to the island of Margarita.

There, after some time, they were joined by Ana de Ayala and twenty-five others, but not her husband. She reported that Orellana had not succeeded in finding the main channel of the Amazon, and that in consequence of his becoming ill, he had decided to abandon the project of founding New Andalusia. He had made up his mind to seek gold and silver instead. But when, more prosaically, he was looking for food, he and his expedition were attacked by Indians in canoes. They bombarded the Spaniards with arrows. Seventeen of them died. Orellana also died shortly afterwards, whether from grief over this loss or from his fever was quite unclear. That was in November 1546.

Of the whole expedition that had set out from Sanlúcar in May 1545, only forty-four survived. The forty-four included Orellana's widow, Ana. New Andalusia was not to be. But all the same, Orellana is remembered as the involuntary architect of the geographical unity of a continent and the heroic survivor of one of the greatest journeys. Gonzalo Pizarro remembered him, too—for other reasons.

29

The Defeat of the Viceroy

Oh Indies! Oh conquistadors full of work in the simplicity of those
times, where you had an excellent name and found eternal fame.

DORANTES DE CARRANZA

Vaca de Castro's apparently calm control of turbulent Peru lasted till a formal
successor, a viceroy, was appointed from Spain. That was in February 1543,
and the nominee was Blasco Núñez Vela, whose earlier life had been spent as
a captain of the fleet in several voyages to the Indies. He had also been
corregidor of Cuenca and of Málaga. His maritime qualities may have been
superlative; he may have been privately enchanting, for he was known to
have been passionate in his feelings; he may have been a good administrator;
but he was politically inept. The Council of the Indies made an error in
nominating him to such an important post. When he was named viceroy, it
became immediately known that it would be his responsibility to carry into
effect in Peru the New Laws on the administration of the empire and the
benign treatment of Indians. (For the New Laws, see chapter 44.)

This news shocked the old conquistadors of Peru, above all the *encomenderos*. These men, often rich and comfortable, turned to the last of
the Pizarros, Gonzalo Pizarro, to represent and to lead them. Since his return from the Amazon, Gonzalo had been living in luxury on his property
in Charcas, in what is now Bolivia. He had planned an expedition in 1542
but had been distracted from that by his wish to avenge his brother Francisco. The next year, 1543, with his son Francisco he set out to deal with the
Páez Indians, who had obstructed him on his earlier journey to the headwaters of the Amazon, precisely at Timaná. In his absence, he left Juan

Cabrera as his acting governor. Cabrera then was named to carry out an expedition to the cinnamon forest.

Throughout 1542, however, Gonzalo seemed the man whom the *encomenderos* thought could lead them against the New Laws, which they considered both unfair and absurd. Some friends urged him to seize the opportunity of carrying out a "unilateral declaration of independence," even make himself the first Spanish King of Peru, and to marry an Indian Princess.

In this electric atmosphere, Núñez Vela, the first viceroy, arrived at Nombre de Dios in Panama-Darien, accompanied by new judges of the supreme court of Peru. From Nombre de Dios, the Viceroy traveled overland to Panama, where he liberated many Indians who had been brought as slaves or servants from Peru. There were protests from the "owners," but the Viceroy told them that Charles the Emperor had specifically requested that this should be done.

The rest of the Viceroy's journey was beset with bad luck. First, his judge Ortiz de Zárate could not leave Panama because of illness. Ortiz de Zárate tried, though, to persuade Núñez Vela to enter Peru "*blandamente*" (innocently) and not to try to execute immediately the New Laws agreed in Spain, at the least till the supreme court was in place. Then Núñez Vela could proclaim such laws as he thought right, but even then, if there was opposition, it would be as well to consult the Emperor again. If Charles once again directed the Viceroy to enact the laws, he would by then be in a better position, having since established himself.

The Viceroy was angry at these suggestions, which he thought feeble. Without waiting for the judges, he set off impetuously, going first to Tumbes, then south to Trujillo, insisting on declarations there about the New Laws. The people of Trujillo appealed against him, many of them supposing that their wars had been wasted if they were going to have no slaves to look after them when they were old. But Núñez Vela went ahead and sent a message to the interim governor, Vaca de Castro, ordering him to lay down his authority.[1] By then, "all Peru was full of the Viceroy's harshness," as Garcilaso later put the matter. But Núñez Vela's train continued onward to Lima. The town council decided on a grand reception. But there were to be no Indian slaves present. An unknown wit wrote on the back wall of the main inn in the place, "Whoever seeks to throw me out of my house, I shall throw out of the world."[2]

Núñez Vela was received about ten miles from Lima, where many went out to meet him. These were headed by Vaca de Castro; Bishop Loaisa, not to be confused with his namesake and cousin on the Council of the Indies; the bishop-elect of Quito, Díaz; and the town council, headed by the Basque Benito Suárez de Carvajal, brother of Illán and Juan. The Viceroy publicly swore that he would always act in the interests of all Peruvians. Celebrations followed in the cathedral. The next day, Núñez Vela went to Pizarro's palace and had Vaca de Castro arrested and then placed in the common prison. The Viceroy accused his predecessor of abetting the plots of Gonzalo Pizarro, an unjust accusation. If blame were to be found for such events, the finger rather should point at the Viceroy himself. It was he who was to blame for coming to Peru in such an impulsive and hasty way, publishing all that he was going to do against the *encomenderos*.[3] He seemed an absurd figure in demanding so much ceremony and ritual from his attendants.

Meantime, Gonzalo wrote to the Viceroy on behalf of the cities and the *encomenderos* to protest against the New Laws. The Viceroy seemed obtuse. The judges of the supreme court eventually arrived in Lima. This complicated matters, for they soon took up the cause of Suarez de Carvajal, a factor whom the Viceroy had had killed because a body of soldiers had been seen leaving his house on their way to see Gonzalo Pizarro.[4] The matter was further complicated by the bad behavior of two Almagrists, Diego Méndez and Gómez Pérez, who had escaped Vaca de Castro to go and live in the circle of Manco Capac. They suggested that Manco should be permitted to return to Cuzco, where he could be expected to serve the new Viceroy. Núñez Vela was pleased with that idea. But before he could act, Gómez Pérez and Manco Capac had a dispute over manners. The former threw a ninepin ball at Manco, which hit him on the head and killed him.[5] Life in the new Peru was nothing if not short.

Now those Spaniards who were settled in Peru took the law into their own hands. The settlers of Huamanga, Arequipa, and Chuquisaca all implored Gonzalo Pizarro to be their *procurador* (representative) against the Viceroy. In La Plata, the settlers made a similar request to Diego Centeño, one of Pedro de Alvarado's followers who by now was Gonzalo's deputy. Both went to Lima with armed men and, with the Viceroy in Cuzco, prepared an independent army. Gonzalo recovered the *encomiendas* and other property of his brother Francisco that Vaca de Castro had seized. He also took gold and silver from the royal chest and soon had four hundred settlers and as many as twenty thousand Indians at his behest. He took prisoner those who had sided in recent events with the Viceroy. He hanged several of these, such as Gómez de Luna, another former follower of Pedro de Alvarado, as well as Martín de Florencia, who had been at Cajamarca. Diego Maldonado, held to be the richest of *encomenderos* in Peru and so known as "the Rich," was placed naked on a donkey and tortured by ropes and water.[6] Gonzalo also ordered other injustices, such as the execution of his cousin Pedro Pizarro. But he was talked out of that unwise idea by his experienced, eccentric, and artful master of the horse, Francisco de Carvajal. Gonzalo also permitted Vaca de Castro to escape in a ship to Panama.

Gonzalo Pizarro now sought to order his army in an efficient style. Hernando Bachicao pretended to be a count. He was savage in all his actions, but captained Gonzalo's artillery. That arm was becoming the decisive weapon of war at that time. All Gonzalo's men were powerful independent conquistadors with long histories of achievement. They climbed the great hill of Sacsahuamán, overlooking Cuzco. There they awaited the Viceroy, who had a slightly larger army of six hundred Spaniards, with one hundred horse and two hundred arquebusiers. Its basis was Vaca's army, and many of its men had known their opponents intimately for a generation.

For a time, the two armies fenced with, rather than fought, each other. Gonzalo was despondent at the size of his opponent's force and realized the risk that he was taking in choosing to fight against the Emperor's envoy, an action that could be interpreted as a revolt against the Emperor himself. But he was cheered by the adhesion to his cause of Pedro de Puelles, one of those who came to Peru from Guatemala with Pedro de Alvarado, with forty horsemen and twenty arquebusiers. He was also cheered by the complete confusion in Lima, resulting in charges and countercharges between the Viceroy and judges of the supreme court. Núñez Vela was for a time under arrest as a result of the judges' decisions, then placed on an island two leagues off, allegedly for his own safety.[7] Then he was able to leave for the apparently safe port of Trujillo.

On October 6, 1544, Gonzalo Pizarro entered Lima. It was a triumphant entry. His van was led by Bachicao, and he was backed by no fewer than twenty-two pieces of artillery, carried by Indian porters. This was a colossal array for Peru. There followed thirty arquebusiers, then fifty artillerymen, followed by Diego Gumiel and two hundred pikemen. After them came three companies of infantrymen, who preceded Gonzalo Pizarro riding a fine white horse. Pizarro, in turn, was followed by three sections of cavalry. Gonzalo repaired to the house of Judge Ortiz de Zárate, where that official and his judicial colleagues took his oath. They then went to the council chamber, where Gonzalo was received with due ceremony as procurator general of Peru. No one in Spanish America had had such a grand entry into a city as Gonzalo. There was no battle. The presence of artillery and arquebuses on such a substantial scale was remarkable, and a formidable innovation.

Gonzalo now found himself governor of Peru in view of the rights of conquest held by his brother Francisco and the nomination of the judges. He acted, however, as a monarch more than a governor. He gave satisfaction to merchants as well as *encomenderos*. Of course, there were some settlings of old scores: For example, Diego Gumiel, head of the pikemen in Gonzalo's *joyeuse entrée*, made a minor complaint and was strangled by Francisco de Carvajal. Carvajal declared, with his special black humor: "Make way for Captain Diego de Gumiel, who has sworn never to do it again."[8] Garcilaso commented: "There were no rejoicings without executions and no executions without rejoicings." Yet there were many more conventional celebrations—bullfights, games, jousts—and even some poems were specially written. After a few weeks, Gonzalo Pizarro, a man with no sense of bitterness, gave a general pardon to all who had taken up arms against him. The exceptions were Sebastián Garcilaso de la Vega, an aristocrat related to the poet of that name who had also come to Peru with Alvarado and who hid for a time in a grave in the Dominican monastery, and a Licenciado Carvajal, who fled to the north. Gonzalo sent Dr. Tejada and Francisco Maldonado as *procuradors* to represent his cause in Spain, escorted by Hernando Bachicao as far as Panama. On the only ship, there was Vaca de Castro, still a prisoner, who, with a kinsman, García de Montalvo, seized control before it could leave harbor. In the end, a brigantine was found, and Bachicao and the *procuradors* left on it.

Núñez Vela, surprisingly free and still determined to impose his viceroyalty, was now making for the first Spanish city of Peru, Tumbes, in order to try to raise men. He then went to San Miguel (in modern

Ecuador). He was certain that reinforcements would rally to him, for he was strategically well placed to receive such help. He could not avoid some further skirmishing. Jerónimo de Villegas from Burgos and Gonzalo Díaz de Pineda, acting for Gonzalo, captured one of the Viceroy's men and cut off his head. The Viceroy, in revenge, pursued and dispersed them, Gonzalo Díaz afterwards being killed by Indians as he wandered lost.

Gonzalo Pizarro himself set off in March 1545 to deal, as he supposed, with the Viceroy's challenge, now with about six hundred foot and substantial cavalry. He left behind the ambiguous Lorenzo de Aldana—originally from Cáceres, who like so many had come with Pedro de Alvarado to Peru—in control of Lima with eighty men. There were other ambiguities: Thus Gómez de Luna, in La Plata, unwisely remarked that sooner or later the Emperor would rule again—a comment that led to his execution by Francisco de Almendras, Gonzalo's great friend, who was a native of Plasencia. Friends of Luna, such as Diego Centeño, organized a rising. There was some sporadic bloodshed in Lima as a result, but everyone knew that all depended on the dealings between the Viceroy and Gonzalo Pizarro.

The Viceroy withdrew even farther northward: He fled to Quito, thence to Popayán, which is far into what we think of now as Colombia. There, he built forges and made new arquebuses. He wrote to Benalcázar and Juan Cabrera, asking for their help. Gonzalo put it about that he was planning to withdraw from Quito in order to deal with the rising of Diego Centeño. The Viceroy believed this and made as if to return to Quito. But Gonzalo had made a feint. The Viceroy returned to Quito and was astounded to find Gonzalo still outside the city. All the same, though weary, he prepared for battle. His captains of infantry were Sancho Sánchez de Ávila and Juan Cabrera, while Benalcázar fought for him with Cepeda and Pedro de Bazán as captains of cavalry. The arquebusiers skirmished. Then Gonzalo's evil genius, Francisco de Carvajal, attacked the Viceroy's right. The Viceroy's cavalry, despite the presence of Benalcázar, attacked in no special order and were destroyed by the arquebusiers. Gonzalo rode into the center of the fight with a hundred horsemen. Cabrera and Sancho Sánchez were killed, as was Alfonso de Montalvo on Gonzalo's side. Dressed in an Italian shirt, the Viceroy was knocked to the ground by Hernando de Torres, his execution completed by a black slave. His head was taken to Quito, where it was exposed for months. Two hundred of his men were killed, but only seven of

Gonzalo Pizarro's. Most of these men were buried on the field, but the Viceroy himself and other leaders were interred in the new cathedral of Quito. The wounded were pardoned, Benalcázar was sent back to Popayán, and others went to join Valdivia in Chile.[9] Another who died was Santa Teresa's brother, Antonio de Cepeda. Of the old leaders, Licenciado Álvarez was dead, Tejada had gone to Spain, Ortiz de Zárate was in Lima alone, and Centeño was in the South, but had so few friends with him that his whole force could hide in a cave.

At this time, there were probably some four thousand Spaniards in Peru living in 274 *encomiendas* scattered throughout the colony—probably eighty-six at Cuzco, forty-five at Trujillo and Lima, thirty-four at Huánaco, thirty-seven at Arequipa, twenty-two at Huamanga, and five at Chachapoyas. Perhaps there were 1,550,000 tributary Indians. So at least the census of 1540 suggested.[10] The missionary orders, the Dominicans and the Mercedarians, numbered about one hundred.

These unprecedented political disputes overshadowed some great economic events. Thus in 1542–43 there was a gold rush near Cuzco and another one in 1545–46.[11] Then, in 1545, the silver mines at Potosí were stumbled upon by Don Diego, son of a minor Indian cacique in the region of Cuzco. Don Diego had been first at the mine of Porco, which was no distance from Potosí. Then he found Potosí, and within months seven thousand Indians were working there. It was an event that soon transformed the country—indeed the empire.

The Spanish miners with chains of gold round their necks would spend their new wealth on "fountains in which flowed the best European wines and on dark mestizo girls in silk shoes and pearls for laces, their hair kept in place by rubies . . . and the streets would be covered by silver." Every kind of embroidery, brocade, silk, gold, tapestries, looking glasses from Venice, and pearls from Panama could soon be bought.[12]

30

Gonzalo and La Gasca

No one can foresee the future, which is known only to God. Cowards
may weep over tomorrow's misfortunes, but you know better than I
that brave knights may still gain victory's crown of glory.

Tirant lo Blanc

Gonzalo Pizarro had Peru at his feet. That was certain. But what should he do
with it? His chief adviser was a curious and talented if dangerous individual,
Francisco de Carvajal, an experienced conquistador who had become known
in his old age as "the devil of the Andes." He was apparently born Francisco
López Gascón and took the name of Carvajal since he had been a protégé of
the cardinal of that name in Italy—or he had wanted to be.[1] He was born in
1464 at Rágama, a bleak village in old Castile between Peñaranda de
Bracamonte and Madrigal de las Altas Torres. In the early years of the
sixteenth century, he went to Italy to fight under the command of "El Gran
Capitán," Fernando's most successful commander, Gonzalo Fernández de
Córdoba. Carvajal was said to have been at Pavia in 1525—but then so many
who went to the Indies were rumored to have been present at that legendary
combat. Then he went to New Spain. After a few years there, he was among
those sent by Viceroy Mendoza to help the Pizarros in Peru against Manco
Capac. He seems to have conducted himself well and had risen to be a
magistrate in Cuzco by 1541. He later fought effectively for Vaca de Castro as
captain of the pikemen at Chupas and, as we have just seen, for Gonzalo
Pizarro at Quito. By then he was well into his seventies.

Carvajal had a formidable reputation as a witty, cruelly courteous, and
competent soldier who was never shocked by his own or other men's bru-

tality. He killed men pitilessly but accompanied his actions with jests and humorous sallies. On one occasion, he said that since a doomed man was so rich, Carvajal would allow him to choose from which branch of a tree he would like to be hanged. Referring to the citizens of Lima who had fled from him, Gonzalo Pizarro once asked him to "calm these people down." Carvajal replied, "I promise your lordship that I'll quieten these men down so effectively that they will come out to meet you." Their bodies were soon hanging on poles on the road into Lima.[2] Carvajal dressed always in a purple Moorish burnous, and a hat of black taffeta.

Now in 1546, after the death of the Viceroy Núñez Vela, Carvajal is said to have addressed Gonzalo Pizarro in Lima along the following Shakespearean lines:

Sir, when a viceroy is killed in battle and his head is cut off and placed on a gibbet and the battle is fought against the royal standard, there is no pardon to be hoped for and no compromise to be made, even though your lordship may make ample excuses and shows himself more innocent than a suckling or a babe. Nor can you trust their words or promises, whatever assurances they give, unless you declare yourself to be king and take the government on yourself without waiting for another to give it to you and put a crown on your head and allocate whatever land is unoccupied among your friends and supporters. And as what the King gives is adequate for two lives, you should give it as a perpetual title and make dukes, marquesses and counts and set up military orders, with similar names and titles to those in Spain, and name other saints and patrons and insignia, as you think fit. Give the knights of the new orders incomes and pensions to keep themselves and to let them live at ease. With this approach, your Lordship will attract to your service all the Spanish nobility and chivalry in this empire, fully rewarding those who have conquered it and who have served your lordship. And, to attract the Indians, and make them so devoted that they will die for your lordship, as they would have done for their Inca monarchs, take one of their princesses to wife and send ambassadors to the forest where the heir of the Incas lives and bid him come forth and recover his lost majesty and state, asking him to offer you as your wife any sister or daughter whom he may have. You know how much this prince will esteem kinship and friendship with you and you will gain the universal love of all the Indians by restoring their Inca and, at the same time, make them genuinely willing to do whatever their king orders them on your behalf, such as bringing supplies, etc.

In short, all the Indians will be on your side and, if they do not help your enemies with supplies and porters, no one can prevail against you in Peru . . . The Inca will govern his Indians in peace as his ancestors did in the past, whilst your Lordship and your officials and captains will govern the Spaniards, and have charge of military affairs, requiring the Inca to tell the Indians to do whatever you command. Your Lordship will receive all the gold and silver which the Indians produce in this empire, for they do not regard it as wealth . . . With all the gold and silver which they are reputed to have, your lordship can buy the entire world if you want to. And pay no attention if they say you are a traitor to the King of Spain. You are not. For no king can be a traitor. This land belongs to the Incas, its natural lords and, if it is not restored to them, you have more right to it than the King of Castile, for you and your brothers conquered it at your own expense and risk. Now by restoring it to the Inca, you are simply doing what you should have by natural law [*ley natural*] and in seeking to govern it yourself as its conqueror and not as a vassal and subject of another, you are doing what you owe to your reputation, for anyone who can become a king by the strength of his arm should not remain a serf. It all depends on the first step and the first declaration.

I beg your lordship to consider the import of what I have said about ruling the empire in perpetuity so that those who live and shall live will follow you. Finally I urge you, whatever may happen, to crown yourself and call yourself king, for no other name befits one who has won an empire by his strength and courage. Die a king and not a vassal.[3]

This was the speech of Carvajal as reported by Garcilaso. It may owe much to imagination. But it was perhaps the approximate truth.

Carvajal was supported in this appeal by three men high in Gonzalo Pizarro's favor at the time: Pedro de Puelles, Hernando Bachicao, and Diego de Cepeda. We have learned of them earlier, but now was their hour.

These three are said to have repeated the theme of Carvajal's speech: Won at their own expense, the land of Peru was theirs to share. They would ally with the Turks if Gonzalo was not given the governorship of Peru and Hernando Pizarro not released from his prison in the Castillo de la Mota, in Medina del Campo.

Gonzalo himself was tempted by the ideas of Carvajal, but he still hoped that Charles the Emperor would make him governor of Peru.

In these months, he seemed to have no enemies in Peru; he treated everybody so kindly, referring to all his captains as "brother." He called Carvajal "father." He ate at a long table always laid for a hundred people, with two empty places always beside himself so that he could summon whoever he wished to dine with him.[4]

Yet time was not on Gonzalo's side. His rebellion against the Viceroy disturbed Charles, who was distressed by what seemed an imperial set-back.[5] In Spain, they were considering the dispatch of someone new, a clever man ready for everything, "to put Peru in order." In the Council of the Indies, the name that appealed to everyone was Antonio de Mendoza. But that could not be. Mendoza was still fully occupied in his current post as Viceroy of New Spain. In the council, the Duke of Alba supported the idea of pursuing the rebels without quarter. The Duke and Dr. Guevara thought it essential to send some gentleman to Peru in whom the King would have personal confidence because of his family and blood. A Velasco or a Mendoza would be ideal. But the majority of the council thought a *letrado,* a man of the pen and one of learning, was the right person.[6] The latter argument won the day. At the end of May 1545, the council decided in favor of sending to Peru Pedro de la Gasca, a lawyer who was at that time visitor-general of public officials in the kingdom of Valencia, where he was concerned with the incursions of Muslim pirates from the north of Africa. He had successfully defended Valencia against the Turkish admiral Barbarossa. He was known as a hard man, and he had political experience. He was a protégé of the powerful secretary Cobos and had always been favored by Cardinal Tavera. He was already in his late fifties and would celebrate his sixtieth birthday before he reached Peru.

La Gasca was a typical bureaucrat of the age of Charles the Emperor, for like so many, he derived from a family of public servants. He took his name from his mother's family, his maternal grandfather having been *corregidor* of Congosto (León). Until he agreed to go to Peru, Pedro de la Gasca's career was also a characteristic one. He had attended Cisneros's famous university of Alcalá de Henares and had taken part in the war of the *comuneros* on the royalist side. He had been taught by the great grammarian Lebrija. In 1528, he became rector of the University of Salamanca but he was there for a short time only, because of some mysterious controversy, which turned out to be less an ideological matter than an affair of personalities. He had several other lucrative assignments before becoming in 1540 judge of the Council of the Inquisition in Valencia.[7] In Valencia, he had shown the qualities of efficiency and leadership that were to serve him well in Peru.

La Gasca, to look at, was a person of no importance. But Garcilaso rightly wrote of him that he was "a man of much better understanding than his appearance suggested."[8]

La Gasca studied Peru carefully before he agreed to accept the commission. He made unusual requests, which were, unusually, granted. He wanted full powers, including the right to grant life and impose death. He wanted to be free to name new men for the right places. He wanted to be able to concede *encomiendas*.[9] He wanted no salary but insisted all his expenses had to be paid.

He set off, visiting on the way his brother Abbot Francisco Jiménez de Ávila, his mother in El Barco de Ávila, then his brother Juan, the *corregidor* in Málaga. He took with him a suite of thirty, including two new judges, Licenciado Andrés Cianca of Peñafiel, Valladolid, and Íñigo de Rentería. The first would become La Gasca's chief legal adviser; the second was an old friend, having been with him in the 1520s in Salamanca. There were also Alonso de Alvarado, whom we met earlier as a captain of the Pizarros against Almagro, and Pascual de Andagoya, the first Spaniard to go to Peru, even before Pizarro became interested. He had been a long time recovering from his near drowning in 1522 and in the interim had performed other tasks, such as being deputy governor in Panama.[10] Also with La Gasca was Francisco Maldonado, who had gone back to Spain on Gonzalo Pizarro's behalf to explain what he had done or was doing and seems then to have changed sides. La Gasca was likely to be well advised once he got to Peru.

La Gasca's party left Sanlúcar on May 26, touched at La Gomera in the Canaries, as was then usual for America-bound ships, and made landfall at Santa Marta, where they were all well received by the governor of New Granada, Miguel Díaz de Armendariz. They then went on to Nombre de Dios, where they arrived on July 27 with little display, crossing the isthmus to reach Panama on August 13, where they learned for the first time of the death of the Viceroy. One of Gonzalo's captains, Hernán Mejía, offered to bring many of his colleagues over to him.[11] But La Gasca also met a small delegation of high-placed churchmen and others who were on their way to Spain to request the Emperor to make Gonzalo governor. They, too, changed sides, after meeting the new royal emissary, who, despite his feeble appearance, clearly had nerves of iron and real qualities of leadership.

These churchmen were important. Fray Jerónimo de Loaisa had been archbishop of Lima since 1545 and was the brother of the new archbishop of Seville, the *inquisidor general* and sometime president of the Council of the Indies; Fray Tomás de San Martín was the provincial of the Dominicans in Lima and had already once been acting governor of Peru; and Lorenzo de Aldana had accomplished much since he, with so many other grand captains, had arrived in Peru in 1534 with Alvarado. Gonzalo had made him governor in Lima in his absence in the north. La Gasca shortly thereafter made him commander of his navy. Another churchman with them who made this act of royal loyalty was Martín de Calatayud, bishop of Santa Marta, near Cartagena. Finally, among these eminent turncoats was Gómez de Solís, who had been majordomo to Gonzalo.[12] These men were influenced by La Gasca's decision to declare a general pardon and his undertaking to delay implementation of the New Laws; thus they deserted the leader "who had raised them up," in Garcilaso's words.[13]

One of those who came with La Gasca was Pedro Hernández Paniagua Loaisa, a cousin of both Cardinal Loaisa in Spain and of the archbishop of Lima. He had been on the municipal council of Plasencia in Castile and now was sent by La Gasca to take a letter to Gonzalo Pizarro. This missive explained that he had heard of the late viceroy's intractability over the New Laws. He also said, "We are assured that neither you, nor any who has followed you, has any inclination to be disloyal to us."[14] In another letter, La Gasca told Gonzalo that he was certain that it would be impossible for him to resist the attack of a powerful army formed in the name of the Emperor.

Another clever letter from La Gasca to Gonzalo declared, "His Majesty and the rest of us in Spain have never regarded what you have done as rebellious or disloyal to the King but simply as a defence of your just rights." Henceforward, though, Gonzalo should fulfill His Majesty's demands, "thereby performing what was due also to God."[15]

Gonzalo discussed these missives with Francisco de Carvajal and with Cepeda. Carvajal thought the letters excellent and thus became in favor of collaboration with La Gasca. Cepeda thought that they were deceitful documents, being a way of securing Gonzalo's surrender without the use of force: Thereafter, trials and executions could begin.

Gonzalo was foolishly in favor of Cepeda's view. All the same, he thought it right to have a meeting of eighty settlers, a majority of whom supported Carvajal. One or two told Hernández Paniagua that they would now support La Gasca in any discussion or dispute. Hernández Paniagua thought that La Gasca would have confirmed Gonzalo in the governorship of Peru if he had had real evidence that the majority of settlers wanted it. But there were difficulties: One of La Gasca's representatives, Fray Francisco de San Miguel, was detained at Tumbes by Gonzalo's men. These men told the friar that the King was bankrupt and needed their money. Paniagua spiritedly replied, "The city of Naples alone is worth more than three Perus."[16] He left Lima with a bland reply from Gonzalo to La Gasca in which the former pledged anew his loyalty to the emperor Charles and described how "for sixteen years he and his brothers had worked for the royal crown of Spain to whose glory they had added so much."[17] At the same time, sixty Spanish residents wrote to La Gasca suggesting that he go home because, they said, they had no need of his presence; nor did they need any royal pardon from him since they had done nothing wrong.[18]

La Gasca could now see that the surrender of Gonzalo would be a complex matter. He set about organizing the skeleton of an army and, on April 10, 1547, set off for Peru from Panama with 820 soldiers in eighteen ships and a galliot. Despite bad weather and heavy winds, the new army reached Manta on May 31 and went on to Tumbes on June 30. Several groups of settlers in nearby towns proclaimed their loyalty to the Crown and told La Gasca so. After waiting a month at Tumbes, La Gasca wrote to Charles the Emperor suggesting that a new viceroy immediately be named. He again proposed Antonio de Mendoza, the Viceroy in New Spain.[19] Then La Gasca continued down the coast as far as the mouth of the river Santa before starting into the mountains.

He was all this time accompanied by both Alonso de Alvarado and Bishop Loaisa, who knew the land so well by now. La Gasca had before that named Pedro de Hinojosa as the commander of his forces. Hinojosa came from a notable family from Trujillo; he had been among those recruited by Francisco Pizarro in 1529 and had been for a time Gonzalo Pizarro's naval commander.

On July 20, Gonzalo Pizarro wrote to the Emperor saying that if there were any fighting, the fault would be all La Gasca's, not his, because Gonzalo would never do anything that His Majesty would dislike as a disservice.[20] But now Gonzalo had begun to find that his position was falling apart. As soon as they heard that La Gasca had at least delayed if not canceled the New Laws in Peru and had proclaimed a pardon, many of Pizarro's leading supporters made it evident that they would repudiate the leadership of Gonzalo.

Still, the latter arranged his army. Carvajal was the overall commander, to whom a company of arquebusiers was attached. His captain of cavalry was the ex-judge Cepeda. His standard was borne by Antonio de Altamirano, a member of a famous family in Mérida and related to the great Cortés. Some captains had chosen as their heraldic devices Gonzalo's name surmounted by a crown. Carvajal insisted that each soldier should have a badge indicating to what company he belonged. Cepeda drew up a document insisting that Pedro de Hinojosa had committed treason in giving Gonzalo's ships to La Gasca, and La Gasca was accused of the same for having received them. He announced that both would be hanged, drawn, and quartered when they were captured.

As this army took shape, there were some terrible moments for Gonzalo. Thus the standard-bearer, Altamirano, was killed by Carvajal personally on suspicion of desertion. Pedro de Puelles deserted and was killed by a gang of Spaniards led by the hunchback Diego de Salazar, who then himself crossed to La Gasca. Gonzalo hanged a common soldier whom he observed wearing two shirts, which he interpreted as a sign that he was ready to desert. Gonzalo announced that even if only ten friends stood by him, he would reconquer all Peru. But every day brought a new setback: Lima declared for La Gasca, and some of Gonzalo's men began to think that they could preserve their lives only by fleeing to the forest of Anti or going to join Valdivia in Chile. Gonzalo had also sent some of his best men against Diego Centeño, who was still sheltering near Lake Titicaca. Reading of these and other maneuvers is like hearing of an elaborate game whose rules had not yet been decided.

Gonzalo and La Gasca fought two battles. The first, at Huarina on the shores of Titicaca, was won by the former. Carvajal was Gonzalo's commander as usual, and he still had with him four hundred skilled fighters, among them Juan de Acosta and the experienced Hernando Bachicao. For once, his arquebusiers had a decisive effect, though the cavalry of the two sides fought fiercely. Bachicao seems to have changed sides in the middle of the battle, but then changed back again. Gonzalo's camp was sacked, but Centeño's infantry was too busy doing the sacking to be able to fight afterward. Then the victorious captains returned to Cuzco to seek supplies and reinforcements. There they were diverted by feeling that they needed to execute—in some cases brutally—Spaniards and Indians whom they thought not in favor of Gonzalo.

In these moments of hesitation, La Gasca recovered. He sent Alonso de Alvarado back to Lima to seek artillery, clothes, arms, craftsmen capable of making arquebuses, powder, pikes, and helmets. He dispatched two commanders to assemble the remains of Centeño's forces; he captured one of Gonzalo's friends, Pedro de Bustamante, and had him strangled. He then organized a new army in which the commanders were the same as they had been before but whose captains included such old stagers as Gómez de Alvarado, of Mexican fame, and Pascual de Andagoya. Rojas was his captain of artillery. Equipped for war, La Gasca had with him Loaisa, the archbishop of Lima, as well as the bishops of Cuzco and Quito, not to speak of the heads of the order of Saint Dominic and of the Mercedarians.

La Gasca left Jauja, making for Cuzco, on December 29, 1547, with about 1,900 men, including 400 horse, 700 arquebusiers, and 500 pikemen. This was the most formidable army that had yet been assembled in the New World. They spent the three months of the Peruvian winter at Antahuailla. Many of Gonzalo's men joined him, and La Gasca was especially pleased by the adhesion of Pedro de Valdivia from Chile. La Gasca said that he valued Valdivia more than 800 good soldiers. La Gasca wrote a long letter to Gonzalo on December 16, 1547, with a meticulous response to all the comments made by Pizarro to the Emperor in his letter of July 20.[21]

Given this swelling success, Gonzalo's friend the ex-judge, Cepeda, suggested to his leader that he should accept peace terms with La Gasca. Gonzalo consulted several of his captains. Bachicao, Juan de Acosta, Diego Guillén, and Juan de la Torre considered themselves invincible and advised Gonzalo not to treat. Carvajal then returned and had Bachicao strangled for deserting in the middle of the Battle of Huarina. He also had strangled María Calderón, who had railed against Gonzalo's intransigence. Her body was hung outside her window.

For the moment, Gonzalo seemed well enough. He entered Cuzco triumphantly—with flowers, bells, Indians greeting him as the Inca, and trumpets. The chronicler Garcilaso de la Vega saw it all as a boy. He also observed Carvajal, old but indomitable, entering the city on a large dun-colored mule.

Gasca moved toward Cuzco with his great army, and reached the river Abancay. Then he faced the river Apurímac. Where should the army cross? There were three or four bridges. The road was almost impassable for men in any kind of formation, because of the sharpness of the mountains on both sides of the river. Advised by the imaginative Valdivia, La Gasca pretended to build bridges at four new places so that Gonzalo would not know which section he would use. Carvajal is said to have commented: "Valdivia is in this land or else it is the devil." Carvajal had known Valdivia in Italy, perhaps even, heroically, at Pavia. La Gasca decided to cross the river at Cotapampa.

Carvajal advised Gonzalo how to destroy everything living on the northern bank of the river and, playing on the inexperience of half of La Gasca's army, fall on them while they were crossing. But, for reasons now difficult to understand, Gonzalo preferred to rely on the counsel of Juan de Acosta, who had accompanied him on his cinnamon journey and who now lazily permitted the enemy to cross at night while he slept. Had Carvajal's advice been followed, Gonzalo would have had a chance of victory. Now, however, there was little that he could do. He fell back on Sacsahuamán, where La Gasca could attack only from the front and where he hoped to be able to destroy his enemy by heavy artillery fire. Gonzalo had become bemused by the effectiveness of artillery. At the end of March, he wrote desperately to Father Francisco de Herrera, then a priest in his own *encomienda* of Charcas, "God is fighting for us, your excellency must believe that, we can conquer the world."[22]

At Sacsahuamán, the battle was not to be, for Gonzalo's army was melting away. Even Diego de Cepeda (of all people) abandoned Gonzalo, as did Garcilaso de la Vega. The pikemen dropped their weapons and took to their heels; the arquebusiers copied them with their weapons. Carvajal was for once uncertain what to recommend. Gonzalo took the hint. He rode toward the enemy and, coming up with Villavicencio, said, "I am Gonzalo Pizarro, I wish to surrender to the Emperor." He preferred to surrender honorably rather than to flee in dishonor. He was taken to La Gasca who asked Gonzalo if he thought it right to have stirred up the country against the Emperor and to have made himself governor against the will of His Majesty, as well as to have killed a viceroy in a pitched battle. Gonzalo replied that the judges of the supreme court had bidden him become governor and he had himself authorized these actions in light of the power vested by His Majesty in his brother, the Marquess. As to the viceroy Núñez Vela, the judges had ordered him to be expelled from Peru. He, Gonzalo, had not killed the Viceroy. But the relations of those whom the Viceroy had killed had been obliged to seek revenge. Everything he had done had been at the insistence of his fellow residents.

La Gasca replied that Gonzalo had shown himself most ungrateful for the grants that the King-Emperor had made to his brother Francisco. Those grants had enriched them all, though they had been poor before. They had raised them from the dust. In any case, Gonzalo himself had done nothing in respect of the actual discovery of Peru.

Gonzalo replied: "My brother alone was enough to discover the country, but all of us four brothers were necessary for its conquest. We and our relations and friends did what we did at our own risk and expense. The only honour which His Majesty gave to my brother was to make him a marquess. He did not lift us from the dust since the Pizarros have been noblemen and gentlemen with our own estates since the Goths came to Spain. If we were poor, that explains why we ventured out into the world and won this empire and gave it to His Majesty, though we might have kept it, as many others have done who have won new lands."

La Gasca considered and said to his advisers, "Take him away, he's as much a rebel today as he was yesterday."[23]

Meanwhile, Carvajal, seeing the game was up, fled on a pony. It fell into a stream, pinning one of its rider's legs under it. Some of his men who were also fleeing found him and took him to La Gasca in the hope that he would pardon their misdeeds if they handed in a prisoner such as he.[24] Carvajal was taken to a makeshift jail. His guards at first put lighted torches between his shirt and his back, but Diego Centeño, who had known him well, put a stop to that torture.[25]

The following day, April 10, 1548, Gonzalo Pizarro, Carvajal, Juan de Acosta, Francisco Maldonado, Juan Vélez de Guevara, Dionisio de Bobadilla, and Gonzalo de los Nidos—all the leaders of the Pizarros who had not deserted—were executed. Carvajal was treated especially harshly. He was dragged from prison to an execution yard by a horse and there hanged. The heads of the dead were cut off and sent for exhibition to numerous places in Peru. Gonzalo's body was buried in the Mercedarian church in Cuzco, alongside that of Almagro. His house was razed. Of course, his heirs lost all his valuable *encomiendas*. Another whom La Gasca executed was Francisco de Espinosa, nephew of the famous Licenciado Espinosa who had served as Gonzalo's *maestresala*.[26]

La Gasca was shortly received in Cuzco with the ceremonies usual for the reception of great men, which had included Gonzalo Pizarro only a short time before. There were bullfights and shows of tilting. Alonso de Alvarado and the judge Andrés de Cianca punished all Gonzalo's supporters if they had not given themselves up. Some were hanged, some quartered, some were condemned to serve in La Gasca's galleys, some were flogged.[27] The last caused a scandal, for the Indians, still secretly worshipping their dead, had not seen Spaniards beaten before.

Soon the Spanish victors would turn their imaginative attention to the Peruvians, whom they had so roundly defeated. In the 1550s, Juan Polo de Ondegardo, a Spanish magistrate, would begin profound inquiries into the nature of the Inca religion. He established that the Incas worshipped at more than four hundred shrines in or near the city.[28] He found in 1558 that the descendants of the Inca were still worshipping their ancestors' mummies.

One element in La Gasca's success should not be ignored: "The desire of the Spaniards to see the things of their own land in the Indies has been so desperate," wrote Garcilasa de la Vega, "that no effort or danger has been too great to induce them to abandon the attempt to satisfy their wishes."[29]

As they wanted wine, oranges, horses and dogs, guns and swords, wheat bread and salt beef, a real break with the old Spain was inconceivable.

La Gasca hoped to persuade the heirs of Manco Capac, headed by the five-year-old Sayri-Tupa, to come out of their secret encampment in the jungle at Vilcabamba, and he made some headway in this.

31

Valdivia and Chile

> Are you not aware, Christian Soldier, that when you were initiated into the mysteries of the life-giving feast, you enrolled in the army of Christ?
>
> ERASMUS, *Enchiridion*

We have run ahead of the story. For in April 1539, Francisco Pizarro—apparently triumphant in all Peru over the Indians of the region and his Spanish rivals—made a journey of exploration to Charcas and Lake Titicaca. Among the followers and friends with him was Pedro de Valdivia, who had recently been his chief magistrate and who had been asked to lead the army against Almagro. After his victory at Las Salinas, Pizarro gave Valdivia the valley of Canela, "the cinnamon valley," in Charcas as an *encomienda* and the rich silver mine of Porco. Pizarro probably thought of him as an entirely reliable captain who could be counted upon in all circumstances. It was, therefore, probably an unwelcome surprise when Valdivia asked for permission to explore and conquer the land to the south that had been abandoned by Almagro. But Pizarro, wrote Valdivia himself, "seeing my determination graciously opened the door."[1] Pizarro also took away his grants in Peru, but Valdivia did not seem to mind.

A military man and the descendant of military men, Valdivia was the son of Diego de Valdivia and came from a village named either Castuera or Campanario in the beautiful valley known as the Serena in Extremadura. His hometown was about twenty miles from Cortés's birthplace, Medellín, and so not far from the hometowns of all the great conquistadors. He entered the army about 1520 in Italy, where he fought under Henry of Nassau, then Prospero Colonna, finally at Pavia under the immortal Pescara. Valdivia seems in those campaigns to have been a simple soldier. He married Marina Ortiz de Gaete of Zalamea, also in the Serena, and lived an impoverished life with her, without children. He apparently met Pizarro in Trujillo, in Extremadura, in 1529.

Valdivia left Spain in 1535 and spent an unprofitable year or so with Federman in Venezuela. He then went to Peru and earned the nickname of "the perfect captain," for he inspired high regard among his men. His motives in wishing to go to Chile seem simple. He later wrote to the emperor Charles: "I have no other wish than to discover and to settle lands for Your Majesty and no other interest, together with the honours and favours which you may be pleased to grant me, than to leave a memory and the good report which I won in war as a poor soldier in the service of an enlightened monarch who, putting his sacred person every hour against the common enemy of Christianity and its allies, has upheld, and upholds, with its unconquered arm its honour and God's." Valdivia said that he aspired to be a governor, a captain, a father, a friend, a geometrician, an overseer, "to make channels and share out water, a tiller and a worker at the sowings, a head shepherd, a breeder, a defender, a conqueror and a discoverer."[2]

From the beginning, Valdivia had difficulties with the nature of his command, for he owed his commission to Francisco Pizarro, not to the King nor to the Council of the Indies. Pedro Sancho de Hoz, who had joined Pizarro in Panama and been at Cajamarca, where he received one full share of gold, together with a quarter share for secretarial work (he was for a time Pizarro's secretary), was a rival. Sancho de Hoz had been concerned in all the great dramas in the conquest of Peru: as a clerk at the execution of Atahualpa and a notary at the creation of the new Spanish city of Cuzco. He wrote the texts of many grants of the *encomiendas* in that city and himself had one. Pizarro seems to have dismissed him as a secretary in early 1535, for Sancho had told Fray Tomás de Berlanga—the Dominican vice-provincial and later bishop of Panama and then Peru—that Pizarro had not paid the King's one-fifth on the silver that he had used to buy Pedro de Alvarado's ships. Sancho was a good writer. His account of the Spanish discovery of Cuzco is second to none.[3]

Sancho de Hoz was back in Spain in 1536 and seemed as rich as all those who had been at Cajamarca. He went to live in Toledo and married Guiomar de Aragón, who was perhaps a child of a royal bastard. Then Sancho persuaded the Council of the Indies to make him not only chief notary of mines in Peru, but also governor of the territories leading to the Straits of Magellan, and to give him permission to penetrate south of Peru in general, making him captain-general "of the people who go on the expedition and those found in the discovered territory." He returned to Peru to find Valdivia had also been given the right to penetrate the south. Pizarro commented, "Pedro Sancho has come back from Spain as stupid as when he went." But Sancho was persistent in his demands and caused no end of difficulty.

Pizarro sought to be the mediator between Valdivia and Sancho de Hoz. He adopted a twentieth-century solution by asking them both to lunch. Pizarro asked Sancho to show his credentials. These indicated that he had indeed been asked by the Crown to explore the seas, the coasts, the ports to the south of Peru but—and this was a most curious qualification—"without entering into the confines and territories of those portions which have been given in government to other persons."[4] Pizarro was tactful (his capacity for tact was one of his remarkable characteristics). He pointed out that, in any expedition, Valdivia's capacity to lead men in battle would be most helpful; and he thought that Sancho de Hoz could contribute to the success of the enterprise because of his wealth and his capacity for administration. He asked them to form a partnership. They agreed, though it was said that Pizarro gave Sancho de Hoz too much wine. The agreement read: "I, Pedro Sancho de Hoz will go to the city of Los Reyes [that is, Lima] and from there I shall bring fifty horses and mares . . . and I will bring two ships loaded with necessary things . . . including 200 shields. And I, Captain Pedro de Valdivia, say that, in order to serve His Majesty better in the expedition which I have begun, I accept the said company."[5] But despite this agreement, there was always ambiguity. Was Valdivia the subordinate of Sancho de Hoz? Or was Sancho his subordinate? Pizarro gave the latter some kind of document, but its contents are unknown. Perhaps it was destroyed by Valdivia when Sancho de Hoz tried to kill him.

In January 1540, Valdivia set off on his expedition. He seems to have been accompanied by only seven men. These included Luis de Cartagena as his secretary, perhaps a member of the famous converso family of that name. Others were Juan Gómez de Almagro, the *alguacil mayor* (chief constable) who had married Colluca, daughter of Atahualpa. His father, Diego de Almagro's brother, Alvar, also traveled. Valdivia brought with him his beautiful and resolute mistress, Inés Suárez. Pizarro had asked Valdivia what he planned to do with her when he left for Chile. "I will carry her with me if your excellency gives me leave." "How will you manage that if your wife is still living in Spain?" asked Pizarro. "Inés is my servant," Valdivia answered. In fact Valdivia's relation with Inés was based on more than love. Valdivia had always been a gambler and was wont to go to Francisco Martínez de Peñalosa's bar in Cuzco. Here he saved Inés, then a widow from Palencia, who was being molested by a certain Fernán Núñez. She had come to the Indies to look for her husband first in Venezuela, then in Peru. She had obtained a small *encomienda* in Cuzco. She turned out to be brave, intelligent, and resilient.

In addition to his seven Spaniards, Valdivia took a large escort of Indian servants; there was a rather gloomy send-off, with a complete absence of the shining armor, the plumes, the banners, and the trumpets frequent on such occasions. This absence, coupled with the presence of a servile people who were jaded, dust covered, and sweaty, left the impression of a drove of slaves guarded by a few horsemen of low rank, instead of an expedition marching to conquer one more kingdom for the European emperor Charles.

One companion who was not present was Sancho de Hoz. The explanation was that he was in prison in Lima for debt. The rich often suffer from financial conundrums. So his two ships with their horses and shields were naturally missing.

The route taken by Valdivia was the one by which Almagro had returned. They traveled about twelve leagues a day. Almagro's brother Alvar fell from his horse and died. There were other difficulties. But as Valdivia went south, he was joined by others: For example, at Arequipa, Fray Juan Lobo and Alonso de Monroy, a member of that remarkable family of Extremadura from whom Cortés descended, attached themselves and their destinies to him. At Tarapacá, seventy soldiers came in from the sea, including two new priests, one of whom was Fray Rodrigo Marmolejo, and two Germans, Juan Bohon and Bartolomé Flores.

After leaving Arequipa, Valdivia was soon in the desert of the north of Chile. The story of the expedition's crossing of this famous obstacle was, according to one historian, "an epic not yet well written. Historians have gathered a thousand details but have not yet captured its spirit."[6] Valdivia adopted the technique of sending out little troops of his followers to break up any band of Indians that might be forming and to seek Spanish reinforcements.

The difficulty at this stage was not so much the Indians as Sancho de Hoz, who arrived at Valdivia's headquarters by riding fast and light with a few horse, some of his wife's grand relations, and some friends. This group had all determined to kill Valdivia when they caught up with him. But when they reached Valdivia's camp near Atacama, they found that their enemy was away on a reconnoiter and only the capable Inés Suárez was there. She gave the newcomers dinner and discussed with her own friends what should be done. They learned that Sancho de Hoz planned to seize and to kill Valdivia. Next morning, Sancho de Hoz told Don Benito that the site had been badly chosen for a camp. "Who are you to say this to me?" asked Don Benito. "For I am in command by order of Captain Valdivia." Next day, the latter appeared with ten horsemen, and he was immediately apprised of Sancho de Hoz's arrival and how they had heard that they planned to kill him.

Valdivia went to Sancho de Hoz and said, "You repay badly, friend Sancho, the affection that the marquess Pizarro and I hold for you." He arrested him, and there was a brief trial. Sancho was imprisoned, while his comrades were ordered to return to Cuzco with neither horses nor arms. The two Guzmán brothers (who were relations of Sancho de Hoz's wife) and Juan de Ávalos, an Extremeño from Garrovillas, accepted the compromise and did in fact make their way back on foot and then by sea. They were fortunate, since Valdivia's first idea had been to hang them, and he even had gallows built for the purpose.[7] Sancho was kept under guard, and for a time in handcuffs, for the rest of Valdivia's journey. Valdivia would have liked to have executed him, but he did not want to kill someone whose relations could claim that he was the Crown's representative. But Sancho de Hoz did sign a declaration that released Valdivia from any partnership with him, though he paid for the horses that Sancho had sold him.[8]

The expedition continued across the desert of Atacama. There was a constant shortage of food and even more so of water till Inés Suárez's white horse by accident ate a prickly pear, the red fruit of which cactus became a major source of sustenance. It was also her horse that found a spring in an unpromising desert zone. There was a fierce wind, sometimes stinging sleet, once a dust storm. Then they found at last the green valley of Copiapó. There the army rested two months. Valdivia took possession of the land to the south of it and gave it the promising name of New Extremadura.[9] They raised there a large wooden cross, and Valdivia told the nearby Indians that he was going to instruct them in Christianity.

Several stragglers caught up with the expedition. These included men such as Gonzalo de los Ríos and Alonso de Chinchilla. Some of these newcomers seemed ready for a new rebellion, as Inés Suárez and some others told an unbelieving Valdivia. Juan Ruiz de Torbillo was heard to say: "If it had been left to me to do, I should have killed Pedro de Valdivia by now." He was arrested and hanged.

Then Valdivia was again absent one day reconnoitering. Chinchilla and Gonzalo de los Ríos rode into the camp at the head of twenty horsemen and announced that they had come to kill Valdivia. Sancho de Hoz was delighted, but the redoubtable Inés arrested both leaders. On his return, Valdivia gave them a choice: continuing under guard or going back to Peru. Astonished at that merciful concession, Chinchilla cravenly told all his plans, and he was held with Sancho de Hoz till they reached their journey's end. The expedition continued, but there were more and more Indian attacks on stragglers, sometimes killing horses or more often Indian bearers. Valdivia forced a pass into the valley of the Mapocho in mid-December 1540. It was December 13, Santa Lucía's Day, and they called the hill that defended that place by that name.[10]

A good analysis has been made of the 154 companions who in the end accompanied Valdivia. There were twenty-six Andalusians; seventeen were Extremeños; sixteen came from New Castile, fifteen from León, while twelve were Basques and one was from Asturias. Forty-one, or more than a quarter, were illiterate. Eleven were called hidalgos *de solar,* gentlemen with property; twenty-three were ordinary hidalgos. Fourteen had been with Almagro in 1535.[11] None of these things was surprising except that it is strange that there were no Gallegos. The geographical breakdown is very similar to that in Peru and in Mexico.

No sooner had Valdivia decided that the valley of the Mapocho was the obvious place for his capital city than he suffered a serious attack by Indians, whose numbers seemed at first to compensate for the Spanish swords and horses. The Spaniards were almost defeated till the Indians threw down their arms and fled due to the arrival, so legend tells, of a new conquistador on a white horse who came out of the sky with a naked sword: Santiago![12]

The subsequent victory meant that Valdivia could establish himself at the foot of Santa Lucía. He adopted a clever technique of sending out horsemen regularly in all directions so that, as he told the emperor Charles, the Indians "believed that the Christians were many, so most of them came in and served us peacefully."[13] They even helped the Spaniards to carry logs and clay to build their first houses.

Valdivia finally founded Santiago de Chile on February 12, 1541. The municipality of the new city proclaimed Valdivia captain-general and governor of the city, thereby detaching itself, and him, from Pizarro. There was quite a ceremony. The whole camp gathered; Valdivia appeared in full armor, carrying in his left hand the standard of Castile. He took possession of the place in the name of the Emperor and King. Galloping cavalrymen passed. Valdivia declared that anyone who challenged his claim to be governor should give him battle, and he would defend his right to the title with his life. He drank water from the river Mapocho, offered it to his senior captains, and tossed what was left in the air. He then planted a cross, before which all knelt in thanks. The scene was like one from *Amadís*. They were over 1,500 miles from Lima.

The only one of Valdivia's captains who was absent on this startling occasion was the German conquistador Bartolomeus Blumenthal, who, in Spanish circles, called himself Bartolomé Flores. He came in some days later to say that he had engaged in battle an Indian cacique named Talagante. He had captured a son of that potentate, whom, in keeping with Valdivia's chivalrous rules, he had handed back. Talagante had been pleased and had asked Flores to go back and visit him. Talagante gave him four Princesses, one of whom was his daughter, perhaps his heiress. Inés took charge of these ladies and had them baptized. They lived with or married Spaniards.

The building of Santiago de Chile began on February 20, 1541. The designer, or architect, was the one-eyed Pedro de Gamboa. There were nine streets, each about twelve *varas* (a *vara* is about 835 millimeters) wide, in blocks 138 *varas* wide. Each block was divided into four lots (*solares*). One block, though, was reserved for a square on the west side of which there would soon be a church—a cathedral. This was traditional Spanish urban practice. On the north side of the square, there would be both the governor's house and the prison. A municipality (*cabildo*) with a headquarters on the south side was formed in March 1541, with two magistrates, six councillors, a *mayordomo*, a notary, and a *procurador*. All these were men with well-known names, the chief magistrate being an old associate of Valdivia's, Francisco de Aguirre.

Though his name was Basque, Aguirre came from Talavera de la Reina. A man of great energy, he was proud and irascible, if cultivated, and he liked to live, so we are told, *rumbosamente,* which perhaps we can translate as "grandly." He had in the end fifty mestizo children, to whom he gave exotic names: Marco Antonio, Eufrasia, Floridan. He eventually married his cousin, María Teresa de Meneses.

One of the first councillors was one of Valdivia's Germans, Juan Bohon. Luis de Cartagena was the notary, as he had been of the expedition. Valdivia, as ever disdainful of danger, or not believing that it existed, made councillors of two friends of Sancho de Hoz: Antonio de Pastraña (*procurador*) and Martín de Soller. The council took their oaths on March 11, and municipal life began.

Valdivia sought to make the survival of Santiago easier. "At once," he said, "I set about coming to speak with the chiefs of the land and, owing to the diligence with which I moved about it, whereby they believed that there were many of us Christians, most of them came in peacefully and served us well for five or six months . . . and they built us wooden and grass houses on the flat land, which I gave them." But, Valdivia had learned, Manco Capac "had sent to warn them, the people of Chile, that they should hide all the gold, sheep, clothing stuffs and food, for since we sought all this, [they thought] that, if we did not find such things, we would go away. And they did this work of obstruction so thoroughly that the sheep were eaten and the gold and all the rest hidden or burned; and they did not spare their own clothing but left themselves bare."[14]

Sancho de Hoz's friend Antonio de Pastraña urged Valdivia to accept the nomination as governor by the municipality. He thought that that would be a way of eventually ridding Santiago of Valdivia, because he would, if he accepted the nomination, be seen in Spain as committing treason. On June 10, Pastraña's plan seemed to work. For Valdivia called an ex-

traordinary meeting of the town hall (a *cabildo abierto*) at which he presented a petition signed by nearly all the inhabitants of Santiago demanding that he should become governor. This document was presented to the
"perfect captain" as he was leaving Mass. Valdivia said at last: "Since you
have seen my replies and are not satisfied with them . . . you in one voice
say it and I alone contradict it, so I might be mistaken . . . And so I accept
the office of governor elected by the town hall and so I shall entitle myself
until His Majesty commands something else."[15]

Thus Antonio de Pastraña's cynical plot was, in the short term anyway,
a success. Valdivia, however, went to the notary, Luis de Cartagena, and had
him write down, "This election was not of my wish and since I do not know
if in doing it I am doing a disservice to my King, let everyone be a witness
for me in what way I have accepted it. Nor do I reduce the obedience that I
owe to the illustrious marquess Don Francisco Pizarro if he lives."[16] Valdivia later explained what had happened to the emperor Charles in a letter,
which seems accurate in its summary.[17]

Despite the ceremony with which Valdivia had welcomed his being
hailed as the chief ruler in Santiago in February, he was still not governor
and captain-general in the reckoning of the Council of the Indies. The
rumor, and then the news, of the death of Francisco Pizarro affected Valdivia's position in Chile, for Pizarro had been his first stay and protection.
He regarded himself as the lieutenant of Pizarro. As soon as he had confirmation of Pizarro's death, Valdivia rather curiously wrote to the Emperor
suggesting that he should take care to ensure that Pizarro's children "could
support themselves as such."[18]

Soon after this, the Indians made a major onslaught on the new Spanish town of Santiago. The attack was made under two leaders coming from
two directions. Valdivia himself wrote one of his excellent letters to the
emperor Charles about his exertions. He himself dealt effectively with the
large attack with ninety men, but in the second battle, with Alonso de
Monroy in command, the Indians burned the new Santiago entirely and
killed all the animals. Valdivia wrote: "We were left only with the arms at
our sides and two small pigs, one suckling pig, a cock and a hen, and about
two handfuls of wheat. In the end, when night came, the Christians gathered so much courage, together with what their commander Monroy put
to them, that, though all were wounded, with the good wishes of Santiago

himself, they found the energy to fight and kill many. . . . And with this, the war began in earnest."

Valdivia continued: "Seeing the plight we were in, it seemed to me that, if we were to hold onto the land and make it Your Majesty's forever, we must eat of the fruits of our hands as in the beginning of the world [*la primera edad*]. So I set about sowing. I divided my men into two groups. We all dug, plowed and sowed, being always armed and the horses being saddled always by day. At night one half of us kept watch. And I with the other half moved at the time eight to ten leagues [twenty-four to thirty miles] around the town breaking up bands of Indians . . . [till] I built up the town again."

One of these expeditions in the neighborhood of Santiago captured the local *toqui,* or cacique-in-chief, Michimalongo. To save his life, Michimalongo led the Spaniards to some gold mines, in the so-called Malga district. It was from those mines that the people of the Mapocho had dug the gold that they paid to the Incas. The Spaniards were delighted, and they began to calculate how many sacks they would need; and some put on airs as if they were already rich people, thinking that, in a short time, they would be able to go to Spain, establish a country estate, and—who knew—obtain a Marquessate.

Work began at Malga, with a hundred Indian workers (*yanaconas*) obtained from Santiago. Michimalongo offered his own army of miners, which numbered 1,200 (there were also many women). Valdivia left there two Spanish captains, Pedro de Herrera and Diego Delgado, who had engaged in mining in Peru, together with fifteen soldiers, under Gonzalo de los Ríos. Then Valdivia went down to the coast near Santiago to seek a place where he could conveniently build a brigantine, with which he could communicate with Peru by sea. He found a likely harbor at the mouth of the river Aconcagua at Concón, where there was also plenty of wood. Work on a brigantine began.

Two crises arose for Valdivia. First, Alonso de Monroy sent a message to explain that yet another plot was being planned by Sancho de Hoz. The idea was to kill Valdivia, Suárez, Monroy, and all their friends. Sancho would then seize the gold of Malga and return to Peru to join Diego de Almagro, who had now, it seemed, triumphed over the Pizarros. Valdivia made light of the rumor. But then a confused quarrel occurred in the house of Monroy. The lamps were destroyed. Inés Suárez brought another light, which showed Sancho de Hoz being held by Monroy himself, Chinchilla engaged in a duel with one of Valdivia's captains, and the priest Fray Juan Lobo defending himself with a stool against Pastraña.

As if that fracas were not enough, Gonzalo de los Ríos and a black slave named Valiente at this moment rode in from the gold mine at Malga to say that the Indians who had been working in the mines had risen, had killed all the Spaniards there except for themselves, and then had gone down to the coast and thrown the gold that had been mined into the sea.

Valdivia feared another general assault—with good reason, since the woods near Santiago were reported to be full of Indians bent on his destruction. Valdivia went to the north of his city and captured seven caciques. They confirmed that an attack was probable. Since Valdivia was away and could not return in time to Santiago, Inés Suárez and Monroy organized the resistance. The Spaniards were pressed back to their main square, most of their houses were soon on fire, and a majority of the Spanish population were wounded—but Inés Suárez cut off the heads of the seven caciques whom Valdivia had captured, and exposed them. The gory heads of their leaders inspired dismay in the attackers, who held off their attack. Sancho de Hoz seemed to redeem himself by fighting well with a lance, even if he had to do so manacled. Afterwards, he was pardoned.

Valdivia returned, and the Indians withdrew. There was, however, practically no food. Some argued for the abandonment of Santiago and a withdrawal to Peru, but even that retreat did not seem feasible without supplies. The recently established fields of maize were caused to work at double pressure. A harvest of twelve *fanegas* (bushels) of wheat was also forthcoming, but these were immediately put back into the soil. Starvation was the characteristic of this first year at Santiago.

The old Spanish houses were swiftly rebuilt, but this time—to avoid the effects of fire—not with wood and straw roofs but with adobe bricks. A fort, too, was built—1,600 feet square, needing two hundred bricks three feet long and a handsbreadth high. In the event of another Indian attack, the children of the Spaniards and their Indian servants could take refuge there.

The likelihood of another attack was assumed to be considerable by everyone concerned.

32

Valdivia's Consummation

> Can it be that only the design for a holy life is without the benefit
> of a system of rules? Indeed there is in general an art and a
> discipline of virtue, in which those who exercise themselves
> diligently will be inspired by the Spirit.
>
> ERASMUS, *Enchiridion*

In December 1541, Valdivia sent back to Peru his most reliable subordinate, Alonso de Monroy, presumably a cousin of Hernán Cortés, to seek new clothing, men, horses, ammunition. He went by land with five men, taking the best horses with new horseshoes. Some of these horseshoes were made of gold because iron was so short. Valdivia wrote to the Emperor: "Since I know that no man would stir to come to these lands owing to its bad report, unless someone would go from here to bring them and take gold to buy men . . . And since the land they had to traverse was at war and there were great wildernesses, they would have to go lightly equipped and unsheltered by night, I have arranged . . . to send [to Peru] no less than 7,000 pesos of gold"—gold from Malga—to impress the Peruvians. Valdivia also wrote a letter that Monroy was to take to Pizarro.[1] Then, reported "the perfect captain," "we went through the next two years in great want. Many of the Christians had sometimes to dig up roots for food . . . There was no meat and the Christians who found fifty grains of maize a day thought themselves well off. And he who had a fistful of wheat did not grind it to take away the husks . . . I chose to have thirty or forty mounted men always about the plain in winter; and when the food which they took with them was finished, they came back and others went out.

And so we went about looking like ghosts and the Indians called us '*cupias,*' which is the name which they give to their devils for, whenever they came in search of us (and they know how to attack at night), they found us awake, armed and, if need be, on horseback."[2]

Monroy and his party of five men meantime journeyed on to Peru till they reached the valley of the Copiapó. There, early in 1542, they were surprised by Indians, and four of the six were killed. Monroy and Pedro de Miranda survived, and were made prisoners. They were led to the cacique Andequín, who had a Spanish adviser in Francisco Gasca—earlier one of Almagro's men, who had been captured some years before. Gasca had won the admiration of the Indians by playing the flute well, and so he was allocated three wives, who gave him many children. Gasca ensured that Monroy and Miranda were well treated; their lives were saved, if not their possessions. After several months, Monroy and Miranda began to teach Andequín to ride. One day, they drew farther and farther away from the Indian settlement, then Miranda stabbed the cacique, and he and Monroy forced Gasca to escape with them to help them on their way—three men on two horses[3]—but he soon escaped.

After further difficulties, Monroy and Miranda reached Cuzco in September 1542. By that time, Vaca de Castro was in power, but his authority was fragile. He received Monroy well, but he had no money nor indeed time for them: "Being so busy, trying the guilty, bringing peace to the land, rewarding services, sending out captains to make further discoveries, he could do little." Vaca de Castro promised to send a ship of supplies to Valdivia once he had restored order in Peru, but that moment was a long time coming. Monroy, with the persistence of an Extremeño, did meet two rich men who were interested in his story. One was a merchant who had been in the Indies since 1531 and who offered 5,000 castellanos to equip seventy horsemen. The other was a priest who lent Monroy a similar sum, with which he returned to Chile.

On his journey back, Monroy stopped at Arequipa where he met an old friend of Valdivia's, Lucas Martínez Venegas, who was also willing to help him. "Look for a ship, Señor Monroy," he said, "in which to put the things most needed by your governor. I have only one ship, the *Santiaguillo,* and I would rather not give that to you since I need it for my mines. But if you do not find a ship on the nearby coast, I am prepared to give it to you even although I should lose much by it."[4] Monroy was not one to hesitate: He took the *Santiaguillo*, and filled it with arms, ammunition, ironware, clothing, food, and wine. They left for Chile in May 1543, but thanks to adverse winds and ignorance of the route, they did not arrive in Valparaíso till September.[5] They found 118 Spaniards there, near skeletons they seemed. But what a wonderful change the *Santiaguillo* brought about.

Monroy, who part of the way traveled by land, did not reach Santiago till December. His arrival was another infusion of life into the moribund colony. But they brought back no confirmation of Valdivia as governor: To his frustration, he remained just the lieutenant-governor.

Thereafter, Valdivia told Emperor Charles that the Indians did not attack anymore, "nor came within four leagues [twelve miles] round this town and they all withdrew to a remote province and would send daily messages bidding me to come and fight them and bring the new Christians who had come, for they wanted to see if they were as brave as we were; and if they were, they would submit to us but if not, not.[6]

"When all the men and horse of Monroy had recovered, I went forth with them to seek the Indian strongholds. I found them but the Indians all fled. . . . leaving all their villages burned down and abandoning the best stretch of land in the world so that it looks as if it never had an Indian in it."[7]

Soon after, still with no further communication from Peru, Valdivia began to grant *encomiendas*. In order to make that easier, he founded a second settlement in the north where colonists coming in from Lima or Cuzco could rest on the last stretch of their journey. The need for this was confirmed by the fate of a ship belonging to an Italian, Juan Albert. He sent a boatload of men ashore to seek freshwater at Copiapó, but all these men were killed. Juan Albert sailed on south, passed Valparaíso, and somewhere south of that port, all his crew were killed by Indians—as was a black slave who was scrubbed to death to see if he washed white.[8] Valdivia meanwhile sent the German Juan Bohon and thirty horsemen to found a settlement in the Coquimbo valley, in the north, near the Andacollo mines. Valdivia himself joined him, and they called the place La Serena, after everyone's happy memories of that magical valley in Spain. They found there a good pitch, which was yielded by certain plants, like a wax. It could be used for careening boats.[9]

The colony was further reinvigorated by another arrival from Peru: This was Juan Calderón de la Barca in the *San Pedro*, a vessel owned and piloted by Juan Bautista de Pastene from Genoa, who afterwards would be a strong adherent of Valdivia. Valdivia sent Pastene down the coast to explore the land south of Magellan's strait. This was seen as an important extra journey: Pastene, a treasurer, and a chief clerk (Juan de Cárdenas Alderete and Cárdenas) were to take possession of all the land in the name of the Emperor. They were to give names to ports and rivers, islands, and districts (Valdivia, Concepción, and Osorno—the latter after the acting president of the Council of the Indies) and load the ship on return with sheep and food. The *San Pedro*'s voyage would be followed by that of the *Santiaguillo*, which would sail to the river Maule to assist Valdivia in a more local contest. Both expeditions brought back good news of the fertility of the land in the South, the number of natives, the crops grown, the size of the towns, and the good harbors.

Valdivia was concerned with the gold mines, too: He used Peruvian Indians to work in them, guarded by a Spanish contingent of armed men. In the next nine months, they would produce 60,000 castellanos worth of gold. Valdivia sent one of his would-be assassins, Antonio de Ulloa, back to Spain to represent him before the monarch in the Council of the Indies—a very odd designation by the naïve Valdivia, one cannot but think, for Ulloa was a close friend of Sancho La Hoz's. Valdivia also dispatched Monroy again to Peru by land, and Pastene by sea for more supplies. Valdivia had further dealings with the equally naïve Michimalongo, to whom the still determined Inés Suárez offered looking glasses, combs, Venetian glass, beads, and trinkets. In reply, Michimalongo presented Inés with a white feather from a bird that lived high up in the snows; the feather did not burn if passed through a flame.

It was at this stage, on September 4, 1545, that Valdivia sent Charles the Emperor a very enthusiastic description of Chile. "This land," he insisted, "is such that there is none better in the world for living in and settling down in . . . it is very flat, very healthy and very pleasant . . . it has four months of winter [but] it is only when the moon is at the quarter that it rains for a day or two . . . on all other days, the sun is so fine that there is no need to draw near the fire. The summer is so temperate with such delightful breezes that a man can be out in the sun all day long without annoyance. It is a land most abounding in pastures and fields and yielding every kind of livestock and plant imaginable; much timber and very fine [too it

is] for building houses, endless wood for use in them; the mines being rich
in gold, the whole land being full of it. And whoever wants to take it, there
they will find a place to sow and a site to build on and water, grass and
wood for their beasts." He added that, as a result of the expedition of Almagro, Chile had received an evil name but it did not deserve it.[10]

Valdivia wrote too a curious letter to Hernando Pizarro (also dated
September 4, 1545) telling him that there were fifteen thousand Indian
families between Copiapó and the Río Maule valley. Assuming an average
of five persons in each family, the total population would accordingly have
been seventy-five thousand. But Valdivia added that an equal number had
died in the intervening years since the conquest of Chile had begun. So one
might assume that the total population would have been 150,000 in 1540.
But these are guesses. No one knows how accurate Valdivia was, and no one
knows how many are to be recognized in a single family.

In early 1546, while Gonzalo Pizarro was still dominating Peru, Valdivia
was driving down to conquer the immediate south of his new country. He
had sixty horsemen, 150 Indians as porters, and a black ex-slave, Juan Valiente, as doctor. South of the Río Maule, they encountered hostile Indians.
Many who were captured were asked to put to their fellows a request that
they come in and surrender to Valdivia, but instead, three hundred Indians
came to bar the Spaniards' path. The conquistadors fell on them and killed
fifty. Later that day, Valdivia said that they reached Quilicura, where they
found that a surprise attack was being mounted by seven thousand Indians. The onslaught was cleverly foiled by the Spaniards, but the Indians
fought well, "packed together as if they had been Germans." Rodrigo de
Quiroga killed the cacique and routed this force, with the loss of two
horses, though with many Spaniards wounded. Having reached the river
Biobío, they returned to Santiago at the end of March 1546.[11]

There they found some disquiet. The settlers there, fully expecting Valdivia to have established a new city in the South, had been busy reassigning
the encomiendas locally. Now Valdivia ordered all property to be replaced
in the hands of those who had had it before his departure. This caused
much grumbling.[12] Valdivia worked anew on the divisions, and some
twenty-eight persons found themselves actually dispossessed, the number
of encomenderos being cut from sixty to thirty-two. The gainers were the
men of the cabildo (the town council), the church, the most powerful con-

quistadors, and Inés Suárez. The dispossessed were assured that they would be assigned wonderful property in the beautiful South, but only when it was conquered.

Sancho de Hoz was among those dispossessed. Still longing for authority in Santiago, or the *vara de dos palmos* (the symbol of mayoral authority), he approached and won the sympathy of several other discontented men. Thereupon, he sent a message to Valdivia to tell him that he was dying and begging him to visit him. The plan was that once Valdivia had entered Sancho's house, a friend of Sancho's would stab him. Valdivia agreed to go but insisted on taking several of his friends. Sancho de Hoz asked Pedro de Villagrán to join his conspiracy. He went to Inés, who immediately informed Valdivia, who in turn at last arrested Sancho.

Soon afterwards, the German Juan Bohon rode in from La Serena to inform Valdivia of further treachery, for Pastene, the Genoese friend of the "perfect captain," had just arrived back in the port. Bohon said, and Pastene confirmed it, that on their outward journey to Peru, their ship had reached Los Reyes (Lima) in the record time of twenty-four days. There they had news of the war between Núñez Vela and Gonzalo Pizarro. When they arrived, the faithful Monroy died and Antonio de Ulloa, instead of going to Spain, had gone rather to Gonzalo Pizarro. Ulloa had torn up the letters and papers that had been given him by Valdivia for the emperor Charles. He also obtained an order from Gonzalo's chief justice, Aldana, which enabled him to seize all the gold that had been carried for the Viceroy by the now deceased Monroy. Pastene, the loyal Genoese, had been restrained from leaving Los Reyes. Ulloa gained permission to make off with what was being held of Valdivia's money in Pastene's ship. But Pastene was saved by Gonzalo's evil genius, Francisco de Carvajal, whom he had known—as he had known Valdivia—in Italy.

Ulloa arrived in Gonzalo's camp just in time to take part in his rebellious activities at the Battle of Añaquito. But by then Carvajal had heard of the plans of Aldana and Ulloa to carry out a *maldad galalonesa*—that is, a crime of the style of Galalón in the chivalric novel *The Twelve Peers*. Carvajal might be a scoundrel, but he was a literate scoundrel. He told Pastene, "Aldana and Ulloa are aiming at . . . Valdivia's death so that they [and their friends] may govern. And they want to make use of my lord the governor's friendship with Pedro de Valdivia to gain what they want."[13] Carvajal sent

Pastene to Quito to see Gonzalo Pizarro, who authorized him to collaborate with the treacherous Antonio de Ulloa in search of supplies.

Pastene returned to Los Reyes (Lima) where he found Ulloa busy loading the *San Pedro*. He showed Ulloa his letter from Gonzalo Pizarro. But, despite that, Ulloa sailed down to Arequipa, forcing Pastene to buy another vessel for 1,000 pesos, which left him with the responsibility to pay another 7,000 once he rejoined Valdivia. Valdivia's name stood so high that the seller of the ship knew that even a debt of that size would be sure to be honored. Pastene found thirty men to sail with him and went down to Tarapacá. Ulloa had already sailed south, planning to kill Valdivia and rearrange the *encomiendas* under Gonzalo's rule. Pastene overtook Ulloa, who invited him to confer, but Pastene, realizing that he would be killed, declined the invitation. Ulloa then returned north in order to fight on behalf of Gonzalo.

Valdivia, still preoccupied by his legal position (was he governor or lieutenant-governor?), sent Juan de Ávalos, from the family of the victor of Pavia, an old friend, north to Peru to clarify matters. He took with him, as any responsible well-to-do conquistador then did, 60,000 castellanos in gold, as well as copies of the letters that Ulloa had seized and torn up.[14] A little later, having received no answer, Valdivia realized that he ought to return to Peru himself. He left Francisco de Villagrán as his deputy and Francisco de Aguirre as the administrator.

Valdivia had been away from Peru for seven years and was determined to resolve the question of his gubernatorial status. He left Valparaíso with as much money as he could secure. He is supposed to have told all Spaniards who wanted to return to Spain with what they had accumulated in Chile to put their possessions on board his boat. They did so. He gave a dinner on the shore before departure, and then, with Jerónimo de Alderete and Juan de Cárdenas, he left for the ship to take their possessions to Peru, leaving the diners aghast. One of them, Juan Piñelo, outraged, swam after the boat, but was thrown back into the sea. The defenders of Valdivia argued that this was just a change of plan, and that view was sustained by La Gasca in a later enquiry. But the money seized thus came to be known as the "80,000 dorados [gilthead]," netted by Valdivia, "as easily as St Peter brought up his net so full of fish that it broke."[15]

Valdivia intended to go back to Spain to establish his position. On leaving Santiago, the city he had founded, he wrote to the *cabildo* there: "I am leaving for the court of His Majesty, to present myself before his exalted person . . . to tell him all that his subjects and I in these provinces have done for him; and to ask and request that it be to his service to grant to me this government in order to be better able to serve him and to reward the persons who have helped me conquer this land."[16] There were, however, a few who thought that he might instead be going to Portugal "to live off the gold which he had stolen." That would have been out of character, but not impossible to imagine in the extraordinary circumstances.

Valdivia set off for Peru with a handful of loyal friends. At La Serena, he received the news that Gonzalo Pizarro had won the civil war in Peru. But a little more to the north, at Tarapacá, he heard that La Gasca was recapturing the country. Valdivia had no doubts about siding with the Crown, despite his old friendships with Carvajal and Gonzalo Pizarro. As we read in chapter 30, Gasca was delighted to welcome him, "knowing him to be a man of great diligence and experience and courage and to whom great credit is given in this land in matters of war." The "perfect captain" became one of the three most important members of La Gasca's army, alongside Alvarado and Hinojosa and, as we have seen, it was he who was concerned in deciding the crossing of the river at Jaquijahuana and rebuilding the bridges broken by the Pizarrists.[17] This was a decisive contribution to La Gasca's triumph.

Valdivia's participation in the battles against Gonzalo Pizarro led to his tardy but welcome nomination by La Gasca as governor and captaingeneral of New Extremadura, by which was to be understood Chile (April 23, 1548). His dominion was declared as lying between Copiapó at 27° in the north and 41° in the south, which gave him not only Santiago but the towns of Concepción, Valdivia, and Osorno, too, as well as nearly one thousand miles of seacoast. In the interior, the concession was for one hundred leagues (three hundred miles), which would give him the entire southern Cordillera of the Andes and much of the flatlands of what would become Argentina.

Valdivia left triumphantly for Santiago. La Gasca gave him two ships, unprecedented largesse from the effective authority in Peru. Valdivia loaded them and sent them by sea under Jerónimo de Alderete down to Atacama, where he planned to greet him himself. Valdivia set off for there with 120 men but was overtaken by Hinojosa, his fellow general, who compelled him to return to Peru to face charges made by the treacherous Pizarrist Antonio de Ulloa, who had successfully maneuvered himself into becoming commander of La Gasca's ports. The accusations were that Valdivia had taken some Indian servants (*yanaconas*) with him from Peru and that he had also taken with him some ex-Pizarrists who had been condemned to perpetual imprisonment or to the galleys; Valdivia had also refused to allow Ulloa to inspect his ships.

Valdivia returned and met La Gasca at Callao on October 20, 1548. His bizarre investigation then began. Almost immediately, a letter from the *cabildo* at Santiago reached La Gasca to tell him that, in the prolonged absence of Valdivia, they would like Francisco de Villagrán to be named as governor. But they preferred Valdivia. If he were alive, "please do us the favour of sending him back to us as soon as possible, because it is conducive to the peace and tranquillity of this land; and if Your Excellency does not favour us by sending him, our loss would be great."[18]

In Valdivia's absence, the ineffable Sancho de Hoz, the thorn in his side in Santiago for so long, had sought to take advantage of the discontent caused by the rearrangement of the *encomiendas*. He had been living outside Santiago, but he had friends in the city, such as Hernando Rodríguez Monroy, who committed the unwisdom of making a new plot with Fray Lobo and Alonso de Córdoba. They went immediately with their news to the subgovernor, Villagrán, who, more determined than Valdivia had ever been in matters of rebellion, arrested Sancho de Hoz and his friend Juan Romero and had them both executed there and then. Valdivia would probably have hesitated and given them a pardon again.[19]

Despite the death of Sancho de Hoz, there remained friends of his in the *cabildo* in Santiago and also some in La Gasca's circle in Peru. They accused Valdivia of murder, immorality (living with Inés), and sometimes of tampering with the royal box with three keys. La Gasca talked to some of these conspiratorial spirits.[20]

Most admitted that there was discontent in Chile. Some thought that Sancho de Hoz had had a good claim to much land. Others thought that Valdivia had been excessively generous to Sancho de Hoz, and yet others that his eventual execution had brought peace. Some said that Valdivia had given them a charge on his land in return for his seizure of their gold. Six

out of eleven witnesses considered that Valdivia's return would benefit
Chile. Bernardino Mella, who had ridden back with Monroy to Chile in
1543, said that La Gasca ought to send Inés Suárez back to Spain because she
was mad. Other accusations were levied against Valdivia. He defended himself well, saying that Inés was his maid and that Pizarro himself—Francisco,
not Gonzalo—had given him permission to take her.

La Gasca's judgment was solomonic: Valdivia was confirmed as governor and captain-general, but within six months he had to break his relation
with Inés. He had to either send her away or marry her to someone else. He
had within a year to pay off all loans forced by him; he had to permit all who
wanted to leave to do so; and he had to ensure that all *encomiendas* had
enough Indians to support them and that anything borrowed from the
King's box was replaced. Except for the clause about Inés, the punishments
were logical. Some of Valdivia's friends tried to persuade him to act against
La Gasca. Valdivia refused and went overland to Arequipa. There he became
ill but recovered, thanks to two later-notorious nurses. He went thence to
Aruca and took a ship to Valparaíso, where he arrived in April. There he remained till June.[21]

He discovered immediately that La Serena, his port of entry 250 miles
north of Santiago, had been destroyed. All Juan Bohon's men and settlers
had been massacred. The Indians had entered the town at night and placed
an assassin in front of every door. When the alarm was given, the Spaniards
were killed on their doorsteps. Only two survived, who explained how not
only the settlers but also their animals were killed.

Villagrán was sent back to La Serena to recover the place with sixty men
and thirty horse under himself by land, and thirty arquebusiers by sea
under Diego Maldonado. The sea party arrived first but were forced back
onto their ships. Villagrán arrived next day, and the two groups were able
to hold back the Indians. The rebuilding of the town began. The loss had
inspired consternation in Santiago. There was a general fear of an Indian
attack, especially in the mines of Malga. The miners wanted six armed
horsemen; Valdivia sent four, and the mines were closed.

Valdivia's return to Santiago had many bizarre characteristics. His
friends were now established in the town council, since Alderete had become treasurer again, Esteban de Sosa was accountant, Vicente del Monte
was overseer, and Pedro de Miranda was spokesman. Valdivia himself,

through his agent Juan de Cárdenas, had already sworn to respect the laws and rights of all settlers, and he now made a triumphal entry with Indians carrying myrtle and cinnamon before him. He found that Inés Suárez, evidently hearing of her condemnation by La Gasca, had left Valdivia for Rodrigo de Quiroga, whom she subsequently married.[22]

Just as soon as Valdivia had returned to Santiago, another hundred men under well-established leaders appeared in the capital, led by Francisco de Villagrán. Valdivia was then tempted by a new idea for an attack in the South. But first he sent Francisco de Aguirre to assist in rebuilding La Serena. Then he set off himself for the south in a hand chair carried by Indians, because he had broken his hip when his horse fell. With Alderete as his second-in-command, he as usual sent small units ahead to find the lay of the land. Then he moved down to attack the Indians on the rivers Laja and Biobío, both of which flow into the Pacific, and at what would become Concepción, where a fort was now established (March 3, 1550). There was a ferocious reply by the Indians. Alderete responded successfully, and many prisoners were captured, whose noses Valdivia, in a break from his usual policy of reconciliation, cut off.[23]

Valdivia was supported by his Genoese ally Pastene, who arrived with food at his fortress. Pastene went in search of further supplies and information, and reached as far as the island of Santa María, off Talca and close to Concepción. Valdivia's land party then continued, founding a new settlement at what became La Imperial and then at Valdivia itself, a new town also, and like almost all those founded by the governor, on the coast. The towns mentioned survive till the present day in much their old sites. Valdivia also founded Villarrica, between Concepción and Valdivia, in April 1552. In March 1550, Valdivia wrote that he had defeated the Araucanian Indians—"the finest and most splendid Indians that have ever been seen in these parts." Some 1,500 or two thousand had been killed, and he had cut off the noses and hands of another two hundred for "their contumacy in rejecting his offers of peace."[24] He continued his advocacy of Chile as the best place in Charles's American empire: "The land has a fine climate and every kind of Spanish plant will grow in it better than [in New Spain]."[25] He thought that southern Chile was "all a town, a garden and a gold mine." He argued, too, that there were "more Indians in southern Chile than in Mexico."[26]

Obviously Valdivia was hoping to establish Spanish imperial control over the whole of the southern part of the continent. He was, he wrote, sending the faithful Francisco de Villagrán from Villarrica across the Andes to "the northern sea," the Atlantic. He had also sent Francisco de Aguirre to the north to add El Barco to the empire. He himself had been recently into the mountains and discovered there a high lake, presumably Lake Ranco. He was also thinking of sending Alderete to explore the Strait of Magellan from the South.

Then Valdivia returned to Santiago to speed the departure for Spain, precisely of Alderete: He was instructed by La Gasca to try to bring to Chile Valdivia's wife, whose presence had been demanded.

Villagrán's journey to the Atlantic was not a success. He crossed the Andes near Villarrica, but he found his way ahead was blocked by two rivers (perhaps the Almuinó and the Limay), so he returned to Villarrica. There he learned that the Indians had risen. He sought to save the garrison, though the commander Alonso de Moya was killed. From Villarrica, Villagrán went down to Concepción, where he found Valdivia, to whom he gave an account of his journey. Everyone else was engaged in a minor gold rush since that intoxicating metal had just been discovered nearby.

Back in Santiago, Valdivia wrote to the emperor Charles: "Most sacred Caesar, Your Majesty being so taken up with the service of God and the defence and the upholding of Christianity against the common enemy the Turks and the Lutherans, it would be more fitting to help by deeds rather than distract by words. Would to God that I could find myself in Your Majesty's presence with much money and that you might use me in your service, even though I am not useless where I am."[27]

This was the last letter that the "perfect captain" wrote to Europe. He soon returned to the south of Chile, where he considered his mission was to bring the entire land to submission. He founded Los Confines, between Concepción and La Imperial. Then he built forts at Purén and Tucapel, where his captain Alonso Coronas advised him that another general rising of Indians was about to begin. He also reported that a onetime stable boy, Lantaro, an Indian who had worked with the Spaniards, was teaching his compatriots how to fight on horseback. Captain Martín de Ariza was obliged to abandon the fort at Tucapel by Indians who hid their guns in bundles of grass brought in precisely for the horses. Tucapel was burned.

On Christmas Day 1553, there was one of the few battles on fixed lines between Indians and Spaniards, outside Tucapel. Lantaro had arranged to follow Valdivia's route carefully, then to force the outnumbered Spaniards into the marshes. Valdivia drew up his men in three companies. He ordered his first unit to charge and rout the Indians. They held firm. Then he sent in his second company. Still the Indians did not flee. Leaving ten men to guard the baggage, Valdivia then led his own company against the enemy. Their ranks held. "Gentlemen," asked Valdivia of his captains, "what shall we do?" "What does your lordship wish us to do except fight and die?" they replied.

Valdivia withdrew his horsemen from the baggage, hoping that the enemy would be distracted by the chance of loot. It was usually a success-ful tactic, but Lantaro had anticipated that move, and there was still no weakening on the Indians' part. The Indians advanced, pressing the Spaniards into the nearby marsh. They were killed one by one. Valdivia had a strong horse and might have escaped, but he refused to abandon Fray Bartolomé del Pozo, who was on foot. Both were captured.[28]

According to Góngora de Marmolejo, Valdivia was disarmed and un-dressed and then tied up by the Indians. They built a fire in which they roasted slices of his arms cut off with mussel shells, and then they ate them. Other torture followed till they finally cut off his head.[29]

Thus died the "perfect captain," among a group of very hard men, one of the most humane and tolerant of the conquistadors, and the father of Chile, a society which, being buffered behind the *despoblado* desert of Ata-cama, was more free of the diseases of Peru and the north than elsewhere on the continent. But the country was to be at the mercy of both famine and pestilence in the late 1550s.

Book III

❧❧❧

COUNTER REFORMATION, COUNTER RENAISSANCE

33

Carolus Africanus

The best remedy would seem to be a good war. How can we arrange that? I have no means of sustaining my army. . . . The King of England does not look on me as a true friend and does not advise me adequately as to what he is going to do.

CHARLES V, AUTOBIOGRAPHICAL NOTE, FEBRUARY–MARCH 1525

News of the thunder and the fury of all these conquests and battles, these slaughters and sufferings, these arguments and these denunciations in the New World eventually reached Europe and were absorbed by those who served the Crown in the matter of the Indies. But these officials had different priorities. The decision of the Emperor's brother, Fernando, to become King of the Romans in 1531 was seen by many as the end of the idea of universal monarchy. But this had an impact on American policy. The frame of the extraordinary achievements in the Americas was provided by the Crown, after all. Charles V might be at Innsbruck or Augsburg, in Toledo or in Valladolid, Rome or Bologna; he might be on the Mediterranean or in a palace in Flanders; he might be considering the Turkish threat (was Erasmus right to argue that the true victory over the Turks would be to make them Christians?),[1] or how he could outmaneuver that "monster" (that "*bellaco*" as Diego de Ordaz, the conqueror of the Orinoco, put it) Luther, or how he could defeat the German princes—but at any moment, the Emperor might be interrupted by his faithful secretary Cobos with a request for a contract for a new adventurer from Seville or Extremadura who wanted to go to the Indies to conquer and settle a new desert or jungle, to be called, say, New Extremadura or even New Badajoz. Charles might want to concentrate on the question of how to persuade the pope to call a general council of the Church, but more news from New Spain might interrupt his consideration of episcopal and religious reform.

Charles traveled continuously—surely no ruler has ever traveled so much. Gout already tortured him, but the Council of the Indies was always in communication, and other informal advisers were always writing to him. So were conquistadors themselves, such as Valdivia or indeed the great Cortés. Decisions affecting the Americas had to be made. Of course, Charles decided to give the island of Malta to the knights of Saint John, who had been expelled by the Turks from their old home at Rhodes. That was an easy decision. More difficult was deciding who should be sent to Peru to face and defeat Gonzalo Pizarro. A lawyer or a gentleman?

Charles is often held to have had no profound interest in his marvelous American empire. That was only half the case. True, his first attention was always paid to the cause of Germany, the Protestant revolt as well as the growing disorganization in the Low Countries. But all the same, from the moment that Charles saw the shivering Totonaca sent from Mexico to Andalusia by Cortés in 1520, he was concerned with the health of his new subjects. Charles had often listened to Las Casas's pleas, and he was very interested indeed in the provision of gold and silver from the Indies, which helped to finance his wars in Italy. Charles was also "most fond" of maps, as Ambassador Dantiscus reported.[2] So even though preoccupied by the Diet of Augsburg in 1530, the Empress signed the decree of August of that year that forbade any new enslavement in his realms: "No person shall dare to make a single slave whether in peace or in war . . . whether by barter, purchase, trade or on any pretext or cause whatsoever";[3] and Charles advised his son Prince Philip, in 1544 and 1548, always to concern himself with the quality of governors and Viceroys: "Do not cease to keep yourself well informed of the state of these distant lands, for the honour of God and for the sake of justice. Combat the abuses which have arisen there."[4] The twentieth-century Spanish historian Ramón Carande, however, pointed out that "without the Indian payments, his adventures [in Italy] would have been few."[5]

In 1534, the Moorish admiral Barbarossa had captured Tunis. Charles, who had some knowledge of strategy, thought that that threatened the entire western Mediterranean, Spain as well as Italy. He thereupon began to gather a considerable army and navy, and called a meeting of the *cortes* in order to look for more money. He remained in Madrid all the winter of 1534–35, meeting the controllers of his military orders in hopes of financing this conflict.

While these preparations were being made, the news came in September 1534 of the death of Pope Clement VII, a great relief to Charles. He was succeeded by Cardinal Farnese, the oldest of the cardinals and the only one to date his cardinalate to the days of Alexander VI. Farnese was proclaimed Pope Paul III, and he immediately announced his support for Charles's plea for a general council of the Church.

Two senior counselors, Tavera and Cobos, opposed Charles's proposed campaign against Barbarossa, but their protests were ignored. Charles had, after all, a new source of finance—namely, Peruvian gold. For, as we have seen, Hernando Pizarro had returned in the winter of 1534 with his extraordinary news and presents from Peru. One hundred and eighty-five thousand ducats of the treasure of Pizarro were held in the castle of La Mota at Medina del Campo (a castle that Hernando, ironically, would come to know only too well). Cobos said that the King could also count on 800,000 ducats seized from private people who had brought that sum from the New World. Twenty-two cartloads of gold in bars arrived on April 29 in Barcelona, where the expedition to Tunis was being planned. Another twenty heavily laden mule trains arrived on May 22.

On May 13, 1535, all the forces that Charles was committing trooped past the Emperor outside the gate of Perpignan at Barcelona, while the royal treasurer, Pedro de Zuazaola, and Juan de Samano, the secretary of the Council of the Indies during most of the long reign, sat at a table writing down names and numbers. Never before had Charles seemed the leader of a real crusade. He himself unfurled a banner of Christ crucified and called to the assembled men, noblemen, soldiers, and camp followers: "Here is your captain-general, I am your standard bearer." Seventy-four galleys, thirty minor ships, and three hundred transport then sailed under the command of Andrea Doria, the brilliant admiral of Genoa, assisted by his young Spanish disciple, Álvaro de Bazán. The Marquess de Vasto (son of the Marquess de Pescara, of Pavia renown) commanded the troops in Doria's fleet, Charles agreeing to submit himself to that command.[6]

On June 10, the great fleet set out for Africa. Five days later, it lay at anchor before the ruins of Carthage. On July 14, the fort of La Goleta was stormed. That was Charles's baptism of fire. Was he in a melée, was his horse killed under him? Such details are obscure. We know, though, that on July 21, Charles entered Tunis, triumphantly releasing twenty thousand Christian captives. He captured eighty-two vessels of Barbarossa's fleet. Next month, he returned Tunis to his friend Muley Hasán, whom Barbarossa had dispossessed as king. The King-Emperor returned to Sicily on August 22, greeted as "Carolus Africanus." A banner spoke of him as "Champion of Europe and of Asia," and another proclaimed, "Long live our victorious Emperor, conqueror of Africa, peacemaker of Italy." Much booty was obtained. People began to talk of Charles as if he had become a combination of Saint Louis, Scipio, and Hannibal. Turkish fashions had a short vogue.

Charles was in Palermo for a month, leaving on October 13 to make a triumphal entry into Naples, where he stayed the winter. Splendid sculptures welcomed him at the Porta Capuana (Giovanni da Nola building on the work of the Florentine Giuliano da Maiano). The leaders of Europe flocked to congratulate him.[7] There were dances, masked balls, even bullfights. Cobos in December gave a dinner in Naples for the collector Paolo Giovio, and it was presumably at that point that he gave Giovio a preconquest codex from New Spain, which may have been a present to him from Cortés. A treasure from the New World thus won pride of place in the city of Stupor Mundi.[8]

While Charles was still in Naples, the Council of the Indies recommended that the trade in African slaves in the New World should be thrown quite open, relieving the practitioners of all rules save payments of taxes.[9] Charles considered that, but he was preoccupied: On April 2, 1536, he met the pope at Sermoneta, the most southerly town of the Monti Lepini. Two days later, the Emperor celebrated a triumphal entry into Rome "*con gran demonstración de alegría*," Charles reported to the Empress in Spain.[10] More than two hundred houses and even three or four churches were pulled down to make possible *la grande entrée*.[11] The vicar of the pope came to meet the Emperor. Then, surrounded by noblemen such as the Dukes of Alba, Guasto, and Benavente, Charles rode down a new street (now the Via di San Gregorio) to the Arch of Constantine. He crossed the bridge over the Tiber to be greeted by the pope at St. Peter's. The two talked. Though Charles failed to persuade the pope to side with him against France, a special congregation of cardinals at last agreed to summon a general council. Charles was so pleased that he arranged to thank the pope formally on April 17.[12]

On that day, Charles met the pope, the cardinals, the ambassadors, and other Roman officials, and harangued them for an hour in Spanish without notes. He launched a real challenge to the King of France.[13] He promised again that, if the King of France wanted him to fight personally, he could do so, armed or unarmed, "in shirt sleeves or in armour, with a sword or with fists, on land or on sea, on a bridge or on an island or in a closed place, in front of our armies or wherever he liked."[14] The prize would be Burgundy if he, Charles, won; Milan, if Francis won. Cobos and Granvelle were not consulted before their master made this chivalrous gesture.[15] They were dismayed. If such challenges could be made in Europe, what if a Peruvian made the same in the Americas? The French bishop of Macon said he could not understand what was said: Charles made a defiant reply about the virtues of the Spanish language.[16]

The speech by Charles was seen everywhere as aggressive because of its Spanish vocabulary. The twentieth-century scholar Ramón Menéndez Pidal argued that it proclaimed Spanish the common tongue of diplomacy,[17] but there was no such purpose in Charles's declaration.

Though this occasion seems to have settled the issue of war against France, there was agreement on the need for a general council of the Church, which on June 4, 1536, was summoned to meet at Mantua in May 1537. But when the Protestant Germans refused to come to a meeting in Italy, the scheme was canceled. Alas, if the Protestant community had only brought themselves to make the journey to the enchanting Palazzo del Te at Mantua, the unity of Christendom might have been preserved!

Instead, war with France was decided. The Emperor moved up to Sarzana, the first Genoese town to the east on the Gulf of Liguria, the city of Pope Nicolas V, who had given Portugal its great place in Africa and India. There, Charles was greeted by Doria, who had decided to fight for him. The plan was for a joint land and naval attack such as had been so successful at Tunis the year before. Anselmo de Grimaldo came out to meet Cobos and Granvelle, and a few weeks later, Cobos and another Genoese banker, Tomasso Forne, arranged a loan with Grimaldo for 100,000 scudi.

Even in these fraught circumstances, the news from the Indies re-mained insistent. Thus on May 30, 1536, Granvelle—in effect now chan-cellor of the empire without the name—wrote: "*Tout se porte bien en Espagne et y attend l'on merveilleuez nombre d'or des Indes.*"[18] In July 1536, Charles crossed into France, but it was a disastrous campaign thanks to Constable Montmorency's scorched-earth policy. Aix-en-Provence was be-sieged, but the attempt to take it failed.[19]

In September, Charles decided to withdraw. Montmorency, always in favor of an alliance with the Emperor against the heretics, wrote to Granvelle that Francis was prepared to seek a lasting peace. Though Charles returned to Genoa, no peace was signed. On November 14, 1536, Charles also admitted how much he was relying on the gold from the In-dies: "*Et sommes attendant et en espoir qu'il viendra du côté de Perou, qui pourra servir au propos* [and we are awaiting what comes from Peru which will be well deserved]."[20] Considering the significance of Genoa in opening the New World, it was appropriate for the Emperor to be there. Two days later, the court sailed for Palamós, in Catalonia, where they arrived on De-cember 5. There, the remorseless succession of decrees affecting the New World continued.

Charles gave his assent in January 1536 to the dispatch of a press and type to enable a son of Cromberger to set up a branch of his successful family business in Mexico, even if for a time only government printing and Christian textbooks were undertaken.[21] The initiative to establish a branch of the printer Cromberger in Mexico was largely that of Bishop Zumá-rraga. As a Franciscan, he had had much to do with the Crombergers be-fore he left Spain. In 1529, we find him owing Jacob Cromberger money, and in 1528, Jacob authorized him and Licenciado Marroquín to take over the fortune of a certain Diego de Mendieta in Mexico. Zumárraga soon de-cided that the establishment of a printing press would greatly assist the business of evangelization. Back in Spain in 1533, Zumárraga talked with the Council of the Indies of the plan, and in 1534, the Emperor gave per-mission to the bishop to spend a fifth of the income of the diocese for three years to establish a printer.[22] The nucleus of this would be the already pub-lished books of Cromberger. As for the printer in Mexico-Tenochtitlan, the Crombergers sent an Italian from Brescia, Giovanni Paoli (Juan Pablos) to establish their branch.[23] He set himself up in one of the houses owned or controlled by the bishop. There, Juan Pablos was formally registered as a citizen of Mexico; there, in 1540, he supervised the publication of *Manual de adultos,* the first volume that we know for sure was published in Mexico.[24] The Cromberger family soon acquired other interests in Mexico, principally in the silver mines of first Taxco and then Zacatecas.[25]

But in Europe, the battles for peace continued. At the end of 1537, talks about ending war were held at the little town of Fitou, on the French frontier between Leucate and Salsas, with Granvelle and Cobos on the one hand, and Montmorency and Jean, cardinal of Lorraine, on the other. Charles was at Perpignan, Francis at Montpellier. The officials' discussions centered on the restoration to the empire of Savoy, Milan, and Hesdin, in the Pas-de-Calais, which Charles had wanted given to him as a preliminary to further discussion. Later, there was also discussion of Navarre, Tournai, and even Asti. The discussions lasted till 1538. The Emperor again suggested a personal meeting between himself and the French King Francis. But Francis was reluctant. The commissioners met for the last time at Fitou on January 11, 1539. By January 20, the Spanish court were on their way back to Barcelona, the French to Lyons. Of the nobles accompanying Charles, the Duke of Nájera gave balls and jousts.[26] But there was no meeting between Francis and the Emperor.

On December 21, 1537, Bishop Zumárraga wrote to Charles from Mexico urging that a large college (say, for five hundred boys) should be established in each diocese in New Spain and a second one for girls. The instruction for boys should be extended to include Latin grammar, while girls should be educated from six to twelve, when they should be married.[27] Certainly the nineteenth-century historian Lord Macaulay would have approved. So did Charles after a time.

As far as officials in Seville are concerned, we are aware of a constant pressure on the Emperor to control and limit the scale of operations. Thus in 1538, we read of a decree on the petition of the officials of the Casa de la Contratación and the merchants of Seville that made the rules to exclude foreigners from navigation to the Indies more strict.[28]

The pursuit of an understanding between France and the empire continued: In May 1538, the Emperor arrived at Villefranche, near Nice, as usual in his friend Doria's fleet. He sent a courtier, M. de Bossu, with thirteen galleys, to Savona, Columbus's town, where the pope was waiting. The pope then went to the Franciscan house of Les Cordeliers, near Nice; the next day, Charles had an hour's talk with him there. They met again in a pavilion built between Nice and Villefranche. On May 28, Francis arrived at Villeneuve, west of Nice, with his son Henry's consort, Catherine de' Médici; Queen Leonor, Charles's sister; and a bodyguard of ten thousand Swiss. On May 29, Cobos, Alburquerque, and Granvelle called on King Francis and met Queen Leonor, and there was a similar courtesy visit by Montmorency and Cardinal de Lorraine to the Emperor. Then, on June 2, Francis had his first meeting with the pope, in a house that had been specially prepared for him, between Nice and Villeneuve. On June 4, the French and imperial commissioners met the pope for the first time, and later, the Queen visited Charles. The pier collapsed and many grand men and women fell into the water (including the archbishop of Santiago). Even the Emperor was temporarily thrown in, but he saved his sister Queen Leonor; and while Charles still did not meet on that occasion the French king, the pope did arrange a ten-year truce.

Leonor eventually persuaded Charles to meet Francis at the castle of Aigues-Mortes on a lagoon near Montpellier. They talked a long time, while a dance went on outside. Perhaps they could arrange a crusade together? Francis embraced the proposal with the same exaggerated enthusiasm that he had shown before for the idea and then quickly forgot about it.

All the same, there was a celebration in Mexico to mark the end of the war with France. This took place in the royal palace in Mexico, whose corridors "were transformed into bowers and gardens and, for each course, there were stewards and pages and a full and well-arranged service . . . together with much music of singers and trumpetry, and all sorts of instruments, such as harps, guitars, vihuelas, flutes, dulcimers, and oboes . . . huge pastries were full of live quail and rabbits, whose escape afforded much amusement. There were also jesters and versifiers, and fountains of white wine, sherry, and red wine. Over 300 men and over 200 women were present and the banquet lasted till two hours after midnight when the ladies cried out that they could no longer stay at the table and others that they were indisposed." Everything was served on gold and silver, none of which was lost since the authorities placed an Indian guard next to every dish. But silver salt cellars, tablecloths, napkins, and knives did disappear. These fiestas were organized by Luis de León of Rome. The Viceroy Antonio de Mendoza and Cortés, the Marquess del Valle de Oaxaca, now on reasonable terms, celebrated together. Thus, less than twenty years after the great conquest of New Spain, did the New World give a full recognition of the old one.

34

The Indies Finance Europe

I wished your Highness to know all the things of this land which
are so many and of such a kind that one might call oneself Emperor
of the Kingdom with no less glory than of Germany which by the
grace of God Your Sacred Highness already possesses.

CORTÉS TO CHARLES V, 1519

Charles the Emperor was in Spain in mid-1538, first in Burgos, then in
Valladolid, and there he or the Empress issued numerous decrees—for
example, one to encourage bachelors in the Indies to marry, giving
preference indeed in *encomiendas* to those with families. Another royal
decree ordered an ecclesiastical tribunal to examine a Tarascan catechism
used in central Mexico and to take special heed that the terms used did not
present difficulties for the teaching and practice of the Christian religion
among the Indians.[1] It almost began to seem as if the American empire was
becoming a priority among the imperial authorities.

Charles had to preside over the death of his beloved wife, the Empress
Isabel, who died in childbirth in 1539. Her death was the tragedy of
Charles's middle life. But the Emperor in Spain was also as busy with difficult noblemen as he had been in Germany. Thus, in October 1538, he summoned the *cortes* of Castile at Toledo. Charles had with him not just the
procuradores of the towns but also the nobility and the clergy. He explained
that the total revenue of the realm was just over a million ducats, but more
than half was mortgaged in advance. The Crown had decided, therefore, to
levy a new tax, the *sisa,* which would be paid by everyone. The very rich
Duke of Béjar, son of Cortés's great friend and benefactor, was the leading
opponent, and in the end, Charles dropped the idea.

This meeting of the Castilian *cortes* was notable for bad tempers on all sides. Ninety-five grandees and nobles attended. The three estates assembled in different buildings in the city. The nobles refused to accept the secretary designated by the court, and whenever he appeared in the chapter house of the monastery of San Juan de los Reyes, he was expelled by angry noblemen crying: "Leave us, leave us, here we have no need of any secretary."[2]

It was here, according to Sepúlveda, that Charles said, "It's now that I understand the little power that I possess."[3] Sandoval reported that Charles said to Velasco, the constable of Castile, "I should like to throw you out of the window," to which the constable replied: "Your Majesty should take care for, even if I am small, I weigh a lot."

At this time, the idea of fighting the Turks so filled Charles's mind that he hastily worked to solve all other problems.[4] He was not deflected by a letter of good advice from his sister Mary, the regent in the Netherlands: "Your Majesty is the greatest Prince in Christendom but you cannot undertake a war in the name of all Christendom until you can be sure to carry it to victory. Such an enterprise could not be carried out save over many years and would cost inexhaustible money. Where could this come from? France, Venice, Naples, the Netherlands? Could you really go and leave us unprotected? The Turks cannot be conquered unless their whole empire falls. So great a Prince as you must only triumph. Defeat is the ultimate crime. Win the love of the German princes, make France a friend, not an enemy. March across France, settle your last accounts with the King there, then visit your Netherlands, then Germany and at last Italy. Gain the support of all! This is the advice which in all humility I offer you."[5]

Yet Charles still had to decide such tedious matters as the rivalries between the Casa de la Contratación, the Council of the Indies, and the city council in Seville.

In civil cases relating to the Indies, the petitioner could choose between the Casa de la Contratación and the municipal court, always supposing that the accused was in Seville. Criminal cases had to be heard first by the Casa de la Contratación, except for criminal cases involving death, which would be heard by the Casa and passed to the Council of the Indies for sentencing.[6]

These considerations did not prevent Charles from planning once more to leave Spain for Flanders and Germany, leaving the reliable Cardinal Tavera as regent.

We follow Charles in 1541 to the Diet of Regensburg, where the German princes had assembled. He was also in Ghent for the beheading of the leaders of that city's dangerous revolt that year. There the Venetian Cardinal Contarini, dominating the Catholics, spoke with the authority of one experienced in the affairs of the Indies because of his old *nunciatura* in Spain. There was, too, the new prophet of intolerant Protestantism, Jean Calvin, from Geneva. There were some good signs. The German reformer and collaborator of Luther, Philipp Melanchthon, for example, was conciliatory. Charles, longing for a reconciliation, which he still believed possible, intervened often. But still, in the end, there was no peaceful solution. Charles withdrew and eventually saw the pope at Lucca in the bishop's palace. He received papal blessing for a new expedition against the Ottomans, which had long been his dream.

For this an armada of sixty-five galleys and 450 other ships was made ready with twenty-four thousand troops, including, astonishingly, none other than the Marquess del Valle de Oaxaca, Cortés himself. He had talked his way into being accepted by Charles. But he had no command. How could a conquistador command European troops? The Duke of Alba assembled the fleet in Majorca under Doria, the troops under Ferrante Gonzaga. They left Majorca on October 13, 1541, and arrived off Algiers on October 20. On October 23, Charles began to disembark his troops on a treacherous spit of land to the east of that city. The infantry was landed, but bad weather prevented the cavalry and artillery from following them. A storm blew up on October 24–25, and there seemed no way of saving the ships without throwing overboard food and armaments. Even so, fourteen galleys were lost. Charles landed again, to the west of Algiers. But the disembarkation of provisions seemed impossible. Cortés told Charles that if he turned back, he personally could show the monarch how to conquer the city. If it had not been for the storm, Algiers could easily have been captured, but Cortés, for all his astounding talents, was not a master of the weather.

On November 2, Charles now ordered his half-starving troops to be reembarked.[7] He was held up for days at Bugia, west of the city. He returned to Cartagena on December 1, then to Valladolid via Ocaña, Toledo, and Madrid.

When Charles was back in Valladolid, he found the Council of the Indies again in bad morale. The trouble was that various Spanish cities, such as Córdoba, Madrid, and Guadalajara, had complained of the slow pace with which the council dispatched its business. In the *cortes,* someone had written, perhaps under the influence of Las Casas: "We beseech His Majesty that he remedies the cruelties which are done to the natives in the Indies and, in that way, God will be served and the Indies preserved."[8]

Charles, contemplating these problems, held a new *cortes* in February 1542, this time at Valladolid. Most towns yielded to royal pressure and granted a subsidy of 400,000 ducats a year for the purpose of financing a crusade against Islam, substantial bribery probably being used to achieve this.[9] Charles told the *cortes* what he had been doing. He saw Las Casas, who came on the recommendation of Bishop Zumárraga. Of course, Charles had met him often in the days of his first visit to Spain in 1517–18.[10] But their present encounter was equally important. Las Casas again made a profound impression, not only on the Emperor, but on all to whom he talked. After all, he had been to the places which they only discussed. The Emperor was shocked by Casas's new *memorials* about the condition of Indians. Those documents led to the reorganization of the Council of the Indies and then to the New Laws, essentially a Las Casasian project.[11]

At that time, Spain alone of Charles's dominions was at peace. Taxes remained high. Sometimes there were extra revenues, such as the dowry paid by the King of Portugal for Isabel; or the King of France's ransom of his sons for a million ducats. In 1540, the 282,000 ducats that derived from "Indies treasure" was a major item in the Crown's total income of 1,159,923 ducats.[12]

But there was never enough money at the start of a war. Bankers were called in; loans were raised at high interest. Crown lands and some sources of revenue were mortgaged. The future income of the Crown was crippled. Charles contracted debts haphazardly as the need occurred. That is why the Spanish Crown was coming to think of the Indies as a new treasure trove to finance their European designs. The Crown seems to have raised as much as two-thirds of its entire revenue from the Indies in 1543.[13] This was exceptional, but it was an indication of what might be expected in the future.

There were, however, obstacles to the Indies being able to confirm this weighty financial contribution. In consequence of the accusations of corruption, the Council of the Indies suspended its activities till February

1543. Dr. Juan de Figueroa carried out an investigation. He was, Cobos said, "a man of sound learning, very honest and, in official matters, nothing will deflect him an iota from that which is right."[14] Figueroa found that the only permanent long-term member of the council, Dr. Beltrán, was flawed. He had requested benefits in Peru from the Pizarros for his two sons, Antonio Beltrán and Bernardino Mella. The latter received the post of chief constable (*alguacil mayor*) of Cuzco, while the former received good Indians in an *encomienda* in Arequipa. Those benefits were illegal. Beltrán also admitted that in return for support or for favors, he had in his time received money from Almagro, Cortés, and Hernando Pizarro, and from Gonzalo de Olmos, a cousin of Beltrán's wife, two emeralds and two beakers of gold.[15] The emperor Charles was outraged.

Beltrán defended himself: The money that came from Almagro had not been for him but for someone else, to whom he had given it. The bribes of Cortés had gone astray, and he then denied those of Hernando Pizarro. The presents of Olmos, he claimed, were worth only 220 ducats. But these defenses were not believed, Beltrán contradicted himself several times, and finally he was condemned to deprivation of office and salary. He lost all his special grants, and he was condemned by the magistrates of the court to pay a fine of 17,000 ducats, which almost ruined him. (It was twice what he was said to have received in bribes.) Suárez de Carvajal, bishop of Lugo, was also condemned, but the papers of this inquiry have been lost, so it is not clear of what he was accused. But he was deprived of his bishopric and fined 7,000 ducats.[16] The emperor Charles strongly opposed tolerance in both these circumstances.

So in the winter of 1542–43, Beltrán withdrew to the monastery of Our Lady of Grace in Medina del Campo. There this first civil servant of the Indies made an appeal, but no one wanted to listen. Juan de Samano, with whom Beltrán had collaborated for twenty years, said he could do nothing. A newly reconfigured council wrote to the Emperor asking for tolerance, but the Emperor instructed the magistrates to maintain their sentence.

Afterwards, for the first time, the council received rules. These were prepared by Cardinal Loaisa, Dr. Figueroa, and Dr. Fernando de Guevara (speaking on behalf of the Council of Castile), with the help of Fray Domingo de Soto, Granvelle, and Cobos. The rules were publicly announced in a contract signed by Charles, among others, on November 20, 1542.[17]

Another important innovation came in 1546: From then on, on the express petition of merchants in Seville, ships bound for the Indies were to sail together in convoys for safety. No vessel less than ten tons was to be cleared for departure to the Indies. The minimum fleet was ten vessels, and two such fleets would leave a year, one in March, one in September. This, to begin with, was only in time of war, but given that French pirates were active at all times, the idea was maintained in peace. In January 1546, all merchant vessels, not just those for the Indies, were instructed to sail in convoys and were to arm themselves.[18] Over the years these arrangements would be further developed.

Alas for the papal hopes of peace with France. On July 10, 1542, that country declared war against Charles, an act inspired by the Emperor's designation of his son Philip as Duke of Milan. That caused a crisis in the Netherlands. Queen Mary of Hungary as regent led the defense herself, with the Prince of Orange. Antwerp beat off a rebellion of Gelderland, but there was much destruction. Then the French mysteriously withdrew, even as the Netherlands suffered from the lack of a general.

Charles left Monzón in October for Barcelona. He had written to Pope Paul hoping that the Pontiff would cease dealing with France and the Empire as if they were equal powers. At Barcelona, Charles welcomed his son Philip for his first visit to the city. On November 8, 1542, Philip made a formal entry into the Catalan capital (having arrived secretly and in disguise the previous night). On November 9, Philip received the homage of the councillors, as of the multi-competent Francisco de Borja, still the Viceroy of Catalonia. In May, Charles left for Genoa, leaving the sixteen-year old Philip as regent, to be advised as before by Fernando de Valdés, archbishop of Seville, a hard and unbending churchman from Asturias who was also *gran inquisidor*. The Council of the Indies would be still chaired by García de Loaisa but in his frequent absences, the experienced ex-judge of the *audiencia* in Santo Domingo and Mexico, Ramírez de Fuenleal, would preside.

Charles's two letters from Palamós to Philip as to how to conduct himself as regent have a deserved place in history. It was now that Charles told his son not to give himself over too much to the pleasures of marriage (Philip had married his first cousin María of Portugal in November 1543). In respect of the American empire, Charles enjoined Philip to "remember how many lands you will be called on to govern, how far apart they are, how many different languages they speak . . . and you will see how needful it is to learn languages." Latin, Charles insisted, was indispensable, though he himself had never mastered it.

In August 1543, Cobos wrote to the Emperor: The difficulty of finding money was so great that there had never been anything like it. He assured Charles, "There is no way that it [more money] can be found, for there is none . . . To find 18,000 ducats every 30 days for the defence of Perpignan, Fuenterrabía, San Sebastián and Navarre, as well as Malaga and Cartagena has been, and is, extremely difficult . . . I am very truly perplexed." In the end, he raised 420,000 ducats, much of it from a shipment of gold and silver from the Indies, and there were some loans from private persons. Tavera lent 16,000 ducats, Cobos himself advanced 8,000, but other rich men refused. The Duke of Alba said that he would serve the Emperor "pike in hand" but in no other way.[19]

Such difficulties did not act as a brake on Charles, who in July 1544 led his armies under Orange, Este, Gonzaga, and Granvelle into French Burgundy. He besieged Saint-Dizier on the way to Vitry-le-François. King Henry VIII of England was ready at Boulogne. Charles proceeded with the slogan "On to Paris." He did not besiege any city but drove on. There was panic in the capital. The cardinal of Lorraine, a Guise before he was a churchman, indicated that France was interested in negotiation. On August 31, a conference at Saint-Amand, to the north of the Marne, articulated a serious effort to make peace. This led in September to the Peace of Crépy. The public terms included: first, France would send ten thousand men, of whom six hundred would be cavalry, against the Turks. Second, both sides would restore all conquests made since the Truce of Nice of 1538. Third, Stenay, in the Ardennes, was to be given back. The French king's son Charles, Duke of Orléans, was to marry the Infanta and inherit the Netherlands on Charles's death; or he could marry the archduchess Ana and have Milan. More important, France would abandon its policy of encroaching on Spain's empire in the new world and would not attack any more treasure fleets.

There were also secret clauses: Francis would help Charles to reform the abuses of the church; France would support the planned general meeting of the church at Trent; France would do what it could to encourage the return of the German princes to the Catholic fold; Francis would give

Charles the diplomatic help that he had promised against the Turks; France would support the return of Geneva to the Duke of Savoy; and Francis promised not to make any peace with England from which Charles was excluded. If Charles were to go to war with Henry VIII and England, France would support him.[20]

On September 14, 1544, treaties along these lines were signed in the abbey of Saint Nicolas in the vineyards of Soissons. The peace was to be confirmed by a visit in October of the Queen of France, Charles's sister Leonor, to Brussels, her birthplace, accompanied by her stepson (the Duke of Orléans), whom the Emperor already treated as a half son, and by Madame d'Estampes, the French king's mistress. Charles had with him his sister Queen Mary of Hungary and his Austrian nephews, the archdukes Maximilian and Ferdinand. Also present was Ottavio Farnese, his son-in-law, the pope's son who had married his illegitimate daughter, Margaret of Flanders. There were balls and tournaments: "At the reception, it seemed as if they [the Emperor and his sister] would never have done with kissing and embracing each other."[21]

These celebrations were followed by discussions in Spain as to whether Charles should maintain himself in Milan or in the Low Countries. The Italian party was headed by the Duke of Alba, who was the new governor of Milan, supported by the Count of Osorno, who saw in Milan the essential point of entry to Germany, as well as the key to the defense of Naples, while Flanders was difficult to govern, easily open to French attack, and had never done anything for Spain. The opposing view was held by Tavera.[22] Nothing was decided. Spain continued with pretensions to both territories.

Another consequence of Charles's continued preoccupation with war was that when at last that so-much-desired general council of the Church opened at Trent, in the far north of Italy, in the winter of 1545, his representative—Francisco de Toledo, a disciple of Fray Domingo de Soto and a lecturer at Salamanca—had a free hand to decide what he thought best.

Cobos wrote sycophantically of Philip to the emperor Charles: "King Philip . . . is already so great a monarch that his knowledge and capacity have outstripped his years [he was then sixteen], for he seems to have achieved the impossible by his great understanding and his lofty comprehension. His diversions are a complete and constant devotion to work and the affairs of his kingdom. He is always thinking about matters of good government and justice, without leaving room for favouritism nor for idleness, nor for flattery nor for any vice . . . Where it is necessary to hold meetings, he listens to the opinions of each one with the greatest gravity and attention . . . He is frequently closeted with me for hours at a time . . . afterwards, he does the same thing with the president of the council [the *inquisidor*] Valdés to talk about justice and the Duke of Alba to talk about war . . . I am astonished at his prudent, well considered recommendations."[23]

Charles wrote in 1546 to his son Philip that he was determined to take the field against the German princes. He proposed to borrow the money needed for these campaigns from bankers in Nuremberg, Augsburg, Genoa, and Antwerp. The security? Why, the shipments of gold and silver from the Indies of 600,000 scudi. He hoped that Cobos would undertake the negotiations. He was optimistic: The Emperor's fifth in 1545 had been 360,000 ducats.[24]

Cobos acted quickly: On May 22 he and the Castilian Council of Finance signed a contract for a loan with the Fuggers' agent in Spain. The Fuggers were still the richest bankers in Germany, and the requested funds needed to be explained and justified. Cobos also raised money by diverting some already allocated elsewhere. Still, he wrote to the Emperor that the financial situation remained difficult: "We are at the end of our tether unless God our Lord in His mercy and Your Majesty can find a remedy." Cobos suggested "a counsel of despair": to seize all the cash in Spain and ship it to the Emperor by galleys. That would provide ready money in Genoa, where it was so needed. This mad plan was approved by Philip and the council. Philip then wrote to his father: "These Kingdoms are so bare of gold—you cannot find a *scudo*—that there will be no lack of complaints and outcries." But somehow they did manage to gather 180,000 scudi by October 10.[25]

Long before that, in June, Charles had written despairingly to his sister Mary about his efforts to rein in the rebellious Protestants:

All my efforts . . . have come to nothing. The heretic Princes and electors have decided not to attend the Diet in person; indeed they are determined to rise in revolt immediately the Diet is over, to the utter destruction of the spiritual lords and to the great peril of the King of the Romans and ourself. If we hesitate now, we shall lose all.

Thus we are certain, I, my brother and the Duke of Bavaria, that force alone will drive them to accept reasonable terms. The time is opportune, for they have been weakened by recent wars. Their subjects, the nobility in particular, are discontented . . . Over and above this, we have good hope of papal help of an offer of 800,000 ducats or more. Unless we take immediate action, all the estates of Germany may lose their faith and the Netherlands could follow.

After fully considering all these points, I decided to begin by raising war in Hesse and Saxony as disturbers of the peace and to open the campaign in the lands of the Duke of Brunswick. This pretext will not long conceal the purpose of this war of religion but it will serve to divide the protestants from the beginning. Be assured I shall do nothing without careful thought.[26]

Charles's letter to Mary was an implicit order to the Netherlands to mobilize.

35

Federmann and
Jiménez de Quesada

Between the province of Santa Marta and that of Cartagena, there is a river which divides these territories, it is called the Magdalena and it is known because it is a great river and also because it runs with great fury and impetus into the sea, carrying sweet water out for a league's distance.

GONZALO JIMÉNEZ DE QUESADA, 1536

In 1529, there were several German subjects of the Emperor in Venezuela connected with the banking house of Welser. These were Ambrosio Alfinger, Nicolás Federmann, and Sebastian Rentz, from Ulm; Jorge Ehinger, from Konstanz; and Juan Seissenhofer, often known as Juan Aleman, who came from Augsburg. Alfinger was formally the governor, but being on an expedition in the Andes, he allowed himself to be briefly substituted by Seissenhofer. Upon his return, he handed authority over to Federmann while he went, at the end of July 1530, to rest in Santo Domingo.[1]

Federmann, who was, of course, a citizen of Ulm, had courage, energy, and originality. He spent the early days of his new responsibility looking for pearls off the peninsula of Paraguaná. Then, a month later, he set off on his own expedition into the interior, leaving Bartolomé de Santillana as his deputy. Federmann's object in exploring the interior was to seek the Mar del Sur (the Pacific), by which route it would surely be a short distance to the Spice Islands. He set off on September 13, 1532, with a hundred

Spaniards on foot, sixteen on horses, and about a hundred porters from the nearby tribes. Federmann's activity clashed directly with the instructions of Alfinger to stay where he was.

Federmann's aim was to go due south from Coro. He journeyed through the territories and villages of three new and unknown peoples, the Xideharas, the Ayamanes, and the Xaguas. Of these, the Ayamanes were so small that they seemed to be dwarfs. The illness of many of his men caused them to travel in hammocks, "more like hospital patients than men of war."[2] In those humid valleys, he strove to ensure that his sick colleagues were treated as if they were great lords. He wanted the Indians to think the Spaniards were immortals, immune to all diseases.

As usual with Spanish adventurers of this kind, he met many difficulties. For instance, his accountant, Antonio Naveros, made an unwise comment criticizing him.[3] He was sent back in chains to Coro and was killed on the way by a poisoned arrow in his throat. That was a serious setback to the Welser cause in Venezuela, for Oviedo had looked on Naveros as an excellent person, and it was said that he had a calm disposition.[4]

On his way south, Federmann reached the large pueblo of Acariagua, on the river Tocuyo. There he had a serious battle in which almost all the Spaniards were wounded. He then returned to Coro. Alfinger, who by then had returned from his rest in Santo Domingo, was furious with Federmann for undertaking a grand journey without his permission. He decided to send Federmann back to Europe, and he accordingly went home to Seville in the company of his friend, Sebastian Rentz. He even made his way back to Augsburg, where he wrote his *Historia Indiana* to inform the Welsers what was happening. At first he was requested to stay away from the Indies for four years, but he then negotiated a new contract for seven years in Venezuela, for which he would receive a small salary. When news came that Alfinger had been killed by Indians near Lake Maracaibo, Federmann was named his successor in July 1534, with the titles of governor and captain-general of Venezuela.

Alfinger had made another fruitless journey west to find the elusive strait to the Southern Sea, for he remained convinced of the strait's existence. He went to Lake Maracaibo, he went to the mountains of Perijá, and he reached the banks of the great river Magdalena. But there was no strait; and Alfinger was killed by Indians.

Federmann's rise to the governorship was confused by the fact that for a time he had a rival in Venezuela, another German, Georg Hohermuth von Speyer (known among Spaniards as Espira), from the ancient ecclesiastical city of Speyer. But Federmann was restored before he left Spain.

Federmann's second departure for Venezuela from Sanlúcar was attended by an astonishingly lavish ceremony: There were shawms and bagpipes; processions of priests with candles; bandsmen with trumpets and trombones; Dominican friars, barefoot Franciscans; drummers; soldiers with fighting dogs, eleven columns of horsemen, soldiers with axes, arquebusiers, shield-bearing captains, and soldiers in deerskin to ward off poisoned arrows. There followed flags, units of infantrymen, shoemakers, tailors, builders, and then the whole troop of Federmann's army. This included Flemings, Englishmen, Albanians, even Scots, as well as Germans and Castilians. They went as a procession to the convent of the barefoot friars to swear loyalty to the Emperor, as well as the governor.[5] Provisions on the journey would be generous (a pound of meat three times a week, on other days fish).

The expedition reached Santo Domingo and then made for Coro. For a year or two, Federmann negotiated his way more or less successfully through a jungle of conflicting interests in northern Venezuela. Espira then set off for the interior and was not seen again for three years. The municipality of Coro clashed with Federmann, whose activities they sought to limit. Federmann, like other German governors in Venezuela, looked on his post primarily as one that could give a justification for journeys of discovery: Espira was looking for the apparently rich territory of Xeriva; Antonio de Chaves, another Spanish adventurer, made his way along the coast to the mouth of the Magdalena; Federmann himself tried to found a port on the Río Hacha, on the way to the coastal city of Santa Marta, beyond Maracaibo. Life in Coro declined severely; the population of this new Spanish "city" fell to a mere 140, of whom two-thirds were ill. Bishop Bastidas, son of Rodrigo, who came from Santo Domingo as acting governor in the absence of the Germans, gave a gloomy picture: "It was part of my infirmity to have to see the place's great poverty. And we went to our church and there found poverty and ruin. Everything both smelled and appeared of sovereign impoverishment. . . . The *pueblo* has fifty cottages, or a few more, and there are not four *bohíos* which could be described as reasonable. The church is covered with the poorest kind of straw . . . and at present people do not have shirts with which to dress themselves."[6] There were later denunciations of cruelty: For example, Federmann was accused of transporting his Indians in a long chain with their necks in irons, and of cutting off their heads when they were ill or tired. This evidence emerged during a later *residencia,* which had to be interrupted by the judge because he ran out of paper.[7]

In 1539, Federmann resolved on an extensive new journey of discovery. This would go due south from Coro along roads where he had been before, but then seek a crossing of the Andes a long way to the south of his last expedition's concluding point. Again the aim was partly or perhaps wholly the search for "the strait."

Federmann set off with about two hundred men and five hundred bearers. His first stage was the eastern foothills of the Andes to the valley of the river Tocuyo. Here he encountered troops of Juan Fernández de Alderete, who had rebelled against Governor Dortal in the Paria territory. They were seeking what they had heard, from the survivors of the late Diego de Ordaz's expedition, were the rich lands of the valley of the Meta. Federmann took over these troops and seized the goods of the leaders, whom he sent back to Coro. He had a similar encounter with an expedition of Diego Martínez, who had explored the rather more remote peninsula of Guajira. His goods, too, were seized.

Federmann crossed the river Pauto, a tributary of the Meta, and then sent a lieutenant, Pedro de Limpias, to seek a pass over the Andes to the west. He could not find one. Federmann divided his little army into three but they were united again at Aracheta, the future San Juan de los Llanos. The rumor was that, between the rivers Meta and Guaviare, an entrance could be made to a magical territory known as El Dorado, where all Spanish dreams would be fullfilled.

In February 1539, Federmann, with the three sections of his force reunited, was on the upper river Guaviare. Here he found many objects of gold and realized that these came from "the other side of the sierra"—that is, from the Indians who inhabited the Chibcha high plateau. This realization gave Federmann an even stronger motive to seek to scale the cordillera of the Andes. He performed this feat in forty days, of which twenty-two were through barren country, including a wide plain of intense cold where seventy of his Indians died as well as forty of his 130 horses. When he reached the summit, he had only 160 soldiers and seventy horse. Here, he assumed, was the land of his expectations. It was not "the strait" to the Southern Sea. But it was a magic land of gold. Alas, the land could not be Federmann's, not without argument at least. For he discovered that the territory had been occupied for two years by another Spanish expedition from Santa Marta, under the leadership of Gonzalo Jiménez de Quesada.

Gonzalo Jiménez de Quesada was a native of Córdoba, a city that gave fewer conquistadors to the Indies than any other large city of Andalusia. Jiménez de Quesada's father was a lawyer and his mother came from a famous family of dyers. A maternal uncle, Jerónimo de Soria, had been President of the dyers' guild in Córdoba, but had difficulties when he started using a cheap dye that, it was said, damaged the good cloth of the city. So Gonzalo Jiménez de Quesada, with his brothers Hernando and Francisco, decided to go to the Indies to recover their fortunes. Perhaps they were conversos. The "evidence" for that, such as it is, derives from a quarrel that Gonzalo once had with Lázaro Fonte, who accused him of being Jewish. When he sought to become governor in the Indies, the Council of the Indies even said that one reason against him was that he was descended from people who had been "reconciled."[8]

Gonzalo, like his father, was by education a lawyer. Probably he had attended the University of Salamanca, and certainly for a time he worked in the supreme court of Granada. He then went to Santa Marta. Probably it was about 1534.

Jiménez de Quesada found Santa Marta in bad shape. There was a shortage of horses, arms, food, and houses. The inhabitants received supplies on a modest scale from the cacique of Bonda. The governor, Pedro Fernández de Lugo, seemed incompetent, greedy, and miserly, even though he came from a family of conquistadors (who were probably also conversos).[9] He gave Jiménez de Quesada a characteristic contract (*capitulación*) on January 22, 1535. This was in the first instance bounded in the east by the meridian line that crosses the Cabo de la Vela; in the west, by the line that runs from the mouth of the Magdalena; and in the south, by the unknown coast of the Southern Sea. Jiménez de Quesada was named as commander and captain-general. His brother Hernando was named chief magistrate. Provision was made as to who should succeed Gonzalo if he were to die.

His expedition left Santa Marta on April 5, 1536, with six hundred men, including seventy mounted. Another two hundred men were to sail up the Magdalena in support, on three brigantines and a pinnace (*fusta*). But this little fleet was dispersed on the open sea before it even reached the Magdalena. The pinnace was sunk, and its crew drowned. The brigantines took refuge in Cartagena. A hundred miles up the Magdalena, Jiménez de Quesada waited fruitlessly for these ships. He had placed his supplies on them. In the end, his men had to continue without food, eating herbs and berries as best they could. As usual, the mangrove swamps extended down to the river's edge, and the continual difficulty posed by tributaries of the Magdalena, as well as the mosquitoes, combined with the lack of food, made the journey very difficult. About two hundred miles up the river, they were met by two new brigantines sent up under Diego Hernández Gallego by the governor, Fernández de Lugo, when he heard of the setbacks met by the other three vessels.

Reaching La Tora, at the point of confluence of the rivers Magdalena, Opon, and Carrare, the expedition followed the second named. Jiménez de Quesada sent a mounted expedition ahead to find out the nature of the territory and where the Opon rose. This little unit, captained by Juan de Céspedes, a Sevillano,[10] and Juan de San Martín, came back to explain that the land was well populated. The whole force then camped in La Tora. They then numbered only 230 foot and seventy horse, for more than three hundred had already died or otherwise fallen by the way. Most of the survivors ascended the Opon, leaving the ships below under Hernández Gallego, with thirty-five healthy men and twenty-five sick ones. About fifty miles up, they were welcomed by the first Chibchas. Dressed in cotton cloaks, the Indians offered them food. They entered the valley of the Opon, where they came upon abundant food and even some gold. In the far distance, they could see the Chibcha plateau.

While they seemed well enough, the news brought them from the valley was that Diego Hernández Gallego had been attacked by Indians. After he lost a brigantine and half his men, he had decided to return to Santa Marta. A new (interim) governor, Jerónimo Lebrón, sent a new flotilla of four brigantines with food to restore Jiménez de Quesada, but they never found him. By then he was enriching himself on the Chibcha plateau.

For on reaching La Grita in March 1537, Jiménez de Quesada found in one day over 1,000 pesos of fine gold and 73 of a lower grade. Two or three days later, his party reached Guachetá, where they found their first emeralds. Moving southward, meeting every day new peoples, such as the Lemguarque, the Conumba, and the Suesca, they found more gold and emeralds, and then on March 22, they even discovered salt—another and equally important item of commerce. On March 28, they skirmished with natives sent by a chief known as Bogotá, but they went ahead, first to besiege, and then to enter, the capital that had the chief's name. The chief fled with his main treasure to mountains nearby, where he was later killed. By that time, the Spaniards had seized about 4,600 pesos of good gold as well as more than five hundred emeralds. Jiménez de Quesada then dispatched Pedro Fernández de Valenzuela to the emerald reserves of Somondoco.

Jiménez de Quesada meantime began to explore the cordillera of Tunja, where a rich chief was said to be. On August 20, the Spaniards found there another 140,000 pesos of fine gold, 280 emeralds, and 14,000 pesos of low-grade gold. In October, they seized even more: nearly 200,000 pesos of fine gold, 30,000 of low-grade ore, and more than eight hundred emeralds. The story then reached them that to their southeast, there was a rich region called Neiva, which was abundant in gold mines. The Indians of Pasca were said to descend there to trade their many products for gold. The Spaniards abandoned Tunja, though part of their army under Jiménez de Quesada's brother Hernando remained. The rest went on under their established commander to Pasca and the plateau of Sumapez, to camp in Neiva, where they were offered gold, though not in the quantity that they had anticipated.

Now came a division of the booty. This was decided by the commander, Jiménez de Quesada, and the inspector, Juan de San Martín. It was a great moment for all concerned, since the wealth almost equaled the great riches found in Peru. The army was divided into captains, horsemen, and soldiers. There were also payments to the surgeon and for the cost of arquebuses. Jiménez de Quesada insisted on contributions being made to the two dilapidated churches of Santa Marta—La Mayor and La Merced.[11] The royal fifth was decided as being 38,259 pesos of fine gold, 7,257 of low-grade gold, nearly 4,000 of scrap (*oro de Chatalonia*), and 360 emeralds of varying sizes. There remained over 150,000 pesos of fine gold, 30,000 of low-grade gold, and 1,450 emeralds to be divided among the conquistadors. All debts were paid out of the scrap gold. In the end, there were 148,000 pesos of fine gold, about 17,000 of lower-grade gold, and 1,455 emeralds to be divided. Those who had come up the Magdalena under Diego Hernández Gallego were excluded, since they had not participated in the extraordinary struggles along the great river.

Each share of the treasure, it was determined, would be worth 510 pesos of fine gold, 576 of low-grade gold, and five emeralds.

The leaders decided that the absent governor in Santa Marta would receive ten shares, Jiménez de Quesada nine, his captains four, the sergeant major three, the lieutenants two, each captain's lieutenant half, lieutenants of horse three, horsemen and clerics two, arquebusiers one and a half, and one each for the *macheteros* and the infantrymen. Those who had died on the journey were allocated nothing, nor would their heirs receive anything; however, 200 pesos were allocated to pay for the Masses for the five hundred who had died since the expedition had begun.

Jiménez de Quesada decided that he wanted to settle this high territory and establish himself and his soldiers there. He decided to go home to Spain to have himself proclaimed *adelantado* of the area, taking with him his own money and the royal fifth. He would leave his brother Hernando in command. He first, however, allowed himself to be diverted by a cacique, Sagipa, who came to ask Spanish assistance against his old enemies, the Panches. Jiménez de Quesada set off with a group of horsemen and some infantry, promising his help in return for being told the whereabouts of the dead cacique Bogotá's treasure. Sagipa agreed and presented Jiménez de Quesada with many presents such as plumes, snail shells (*caracoles*), and bells of bone (*cascabeles*). But no gold came. Jiménez de Quesada, disillusioned, chained up Sagipa, though giving him free access to his people. Nothing transpired. The conquistadors, in a democratic impulse, elected Gonzalo de Luza as their *procurador*. Through an interpreter he told the cacique Sagipa that he would be tortured if the treasure did not appear. Gonzalo de Luza said that he needed 10 million pesos in gold, and ten thousand emeralds. Jiménez de Quesada named his brother Hernando as the defender of the chief. But having heard the arguments, he nevertheless sentenced Sagipa to torture, and the cacique was raised by a beam to which his hands were tied. This was twice repeated ("lightly" apparently and "only twice"). But Sagipa returned in a bad condition to his prison. There was then a fire in the improvised Christian section of Bogotá, which was attributed to Sagipa, who in order to save himself from further torture, agreed to lead Jiménez de Quesada to the place where he believed that the cacique Bogotá had buried his gold. But there seemed to be nothing there.

Jiménez de Quesada lost his temper and submitted Sagipa to further tortures, such as burning his feet, a favorite torment of the conquistadors at this stage, as we saw in respect of what happened to Cuauhtémoc in New Spain. The consequence was that in a few days, after returning to the camp, Sagipa died. Later, there were inquiries as to whether Jiménez de Quesada had tortured poor Sagipa to death.[12] There was real doubt about this: A witness of Jiménez de Quesada's, "Don Gonzalo Indio," said that he had dined with Sagipa the night before he died and that all that he complained of was a headache.[13] Jiménez de Quesada gave a document to two of his colleagues, Pedro Fernández de Valenzuela and Diego de Segura, which enabled them to mount a lawsuit at the Council of the Indies on behalf of the cacique Sagipa.

That was a matter that would be debated for many years. In the meantime, Jiménez de Quesada still hoped to return to Spain to confirm his status as an independent governor and *adelantado,* but he had to postpone his journey again, for two reasons: first, because of the battles that he had to fight against a ferocious and indeed apparently indomitable tribe, the Panches; and second, because, in the middle of that year, 1538, he received astonishing news—not only that Federmann had reached the eastern cordillera, no distance away, but also that the even more threatening Sebastián de Benalcázar was in Neiva, about 150 miles south of Bogotá. Benalcázar had driven up from Peru, his reputation as a fighter second to none. Jiménez de Quesada, isolated and even incommunicado for three years, now found himself confronted by two Spanish armies, both of which were well furnished with arms and horses, while he had little fighting capacity except for his swords.

Benalcázar had left Quito early in 1538 and made his way north with about five hundred men well equipped for war. He reached what is now Popayán, then climbed up modern Colombia, along the river Magdalena to

Neiva. He had a tiny force, perhaps only thirty or forty men, to which his own great name, as one of the conquerors of Peru, added much. On the way, he had founded four towns, including a settlement at Popayán, where he had left altogether three hundred men. From Neiva, hearing of Federmann's journey, he sent messengers to Jiménez de Quesada hoping to concert action with him against the unexpected German from Venezuela.

For Federmann, it was a hard blow to find at the end of an atrocious journey of two years that the territory which he, on the Welsers' behalf, had coveted as part of Venezuela was being occupied by others. But he was realistic. He made a remarkable concession. For he subscribed to an agreement by which he would leave his men under Jiménez de Quesada's control, or that of his brother Hernando, but he and the former would go to Spain, on the same ship, to seek judgment from the Council of the Indies as to who would rule the country. The Welsers later thought that for Federmann to have left his men in New Granada exceeded his authority. But Bogotá was an advantageous place, and some of Federmann's men had anyway come from Santa Marta or, as we have seen, from Paria. Federmann thought that his men would not have accepted an order to return to Coro by the way that they had come. The decision was a good one even if Federmann would probably have won in a pitched battle against Jiménez de Quesada in the style of the Spaniards in Peru. Jiménez de Quesada's army was in poor shape. Federmann's men would now help to establish a sound nucleus of Spaniards in Bogotá, with magistrates, councillors, notaries, and other officials.[14]

Jiménez de Quesada soon also reached an agreement with Benalcázar, the text of which is lost. Benalcázar went on to Bogotá—Santa Fe de Bogotá, it had become—met Federmann on June 20, and set off with both his rivals in a brigantine down the Magdalena. They first went to Cartagena, where they met a judge, Juan de Santa Cruz, who had been appointed to carry out a *residencia* of Pedro de Heredia, governor of that port, and the three conquistadors gave him much information about the Indians whom they had encountered, and whom Jiménez de Quesada believed that he had conquered. They also explained how they had granted *encomiendas* to fellow conquistadors in Bogotá, and how one or two chiefs had been similarly favored, as if they had been Spaniards. For example, the chief Quencubansa had been allotted a town in the Panche province of Tamanjuaca.

In Cartagena, the three conquistadors of Bogotá awaited a ship to take them to Castile. While they waited, Jiménez de Quesada found himself in a lawsuit with his ex-subordinate, Diego Hernández Gallego, in respect to the first flotilla of brigantines that had sailed up the Magdalena without finding his army. But eventually the three returned to Spain, Jiménez de Quesada and Benalcázar going together directly, Federmann traveling via Jamaica. The first named took with him 11,000 pesos de oro in twenty-one bars, as well as nine boxes of emeralds and one fine necklace of emeralds.

The circumstances of the return of these conquistadors were highly discouraging. Bartolomé de las Casas was at that time winning his debates against the *encomenderos*. Jiménez de Quesada also found that he had suits mounted against him by Alonso Fernández de Lugo, the heir of Pedro Fernández de Lugo, a brutal but influential proconsul himself, being the brother-in-law of Cobos no less. The treasurer of Santa Marta, Pedro Briceño, and the new governor there, Jerónimo Lebrón, sued Jiménez de Quesada, and he was ordered to pay them 5,300 pesos of gold and some emeralds. Till he had paid it, he was to remain in the Casa de la Contratación's prison in Seville. In addition, Jiménez de Quesada was to pay 1,000 pesos as taxes to the King. He appealed through his skillful lawyer, Sebastián Rodríguez, to the Council of the Indies, but when he appeared before that august body, he was further accused of bringing into Spain 150,000 pesos of gold illegally and of having had his own secret supply of emeralds. To his astonishment, he found that he had numerous creditors, such as Marcos Griego, who owned a boat that had been used by Pedro Fernández de Lugo and Martín de Orduña, the factor of the Welsers in Santa Marta.[15]

Eventually, Jiménez de Quesada's uncle offered bail, and Jiménez de Quesada was released, still in possession of his gold and emeralds. The Council of the Indies at first decided in favor of the conqueror of Bogotá as the next governor there, but then reversed themselves, supported by the Emperor. It was at this point that the question of Jiménez de Quesada's supposed Jewish blood was brought up.

How disillusioned that conquistador must have been, thinking that he was going to return home as a great conqueror of new territory but to find himself tied down by petty denunciations. All the same, his new province took shape in his absence. Santa Fé de Bogotá was named a city, and the

Dominicans agreed to send friars. Jiménez de Quesada then went to France, apparently (or so his enemies said) to sell his emeralds. He did not return to Spain till the end of 1545. He busied himself with his defense of Charles V, *Antijovio*—a denunciation of the Italian historian Paolo Giovio.

New accusations were soon made against Jiménez de Quesada. He was not praised for conquering a rich territory. Instead, he was denounced with his brother Hernando for bringing about the deaths of the caciques Bogotá and Sagipa, as well as for other cruelties against the Indians. In Bogotá itself, Alonso Fernández de Lugo appeared as the new governor, and he declared the *encomiendas* and the division of treasure made by Jiménez de Quesada to be illegal. He sent Hernando Jiménez de Quesada home to Spain, and Francisco (who had joined them from Peru) was dispatched under guard. New legal disputes followed. But events in Santa Marta and Cartagena were nothing compared with what was brewing in Castile.

Jiménez de Quesada received numerous accusations about his emeralds. In return, many witnesses appeared before him, including his interpreter in the Chibcha plateau, an Indian now known as Don Gonzalo de Huesca, who had by then mastered Spanish perfectly. In his own defense, Jiménez de Quesada presented an interesting questionnaire in which there were sixty-three questions. In question 22, we hear that the cacique Bogotá had made "a very cruel war" against Jiménez de Quesada. Question 41 offered a chance for a friend of the conqueror's, Antonio Díaz Cardona of Seville, to say that Jiménez de Quesada had "treated the Indians of the new realm of New Granada very well indeed and that witness never saw or knew of or heard talk of such cruelties administered to the Indians except in war."[16]

On February 5, 1547, the trials seemed at an end, and Jiménez de Quesada was found innocent of all the serious charges. Among the "modest" charges, he was found guilty of asking his soldiers for money when he was contemplating a return to Spain, a "crime" for which he was condemned to pay 100 ducats and have his offices suspended for one year. For the torture and subsequent death of Sagipa, he was fined another 100 ducats and called on to accept the suspension of all his offices for another seven years, as well as being sent into exile for a year. An accusation that he had thrown two Indian principals to be devoured by dogs was left undiscussed for the time being. The heirs of Sagipa would be able to sue Jiménez de Quesada for all the trouble that that death had caused them.

Juan de Oribe, a skillful lawyer, appealed against these judgments and persuaded the Council of the Indies to reduce the fines from 100 to 50 ducats. There remained outstanding only the accusation that Jiménez de Quesada had somehow secreted 12,000 ducats. That accusation dominated the rest of his life—and that of his heirs.

In July 1547, a supreme court (*audiencia*) was established for the new realm of New Granada. At last triumphant in his own country, Jiménez de Quesada was named marshal (*mariscal*), as well as receiving a coat of arms. He became *adelantado* on the death of Fernández de Lugo. In April 1548, he was allowed to introduce fifty black slaves into his new country to work for him only. He was granted an income of 2,000 ducats a year, and also received three large *encomiendas* with a promise from the Council of the Indies that they would be perpetual grants to continue to his children. His prohibition on working in any official position was cut from seven years to two.

Having written his *Epítome de la Conquista del Nuevo Reino de Granada* for the Council of the Indies, he returned to New Granada at the end of 1550. The *Epítome* is the best account of a conquest in the New World after the letters of Cortés and Valdivia.

Meantime, Jiménez de Quesada's colleague (as he now had negotiated himself to be), Nicolás Federmann made his way by land to salute Balthasar Welser, his supposed leader, then continued to Ghent. It seems that he wanted to be named governor of Venezuela by the Emperor himself rather than by the Welsers. But the return of Las Casas to imperial favor removed that possibility. Instead, Federmann had to negotiate a new agreement with the Welsers, for his first one had been for ten years; his time would soon run out. The Welsers also demanded accounts. At that time in Flanders, it was supposed that all new conquistadors came back vastly rich from the Indies, but they would never concede the size of their colossal wealth. Federmann refused to present any accounts.

The ensuing drama marked an astonishing transformation in Federmann's life. First, he was seized in his house in Ghent. Then he was imprisoned in Antwerp, and his goods were confiscated. His case passed from one court to another, ending up in the Council of Flanders, where the procedure was carried out in either Latin or Flemish, with Spanish and German ignored. Everything was done to favor the Welsers. Federmann sought to have his case transferred to the Council of the Indies, and in that the Crown of Castile supported him. After some further changes of position, Federmann was freed from prison in Antwerp on a bail of 8,000 ducats. The Flemish authorities refused the order of release and demanded that Federmann hand over to them an emerald worth 100,000 ducats as well as 15,000 ducats in gold, which they claimed that he had received from Jiménez de Quesada. Federmann denied that, but the consequence was the continuation of the Flemish holding of his goods and his continued imprisonment. But everything that Federmann was said to have brought from the Americas was apparently deposited in the bank of Cristóbal Raizer, the factor of the Fugger family in Seville.[17]

On September 22, 1540, the president of the Council of Flanders appeared in the prison of Antwerp and asked Federmann if he could substantiate his statement that the Welsers had committed a fraud in the New World. If he did not prove the declaration, he would have to be physically beaten by one of the Welsers. Federmann accepted the charge. Immediately, the Emperor, who had learned of Federmann's astounding triumphs, ordered that the prisoner be sent to Spain. Federmann arrived in Madrid in February 1541. The Council of the Indies then insisted that they had exclusive competence in relation to the suit between the Welsers and Federmann. The Welsers complained and demanded the return of the accused to Flanders. That was refused. Federmann was given a new delay, till the end of 1541.

In August 1541, Federmann admitted in Madrid, at a court where the King's regent Philip presided, that his complaint against the Welsers had been made only to secure his departure from the prison in Flanders. He then had transferred to him the income from an *encomienda* in Bogotá, which had been allocated to him by Jiménez de Quesada. He was by then in Valladolid, where he was kept under house arrest. There death from a wasting disease surprised him in February 1542.

Thus the conquest of the plateau on which Santa Fé de Bogotá was established brought almost as much tragedy to the conquerors as to the conquered. The long years of exile of Jiménez de Quesada were a sad commentary on his remarkable achievements. The lawsuits against Federmann were more personally destructive to him than the jungles of the eastern Andes. Of the three conquerors who met so unexpectedly in Bogotá in 1540, the only one to survive and prosper thereafter was Benalcázar. He was named governor of Popayán. His great fame as a conqueror of Peru ensured him that designation. Illiterate but brave, he was one of the great survivors of the age of the conquests.

36

The Return of Cabeza de Vaca

The Myth of the Giant admonishes us not to do battle with the forces of Heaven.

ERASMUS, *Enchiridion*

Cabeza de Vaca seemed to be the only remaining conquistador from Narváez's expedition of 1528. He had become famous among the Indians of the delta of the Mississippi. He acted for many months as a trader of shells (which were used as knives), of hides, of ocher used by Indians to paint their faces, flints for arrowheads, tassels of the hair of deer, glue from pine trees, and dried reeds. He was also considered a doctor. He was always planning to move on to Pánuco (about seven hundred miles southwest of the Mississippi estuary) and New Spain, but the companionable presence of Lope de Oviedo constrained him. Lope de Oviedo was a strong and vigorous conquistador, and Cabeza wanted him to accompany him westward. Lope de Oviedo was always saying that he would indeed eventually go one day but could not think of doing so till the following year.

Eventually, they set off and crossed the Mississippi. Once they were on the western bank, they encountered Indians, who assured the Spaniards that they were then close to a band of Christians who had been living there for some years. These Christians turned out to be Andrés de Dorantes, Alonso del Castillo, and the slave Estebanico, also survivors of Narváez's expedition. Dorantes was a native of Béjar, in northern Extremadura, the town where Cortés had married, while Castillo came from Salamanca. Being the son of a doctor, Estebanico was probably a Berber. The five planned to set off for Pánuco, but just before they started, Lope de Oviedo said that he had to return to bring with him some of his favorite Indian women. He left his friends, and no one saw him again. Presumably the women persuaded him to stay.

Cabeza de Vaca and his party were held as slaves for several months by a family of one-eyed Indians (as he explained it). Many times, he recalled, these one-eyed people "said that we were not to be sad because soon prickly pears would be brought and, in the end, they did come." These people had many strange characteristics; for example, they would set the forest afire to force lizards and other such to come out, which they would kill and eat. They would also trap deer by surrounding them with fires and depriving them of grazing places so that their needs would force them to go where the Indians wanted. They would make fires against mosquitoes, though they were bitten by them all the same. From deerskin, they would make cloaks, shoes, and shields.

Cabeza, Estebanico, Castillo, and Dorantes agreed to escape from their Indian masters one day of a new moon. They did so and entered the territory of the Marcame Indians, whose language they seemed to be able to speak. The night when they arrived, some Indians came to Castillo and said that they had dreadful pains in their heads. They implored Castillo to cure them. After he had made the sign of the cross and commended them to God, the Indians said that all their pains had left them. The same occurred on other occasions. This comforted the Spaniards as much as it did the Indians, for it reinforced their beliefs. "It inspired us to give many thanks to Our Lord that we might more fully know His Goodness," recalled Cabeza, "and have the firm hope that he would free us and bring us to where we might serve Him. For myself, I always had faith in His mercy that he would release me from that captivity." Cabeza also carried out a comparable medical feat, for he removed an arrow of deer bone which was close to one Indian's heart. "This cure," Cabeza recalled, "gave us fame everywhere in the land."

Cabeza also recalled that the Indians told of an evil spirit named Mala Cosa who would come to houses with a firebrand and take what he wanted and sometimes, with a sharp knife, tear out the entrails of people whom he did not like. Sometimes Mala Cosa would appear at dances, sometimes dressed as a man, sometimes as a woman, and he could lift up a house and let it crash when he wanted. He was often given food, but he never ate anything, and it was said that he lived in a crack in the earth. The Spaniards told the Indians that if they could only believe in God, demons such as Mala Cosa would never return, and indeed, as long as they were in the town, no one saw him.

Cabeza de Vaca and his three friends moved on. They were always hungry and always naked—except at night, when they had deerskins to keep them warm. They shed these skins twice a year, as if they had been snakes.

The journey of the three Spaniards across what later became Texas must have lasted a year. Remarkably, a large body of Indians attached itself to them. Each Indian carried a club. Eventually, Cabeza wrote in his later work, they began to find villages where there were permanent houses, whose inhabitants ate squash, beans, and maize, as well as deer or hare. One day, Alonso del Castillo saw a buckle from a sword belt hanging round the neck of an Indian, with the nail of a horseshoe sewn onto it. Where did it come from? Castillo asked. "From heaven" was the reply. They asked more questions, and after a while, they learned that "those who had brought it were men who wore beards like us and who had come from Heaven and reached the river [the Mississippi] and that they had horses, lances and swords and they had wounded two of their people with lances. Where had they gone? They said that they had gone to the sea and thrust their lances under the water, and that they had followed them and later the Indians saw them floating in the water going towards the sun."

After that, Cabeza de Vaca's expedition heard again and again of Christians. They saw many a place deserted because "the people there feared the Christians, even though it was fertile and beautiful."[1] "They brought us blankets which they had hidden for fear of the Christians and gave them to us and even told us how, on many occasions, the Christians entered the land and destroyed and burned the villages and carried off half the men and all the women and children and that those who had managed to escape were wandering and in flight. We saw that they were so frightened, not daring to stay in any place and that they neither wanted nor were able to sow crops nor cultivate the land but rather were determined to let themselves die, for they thought that was better than waiting to be treated with such cruelty as they had endured."[2]

After a few more weeks, Cabeza de Vaca and Estebanico, going ahead but accompanied by eleven Indians, encountered Lázaro de Cárdenas and three mounted Spaniards at Los Ojuelos, a day's journey from Tzinaba on the river Petatlan, somewhere in what is now the northwestern Mexican state of Sinaloa. Cabeza had thus crossed the entire modern Mexican peninsula. Cárdenas took the walkers to meet his own captain, Diego de Alcaraz. Estebanico was sent back to fetch Andrés de Dorantes and Alonso del Castillo, who arrived with an escort of six hundred Indians. Cabeza de Vaca had many arguments with Alcaraz, who at first wished to enslave the Indians that Cabeza had brought. In the end, they sent the Indians home and promised that they would not be attacked.

The great walkers then went to Compostela, farther south. News of their coming began to circulate. They reached Mexico-Tenochtitlan in July, where they were sumptuously received by Cortés and by the Viceroy Mendoza, though for months they were unable to wear clothes and preferred to sleep on the floor rather than in beds. Celebrations included jousting with canes and bullfights. After spending the autumn and winter of 1536 in the capital, they went down to Veracruz in the spring of 1537. They boarded a ship to Spain on April 10, stopping at Havana, Bermuda, then the Azores, and finally Lisbon, before reaching Sanlúcar. They had some difficulties with French pirate ships, but they reached Castile at last. They were in time to greet and wish "godspeed" to Hernando de Soto, a veteran of Peru who was resolved to return to the New World and to conquer as much of North America as he could.

37

Soto in North America

> The rarest thing of all in men who have made history is greatness of soul.
>
> JACOB BURCKHARDT, *Reflections on History*

The most glittering of expeditions led from Spain in the late 1530s was that of the Peruvian conquistador, the reckless, brave, and enterprising Hernando de Soto. It was he who had been in the vanguard of Pizarro's triumphs and who secured a contract in Spain in April 1537 to conquer and settle the land between the Río de Palmas in Mexico and the southernmost keys of Florida. He would be named the governor of Cuba. As *adelantado* of Florida, he would be allowed to take 1,500 men with him. He would receive 500 ducats a year from the Spanish government. In addition, Soto had his 180,000 cruzados from the treasure of Peru. He would take a large household with him, among whom were several Peruvian veterans. Soto took with him, too, his new wife, Isabel de Bobadilla, a daughter of Pedrarias.

Cabeza de Vaca had recently come back to Castile to explain that Florida was the richest of countries. He also said that, though he wished Soto well, neither he nor Andrés de Dorantes could accompany him, because they "did not wish to divulge certain things which they had seen lest someone might beg the government in advance."[1] No one knew what that mysterious message meant. Some of those who decided to go to the Indies with Soto (Baltasar Gallegos, Cristóbal de Espíndola) told Cabeza de Vaca that they undertook the journey because of his strange words.

The court smiled on Soto. Many close to the monarch planned to accompany the expedition: for example, the Osorio brothers, Francisco and

Antonio. Soto spent a great deal on outfitting: Indeed, the 130,000 castellanos that he lavished on his expedition was six times what Pedrarias had spent twenty years earlier. Soto himself paid for many of the men. He bought the galleon *La Magdalena*, of eight hundred tons, for 1,212 ducats from a famous shipbuilder of Triana, and the galleon *San Juan* for 1,410 ducats. He took eight hundred quintals of biscuit and a quantity of salt beef. His ships were well stocked with olive oil, water, and wine, as well as "steel, iron for bridles, spades, mattocks, panniers, ropes, baskets, arquebuses, gunpowder, crossbows, swords, chain mail, bucklers, boots, sacramental vessels for use at mass, beads and other goods for presents, and iron chain links and collars for slaves."[2] Horses, seed, and other provisions would be bought in Cuba.

Soto had an outstanding gathering of commanders: His infantry would be commanded by Francisco Maldonado, the cavalry by Pedro Calderón. Soto had a personal guard of sixty halberdiers, led by Cristóbal de Espíndola, a future official of the Inquisition in New Spain. (The halberdiers carried two-handed pole weapons.) Probably Soto expected to conquer all the lands to the north in America.

The expedition sailed from Sanlúcar in April 1538, leaving in great style. As usual in expeditions like this, they stopped for a few days in the Canaries, where they were greeted by the governor, who was dressed in white, and where the governor's daughter, Leonor de Bobadilla, joined them. She traveled as lady-in-waiting to her cousin, Isabel, the wife of Soto. (Leonor was soon seduced by Nuño de Tovar, one of Soto's senior captains, who later married her and was rather curiously dismissed by Soto in consequence.)

Soto reached his Cuban governorship in June 1538, making landfall at Santiago. There the flagship, the *San Cristóbal*, hit the shoals of Smith's Key, and it was supposed that all was lost. Many left precipitately in small boats, some distinguished men in panic, thinking that "it was no time for gallantry." But only the wine was lost.

Soto landed in Santiago on June 7, amid much celebration. He and his friends were pleased by what they saw, for the Spaniards lived in well-built houses, of which some were of stone and some roofed with tiles. Most had walls of board and dried-grass roofs. The many country houses nearby often boasted fig trees, pines, guava, bananas, and sweet potato, from which

Bartolomé de las Casas, the apostle of the Indies

Portable altars were used everywhere in the New World.

A bust of Francisco Pizarro, above that of his mistress, in the Palace of the Conquest, built by Hernando Pizarro

Hernando Pizarro, second in command to his brother Francisco in the conquest of Peru, kneeling in the Palace of the Conquest

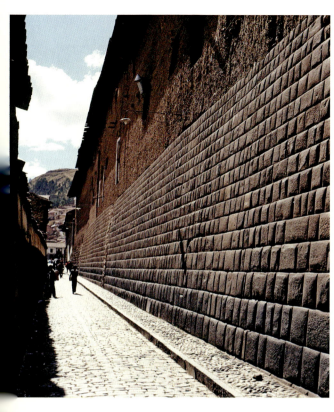

(Left) Inca architecture: a street wall built to last, in Cuzco

(Below) Inca walls: the fortress of Sacsahuamán, Cuzco, whose stones were put together with immense skill

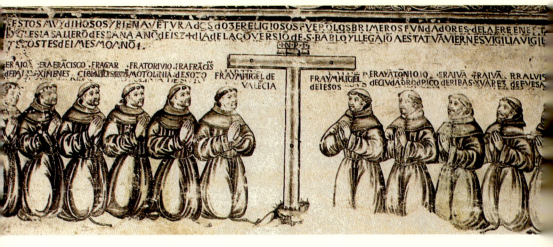

The barefoot friars who walked to Mexico from Veracruz, 1524.
Mural in the Franciscan monastery at Huejotzingo.

Augustinian monastery of Acolman, completed in 1560, with
plateresque façade and open chapel in the center

The Franciscan monastery in Quito, built in 1533–81,
was an inspiration for all the New World.

San Pablo, Valladolid, where Philip II was christened, where the nobility took an oath of loyalty to Charles V, and where Las Casas debated with Sepúlveda

Philip II, regent of Spain in 1542, king in 1556 *(Moro)*

Charles V at Mühlberg: the great battle picture of Charles V, who was always at war *(Titian)*

The Jeronymite monaster of Yuste in the Gredos mountains, where Charle retired and died

bread was made. Some had groves of orange trees, and there were wild cattle. Already Santiago and Havana (in the west of the island) had seventy or eighty Spanish households each; another six towns had thirty to forty dwellings in each. All had not only a church but a priest. In Santiago, there was a small Franciscan convent. While Soto was in Cuba, a tax was introduced for "defence against rebels, wild Indians and the French."[3] This demand was much resented.

In Santiago, then the capital city of Cuba, Soto presented his credentials as governor to the city council, and so there were the usual celebrations: balls and masquerades, horse races, and bull-running. A new bishop, Diego Sarmiento, reached Santiago at much the same time as Soto. He had previously been rector of the Carthusian monastery of Las Cuevas, in Seville. He, too, was fêted. After some weeks, the new governor rode to Bayamo, eighty or so miles to the west, on a new roan horse, a present from the people of Santiago. Then he rode on to Puerto Príncipe, another 150 miles farther west, where Vasco de Porcallo de Figueroa, an unprincipled adventurer who had been in Narváez's expedition to New Spain, joined him as captain-general. Soto went on by land to Havana, which would later be his point of departure and which had already been established for ten years on the north coast of the island (not the south, where it had originally been founded). Las Casas recalled that at that time, the forest was so intense that one could ride from one end of the island to the other without leaving the shade.[4] At Havana, Soto's wife, Isabel, joined him after a rough journey by sea from Santiago.

Soto was convinced that the expedition was going to make him the richest man in the world. He left nothing to chance. Thus he sent ahead Juan de Añasco, his accountant, who was a good geographer and from one of the good families of Trujillo, in Extremadura, to explore the coast of Florida. Añasco went with fifty men in two pinnaces. Avoiding the swamps on the southern tip of Florida, Añasco made for places on the Gulf of Mexico such as Charlotte Harbor (then referred to as La Bahía de Juan Ponce de León) or Tampa Bay (Bahía Honda). In the second of these, Añasco kidnapped four Indians, who were later to serve as interpreters. They assured their eager and gullible captors that "much gold existed in Florida."[5]

Meantime, Soto was shown something of the reality of the Caribbean by a rising of Indians near Baracoa, in eastern Cuba, some African slaves joining them. Bartolomé Ortiz, the chief magistrate of Santiago, dispatched a small force to crush the revolt, but these men were murdered by their Indian guides. It took some time for the rebellion to be reduced.[6]

Soto was busy in Havana organizing the details of his expedition. He was short of ready money, and in consequence he sent a request for 10,000 ducats to an old friend in Panama, Hernán Ponce de León, who had done so much to assist the conquest of Peru. Alonso de Ayala sold a ranch in Panama belonging to Isabel de Bobadilla for 7,000 pesos. Ponce de León took ship to Havana, where he remained for a time as the virtual prisoner of Soto, who extracted 8,000 castellanos from him as well as a pair of silver stirrups. Ponce de León then left for Seville, where he concealed what remained of his treasure to avoid tax, and bought a large house. Soto also was investing in land, in Cuba, where he established plantations in Cojímar and Mayabeque, both close to Havana.

Soto finally set off on the last stage of his great journey to Florida in May 1539. He had nine ships (five *naos,* two caravels, two pinnaces), in which he carried six hundred men as well as about 130 sailors. Among the six hundred, there were about 240 horsemen. Vasco de Porcallo de Figueroa, who had first gone to the Indies with Pedrarias and who had been a close friend of Diego Velázquez as well as a companion of Cortés with Narváez, became deputy leader. The supplies seem considerable: three thousand loads of cassava, 2,500 shoulders of bacon, and 2,500 *fanegas* of maize. Soto left his wife, Isabel, as deputy governor in Cuba, with the experienced, if elderly, Juan de Rojas as her deputy. It was this Juan de Rojas who, years before, had glimpsed the treasure that Cortés's friends Francisco de Montejo and Hernández Portocarrero were taking back from Veracruz to Spain and who told Diego Velázquez of its quality. Rojas had also invested in Cortés's expedition in 1519 and had been largely responsible for moving the town of Havana from the south to the north coast of Cuba in the late 1520s. These Spaniards and Bartolomé Ortiz, the chief magistrate of Santiago, found themselves in a bitter dispute with the settlers of Cuba, for the Crown wanted to set all the Indians free, while the latter tried to prevent it.

On May 25, Soto's fleet saw the land of North America, and on May 30, they reached what seems to have been Tampa Bay, which they named Bahía Honda.[7] This was not uninhabited land. It was only two leagues (six miles) from Espíritu Santo, the town of the Indian chief Ucita, established where there is now the town of Ruskin, Florida. All the horses were safely disembarked.

Soto's deputy, Vasco de Porcallo de Figueroa set off immediately on a reconnoiter. Finding six Indians who sought to resist him with bows and arrows, he killed two of them, but the others fled into marshes in which the horses could not survive. Soto set off himself in a pinnace and established himself in another small town, Ocoto, whose inhabitants had fled. At the same time, the Indians who had been captured by Añasco to be guides or interpreters fled, too. Ocoto was characterized by seven or eight houses made of timber but covered with palm leaves, all built on a rise, apparently to facilitate defense. There was a temple, from whose summit a wooden chicken gazed out through golden eyes. Within the building, there were rough pearls. Soto and Porcallo, with Luis de Moscoso, slept in the chief's house. To ensure defense, the rest of the Spanish force cut down the nearby wood within a crossbow shot. They began to build a palisade of earth and timber.

The natives who had fled from Soto's first settlement and who had earlier attacked were Timúcan Indians. They worshipped the sun, they built their chief's palaces on high earth mounds, they tattooed their bodies with pictures of birds and snakes as well as geometric designs, and they were led by chiefs who ruled clusters of townships. Most had black hair, brown skin, strong arms, and black, cheerful eyes. They were excellent runners. They fought with six-foot longbows, with which they fired deadly arrows of cane or reed tipped with sharp stones or even fish bones capable of penetrating chain mail and shields.

In June 1539, the expedition had an unnerving experience. Baltasar Gallegos, the chief constable of the expedition, set out with about forty horse and eighty foot to explore the land to the north of Ocoto. They encountered twenty red-painted Indians wearing plumes and carrying longbows. These warriors the Spaniards began to cut down. But one of them suddenly proclaimed himself to be Juan Ortiz, of Seville, a veteran of Narváez's expedition, who had returned to Cuba but then returned to Florida. There he was captured by Indians, who placed him on a grill and started to roast him. But he had then been saved by the daughter of the chief. Ortiz had lived with the princess for nine years, becoming Indianized. He wore a grass skirt and a breechcloth. He had had himself tattooed, and he carried a longbow.

Ortiz successfully reestablished himself as a Spaniard and became Soto's chief interpreter. He begged Soto and his colleagues not to pursue his Indian friends as if they were deer, since they had "given me my life." He also gave the unexpected news that there was no gold, so far as he knew, in Florida. This disquieting information had a predictable effect on Porcallo's commitment to Soto, and he soon returned to Cuba.[8] His first aim had probably been to find slaves for his plantations in Cuba, but he left his son Lorenzo Suárez to continue with the expedition.

With Ortiz's bad news in the forefront of his mind, Soto now left on a new journey of investigation. His aim was still to find a good place for a settlement of Spaniards that would also be rich in, above all, gold. Espíritu Santo did not seem the ideal candidate for that destiny. But the chief of a nearby town, Urriparacuxci, assured Soto that at Ocala, some way to the north, the Spaniards would find all the treasure that they could carry. The chief added that at Ocala, the Indians even wore hats of gold when they made war. Baltasar Gallegos was skeptical, but Soto, a simpler soul, became enthusiastic. Spaniards in the New World were always being deluded by such aureate dreams.

Soto left half his men with Pedro Calderón in Espíritu Santo and set off through Florida in a northwesterly direction. Ocala turned out to have maize but no gold. Eventually, Soto and his friends found themselves in the territory of the Apalachee Indians, whose main settlement lay in what is now Tallahassee. The Apalachee, like most of the native Indians in the New World before the Christians came, worshipped the sun, grew maize, ate shellfish, built cities with pyramids on which they placed temples, and lived in round houses. There may have been one hundred thousand Apalachees. They played a kind of pelota with a hard buckskin ball, the purpose of which was to secure entry to a goal on top of which a stuffed eagle was placed. If a player hit the eagle, he scored two points; if he hit the post, one. Here Soto reassembled his forces. Calderón came up from Espíritu Santo. The Spaniards were delighted with the fertility of the Apalachee territory, even if the promised gold was not to be seen. So Soto sent back a message to Havana with orders to restock him with supplies and then come back the next year to meet him in the vicinity of Tallahassee. If they found nothing, Soto made evident that he would keep cruising as far as the Mississippi, of which he knew from previous journeys of discovery.[9]

On March 3, 1540, Soto and his little army turned their backs on the known world of the Gulf of Mexico and set off for a newly described magic Kingdom named Cofitachequi. This was a long way to the northeast, across the rivers Ochlockonee and Flint, in what is now south Georgia. The Spaniards crossed these waterways with difficulty, using chains of Indians to haul them over rivers on rafts. They stopped at Capachequi, where the Indians attacked stragglers. Then they met Lower Creek Indians living in large and quite comfortable towns built along the rivers and surrounded by palisades. They had a well-developed agriculture and made good pottery, baskets, jewelry, and even statuary. These Indians often lived in good houses constructed from trunks of cedar or pine wood. The women wore blankets woven from fine thread; jeweled necklaces, earrings, pendants, and amulets; and beads made from shells, bone, and wood.[10]

The apparently civilized town of Toa was deserted when Soto arrived. The king of the place ordered his men to offer the Spaniards lodging as well as food. Soto now found some complaints among his men. Some were restless at the endless journeys. Where were they going? Soto would explain that he had come to teach the Indians "to understand the sacred faith of Christ . . . that they should know Him and be saved."[11] He also asked the Indians to give obedience to the Emperor and King of Castile and to the pope, the supreme pontiff and vicar of Christ. Soto added comfortingly that he was himself the Son of the Sun.[12]

Brightly dressed Ichisis Indians led Soto's expedition toward their capital, probably Lasmar, near what is now Macon, Georgia. Rodrigo Rangel, Soto's secretary, recalled that here they were greeted by innumerable women in white who gave the Spaniards omelets made of maize and spring onions. Several hundred Indians, Mississippians, seem to have lived here in a town encircled by a log palisade about 1,200 feet long. On this, Soto raised a large wooden cross.

Soto moved on to the river Oconcee, where he was met by some Indians from Atamaha. A ruler named Camumo received the adventurers in his capital, which seems to have been close to what is today Milledgeville, Georgia. Soto gave him a feather that had been colored silver. Camumo said: "You are from heaven, and with this feather that you give me I will eat,

I will go to war, I shall sleep with my wife." Camumo then asked to whom he should give tribute, to Soto or to Ocute, who was a king on the river of that name to the north. Soto rather surprisingly said that Camumo should pay tribute to Ocute. Then he went on to the town of Ocute, where the chief there gave the Spaniards rabbit, partridge, maize bread, hens, and many small dogs. He also provided several hundred porters, who were loaded with food. Then they moved on to Cofitachequi, guided by an Indian who claimed to be taking them to a new El Dorado in the north. They soon reached the river Savannah, "broader than the shot of an arquebus." The army crossed, the men tied to one another. It is astonishing that Soto was able to maintain discipline and order. Not only that, he asked four of his captains to lead eight horsemen each to go in different directions, to establish exactly where they were. In their absence, Soto killed his pigs, which enabled him to allow each man half a pound of pork every day for a short spell.

Juan de Añasco returned to Soto's headquarters to say that he had found a good town some thirty-six miles away. He brought back grain and some horns of cattle, as well as an Indian girl and boy. This town was Himahi, which may have been near Columbia, South Carolina. They found there fifty *fanegas* of maize, some mulberries, and other fruit, as well as roses. They then continued their way to the mysterious Cofitachequi, about twenty miles east of Himahi, near what is now Lugoff, South Carolina, where Soto met a Queenly ruler of the tribe. This lady is said to have come out to meet Soto in a canoe with an awning. She gave Soto some pearls as large as hazelnuts. Garcilaso characteristically insisted that she was a beauty. Soto gave her a ruby ring that he had the habit of wearing on his finger. In return, she offered food and lodging. The Spanish expedition, so quickly moving from pessimism to joy, became optimistic again.

It turned out that Cofitachequi had recently experienced a serious plague, which had much reduced the population (this seems not to have been the direct responsibility of European invaders). The Queen apparently controlled the land between the Blue Ridge Mountains and the Atlantic. Her people wore "excellent hides which had been very well tanned" as well as "blankets of sable." They also wore breeches and buskins with black garters, tied by laces of white hide. They were, wrote Elvas, "more well-mannered" than the other Indians whom the Spaniards had met in

Florida. The soldiers of this principality are said to have worn breastplates made from raw and hairless hides, perhaps buffalo. Rodrigo Rangel recalled seeing a substantial temple on high ground at a town called Tamileco. This, Garcilaso commented, was well decorated with giant figures carved from wood. There was also, Rangel recorded, "a large, tall and broad palace."[13] The Queen gave Soto the town of Ilap, about fifty miles northeast of the modern town of Cheraw—a generous gesture, considering that she herself was short of food.

Alas, the "gold" in the Queen's palace turned out to be copper, the emeralds were glass, and the "silver" was mica. The best treasure was some Castilian iron axes surviving from Vázquez de Ayllón's expedition there.

Some Spaniards would have liked to have established a colony here in what one day would become South Carolina. But, Elvas commented, "the Governor's purpose was to seek another treasure like that of Atahualpa" and "he insisted that they keep going." For "he had no wish to content himself with good land and pearls."[14] Many wondered whether Soto had lost his senses. But his magnetic attraction as a leader remained, and no one would oppose him, even when he now insisted on going on to Chia, a territory that was either Hickory in North Carolina or Dandridge, Tennessee. They saw then the Appalachian Mountains, which seemed to Soto a sure sign that gold was close at hand. In these foothills, the expedition rested for three weeks. Soto asked the chief in Chia for women. The population fled. In the end, the chief supplied porters but not women.

At this point, the Spaniards still numbered about 550, with a large army of carriers, most of whom were treated more as slaves than as servants. During the summer of 1540, they slowly headed for what they believed to be the southern coast, in what is today the state of Alabama. The ruler of the Coosa also assisted them with porters, thinking—probably correctly—that that was the best way to rid himself of such demanding visitors, who for a while kidnapped him.[15]

How to treat Soto was also much on the mind of the next ruler whom they met, the giant Tuscaloosa of the Atahachi, in southwest Alabama. Tuscaloosa knew something of Spaniards from a Greek, Doroteo Teodoro, who had fled to him many years before from the expedition of Narváez. Soto's tactic in these days was to insist on being received by a ruler; kidnap him; demand food, porters, and women; and then move on. The technique worked well across Alabama. But Tuscaloosa was of a different mold than other monarchs. He seemed to have hundreds of servants. A nobleman always stood in front of him with a sunshade on a pole as, in his vast headdress, he addressed large audiences from a balcony, almost as if he were a modern Mexican politician.

On October 10, Soto reached the outskirts of Atahachi with his host. He sent Luis de Moscoso to greet Tuscaloosa. Moscoso made a successful display of horsemanship, and then Soto arrived. Tuscaloosa offered dinner. Afterwards, Soto requested the king to give him women and porters in order to carry their burdens onward on the next stage of the journey. Tuscaloosa declined, explaining that he was not accustomed to serve anyone. At that point, as Doroteo Teodoro should have told Tuscaloosa would be likely to occur, Soto detained him. The two then rode through Atahachi, the king in his litter, the conquistador on his horse. Tempers were worsened by the death of two Spaniards at the hands of Indians, and Soto was even more angry when he was informed that the Indians were preparing an attack at Mabila, their next port of call.

The Spaniards went there with Tuscaloosa remaining in virtual freedom. Three to four hundred Indians in ceremonial feathers were ready to greet them. It was a substantial town, for there were eighty large houses, and stockades with towers. Soto and Tuscaloosa walked to a place of honor in a square, most of the former's army being left outside. Tuscaloosa succeeded in meeting his captains, and they decided to act right then and there against Spain. Cristóbal de Espíndola observed that the houses around the square were full of soldiers, and Baltasar Gallegos tried to persuade one of Tuscaloosa's captains to fetch the king. He refused, and Gallegos cut off his arm. At that, Tuscaloosa gave the signal to move against the Spaniards.

Soto was trapped in a fortress-like town with his horsemen unable to move freely. Five of his guards were killed instantly; Gallegos was wounded. All the porters deserted. But Soto managed to find a mount and escape. This became the most serious battle in which the Spaniards had been engaged since their landing in North America. But with Soto outside, the Spaniards were able to besiege the town, and they did so, setting on fire the houses nearest to them. In this combat, it seems that Tuscaloosa and his son and heir were burned to death. About twenty Spaniards were killed, and 250 were wounded. Twelve horses were killed, and almost all the baggage was lost. Soto remained outside this fatal city of Mabila for several weeks, his men forced to cover themselves in native blankets, not Spanish dress.

Next, the expedition went south again, crossing the river Alabama. They found maize at Talicpacam but not enough. At Mozulixa, the Indians disappeared without leaving any food. Soto seized food at two villages belonging to the Apafalya people, capturing a chief, whom he afterwards used as a guide. Crossing the cold river Tombigbee, the Spaniards reached the capital of the Chickasaws, which had twenty houses and was full of maize. The people fled; the chief presented Soto with 150 rabbits, some skins, and blankets. This friendly tactic was a ruse, for the Chickasaw Indians sought to steal Soto's pigs and horses. In fact, they did kill about four hundred pigs and nearly sixty horses, as well as eleven Spaniards. It took two months for Soto's 450 Europeans to organize their defenses once more.

Shortly thereafter, they reached the Mississippi, near what is now Memphis. The mouth of that great waterway had been observed years before, in 1520, by Alonso Álvarez Pineda. Here, Soto saw a fleet of canoes with painted warriors on board wearing white plumes in their hats, led by a chief from a town called Aquixo. This dramatic appearance suggested once again to the credulous invaders that they might be on the edge of a land of gold.

On June 18, 1541, Soto carried his men across the Mississippi, going first to Aquixo, then to Casqui, where they found buffalo, maize, walnuts, plums, and mulberries. Soto was making for Pacaha, which he besieged and then broke into while it was being abandoned. The chief escaped and hid successfully, leaving Soto to observe the fine pottery made in the place, the elaborate system of irrigation, the blankets and deerskins, the shirts, the leggings of hide, and cassocks. Soto stayed in this town for a month making local forays. They were probably then near what is now Helena, fifty miles south of Memphis.

They continued down the Mississippi, reaching the river Arkansas in mid-September, and finding in Tula a people who deformed their heads at birth to make them longer. They also pricked their faces and lips with flint needles in order to color them black. They used long lance-like poles against buffalo and as defensive weapons. They had the eccentricity of weeping profusely as a greeting.

Soto and his army spent the winter of 1541–42 near Redfield, on the river Arkansas, where they had gone because rumors of wealth in that territory had reached them. There were, however, only beans, dried plums, and nuts. In the spring, they went south again, to follow the Mississippi. Soto sent Juan de Añasco ahead to report how far off the sea might be. He rode fifty miles down the river but saw no sign of it. Unlike Orellana in somewhat similar circumstances on the Amazon, he returned. Soto was gloomy at his apparent isolation. He again told a local chief that he was the Son of the Sun, at which the chief replied that if Soto were really a god, he should dry up the great river.[16]

In the spring of 1542, Soto abandoned his mission. He died soon after. Did he die from exhaustion, or was there a fever or other infirmity? It is impossible to say, but he was not old. We hear, though, that Baltasar Gallegos sought to console him by speaking of the shortness of life in this world, attended as it was by so many afflictions. God showed particular favors to those whom he called away early. Sweet were the uses of adversity. Elvas commented that Soto "died in a land and at a time that could afford him little comfort in his illness."[17] Before he died, Soto named Luis de Moscoso as his successor.

Moscoso buried Soto first at the gate of the town, but then, to avoid questions from Indians, his body was committed to the great river. Moscoso told the local chief that Soto had not died but had gone to the skies. All the same, he immediately set about selling the mobile property of Soto: two male slaves, two females, three horses, and seven hundred swine. Moscoso himself made evident that he had no more interest in Soto's enterprise. On the contrary, he longed "to be again where he could get his full measure of sleep rather than govern and go on conquering a country so beset for him by hardships."[18]

It appeared sensible to all to march westward. In that direction, as all knew, lay New Spain. They were surprised not to find the gold, silver, and cotton that Cabeza de Vaca had assured the emperor Charles was to be found on the way, but they concluded that that was because they were marching into the interior, whereas Cabeza had gone along the coast. Some grieved to return to civilization. They would rather have continued to live in peril than leave "Florida" poor.

Moscoso hoped to reach New Spain in the summer of 1542. But they found the country in Texas too dry to maintain the army, so they returned to the Mississippi, near Guachoya, where Soto had died. There they spent the winter making rafts to float down the river.

The expedition eventually reached Pánuco by boat in September 1543. They numbered 311. The viceroy Mendoza welcomed them and gave orders that they should be fed as they required. The news was soon taken to Havana. Thus what had been assumed there was confirmed. Soto was dead, and Isabel, his widow, was in consequence disconsolate.

Soto's expedition was one of the oddest of the Spanish adventures in the New World. It would have seemed heroic had it had a true destination. As it was, Soto and his constantly dwindling band of experienced Spaniards and their horses traveled on and on, always expecting to find a new Peru or a new Mexico, with Soto himself and his senior colleagues always believing in stories that fifty leagues ahead, there was just such a realm with vast resources of gold—not just maize and persimmon, or other delicacies such as watercress or cabbages, or chestnuts and grapes, not to speak of the "symmetrical and tall" girls of the Macanoche tribe or the robust Mochila ladies. Many self-deprecating comments had been made to the Spaniards: "I entreat you to forgive me for the error I committed in not waiting to greet and to obey you since the occasion should have been for me (and is one) a matter of pride,"[19] or "Very high, powerful and good master. Think what must be the effect of me and mine of the sight of you and your people . . . What pride was ours when the fierce brutes of your horses entered with such speed and fury into my country . . . I hope you will tell me who you are, whence you come, and what it is you seek."[20]

The Spaniards were often cruel: We read "of those made captive, the governor sent six to the chief with their right hands and their noses cut off." Or, "the governor having been led for two days out of the way ordered that the Indian [guide] should be put to the torture, when he confessed that his master, the chief of Nondaco, had ordered him to take them in that manner . . . He was commanded to be cast to the dogs." Sometimes the distress was caused by "the intolerable torment of a myriad of mosquitoes." The sails of Spanish vessels might seem covered with insects at daylight. It is hard to sympathize with Hernando de Soto. Yet his plight was genuine. We cannot forgive him his brutalities, nor can we forget his multiple tragedies.

38

The Magic Lure of the New World

I could not die in peace without having seen the Indies.

PHILIPP VON HUTTEN TO BISHOP MAURICE VON HUTTEN

We are in Venezuela. The great expedition of Federmann had long before vanished into the Andes. The few Spanish settlers at Coro maintained an austere life, interrupted from time to time only by demands for more slaves from the Caribbean islands, which they could not meet.[1]

Coro remained important, however, as a place from which expeditions could be mounted. Hence the arrival there of Philipp von Hutten. His temperament was one that seemed to have been formed by an excessive diet of romantic novels. He was the second son of a powerful family in Frankfurt. The young Philipp's benefactor in his early youth had been the Emperor's friend Henry of Nassau, and he was for a time a companion of the prince, later emperor, Ferdinand. Still in his twenties in 1535 (he had been born in 1511 at Birkenfeld, Frankfurt) he went to the New World in search of honor: "After having passed a great part of my life among friends, I want to come back with my name and my family honoured, so that no one laughs at me."[2] He had a lot to live up to. A Hutten had led the army of Emperor Frederick Barbarossa against the Hungarians; he was a cousin of the humanist reformer and rebel Ulrich von Hutten, who had died so young so recently; and his elder brother was Maurice, bishop of Eichstatt. The Indies were for Philipp the curtain against which he hoped to display his personality, the ideal of a Renaissance man. "God is my witness," he wrote to his brother the bishop, "that, in this journey, I have not been for a second moved by a desire for wealth, rather I have been affected by a strange dream. It seemed to me I could not die in peace without having seen the Indies [*No hubiera podido morir tranquilo si no hubiese visto las Indias*]."[3]

He went on Federmann's (first) unfortunate expedition to the plains, in which three-quarters of the soldiers died. Hutten came to admire Federmann, whom he had met in Seville. "I believe," he wrote, "that the future of this province depends on him." He wrote to his brother the bishop: "I ask you to think that it would be an honour for you and for our friends if I came back heavily laden with debts for, for the moment, I cannot expect to bring any other booty."[4] His letters then take on a darker character: "If you could know what an effort and danger the riches from here entail, and how many thousands of Christians the Indies have cost and how many fleets one loses before one finds a Peru . . . !" He added, "It is a great comfort to those who are here in the desert [a green desert of jungle, not of sand] to receive a letter from home . . . I well know that, with this long drawn out journey, I have given my parents a sad and restless old age . . . You cannot believe what a good cook hunger makes. Please wish me a glass of wine which I have not drunk for almost four and a half years, except for the drop I receive in the chalice when I take communion."[5]

Hutten achieved some success in Venezuela. Thus in 1540, he was in Barquisimeto when he received the news of the death of Espira. Hutten had been a part of the little army led by Lope Montalvo de Lugo, Espira's favorite captain. He returned to Coro, where he met Bishop Bastidas, who had brought two hundred men, including 150 horsemen. Bastidas named Hutten captain-general to pursue the plans of Espira. The nomination was received by Hutten with much happiness, though just then he also heard from Germany that his father had died.

He set off in August 1541 for what he fondly expected would be El Dorado, the source of fabulous gold supplies, with a hundred horse and a few foot. He took with him as his second-in-command Bartolomé Welser the Younger, the innocent son of Bartolomé Welser, as well as Fray Frutos de Tudela. He expected to join or indeed absorb the army of Montalvo de Lugo, but that captain, horrified by the nomination of Hutten as captain-general, had left for New Granada. So Hutten and Welser went ahead by themselves.

They crossed the river Opia by canoe and entered the territory of the

Guaypiés Indians. Hutten went along the base of the Andes, and they were soon at San Juan de los Llanos, where they supposed that Jiménez de Quesada had been. They moved west and seem to have found the source of the river Uaupés, a tributary of the great Amazonian river Negro. Pedro de Limpias, a skilled linguist and experienced explorer, who could not bear being considered in an inferior position to the spoiled Bartolomé Welser, went for a three-month reconnaissance down the river Guaviare, which eventually joins the Orinoco. The entire expedition then went on to a town that seemed to be called Macatoa. There the chief told Hutten that "alongside a certain range of mountains which could be observed on clear days, there were vast towns of rich people who possessed enormous wealth."[6] Once again, an Indian chief was seeking to divert a potential conqueror with a tale of wealth just round the corner; and as usual, the diversion worked, for Hutten and his army made for where they had been directed.

This was the town of the Omagua people, and Hutten and his company saw in the center of it a fine house, in which, they were assured, were wonderful objects, including a woman made of gold who was their goddess. With a friend, Arteaga, Hutten went to seize two Indians who, however, defended themselves well. They wounded both the conquistadors. The Europeans retreated to the jungle, where Diego de Montes operated on the two captains to save their lives (he investigated the interior of an Indian to see how such wounds affected the body). Hutten then reached the conclusion that he did not have enough men. He resolved to return to Coro to recruit reinforcements.

The return was nearly one thousand miles, and the journey took them from January to May 1545. They reached the Río Pauto, whence Hutten sent on Welser in command of twenty men, alongside Pedro de Limpias, who had been on one of Federmann's journeys. But relations between Welser and Limpias were still bad, and anyway, the former did not want to go to Coro: He suggested that they go to Cubagua, where there were by then good houses and whence they could return to Santo Domingo and escape forever the fortunes of Venezuela.

In Hutten's absence, there had been both natural and human catastrophes on the coast of Venezuela. In 1541, a hurricane had destroyed Cubagua, which had become prosperous because of the pearls found there.

Two years later, in July 1543, French pirates in five big ships fell on the ruins and seized what remained there.[7] But in addition, a decision had been taken in the Council of the Indies to take a *residencia* in Coro and in particular of the actions of Hutten. A judge of Santo Domingo, Cervantes de Loaysa, was appointed. But illness prevented him from going there. Instead, he sent Juan Frías, prosecutor of the supreme court in Santo Domingo, to be governor of Venezuela once the *residencia* was over; and Juan de Carvajal, one more member of the vast family of that name who played such a part in the history of the Americas, and *relator* (rapporteur) of the *audiencia,* would be his lieutenant in Coro. He accompanied the nomination with a sensible proviso: Carvajal was not to be allowed to go into the interior of Venezuela, as so many governors or their lieutenants had done.

Carvajal went to Coro, to find the place utterly miserable. This must have played a part in his reaction, for the settlers seemed primarily in pursuit of Indians, particularly Caribs, so that they could send them to be sold as slaves in Santo Domingo. The few remaining natives had, unsurprisingly, an implacable hostility to all Spaniards.

Unable to survive there, Carvajal went by ship eastward along the coast, so far as to enter the valley of the Tocuyo, where he founded a new town, Nuestra Señora de la Concepción de Tocuyo, more or less at the mouth of the river. This was a more fertile region. He even felt able to grant *encomiendas,* which he did with the help of the skillful Juan de Villegas.

Limpias, meantime, bade Welser goodbye at Barquisimeto and, with five friends, went immediately to the camp of Carvajal, where he was given a safe-conduct as well as a pardon for breaking with Hutten. But both Hutten and Welser followed Limpias and clashed violently—in words, that is—with Carvajal. At first, it is true, they dined together, and they even observed a play of canes. Carvajal suggested that Hutten suspend his march to Coro and that they both collaborate in the government. Then Carvajal said that he wanted to go to the so-called valley of Pamplona, said to be full of riches. He suggested to Hutten that he for his part go to the island of Margarita, the center for pearls, and that he buy some horses there with money borrowed from his own soldiers. Hutten refused and said that he had to go to Coro in order to report to the Crown what had been done. Carvajal then held another dinner, but he suspended the play of canes and asked Hutten to present himself at his camp tent. The sympathies of his soldiers for Hutten were confused, for they had suffered great privations without much reward. They saw in their mind's eye the possibility of having to go again to distant lands in search of mythical El Dorados. The Germans seemed to bring bad luck. Carvajal seemed better organized. At least he could provide food.

Carvajal asked Hutten to place himself at his, Carvajal's, orders. Hutten replied: "Señor governor, already you know that I and these gentlemen and brothers have been marching for five years in order to carry out the full discovery of this territory, where we have lost many friends, horses and clothes. And we come here ruined and poor, sick, tired and indebted; and as my followers have been friends, I would like them to go with me to the port whence we set off [Coro] and there we can recover, for there is the judge of the *Residencia*. I wish to give my testimony and give an account to His Majesty and to the Welsers who have this government. I beg your excellency not to disturb us."

Carvajal said to the soldiers: "I hope you will be a witness of the fact that this is the government of the Emperor. Here the Welsers are nothing, it is His Majesty who rules."

Hutten replied: "Already I have said that these [the Welsers] hold the land on behalf of His Majesty."

Carvajal responded with: "Stop talking." He said to the notary: "Take heed that I order that he goes a prisoner to his tent and does not leave it."

Hutten answered: "Take heed that I stand by what I have said, which is that I do not recognise Señor Carvajal as the judge, for I am the captain-general of His Majesty." He insisted again that he had to go to Coro in order to make a report about his journey to the King and to the Welsers.

Carvajal said: "To the King you have to tell this story and not to the Welsers."

Hutten returned: "To the King I say I shall give my first account and then to the Welsers."

Carvajal replied: "You are not captain-general, indeed you are nothing where I am and, therefore, both you and Captain Bartolomé Welser must go as prisoners to your tents and treat them as a prison."

Hutten then said that Carvajal had powers only because it was believed that he, Hutten, was lost and dead in his expedition.

This remark caused an uproar. Carvajal went forward to seize the two Germans himself, but they, supported by ten of their soldiers, drew their swords to defend themselves. Carvajal withdrew, and Hutten and Welser went to their lodgings. They were soon surrounded by Carvajal's men. Lance in hand, Welser attacked Carvajal, but only his horse was killed. All the same, the Germans, with some supporters, set off that night on the hundred-or-so-mile journey to Coro. On the way, an agreement was reached between Carvajal, Hutten, and Welser: The latter were to be permitted to go to Coro. This was arranged by Carvajal's notary, Juan de Villegas. But on the second night of their journey, Carvajal attacked and seized Hutten and Welser in their hammocks. He ordered an African slave to cut off their heads with a machete, refusing them the rite of absolution. "They can make their confession in heaven," he grimly commented.[8]

So ended the brutal implication of Germany in the Spanish empire.

The conclusion of this chapter of tragedy is quickly told. At the end of 1545, Licenciado Frías at length reached Coro to carry out his task as judge of the *residencia*. He found the port practically deserted, food almost nonexistent. But at the same time, the Council of the Indies had changed their policy, for they had named Juan Pérez de Tolosa, a *licenciado* of Castile, in Juan Frías's stead, at a salary of 645,000 maravedís a year. All other governors, lieutenant-governors, and chief magistrates were suspended. The *residencia* was to be completed in ninety days.

Pérez de Tolosa reached Santo Domingo on May 27, 1546. There he was told that Venezuela was in chaos. On June 9, he arrived to see for himself. He found Coro, as Frías and indeed Carvajal had found it, in a deplorable state, for there were only fifteen settlers there. The rest had gone to Santa Marta or to Bogotá. He wrote: "The poverty of those who are to be found in this city . . . is so great that if it were not for the little I have brought of clothing and footwear I could do nothing. There is no gold, nor silver, nor money and no food except for fish and good things obtainable from hunting."

Three weeks after Pérez de Tolosa arrived, he began his investigation of Carvajal, using Juan de Eldua as magistrate. Carvajal was accused of conducting himself as a governor and a captain-general without authority, of removing the colony from Coro to Tocuyo without permission, of robbing peaceful Indians of their goods, and of executing Hutten and Welser without trial. Pérez de Tolosa had Carvajal arrested, and his men accepted the new judge as the new governor. Carvajal presented a long questionnaire with witnesses. He explained that the executions of the Germans were the consequence of their disobedience to his government. He did not improve his cause by saying, "If Prince Philip had committed the crimes of Philipp von Hutten, he would also have had his head cut off." But he also admitted to saying that "no one in these parts who has a house can do without having women, Spaniards or Indians, it does not matter which."[9]

Carvajal did everything he could to save his life, but on September 16, he was condemned to be "taken from the public gaol where he is to be tied to the tail of a horse; and from this square, he will be taken to the pillory and the gallows; and there he will be tied from the neck with a cord of esparto grass . . . so that he would die naturally."[10]

The Hutten and Welser families thought that it had been the desire of Carvajal and his friends to rob the two Germans of the riches that they had brought back from El Dorado and that that had obviously been the motive for their arrest and execution. Bartolomé Welser's father, also Bartolomé, told Bishop Maurice von Hutten that they had brought back great riches.[11]

Thereafter, the government of Licenciado Pérez de Tolosa confirmed Carvajal's *encomiendas* in Tocuyo and organized several journeys into the interior. Pérez de Tolosa sent his brother Alonso on one of these to the Sierra de Mérida, as it is now known, but he took care not to go himself. He declared Juan de Villegas free from blame in relation to Hutten and Welser, and sent him in mid-1547 to the Valle de las Damas in order to see if a settlement could be established there; and the explorer did find a new route from the interior to the coast. Pérez de Tolosa took a close look at the coast of Venezuela but left his brother and Villegas to investigate the interior. When he died in 1549, Villegas became his successor, and in most senses, the latter inaugurated the colonial era in the country. He founded a road to New Granada, which passed over the headwaters of the rivers Apare and Sarara, and Río de Oro. There were no further disastrous expeditions into the southern jungle. Tocuyo became in effect the new capital.

Perhaps the best memorial of this era in Venezuela is to be found in the German town of Arnstein, near Würzburg, in Bavaria. There Philipp von Hutten is nobly remembered in the church of Maria-Sondheim in a tomb ordered by his responsible brother Bishop Maurice. He was a victim of his own generous illusions. Nothing in his tragic life shows more vividly the extraordinary connection between the new and the old worlds, and the contrast between reality and the world of fantasy as expressed in the chivalric novels.

39

Buenos Aires and Asunción:
Pedro de Mendoza and
Cabeza de Vaca

Some day things will be as God wills and the Twelve Peers will rule.
Just as the wild olive shoot is grafted onto the olive tree, out of this
Moabite was made an Israelite, and out of a demon-worshipper a
handmaiden of the living God.

ERASMUS, *De Vita Christiana*

The capital of the Portuguese colony in Brazil would soon be Olinda, a
name taken straight from that of a princess in *Amadís de Gaula*. Yet the
Spaniards were slow in developing relations with, much less conquering
and settling, the territory they believed to be theirs that lay beyond the
Portuguese colony in Brazil. Their interest there had, however, been
awoken by the ill-fated journey of Vespucci's successor as *piloto mayor* in
Seville, Juan Díaz de Solís, in 1515. Like so many adventurers who followed,
Díaz de Solís had been looking for a strait to the Southern Sea; and like
them, he found many other things while not finding the strait. Díaz de
Solís, as we have learned before, was captured on the banks of the river
Plate (Río de la Plata, the river of silver), though that was not yet its name
in 1515. His captors were the Querandí Indians. With those companions
who had landed with him on the island of Martín García, he was killed and
then eaten, slice by slice, in full view of those who remained in the boats.
Those survivors of the expedition understandably did not choose to

continue their search for the strait and returned home as fast as they could. The Plate was then named by the Spaniards the Solís.

The next to risk those waters was Sebastian Cabot, who sailed from Sanlúcar in 1526. He was himself *piloto mayor* in succession to Díaz de Solís, and now that Magellan had shown the way, it was thought right that Cabot should direct a new expedition to the Spice Islands by Magellan's route. The expedition of García de Loaisa had made an effort to do so but had been a failure. Cabot left Sanlúcar on April 5, 1526, with three *naos* and a caravel. He explored the estuary of the river Plate, as well as the Paraná River, and on the Carcaraña River, he built a fort near where is now the town of Rosario. He sent some silver home to the King, hence the name of the great river. Río de la Plata it had become by 1530, and so it has remained, though the English mistranslated the word "plata."

Cabot carried out several minor expeditions up the rivers of this territory, and these remain his great achievement. But he was supposed to be heading for the Spice Islands, in what is now Indonesia, and these he did not approach. Indeed he never went farther than the estuary of the Plate. This was partly because of the arrival in that estuary of another Spanish expedition, that of Diego García of Moguer, with two caravels. García claimed to have secured the right to explore and colonize the whole region. The quarrels between Cabot and García brought an end to both expeditions, for the two returned to Spain to engage in a lawsuit. Since Cabot had been expected to go to the Spice Islands, he found himself in disgrace, and he was sent for two years' exile in Oran.[1]

After such small expeditions whose aims had been far beyond the Río de la Plata, it was notable that in 1535, a major expedition should at last be sent to the region under the leadership of Pedro de Mendoza. It must seem right that the conquistador who first established himself in a permanent fashion on the Plate and founded a colony, which has eventually become a great nation, should have been a Mendoza, a member of the family that dominated Spanish history in the early sixteenth century. It is, however, obscure from which branch of the family of the Dukes of Infantado Pedro de Mendoza derived. He probably was an illegitimate son of Íñigo López de Mendoza, count of Tendilla, for he was born in Guadix while Spain was still at war a few miles away in Granada.[2] He seems to have lived a good deal at court and to have served in Italy, being present in his thirties in 1527 at the sack of Rome, where he is said, probably falsely, to have increased his fortune. His interests were extravagant, and without proving his capacity for such a mission, he succeeded in having himself named *adelantado* of the region: "to go and conquer the lands and provinces which there are in the river Solís which is called La Plata where Sebastian Cabot was." One can sense the proximity of Mendoza to the court by the terms with which the King addressed him: "You, Don Pedro Mendoza, *mi criado y gentil hombre de mi casa.*" He had no knowledge of where he was going.[3]

Mendoza left Sanlúcar in September 1535 with fourteen ships and no fewer than 2,150 men. His expedition was full of high-ranking persons known at court, such as the sea captain Juan de Osorio; the chief magistrate Juan de Ayolas, who came from Briviesca, Castile; the Cáceres brothers; and Pérez de Cepeda de Ahumada, a brother of Saint Teresa of Ávila, who left Spain to avoid persecution as a converso. More important still was Diego de Mendoza, Don Pedro's brother, who acted as admiral of the fleet. Various wives, daughters, and sisters of the adventurers sailed, too. Oviedo wrote that the expedition was fit to make a "goodly show in Caesar's army in any part of the world."[4] One ship belonged to Flemish merchants established in Seville, on which traveled Ulrich Schmidt, who wrote an unreliable account. Another vessel was hired by the Welsers, and it carried Sebastian Neidhart, a German from Nuremberg, the captain and factor being another German, Heinrich Paeime.[5]

The expedition encountered a storm halfway across the Atlantic, and the ships were dispersed. Some went to Rio de Janeiro instead of the Río de la Plata. But most of the expedition had reassembled on the Río de la Plata by New Year's Day, 1536. On February 22, Mendoza, in the name of the Emperor, established the first serious settlement at what he named El Puerto de Nuestra Señora del Buen Aire. One of the most remarkable Spanish cities thus had its beginning. The name derived from the Virgin of Buenos Vientos, protector of sailors, a figure of whom used often to be placed in caravels in the center of the compass.

Some months passed, during which the Spaniards began to establish their settlement. The Indians who had eaten Díaz de Solís appropriately gave them some food, but ceased doing so by May. In June, Mendoza sent his brother Diego to "punish" the Querandí Indians for this omission. There was a fierce battle. The Spaniards won, but Diego de Mendoza was killed, along with four nephews of his and Pedro's. Soon after, the settlement itself was attacked by an army of natives. They were driven off but not before they had burned four of the *adelantado*'s ships. Mendoza then had the settlement resited, with new buildings built along the entry of the river Riachuelo into the estuary. He also went to rest at a site found by his lieutenant, Juan de Ayolas, and which he named Buena Esperanza. There he left two lieutenants, one characteristically being an Alvarado (a nephew of Pedro) and the other a Dubrín, and there his kinsman Gonzalo de Mendoza, who had arrived from Brazil, brought an ample supply of food as well as another 150 men. (Gonzalo had been with Pedro at the beginning. He had gone to Brazil in search of supplies the previous year.)

Now the rule of Pedro de Mendoza was approaching its conclusion. Illness seized him, and he decided to return to Spain. He took two ships. He left one hundred Spaniards in Buen Viento (Buenos Aires) under Juan Ruiz Galán. At the same time, Alvarado and Dubrín were in the Pampas at Buena Esperanza while Juan de Ayolas had been sent up the river Paraguay—successfully, since he reached a place on the Candelaria where he established a settlement, soon to be called Asunción since it was formally founded on the day of that feast, August 15, 1536. Ayolas left behind there as the interim governor Domingo Martínez de Irala, a Basque from Vergara who, like him, had come out with Mendoza. Ayolas was unfortunately killed by Payaqueses on his way back to Buenos Aires. Pedro de Mendoza, too, died at this time, not at the hands of Indians but of a fever on his ship on the way back to Spain, in May 1537.

The achievement of Mendoza was modest because soon after he left, Buenos Aires was attacked by Indians twice and burned. In 1541, the place was abandoned, and the inhabitants left for Asunción. All the same, Pedro de Mendoza was the founder of the new colony, which eventually was looked upon as a jewel in the Spanish diadem.

It now seemed necessary in Seville to appoint a new governor in the far south of South America, and the man of the hour in Castile was Álvar Núñez Cabeza de Vaca, hero of the extraordinary walk across North America, who had just published his account of his journey. He also plainly wanted to return to the Indies. Probably he had been adversely affected by his experience, but then he had always been persistent if tactless. His affection for Indians was proverbial and at the time of his nomination to succeed Mendoza, seemed to be fashionable—in the mode of Las Casas.

Cabeza de Vaca at first expected to be able to gain the position of *adelantado* of the region between Florida and New Spain. But Hernando de Soto had obtained that grant. Cabeza, therefore, devised a new territory for himself. It would be the unknown land between the Río de la Plata and Santa Catalina—that is, the part of the continent of South America that lay south or southwest of the Portuguese dominion that would become Brazil. Cabeza de Vaca had never been to this territory, but all the same, he secured nomination as "*adelantado,* captain-general and governor" as well as "chief magistrate" of it. The King-emperor Charles signed this *capitulación* on March 18, 1540.[6]

Eight months later, Cabeza de Vaca left Sanlúcar de Barrameda with three ships and four hundred men (this was in November). There was a storm, however, and the fleet was delayed, leaving Cádiz only on December 2.

The journey was longer than usual, but then they were going to unknown places. They stopped on the way in both the Canary and the Cape Verde Islands, where Cabeza de Vaca secured some supplies without paying for them. They arrived at Santa Catalina, off Brazil, at the end of March. To Cabeza de Vaca's astonishment, he found on the island a Franciscan, Fray Bernaldo de Armenta, living alone, having come there from Buenos Aires. Cabeza de Vaca sent a small expedition to Buenos Aires to assist its revival as a Spanish dependency; but since it was already the South American winter, it seemed unsuitable to travel far by the Río de la Plata, so they pusillanimously returned. Their return coincided with the arrival of nine further Spaniards who had successfully come up from Buenos Aires.

Cabeza de Vaca now discovered that most of those Spaniards who had survived from Mendoza's expedition had established themselves high up the river Paraguay at Asunción. He sent ahead his friend Pedro Dorantes from Béjar (presumably a cousin of that Dorantes, Andrés, with whom he had crossed America) to find out what the territory was like, and he began a journey to Asunción with 250 men and twenty-six horses.[7]

This was another great walk for Cabeza de Vaca, for he took four months to reach Asunción from Santa Catalina. He attained his destination without losing any man or horse. On the way, they saw extraordinary sights, such as the waterfall of the river Iguazú.[8] In Asunción, Cabeza conducted himself as a man of the new enlightened era of Las Casas, and tried to make his fellow settlers pay taxes and treat Indians as human beings. This caused fury, and he was opposed by Martínez de Irala, who had been serving as interim governor. At one point, Cabeza and his followers lived off worms: "In the hollows of these [bamboo] reeds there were white worms, *calandra palmarum,* about the length and thickness of a finger. The people eat these, obtaining enough fat for them to fry them very well."[9] The position was rendered more complex by the fact that Cabeza de Vaca was attracted, even seduced, by stories of fabulous wealth in the South American interior. The myth of Alejo García and his journey to the fabulous white chief was current, almost as if it had been a real chivalrous novel. Cabeza organized a new expedition into the interior after hearing promising news along those lines from Martínez de Irala. They sailed up the river Paraguay from Asunción, almost to its source. But they found nothing, and the white chief was notable for his absence. They went back after a year, ill, poor, and unhappy.[10]

On their return to Asunción, the quarrel between Cabeza de Vaca and Martínez de Irala became a public one, and basing himself on his local authority, which Cabeza had never replaced, the latter arrested his governor and sent him home to Spain in chains on a caravel, accompanied by his notary, Pedro Hernández. Several of the officers on board the ship thought this too great a dishonor for Cabeza de Vaca, who was not only the hero of North America but had, after all, been named governor by the King. At least Cabeza de Vaca could return as a free man. They reached home on August 15, 1545.

In Spain, things continued badly for him. After some months' delay, he appeared before the Council of the Indies. There he was accused of robberies of food and horses in the Canary and Cape Verde Islands on his way out to South America. The prosecutor, Marcelo Villalobos, also presented a series of accusations made by the settlers in Asunción. They spoke with one voice about Cabeza de Vaca's hard attitude to taxation and soft one toward Indians. Cabeza de Vaca suddenly found himself not a hero of the empire but an accused prisoner. He said that he was "poor, lost and bankrupt." He was duly arrested, and though released with provisional freedom after a mere month in jail, he never recovered his health or his morale. Living in

Madrid, he devoted his time to collecting material for his defense. Three years passed.

The Council of the Indies eventually found against Cabeza de Vaca. As punishment, he was stripped of the grandiose titles granted him in 1540 and prohibited from returning to the Indies, and it was ruled that settlers in Asunción could pursue private petitions against him. He was also, remarkably for the national hero that he really was, condemned to forced labor in the galleys of Algiers. This last he appealed against, and he secured the removal of that punishment. He died poor in Valladolid in 1556, leaving behind only the memory of his astonishing achievements, nevertheless a victim of his weaknesses.

Domingo Martínez de Irala, now established in Asunción, very far indeed from Buen Viento (Buenos Aires), was the master of the field in the region of the river Plate. He had come to the Indies for the first time with Mendoza. Then he had accompanied Ayolas up the Paraguay, and was with him at the moment of the foundation of Asunción. At Ayolas's death, he was named governor—nothing more, no *adelantado*-ship or captaincy-general—of the Spaniards on the Río de la Plata. He was unceasingly active in the fortification of Asunción, naming a town council and controlling the countryside. The arrival of Cabeza de Vaca, of course, had confused him, even if the great walker was tolerant to him and named him his *maestre de campo*. Eventually, Martínez de Irala felt that he had to act against what he argued to be an improperly designated governor, whom, as we have seen, he sent home in ignominy.

Another Spanish proconsul, Diego de Sanabria, soon came with orders to establish himself in the Spanish ports on the Atlantic coast, to the south of the Portuguese colony of San Vicente, where many Spaniards had taken refuge.

Later, Martínez de Irala had to contend with a new rival for authority in those remote plains, namely, Gonzalo de Mendoza, and then Diego de Abreu. But Martínez de Irala survived these difficulties—though it seems probable that he had Abreu assassinated when he saw that he could not control him peacefully. For some years afterwards, though, this tiny colony lived in approximate peace—untouched by the journeys through what became northern Argentina of some conquistadors from Peru led by Diego de Rojas, Felipe Gutiérrez, and Nicolás de Heredia, including some two hundred wanderers in search of riches and fertile land. These expeditions included women, slaves, and Indian bearers. But Rojas was killed, Gutiérrez was discredited, and Heredia, a notary, eventually died in the Peruvian civil war, so nothing came of that initially promising incursion. Martínez de Irala, the least remarkable of all these conquistadors in the southeast of the continent, proved the most enduring. His grandson, Ruy Díaz de Guzmán, wrote the first authoritative history of his achievements.

A characteristic of his government was the swift development of a mestizo society based on the fact that Spanish women were rare and unusual. The percentage of natives who acted as wives to the conquistadors was far higher than anywhere else in South America. The mestizos were, therefore, increasingly numerous.[11]

40

New Spain with Antonio de Mendoza

> To the third question, he answered that "after the said lord Viceroy came to this New Spain, this witness used and exercised an authority from the accountant Rodrigo de Albornoz, that is the office of chief financier, for about two years more or less."
>
> JUAN DE BURGOS, *Información de servicios y méritos*
> OF ANTONIO DE MENDOZA

In April 1535, Antonio de Mendoza was named viceroy of New Spain. He would also be president of the supreme court (*audiencia*) in succession to the wise Ramírez de Fuenleal. Cortés, the conqueror who had made New Spain possible and had given the place its name, would remain captain-general at the Viceroy's pleasure: a title without weight in these strange circumstances.[1]

Mendoza was to represent the person of the monarch, to administer equal justice to his subjects of all races and his vassals, and to be active in everything to ensure the "peace, quiet and prosperity" of the Indies. He was to help in the conversion of Indians to Christianity, and govern his viceroyalty according to his best understanding. He was to have general authority over all appointments to ecclesiastical positions within his viceroyalty, even bishoprics, as the pope had agreed. He was to visit all the towns of New Spain so far as he could. He should make a census. Existing indigenous temples, "heathen" temples, should be sought out, for who knew whether they had gold and silver there. Abuses of the Indians should be, however, investigated and punished.

Mendoza's salary would be 3,000 ducats as viceroy and 3,000 as president of the supreme court. This was a substantial increase in comparison with what was paid to Guzmán or to the governor of Cuba. Numerous grants of land, wood, water, and grazing rights completed his perquisites. As he was not formally a *letrado*, a university-educated man, he could not vote in the supreme court of which he was president, but all the same, his signature was necessary to make decisions of the court binding.

In her letter of appointment to Mendoza, the Empress suggested various ways of increasing the royal income of New Spain. Gold and silver could be sought more than they had been theretofore. To avoid having to pay civil servants to count what was due to the great institution, there should be payments of tithes directly to the Church. Perhaps silver mines might be directly run by the Crown, instead of it taking a fifth from those privately run. The Viceroy was also to help two German entrepreneurs, Enrique and Alberto Girón, to develop saffron and blue dyes.[2]

Defense also had to be considered. The Spaniards were always to be concentrated in one part of the city of Mexico, and a second fortress was to be considered for the causeway to Tacuba, to balance that existing in the shipyard to the east of the city. Mendoza should establish a mint.[3] The Viceroy could distribute *encomiendas* if he thought fit.

The beneficiary of all these provisions, Antonio de Mendoza, was the son of Íñigo López de Mendoza, the count of Tendilla, who had been a successful ambassador to the Vatican and then a most effective, if liberal, governor of Granada. It would seem certain that his father's determined tolerance and grand style influenced Antonio. Viceroys in Mendoza's view had to live like kings—but wise kings. His mother, Francisca Pacheco, was the daughter of Juan Pacheco, the Marquess of Villena, who was the dominant nobleman in the reign of King Enrique IV of Castile. Antonio de Mendoza's brothers and sisters included the all-too-famous María who married the hero of the *comuneros,* Juan de Padilla, and she herself was a heroine of that war after her defense of Toledo against the Crown; his brother Francisco was an ambassador and Viceroy of Naples; and another brother, Diego Hurtado de Mendoza, would be the accomplished ambassador to Venice and Rome and would write a history of the last Spanish war against the Moors, in the Alpujarra mountains in the 1560s. Probably he was half brother of Pedro de Mendoza, the father of Argentina. Of course, the Viceroy's paternal grandfather was the famous Íñigo, first Marquess of Santillana, grandfather-in-chief to the Spanish aristocracy in its golden age.[4] The memory of the great cardinal Rodríguez de Mendoza survived.

Antonio de Mendoza was born in 1492 in Alcalá la Real, a picturesque town between Jaén and Granada, built on a conical hill. Being taken from the Moors by Alfonso XI in person, it acquired the epithet *Real* ("royal") in 1340. Visitors are shown a tower, La Mota (El Farol), which Antonio's father built to be a light guiding those Christians who had escaped from Granada. This town was the headquarters of the Spaniards fighting the Moors, and when Antonio was born there, it was at "the front."

Mendoza's childhood was mostly passed at Granada just after its conquest by the Castilians. Eminently an aristocrat, he was brought up to despise the *letrados* who, as civil servants, increasingly dominated the Spanish government. In 1521, Mendoza was at Huéscar with five hundred foot and one hundred horse and defeated the *comuneros* there. In 1526, he went to Hungary as an emissary of the emperor Charles to his brother, Ferdinand, the King of the Romans, just after the terrible Battle of Mohács, with some letters of credit worth 100,000 ducats. He was in England in 1527 and encountered King Henry VIII at Greenwich. He later became chamberlain of the Empress, to whom Mendoza said that he would be interested in going to Mexico. In 1530, he went as the personal messenger of the Empress-Regent to the Emperor, who was then at Bologna. He was named viceroy in April 1535, an appointment of Isabel's.

The country for which he assumed responsibility was in a far better condition than it had been when the second supreme court had taken over. Then it had seemed as if the president of that body's predecessor, Nuño de Guzmán, had been seeking to link the province of New Galicia, which he was busy conquering, with his old responsibility of Pánuco in order to create a big new realm for himself. The disorder in the city of Mexico was considerable—despite its illegality, the trade in slaves in Pánuco was out of control.[5]

Because Guzmán had seized 10,000 pesos from the treasury of the city of Mexico in order to conquer New Galicia, the second supreme court confiscated all Guzmán's property in the capital. All his property in Pánuco was also seized. Many settlers in New Spain thought that Pánuco should be merged with New Spain as a province. This business of the disentangling of

Pánuco from its union with the rest of Guzmán's realm occupied much of the early 1530s.

The second supreme court had found itself immediately in difficulties over recent decisions in Spain. For example, on August 2, 1530, an ordinance had been proclaimed in Madrid on the subject of enslavement. It was resisted by all officials of the Spanish Crown in the Indies. It stated that no person should venture "to make a single new slave whether in peace or in war . . . whether by barter, purchase, trade, or any pretext or cause whatever." The penalty for a breach of this law would be the loss of all wealth and of Indians so enslaved. Within thirty days, everyone who owned (Indian) slaves was to register them and prove that they were true chattels. After that, there was to be no more enslaving.[6]

In August 1531 the supreme court of New Spain wrote to the Crown saying that if the law about slaves was enacted, the colonies would be in rebellion once the Indians learned of their freedom. No Spaniard would want to help to put down such a rebellion, for there would be no reward for his efforts. The Council of the Indies, therefore, hesitated over its policy.

There had, however, been some positive new policies during this uneasy period before Mendoza's arrival. One was the foundation of Puebla de los Ángeles, in Tlaxcala, in 1531. It was to be a city of workers, not of *encomenderos.* The creator there was Alonso Martín Partidor, who had arrived in New Spain in 1522 and married a *conquistadora,* María Estrada Farfán, who had accompanied Narváez and, indeed, had been in the classic battles on the Causeways and at Otumba.[7] She was first married to Pedro Sánchez Farfán, who had died, and she inherited herself his *encomienda* of Tetela del Volcán.[8] In his endeavors, Martín Partidor received the enthusiastic help of 7,500 Tlaxcalteca. To encourage people to live in this new city, the Crown gave numerous fiscal benefits to settlers there so that by the time of Mendoza's arrival as Viceroy, there were eighty-two citizens in Puebla, among them thirty-two conquistadors of the first wave.[9]

In 1533, a large Augustinian convent was built in the city of Mexico, reflecting the arrival in May of that year of seven friars of that order. The Mercedarians also built their own refuge, appropriately, considering the role played by the Mercedarian friend of Cortés, Fray Bartolomé de Olmedo, in the conquest of New Spain.

Dr. Ramírez de Fuenleal had reached New Spain only in September

1531, but his arrival brought an immediate transformation in how political matters were managed. The new judges petitioned the Crown for their number to be increased, for, they said, they found that their work needed twelve hours a day, the *residencia* of their predecessors was itself a Herculean task, and they were absorbed all the time by the conversion of the natives, as they were by the regulation of relations with the Church.

The supreme court, it is true, made some astonishing reforms. For example, Indians were formally to have equal rights with Spaniards, and they were to be trained in Spanish methods of administration. The two "republics," as it was put at first, were to be treated equally. Of the judges, it seemed that only Vasco de Quiroga was up to the burdens, and even he was more interested in the problems of the Church than those of general administration. The other judges, Alonso de Maldonado, Juan de Salmerón,[10] and even Fuenleal, were old and tired. Still, they maintained themselves. Perhaps the most surprising innovation was a decree of December 10, 1531, by which officials in New Spain were instructed to keep a ledger in which they were to strike a balance between good and bad conduct of each *encomendero* every two years.[11]

Of the members of the second *audiencia*, the most remarkable was Vasco de Quiroga, or Tata Vasco as he was universally known, a son of a Gallego nobleman who had become governor of the Priory of San Juan, in Castile.[12] Tata Vasco, who was born in Madrigal de las Atlas Torres in the late 1470s, had been at the University of Salamanca; he had been a *letrado* and was a judge. He lived at the court, where he became friendly with Juan Bernal Díaz de Luco, a Sevillano who became bishop of Calahorra, a protégé and then secretary of Archbishop Tavera, and later a member of the Council of the Indies.[13] With Díaz de Luco, Quiroga is said to have discussed the role of Spain in the Indies in the criticism included in Antonio de Guevara's *El Villano en el Danubio*.[14] (Here an uncivilized peasant astonishes the senate by his wisdom in condemning the greed of his conquerors.) Perhaps it was Díaz de Luco who suggested him as a possible judge in New Spain, but the Empress also favored him.

Quiroga went to a monastery to obtain divine guidance as to whether he should accept his nomination. The voices of the friars spoke favorably for going ahead. Once in New Spain, Tata Vasco set about planning his first pueblo-hospital, of Santa Fe, at Tacubaya. His aim was to create a place where Indians would be educated by friars to live in a Christian way, to carry out conversions and to effect benevolent missions among the sick. He explained all this in a letter to the Council of the Indies in August 1531.[15]

We need to recall that this was the era of the humanist Juan Maldonado, who, from a tower on the walls of Burgos in 1532, evoked a Christian America in his writings. The worst savages would acquire in ten years the purest of orthodox faith. Being blessed by nature, they could live an idyllic life free from both fraud and hypocrisy. There would be no false modesty or decorum, only shame for morally reprehensible actions. Men and women would mix together in games, like brothers and sisters. The shops would be so well supplied that the customers could help themselves. Such heavy agricultural labor as was needed would be carried out by all. Quiroga had a similar view, since he said: "Not in vain but with much cause and reason is this called the new world because in its people and in almost everything it is like the first golden age."[16]

In 1533, still a member of the supreme court, Quiroga went up to Michoacán. He reported how surprised he was to find the natives so capable of juridical expression and to find the conquistadors so evil, for they were already exploiting indigenous people in copper mines. So he founded his second pueblo-hospital in Santa Fe de la Laguna, near Tzintsuntzan, the old capital of Michoacán. There was a protest by *encomenderos*. For example, Juan Infante said that he had received land there from Cortés himself.[17] There, in 1535, Quiroga would say firmly, "The people of this land and of the new world generally are almost all of one quality, very mild and humble, timid and obedient. They should be brought to faith by good Christian influence not by war and fear." He strongly opposed the use of Indians as slaves; he thought slavery an invention of the devil. He said: "Those who allege Indian vices have their own profit in mind. I have never seen the abominations charged by those who desire to defame them . . . [but] persons who have Indians serving them use them not as men but as beasts and worse."[18] Thus Quiroga began his mission in a quite new mood. By this time, he had already written to the Council of the Indies suggesting that the life of the native Indians should be regulated by placing them in villages, "where by working and tilling the soil they may maintain themselves with their labour and may be ruled by all good rules of policy and by holy and good and Catholic rules; where there may be constructed a friar's house, small and not costly, for two or three or four brothers who may not leave their task till such time as the natives have acquired the habits of virtue." Quiroga wanted to establish "a priest in each district." He talked hopefully of "the simplicity and humility of the aborigines; men who went barefoot, bare-headed but long-haired as the Apostles were."[19]

At the end of 1531, in Mexico there had been a remarkable occurrence, which affected forever all relations between Spaniards and Indians. The Indian Juan Diego met the Virgin Mary on the hill of Tepeyac, just outside Mexico-Tenochtitlan, on the north of the town. Our Lady of Guadalupe, as she became known, left a picture of herself on a shroud, which was taken to Bishop Zumárraga, who organized a chapel there. She appeared three times. Cortés supported Zumárraga in his identification. The consequent cult soon began to seem of the greatest importance for the Christian faith of the Indians. It remains so. No matter that the skeptics included Franciscans and their brother fraternities, the Dominicans and Augustinians, who pointed out that the hill of Tepeyac had been a Mexican site of worship before the conquest. The idea caught on and transformed Mexican and Christian history.

There were also more practical ideas afoot. Early in 1533, Gaspar de Espinosa, the richest and most influential settler in Panama, later a great entrepreneur in Peru, suggested to the Council of the Indies that a canal might be dug from the Pacific to the Atlantic. This would be at the level of the river Chagres, near the line of the canal that was eventually built by Ferdinand de Lesseps in the twentieth century. But Espinosa died before he could do anything to help to carry that great project into being.

In July 1532, the supreme court in New Spain informed the Empress that they were sending a description and account of the land and the people of the conquistadors and settlers. The viceroyalty, they considered, should be divided into four provinces. In November 1532, ex-judges Matienzo and Delgadillo sailed for Spain, taking with them a wooden box that had within it the depositions of the supreme court and descriptions of the land. In a legal brief of 1535, Quiroga proposed that "the Indians be brought together in cities."[20] He suggested that the laws of which he had read in Sir Thomas More's *Utopia* should be introduced. Thus a city of six thousand families—

each composed of between ten and sixteen couples—would be ruled, regulated, and governed as if it were a single family. Each magistrate would control thirty families, and each governor would preside over four magistrates. These magistrates could be chosen by a method copied from *Utopia*. The supreme court would appoint a mayor-in-chief (*corregidor*).²¹

Such was the New Spain to which Antonio de Mendoza, now forty-three years of age, would devote the next fifteen years—in effect, the rest of his life. He arrived at Veracruz in October 1535 with a large number of followers and relations. It was as if he were really a monarch. Spanish viceroys in Galicia, Navarre, or Naples, though they had that title, never had enjoyed such a style. Mendoza then went up to the city of Mexico, as it was already being called, and there, on November 14, 1535, he was greeted by trumpets, acrobats, the public crier, and the whole of the town council. Indigenous Mexicans made very good acrobats, as is evident to this day.

The Viceroy was an absolute monarch. His rule seems to have been supposed to extend throughout the Spanish Indies as far as the northern frontier, if that is not an inappropriate word, of Peru—that is, it included Colombia and Venezuela. His domain thus in theory included all of Central America, Florida, California, the Antilles, and the north coast of South America from Urabá or Darien to the mouth of the Amazon.²² But absolute monarchs have their limitations, and this was provided in the Viceroy's case in the shape of the supreme courts.²³

In Mendoza's day, the supreme court in New Spain sat daily from eight A.M. till eleven A.M. On Mondays, the Viceroy would attend all day. On Mondays, Wednesdays, and Thursdays, there were also sessions in the evenings, from two to seven o'clock, mostly given over to the affairs of the Indians. There were then hearings until ten P.M. (on Saturdays till nine P.M.), after which there would be a visit to the prisons. On Tuesdays and Fridays from eight A.M. till eleven A.M., the Viceroy would be present as the informal president of a court, as also would be the rapporteurs; and every day, the last hour would be given over to petitions. On Tuesdays, Wednesdays, and Thursdays, the judge would receive petitions from Indians in his own house, working with a notary and a translator. There were a vast number of the last named. The judges were all men well connected in Castile and would bring their wives and children with them. They would be expected to conduct themselves as if members of an aristocracy.

Mendoza's arrival in the city of Mexico coincided with a decision by the Empress and the Council of the Indies that settlers in New Spain would henceforth be able to buy land in Mexico from indigenous owners. The conquistador had first to establish that the land was empty but, if he did that, he could purchase innumerable acres for very little. This decision in Valladolid of October 27, 1535, was the real beginning of the history of the great estates of New Spain.[24]

One limitation on the Viceroy's power was that he could not grant sites for building in established cities. That was for the council of that place. He could not even give permission to build churches or monasteries. Nor could he grant titles of nobility. He could not increase salaries, certainly not his own, nor could he extend his own term, although that term was without a date of completion.[25]

The supreme court had become the most important institution before the arrival of Mendoza, but now it lost much of its political power and became largely judicial. The court, with each judge being paid 500,000 maravedís a year, was still supposed to control the actions of the Viceroy, but it did not do so in the days of Mendoza. He conducted himself as a benign monarch more than a public servant. Mendoza's court had to take the *residencia* of its predecessor, but there were no complaints except, bizarrely, against Quiroga, who was accused of having built his two hospital villages of Santa Fe on land belonging to Indians. But he was easily able to prove the benefit to the indigenous people.

In Santa Fe the bishop established the common ownership of property, the integration of large families, the systematic alternation between urban and rural people, work for women, the abandonment of all luxury, the distribution of the products of common labor according to the needs of the people, and the election of judges by families.[26] Of the new judges, Tejada was once described as the first great promoter of land values in the New World. He was especially concerned in flour mills in Otumba.[27]

Beneath the Viceroy and the supreme court there was no administration except the municipalities, which in character were transplanted direct from old Spain. They were usually known as *cabildos*. They had a variable number of councillors, but in the city of Mexico, there were twelve of them, six elected each year. There were also two magistrates (*alcaldes*) while the councils themselves would name the others.

Mendoza had at first hoped to leave exclusively Indian towns to their native lords, but there was much confusion in this regard because some of them had their power from before the conquest, while others had been nominated by *encomenderos* or churchmen. It also seemed that such indigenous lords—in the spirit of Montezuma's encouragement to his subordinates to be harsh—often treated their people worse than the conquistadors did.

On Mendoza's arrival, the dominant figure in New Spain was the bishop of Mexico, Juan de Zumárraga, whose early life and struggle against Guzmán and his circle we have already discussed. He was high-minded and resolute, and he and Fray Martín de Valencia destroyed more than five hundred temples in New Spain and smashed twenty thousand idols.[28] Valencia noted that there were already twenty Franciscan convent houses in New Spain, even if most were no more than large huts.[29] By 1532, on the other hand, the first cathedral of Mexico was completed, the builders using much of the stone of the old pyramids in the construction. Martín de Sepúlveda, the architect (he had worked on the rebuilding of Tenochtitlan as a master of works, having originally come with Narváez to Mexico), had built an aisled rectangular building with a flat wooden roof and wooden supports.[30]

Perhaps this explains the enthusiastic attitude that the supreme court had toward the Indians' capacity for Christianity. At the first ecclesiastical junta in the city of Mexico—at which Ramírez de Fuenleal had presided, with Zumárraga in attendance—the learned good men proclaimed that there was no question but that the natives had sufficient capacity, that they greatly loved the doctrine of the faith, and that they were "able to carry on all mechanical and agricultural arts." The Indian, they thought, was a rational being entirely capable of governing himself.[31]

The first radical decision taken by Mendoza was one to suspend a dispatch to New Spain of a large new consignment of black slaves, which had been ordered and which he had wanted. The reason was not altruistic: The explanation was the discovery of a conspiracy of black slaves such as had led to ferocious rebellions in Puerto Rico in 1527, in Santa Marta in 1529, in Santo Domingo in 1522, and in New Spain itself in 1523. That last-named occasion had seen a threatening alliance of Zapotecs in the neighborhood of Oaxaca with the blacks. This was none the better for having been seen by some romantically minded Spaniards, such as the poet Juan Castellanos, as idealistic. Castellanos later wrote a poem in which figures the line "Skillful are the Wolofs and very combative, with a foolhardy presumption to be gentlemen."[32]

Some black slaves fled their masters, and the viceroyalty of Mendoza saw the establishment of a small colony of escaped Africans in the forest near the mines of Tomacustla, in Veracruz.

The key to Mendoza's rule in Mexico was his court of thirty to forty gentlemen (*caballeros*), who served as both his bodyguard and in his private office. This was headed by Agustín de Guerrero, his majordomo and also the chancellor of the supreme court, the keeper of the official seal, which could not be removed from the courtroom and without whose stamp no document could be looked on as legal. His assistant, Juan de Salazar, became almost as powerful. Luis del Castillo, a descendant of King Pedro the Cruel in the male, if illegitimate, line, was also a constant assistance to the Viceroy. Castillo had first come to New Spain in 1529 as a companion to Juana de Zúñiga, Cortés's second wife, his distant cousin. Earlier, he had fought against both the *comuneros* and the French. He received an *encomienda* at Tututepec in 1534 and lived sumptuously, as perhaps a king's bastard cousin should: "Even the servants drank from silver," commented Dorantes de Carranza admiringly.[33] But Castillo gave away a great deal to the poor, especially to the Spanish poor in New Spain.

Mendoza had sixty Indian servants. He received the harvests from numerous ranches: one in the valley of Matalingo; five near Marabatio, in Michoacán; two near Tecamachalco, including the site of Cortés's victory after the Noche Triste at Otumba; and one, a ranch for horses in the valley of Ulizabal. These ranches produced the meat and the wool needed in the Viceroy's household.

Mendoza lived in the city of Mexico in the great house of Axayactl, which Cortés had converted into a Spanish palace, next to the onetime sacred precinct of the ancient Mexica. He lived there with his son, Francisco, and his sister. Mendoza's wife, Catalina de Vargas y Carvajal, seems to have died before he left for Mexico. Mendoza himself rose early and would listen to petitioners at all hours, not just those prescribed by the supreme court. He was always friendly, if always brief. He traveled continually. He insisted that his Indian servants were taught music, and everything to do with "minstrelsy." He was able to grant *corregimientos, encomiendas,* and the services of Indians, so he was powerful. No act of a town hall had validity unless he approved. He could proclaim laws and, in that respect, was dependent only on the approval of the distant Council of the Indies.

From all these discussions, Cortés the conqueror was excluded. Mendoza as viceroy found the overpowering personality of that great conqueror difficult to manage. But he had also been previously excluded from consideration at court in Spain. He had been made a Marquess, he had married an aristocrat, he had a family, he had become rich. What more, people asked in Valladolid, did he want? There was a sense that the court was afraid of Cortés. He had done too much to be easily pleased by a second-rate position. Cortés's resentment at this was expressed by him in a memorandum to Charles the Emperor in June 1540: Having alluded contemptuously to an expedition northward led by Fray Marcos de Niza, he went on to talk of his own discovery and conquest of the land and how he had sent four fleets at his own cost (300,000 ducats) in order to discover the north.[34]

It was not just Marcos de Niza whose plans offended Cortés. There was the fact that Pedro de Alvarado had also secured a contract to discover islands—those of the Santa María, off Puerto Vallarta (as it later became). He took six hundred men and twelve ships from Guatemala, met and negotiated with Mendoza's friends Luis del Castillo and Agustín de Guerrero, and worked out an agreement whereby Alvarado would have a quarter share in the profits of the Viceroy's expeditions, while Mendoza could have a half interest in Alvarado's fleets. This looked like an effective prohibition on Cortés from making further conquests.

Cortés's protest was serious, but the Viceroy had his own problems. For example, there was the Mixton War. This was a serious rebellion of Indians. It was probably inspired by the brutality of many *encomenderos* in the north of New Spain. The Viceroy, who had been preoccupied by new plans of Francisco Vazquez de Coronado and Marcos de Niza, thought that the new religiosity and rebellion was one of wild Chichimeca Indians from the far north, with a new religion of a kind, brought to them by "messengers of the devil."[35]

There was also much brutality attached to work in the mines, such as those at Oaxtepec, where Fray Motolinía—who, it is true, often exaggerated—said the work was so destructive that for "half a league around it one could not walk without stepping on dead men and bones and so many birds came to scavenge that they darkened the sky."[36] The tale told was that Indians were dancing round a pumpkin when a gust of wind carried it away. Their sorcerers said that that meant that the Indians should rise against the Spaniards.[37]

In this region to the north of the viceroyalty, ancient rulers and some of their families assembled on the hill of Tepetiquipaque and revived some of their ancient religious practices, including human sacrifice. Several local *encomenderos* were forced to leave; some were wounded and fled to Tlatenango, where Diego de Ibarra sought to establish an armed force to fight the rebellion, assisted by four Franciscans.[38] There ensued the most serious conflict between Christians and Indians since the conquest.

The indigenous rebels were cheered by supposed messages from the alleged devils of the old days. For example, in the valley of Tlatenango, a rebel leader declared: "We are the messengers of Tecoroli [the devil, according to the Spaniards]. Accompanied by his ancestors, whom he has revived, he is coming to seek you. He will make you believe in him, not in [the Christian] God, on pain of never seeing the light again and being devoured by wild beasts. Those who believe in Tecoroli and renounce the teaching of the friars will never die, but will become young again and have several wives, not just one, as the friars order and, however old they may be, they will beget children. Whoever takes only one wife will be killed. Tecoroli will come to Guadalajara, Jalisco, Michoacán, Mexico and Guatemala, in fact wherever there are Christians, and will kill them all. After that, you will be able to go home and live happily with your ancestors, suffering no more hardship or pain."[39]

Among the leaders of the rebels was Tenemaxtli, who had once had a mission to take the catechism to the converted. Under his leadership, the rebels burned the churches at Tlatenango and at Cuzpatelan. They also burned the convent at Juchilpa. Christian Indians were made to do penance for the time that they had been Christians, washing their heads to free themselves from the memory of the cross. They killed Fray Juan de Esperanza at Tequila, outside Guadalajara; they killed Fray Juan Calero near Etzaltán; and Fray Antonio de Cuéllar was assassinated near Ameca.[40]

Diego de Ibarra, an able conquistador, was persuaded to face the rebels.

He had only seventeen Spanish horsemen, but he had about 1,500 Tonalá Indians, who had always opposed the Mixton people, and he also had the more doubtful support of some Cascan Indians. Some of the Tonalá told of a planned ambush by the Cascanes in a cedar-lined gully where the Spaniards would be unable to use their horses very well. Ibarra had several Cascanes executed, but all the same they attacked, wounding Ibarra and some others, as well as some of the precious horses. The Spaniards retreated first to Suchilpala, then to Guadalajara, rescuing numerous fellow countrymen en route. By then the rebels were established throughout the area of the river Tololotlan.

Mendoza at first thought that this rebellion was a local affair. Then he realized that the threat was colony-wide, and he hastened to Guadalajara. There he sent out a peace mission headed by Fray Martín de Jesús and guarded by Ibarra. Its failure convinced Mendoza that force had to be used. He assembled a council in Guadalajara, where there were Licenciado Francisco Marroquín, the bishop of Guatemala; Ibarra, who was recovering; and Cristóbal de Oñate, who had been Nuño de Guzmán's deputy in New Galicia and had founded Guadalajara in 1531, naming it after Guzmán's birthplace. They resolved to dispatch Oñate with fifty horsemen against the Mixton camp on a hillock. The Indians fought well, thirteen Spaniards being killed as well as six black slaves and a large number of Indian allies. This battle was the signal for many further revolts throughout New Galicia and Jalisco.

This threat persuaded Mendoza to call on Luis del Castillo and Pedro de Alvarado to abandon their planned journeys of discovery in the Pacific. They landed near Colima and made for Guadalajara with one hundred horse and an equal number of foot. That put paid to any Indian advance on that city. Mendoza also sent a hundred men from Mexico under Íñigo López de Anuncibay and ordered another member of the large Alvarado family to move in from Michoacán with thirty horse and a huge number of Mexican foot, perhaps five thousand.

There followed a meeting under Oñate's direction in Guadalajara to formulate a plan of action. Pedro de Alvarado, impatient to return to his voyage of discovery, told his colleagues that they were children in their timidity and declared that, with his experience, he would soon personally defeat these Indians. Oñate sought to dissuade Alvarado, but the latter reminded all his comrades of their lack of experience in comparison with his. Alvarado set off for the hill of Nochistlán and reached there on June 24, 1541, refusing Oñate's offers of help and certainly not waiting for support from Mexico.

Alvarado had with him a hundred foot soldiers, a hundred horsemen, and several hundred Indian allies. He first sought to negotiate his enemy's surrender, then mounted a direct assault, which was repelled with losses. Alvarado rallied, his infantry attacked without the help of cavalry, and the rebels attacked then with great force. Alvarado tried unsuccessfully to rally his men again, and he dismounted to prevent a headlong retreat. It was raining, and the ground had become a bog. Alvarado led his horse backward, but his secretary slipped, leaving Alvarado to be flung into a ravine with his horse on top of him. Watching from a nearby hillock, Oñate saved the day, prevented a complete catastrophe, and carried the wounded Alvarado back to Guadalajara. There Alvarado went to the house of his cousin Juan del Camino, and there, victim of the impetuosity that had always been his hallmark, he died of his wounds in June 1541.

The first great ally of Cortés in his conquest of Mexico was thus removed, leaving a reputation for success in spite of danger; bravery in spite of cruelty; and good looks, which even his enemies admired, in place of prudence.

The Indians besieged Guadalajara. The assault of fifty thousand Mixton Indians was beaten off with difficulty. Beatriz Hernández, surely the same *conquistadora* who had come to New Spain from Cuba with the great Cortés, was the heroine of this siege. There were several successful sorties, including one in which the tireless apostle Santiago was said yet again to have appeared on his white horse to save the Spaniards from defeat.

Mendoza sent the judge Maldonado to report on the situation in Guadalajara. He returned to say that Mendoza himself was needed. Though he had little military experience, except in the war of the *comuneros,* it was assumed that a Mendoza could automatically command men in battle. The Viceroy did go up to Guadalajara with 180 horse and a large number of friendly Indians, perhaps several thousand, and also a good quantity of artillery, the new weapons of the day. This was the great challenge to, or test of, his viceroyalty.

The innovation of Mendoza's army was not only the substantial number of guns, but the fact that friendly Indian noblemen, of Mexican origin, were encouraged to use Spanish weapons, including swords, and to ride on horseback.

Mendoza traveled via Michoacán. He met Ibarra and Juan del Camino at the Tlazazalca tower, near Cuina. Mendoza surrounded that fortress, then feigned flight, returned to the hilltop, defeated the enemy easily, and condemned the Indians whom he captured to death or to slavery. He seems to have felt an exemplary series of punishments was essential: "Many of the Indians taken in the conquest of the said hill were put to death in his presence and by his orders. Some were placed in line and blown to pieces by cannon. Others were torn to pieces by dogs while others still were handed over to negroes [sic] to be put to death. These killed them by knife thrusts."[41]

After this repression, Mendoza was able at Acatic, Istlean, and Cuyutlán to negotiate peace. He moved on to Nochistlán. Fray Juan de San Román, Fray Antonio de Segovia, and Diego de Ibarra sought a truce, without success. Mendoza settled down to a siege, cutting off the supply of water and battering down the obstacles with artillery. The Indians offered peace at last, but Mendoza chose to launch an assault, reasoning that anyone who offers peace can be more easily defeated. He triumphed. He moved to Mixton hill, where the bulk of the enemy had gathered. Ibarra and Francisco Maldonado made a new offer of peace, but they were rejected. Mendoza then moved to Suchilpala, where eight hundred Indians appeared in order to sacrifice chickens to the rain god Tlaloc and to sing hymns. He again sent Ibarra to propose peace, but he was again rejected.

Mendoza spent the next three weeks besieging the Mixton camp. There were daily proposals of peace and also daily enfilades of artillery. The Indians on Teul deserted, and betrayed an oath to indicate a secret way to the top of their hill. The hill soon fell; the Viceroy's horsemen made their presence powerfully felt on the summit. They purposely permitted the Indians to escape, hoping to save lives and so spare the encomenderos the loss of all their Indians. This broke the back of the revolt. The captives were divided up as slaves, and the war ended with the capture of Ahuacatlán. Mendoza returned to Mexico, where his victory was celebrated solemnly, with rejoicing and many festivities. A general rising of Indians, which had seemed for a time a real possibility, was thus avoided. The Viceroy was afterwards accused of causing unnecessary cruelty, a charge that he successfully fended off.

During these celebrations, the news came that Diego de Almagro the younger had rebelled in Peru. Mendoza wrote, "It would appear that the marques del Valle [Cortés] would be a very good person to remedy the problems down there, because of the experience he has of that kind of matter and I would help him as much as possible."[42] It would seem that the Viceroy was seeking a way to rid himself of the brooding Marquess. But if that was so, he was unsuccessful. The crisis in Peru proved anyway to last a short time only. Cortés remained in New Spain.

Mendoza's victory over the Mixton Indians coincided with many steps taken to demonstrate that the Spanish presence in New Spain was no ephemeral phenomenon. Nothing, for example, could be less transitory than the beginning of the great cathedral of Pátzcuaro, whose inspiration was Bishop Quiroga. He sought to create a building as big as the cathedral of Seville and on the model of the cathedral of Granada. The plan that Quiroga requested of Hernando Toribio de Alcázar was to have five naves culminating in a great central chapel. The construction began and went on for twenty years, but thereafter the pace of building declined.

Another confirmation of Spanish grandeur was Mendoza's insistence on sending Ruy López de Villalobos on an expedition from Acapulco to the islands off Asia discovered by Magellan, who had died there.[43] Villalobos's expedition was intended to establish a colony in that archipelago. They and their friends did establish themselves in a land that was claimed by Portugal and the Emperor. Eventually, Charles told Mendoza that he accepted the Portuguese mapmaking and that he would have to abandon the settlement. Mendoza wrote to Juan de Aguilar that he hoped that one day he or one of his sons might be permitted to stand on the line of demarcation armed with a sword in order to demonstrate what belonged to them.[44] A Spanish ship from this expedition under Álvaro de Saavedra landed in Hawaii, and two Spaniards are said to have survived to marry into the royal line of those islands. All the same, Villalobos gave the Philippines their name in honor of the King's heir, Prince Philip.

Another expedition was dispatched by Mendoza up the west coast of California, under a Portuguese, Juan Rodríguez Cabrillo, with a Valencian, Bartolomé Ferrelo, as chief pilot. They left Navidad in June 1542, were at Cabo San Lucas on July 3, and by the end of September, were in what is now San Diego (which they called San Miguel). They continued north, dropped an anchor in Cuyler's Harbor, and rounded Port Concepción in early November, being already north of San Francisco, whose superb harbor they did not see. Their farthest northern point was approximately Fort Ross, where they turned south again, resting in Cuyler's Harbor, where Rodríguez Cabrillo died in early January 1543. Ferrelo took over and determined to sail north again. He sailed as far as the river Rogue, halfway to what is now Canada. This was a triumph of navigation, for they had returned successfully to Navidad by April 14, 1543.[45] We can look on it as one more triumph by Viceroy Antonio de Mendoza.

Meantime, Vasco de Quiroga—a bishop after 1537, and consequently richer—was still busy in his attempts to use *Utopia* as a guide to good governance. We know a good deal of Tata Vasco's thinking, since he was never silent about his meditations. Thus we hear that after his first reading of *Utopia,* Quiroga came upon the account by the philosopher Lucian (born about A.D. 120) in the form of a dialogue about the *Saturnalia,* as translated by More with the help of Erasmus. This led Quiroga to suppose that "the simple people of New Spain would be found capable of dwelling in the state of innocence of the golden age" as indicated by the sophist Lucian. These people were ready for whatever one might make of them. The task of civilization in the New World should therefore consist not in transplanting the old culture among the newly discovered peoples but in raising them to the standards of primitive Christianity. More's *Utopia* would be the instrument of the elevation.[46]

41

Coronado and the Seven Magic
Cities of Cibola

There are guileless people who think that there can be no lies in
print.

FRANCISCO RODRÍGUEZ LOBO, *Cortes en aldea y
Noches de Invierno*

By the late 1530s, successive expeditions by conquistadors had revealed an
outline of the geography and much of the social organization of New Spain
and Guatemala on the one hand, and Panama on the other. Those one
thousand miles of isthmus, mountain, and lakeside no longer held grandiose
secrets. It was quite different with the territory to the north.

So it was logical that the viceroy Mendoza, as intelligent as he was curious, should seek an expedition north of New Spain, and north of New
Galicia, and of anywhere known to the conquistadors.

Unusually enough, the first such expedition was led by a clever Franciscan. This was Fray Marcos de Niza. Born in Nice (hence his name), he went,
already a member of his order, to the New World in 1531. First in Santo
Domingo, then in Nicaragua and Guatemala, later he went to Peru with
Pedro de Alvarado. There he was the leader of the first Franciscan mission
and returned soon after to Guatemala. He became vice-commissioner of the
Franciscans in New Spain.

In 1536, Fray Marcos de Niza was sent by the Viceroy as head of a small
expedition of discovery to the north. The main part of his group remained
in Culiacán while he went on with the legendary Estebanico, Cabeza de

Vaca's Berber companion, and a lay brother, Onorato, across half the continent. They left Culiacán with some Indian bearers on March 7, 1537.[1] Onorato became ill and was left behind. Estebanico went on ahead. He found interesting places such as Hawikuh, in what is now New Mexico. He found two large crosses there and reported the place to be one of the Seven Cities of Cibola, a legendary concept that had come to dazzle settlers in New Spain. *Cibola* is a word used normally by Spaniards as a translation of "bison," but in the hands of the citizens of New Spain, it signified something magical—an echo of the fantastical novels that played such an important part in forming the conquistadors' imagination.

Estebanico, though a man of extraordinary resilience, was not one of any delicacy. He mistreated all the Indians with whom he came into contact. His ruthless insensitivity now led to a rebellion in the expedition, causing the murder of his group, including himself, except for three members who escaped by accident.

Fray Marcos was informed of these developments and himself went ahead in Estebanico's footsteps. He wrote back to the Viceroy: "Judging by what I could see . . . the settlement [of Hawikuh] is larger than the city of Mexico. It appears to me that this is the best and largest of all the lands which have been discovered."[2] The Viceroy and monarch should by that time have been used to such extravagant commentaries about new places. But like everyone else engaged in the expansion of the empire, they had an unfailing appetite for good news. Hawikuh was actually a hamlet in comparison to Tenochtitlan.

At all events, the myth of Cibola was now launched. The Indian settlements concerned were the villages of the ancestors of the Zuni Indians in New Mexico.

In order to stay alive, Fray Marcos divided all the goods that he had with him among his Indians and persuaded, or induced, them to remain with him till he reached the village where Estebanico had been killed. There Fray Marcos raised a cross, and then he returned to Culiacán.

At the end of 1539, the Viceroy decided to follow up this voyage of enquiry with another more powerful one, at whose head he placed a great friend, Francisco Vázquez de Coronado, a man who seemed "wise, skilful and intelligent."

Vázquez de Coronado was a native of Salamanca and had come to the

New World with Mendoza himself. He soon set about marrying the beautiful and rich Beatriz de Estrada, daughter of the treasurer Alonso de Estrada. Vázquez de Coronado had first of all been named investigator in the affair of Nuño de Guzmán in the *residencia* mounted against him as governor of New Galicia.

The expedition that Viceroy Mendoza wanted Coronado to lead was elaborately organized. He had, for example, Lope de Samaniego, an experienced old hand in New Spain, as his general. Samaniego had gone first to New Spain as agent or representative of Peter Martyr and had returned to Spain as guard of the famous silver phoenix of Cortés. The captain of Coronado's infantry was Pablo de Melgosa; his captain of horse, Hernando de Alvarado—probably a nephew of the great Pedro. Coronado had altogether about 580 conquistadors with him and perhaps two thousand Indians, most of them camp followers, porters, or cattle- or swineherds. Fray Marcos de Niza would travel as the priest-in-charge. Among the captains was Juan de Zaldívar, a pioneer of New Granada, a future pioneer, too, of silver mining in Zacatecas. His house in Mexico was one of the best in New Spain and was always full of guests and visitors.

Mendoza ordered an expedition by sea to escort Coronado, and he asked his chamberlain, Hernando de Alarcón, to lead it. He did so, sailing up to the extreme north of the Gulf of California with three ships, the *San Pedro,* the *Santa Catalina,* and the *San Gabriel.* He set off up the river Colorado, hoping there to meet Coronado. He did not find the latter, but he probably reached as far as Yuma, some fifty miles inland, before he turned back. He then returned to Guatemala, having at the least established that the land called California was not an island.

Coronado's expedition set off on February 23, 1540, Viceroy Mendoza giving his blessing by accompanying it for the first two days. They set off gaily, pennons and lances to the fore. At Chametla, Samaniego was wounded in the eye by an arrow, but his men were rallied by Diego López of Seville. At that stage, the danger seemed to be the cold, rather than the Indians. The vanguard of Juan de Zaldívar, for example, reported that the excessively low temperature had frozen to death some of the Indians with him. Reaching Culiacán, Coronado determined to press ahead with Tristán de Arellano, one of his highborn captains, and fifty horse. He left the main body of the army under Fernandarias de Saavedra. Pressing on, Coronado captured Fray Marcos de Niza's town of Hawikuh, while Pedro de Tovar and García López de Cárdenas seized several villages belonging to the Moqui Indians. They became the first Europeans to look into the Grand Canyon. López de Cárdenas spent several days seeking a passage down to the river, which from above seemed to be a mere six feet across, but, when they descended into the valley, proved to be half a league wide.

After three days, Pablo de Melgosa, with Juan Gallego and another who was among the lightest and most agile of the men, made an effort to go down at the least difficult place and "so continued till those who were above could not see them any more. They returned about four o'clock in the afternoon on account of the great difficulties, because what seemed to be easy from above was not so."[3]

The whole army marched on to winter in the valley of the Rio Grande, in the country of the Tiguex tribe. On the way, they passed Chichilticale, "where the wilderness begins," recalled Coronado.[4] This town was expected to be one of the magic cities of Cibola but it turned out to be "full of tumbledown houses of red earth" without roofs.

In the spring of 1541, the army of Coronado set out for the city of Cibola, as they supposed it to be. When they arrived, Melchor Díaz would remain in charge while Juan Gallego would return to Mexico-Tenochtitlan with a report for the Viceroy. Fray Marcos de Niza and Tristán de Arellano would remain in the town of Señora with the weakest men, while Melchor Díaz took twenty-five strong and competent soldiers into country that turned out to be very cold indeed. There were said to be giants there, also, one hundred of whom, young and old, slept in one large cabin, each carrying a firebrand as he moved about. They found a message from Hernando de Alarcón buried near a tree fifty miles up the Colorado River, which for a time they called the Tison (firebrand). At Chichilticale, they also saw Rocky Mountain sheep and prickly pears, then they were caught in a tornado that turned to snow, and finally they reached the presumed magic city, their destination, Cibola of their dreams.

Coronado sent into the place a small troop headed by Pedro de Tovar, with Fray Juan de Padilla. The natives offered them presents of copper, cloth, dressed skins, pine nuts, and turquoise mosaics, "but not many." The place seemed to be governed by an assembly of the oldest men. The Spaniards found the place poor and small, for it was no more than "a crowded village of small houses, one piled on top of the other without courtyards," which looked as if they had been scrambled together. "Such were the curses that some hurled at Fray Marcos de Niza that I pray that God will protect him from them,"[5] Fray Juan de Padilla added, "To tell the truth, I do not know why we have come here." It is true that there was some food, which the Spaniards seized; and there were about two hundred native soldiers, who did nothing.

The expedition, sadly disillusioned, continued with other adventures. They reached a town on the river Sonora, which Cabeza de Vaca, passing that way, had called Corazones because the Indians there had offered him the hearts of animals. Rodrigo Maldonado went to look for Hernando de Alarcón's ships but found only the very tall Indians ("giants") of whom mention has been made. Hernando de Alvarado, accompanied by Fray Juan de Padilla, made a special journey to see the bison of Cicuye, of which he had been told. He took twenty companions via Acoma (Acuco), a large village on a rock, where he was offered corn, pine nuts, deerskin, bread made from maize, and cocks.[6] They went on with a chief, whom they nick-named Bigotes (Mustaches), to Tiguex where they were at least welcomed by flutes and drums. An Indian slave whom they nicknamed the Turk, for the simple reason that he looked like one, told Alvarado and Padilla that his country, which lay ahead, was full of gold and silver, so that "they need not look at cows." When they returned to Coronado to tell him this good news, the Turk went on to say that, in addition, in his country, there were rivers with fish as big as horses, canoes with twenty rowers and with sails, and, on the hillsides, golden eagles. Everyone ate off gold plate and the chief lived under a tree with golden bells.

Coronado found this story promising, and they set off for the Turk's country. What can explain such fancies? On the way, they were rejoined by Tristán de Arellano, who had demanded of a local cacique three hundred pieces of cloth, which "he needed" because of the cold. The cacique said that that was impossible because the demand would have to be discussed by each town of the region. In the end, the people seem to have taken off their own cloaks to provide the right quantity of cloths.

The army reunited. Gloom rather than enthusiasm characterized the conquistadors. In one village, a Spaniard was accused of having violated an Indian's wife. That village and others nearby then closed themselves in behind palisades; Spanish horses chased Indians as in a bull-run, and were shot at with arrows. Coronado ordered García López de Cárdenas to surround the village where the violation had occurred. Coronado, Zaldívar, and others seized the upper section of the place. López de Cárdenas did not seem to realize that they had done so, and killed two hundred Indians whom he had made prisoners. There followed a siege of Tiguex for fifty days, with many Indian deaths and some Spanish ones. Here the good faith of the Turk was seriously criticized, for a Spaniard named Cervantes swore that he had seen the Turk talking to the devil, who had appeared in a pitcher of water. The Turk asked Cervantes how many Spaniards had been killed at Tiguex. "None" was the answer. "You lie," said the Turk, "five Christians have been killed at Tiguex." That was the truth, but how could he have known it if he had not been in touch with the devil?

The next adventures of the expedition of Coronado were varied and interesting. They became experts on the way to capture bison; they were impressed by the way that they could be easily herded and by their vast numbers. They also noticed how the women painted their chins as well as their eyes. They suffered from hail, which destroyed tents, battered helmets, broke china plates and cups, and terrified horses. Some Spaniards were lost when they went out hunting on their own. Then they reached Quivira, the Turk's town of Wichita Indians. There the Turk had to admit that he had been lying all the time: There was no gold nor silver to be found, nor, it seemed, had such metals ever been heard of. Coronado sent out captains in numerous directions but "found only roses, muscat grapes, parsley and marjoram." The Turk was promptly garroted, a victim of the conquistadors' credulity as well as of his own fantasies.

But the Spaniards did, in the end, find a territory in what is now New Mexico, where there was treasure in the shape of beautiful glazed earthenware with many figures in different shapes, as well as bowls of shining metals, which looked like silver from a distance.

Coronado now began his return journey and passed the winter at Tiguex, where Pedro de Tovar joined them with letters from Mendoza. They whiled away the time with games. Coronado had a race with Rodrigo Maldonado, but he was thrown so badly by his horse that for a time his recovery seemed improbable. With the men weary of the unpromising search for the magic towns, the return to Mexico began with a minor rebellion deriving from a protest headed by Pedro de Ávila. Fray Juan de Padilla stayed on at the Turk's town of Quivira, and Luis de Escalona did the same at Cicuye. The former was martyred within months, and we must assume that the latter was also soon killed. By June 1542, Coronado and his men had reached Culiacán and went on as fast as they could to Mexico, where the commander, "very sad and very weary, completely worn out and very shamefaced, went to kiss the hand of the Viceroy."[7] Coronado traveled on a litter and reached the capital of New Spain with barely a hundred men, for the rest had deserted.[8] Juan Suárez de Peralta, nephew by marriage of Cortés, recalled seeing the return of the expedition, with the Viceroy receiving his old friend in great sadness.[9]

Yet Coronado had two achievements to his credit: He had learned much of the size of the continent, and he had laid to rest the tales that there were wonderful rich new Perus and Mexicos to the north of New Spain. He later returned to his governorship of New Galicia, but he was soon dismissed because of poor management. A *residencia* later conducted against him by the judge Tejada talked not only of serious abuse of funds but of mistreatment of Indians on a large scale. Coronado pleaded extenuating circumstances; he was arrested but allowed to go free till his appeal was heard by the Council of the Indies. He knew as well as Viceroy Mendoza that it would be a long time before the matter was resolved.

42

Montejo and Alvarado in Yucatán and Guatemala

The ominous thing is not the present war but the era of wars upon which we have entered . . . how much, how very much, that men of culture loved, will they have to cast overboard as a spiritual luxury?

JACOB BURCKHARDT, *Reflections on History*

After the conclusion of Francisco de Montejo's unsuccessful attempts at the conquest of Yucatán, in the early 1530s, for several years the rule of authority remained confused. Montejo continued as titular governor and maintained an interest in the territory, but he spent most of his time in the city of Mexico seeking new support in men and money for his far-reaching ambitions. In 1535, he was named governor of Honduras. Montejo's wish was to exchange that remote territory for Chiapas, then ruled by Pedro de Alvarado as part of his Guatemala. That would enable Montejo geographically to consolidate his interests better. Alvarado, impetuous in politics as in battle, agreed instantly. He had just returned from his humiliation in Peru. The viceroy Mendoza also agreed.

Alvarado immediately went to this, for him, new territory of Honduras. He founded one new town, San Pedro de Puerto Caballos (now San Pedro Sula), a little south of the Gulf of Honduras. He overwhelmed the natives in Zompa. He sent Juan de Chávez to found a city at the remote but remarkable Cape Gracias a Dios, on the extreme east of the peninsula of Honduras. He was not, however, a good peacetime governor, for he permitted every kind of brutality against the Indians. After this, he returned to

Spain in August 1536 to tell of his achievements in New Spain, as Cortés had done earlier. He traveled via the Azores and Lisbon, then made straight for the court. There he seems to have convinced the emperor Charles that it would be good to arrange to send a fleet to sail regularly across the Pacific to the Spice Islands from, say, Acapulco. Álvaro de Paz, a relation of Cortés, said that Alvarado deliberately sought new contracts "for the discovery of the west, for China and for the Spice Islands!"[1] Perhaps he was in fact thinking of an invasion of China. A friend of Alvarado's, Álvaro de Loarca, later recalled that he had said that he would set off for China in consequence of a definite contract he had arranged with the Crown.[2] This may have been a wild embroidery of the truth, but Alvarado was capable of anything.

Alvarado returned to the Indies from Spain in January 1539 with three ships, the *Santa Catalina,* the *Trinidad,* and the *Santa María de Guadalupe.* On board, he had not only a new wife (Beatriz de la Cueva, a sister of his dead first wife, Francisca) but also Andrés de Urdaneta, who had accompanied Loaisa on his abortive journey around the world. Urdaneta was to assist Alvarado in building a Pacific fleet in Guatemala. They stopped at Santo Domingo and reached Puerto Caballos in Honduras in April. For a time, then, Alvarado continued as governor of Honduras-Higueras with Guatemala, though it was known that he was thinking of the Pacific Ocean and of China. But he was distracted and went up to assist the Viceroy in his fatal battle against the Chichimeca in Jalisco, with the disastrous consequences that have been noticed in chapter 40.[3]

Alvarado left Guatemala to his new wife, Beatriz, and for a while, she acted as the first woman governor in Spanish America. It is astonishing that, given the concern in the twenty-first century with women in politics, she is not remembered better. She lasted as governor for a year, till 1542, when she was killed in a flood-earthquake in Santiago, Guatemala, with her daughter Ana.

Guatemala enjoyed a certain continuity of Spanish rule after Alvarado's death. But that was not the case in Honduras-Higueras. There, early in 1542, the town halls wrote to Montejo asking him to take over the governorship, since there was chaos in the territory. The disputes between the town halls had been rendered worse by the nomination of the supreme court in Mexico of one of its judges, Alonso de Maldonado of Salamanca, as acting governor of Honduras as well as of Guatemala. Later, in 1544, he would become President of a new short-lived supreme court, that of *Los Confines* (the Frontiers), a tribunal later briefly established at Gracias a Dios. Maldonado had married the daughter of Montejo, a fellow citizen of Salamanca, and therefore it was not hard to see where his loyalties would lie. He was a man of many interests since, in addition to being a judge, he loved racing and would hold horse races in his garden in Mexico. Maldonado in 1546 would write to the King that it would be for the well-being of the state if Bartolomé de las Casas were assigned to a monastery in Spain rather than a bishopric in the Indies.[4]

In these years, Montejo seems to have dreamed of a large territory at his disposition. This would extend from Yucatán as far as Tabasco, near Villahermosa, in the north, to the Bay of Fonseca in the South, on the Pacific. He hoped that Honduras would become the commercial center of the whole region. Guatemala would presumably adhere in due course. But still, Yucatán itself remained unconquered. Montejo commissioned his son El Mozo to complete this process.

Much had occurred to alter the balance of forces in Yucatán. For example, in 1535 or 1536, five Franciscans went there, headed by the interesting figure of Fray Jacobo de Testera, a well-connected churchman, who was a brother of the chamberlain to the King of France. Testera went to the Indies in 1529; he was custodian of the Franciscan mission by 1533; he visited Francisco Montejo, "el Mozo," in Campeche and, after returning briefly to Castile, sent an enlarged mission to Yucatán, headed by the famous Motolinía, to carry out proselytization there and in nearby Kingdoms. Among Motolinía's twelve followers were four who later made their mark there: Fray Juan de Herrera, Fray Melchor de Benavente, Fray Lorenzo de Bienvenida, and Fray Luis de Villalpando.

Testera himself was powerful because of the strength of his personality more than for his learning. Yet though he knew no Indian language, he preached with Indian pictures (hieroglyphs) and was very effective.[5]

At the same time, the Franciscan Motolinía secured permission from Montejo, then in Gracias a Dios, to let Lorenzo de Bienvenida enter Yucatán by a southern route on foot via the Golfo Dulce in the Pacific. But in the end, Villalpando, Benavente, and Herrera went to Yucatán via Chiapas and Palenque. Four other Franciscans arrived in Yucatán direct from Spain.

Villalpando, meantime, learned Maya and remained in the west of the territory carrying through the conversion of what he claimed were twenty-eight thousand Indians. He also prepared a Maya dictionary and grammar.

In Champoton, on the coast of the Gulf of Mexico, Montejo el Mozo, now a relatively mature conqueror and administrator, received these Franciscans with attention, welcoming them to his house so that the Indians would also respect and worship the Christian deities.[6] El Mozo had a church built for the Franciscans in Champoton and told the natives that the friars had arrived to instruct them in the true faith and lead them to a better life.

This was in keeping with the firm instructions of his high-minded father: "You must strive to see that the people who go with you shall live and act as true Christians, keeping them from evil and public sins, and not allowing them to blaspheme God nor His Blessed Mother nor his saints."[7]

In 1540, Montejo el Mozo was gathering a new army together. Unlike those who had accompanied his father ten years and more before, the new men seemed chastened individuals, knowing that Yucatán, unlike Peru, could boast embroidered cloths though not gold, but that there were honey, wax, indigo, cacao, and slaves—all good exports.[8]

El Mozo returned from his army-raising to Champoton and there met a cousin, Francisco de Montejo, "el Sobrino" (the nephew). They both went up to Campeche, which they reestablished as a Spanish town under the name of San Francisco. They had been reinforced by 250 to 300 well-equipped soldiers and many, perhaps one thousand, Indian auxiliaries. The latter included some Mexicans from Montejo senior's rich *encomienda* near Mexico-Tenochtitlan at Atzcapotzalco.

El Mozo's plan for the conquest of Yucatán was a slow process of penetration by the manipulation of a series of pueblos founded by the Spaniards on Indian bases. Each of these would be self-supporting, with a well-ordered system of supply. Every column that attacked in Yucatán would have a system of communication to avoid isolation. The subjugation of any district beyond existing penetration would not occur till sufficient forces had been gathered. Each town would have the citizens needed to ensure its permanent success. The surrounding district would be brought under control before the town was properly settled.

This "admirably conceived system" was described by the learned North

American historian R. S. Chamberlain as "Roman" in its efficiency. *El Mozo,* as well as his father, the *adelantado,* worked on the strategy. The columns were instructed to advance in three sections: Mounted troops would advance in the center, with on either side well-armed foot soldiers. In pitched battles, the impact was as decisive as ever, for the Maya were never to find any real defense against the horse. The *Relación de Mérida,* a full account of the conquest published later, repeats the old story that "at the beginning, they thought that the man and mount were all one animal."[9] Firearms, swords, daggers, lances, and crossbows ensured the Spaniards their usual superiority. Though they often stood their ground very well, the Maya also never overcame their fear of artillery.[10]

The expedition left Campeche in the autumn of 1541, and a captain was sent to the Indian town of Tihó, which would soon become the city of Mérida. There they founded a new and permanent settlement, the chief receiving them well. They naturally found the remains of the old fortifications, which had been thrown up during the previous Spanish occupation of the 1520s. But those apart, Tihó was a typical Indian town. Though the chief welcomed them, the Indians, reported one of the conquistadors, had "haughtiness and stubbornness in their souls."[11]

The disputes among the Maya themselves had, admittedly, continued unabated in the years between, with the Cocom of Sotuta in what seemed like permanent war with the lords of Maní. The former had also killed many important leaders of the Xiu people. The inhabitants of the peninsula had wasted much of their maize during their endless wars with the Spaniards, and such a famine fell on them that it seems that they were reduced to eating the bark of trees, especially the tender *kumche.* The Xiu offered sacrifices to their gods to escape the persecution visited on them, by throwing slaves into the cenote, the large deep natural well of Chichén Itzá.

All the same, there were some resolute enemies of the Spaniards, such as H-Kin-Chuy, a priest from Pebá, a small pueblo near Tihó, who preached a war of extermination against them—so much so that the Spaniards were told at one stage that "more Indians than a pelt of a deer has hairs" were threatening them.

Still, on January 6, 1542, Mérida was finally founded in the north of Yucatán. The name was chosen because "on its site they found buildings of worked lime and stone and with many mouldings," which, as Extremeños recalled, was the case in the Roman city of Mérida in Spain. Seventy soldiers were named residents, and soon there was a town council. A geometrician, a friend of Alonso de Bravo (who had laid out Mexico-Tenochtitlan after 1521), was asked to design a new town. A Franciscan, Fray Francisco Hernández, was requested to plan the church.

There was an immediate Mayan attack. The seventeenth-century historian Fray Diego de Cogulludo thought that as many as sixty thousand Maya fell on the Spaniards, and "only sword-thrusts could defeat our enemies." The natives who survived, however, fled away and never again offered an open pitched battle.[12]

El Mozo sent out little bands of Spanish horsemen in all directions to carry the war into outlying districts, while the Indians sought to destroy everything that might be useful to the Spaniards. But the battle of Mérida had broken the Mayan resistance. El Mozo occupied Techoh and Dzilam. The local chieftains were now under control.[13]

El Mozo and his cousin next made plans for the general area of Conil in the northeast. They also planned to move against Chikinchel and Ecale, two other regions also on the far northeast of the peninsula. They hoped that Conil would become a center of commerce. Independently, El Mozo moved against interior chieftains such as Sotuta, to whom he read the *Requerimiento*, without, however, much success. He also defeated the proud Nachi Cocom, who was obliged to accept the formal overlordship of the Spaniards. El Mozo allowed him to retain his usual authority, but as a vassal now of the King of Spain (though, as with other natives, whether he really understood the concept must be extraordinarily doubtful).[14]

Meantime, El Mozo dispatched his uncle, Alonso López, to Calotmul and the southeast of Yucatán. Here he encountered more Xiu, who had not followed their kinsmen of Maní into an alliance with Spain. He managed to control Calotmul, though without glory. Then in 1543, El Mozo led a well-equipped expedition into Cochuah, in the east, with a long seacoast. Montejo el Sobrino was more concerned with the northeast, where he established Valladolid in 1543 with a forceful leader named Bernaldino de Villagómez as chief magistrate: He had been El Sobrino's field commander, and he was the younger brother of Jorge de Villagómez, who had been Cortés's chief magistrate in Xochimilco and then in Tlaxcala, where Bernaldino had befriended the son of the old ruler Maxixcastin; he had even accompanied him to Spain with Cortés in 1528. Thus Villagómez was part of the new aristocracy of New Spain. Once more, forty or fifty soldiers were named residents of the new town. This was a successful settlement because, so a *relación* put it, it was healthier and drier than Chuaca: "It is the best town there is in the Indies . . . [It] is surrounded by a large and rough, stony, region covered with bushes . . . There are two wells of fresh water . . . Captain Montejo laid out this town north, east and east–west and gave it broad streets . . ."[15]

The caciques of Saci concerted a new attack on behalf of many towns whose efforts they organized, but Saci itself was seized for El Sobrino by Francisco de Cieza with only twenty Spaniards. An incipient revolt at Mérida was forestalled by Rodrigo Álvarez. El Sobrino then continued through Ecab, where Cortés had first met the Maya in conflict, and then to Cozumel, an island to which he crossed with no opposition. Only a storm gave him reason to complain.

Montejo el Mozo, with his father's agreement, then gave the command in the southeast, Chetumal, first to Jorge de Villagómez, then to Gaspar Pacheco, his son Melchor, and his nephew Alonso. The latter two conquistadors reached Chetumal early in 1544. The Indians resisted, and one of the cruelest campaigns against them began. Gaspar Pacheco and Melchor were successful in reestablishing Spanish control, but they resorted to many acts of savagery. The Montejos were unable to restrain them. The Franciscan Fray Bienvenida denounced the Pachecos: "Nero was not more cruel than this man [Alonso Pacheco]," he reported. "Even though the natives did not make war, Pacheco robbed the province and consumed the food of the indigenous people who fled into the bush in fear . . . since, as soon as this captain captures any of them, he sets the dogs on them. And the Indians fled from all this and did not sow their crops, so that they all died of hunger . . . There were once *pueblos* of 500 and 1,000 houses here, but now one of 100 is considered large. This captain," went on Fray Bienvenida, "with his own hands killed many with the garrotte, saying 'This is a good rod with which to finish these people' and, after he had killed them, he might say 'Oh, how well I finished them off.'"

Contrasting this were acts of education, which must seem now more significant. For example, in the mid-1540s, two thousand Indian boys in the Franciscan school in Mérida were already being taught to read and write Maya in European script. They also learned what Christianity was and how to sing in choirs. A Franciscan house was set up at Oxkutzcab in Maní, the land of the Xiu, the Spanish allies. There was a school attached to it by 1547.

The Spanish military success—as the foremost modern historian of these events, Inga Clendinnen, has explained—was primarily due to "their superb discipline under pressure." They understood the meaning of a light formation, they were aware of the value of every life, but they had the capacity to move through territory with no scruple about the cost of their actions. The crossbows, the muskets, and the mastiffs all counted. Horses enjoyed their usual success when the terrain suited. Nor should one forget the sword of Toledo steel.

The Maya were nevertheless often strong and brave. They were innovative, too. They devised pits to trip up horses. But their traditions were against them in a war with Europeans. For, like the Mexica, they saw the purpose of battle as the taking of prisoners and the seizing of booty. The Spaniards were difficult to deal with partly because they brought new diseases as well as new weapons, and the diseases led to destruction of populations. For example, the town of Champoton, where Cortés had fought and Hernández de Córdoba had been defeated, declined from eight thousand in 1517 to two thousand in 1550. Perhaps the population of Yucatán declined from three hundred thousand in 1517 to two hundred fifty thousand by 1550.

There were four Spanish towns in Yucatán in the late 1540s, the biggest being Mérida, with seventy families. There were forty-five families in Valladolid and forty in Campeche, while Salamanca de Bacalar had twenty. Thus there were then two hundred Spanish families in all Yucatán. They lived in houses with courtyards, Spanish in design, certainly, but with "an ineradicable Indian flavour,"[16] for now the Spaniards on land often slept in hammocks to keep cool and, like the Indians—*their* Indians included—would wake to the sound of women grinding maize on stone slabs. Only the most humble Spaniards would marry Indian women; the others would have Indian mistresses till their real wives, old or new, came from Spain.[17]

Now that the Spaniards seemed well established in Yucatán and the surrounding territories, the work of conversion to Christianity could proceed apace. A great role was played by Bartolomé de las Casas, who was appointed bishop of Chiapas at the end of March 1544. Chiapas at that time comprised Coatzacoalcos, Tabasco, Champoton, and Cozumel, as well as Soconusco, Verapaz, and Chiapas itself. It was thus a large diocese.

Las Casas had traveled from Spain via Santo Domingo.[18] We hear of his arrival in Campeche from the visitor Tello de Sandoval.[19] The captain of the ship on which this great friend of the Indians sailed from Sanlúcar refused to take him any farther than La Española unless he received more payment. But Fray Francisco Hernández, chaplain to El Mozo, gave him money to enable him to go on to Tabasco and then to Ciudad Real de Chiapas. Las Casas was well received in Mérida, however, and stayed with El Mozo, despite being threatened with death by a disgruntled conquistador from Ciudad Real in Castile: Las Casas in those years made no bones about saying that the Mexica and the Incas were as intelligent as the Greeks and the Romans. In 1544, he argued that the discovery of America was a providential decision to provide American Indians with the means of salvation. From the moment that he arrived in Yucatán, he set about preaching the faith without any consideration of the need for conquest. He infuriated the colonists by his decisions in favor of the Indians—his pastoral letter of March 20 had been a striking innovation along those lines. He even refused to confess Spaniards unless they said that they were willing to hand back land taken from Indians. He would advocate the complete enforcement of the New Laws of 1542 for the protection of Indians and continued to admonish the colonists in unmeasured terms. The colonists of Yucatán refused to recognize Las Casas's spiritual jurisdiction over their peninsula and tried to cut him off from food. They also refused to pay tithes. Las Casas was thus encountering the greatest difficulty in the most important part of his diocese.[20]

Then disaster struck. In November 1546, a great Mayan revolt erupted. It had been carefully coordinated by the caciques of the Cupul (the heart and soul of the revolt) the Cochau, Solita, and Vayonil-Chetumal Indians. All these peoples had formally accepted Spanish masters, but only after much protest, and all longed for the day of revenge. The Mayan priests especially dreamed of that. They found the *encomienda* system, with its obligations of the Indians to work a certain number of years for the conquistadors, unacceptable.

At full moon, on November 8, 1546, the Maya of Yucatán rose with violent fury. The greatest attack was against the Spaniards in the new city of Valladolid. There, conquistadors, their wives, and their children were slaughtered, some being crucified, some being roasted over copal, some being shot to death by arrows as if they had been Saint Sebastian, some having their hearts torn out as in a Mexican sacrifice. Bernaldino de Villagómez, the chief magistrate of the town, was dragged by a rope through the streets over which he had so recently presided, and then his head, legs, and arms were cut off. Those vital members were carried throughout the peninsula by swift Indian couriers in order to excite their friends to greater fury. They killed not only the Spaniards but all who had worked for them, as well as those Indians who would not join the rebellion. They slaughtered animals owned by Spaniards—horses, cattle, chickens, dogs, and cats. They uprooted European plants and trees.

Some *encomenderos* were found on their properties. The rebels seized them and killed many, along with their families. They smoked some to death as if they had been dried meat.

The Spaniards came together as best they could. Thus even in Valladolid a few organized resistance under Alonso de Villanueva, while the council of Mérida raised as many as they could to go to help Valladolid under the leadership of Rodrigo Álvarez, the reliable secretary of Montejo el Mozo. Francisco Tamayo Pacheco took forty men and five hundred loyal Indians from there to Valladolid and relieved the garrison. Francisco de Bracamonte moved against the Indian chief Sotuta, but waited at Cheguan for reinforcements. El Sobrino also set off for Valladolid, where Tamayo Pacheco was now the commander. He sought to break the siege and eventually did so, while Juana de Azamar, wife of Blas González, acted as the nurse of the garrison, after her brother and all his family had been killed on their *encomienda*: "I being of but slight age was with my husband, living in our home which we refused to abandon. I gathered into our house many wounded and ill soldiers and, with great care, I healed them and cared for them till they were cured . . . for there were then no doctors in this town. I likewise encouraged them not to leave this land but to remain for the service of His Majesty."[21]

The three Montejos, El Padre, El Mozo, and El Sobrino, met in Champoton to discuss how to crush the rebellion. El Mozo assumed general responsibility for a broad military answer, while El Sobrino would be concerned with reconquering the district of Cupul, the heart of the revolt. He and Tamayo Pacheco stormed the religious center of Pixtemax, whose fall was to prove decisive for the eventual Spanish recovery. El Sobrino then turned against the province of Cochant with a relatively large force, which brought it under Spanish control. Juan de Aguilar was sent to relieve the Spaniards in Salamanca de Bacalar: He was told, "If it should prove that the natives greet you in peace, receive and protect them in accordance with how His Majesty commands."[22] Aguilar relieved Salamanca de Bacalar, the settlers there naming him their military captain, and he and they then moved against the island fortress of Chamlacan. Aguilar persuaded the chief there to surrender and to accept Spanish authority.

By March 1547, after a winter of fighting, the revolt had been quelled. Hundreds of Indians had been burned at the stake; the caciques and priests believed most responsible had all been captured and executed, among them Chilam Anbal, a priest who had claimed that he was the son of God. Only Chikinchel remained to be conquered, and Francisco Montejo the senior sent Tamayo Pacheco—who had proved such a successful commander—to bring that province to obedience.

The campaign to suppress the revolt was carried out more brutally than previous ones mounted by the Montejos. Even the usually just Montejo el Sobrino committed acts of cruelty, for he used dogs and killed some Indian women. But after the end of the crises, the elder Francisco Montejo took legal action against some intemperate captains.[23] After the revolt, El Sobrino summoned the surviving chiefs and addressed them, first assuring them that he would rule with justice and for the benefit of the whole province and, second, asking them why they had risen in rebellion. They replied, no doubt accurately, that it had been the responsibility of their priests.[24]

The Montejos then mounted a serious campaign to capture anew the loyalty, "the hearts and minds," of the Indians. They invited the chiefs to their houses and sought in a hundred ways to gain their goodwill. Fray Villalpando preached in Maya about the essentials of Christianity and invited these lords to send their sons to Christian schools. This educational revolution was among the most noble and successful of Franciscan enterprises—and one that had no obvious precedent in the Old World. That initiative seems to have been successful. Some important chiefs became

Christians. Villalpando and Benavente thereafter went to Maní, where in the monastery they established another similar school.

These moves at last helped to secure the political tranquillity of Yucatán. There were still difficulties to be resolved in the Golfo Dulce, where the different competences of the Montejos, the supreme court of "the Frontiers," and the Franciscans seemed certain to lead to conflict. But though there were many complexities, they were resolved eventually in 1550.

Montejo senior has received high praise for what he did in Yucatán. Professor R. S. Chamberlain, the best student of the conquest of the last generation, wrote: "He was a great conquistador and had all the qualities of a good administrator. He could fight implacably but he could negotiate. He could be both magnanimous and stern. He was far from ruthless. He always sought good relations with the Indians."[25] In addition, he introduced sugarcane into Yucatán.

His daughter-in-law Andrea del Castillo, the wife of El Mozo, is remembered for her comment: "No less of a *conquistadora* can I say that I am; and, many times, the principal women of my quality when they find themselves in such conquests are as good fighters as men are."[26]

Book IV

❦❦❦

THE INDIAN SOUL

43

Las Casas, Pope Paul, and the Indian Soul

> I have the hope that the Emperor and King of Spain our lord and master Don Charles V of the name who began to understand the cruelties and treasons which have been committed against these poor people . . . will extirpate the ills and give them a remedy in this new land which God has given him.
>
> BARTOLOMÉ DE LAS CASAS, *The Destruction of the Indies*, 1539

The Trans-Isthmian Highway had by now become the vital link in transport between Peru and Spain, the goal of pirates, but it remained for a long time nothing but a primitive mule path maintained by fifty black slaves. To build and maintain forty miles of road over mountains covered with tropical forest, through swamps and jungles, in one of the most deadly of climates imposed a big demand on a new community. The inhabitants of Panama suggested that goods might be best carried five leagues to the upper reaches of the river Chagres and then floated down to the Caribbean, eighteen leagues (fifty miles) from Venta Cruz to the river's mouth. These inhabitants urged that the settlement of Nombre de Dios be moved west toward the mouth of the river. But even the river Chagres was only explored for the first time in 1527.

In 1534, a new governor, the persistent Francisco Barrionuevo, ordered a warehouse to be built where the river joined the sea. A third of the cost would be borne by the King, the rest by a tax on local merchandise. Efforts were also made to improve the overland route, at least in summer, and much hope was placed in the efforts of Bernardino Gozna and Diego de Enciso, who were to be allowed an unlimited export of wool from Peru to Spain provided that they contributed to the maintenance of the Trans-Isthmian Highway. When the level of the river Chagres was high, the transit could be accomplished in three or four days, but at other times, eight to twelve days were needed. To transfer goods from the mouth of the river to Nombre de Dios was only a matter of eight to ten hours.

The so-called Tierra Firme fleet carried cargoes to Nombre de Dios even if that port, a little to the east of what is now Colón, was never more than makeshift. The bay was shallow, full of reefs, and open to the sea; the town of Nombre de Dios was not walled. There were 150 wooden houses. There was a sandy beach before it, the jungle lay behind, fever raged. Between the comings and departures of fleets, the population was reduced to about fifty households. The east side provided the best natural harbor on the Caribbean side of the isthmus, but it was just as unhealthy. The removal of the port from Nombre de Dios took ten years because of the need to reroute the road from Venta Cruz.

The river San Juan was mapped in 1521 by Alonso Calero, but its direction was west to east, so it linked Lake Nicaragua to the Atlantic but not the Pacific. Alonso de Saavedra proposed an enlightened scheme for a canal, it seems, but the project was left aside for the attention of a future generation.

Panama in the west had most of its three to four hundred buildings still built of wood, even the churches. Most of the five hundred inhabitants were of Andalusian origin and were merchants or transportation agents, the few exceptions being engaged in pearl fisheries or ranching or agriculture. The carrying of goods across the isthmus provided most of the income of the city. Some merchants maintained stables of pack animals for use on the highway to Cruces and Nombre de Dios; others had large flatboats on the river Chagres, directed by slaves. There were probably four hundred blacks. The cathedral of 1521 had but one canon, even if there was a supreme court in the town.

There were in 1521 three convents, but together they had only eighteen inmates. Prices were high. By 1607, there were five convents and a hospital, with forty-five monks and twenty-four nuns. There were still no more than 372 dwellings, of which only eight were of stone (these were the town hall and the council chamber and six private dwellings). In 1607, there were 550 European households (of which fifty-three were not Spanish, being mostly

Portuguese or Italian), together with a hundred thatched huts occupied by about 3,700 black slaves, of whom one thousand were concerned in transport. There were sixty-three colonists of Creole birth.

But fleets by then came only every two or three years. Brokerage licenses sold in 1580 for 6,550 pesos were worth only 4,200 pesos in 1607. The town crier, who in 1575 was hired for 2,200 pesos, only received 150 pesos in 1607. The rents of the main meat market had fallen from 700 to 200 pesos a year. There were only 250 or so foot and eighteen horses available for the militia. The harbor in Panama was shallow and exposed, the tides being so great that all larger ships resorted to nearby Perico, two leagues to the west, which was partly enclosed. In 1575, sixty-ton vessels could approach at high tide, but in 1607, even small boats had difficulties.

Such was the frame against which the high dramas of Las Casas's middle career were played out.

Bartolomé de las Casas, we should remember, went into the Dominican convent in Santo Domingo after his disappointments in South America in early 1523. He had become a Dominican in 1522. He then spent nine years in meditation and preparation for the next stage in his extraordinary life. He also began his *History of the Indies,* which remains among the finest, as well as the most personal, of sources for events in the Americas between 1492 and 1525.

The convent was at Puerto Plata, on the north side of La Española. Las Casas emerged, about age fifty, from his self-imposed silence in 1531, and on January 1 of that year, he wrote a pamphlet in favor of peaceful conversion of Indians: "That is the true path, gentlemen, that is the way to convert the people in your charge. Why, instead of sending among them peaceful sheep, do you send hungry wolves?"[1] He wrote to the King along those lines a few weeks later.[2] He went as a visitor to the Dominican house in Puerto Rico and then accompanied Dr. Ramírez de Fuenleal, the new president of the supreme court of New Spain, to Mexico. But he was soon sent back to Santo Domingo, where he returned to his convent at Puerto Plata.

Sometime about then, he met Oviedo, who then lived in Santo Domingo as the official historian of the Spanish empire. Despite living most of his life in the Caribbean, Oviedo thought that the thick skulls of the inhabitants of La Española indicated a bestial and ill-intentioned mind, and he saw no chance of their being able to absorb Christianity: To think otherwise was to beat one's head against a wall.

Oviedo devoted a polite chapter to Las Casas in his own history, in which he said that he was a fine man but had been accused of some financial irregularities.[3] It seemed that Las Casas had quarreled with an old friend, Pedro de Vadilla, who had wanted to contest the will of an uncle who had left a fortune to the indigenous people. Las Casas found himself temporarily back in the cell of his convent, but then he went out to meet the Indian rebel Enriquillo and Tomás de Berlanga, then on the first stage of his journey to Guatemala as bishop. Las Casas went to the Dominican house of Granada in Guatemala. There Licenciado Francisco Marroquín, bishop of Guatemala, asked Las Casas to assist him in the peaceful conversion of Tuzuhitlan, which he did, setting a text about the splendor of Christianity to music. Las Casas then finished his pamphlet *De unico vocationis modo*, whose main thesis was that to evangelize was the only way to secure real victories over the Indians. Fray Bernardino de Minaya, who, as a deacon, had helped to found the glorious gilded Dominican convent in Oaxaca, New Spain, sent Las Casas's ideas to the newly elected Pope Paul III.

This was a time when churchmen were beginning to advocate seriously the cause of Indians.

In 1533, Julián Garcés, bishop of Tlaxcala, every year more Erasmian, made a remarkable announcement: The time had come, he said, to speak out against those "who have judged wrongly these poor people, those who pretend that they are incapable and claim that their incapacity is a sufficient reason to exclude them from the church ... That is the voice of Satan ... a voice which comes from the avaricious throats of Christians whose greed is such that, in order to slake their thirst for wealth, they insist that rational creatures made in the image of God are beasts and asses."[4] He added that the children of some Indians spoke better Latin than the children of many Spaniards. Erudite and well-read, Garcés had once been confessor to Rodríguez de Fonseca. He had founded a hospital in Perote and had always concerned himself with the sick. His personality had evolved remarkably.

Bishop Garcés wrote to the pope asking him to take up the cause of the Indians; and at the same time, Dr. Rodríguez de Fuenleal wrote letters to protest against statements that he had heard in Mexico claiming that Indians were incapable of assimilating Christian doctrine.

The first time that Bartolomé de las Casas was engaged as a Dominican in controversy as to how to treat natives was in 1533, when the judges of Santo Domingo complained to the Council of the Indies that the friar had been refusing absolution to *encomenderos*. Then, the same year, Las Casas, still in his convent of Santo Domingo, protested about two slave expeditions from Puerto Plata to the South American mainland, one dispatched by Judge Zuazo (that was financed by the royal accountant, Diego Caballero) and the other by Jacome de Castellón, one of the many Genoese-Spanish sugar merchants. The supreme court supported Las Casas. Two hundred fifty or so Indians brought back from northern South America were distributed as *naborias* (servants), and afterwards, it was understood, they would be freed.

But Las Casas or no Las Casas, these slaving expeditions continued all through the 1530s along the north coast of South America. Slaving in those days was still what brought the most profit of all commercial undertakings. With the sale of Indians, the purchasing of ships, armaments, tools, and provisions for expeditions into the interior of the continent could be financed. There were already thirty-four sugar mills in Santo Domingo, whose efficient working required labor. Black slaves were thought to work harder than Indians, something especially noticeable in the hot climate. But they were not easy to secure and, where there was a shortage of Africans, Indian slaves could serve.

By then, letters between the senior Dominican thinker Fray Francisco de Vitoria and Fray Miguel de Arcos regarding the former's concern about the treatment of natives in Peru had begun to be exchanged. Erasmus himself was not silent. In 1535, his *Ecclesiastes* pointed out that those who talked of the decay of Christianity could be reminded of the great new Christian territories in Africa and Asia. He added, "What should one say of the countries hitherto unknown, which are being discovered in the Americas every day?"[5]

Vitoria, probably born about 1480, was the decisive leader in a new Thomist revival. Vitoria entered the Dominican order in 1504 and then went to the Collège de Saint Jacques in Paris. He was there for nearly eighteen years, first as a student, then as a lecturer on Aquinas's summary of theology.[6] In 1523, he went back to Spain and was soon elected to the prime chair of theology in Salamanca, a position he held till his death in 1546. Since Vitoria published nothing, his views can be discovered only by reading his manuscript lecture notes. But he had an immense impact as a teacher. When he died, thirty of his students held professorships in Spain.

In 1535, Las Casas was heard complaining about what he had heard of "the Germans'" actions in Venezuela: "This is not the path, my lord"—he was writing to someone at court in Spain—"which Christ followed. This is . . . rather a Muslim practice, indeed worse than what Muhammad did."[7] His comments perhaps reflected the attitude of the clever, benign, and beautiful Empress-Regent Isabel. After hearing that many Indians from the region of Coro, Venezuela, were being kidnapped and sold in Santo Domingo, she ordered them to be returned. However, the German controllers of the "colony" of Venezuela did nothing to put the royal order into effect. These complaints had to be judged against the impression made by the publication in 1535 of Oviedo's history, much of which gave a negative picture of the Indians' capacity.

At this moment, Pope Paul III, Alessandro Farnese, took an important stand. He was obstinate but shrewd. He was surrounded by his family and was ambitious for them. His lovely sister, Giulia, was the chief cause of his rise at the court of Alexander VI, for "it is certain that Alexander VI had given the dignity of cardinal not to him but to his sister."[8] Paul III enjoyed the life of a Renaissance prelate, and his papacy was a time of remarkable tranquillity. Titian's painting of him shows him with two grandsons, of whom one, Ottavio, duke of Camerino, married Margaret, an illegitimate daughter of Charles V by a Dutch girl; the other became another Cardinal Alessandro Farnese.

When elected pope, Alessandro Farnese was then the oldest cardinal. Guiccardini says that "he was a man gifted with learning and, to all appearance, good morals, who had exercised his office as cardinal with greater skill than that whereby he had acquired it." He completed the Palazzo Farnese in Rome, "with the cornice of all cornices," with the help of Antonio da Sangallo. Pasquino the pamphleteer put up a notice in the Vatican: "Alms are requested for this building." He also built a palace for the popes in the garden of the friary of the Franciscans facing the Corso, now, alas, replaced by the monument to King Victor Emmanuel. His first action had been to offer Erasmus a cardinal's hat, which he declined.[9]

The pope was influenced by correspondents in the New World, by Fray Minaya but also by the bishop of Tlaxcala, Julián Garcés.

Influenced by these intelligent and humane men, Pope Paul recalled, in his bull *Sublimis Deus* of 1537, that Christ had said, "Go ye and teach all nations." Pope Paul continued: "He said all, without exception, for all are capable of receiving the doctrines of the faith. The said Indians, and all other peoples who may be discovered by Christians, are by no means to be deprived of their liberty or of their property, even though they may be outside the faith of Jesus Christ; and . . . they may, and should freely, and legitimately, enjoy their liberty and the possession of their property; nor should they be in any way enslaved; should the contrary happen, it shall be null and of no effect . . . the said Indians should be converted to the faith of Jesus Christ by preaching the word of God and by the example of good and holy living."[10]

This bull, despite its benevolence, infuriated the emperor Charles. He thought that it infringed his powers. But Paul's motive was benign. His subsequent bull *Altitudo divini consilii* found the Franciscans at fault when they did not administer the complete ceremony of baptism to the Indians. Henceforth, the pope declared, they should not omit the smallest parts of the ceremony except the rites of salt, the ephphatha,[11] the wearing of white robes, and the candles. For it was good that the Indians should be impressed by the grandeur of the ceremony.[12]

Pope Paul's interests in these matters, whatever his motives were, helped to dictate events.

In early 1540, Cardinal García de Loaisa, the long-serving president of the Council of the Indies, held a meeting in Valladolid to discuss seriously how to treat Indians. He had with him Dr. Ramírez de Fuenleal, who, as we know, had been a successful and noble president of the *audiencias* in both Santo Domingo and Mexico. He was now bishop of Tuy, a pretty city in Galicia on the riverine frontier with Portugal—about as far as anyone could be from anything to do with the Indies. Also attending were the commander Juan de Zúñiga, younger brother of the Count of Miranda, Prince Philip's *mayordomo,* and a great friend of the emperor Charles, whom he served well;[13] the Count of Osorno (García Fernández Manrique), who had been acting president of the Council of the Indies for much of the 1530s; Licenciado Gutierre Velázquez, a kinsman of the first governor of Cuba, Diego Velázquez, and related, too, to the great chronicler Bernal Díaz; Cobos; and the eternal and corrupt bureaucrat Dr. Bernal.[14] By then,

Fray Bartolomé de las Casas was again in Spain, and he sent a memorial to García de Loaisa about how to bring to an end the "vexation of the Indians," proposing the end of all *encomiendas*.

The discussion, led by García de Loaisa, lasted off and on almost two years. It began with six interesting questions put by the President, who, it will be remembered, was for many years confessor to the King: How should those who had treated Indians badly be punished? How could Indians best be instructed in Christianity? How could it be guaranteed that Indians would be well treated? Was it necessary for a Christian to take into account the welfare of slaves? What should be done to ensure that governors and other officials carried out the government's orders to be just? And how could the administration of justice be properly organized?

At that time, there were many royal orders in Spain designed to assist or, where necessary, complete plans for peaceful conversion. For example, the Franciscans had been asked to provide Las Casas with the names of Indians who had musical talent.

An equally important development was the extraordinary experiment associated with the new Franciscan house at Tlatelolco, the town that had been Tenochtitlan's immediate neighbor on the island to the north. It had been independent till the 1470s and then had been effectively absorbed by the Mexica's capital till the conquest. There had been a good deal of fighting there in 1520–21. The dedicated and meticulous Franciscan Fray Bernardino de Sahagún presided over an attempt to educate the sons of Mexica noblemen. This was the Colegio Imperial de Santa Cruz de Santiago de Tlatelolco, founded on January 6, 1536. The other Spaniards and friars from other orders who observed the founding of this institution "laughed broadly and jeered, thinking it beyond all doubt that no one could be clever enough to teach grammar to people of such small aptitude. But after we had worked with them for two or three years, they had attained such a thorough knowledge of grammar that some understood, and not only spoke and wrote Latin, they even composed heroic verses in it . . . It was I [Sahagún] who worked with these pupils for the first four years and who introduced them to the Latin language. When the laymen and [regular] clergy were convinced that the Indians were making progress, and were capable of prospering still more, they began to raise objections and to oppose the enterprise."[15]

This school was not comparable to Pedro de Gante's institution, which was concerned with apprenticeship. It was a center of learning comparable to the Jesuit College in Goa. It was from the beginning trilingual (Spanish, Nahuatl, and Latin). It had the support of Bishop Zumárraga. The syllabus reflected the seven liberal arts, and the teachers were enlightened Franciscans. The aim was to educate the future elite of the indigenous population in both European culture and Christian theology. Another intention behind Santa Cruz was to serve as a seminary for indigenous priests. Bishop Zumárraga wrote in 1538 that he had "sixty Indian boys already able to do Latin grammar and who know more grammar than I."[16] But the indigenous priests did not, as a rule, want to become Catholic priests, because they did not wish to renounce marriage.

There were some Spaniards who were seriously perturbed by the consequences of this program of education. They argued that the case of Don Carlos Ometochtl, a Mexican condemned for seeking to revive the ancient religion, showed the risks. (Ometochtl was executed in 1540.) These Spaniards did not include Viceroy Mendoza who, on December 10, 1537, wrote to the Emperor that not only had the old indigenous lords accepted this innovation but that he, the Viceroy, had decided to reestablish— Christianized and Hispanized—the solemn ceremonies by which they, the "Tecles," became aristocrats or leaders.[17] Mendoza even founded an "Order of Tecle Knights," which would regularize the method of education for these Indian *señores*.[18] These new Indian aristocrats would be transformed into a new rung of the Spanish social hierarchy.

The emphasis given to conversion by the three main orders in these years was notable. The Franciscans were more concerned with linguistic and even ethnographic studies, for that is what Sahagún's great book really was (*The General History of the Things of New Spain*). It was written between the 1550s and the 1580s. The Franciscans were optimistic about the possibilities of training Indian clergy. The Dominicans were more doubtful, though they were generally more pessimistic about the capacities of Indians. The Augustinians were more concerned with building monasteries and were perhaps more competent at organizing indigenous communities, and even more interested in securing for their novices real training.[19] All the same, the three orders could collaborate, and in New Spain, on the suggestion of Bishop Zumárraga, they met regularly to discuss their different experiences.

Zumárraga was a man of great interest, because at the same time as being the promoter of the College of Santa Cruz, as later of the University of Mexico, and an admirer of Thomas More, as of Erasmus, he was also a fierce opponent of indigenous religions. Several challenges were made that put Zumárraga on his mettle: not simply that of Don Carlos, earlier mentioned, but also one from Marcos Hernández Atlaucatl, judge of Tlatelolco. These were met with firmess, decision, and ruthlessness.

From this time on, there were few years that did not see some kind of publication in Spain by Las Casas. In 1542, for example, he completed his *Remedy for Existing Evils*. In this, he insisted that the pope had wished to do the Indians a favor, not do them harm, by granting them to the King of Spain. The Indians, he said, "are free and do not lose that status on becoming vassals of the King of Spain."[20] The same year, he completed the most famous of his works, *A Very Brief Account of the Destruction of the Indies*. Las Casas claimed that fifteen or twenty million Indians had been killed by the Spaniards. That was a vast exaggeration. Yet the book was presented to the emperor Charles and became the most famous of Las Casas's works, being translated into all the main European languages, often with horrifying illustrations. In this, he argued that the pope had had no right to give the Indies, much less Indians, to the Christian rulers. There was no justification for the numerous aggresive *entradas*: "All wars which are called conquests are and were very unjust, and are characteristic of tyrannies, not wise monarchies. All the lordships of the Indies we have usurped. For our Kings to achieve their principality in the Indies validly and correctly, that is without injustice, would necessarily require the consent of the Kings and the people concerned."[21]

Cieza de León, the best of the chroniclers of the conquest of Peru, was in rough support. "I knew from experience," he said, "that there were great cruelties and much injury done to the natives . . . All know how populous the island of Hispaniola [Santo Domingo] used to be and how, if the Christians had treated the Indians decently, and as friends, there would be many more of them there now . . . There remains no better testimony of the country having once been so peopled than the great cemeteries of the dead and the ruins of the places where they lived. In Tierra Firme [Venezuela, in the region of Coro] and Nicaragua there is not an Indian left. Benalcázar was asked how many Indians he found between Quito and Cartago . . .

'There are none.' "[22] Did the King ever consider abandoning the Indies? That was improbable, especially after Francisco de Vitoria had begun to insist that "Spain should not leave the Indies till they are capable of being maintained in the Catholic faith."[23] Even cities accepted that Spain had a role to fulfill.

From the middle of 1542, there ensued a string of humane regulations. Thus on May 21, 1542, a royal decree forbade "any captain or any other person to make slaves of Indians, even if they were captured in a just war. No one was to be sold at all." Then a special section of that decree condemned practices that might lead to the death of slaves "*así indios como negros*"—a very rare reference at that time to black slaves—while looking for pearls off Venezuela. The decree insisted that the life of those slaves was more important than any benefit that might be gained from the pearl fisheries.

This order clashed with the views of the noble Vitoria, who in his *Reflexiones de Indios* of that same year wrote that the capture of Indians in a just war could result in slaves. Yet also in 1542 there came the Franciscan Fray Alonso de Castro's treatise *Utrum indigenae novi orbis*,[24] which argued that Indians should receive higher education. He added that the Bible should become generally available to Indians, a view he shared with Bishop Zumárraga, who, in his eloquent *Conclusión exhortatoria*, had urged that the Bible should be translated into the Indian languages so that it might be studied by everyone who could read in Mexico. After all, "no one could be called a Platonist if he had not read Plato. So no one could surely be called a Christian unless he had read the doctrine of Christ."

Castro wrote his *Utrum*, incidentally, at the request of the Crown in consequence of arguments about the school at Tlatelolco.[25] That treatise was praised by all the prominent theologians of the day. Then Fray Luis de Carvajal commented, "It is ridiculous to admit [the Indians] to baptism and to absolution and the forgiveness of sins but not to a knowledge of the scripture."[26]

At that time, Las Casas was back in Spain seeking to inspire new laws about the treatment of Indians; he was accompanied by Fray Jacobo de Testera, who had come from New Spain with a letter from Bishop Zumárraga on the subject, as well as letters from several enlightened Dominicans. There were continual discussions on the matter in the Council of the Indies, where the president, García de Loaisa, was as cautious as always, though he clearly realized that the majority of his colleagues were against *encomiendas*. When Las Casas saw the emperor Charles again in Germany in 1541, his strong, attractive personality had an effect on his master, as it had before, in 1517.[27] Charles was a seriously religious man and could be easily persuaded by Las Casas to act in favor of the Indians.[28] Las Casas would also see Prince Philip very shortly.

Sometime in the early part of 1542, a further series of meetings was held between Cardinal García de Loaisa and Cobos. Probably other advisers were at the meetings: for example, Granvelle, a good Latinist and linguist from Burgundy, who had become de facto chancellor of the empire, though he never had the title, and Dr. Juan de Figueroa and Dr. Antonio de Guevara, both of the Council of Castile. Dr. Ramírez de Fuenleal, with his experience in both Santo Domingo and New Spain—and, as we have seen, now as bishop of Tuy—was also called on to advise. They produced the so-called New Laws of the Indies.

These laws deserve much consideration—first, because they were just, and second, because their proclamation in Peru and Mexico, as well as elsewhere in the Spanish imperial dominions, caused a crisis, as we have seen.

The laws began with a personal statement by Charles. For years he had wanted to involve himself with greater intensity in the organization of the affairs of the Indies. Now he had settled to do so. We must assume that, though most of the rest of the text was written by Cobos and García de Loaisa, the Emperor himself made a contribution.

In the text, dated November 20, 1542, there are forty paragraphs.[29]

Paragraphs 20 to 40 constituted the heart of the new legislation, and it was these that caused such difficulties in the empire. The Indians were declared free if they were vassals of the King, as had been specifically urged by Las Casas in *Remedy for Existing Evils*. In order to free the natives who had been enslaved against all reason, the law now would provide that the supreme courts should act summarily and with true wisdom if the masters of Indian slaves could not show that they possessed them legitimately. The supreme court was to "enquire continually into the excesses and ill treatment which are (or shall be) done to [natives] by governors or private persons . . . henceforward [and this was a passage that caused outrage throughout the empire] for no cause of war nor in any other manner can an Indian be made a slave and we desire that they be treated as [vassals] of the Crown of Castile, for such they are." Indians who "until now have been enslaved against all reason and right were to be put at liberty." Indians were not "to carry heavy loads unless absolutely necessary and then only in a manner that no risk to life or health of the said Indians" may ensue.

As for *encomiendas,* those who held them without a proper title would lose them, and those who held an unreasonable number were also to lose them. Those who had been engaged in Peru in the "altercations and passions" between Pizarro and Almagro would have their *encomiendas* confiscated, as would all royal officials and churchmen (including bishops) and institutions. There would be no new *encomiendas* and, when the present *encomenderos* died, their lands would revert to the Crown. Their children would be looked after since they would be granted a sum drawn from their fathers' revenues. That was a very complicated compromise.

All Indians placed under the protection of the Crown would be well treated. "First conquistadors"—that is, those who had first been involved in the conquest of the place concerned—would be preferred in royal appointments, all new discoveries were to be made according to certain rules, no Indians were to be brought back as loot to Spain or New Spain, and the scale of tributes imposed on new Indians would be assessed by the governor. Indians living in Cuba, La Española (Santo Domingo), and San Juan (Puerto Rico) were no longer to be troubled for tribute but were to be "treated in the same way as the Spaniards living in those islands." No Indians would be forced to work except where no other solution was possible.[30]

These laws, proclaimed in Spain in November 1542, were published in July 1543 and were received with *desasosiego* (disquiet) in New Spain. Even before they were published, they caused "a true panic."[31] So a series of visitors (*visitadores*) were sent to the New World to explain the Crown's thinking: Alonso López Cerrato would go to the West Indies and then to Venezuela and the Gulf of Paria; Miguel Díaz was to go to Santa Marta, Cartagena, Popayán, and the Río San Juan; Blasco Núñez Vela would go to Peru; and Francisco Tello de Sandoval would go to New Spain. In addition to publishing and enforcing the laws, these officials were empowered to take a *residencia* of all royal officials and to act as judge on the supreme court concerned, and were given a papal bull conferring the power to extend or restrict bishoprics and to hold meetings of bishops to consider the welfare of the Church.

We know what happened to Blasco Núñez Vela. Tello de Sandoval was much more prudent, and the Viceroy in Mexico had already begun to educate the colonists in what they should do and think. Tello ordered the New Laws to be proclaimed (*pregonado*), but he delayed their introduction.

Still, Jacobo de Testera, the "custodian" of the Franciscans in New Spain, who had been recently to Spain itself and who had undoubtedly influenced the text of the laws, was received in Mexico with vast enthusiasm by a large crowd of Indians "who bestowed gifts, erecting triumphal arches, sweeping clean the street which Testera was to pass [as if he had been Montezuma, who had been treated like that] and strewing on him cypress branches and roses, bearing him in a litter because he and the other Franciscans had informed the Indians that they had come to free them and restore them to the state in which they had been before they were placed under the rule of the King of Spain . . . the Indians went forth to receive Friar Testera as if he had been the Viceroy."[32]

It may be to emphasize the accidental more than is necessary to realize that 1542 saw the foundation of the Archivo Nacional de Simancas and also the publication of Copernicus's *De revolutionibus orbium coelestium*. Lovers of literature will insist that the publication of the collected poems of Boscan and Garcilaso de la Vega was as important as those events since, by introducing Italian verse forms, a large flood of new Spanish poetry was opened up. To those concerned with romantic geography, the publication of *Felix magno* by Claudia Demattè in Seville should be remembered because it speaks again of Califa, the mystic Queen of California. More realistic monarchists were pleased that the Infante Philip announced his marriage to the Infanta María de Portugal.

Still, we are concerned with Dominicans as well as with treasure. Among the disciples of Francisco de Vitoria was Fray Domingo de Soto. He became a convert to Vitoria's version of Christianity.

After studying with Vitoria at the University of Paris, he followed Vitoria back to Salamanca in 1526. He took over some of Vitoria's lectures when the latter was ill, and in 1532, he was elected to be professor of theology at Salamanca. He lectured there till 1545, when he resigned his chair to go to the general council of the Church at the request of the Emperor. Soto played an important part in the first years of the work of the Council of Trent, both as imperial adviser and as representative of the Dominicans. It is comforting to realize that this great Catholic thinker, with his knowledge of the New World, was present at the council's meetings. Returning to Spain, he was professor again at Salamanca in 1551, a position he held till his death in 1560.

Controversy at Valladolid

One of the guardians, a horseback rider, explained that they were slaves condemned by His Majesty to the galleys and so there was no more to be said.

MIGUEL DE CERVANTES, Don Quixote

Las Casas returned to Spain in 1547 and went to stay at the monastery of San Gregorio in Valladolid, the splendid palace-convent next to the church of San Pablo. He came with Fray Rodrigo de Andrada, who represented the Indian tribes of Oaxaca and Chiapas, and who wanted to represent them before the Council of the Indies. Las Casas had something more to his taste in his agenda: a riposte to the able lawyer and polemicist Juan Ginés de Sepúlveda's latest Socratic dialogue, *Demócrates segundo.* Las Casas insisted that that book should be examined by the universities of Alcalá and Salamanca.

Sepúlveda was an accomplished, if conventional, scholar with conservative views. He had just finished a great translation of Aristotle's *Politics.* He had also completed a new tract about how to treat Indians. It was rejected by the Council of the Indies, but then it was transferred for approval of the Council of Castile—which, as Las Casas said, knew nothing of the New World. Las Casas supposed Sepúlveda thought that "men who knew nothing of Indian affairs would not notice the poison." In fact, the Council of Castile referred Sepúlveda's latest treatise to the theologians at Salamanca and Alcalá, where they discussed whether to publish it on many occasions. On mature consideration, they found that the work was unworthy since the teaching in it seemed unsound. Dr. Diego Covarrubias at Salamanca gave lectures criticizing the idea that the Indians' low culture justified the wars against them. He doubted whether American Indians should be looked on as among those people born to obey.

One who surprisingly seems to have remained on the sidelines in the controversy was Bishop Quiroga, who in 1548—while still bishop of Pátzcuaro, the onetime capital of Michoacán—returned home to work out the boundaries and rights of the bishoprics of New Spain. While in Castile, he wrote a treatise (now lost), *De debellandis Indis,* about whether it was ever just to make war against the Indians. Quiroga, in contradictory fashion, thought that war was usually just since it brought Indians closer to Christianity.[1] Some Muslims had said much the same of slavery.

Sepúlveda wrote to Prince Philip asking for a meeting of theologians to discuss his book. But Philip had left Valladolid for a European tour before he had time to answer, and Sepúlveda instead went to Rome, where, for good or evil, his book appeared. In April 1549, King Charles issued the extraordinary ruling that all conquests and expeditions (*entradas* included) were to be suspended till the dispute between Las Casas and Sepúlveda had been decided and it had become clear whether they were to be looked upon as legal. A declaration of April 1549 entitled "The manner in which new discoveries are to be undertaken" elaborated on this matter. Churchmen were to explain that they had come to the New World principally to secure the friendship of the Indians and to secure their acceptance of their subjection to the Emperor and to God. Conquistadors had been enjoined not to seize Indian women and were to pay for everything that they took from Indian properties, at the low prices set by men of the Church. No force was to be used by Spaniards except in self-defense and then only in proportion to needs. Any breach of these rules would be severely punished "inasmuch as this matter is so important for the exoneration of the royal conscience and of the persons who undertake these conquests, as well as for the preservation and increase of these lands." Perhaps this remarkable declaration was drafted by Las Casas.[2] Whether that was so or not, the very next month, Las Casas was found writing to Fray Domingo de Soto, now at the forefront of Spain's theologians and much preoccupied by the matter of how to treat the Indians.

Las Casas agreed that the New World was far away but the issues involved were close. He regretted that even pious missionaries offered conflicting advice as to what to do. He said that some friars had been suborned

by money from conquistadors, others did not learn the languages necessary to progress in conversion (Las Casas included!), and still others knew
nothing of what had happened. One friar (perhaps de Soto) had eaten the
paper on which he had previously signed his support of the perpetuity of
the *encomienda*. "Where else in the world," Las Casas continued, "have rational men in happy and populous lands been subjugated by such cruel
and unjust wars called conquests, and then been divided up by the same
cruel butchers and tyrannical robbers as though they were inanimate
things . . . enslaved in an infernal way, worse than in Pharaoh's day, treated
like cattle being weighed in the meat market and, God save the mark,
looked on as of less worth than bedbugs? How can the words of those that
support such iniquities be believed?"[3]

On July 4, 1549, the aristocrat Luis de Velasco was appointed as Mendoza's successor as viceroy of New Spain (the King had quietly pushed
aside Mendoza's suggestion that his own son Francisco might be temporarily named in succession). Velasco was worthy of the charge, being of
the family of the constable of Castile. He had been Viceroy of Navarre and,
like so many, had married a granddaughter of the first duke of Infantado.
Thus he was accustomed to grandeur and would soon establish a tradition
of having forty people to dine every day.

Mendoza wrote to Velasco about the mission that he was leaving him:
Everyone wished the government to conform to his own notions, and the
diversity of views was remarkable. Mendoza would listen to all kinds of advice and usually said the ideas were good and that he would adopt them.
His aim was to avoid sudden changes, especially in respect of the indigenous people, for so many changes had been made already that he wondered
that the populace had not become insane. Though many gave advice, few
gave help. The secret of good government was to do little, and slowly, since
"most affairs lend themselves to being handled in that way and in that way
alone can one avoid being deceived." His chief concern was to maintain
good relations between himself, the judges, and the lesser officials.

Mendoza told Velasco that the Spaniards had respect for nothing said to
them if they were not treated as gentlemen. The wealth from which the
Crown's revenue derived came from them, of course: They had brazilwood,
they had mulberry trees for silk, and they had sheep. The Indians' production was of much less value. That had to be taken into account.

Mendoza also said that the Indians should be treated as sons of the Crown and both loved and punished in that spirit. Services and carrying (porterage) should be done away with slowly, so as not to offend the Spaniards. All the same, many Indians were undoubtedly cunning and mendacious. When a legal case was decided against them, they had a habit of bringing the matter up again once they thought that the judge had moved on or everyone had forgotten the case. He, Mendoza, never punished Indians for telling lies, because he feared that otherwise they would not come to him with their stories at all. He had regular hours for them on Mondays and Thursdays, but he was also ready to see them at any time, notwithstanding their "smell of perspiration and other evil odours. Many people thought that the Indians were humble, abused and misunderstood. Others thought that they were rich, idle vagabonds. Neither view was correct. They should be treated as men like everyone else."[4]

On July 3, 1544, the Council of the Indies had told the Emperor that dangers both to Indians and to the royal conscience were so great that no new expeditions should be licensed without his express permission and that of the council. Also, a meeting of theologians was really needed to discuss "how conquests may be conducted justly and with security of conscience." Although laws had been promulgated on these matters, "we feel certain that these have not been obeyed, because those who conduct these conquests are not accompanied by persons who will restrain them and accuse them when they do evil."[5]

Matters continued thus for several years. Pamphlets were written by Las Casas and others discussing the injustice of these wars (in the Indies) "according to all law, natural and divine." Others were contributed by Sepúlveda and others, to the effect that the conquests were just as well as wise.

On September 23, 1549, Sepúlveda (in Valladolid) wrote to Prince Philip saying that "by falsehoods, favours and machinations," Las Casas had succeeded in preventing his *Demócrates alter* from being published and that any copies that reached the Indies were immediately confiscated. Las Casas—"this quarrelsome and turbulent fellow"—had written a "scandalous and diabolical confessionary" against Sepúlveda. He thought that the case ought to be debated before the Council of the Indies. But Las Casas, Andrada, and several doctors of the Church argued fiercely against the idea and managed to shake the opinions of some members of the coun-

cil. Las Casas was able to delay a decision till the emperor Charles returned
from Germany. Bernal Díaz del Castillo, who came home from Guatemala
to assert the need for the heritability of *encomiendas,* returned to New
Spain with this comment: "In this manner, we proceed, like a lame mule,
from bad to worse, and from one Viceroy to another, from governor to
governor."[6]

A formal visitor, Francisco Tello de Sandoval, reached New Spain in
February 1544. He was a characteristic bureaucrat of the age. A Sevillano,
he had attended the University of Salamanca and afterwards had entered
the bureaucracy of the Inquisition in Toledo. Then, in 1543, Tello joined
the Council of the Indies. His nature was inflexible, and he would eventually become a bishop. He brought with him to New Spain not only an
instruction to explain the New Laws to the settlers but a document author-
izing him to investigate the conduct of almost everyone: viceroy, judges of
the supreme court, treasurer, and their subordinates, down to the most in-
significant officials in the poorest towns. In addition, he was named *inquisidor* of New Spain.[7] Tello arrived with a financial adviser, Gonzalo de
Aranda, who left an account.[8] The colonists wanted to go and greet him to
reproach him for the New Laws, but the prudent Viceroy, still Mendoza, restrained them. No grander reception in the event could have been held in
Seville or in Valladolid. Tello de Sandoval himself repaired then to the convent of Santo Domingo in Tenochtitlan, where Bishop Zumárraga greeted
him and where he installed himself. The very next day, a large number of
the colonists and conquistadors besieged him with their complaints, but
Tello dismissed them for the time being since he had not yet presented his
credentials. Later, he met Miguel de Legazpi, the Basque notary, and some
others of the town council, as well as the chief prosecutor, to whom he
talked reassuringly.

The next month Tello devoted to meeting people and listening to their
anxieties. Then on March 24, Tello instructed the notary Antonio de Tun-
cios to proclaim publicly the New Laws on the treatment of Indians. The
announcement was received with no pleasure. Tello was therefore persuaded by the councillor Alonso de Villanueva to stay the execution of five
of the provisions that especially distressed the settlers until an appeal could
be made. Then the provincials—that is, the leaders—of the three main orders, the Franciscans, Augustinians, and Dominicans, declared in favor of

the *encomiendas*. The same three provincials went to Spain to protest at the high-handed manner with which they were treated, as did three important councillors: Alonso de Villanueva, mentioned above; Jerónimo López, a survivor of the conquest (he had reached New Spain in 1521 with Julián de Alderete); and Pedro Almíndez Chirino, the odious ex-inspector and enemy of Cortés.

The day after the proclamation of the New Laws, Bishop Zumárraga invited all the leaders of the viceroyalty to take part in a Mass that he celebrated in the cathedral. Tello attended this occasion. Zumárraga preached intelligently and eloquently. But, with the announcement of the New Laws, all business came to a stop in Mexico. Wheat rose in price to 11 reales a fanega, maize to five reales. Settlers went about saying that they would be obliged to kill their wives and their daughters "lest they seek a life of shame." The first fleet returning to Spain after the proclamation carried thirty-five to forty families, six hundred people in all. The Viceroy and the supreme court judges distributed charity to the families of conquistadors to prevent their flight.[9]

The Dominicans mounted an effective counterattack to the New Laws. Thus the provincial Diego de la Cruz and the eloquent Fray Domingo de Betanzos, the onetime friend of Las Casas, wrote to the emperor Charles to say that Indians should not be encouraged to study "since no benefit could be expected for a long time . . . Indians are not stable persons to whom one can entrust the preaching of the Holy Gospel. They do not have the ability to understand correctly and fully the Christian faith nor is their language sufficient and copious enough to be able to express our faith without great improprieties, which can easily result in great errors."[10]

So no Indian should be ordained a priest. This document was signed on May 4, 1544, by all the leading Dominicans in Mexico. A similar letter was written by the town council of Mexico. The councillors begged to be heard before the New Laws were put into execution. This letter was signed, too, by several old conquistadors still on the town council.[11] Meantime, the *procuradores* of New Spain reached Castile, and they immediately sought out Sepúlveda, who had become the prop and stay of the opponents of the New Laws. They could not seek out Las Casas even if they had wanted to, since that now-famous preacher had been named bishop of Chiapas and was on his way to his see.

Both Alonso de Villanueva and Jerónimo López argued in the town council that the Indians would be better off if the *encomiendas* were given to the settlers in perpetuity. Surely that would be best too for the land concerned? They also insisted that, since the leaders of the orders had given their views, individual friars should keep silent.[12] But it had become evident that those same leaders of the orders were more opposed to the New Laws than anyone expected. Thus Fray Diego de la Cruz, who had been the Dominican provincial for nine years, agreed that *encomiendas* in perpetuity should be granted, to avoid Spaniards abandoning agricultural projects in the middle of them. He did not think that the Indians would work hard even if the judges ordered it. The Indians were no longer afraid of horses. So he anticipated a revolt.

The Viceroy sent a serene commentary to the Crown. He noted that even Tello had used Indian services, including slavery, when he had been in Mexico. Anyway, personal services had not been invented by Spaniards but had been used by the Mexica themselves. Even if His Majesty cut off the heads of the settlers, he could not make them enforce his laws, which actually damaged his rents and his income, and would in the end depopulate the country, which really needed people.[13]

A meeting of the Council of the Indies was held in Spain to discuss these matters. The Duke of Alba, who came across from the Council of State—every day more important in the Emperor's counsels—having talked to churchmen from Mexico, advised the King to suspend the New Laws. He urged the grant of *encomiendas* in perpetuity, though without legal confirmation, so that "the Spaniards there would always need some favour of the King of Spain." He opposed the idea of pensions for conquistadors. The Indians should be subject to the Spaniards, of course, but they should be treated well and not required to be slaves or even servants. If the troubles continued, they should be crushed by "a large and powerful armada"—Alba's usual solution to political problems.[14]

The archbishop of Toledo, still Cardinal Pardo de Tavera, thought that some reward should be given to conquistadors but that they should not be in the form of *encomiendas*. Licenciado Juan de Salmerón, who had spent several years as chief magistrate in Castilla del Oro and had been a judge in New Spain, thought that the New Laws were neither just nor practical.[15] Dr. Hernando de Guevara, learned and imaginative as well as eloquent, thought that till the council received more information about *encomiendas* and *encomenderos,* the New Laws should not be enforced. The count of Osorno, who had acted as president of the Council of the Indies and whose name is preserved in one of the cities founded by Valdivia in Chile, backed the idea of *encomiendas* in perpetuity, though he thought that the *encomenderos* should have only civil jurisdiction. Cobos said that, though he had no experience himself of the Indies, he had noted that two out of the four members of the council who had opposed giving *encomiendas* in perpetuity had indeed been there. Dr. Ramírez de Fuenleal wanted to consider the New Laws themselves first. The trouble had been caused by individuals, not only by the injustice of the laws. He considered that the heir of a conquistador should receive two thirds of his father's property as an entailed estate.

In the end, Cobos argued simply that *encomiendas* should continue to be given to worthy Spaniards in the Indies and agreed with Alba that the New Laws should be temporarily suspended. Cardinal García de Loaisa also supported the concept of *encomiendas* being granted in perpetuity, which he believed would guarantee an income for the King, the conversion of Indians, and peace. Dr. Bernal, Licenciado Velázquez, and Licenciado Gregorio López (an Extremeño from Guadalupe, whose uncle Juan de Sirvela had been prior of the Jeronymite monastery there) supported pensions for conquistadors and "moderate" pensions for other Spaniards who had served in the Indies for two generations. Conquistadors should not collect tribute and should not own property in Spain "so that they would identify themselves with the [new] land."[16]

All these views were passed on to the Emperor, at the time in Germany, and some representatives of New Spain went there to present their views in person.[17] The prince regent Philip wrote to his father that he had talked with representatives of the New World and with "appropriate people" of both the Council of Castile and the Council of the Indies, but "as the matter was so grandiose and of such weight and importance" he, Philip, did not think that he could take a decision which was for his father to resolve.[18]

Philip added, though, that the Council of the Indies evidently wanted someone to put Peru in order. Everyone thought that the ideal person would be Antonio de Mendoza, but all realized that he was too valuable in New Spain to go. Alba and Dr. Guevara thought it essential not to send a *le-*

trado, or university-educated civil servant, but a gentleman (*caballero*), a person in the confidence of the Emperor. But everybody else thought that a *letrado* would be best.[19]

Fray Domingo de Betanzos thought that laws that assumed that sooner or later the Indians would disappear altogether were sound and good. He added that he, like Bishop Zumárraga, longed to go to China, where apparently the "natives were so much more intelligent than those of New Spain."[20]

This decision taken in Malines was against Charles's wishes. He had, however, been much disturbed by the rebellion in Peru of Gonzalo Pizarro, which had been inspired by the New Laws. Las Casas, of course, differed. From Chiapas he sent a message dated September 15 that all who pressed for the revocation of the New Laws should be hanged, drawn, and quartered (*merecen ser hechos cuartos*).[21]

The *encomenderos* in New Spain were breathing a sigh of relief, so much so, indeed, that they set aside the second day of Christmas 1546 for a general rejoicing. But their problems continued: A destructive epidemic of smallpox in 1546 killed thousands; there was a new revolt of black African slaves, which frightened everyone. No doubt the *encomenderos* were pleased that García de Loaisa at last left the presidency of the Council of the Indies when in February 1546 he became *inquisidor general* (he died soon thereafter). He was succeeded by Luis Hurtado de Mendoza, the elder brother of the Viceroy.

Don Luis was one of those noblemen whose education had been formed by Peter Martyr. He was as much a Renaissance prince as his father had been in Granada and as his brother was in New Spain. He had been much concerned in the building of the cathedral in Granada, Spain's most obvious Renaissance cathedral, having been designed by Pedro de Machuca, who was said to have worked with Michelangelo. Luis Hurtado de Mendoza inspired, too, the plans for a Renaissance palace in the Alcázar in Seville, also designed by Machuca. He had been Viceroy of Catalonia and captain-general of Navarre. His father had brought him up in Granada.

When named president of the council, Hurtado de Mendoza was in Regensburg with the court. The Emperor told his new president of the great pressure being exerted on him by *encomenderos.*

The establishment of the Mendoza brothers in the two most important places in the empire articulated perfectly both the importance of their family and the fact that, despite the prevalence of middle-class *letrados* in so many fields, the Emperor preferred aristocrats in the leading positions. The Mendozas' younger brother, the cultivated and creative Diego, was in 1544 ambassador in Venice and would move to the all-important Rome in 1545. It was characteristic of him that, on his journey to Venice, he took both the novels *Amadís* and *La celestina* to read.

No doubt the *encomenderos* of New Spain were also confronted by the open quarrel between the two most prominent friends of the Indians, Las Casas and Motolinía. This occurred because a mere friar such as Motolinía could not at that time legally baptize Indians. He asked Las Casas to act in his stead. Las Casas refused, because he thought that the Indian concerned was inadequately prepared. Motolinía never forgave Las Casas. Motolinía thought that the Christian faith should be disseminated as quickly as possible. This caused Las Casas to lobby against Motolinía's claim for a bishopric.[22]

Actually, in 1546, the Viceroy, Mendoza, was enduring a serious personal crisis, since Tello de Sandoval had presented a list of forty-four accusations against him. The Viceroy was accused of, in particular, favoring his friends, receiving gifts in return for favors, abusing Indians on his ranches, neglecting to send royal revenues, and using the income of certain councils for an improper purpose. Mendoza was accused of forcing his sister María to marry Martín de Lucio, an elderly conquistador who had come to New Spain first with Pánfilo de Narváez.[23] He was also said, more seriously, to have covered up or concealed a murder by a friend of his, Pedro Paco. Mendoza had his replies ready by October 30, 1546. He also drew up a counter-questionnaire of more than three hundred questions, to which most prominent citizens of Mexico replied. Then he successfully carried his case to the Council of the Indies. But, before that, the economy of New Spain had been transformed.

One of the hopeful conquistadors in Mendoza's New Spain was Juan de Tolosa, whom we assume to have been in origin a Basque from Guipuzcoa. At any rate, that is the origin of the surname, and Tolosa has been for generations an important stop on the way from San Sebastián to Burgos. Juan de Tolosa married Leonor, a daughter of the great Cortés by Isabel (Techuipo), the daughter of Montezuma. One day in early September 1546, Tolosa camped at the base of the Cerro de la Bufa, near what became the town of

Zacatecas, in central Mexico, and in return for some meretricious trinkets brought from Spain, he received presents of a few stones, which, according to a metal analyst in Nochistlán, turned out to be high in silver content. The mines nearby surpassed all previous such discoveries. Tolosa founded the town that was later Zacatecas, and he and some others turned the place into a silver town. Of these others, the most important were Cristóbal de Oñate, a hero of the war against the Mixton Indians, and Diego de Ibarra, who had also had a role in that conflict. Oñate soared far ahead of Tolosa in terms of achievement, for in the end, he owned thirteen silver mines, a hundred slaves, and a magnificent residence with a chapel. At last it seemed that New Spain was going to justify the expense that its conquest had entailed. There were, of course, problems—one of which was that there was no river near Zacatecas, so the machinery of production had to be turned by horsepower, or by slaves. All the same, the news intoxicated the colony.

This knowledge arrived just in time for it to become known to the creator of New Spain, then living in a house in Seville, in the Plaza San Lorenzo. In October 1547, Hernán Cortés went to stay just outside Seville in the house of a friend, Juan Rodríguez de Medina, and there on December 2, 1547, having made his will, he died, probably at age sixty-six.[24]

Cortés had transformed the history of Spain and the Americas. Nothing was the same again after his astonishing achievement of leading a few hundred Spaniards to triumph over a powerful indigenous monarchy. Matters might easily have gone differently had the Spaniards been led by a less intelligent commander who did not see, as Cortés did, the importance of interpreters; who did not have the gift of serenity in difficult moments, as Cortés had; who did not believe, as Cortés did, that leaving aside gold and glory (important motives certainly), the Mexica would soon find the Christian God and the attendant saints, not to mention the Virgin Mary, irresistible. Cortés's tactic of kidnapping Montezuma was copied afterward a hundred times, not just in Peru. His skill at transforming the Americas by using a small company of soldiers was an inspiration to other conquerors, who thought that, with a few cavalrymen, they, too, could capture a kingdom.

Yet this great conqueror did not seem quite at ease with his victory, nor did his country help him to be so. The King of Spain, the emperor Charles, never forgot that Cortés had in effect rebelled against Diego Velázquez; so he never gave Cortés the European command that might have transformed the history of Europe. Cortés's life was after 1525 full of disappointment and even sadness.

Several of the contemporaries of Cortés died at much the same time. For example, Cobos, the great secretary for the Indies and for most other things, died in his palace in Úbeda in May 1547. Other advisers, such as Zúñiga, Pardo de Tavera, García de Loaisa, Cifuentes, and Osorno, all vanished for good in the two years prior to Cortés's death. Charles the Emperor must have felt alone in 1550, when he would be faced by some of the most difficult moments of his life.

Las Casas and Sepúlveda

Some qualities are always good in any language.

CASTIGLIONE, *The Courtier*

In August 1550, the epic dispute between Sepúlveda and Las Casas came to a head in a formal confrontation in Valladolid in the monastery of San Gregorio.[1] It was an appropriate year. The best historians of the Spanish world have argued that it marked the culmination of Spanish civilization, though evil memories of the past were not yet quite hidden: In New Spain, for example, a rebellion was mounted by the Zapotecs in Oaxaca by a leader who proclaimed himself to be Quetzalcoatl.

This encounter between Las Casas and Sepúlveda was set on foot by María de Bohemia and Maximilian of Austria, her husband, regents of Spain in the absence of both the emperor Charles and the prince regent Philip.

A junta of fifteen (including seven members of the Council of the Indies, four theologians, two councillors of Castile, and the bishop of Ciudad Rodrigo) had to decide between the point of view of Juan Palacios Rubios, who had said that the pope had full authority and, therefore, so did the Catholic Kings, against the Dominicans, who denied all authority to the pope and therefore indirectly to the Catholic Kings. (The Franciscan Fray Bernardino de Arévalo was ill from the beginning, so the junta was in effect a board of fourteen.)

The Dominican Domingo de Soto put the question: "The purpose for which your lordships are gathered together . . . is in general to discuss and determine what form of government and what laws may best ensure the

preaching of and extension of our Catholic faith in the new world . . . and
to investigate what organisation is needed to keep the peoples of the new
world in obedience to the Emperor, without damage to his royal conscience and in conformity with the bull of [Pope] Alexander [VI]." The
central issue was the justice of making war against the Indians.

Then Sepúlveda spoke for three hours, essentially summarizing his
work *Demócrates alter.* In that book, he had indirectly accused Las Casas of
heresy, for his character Leopoldo was a German "considerably tainted
with Lutheran errors." The character Demócrates was represented as taking
the opposing view.

Sepúlveda's arguments for the legality of the conquests were, first, on
account of the gravity of the sins committed by the Indians, especially their
idolatries and their sins against nature; second, on account of the rudeness
of the Indians' nature which obliged them to serve the Spaniards. Here Aristotle could be cited, recalling his observation that some people are inferior by nature. The Indians were as different from Spaniards as monkeys
are from men.

Sepúlveda then quoted from *Demócrates alter:*

Compare then those blessings enjoyed by Spaniards, of prudence,
genius, magnanimity, temperance, humanity and religion, with
those of the "*hombrecillos*" among whom you will scarcely find even
a vestige of humanity, who not only possess no science but who also
lack letters and preserve no monument of their history except certain vague and obscure reminiscences in some paintings. Neither do
they have written laws, but barbaric institutions and customs. They
do not even have private property.

As to the Spaniards, did not Lucan, Seneca, Isidore, Averroes and
Alfonso the Wise testify to their intelligence and bravery from the
days of Numantia onwards? Did not the brave Cortés subdue Montezuma and his hordes in his own capital? How can we doubt that
those people—so uncivilised, so barbaric, so contaminated with so
many impieties and obscenities—have been justly conquered by
such an excellent, pious and just king as was Fernando the Catholic
and he who is now Emperor Charles and by a most humane nation
and excellent in every kind of virtue?

The third reason for the conquest was in order to spread the faith, which would be more easily done if the natives were first subdued.

Finally, the conquest was to protect the weak among the natives themselves. Here Sepúlveda denounced human sacrifice and cannibalism.

There followed a discussion of the injunction in Luke 14:23 that had so impressed Pope Paul: "Go out into the highways and hedges, and compel them to come in, that my house may be filled."

Sepúlveda argued that the passage justified the prosecution of war to bring Indians into the fold. Las Casas could not say that that was wrong, for many emperors, and indeed popes, had fought for just causes, as they supposed.

When no danger threatened, preachers should go into new lands alone. In dangerous places, fortresses should first be built on borders and then the people would be slowly won over.

Sepúlveda added:

In prudence, virtue, and humanity, the Indians are as inferior to the Spaniards as children are to adults, women to men, as the wild and cruel to the most meek, as the prodigiously intemperate to the continent and temperate, and, as I nearly said, as monkeys to men.[2]

And don't think that, before the arrival of the Christians, the Indians were living quietly and in the Saturnian peace of the poets. On the contrary, they were making war continuously and ferociously against each other with such rage that they considered their victory worthless if they did not satisfy their monstrous hunger with the flesh of their enemies. Their inhumanity was so much more monstrous since they were so distant from the unconquered and wild Scythians, who also fed on human flesh, for these Indians were so cowardly and timid that they scarcely withstood the appearance of our soldiers and often many thousands of them have given ground, fleeing like women before a very few Spaniards who did not even number a hundred.[3]

Sepúlveda argued that, "though some of them [the Indians] show a talent for certain handicrafts, this is not an argument to take seriously . . . since we see that some small animals, both birds and spiders, make things which no human industry can imitate completely." This was an argument later much used by Sepúlveda's friends. We may remember that Burckhardt would write that "insect societies . . . are far more perfect than the human state, but they are not free."[4]

Las Casas appeared on the second day of the debate. His speech was intolerably long and wearied his audience. He read in full his *Argumentum apologiae* (defense), which ran to 550 pages in Latin, in sixty-three sections.[5] He attacked the historian Oviedo almost as fiercely as he attacked Sepúlveda. This speech lasted no fewer than five days.[6] Sepúlveda said that Las Casas only stopped because the jury could bear to hear no more.

Las Casas drew heavily on his *Historia apologética*, in which he argued that American Indians compared very favorably with the European people of antiquity; were in some ways superior to the Romans, being more religious; were better at raising their children (the educational system in ancient Mexico was certainly remarkable); provided a better education for the good life; and had more reasonable marriage arrangements. Indian women were devout and hardworking, and the temples in Yucatán were comparable to those of Egypt. He quoted Aristotle frequently, to outmaneuver Sepúlveda, who, we recall, had translated that philosopher. Evidently, Las Casas agreed with Aristotle that some men were born slaves, just as some men were born with six toes or only one eye; but he did not think that the Indians were in that category. Indeed, he thought, "All the peoples of the world are men . . . all have understanding and will, all have five exterior senses, and four interior ones. All take satisfaction in goodness and feel pleasure with happy and delicious things, all regret and abhor evil . . . No nation exists today nor could exist, no matter how barbarous, fierce or depraved its customs may be, which is not attracted and converted to all political virtues and to all the humanity of domestic, political and rational man."

Las Casas spoke as if the Indians, Mexica, and Peruvians, as well as Tainos and Maya, were all one people. In his *Historia apologética*, Las Casas did, in his universalism, anticipate Rousseau: "Thus we see how they have important kingdoms, numbers of persons who live settled in a society, great cities, Kings, judges, and laws, persons who engage in commerce, buying, selling, lending and the other contracts of the law of nations. So will it not stand proven that Dr. Sepúlveda has spoken wrongly and viciously against peoples like these, either out of malice or in ignorance of Aristotle's real teaching? . . . Even if the Indians are barbarians, it does not follow that they are incapable of government and have to be ruled by others, except to be taught about the Christian faith and be admitted to the sacraments. They are not ignorant, nor inhuman, nor bestial . . . They cultivate friendship and are used to living in populous cities in which they wisely administered the affairs of both peace and war . . . [They were] truly governed by laws which at very many points surpass ours and could have won the admiration of the sages of Athens."

Las Casas then talked of Indians' wonderful "concern about their salvation and their soul." He insisted that the indigenous people had a simple sincerity and were "moderate and meek." He also argued that it had been implied that God had become careless in creating so immense a number of rational souls and had let human nature ("which He so largely determined and provided for") go astray in an almost infinitesimal part of the human race.

Las Casas also declared that even those who lived in highly developed states, such as the Greeks and Romans, could be called barbarians when their conduct was savage. Were the American Indians barbarian because they had no written language? Spanish missionaries had attested to the beauty of the Indian languages. Nahuatl, the tongue spoken by the Mexica, had much grace as a language.

Barbarians were so either because of their wicked character or because of the barrenness of the region in which they lived. They lacked the reasoning and the way of life suited to human beings. They had no laws to live by . . . they lived a life very much like that of brute animals . . . Barbarians of this kind were rarely found in any part of the world and were few in comparison with the rest of mankind.[7]

Human sacrifice? Las Casas almost made a defense of that practice: "Strabo reminds us that our own Spanish people, who reproach the poor Indian people for human sacrifice, used to sacrifice both captives and their horses . . . There is no greater or more arduous step than for man to abandon the religion which he has once embraced . . . There is no better way to worship God than through sacrifice." Thus Las Casas recognized the good faith of the pagan in his religion—even if it was idolatrous and justified his activity of sacrifice—because he was offering his most valuable possession, his life, to God.[8] He added: "That it is not altogether detestable to sacrifice human beings to God is shown by the fact that God commanded Abraham to sacrifice to Him his only son."[9]

After absorbing this remarkable declaration, the judges talked to the two disputants and then asked Fray Domingo de Soto to condense the arguments into a résumé.[10] This he did well, and the text was submitted to Sepúlveda, who replied to the objections of Las Casas. The judges then left, agreeing to meet again on January 20, 1551, after having studied the résumé.

In January 1551, there turned out to be difficulties among the judges. Bishop Ponce de León, for example, found that he had precisely at that time to visit his diocese. Fray Domingo de Soto, advised by the long-lasting council member Samano, wanted to abbreviate the session, and the presence of Fray Melchor Cano and Fray Bartolomé de Carranza was doubtful because they both had to be at the Council of Trent. They wanted to give their opinions by letter.[11]

In early 1551, the judges decided that they needed more time in order to make their judgments. Lent intervened. Soto continued to try to avoid coming at all. Cano and Carranza, as well as Miranda, bishop of Ciudad Rodrigo, remained at Trent.[12] Cano seemed to have the matter of the dispute on his mind there when—on the urging of the Jesuits, led by Fray Diego Lainez, the powerful second general of that order—he supported a resolution at the congress stating that all men, regardless of the color of their skin, have souls capable of salvation.

In mid-April 1551, the second session of the debate at Valladolid finally began. Much of the discussion revolved around the interpretation of the papal bulls of gift to the Catholic Kings. Las Casas had written a considered reply to Sepúlveda in the interim, but the junta had not read it. Sepúlveda, for his part, prepared a paper on the issue of Alexander VI's donation: "Against those who deprecate, or contradict, the bull and decree of Pope Alexander VI which gives the Catholic Kings and their successors the authority to conquer the Indies and subject those barbarians, and by this means convert them, to the Christian religion and submit them to their empire and jurisdiction."

The judges fell into confusion. Las Casas said that the judges had made a decision "favourable to the opinions of the bishop [himself], though unfortunately the measures decreed by the council were not well articulated." Sepúlveda wrote to a friend that the judges "thought it right and lawful that the barbarians of the new world should be brought under the dominion of the Christians, only one theologian dissenting [presumably Soto]." Many of the last session's records seem lost or "at least have not come to light."[13] Both sides claimed victory. Yet it would seem that most of the council approved the Las Casasian rules. So Las Casas seemed to have won.[14]

For months afterward, the Council of the Indies strove to secure the judgments of the judges in writing. None of the written opinions seem to have been preserved except for that of Dr. Bernardino de Anaya, who approved conquest in order to spread the faith and to stop the Indians' sins against nature—provided, though, that the expeditions were financed by the Crown and led by men "zealous in the service of the King, who would act as a good example to the Indians and set off for the good of the Indians, not for gold." He wanted a modern version of the *Requerimiento*.

What Las Casas plainly wanted from the judges was a declaration that "when no danger threatened, preachers alone should be sent to the new world." That is what the Catalan theologian and poet Ramón Llull had thought desirable in respect of the Muslims in the thirteenth century and what Las Casas had tried to encourage in Alvarado's Guatemala—much as what the Jesuits would do in Paraguay or the missions later sent by Spain to California, New Mexico, and Texas. Sepúlveda's doctrine was less clear. He was never satisfied that he was understood.

The Council of the Indies waited for the written statements of the advisers. They waited forever. Perhaps the Crown did not want a clear-cut decision. A compromise might be better.

What happened in practice was that in Spain the benign friars won the intellectual argument but in the Indies, "on the ground," the settlers triumphed. Perhaps no one observed that at the time, since all was subsumed in the quarrels of Europe, the mother continent.

ENVOI

46

The Knight of the Black Eagle

If there is no way to avoid an engagement before I arrive, I cannot
enjoin you too strongly to inform me post haste.

PHILIP II ON THE EVE OF THE BATTLE OF SAINT QUENTIN

War marked Europe in the late 1540s. It was the first time that a major
European war had been fought in Germany. On the one side was a Catholic
emperor standing not only for the unity of Christendom but for universal
Christian power and, on the other, the Protestant states articulating special
particularism. Charles, now a widower[1] and usually melancholy in time of
peace, was happy to be in an army again: "There goes the happiest man in
the world," his brother Ferdinand's ambassador Martín de Salinas had
written in 1536 about Charles and the war in Provence.[2] (It was Salinas who
ensured that Ferdinand received so much information about the Indies.)[3]

On June 26, 1546, the Farnese pope, Paul III, signed a treaty agreeing to
support Charles against the Protestants. But France and England on June 6
had concluded a treaty at Guînes, in the Pas de Calais, then, of course, an
English possession, which freed them both from obligations to Charles. On
July 26, an army of Protestant princes reached the Danube and threatened
to cut off Charles, who, in his litter, marched to the river Inn, and on August 13, joined with papal troops. Next day, the Protestant Schmalkaldic
League formally challenged him, sending him a herald in the traditional
manner. Charles assembled his army of thirty thousand infantry and five
thousand cavalry. He then amalgamated these forces with those of the
Dutch count Egmont, who had five thousand cavalry. The first battle was
on August 31 at Ingolstadt, Charles taking part at the head of his men, sup-

ported by Alba and Egmont. Through his victory there, Charles won control of south Germany by the end of 1546. This was the victory of Alba,
then at his best as a commander.

At Christmas 1546, Charles was at Heilbronn in Württemberg. He was
then weary, having slept in forty different places since August. Next spring,
in April—supported by his brother, Ferdinand, with his son Maximilian,
and by the treacherous Maurice of Saxony—he defeated the elector John
Frederick of Saxony at Mühlberg, near Leipzig, on the Elbe. Charles commented "*Vine, vi y Dios conquistó.*" John Frederick was not aware that
Charles could cross the Elbe at Mühlberg. Alba brought the elector as a
prisoner to Charles, who treated him scornfully. The Emperor then continued north to Wittenberg, the scene of Luther's first challenge, which
John Frederick surrendered on June 4 to avoid a siege. This marked
Charles's greatest triumph and enabled him to summon a diet at Augsburg.
The Battle of Mühlberg is known as the occasion for Titian's masterpiece;
it is a unique example of a great victory inspiring a great picture.

Early in 1548, Charles wrote to his son and regent, Philip, who was then
just twenty-one: "Seeing that human affairs are beset with doubt, I can give
you no general rules save to trust in God. You will show this by defending
the faith . . . I have come to the conclusion that a general council [of the
Church] is the only way ahead . . . Peace will depend not so much on your
actions as on those of others. It will be a difficult task for you to preserve it,
seeing that God has bestowed so many great kingdoms and principalities
on you . . . You know yourself how unreliable Pope Paul III [Farnese] is in
all his treaties, how, sadly, he lacks all [real] zeal for Christendom, and how
badly he has acted in this affair of the council [of the Church] above all.
Nevertheless, honour his position. He is old [he had been born in 1468, so
he was eighty]. Therefore, take careful heed to the instructions which I
have given my ambassador [the clever Diego Hurtado de Mendoza] in case
of a [papal] election . . . France has never kept faith and has always sought
to do me harm . . . Never yield to them so much as an inch . . . Defend
Milan with good artillery, Naples with a good fleet. Remember that the
French are always discouraged if they do not succeed immediately in anything which they undertake. The Neapolitans, remember, are much given
to revolt. Let them be constantly reminded how the French once sacked
their city . . . You can never manage without Spanish troops in Italy . . .

To preserve peace, I have allowed my demands for our ancient hereditary land, for the duchy of Burgundy, to lapse. But do not altogether forget your rights there . . . And do not at any time be persuaded to renounce Piedmont."

It was an emperor who wrote and one who did not forget his more remote possessions. For he went on to advise Philip to keep a watch over his fleet. It was his best defense against pirates in the Mediterranean, and it would also keep the French from interfering in the Indies. Philip should cultivate Portugal for the same reason: "Do not cease to keep yourself well informed of the state of those distant lands, for the honour of God and the care of justice. Combat the abuses which have risen in them." Charles also urged Philip to marry again soon, since he would need more children. (His first wife, María, had died.) He suggested Elizabeth of Valois, daughter of the new king Henry of France, or Jeanne d'Albret, daughter of King Henry of Navarre, who was "very attractive and clever."

"And as for the Indies, take care to keep a good watch to see if the French want to send an armada there, dissimulating or otherwise, and ensuring that the governors of those parts keep a good look out so that, when it is necessary, they can resist the said French; . . . and you should establish good intelligence with Portugal . . . And as for the division of the Indians, about which there have been so many conflicting reports and advice, we have even consulted Don Antonio de Mendoza, the Viceroy of New Spain, so as to be properly informed."[4]

The princely recipient of this letter was, however, himself now on the move. Though quite unconvinced of the need to travel as his father had done, or in the same restless fashion, he had decided to visit his future dominions in the north of Europe. On October 2, 1548, Philip left Valladolid, ignoring the determined opposition of the *cortes* to such a journey. With him there were the Duke of Alba, both his and his father's chief military adviser; Ruy Gómez da Silva, the future prince of Eboli, a Portuguese courtier who would become in effect a chief minister; his longtime secretary, Gonzalo Pérez; Honorat Juan, who had been his tutor in mathematics; the clever and original Fray Constantino Ponce de la Fuente;[5] and Juan Cristóbal Calvete de Estrella, the Prince's learned majordomo, who would write an account of the journey. There were also the musician Luis Narváez and the blind composer Antonio de Cabezón. Vicente Álvarez, the steward, would write an account. They were a strange gathering: Alba represented the hereditary nobility, Silva the *noblesse de robe*; Honorat Juan was a learned preceptor of the Prince from the Borgias' town of Játiva; Ponce de la Fuente was Christophorus Fontanus, an Erasmian preacher, a converso, and one who as a result would die in prison; and Calvete was Philip's teacher in Latin and Greek, who wrote a fine account of La Gasca's triumph over Gonzalo Pizarro.[6]

The Prince's court spent three nights at Montserrat; they stayed at Barcelona with Estefanía de Requessens, widow of Juan de Zúñiga and a foster mother to Philip, and subsequently went to Rosas, in the Ampurdán, where on November 2, 1548, they boarded a vessel in a fleet of fifty-eight galleys commanded by the unconquered Andrea Doria. Then they set off for Genoa, stopping at Cadaqués, Collioure, Perpignan, Aigues-Mortes (where they waited six days because of the wind), Hyères, Savona, and then Genoa itself (on November 25), where Philip was put up by Doria in his palace for sixteen days.

At Savona, Columbus's father's town, the Regent was introduced to the famous bankers Lomellini, Pallavicino, and Grillo—all of whom, or their families, were to become important in the Indies. On December 19, Philip left Genoa for Milan, of which he was already the duke. He was there nineteen days, a time filled with balls, theaters, tournaments, banquets, and local tours, and there he met the painter Titian for the first time. He set off for the Catholic Church's congress at Trent, where he was welcomed by the elector Maurice of Saxony (his father's ally, though a Lutheran) and the cardinals of Augsburg and Trent. The council of the Church had actually gone to Bologna because of plague in Trent. Then, after five more days of celebrations, Philip and his party set off for the Netherlands via Bolzano and Innsbruck. This journey lasted six months. It was a serious education. It was the first time he had visited his northern European dominions.

By February 13, 1549, the princely party was in Munich, with its clean streets and small houses; there was much hunting, and many dinners and picnics. Then at Augsburg they visited the all-important Fuggers. At Ulm, there was a joust on the Danube. At Vaihingen, they were greeted by Prince Albert of Hohenzollern, who escorted them to Heidelberg, a Catholic enclave in a Protestant valley, where the Prince had four days of hunting, picnicking, dancing, and drinking. Then the expedition went on to Speyer,

Luxembourg, Namur, and finally Brussels, where the Prince was greeted by his aunt, the Regent María. There followed a formal reunion with the emperor Charles at the royal palace.

Charles—though, as usual in those days, ill—held many celebrations, balls, hunting parties, and tournaments in honor of Philip. The Spanish Prince met all the grandees of the Low Countries, such as the Prince of Orange and Count Egmont, both fatally associated with him later in life. On July 12, Charles and his son went on a tour of the Netherlands, which lasted till the end of October. There was a formal swearing in of Philip as the heir to the throne, and also a celebration at the beautiful palace of Binche, between Charleroi and Mons, at the end of August 1549. At Binche, Philip saw *The Descent from the Cross* by Rogier van der Weyden, which he had copied by Michel Coxcie[7] and which he bought many years later. Probably he bought other Flemish paintings at this time, including several by Bosch and the popular landscapist Joachim Patinir.

Queen Mary of Hungary had in 1540 held a carnival to honor the Spanish conquest of Peru. But there was now a new chivalric feast in 1549 at Binche, with performances based on the novel *Amadís de Gaula,* characterized by a storming of magic castles and liberation of prisoners. At a later stage in the "chivalrous entertainment," knight after knight failed to defeat a certain "knight of the black eagle," and they were imprisoned in a "dark castle" till a new, unknown gentleman, who called himself Beltenbrós (the name adopted by Amadís during his amorous penance), defeated his adversary and, by drawing forth an enchanted sword from a stone, revealed that he was the knight for whom this adventure was reserved. This unknown, of course, turned out to be Philip.

In September, there were organized for Philip two celebratory processions entering cities: first Antwerp, then Rotterdam.

Next year, 1550, with Philip still in the Netherlands, there were further celebrations. Thus there was a carnival in February at Brussels. Three famous Spanish preachers covered themselves with glory by pronouncing sermons. This was the last night that Philip spent in Brussels: "That night His Highness did not go to bed. He stayed in the main square conversing with the ladies as they sat at their windows. A few gentlemen, young and even some old, accompanied him. The talk was of love, stories were told, there were tears, sighs, laughter, jests. There was dancing in the moonlight to the sound of orchestras which played all night."[8] These were happy days, which were never to recur for Philip in the Low Countries.

An expedition including Charles as well as Philip then went by boat to Louvain, Aachen, Cologne, and Bonn, on the Rhine, though stopping at night on land. They went, too, to Mainz, Worms, Speyer, and Augsburg. In the last named, the imperial Diet met in July 1550. Here or nearby in southern Germany, Philip spent a year. There he commissioned Titian's famous *Poesie*, as well as a portrait of himself by the same Italian master.

There was discussion, too, at Augsburg about the future inheritance of Philip. Charles hoped to leave his son everything, in a last fling of his desire to maintain a Habsburg union, a single constitution, a single confession, and a single ruler. But his patient brother, Ferdinand, the king of the Romans, wanted the imperial throne. Ferdinand's son Maximilian came from Spain, where he was co-regent, to argue his case. Ferdinand and Charles disputed in public. Eventually, in March 1551, a formal agreement (drafted by the adroit Granvelle) between Charles and Ferdinand arranged that, after the former's death, the latter would be emperor, while Philip would be elected King of the Romans and be emperor after Ferdinand. He would make a similar arrangement in Spain for his cousin Maximilian. Thus European power would remain in the hands of the Habsburgs, though it was not quite evident which line it would be.

In July of this same year, Charles wrote to both the young Maximilian and his wife, María, in their capacities as regents of Spain, about the most important matter on his mind: "The fleet which goes for the gold and silver of Peru will set off, we don't know when but we do know that any delay at all is very damaging . . . The people of the Council of Finance write about their problems and costs and what they have to provide this year, taking into account that, in addition to the 200,000 ducats which we permit ourselves to take from the gold and silver of Peru, another 500,000 will be needed for the settling of various other liabilities."[9]

Another letter of this same time dealt with the idea of contracting with the great admiral of Spain Álvaro de Bazan to guard the merchant fleets sent to the New World.[10]

Charles was again talking of gold from the Indies before the end of the year: Thus, on December 30, 1550, he wrote from Augsburg, "La Gasca had brought 200,000 ducats from Peru, of which we will avail ourselves this year. There will be 85,000 ducats which will be remitted and have to be balanced against the fact that costs will amount to 91,716 ducats and another 60,000 ducats which, with interest, will add up to 84,200 ducats and the last slice of 20,000 ducats which, with interest, will make 20,800 ducats which altogether would mean that, from the gold and silver of Peru, we would make either 376,000 or 403,570 ducats."[11] Charles's interest in money was as eternal as his incapacity with dealing with it.

In fact, between 1551 and 1555, the Spanish Crown imported from the Indies more than three and a half million pesos and private people imported more than 6 million.[12] Charles, the mirror of chivalry and the inheritor of the great Burgundian traditions, spent hours puzzling over these figures and sums.[13]

On May 25, 1551, Philip at last left Augsburg for Spain, traveling back via Mantua (where La Gasca explained to him in detail what had befallen him in Peru, with its 346 rich *encomenderos* and about eight thousand colonists). Philip went on to Barcelona, where he arrived on July 12 and as usual stayed with the widow Estefanía de Requessens. He left Barcelona only on July 31 and set off for Saragossa, Tudela, Soria, and Valladolid, his birthplace and de facto capital, which he reached on September 1.[14] No Spanish king had spent so much time abroad, no Spanish monarch would ever know so much of the way of living in other countries, no ruler of Spain was so well prepared to be an international emperor.

On June 23, 1551, the emperor Charles sent general instructions to Philip for the government of the Indies. These included: "That you examine all the offices which become free in the Indies in a spirit of justice, alongside the president and council of that enterprise, except for those in the Casa de la Contratación, the Viceroyalties, the presidents of the *audiencias* and the office of *fundidor* and inspector of forges, as well as the other principal governors I would reserve for myself . . . All the other dignities and benefits should be guaranteed by the Prince." These declarations read like statements in the Emperor's will.

In July, Charles wrote more optimistically from Augsburg: "By letter from Seville on the 12th last, I have gathered that the fleet of the Indies has arrived in Sanlúcar with the galleons coming from all parts [that is, Peru, New Spain, the other Indies, and the islands], and everything on board has been unloaded."

Philip wrote back on November 24, 1551: "And inasmuch as we are talking of the Indies, they say that the latest reports which have been sent are satisfactory and that, from the treasure brought from Peru by the bishop of Palencia [La Gasca], there remains to be taken to Barcelona only 130,000 ducats. And in respect of the other amount from the Indies, that is from Tierra Firme [Venezuela and Colombia], New Spain and Honduras, they say that only 80,765 ducats have yet to be delivered."[15] The letter went into much detail as to how the money from the Indies should be spent. In December, Philip wrote again, from Madrid: "What would be really sensible would be to establish a fleet to guard the coast of Andalusia, from cape Saint Vincent to the straits of Gibraltar, to ensure the safety of the vessels which go to and come from the Indies which is now the main route of the merchants in Seville and Andalusia and where damage can be done by the French. And this fleet could be paid for by a grant which Your Majesty could make and be financed by a tax which could be levied on all merchandise coming from the Indies."[16]

The naval fleet of ships named to protect the merchant ships was always exposed to illegal or even corrupt practice. Thus as much as a quarter of the galleons were carrying goods that overweighed them. The captains of these ships argued that they were rendering their vessels unfit for fighting. But these critics were told that so long as the gundecks were free, a cargo in the hold made the ships steadier. The curious part of this story was that the captains carried their illegal cargoes above decks, where they could easily be seen. Captains sometimes made 100,000 pesos from this illegal freight and more from the sale of offices on their ships to merchants.

In early 1552, Philip was at Madrid, and La Gasca, the victor of Peru, who was becoming an imperial adviser of the first rank, was with the princess María at Linz negotiating for Ferdinand with Prince Maurice of Saxony. Charles's brother, Ferdinand, continued to show concern for the Indies, putting many questions to La Gasca, who received as a present from Ferdinand eight plates richly worked; and Gasca bought a triptych to give to the church of El Barco de Ávila, very close to his birthplace.[17]

Charles, despite his triumph at Mühlberg, did not escape further difficulties—on the contrary. He passed the winter of 1551–52 at Innsbruck, the great city associated with his grandfather Maximilian. In the spring of 1552, he heard that the Protestant Princes, outraged by the Emperor's treatment of their colleagues, would receive the backing of the new king Henry of France, who, with Maurice of Saxony, was ready to fall on the fortresses of Metz, Toul, and Verdun. Charles was on the point of becoming a prisoner. On March 3, 1552, Charles sent a chamberlain, Joachim de Rye, Sieur de Balançon, with instructions to his brother, begging him to try to persuade the Princes to seek peace because the Turkish peril was surely far more grave. But Maurice of Saxony (now known in imperial circles as the "kinglet") nevertheless sent his army against Charles, and on May 23 entered Innsbruck. Charles and what there was of the court only escaped by fleeing south across the Brenner Pass into Italy in driving rain. La Gasca, the Peruvian veteran, was, remarkably, with his master in this crisis.[18]

Charles was now at war with France on every front, and in April, Metz was seized by the constable of France, the brilliant and powerful friend of the late King Francis I, Anne de Montmorency. Metz was a city proud of being a Free Imperial City but it was free within the Holy Roman Empire just as if it were a state. Francis, duke of Guise (*Le Balafré*) as governor ruthlessly pulled down the suburbs and even moved the body of King Louis the Pious from Saint Arnulf's, outside the walls, to the cathedral of Saint-Etienne, within the city.[19] Only in the autumn did troops come from Spain, which enabled the Emperor in person to besiege Guise in Metz; but the duke was a brilliant defender in a siege, and Charles failed to recapture the place.

Philip wanted to help his father. He wrote in May from Madrid: "I have no information about the news that Peru has sent to Panama and Nombre de Dios over 335,000 pesos."[20] He wrote again in June, saying that he was anxious to ensure that the Spaniards who came back from the Spice Islands would be well received: "Let them be good informers about the state of those islands."[21] Then in July, the Casa de la Contratación reported that the treasure brought back by La Gasca amounted to 1,906,082 escudos. Of these, 600,000 would be sent to Germany, 400,000 to the Low Countries, 200,000 to Parma, and only 200,000 to Castile, while 100,000 would be a loan to the pope.[22]

Given the increased reliance of the Spanish Crown on its income from the Indies, the Casa de la Contratación now received new rules of conduct, following the similar reorganization that we have seen of the Council of the Indies. The headquarters would still be in Seville, but there would be a daily

Mass and fixed hours of work. Functionaries who did not attend would be fined. They would have to live in the Casa and take an oath on introduction. The discussions in the afternoons would deal with licenses to go to the Indies. Votes would be by a simple majority. Grave disputes would be referred to the Council of the Indies. Sections 27 to 30 of the new rules forbade officials to receive gifts for any services or to do anything commercial in the Indies. Sections 121 to 126 listed those people forbidden to go to the Indies—Moors, new Christians (*conversos*), and descendants of those punished by the Inquisition—and also merchandise that was similarly prohibited, which would include "profane books and stories, books whose contents are untruthful," with the only books permitted being those that dealt with Christianity and virtue. There was a specific decree repeating the banning of the import of romances into the New World; it was still thought that Indians might doubt the scriptures if they realized that these books were fictional. But this law had little effect.[23]

Scientific books were not banned, but the Council of the Indies wanted strict censorship of both historical and geographical works dealing with the Indies. Sections 144 to the end of the rules of conduct dealt with how ships should sail to the Indies. Two-thirds of the water that was carried should be in well-prepared casks. The rest could go in clay pots or vats or pitchers, which were less good than casks since they sometimes broke and water was wasted.

These rules were signed in August 1552 by Philip and then were widely distributed to colonial officials, a copy being placed on every ship.

On October 7, 1552, Philip wrote to his father from Monzón, where he was attending the *cortes* of Aragon, to say that, in respect of paying the expenses that he had previously listed, "the principal recourse for those necessities is the Indies."[24]

We find Charles replying, from Metz, no less, "Insofar as the perpetuity of the *encomiendas* is concerned, we think that this is not the time to treat of that . . . All the same, we think that we have done well by arranging a contract with Hernán Ochoa for the sale of 23,000 African slaves for the Indies."[25]

On November 12, 1553, Philip wrote again to the emperor Charles that every year more corsairs sailed out of France intending to sack Spanish imperial ports. In the previous July, they had destroyed La Palma, in the Canaries.[26] Yet, had it not been for the sums that now regularly reached Castile from the Indies, Spain would probably have had to abandon northern Europe.

In Spain, Hernando Pizarro, the eloquent victor of Cuzco, seemed a reproach to all. He had been condemned for the illegal execution of Almagro. He was first ordered to be sent to a prison colony in North Africa. That sentence was commuted and Hernando found himself confined in a fortress in Madrid. Finally, he was sent in June 1543 to the Castillo de la Mota, just outside Medina del Campo, city of imagination (Bernal Díaz del Castillo) and of fantasy (*Amadís de Gaula*). Hernando reached there in June 1543, and he remained there till May 1561. He lived comfortably, but confined all the same.[27] At first, he lived with Isabel Mercado of Medina del Campo. Then in 1552, he married his niece, the daughter of his brother Francisco Pizarro, Francisca, who was then aged seventeen. The idea of such a marriage to Francisca had occurred at one time to Gonzalo Pizarro.

Hernando, once married to such a very rich girl as his niece, devoted his time to centralizing the management of his family's estates in Peru, part of which had been managed by royal officials after the final defeat of Gonzalo. When eventually Hernando and Francisca left La Mota, free, in 1561, they went to live at La Zarza. That village outside Trujillo had always belonged to the Pizarro family, of which Hernando was now the head. They embarked there on "a strategy of reconstruction of their finances" and built a new palace in the main square of Trujillo (which still survives). They lived in the shadow of the coat of arms granted to Francisco Pizarro. They had also inherited Francisco's marquessate, which, from 1576, was named as "of the Conquest." Hernando died two years later, a survivor of extraordinary deeds into what seemed a calmer age. Francisca lived until 1598, having married again to Pedro Arias Portocarrero, son of the count of Puñonrostro.[28]

Hernando's fortune was large. In about 1550, it was almost as big as that of the family of Cortés—32,000 pesos a year, in comparison with the family of Cortés's 36,800. Nor does this figure for Hernando's income include the product of his mercantile adventures and mines.[29] In the end, Hernando gained control of most of the estate (including the Porco mines) that the Pizarro brothers had acquired during the conquest.

47

The Emperor at Bay

I shall enter no port other than that of death.

EMPEROR CHARLES V, NOVEMBER 12, 1556

Gold or no, northern Europe notwithstanding, the shadows were darkening for the emperor Charles. Nearly forty years of continuous struggle since 1516 had left him exhausted, and he was forever racked by pain from gout and other maladies. His failure at Metz at the hands of the duke of Guise had been a serious setback. On January 12, 1553, he abandoned the siege, blaming the cold and disease affecting his soldiers. He then retired to Brussels, where he succumbed to melancholy, examining his clocks. In September 1553, a statement about his health was made by Nicolas Nicolai: "In the opinion of his doctors, His Majesty cannot be expected to live long because of the great number of illnesses which affect him, especially in winter . . . the gout attacks him and frequently racks all his limbs and nerves . . . and the common cold affects him so much that he sometimes appears to be in his last straits . . . his piles put him in such agony that he cannot move without great pain . . . All these things, together with his very great mental sufferings, have completely altered the good humour and affability which he used to have and have turned him into a melancholic . . . His Majesty will not allow anyone, lord or prelate, into his presence nor does he want to deal with papers . . . He spends day and night in adjusting and setting his countless clocks and does little else."[1]

The possibility of abdication brought on by ill health became a continual preoccupation. The fact that no monarch of substance had abdicated since Diocletian, also probably in consequence of ill health, in A.D. 305, was on his mind.[2] Charles was only fifty-three but seemed to have reigned for centuries. The realistic, but for Charles tragic, peace of Augsburg of September 1555 sealed his reign: The principle was *"cuius regio, eius religio."* Every state of the empire had the right thereafter to decide its own religion.

Charles, too, was no longer the humane statesman concerned with the well-being of his Indian subjects, with enlightened Erasmian confessors such as Jean Glapion and liberal clergymen such as Alonso Manrique de Lara at his side. Crushed by ill health, he had become intransigent, obsessed by the Protestant heresy, and concerned with the Indies only in respect of the gold and silver that could be drawn out of it, and, it is fair to add, by his own failure to crush heresy and maintain the Habsburg legacy undivided.

The prince-regent Philip, on the other hand, was by then preoccupied with his second marriage. Despite suggestions that he might marry another Portuguese princess (and there were other ideas already mooted in August 1553), Simón Renard,[3] in London, had mentioned the possibility of an English marriage for the Prince to Queen Mary: "She began to laugh not once but several times and looked at me to suggest that she found the idea very much to her liking."[4] She was, after all, the daughter of Henry VIII by Catherine of Aragon and had used to consider the emperor Charles as her guiding light. Once, in 1521, she had even been betrothed to him; "the pearl of the world" she had been proclaimed.[5] Charles obtained Philip's (reluctant) approval and made a formal request for Mary's hand for his son. Mary asked Renard many questions and requested a portrait; a copy of Titian's famous one of Philip in armor was sent to her. If Philip was disposed to be amorous, she told Renard, such was not her desire, for she was "of such an age that Your Excellency knows of and had never harboured thoughts of love. Also she would love and obey Philip but, if he wished to encroach on the government of her country, she would be unable to allow it."[6] It was therefore an astounding decision of Philip's since, at that time, his only heir was Don Carlos, his son by María of Portugal, and he, and the empire, needed more reassurance and, above all, more *Infantes*. The new marriage was not a decision welcomed by Ferdinand, Charles's brother, the king of the Romans, who had already sent a messenger, Martín de Guzmán, a courtier of the Emperor, to propose a marriage of Mary with his own son, the archduke Ferdinand of Tyrol, then in his early thirties. Ferdinand had sent a portrait of him, too, to London.[7]

On October 29, 1553, Mary, however, swore to accept Philip as her husband. He was then twenty-six, eleven years younger than she. He was not enthusiastic, and since the death of his first consort, he had had several pretty mistresses (Isabel Osorio, Catalina Laínez, and, above all, Eufrasia Guzmán). In England, there was also opposition. The House of Commons requested Mary not to marry a foreigner. But she went ahead. On January 12, 1554, a marriage contract was drawn up between Mary of England and Philip. Philip would share all titles and responsibilities with Mary, but would relinquish everything if Mary died first. He would conform to English laws and customs, admit no foreigners to office in England, and not implicate England in his wars. It was an arrangement similar to that of Ferdinand with Isabel in 1479.

On July 13, 1554, Philip left Spain to marry Mary, and this time his sister Juana of Portugal, recently widowed in Portugal, would be regent in Spain.

The Prince sailed from Corunna with seventy vessels, in bad weather; Silva, the Prince of Eboli, said he himself nearly died of seasickness. They were met off the Isle of Wight by Lord Howard of Effingham, the lord high admiral and father of the future English commander against the *armada invincible* in 1588, and entered Southampton on July 20.[8] Philip seems to have had four thousand troops with him. They were greeted by Henry, Earl of Arundel, a Catholic nobleman, who presented Philip with the Order of the Garter. Then they went to Winchester and on July 23 were met at the cathedral by the ambassadorial Stephen Gardiner, the bishop of Winchester, who introduced Philip to the Queen. Though Mary was daughter of Catherine of Aragon, she could not speak Spanish well, but she did speak French adequately. Charles sent, via Juan de Figueroa, a special present to Philip—the throne of Naples—so that he could marry as a king.

On July 25, the day of Santiago, the wedding was held at Winchester. Philip was very affable, talking to the English crowd in the rain, drinking beer, promising to abbreviate his retinue, taking some English nobles into his train, telling his people to try to adapt to English customs. "He has shown such affability and such sweetness of temper as not to be surpassed," reported Soriano, the Venetian ambassador.[9] Then they proceeded slowly to London by water, disembarking there on August 18, and went on to Hampton Court for "what remained of the summer." According to Andrés Muñoz, the Spanish nobles knew that they were in the land of *Amadís de Gaula* (much of which is set in England). "There is more to be seen in England than is written of in those books," he commented, "because of the dwellings that there are in the country, the rivers, the fields, the beautiful flowered meadows, the cool fountains . . . a pleasure to see . . . above all, in summer."[10]

The Spaniards found the English less appealing than their countryside. For they looked white and pink, and were quarrelsome. "All their celebrations seemed to consist of eating and drinking, they think of nothing else . . . They have a lot of beer, and drink more of it than there is water in the river at Valladolid." There were frequent robberies in the streets, the ladies of the court were "quite ugly," and the Queen had no eyebrows, and "though she was saintly, she was short-sighted, and her voice was rough and loud." Some Spaniards said that "they would prefer to be in the slums of Toledo than in the meadows of Amadís." The King acted "as if he were Isaac allowing himself to be sacrificed to the will of his father."[11] Then in November, Mary and Philip presided over a joint session of the English Parliament in which a reconciliation with the Church of Rome was made law. Philip also dealt with imperial affairs. Thus in London he set up a committee of twelve, including the flawed Fray Bartolomé de Carranza and Fray Bernardo de Fresneda, to discuss the matter of *encomiendas*. He told his father that he thought that they should concede these grants in perpetuity.

But there would be shadows in London, too. On February 1, 1555, the first victim of Protestant persecution in England was burned at the stake. Many Spaniards were appalled. The ambassador in London, Simón Renard, wrote to Philip: "I do not think it well that Your Majesty should allow further executions to take place."[12] But the Prince had no power in the English Church courts, even if he inspired his confessor, Fray Alonso de Castro, a Franciscan with a mission to preach to the Prince-Regent from 1553 to 1556, in a sermon on February 10 to criticize the bishops of England for burning Protestants. The initiative was that of the lord chancellor Stephen Gardiner, who reenacted the anti-heresy statute of 1401. Yet he, like Richard Sampson and Edward Foxe, had published acts in defense of King Henry's divorce and royal supremacy in the 1530s.[13]

The year 1555 marked the beginning of the end for Charles the Emperor. On October 22, in Brussels, Charles made Philip master of the Order of the Fleece. Three days later, Charles summoned the authorities of the Low Countries. He abdicated from Burgundy and the Netherlands (leaning on the arm of the Prince of Orange) in favor of his son. Philip came over from England. Charles spoke in elegiac mood of his travels, his troubles, and his triumphs. Through his mind as he spoke there must have passed recollections of Luther at Worms, of Pope Adrian VI in Flanders, and the happy gardens of his childhood with his clever aunt Margaret at Malines. He surely would have recalled meeting Cortés and Pizarro in 1529, Magellan in 1522, King Henry VIII in 1520 and 1522, and all the members of that brilliant Netherlandish court who accompanied him in his first visit to Spain in 1517, above all Chièvres.

He recalled then for his audience his ten stays in Flanders, his nine journeys to Germany, his six stays in Spain, his seven voyages to Italy, four to France, two to England (to see Henry VIII, whom he had admired, to begin with), and two to Africa, not to speak of several voyages in the Mediterranean—his ceaseless journeys, which enabled him to know all the mysterious corners of his European empire as well as his ancestors had known their Spanish kingdoms.[14] He was surrounded as he spoke by the knights of the Fleece, Philip, his royal sisters, Leonor and Mary, both ex-queens, by the young Ferdinand of Austria, by Christine of Lorraine, and by Emmanuel Philibert, the new duke of Savoy. The last named introduced the Emperor. Charles then spoke of his life and how everywhere he seemed to have failed. He warmly commended Philip. There were abundant tears.

Mary of Hungary also abdicated from the Netherlands. She and the former queen of France, Leonor, would follow Charles to Spain, Mary taking with her a fine collection of pictures, books, and tapestries (many of the former would find their way eventually to the Prado). Charles sent to his brother, Ferdinand, a letter of September 12, 1556, that handed him the imperial throne. Early in 1556, Charles gave up Castile and Aragon.

On September 12, 1556, Charles also wrote to explain his decision to all the authorities and municipalities of the Indies. He explained that his bad health made his personal direction of the government impossible.[15] He also abandoned his mastership of the great knightly orders. The abdication was read by Fray Francisco de Vargas, chaplain of the royal family since 1549, in Latin.

Also in January 1556, Philip wrote to the same recipients, accepting the Crown of Castile and León, with everything belonging to it, including the *reinos de las Indias,* his American legacy.[16] The heir to the throne, Don Carlos, son of Philip's first wife, María of Portugal, proclaimed his father in Spain: "*¡Castilla, Castilla por el rey Don Felipe!*"

Charles would retire to Spain in September. The plan was that he would go to live at the Jeronymite monastery of Yuste in the Gredos Mountains. Thus he left Flushing, with 150 followers, on the Basque ship *Espíritu Santo* (known as the *Bertendona*), of 565 tons. Most of Charles's courtiers were made ill by the voyage.

Charles and his court reached Laredo, near Santander, on September 28. It had been a famous port throughout the century. There he was greeted by Pedro de Manrique, bishop of Salamanca, and by Durango, mayor of the court. They went to Burgos, where Charles stayed two days in the famous Casa del Cordón, the house of the constable of Castile, Pedro Fernández de Velasco. At Torquemada, the Emperor was greeted by La Gasca, now bishop of the rich diocese of Palencia; at Cabezón de la Sal, rather gracelessly by his grandson Don Carlos; at Valladolid, by the regent Juana; and at Medina del Campo, by the rich merchant Rodrigo de Dueñas, a financier who gave Charles a gold chafing dish filled with cinnamon from Ceylon— not Amazonian—the extravagance of which gift so infuriated the ex-Emperor that he refused to allow Dueñas to kiss his hand, or so it was said.[17]

Charles then moved to a mansion belonging to the count of Oropesa at Jarandilla, in the Gredos, about ten miles from Yuste. The count was the hereditary protector of the convent of Yuste because of the actions in 1402 of an earlier count in defending the first Jeronymites there against marauding monks from other monasteries. Charles had not been to Yuste before.

Charles remained at Jarandilla three months in 1556 before he moved, on February 3, 1557, to Yuste, which by then had been refurbished by Fray Juan de Ortega.[18] It is in a beautiful spot, surrounded by chestnuts, on the turbulent river Tiétar. During much of the year, the nearby mountains are covered by snow, but the lower valley of La Vera is fertile and productive. The monastery was founded in the early fifteenth century on the site of two ancient hermitages.

The Jeronymites were an offshoot of the Franciscan order. As predicted by Saint Bridget of Sweden, two Franciscan hermits who had been living in the mountains of Toledo presented themselves to Pope Gregory XI at Avignon and obtained the establishment of their new order. The brothers wore white woolen tunics and brown scapulars and mantles, as allegedly worn by Saint Jerome, the symbolic inspiration of the order. Yuste was one of the first of their houses. The Jeronymites were known for the rigor of their observances, the munificence of their alms, and the hospitality of their tables. They emphasized humility. All these attributes attracted the Emperor, for he had always admired them.

Charles had expected to remove himself from all business, but he conducted an active correspondence on many matters, especially those relating to heresy. He employed a staff of fifty, headed by Luis Méndez Quijada, his majordomo. He had with him religious books such as one by Saint Augustine and another by the fluent Fray Luis de Granada, scientific works such as the *Astronomicum caesareum* of Peter Apian, historical works such as the *Commentaries* on Charles's own war in Germany by Luis Dávila y Zúñiga, and Olivier de la Marche's *Le chevalier délibéré*, that "mirror of chivalry" that he had had translated into Spanish. There were also two big books on which had been painted "trees, grasses, men and other things from the Indies," a sign that the Indies were still on the Emperor's mind, though what books they were it is hard to know.[19] He had some clocks, such as one of ebony and sand, another of crystal, and several portraits of his wife, the Empress Isabel, of himself, of Prince Philip, and even one of Queen Mary of England.[20] From his bed in the monastery, he could see the altar of the church and, having positioned himself well, could see the host being raised during Mass.

In August 1558, he became seriously ill with malaria. His gout, which had for so long tortured him, was every day worse. He died on September 21 of that year, at two A.M., his illness having occupied most of the month. He had time to rehearse his funeral. Fray Bartolomé de Carranza was present at the end, as was the count of Oropesa and his brother Francisco, as well as their uncle, Abbot Diego de Cabañas, Luis Dávila (to whom Charles had reserved the bringing up of Don Juan, his bastard son by Frau von Blomberg of Regensburg), and his secretary for correspondence, Martín de Gaztelu.[21] His body was placed beneath the high altar of the monastery of the Jeronymites at Yuste but was removed from there to the Escorial in 1574.

Philip was in Flanders when he received the news of his father's death. On November 17, Mary of England died without heirs. On November 28,

Philip held a glittering funeral service in Saint Gudule in Brussels for his father, and on December 2, another for his wife, the English Queen Mary.

At his death, Charles left his empire in Europe restored. He had Spain, Italy, the Netherlands, and half of Germany under his control or that of his brother, Ferdinand. The empire in the Indies, though no one used that term, was effectively under Spanish direction. Some parts of it were economically successful, especially after the introduction of the use of an amalgam of mercury rendered the processing of silver much easier. Zacatecas and Potosí would become great sources of silver. Then in 1558, the Spanish Antilles produced sixty thousand *arrobas* of sugar to be exported to Seville.[22] Great sums were still regularly paid to the Pizarro family, including the imprisoned Hernando Pizarro, who often received an illegal income through agents. Part of this wealth derived from the cultivation of coca, which was forty times greater than before the conquest.[23]

By the time of the death of Charles V, probably fifteen thousand African slaves had reached the Spanish empire. About five hundred had been bought by Cortés, no less, to work on his sugar plantations in New Spain.[24] Already, too, there was a large subculture of lesser groups; for example, the children of African slave fathers and Indian women, *zambos,* were already making an impact on the society of the empire in both New Spain and Peru. The two large principalities based on those two large regions were the seats of Spanish viceroyalties, and most of the rest of South America, as well as the Caribbean, was governed by Spanish commanders. There were untidy gaps in the texture of the empire. North America, despite the efforts of Hernando de Soto, was far from being a Spanish outpost.

In 1559, another, even more elaborate funeral was held for the emperor Charles in the new cathedral in Mexico. That small edifice had been completed in 1525, on Cortés's orders, using stones from the old pagan pyramids as the foundation. Inside this *iglesia mayor,* as it was known, was an aisled rectangle with wooden supports and a flat wooden roof. It was on the site of its colossal successor cathedral, begun in the 1570s.[25]

The empty sarcophagus in Mexico of the King-Emperor was on two levels, in Doric style. A funeral urn was placed on the first level, and was covered with a black cloth and a cushion on which a crown rested. On the second level, the Austrian eagle spread gilded wings beneath a painted blue sky. This remarkable tribute took the architect Claudio de Arciniega, from Burgos, three months to create. He had been busy since his arrival in New Spain in the late 1540s designing the viceregal palace of the city on the site of the old palace of Montezuma. He had built the first university building in Mexico as well as the beautiful staircase in the hospital of Jesus.

The funeral procession was led by Indian rulers in black cloaks, their hems dragging in the dust, carrying standards with embroidered coats of arms, their own and those of the dead Emperor. There followed the leading men of different towns of New Spain, and many Indian noblemen, followed by four hundred friars and priests, and then by the second archbishop of Mexico, Alonso de Montúfar, a Dominican friar from Loja near Granada (where he had once been *inquisidor* of the Holy Office), attended by the bishop of Michoacán (still the remarkable Utopian Vasco de Quiroga) and the bishop of New Galicia (Pedro de Ayala, a Dominican from a famous family of Toledo).

Quiroga was still firm in his determination to create Utopia in New Spain.[26] He still believed that the Church in the New World could articulate the purity of customs lost among the Europeans, who were victims of ambition, pride, and malice.[27]

At that time, there were nearly eight hundred friars in New Spain, and they had established between them over 150 religious houses. Many of them in their day had converted thousands of Indians. Many of these friars must have been present at this great funeral. So were the six bishops of New Spain (Mexico, Oaxaca, Michoacán, Chiapas, Guadalajara, and Yucatán).

The secular part of the procession was headed by Bernardino de Albornoz, who carried the banner of the city. He had become a councillor of the city and magistrate (commander) of the fortress of Atarazanas. Albornoz was followed by two mace bearers, dressed in black damask and coats of mail on which the royal arms gleamed, in gold and silver. The city's treasurer, Hernando de Portugal, a descendant of the royal house of that country, and a sometime courtier (*contino*) in Spain, carried a crown on a damask cushion. The constable, Ortúno de Ibarra, carried a bare, unsheathed sword, and the inspector, García de Albornoz, brother of Bernardino, a crossbow. Luis del Castillo, the great friend of the late viceroy Mendoza, also a member of an illustrious family, carried an imperial coat of mail.[28] Somewhere in the procession there would surely have been seen Alonso de Vilaseca, possessed of vast cattle ranches as well as rich silver mines in Pachuca, who had endowed a chair of theology at the University of Mexico, a liberal friend of Franciscans on the savage frontiers. Other benefactors of New Spain would all have been present, such as the trustees of the two-story hospital of the Immaculate Conception (later known as Jesus Nazareño) founded so soon after the conquest and maintained by a fraternity (*cofradía*) of which Cortés had been the leading member. There was, too, Bishop Zumárraga's hospital del Amor de Dios. Pedro de Gante would have been present, if only because of his establishment of the hospital for Indians known as Señor San José.

Behind walked Viceroy Mendoza's successor, Luis de Velasco, an eminently noble and dignified figure, a relation of the constable of Castile, whose train was held by a chamberlain. He was married to Ana de Castilla, who had a weakness for the persecuted Archbishop Carranza. There followed other officials, such as the judges of the supreme court, the chief bailiff, the chief of the treasury, and the rector of the new University of Mexico. Velasco had in 1553 introduced a kind of rural guard in New Spain, a Santa Hermandad comparable to what had been created in old Spain under Fernando and Isabel. We cannot doubt that this ceremonial viceroyalty was an advance on what existed before; as the great Burckhardt put it, "the State founded on sheer crime is compelled in the course of time to develop a kind of justice and morality, since those of its citizens who are just and moral gradually get the upper hand."[29]

Thus did Spain carry across the Atlantic ancient ceremonies attended by new aristocrats and recently recognized great men and women. The indigenous population played their part. Had they not done so, the moment would have seemed a self-assertion of nouveaux riches.[30] But they, too, prayed for the soul of the conquering emperor Charles.

Appendix 1

GENEALOGIES

Charles V and His Relations

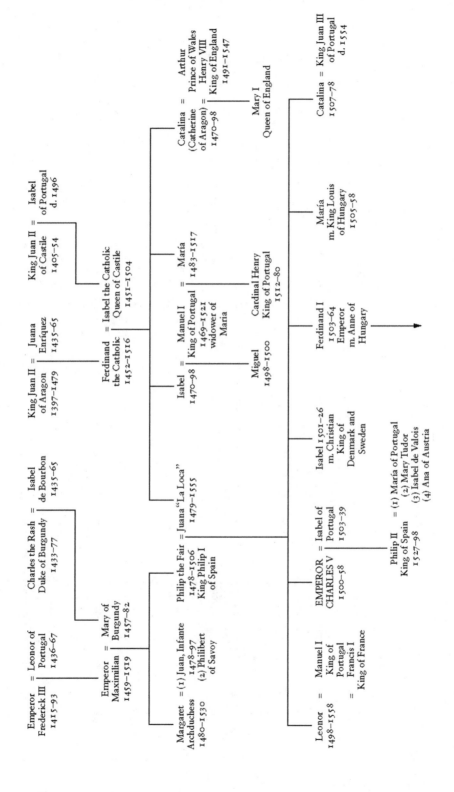

The Montejos

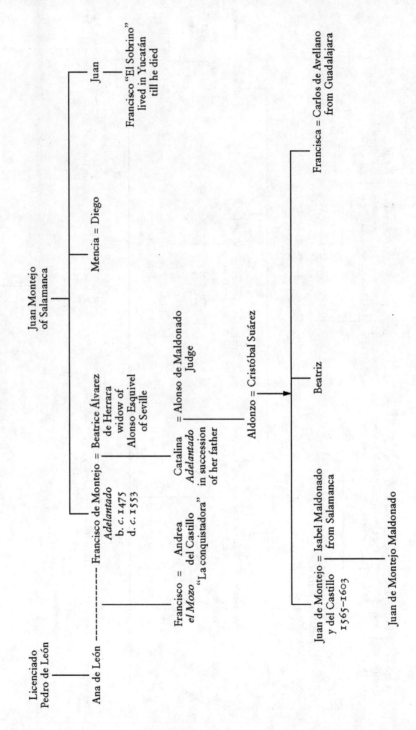

Licenciado
Pedro de León

Ana de León --------- Francisco de Montejo = Beatrice Álvarez
                      Adelantado   de Herrara
                      b. c. 1475   widow of
                      d. c. 1553   Alonso Esquivel
                                             of Seville

Juan Montejo
of Salamanca

Mencia = Diego

Juan

Francisco "El Sobrino"
lived in Yucatán
till he died

Francisco =   Andrea
el *Mozo*   del Castillo
              "La conquistadora"

Catalina
Adelantado
in succession
of her father

= Alonso de Maldonado
  Judge

Aldonzo = Cristóbal Suárez

Beatriz

Francisca = Carlos de Avellano
            from Guadalajara

Juan de Montejo = Isabel Maldonado
y del Castillo   from Salamanca
1565–1603

Juan de Montejo Maldonado

The Velascos

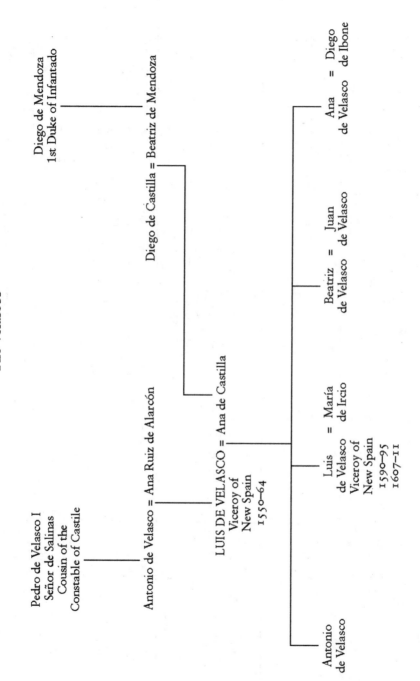

The Pedrarias

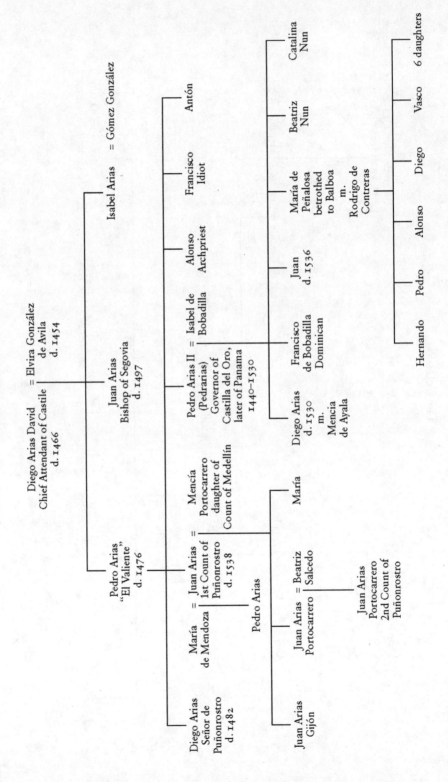

The Pizarros

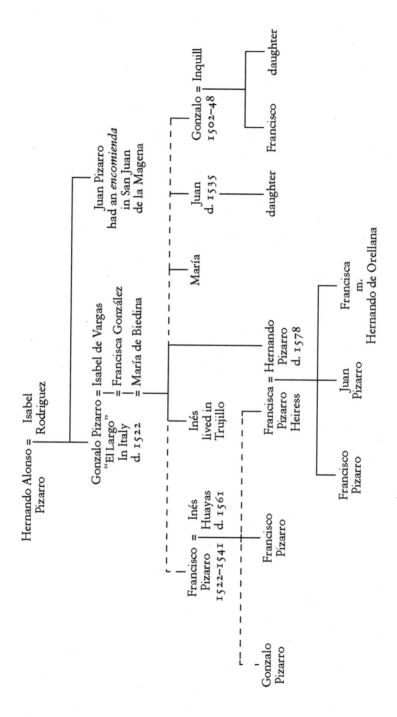

Appendix 2

❦

MAPS

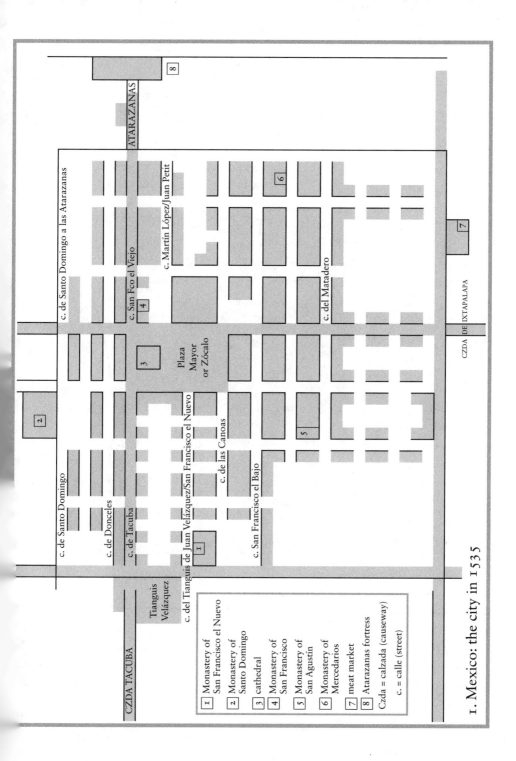

1. Mexico: the city in 1535

CZDA TACUBA

ATARAZANAS

c. de Santo Domingo a las Atarazanas

c. de Santo Domingo

c. de Donceles

c. de Tacuba

Tianguis
Velázquez

c. del Tianguis de Juan Velázquez/San Francisco el Nuevo

c. San Fco el Viejo

c. Martín López/Juan Petit

c. de las Canoas

c. San Francisco el Bajo

c. del Matadero

Plaza
Mayor
or Zócalo

CZDA DE IXTAPALAPA

1	Monastery of San Francisco el Nuevo
2	Monastery of Santo Domingo
3	cathedral
4	Monastery of San Francisco
5	Monastery of San Agustín
6	Monastery of Mercedarios
7	meat market
8	Atarazanas fortress

Czda = calzada (causeway)
c. = calle (street)

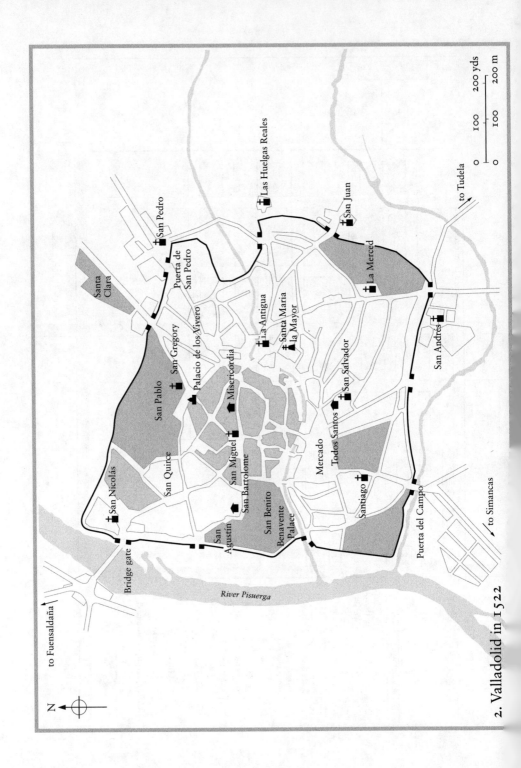

to Fuensaldaña

N

River Pisuerga

Bridge gate

Santa Clara

San Pedro

Puerta de San Pedro

San Pablo

San Gregory

Palacio de los Vivero

Misericordia

La Antigua

Santa Maria la Mayor

Las Huelgas Reales

San Juan

La Merced

San Nicolás

San Quirce

San Miguel

San Bartolome

San Agustín

San Benito

Benavente Palace

San Salvador

Todos Santos

Mercado

Santiago

San Andrés

Puerta del Campo

to Simancas

to Tudela

0   100   200 m
0   100   200 yds

2. Valladolid in 1522

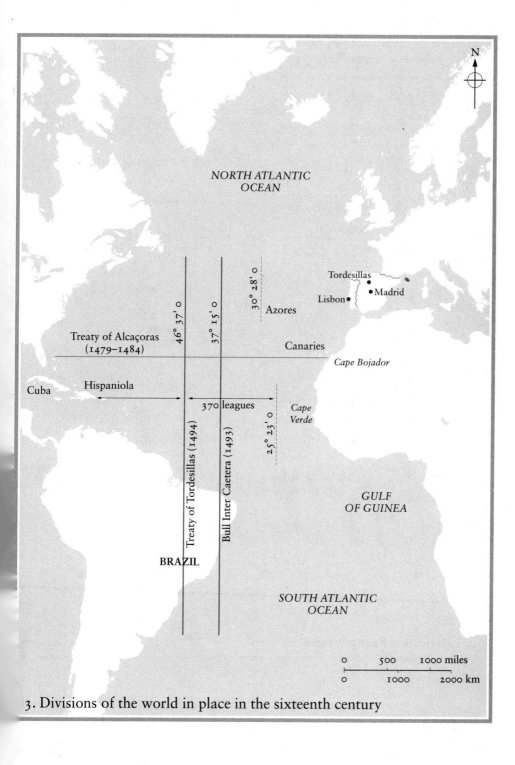

NORTH ATLANTIC
OCEAN

46° 37' O

37° 15' O

30° 28' O

Azores

Tordesillas

Lisbon • • Madrid

Treaty of Alcaçoras
(1479–1484)

Canaries

Cape Bojador

Cuba

Hispaniola

370 leagues

Cape
Verde

25° 23' O

Treaty of Tordesillas (1494)

Bull Inter Caetera (1493)

GULF
OF GUINEA

BRAZIL

SOUTH ATLANTIC
OCEAN

0   500   1000 miles

0   1000   2000 km

3. Divisions of the world in place in the sixteenth century

N

NORWAY

•Christiania   SWEDEN

SCOTLAND

IRELAND   DENMARK   •Kalmar
                           Copenhagen•
                                                  Königsberg•
ENGLAND   •Hamburg
   London•   BRANDENBURG   POLAND
              Antwerp•
              Bruges• GERMAN
                        EMPIRE
                 LUXEMBOURG   Prague•   Cracow•
        Paris•   BOHEMIA

   FRANCE   Vienna•
                                 AUSTRIA HUNGARY

              Savoy   VENICE
              Avignon Milan• •Venice
PORTUGAL   Pamplona•   GENOA   OTTOMAN
                      Marseilles•   EMPIRE
              •Zaragoza   •Florence
•Lisbon Toledo• •Barcelona PAPAL
        SPAIN   STATES
              •Valencia
Seville• •Córdoba   SARDINIA   NAPLES

•Cueta
      Oran•   Palermo•
            ALGIERS   SICILY
                          •Tunis
                                 0   100 200 miles
4. Charles V's Europe, 1522   TUNISIA   0   200   400 km

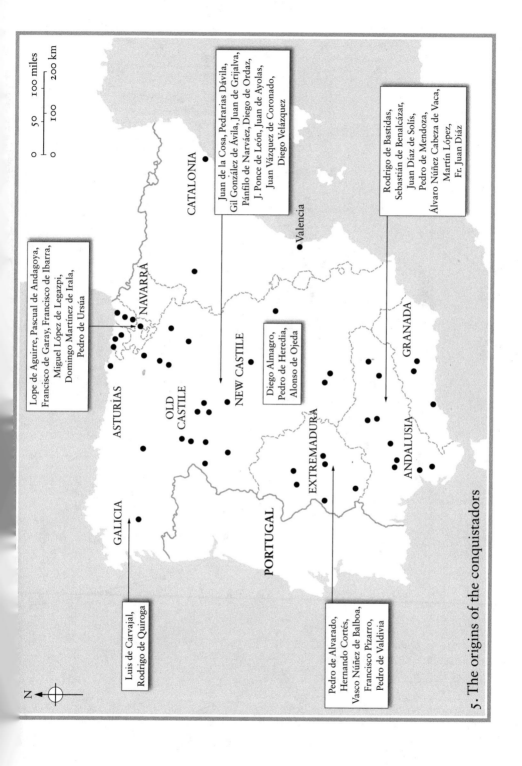

Juan de la Cosa, Pedrarias Dávila,
Gil González de Ávila, Juan de Grijalva,
Pánfilo de Narváez, Diego de Ordaz,
J. Ponce de León, Juan de Ayolas,
Juan Vázquez de Coronado,
Diego Velázquez

Lope de Aguirre, Pascual de Andagoya,
Francisco de Garay, Francisco de Ibarra,
Miguel López de Legazpi,
Domingo Martínez de Irala,
Pedro de Ursúa

Rodrigo de Bastidas,
Sebastián de Benalcázar,
Juan Díaz de Solís,
Pedro de Mendoza,
Álvaro Núñez Cabeza de Vaca,
Martín López,
Fr. Juan Díaz

Diego Almagro,
Pedro de Heredia,
Alonso de Ojeda

Luis de Carvajal,
Rodrigo de Quiroga

Pedro de Alvarado,
Hernando Cortés,
Vasco Núñez de Balboa,
Francisco Pizarro,
Pedro de Valdivia

CATALONIA

Valencia

NAVARRA

ASTURIAS

OLD
CASTILE

NEW CASTILE

GALICIA

PORTUGAL

EXTREMADURA

GRANADA

ANDALUSIA

N

0   50   100 miles
0   100   200 km

5. The origins of the conquistadors

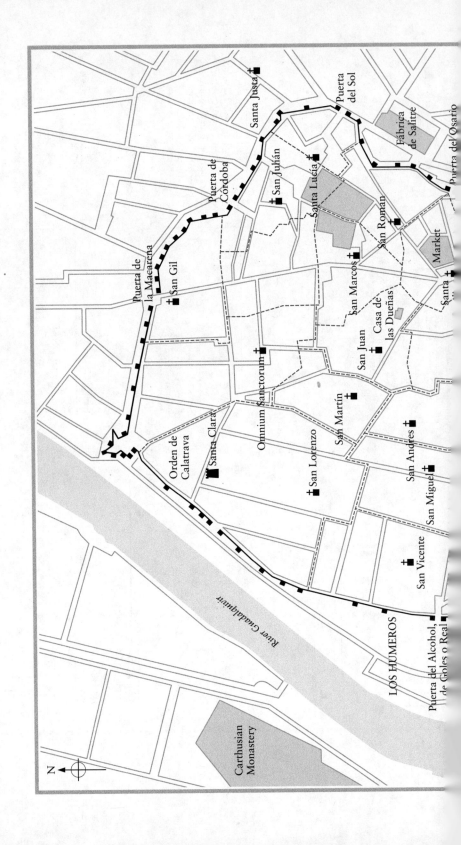

N

Santa Justa

Puerta del Sol

Fábrica de Salitre

Puerta del Osario

Puerta de Córdoba

San Julián

Santa Lucía

San Roman

Market

Puerta de la Macarena

San Gil

San Marcos

Santa

San Juan

Casa de las Dueñas

Omnium Sanctorum

San Martín

Santa Clara

Orden de Calatrava

San Lorenzo

San Andres

San Miguel

San Vicente

River Guadalquivir

LOS HUMEROS

Puerta del Alcohol,
o de Goles o Real

Carthusian
Monastery

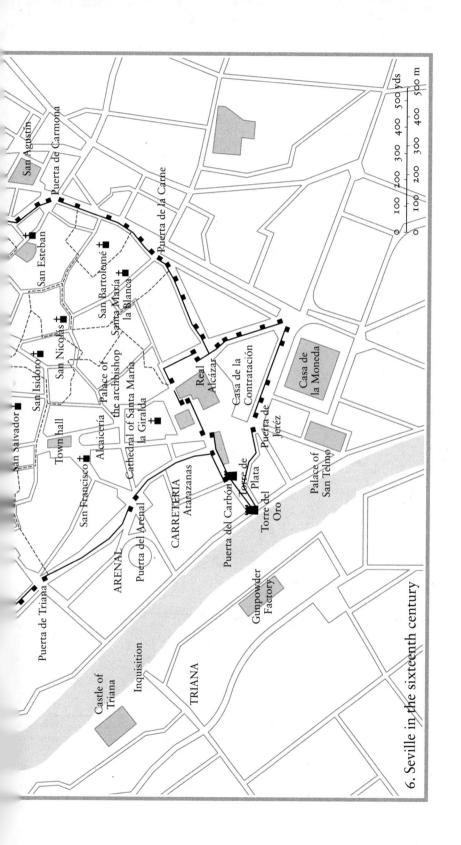

6. Seville in the sixteenth century

San Agustín
Puerta de Carmona
San Esteban
San Bartolomé
Santa María la Blanca
Puerta de la Carne
San Nicolás
San Isidoro
Palace of the archbishop
San Salvador
Town hall
Alcaicería
Cathedral of Santa María la Giralda
San Francisco
Real Alcázar
Casa de la Contratación
Casa de la Moneda
CARRETERÍA
Atarazanas
Puerta del Carbón
Torre de Plata
Puerta de Jeréz
Puerta de Triana
ARENAL
Puerta del Arenal
Torre del Oro
Palace of San Telmo
Gunpowder Factory
Castle of Triana
Inquisition
TRIANA

0   100   200   300   400   500 yds
0   100   200   300   400   500 m

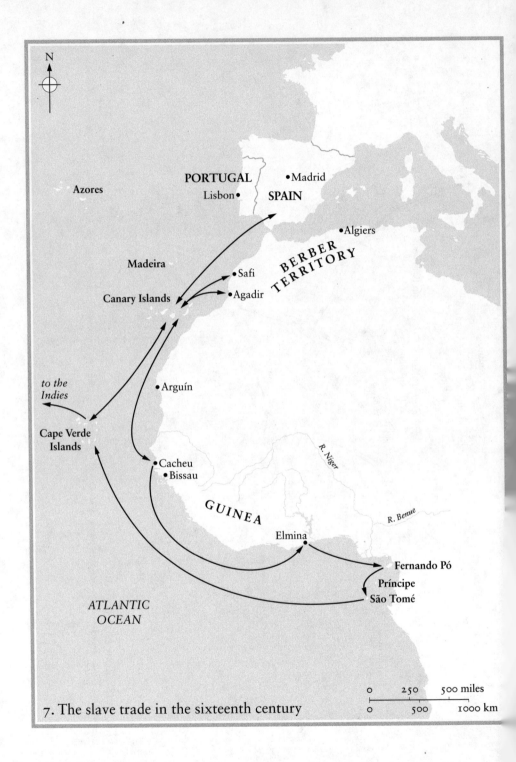

N

PORTUGAL •Madrid
Azores   SPAIN
       Lisbon•

                              •Algiers

                    BERBER
Madeira   TERRITORY
              •Safi
Canary Islands   •Agadir

to the
Indies   •Arguín

Cape Verde
Islands   •Cacheu
                 •Bissau
                              R. Niger

            GUINEA
                              R. Benue

              Elmina
                         •Fernando Pó
                          Príncipe
ATLANTIC   São Tomé
OCEAN

                    0   250   500 miles
                    0   500   1000 km

7. The slave trade in the sixteenth century

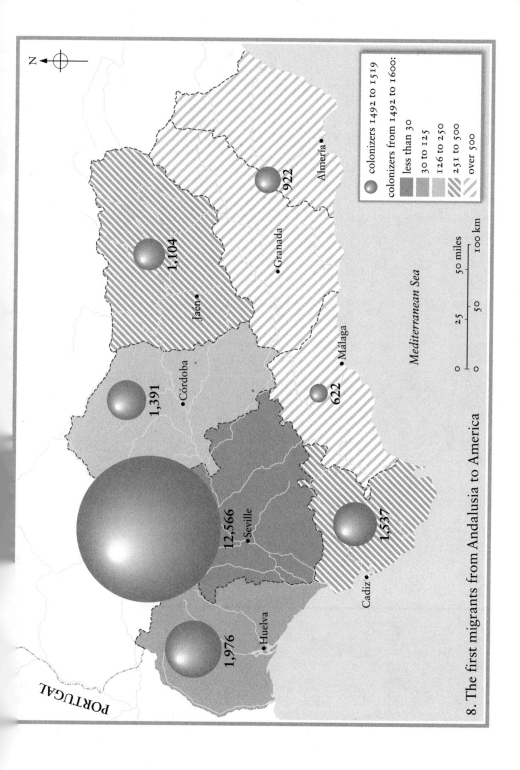

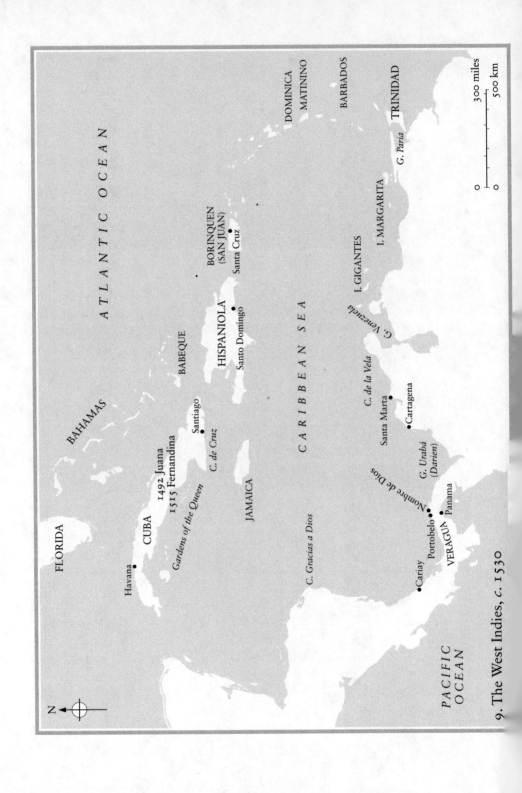

9. The West Indies, c. 1530

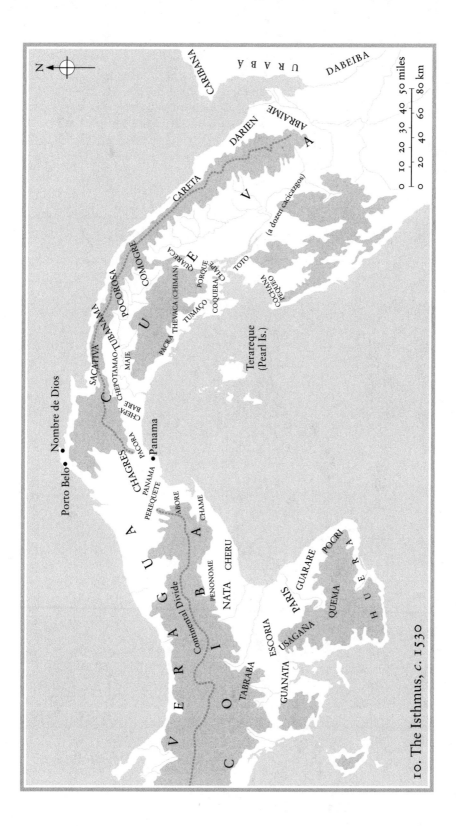

10. The Isthmus, c. 1530

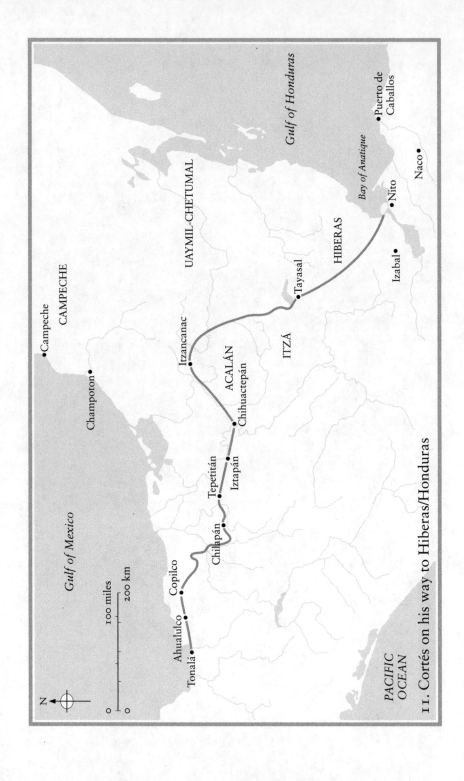

Gulf of Mexico

CAMPECHE

Campeche

Champoton

Gulf of Honduras

UAYMIL-CHETUMAL

Puerto de
Caballos

Bay of Anatique

Naco

Nito

HIBERAS

Izabal

Tayasal

Itzancanac

ACALÁN

Chihuactepán

ITZÁ

Tepetitán

Iztapán

Chilapán

Copilco

Ahualulco

Tonalá

100 miles

200 km

N

PACIFIC
OCEAN

11. Cortés on his way to Hiberas/Honduras

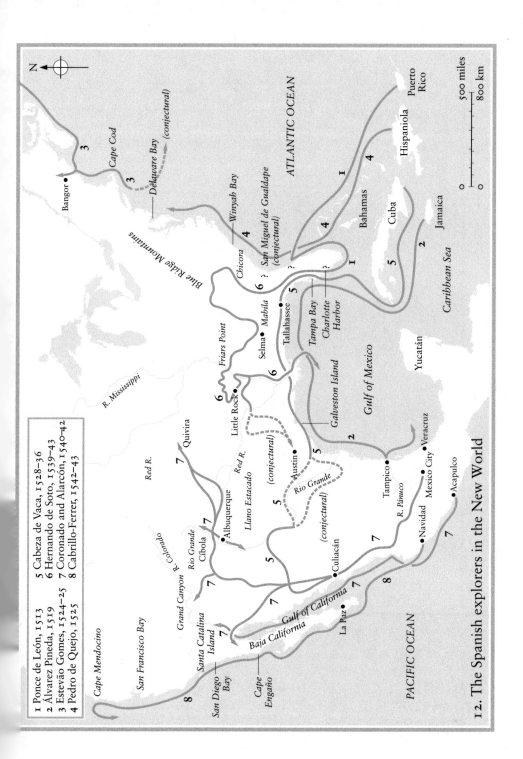

12. The Spanish explorers in the New World

1 Ponce de León, 1513
2 Álvarez Pineda, 1519
3 Estêvão Gomes, 1524–25
4 Pedro de Quejo, 1525
5 Cabeza de Vaca, 1528–36
6 Hernando de Soto, 1539–43
7 Coronado and Alarcón, 1540–42
8 Cabrillo-Ferrer, 1542–43

ATLANTIC OCEAN

PACIFIC OCEAN

Gulf of Mexico

Caribbean Sea

Puerto Rico
Hispaniola
Cuba
Jamaica
Bahamas
Yucatán

Cape Cod
Bangor
Delaware Bay (conjectural)
Winyah Bay
Chicora
San Miguel de Gualdape (conjectural)
Blue Ridge Mountains

Tallahassee
Mabila
Selma
Tampa Bay
Charlotte Harbor
Friars Point
R. Mississippi
Little Rock
Galveston Island

Quivira
Red R.
Red R.
Austin
Rio Grande
Llano Estacado
(conjectural)
(conjectural)

Albuquerque
Cíbola
Rio Grande
Grand Canyon
Colorado R.

Culiacán
Tampico
R. Pánuco
Mexico City
Veracruz
Navidad
Acapulco

Cape Mendocino
San Francisco Bay
Santa Catalina Island
San Diego Bay
Cape Engaño
Gulf of California
Baja California
La Paz

N

500 miles
800 km
0

0

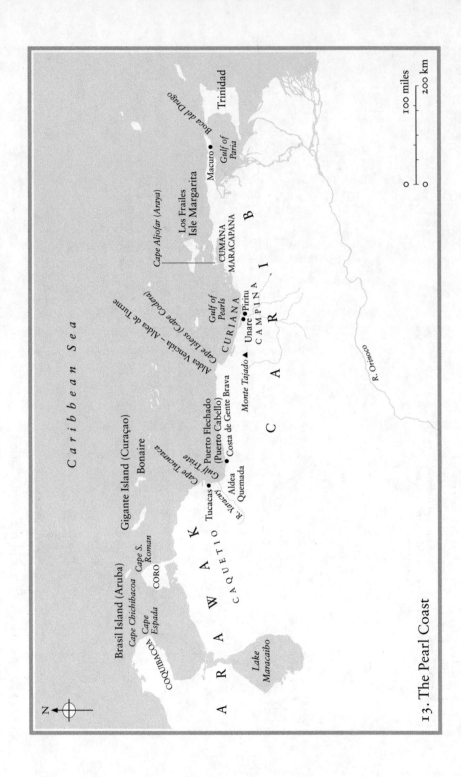

Caribbean Sea

Brasil Island (Aruba)

Cape Espada
Cape Chichibacoa
Cape S. Roman
COQUIBACOA
CORO

Gigante Island (Curaçao)
Bonaire

A R A W A K
CAQUETIO

Lake Maracaibo

Cape Tacuaca
Tucacas
R. Yaracuy
Aldea Quemada
Gulf Triste
Puerto Flechado (Puerto Cabello)
Costa de Gente Brava

Aldea Vencida – Aldea de Tumbe
Cape Isleos (Cape Codera)

Gulf of Pearls
CURIANA

Monte Tajado ▲

Unare ● Piritu
CAMPINA

C A R I B I

Cape Aljofar (Araya)
Los Frailes
Isle Margarita

CUMANA
MARACAPANA
B

Gulf of Paria
Macuro ●

Boca del Drago
Trinidad

R. Orinoco

0 ——— 100 miles
0 ——— 200 km

13. The Pearl Coast

N

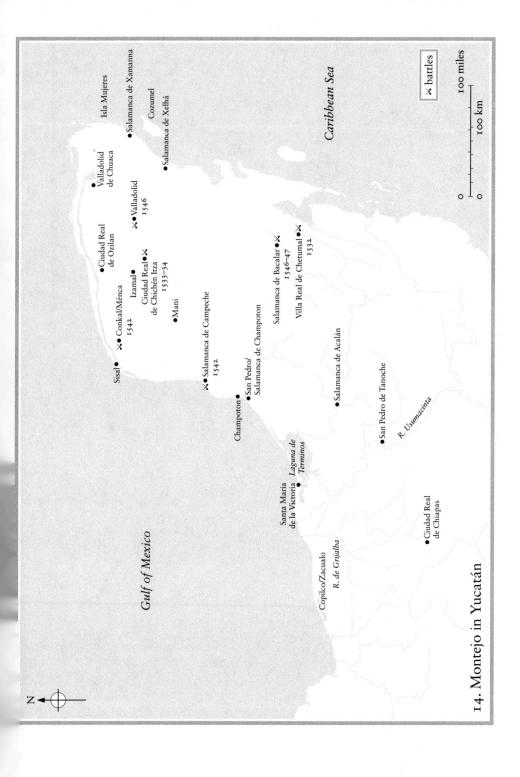

Gulf of Mexico

Caribbean Sea

Isla Mujeres

Salamanca de Xamanna

Cozumel

Salamanca de Xelhá

Valladolid
de Chuaca

Valladolid
Ciudad Real ✕● Valladolid
de Ozilan 1546

Izamal ●✕
Ciudad Real
de Chichén Itza
1533–34

Mani

✕● Conkal/Ménca
1542

Sisal

✕ Salamanca de Campeche
1542

Salamanca de Bacalar ●✕
1546–47

Villa Real de Chetumal ●✕
1532

San Pedro/
Salamanca de Champoton

Champoton

Salamanca de Acalán

San Pedro de Tanoche

R. Usumacintia

Santa María
de la Victoria ● Laguna de
Terminos

Copilco/Zacualo

R. de Grijalba

Ciudad Real
de Chiapas

× battles

0 _____ 100 miles
0 _____ 100 km

N

14. Montejo in Yucatán

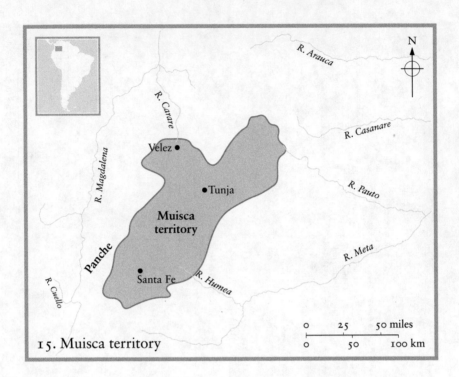

R. Arauca

R. Carare

N

R. Casanare

R. Magdalena

Velez •

R. Pauto

• Tunja

Muisca territory

Panche

R. Meta

R. Cuello

• Santa Fe

R. Humea

0	25	50 miles
0	50	100 km

15. Muisca territory

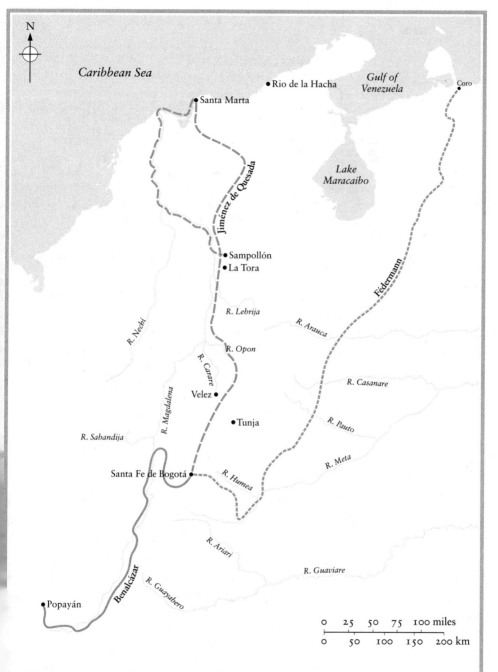

N

Caribbean Sea

Gulf of
Venezuela

• Rio de la Hacha

Coro •

• Santa Marta

Lake
Maracaibo

Jiménez de Quesada

Fédermann

• Sampollón
• La Tora

R. Lebrija

R. Arauca

R. Nechi

R. Opon

R. Casanare

R. Catare

R. Pauto

Velez •

R. Magdalena

• Tunja

R. Sabandija

R. Meta

Santa Fe de Bogotá •

R. Humea

R. Ariari

Benalcázar

R. Guayabero

R. Guaviare

• Popayán

0   25   50   75   100 miles

0   50   100   150   200 km

16. The routes of the great expeditions to Bogotá

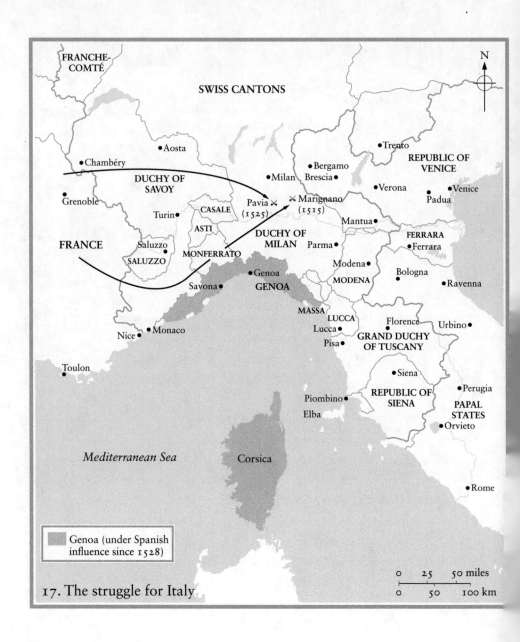

FRANCHE-
COMTÉ

SWISS CANTONS

N

•Aosta

•Chambéry

•Trento

REPUBLIC OF
VENICE

DUCHY OF
SAVOY

•Bergamo
•Milan Brescia•

•Verona

•Venice
Padua•

Grenoble•

CASALE

Turin•

Pavia ×
(1525)

× Marignano
(1515)

ASTI

FRANCE

Saluzzo•

SALUZZO

MONFERRATO

DUCHY OF
MILAN

Mantua•

Parma•

FERRARA
•Ferrara

Savona•

•Genoa
GENOA

Modena•

MODENA

Bologna
•

•Ravenna

Nice •
•Monaco

MASSA

Lucca•

LUCCA

Pisa•

•Florence

Urbino•

GRAND DUCHY
OF TUSCANY

Toulon
•

Mediterranean Sea

Corsica

Piombino•

Elba

•Siena

REPUBLIC OF
SIENA

•Perugia

PAPAL
STATES

•Orvieto

•Rome

  Genoa (under Spanish
  influence since 1528)

0   25   50 miles

0   50   100 km

17. The struggle for Italy

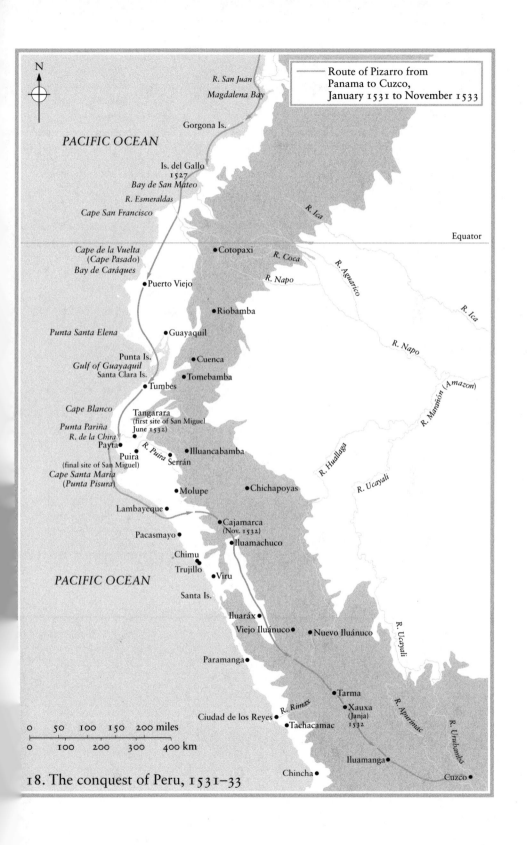

N

PACIFIC OCEAN

R. San Juan
Magdalena Bay
Gorgona Is.

Is. del Gallo
1527
Bay de San Mateo
R. Esmeraldas
Cape San Francisco

Equator

Cape de la Vuelta
(Cape Pasado)
Bay de Caráques
●Puerto Viejo

●Cotopaxi
R. Coca
R. Napo

R. Ica

R. Aguarico

R. Ica

●Riobamba

Punta Santa Elena
●Guayaquil

Punta Is.
Gulf of Guayaquil
Santa Clara Is.
●Tumbes

●Cuenca

●Tomebamba

R. Napo

R. Marañón (Amazon)

Cape Blanco
Tangarara
(first site of San Miguel
June 1532)
Punta Pariña
R. de la Chira
Payta●
Puira
(final site of San Miguel)
Cape Santa María
(Punta Pisura)

R. Puira ●Illuancabamba
Serrán

R. Huallaga

R. Ucayali

●Molupe
●Chichapoyas

Lambayeque ●

●Cajamarca
(Nov. 1532)
Pacasmayo ●
●Iluamachuco

Chimu
Trujillo
●Viru

PACIFIC OCEAN

Santa Is.

●Iluaráx
Viejo Iluánuco ●
●Nuevo Iluánuco

R. Ucayali

Paramanga ●

●Tarma
R. Rímax
●Xauxa
(Janja)
Ciudad de los Reyes ●
●Tachacamac
1532

R. Apurímac

●Iluamanga

R. Urubamba

Chincha ●
●Cuzco

0   50   100   150   200 miles
0   100   200   300   400 km

18. The conquest of Peru, 1531–33

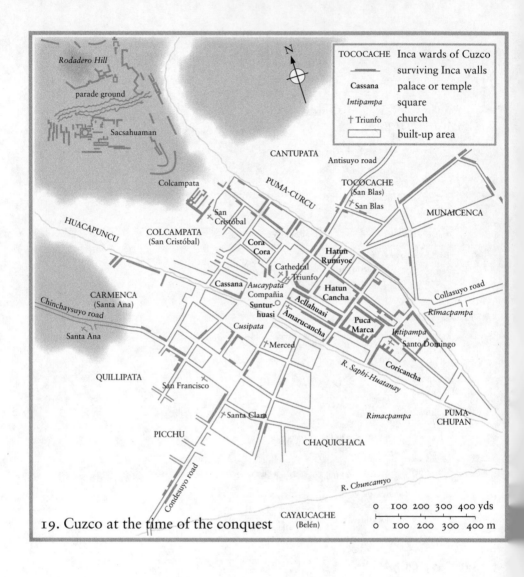

Rodadero Hill

parade ground

Sacsahuaman

TOCOCACHE	Inca wards of Cuzco
	surviving Inca walls
Cassana	palace or temple
Intipampa	square
† Triunfo	church
☐	built-up area

N

CANTUPATA
Antisuyo road

TOCOCACHE
(San Blas)

PUMA-CURCU

Colcampata

San Blas

MUNAICENCA

San
Cristóbal

HUACAPUNCU

COLCAMPATA
(San Cristóbal)

Cora
Cora

Hatun
Rumiyoc

Cathedral
Triunfo

Cassana *Aucaypata*

CARMENCA
(Santa Ana)

Compañia
Suntur-
huasi

Acllahuasi

Hatun
Cancha

Collasuyo road

Rimacpampa

Chinchaysuyo road

Amarucancha

Puca
Marca

Intipampa
Santo Domingo

Santa Ana

Cusipata

† Merced

R. Saphi-Huatanay

Coricancha

QUILLIPATA

† San Francisco

Rimacpampa

PUMA-
CHUPAN

PICCHU

† Santa Clara

CHAQUICHACA

Condesuyo road

R. Chuncamyo

CAYAUCACHE
(Belén)

| 0 | 100 | 200 | 300 | 400 yds |
| 0 | 100 | 200 | 300 | 400 m |

19. Cuzco at the time of the conquest

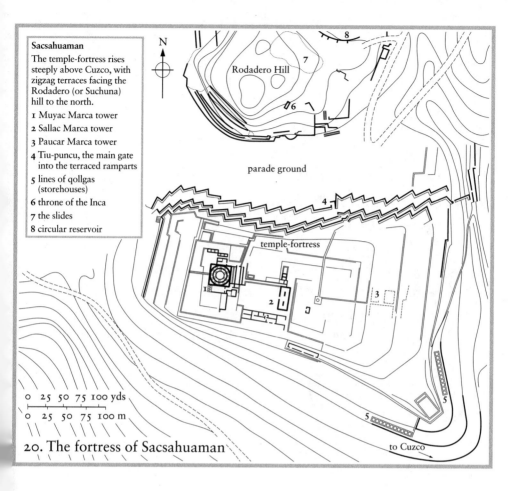

N

Rodadero Hill

parade ground

temple-fortress

0 25 50 75 100 yds

0 25 50 75 100 m

20. The fortress of Sacsahuaman

to Cuzco

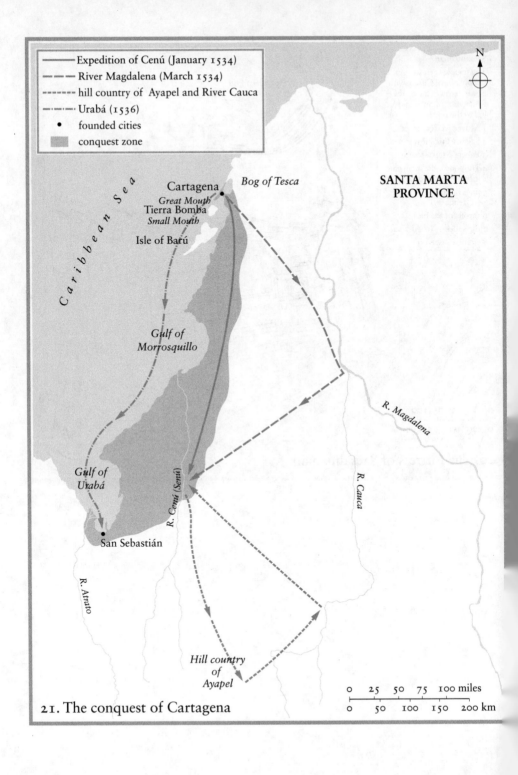

Expedition of Cenú (January 1534)
River Magdalena (March 1534)
hill country of Ayapel and River Cauca
Urabá (1536)
• founded cities
conquest zone

Caribbean Sea

Cartagena
Great Mouth
Tierra Bomba
Small Mouth

Isle of Barú

Bog of Tesca

SANTA MARTA PROVINCE

Gulf of Morrosquillo

R. Magdalena

Gulf of Urabá

R. Cenú (Senú)

R. Cauca

San Sebastián

R. Atrato

Hill country of Ayapel

0   25   50   75   100 miles
0   50   100   150   200 km

21. The conquest of Cartagena

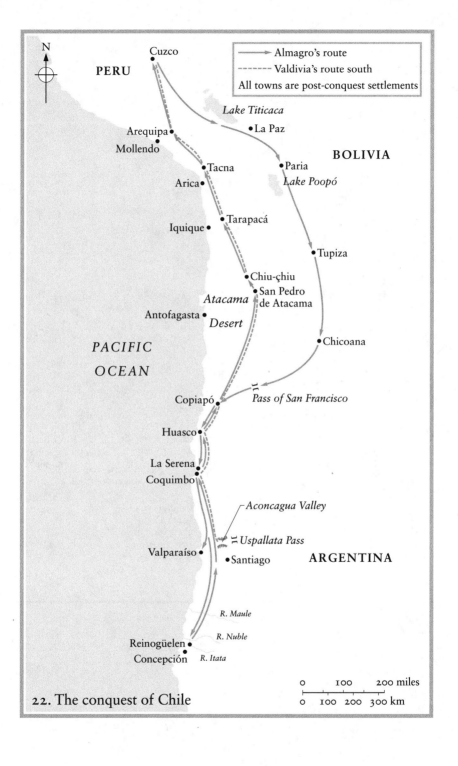

N

PERU

Cuzco

Almagro's route
Valdivia's route south
All towns are post-conquest settlements

Lake Titicaca
La Paz

Arequipa
Mollendo

BOLIVIA

Tacna
Paria
Lake Poopó
Arica

Tarapacá

Iquique

Tupiza

Chiu-çhiu
San Pedro
de Atacama
Atacama

Antofagasta
Desert

PACIFIC

OCEAN

Chicoana

Copiapó
Pass of San Francisco

Huasco

La Serena
Coquimbo

Aconcagua Valley

Uspallata Pass

Valparaíso
Santiago
ARGENTINA

R. Maule

R. Nuble
Reinogüelen
Concepción
R. Itata

22. The conquest of Chile

0   100   200 miles
0   100   200   300 km

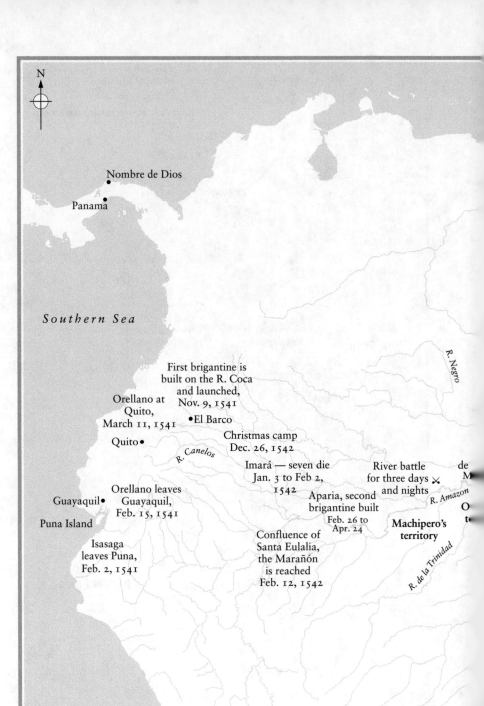

N

Nombre de Dios

Panamá

Southern Sea

First brigantine is
built on the R. Coca
and launched,
Nov. 9, 1541

Orellano at
Quito,
March 11, 1541

• El Barco

Quito •

Christmas camp
Dec. 26, 1542

R. Canelos

Imará — seven die
Jan. 3 to Feb 2,
1542

River battle
for three days ✕
and nights

de
M

Orellano leaves
Guayaquil,
Feb. 15, 1541

Aparia, second
brigantine built

R. Amazon

O

Guayaquil •

Feb. 26 to
Apr. 24

t

Puna Island

**Machipero's
territory**

Isasaga
leaves Puna,
Feb. 2, 1541

Confluence of
Santa Eulalia,
the Marañón
is reached
Feb. 12, 1542

R. de la Trinidad

R. Negro

23. Orellana on the Amazon

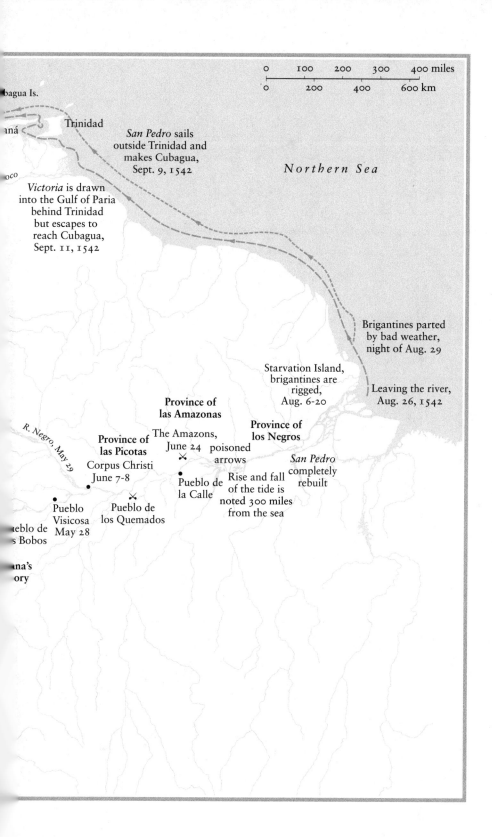

bagua Is.

aná

Trinidad

San Pedro sails
outside Trinidad and
makes Cubagua,
Sept. 9, 1542

oco

Victoria is drawn
into the Gulf of Paria
behind Trinidad
but escapes to
reach Cubagua,
Sept. 11, 1542

Northern Sea

Brigantines parted
by bad weather,
night of Aug. 29

Starvation Island,
brigantines are
rigged,
Aug. 6-20

Leaving the river,
Aug. 26, 1542

**Province of
las Amazonas**

**Province of
los Negros**

R. Negro, May 29

**Province of
las Picotas**

The Amazons,
June 24

poisoned
arrows

San Pedro
completely
rebuilt

Corpus Christi
June 7-8

Pueblo de
la Calle

Rise and fall
of the tide is
noted 300 miles
from the sea

Pueblo
Visicosa
May 28

Pueblo de
los Quemados

eblo de
s Bobos

ana's
ory

0   100   200   300   400 miles

0   200   400   600 km

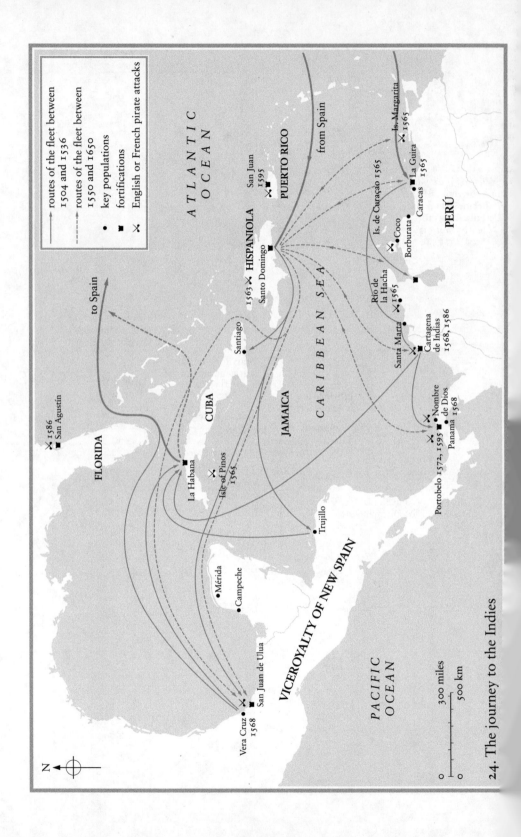

Map legend:

→ routes of the fleet between 1504 and 1536
⇢ routes of the fleet between 1550 and 1650
● key populations
■ fortifications
✕ English or French pirate attacks

ATLANTIC OCEAN

from Spain

to Spain

FLORIDA

✕ 1586 San Agustín

CUBA

La Habana ■

✕ Isle of Pinos 1565

Santiago

JAMAICA

CARIBBEAN SEA

VICEROYALTY OF NEW SPAIN

PACIFIC OCEAN

Mérida ●
Campeche ●

Trujillo ●

San Juan de Ulua ■
✕ Vera Cruz 1568

San Juan 1595 ✕
PUERTO RICO

HISPANIOLA ✕
1563 ✕ Santo Domingo ■

Is. de Curaçao 1565

✕ Is. Margarita 1565

La Guira 1565 ✕
Caracas 1565 ●

Coco ●
Borburata ■ ✕

PERÚ

Río de la Hacha 1565 ✕
Santa Marta ● ✕
Cartagena de Indias 1568, 1586 ■

Nombre de Dios 1568 ● ✕
Portobelo 1572, 1595 ✕
Panama 1568 ■

N

0   300 miles
0   500 km

24. The journey to the Indies

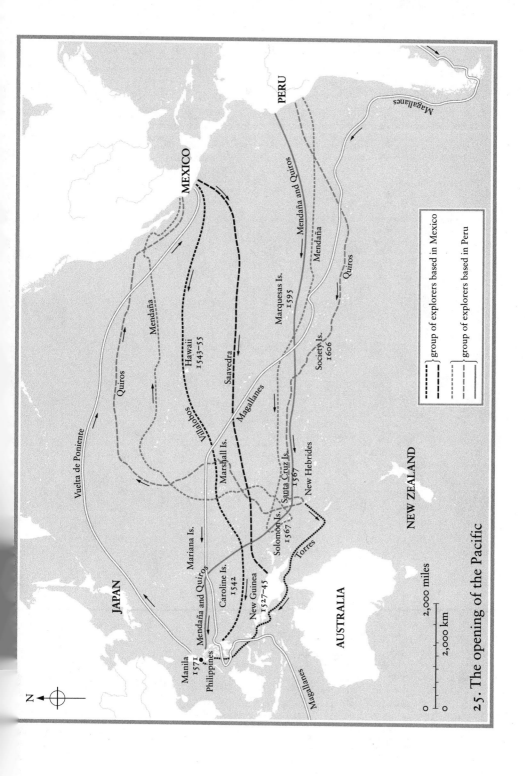

N

JAPAN

Manila
1571
Philippines

Mariana Is.

Caroline Is.
1542

New Guinea
1527–45

AUSTRALIA

NEW ZEALAND

Torres

Solomon Is.
1567

Marshall Is.

New Hebrides

Santa Cruz Is.
1567

Vuelta de Poniente

Quiros

Mendaña

Hawaii
1543–55

Villalobos

Saavedra

Magallanes

Mendaña and Quiros

Magallanes

MEXICO

Mendaña and Quiros

Mendaña

Marquesas Is.
1595

Society Is.
1606

Quiros

PERU

Magallanes

group of explorers based in Mexico

group of explorers based in Peru

2,000 miles

2,000 km

0

0

25. The opening of the Pacific

N

Emden

Groningen

Leeuwarden

11

12

10

Koevorden

Enkhuizen

Alkmaar • Hoorn

Zwolle

9

Haarlem

Amsterdam

6

The Hague

7

8

Delft Rotterdam

Arnhem

Zutfen

The Brill Dordt Schoonhoven

Groenlo

Zierikzee

Geertruidenberg

Den Bosch

Cleve • Emmerik

Wesel

5

Goes

Breda

8

Gelder

Bergen-op-Zoom

Eindhoven

Venlo

Ostend • Sluis

Antwerp

2

Bruges

Ghent

Roermond

Grevelingen • Dunkirk

3 • Malines/Mechelen

Köln

I

Yper

Brussels

Maastricht

St Truiden

Lille

II IV

V Nivelles

4

I

Mons

Namur

Douai

Valenciennes

VI

Arras

Cambrai III

VII

0   20   40   60   80 miles

0 20 40 60 80 100 km

Luxembourg

26. The Netherlands in the 1550s

Bibliography

The reconstruction of Mexico-Tenochtitlan is well analyzed in Lucía Mier and Rocha Terán, *La primera traza de la ciudad de México* (2 vols.; Mexico, 2005), and there is also Jaime Montell's excellent *México: el inicio* (Mexico, 2005). Cortés's time in power, his journey to Honduras (Hiberas), and his later life are to be seen in José Luis Martínez's careful biography *Hernán Cortés* (Mexico, 1990), and four useful accompanying volumes of documents. The Welsers have been magisterially studied by Juan Friede. The Montejos in Yucatán can be followed in Robert Chamberlain's admirable *The Conquest and Colonization of Yucatan 1517–1550* (Washington, D.C., 1948).

On Valladolid in the 1520s, there is Bartolomé Bennassar's *Valladolid au siècle d'or* (Paris, 1967). On Charles V, I still like best the biography of Karl Brandi, translated by Veronica Wedgwood: *The emperor Charles V: The Growth and Destiny of a Man and a World* (London, 1949). But there are also excellent works by Fernández Álvarez (*Carlos V, el césar y el hombre* [Madrid, 1999]), Federico Chabod (*Carlo V e il suo imperio* [Turin, 1985]) and the former's great collection, the seven-volume *Corpus documental de Carlos V* (Salamanca, 1973–82). Now we can also study the remarkable collected works of J. Martínez Millán, ed., *La corte de Carlos V* (5 vols.; Madrid, 2000). Very late I came upon the useful life of the empress Isabel by Antonio Villacorta (Madrid, 2009).

On Pizarro and the conquest of Peru, there is now John Hemming's masterpiece *The Conquest of the Incas* (London, 1970), and his more recent *Monuments of the Incas* (London, 2010), with admirable photographs by Edward Ranney. The work should be supplemented by James Lockhart's remarkable *The Men of Cajamarca* (Austin, 1972) and the same author's *Spanish Peru, 1532–1560* (Madison, 1968). New lives of Pizarro include J. A. Busto Duthurburu's *Pizarro* (2 vols.; Lima, 2001). A work of consummate skill is Guillermo Lohmann's *Les Espinosa* (Paris, 1968). Other important secondary works on Peru include Rafael Varón Gabai's *La ilusión del poder: apogeo y decadencia de los Pizarro en la conquista del Perú* (Lima, 1996), and the same author's *Francisco Pizarro and His Brothers* (Norman, Okla., 1997). Teodoro Hampe's brilliant biography of Pedro de la Gasca, *Don Pedro de la Gasca* (Lima, 1989), deserves translation.

On the conquest of Peru, like my many predecessors in this fascinating field, I have depended a great deal on a series of contemporary accounts such as the works of Pedro Pizarro, Cieza de León, Martín de Murúa, Alonso Enríquez de Guzmán, Francisco de Jerez, Garcilaso de la Vega, Pedro Sancho de Hoz, and even Hernando Pizarro's letters to the judges in Santo Domingo. But I confess I missed the literally hundreds of *informaciones de servicios y méritos* that characterize the similar events in New Spain / Mexico.

Valdivia's life has been well written, and his companions are studied in Thayer's *Valdivia y sus compañeros* (Santiago de Chile, 1950). On Jiménez de Quesada, there is the edition of his own memoir by Demetrio Ramos, *Ximénez de Quesada* (Seville, 1972), and there is also Friede's *Gonzalo Jiménez de Quesada a través de documentos históricos, estudio biográfico, 1509–1550* (Bogota, 1960). See, too, *Vida y viajes de Nicolás Federmann* (Bogotá, 1964). Here we encounter another illuminating work by John Hemming, *The Search for El Dorado* (London, 1978).

De Soto in North America is magnificently recalled by David Ewing Duncan in *Hernando de Soto* (New York, 1995), one of the outstanding biographies of the century.

The extraordinary journey of Álvar Núñez Cabeza de Vaca in the southern United States is analyzed well in *Castaways,* Roberto Ferrando, ed. (Madrid, 1984), and Enrique Pupo Walker (Berkeley, 1993).

Of the many works relevant to the life and work of Bartolomé de las Casas, there is Lewis Hanke's deservedly famous *The Spanish Struggle for Justice in the Conquest of America* (Philadelphia, 1949) and a more recent biography, Luis Iglesias Ortega's *Bartolomé de las Casas: cuarenta y cuatro años infinitos* (Seville, 2007). There is also the astonishing life of Las Casas by Manuel Jiménez Fernández. Its two volumes cover three years but illuminate an age. On ecclesiastical matters, I was guided by the great history of the papacy by Ludwig von Pastor, trans. Mgr. Ralph Kerr (vols. 5 to 20; London, 1898–1930). The challenge of Erasmian thought is marvelously studied by Marcel Bataillon, *Erasmo y España: Estudios sobre la historia espiritual del siglo XVI,* Mexico, translated from the French, 1950.

MANUSCRIPT DOCUMENTS

I have, as in previous works of mine, consulted several *legajos* (files) of the Archivo de Indias in Seville, especially the sections named *Justicia,* where there are the texts of so many *residencias* (inquiries as to the conduct of officials) and *Patronato,* and in particular *legajo* 150, which contains a mass of documents loosely referred to as *Informaciones de servicios y méritos.* Other sections that I saw included *Escribanía de camera* and the magnificently named *Indiferente general.*

I relied heavily on the *Colección de documentos inéditos relativos al descubrimiento . . . de las posesiones españolas en América y Oceanía,* eds. Joaquin Pacheco and Francisco Cardenas (42 vols.; Madrid, 1864–89). What a work! To possess these volumes as I do is a pleasure. The references to them are abbreviated CDI.

I made one or two raids into the Archivo de Protocolos de Sevilla, and I also looked at the Additional Manuscripts in the British Library.

BOOKS AND ARTICLES

This is a list of books and articles referred to in the notes of this volume. A full bibliography will be included at the end of volume 3 of this work.

Aiton, Arthur. *Antonio de Mendoza.* Durham, N.C., 1927.

Albèri, Eugenio. *Relazioni degli ambasciatori veneti al senato,* series 1. Florence, 1839–63.

Alvarado, Pedro de. *Residencia of Pedro de Alvarado.* 1535. Edited by José Fernando Ramírez. Mexico, 1847.

Álvarez, Vicente. *Relation du beau voyage que fit aux Pays-Bas, en 1548, le prince Philippe de Espagne.* Brussels, 1964.

Andagoya, Pascual de. *Relación y documentos.* Madrid, 1986.

Andrés, M. *La teología Española en el siglo XVI.* Madrid, 1977.

Angulo, Diego. *Pedro Berruguete en Paredes de Nava.* Barcelona, 1946.

Arranz, Luis. *Don Diego Colón.* Vol. 1. Madrid, 1982.

———. *Repartimientos y encomiendas en la isla Española.* Madrid, 1991.

Bataillon, Marcel. "Les colons du Pérou contre Charles Quint 1544–1548." *Annales,* May–June 1967.

———. *Erasmo y España: Estudios sobre la historia espiritual del siglo XVI,* Mexico, 1950.

———. "Novo mundo e fim do mundo." *Revista de historia* 18. São Paulo, 1954.

———. "La rébellion pizarriste enfantement de l'Amérique espagnole." *Diogène* 43 (July–Sept. 1963).

Bauer, Brian S. *The Development of the Inca State.* Austin, Tex., 1998.

Bejarano, Ignacio. *Actas del Cabildo.* Mexico, 1889.

Bennassar, Bartolomé. *Valladolid au siecle d'or.* Paris, 1967.

Bernal, Antonio-Miguel. *La financiación de la carrera de Indias, 1492–1824.* Seville, 1992.

Blockmans, Wim, and Nicollette Mout. *The World of Charles V.* New York, 2000.

Bonet Correa, Antonio. *Monasterios iberoamericanos.* Madrid, 2001.

Borah, Woodrow. "The Cortés Codex of Vienna." *The Americas,* 2. vol. 19. 1962.

Brading, David. *The First America.* Cambridge, U.K., 1991.

———. *Mexican Phoenix.* Cambridge, U.K., 2002.

Brandi, Karl. *The emperor Charles V: The Growth and Destiny of a Man and a World.* Translated by C. V. Wedgwood. London, 1949.

Braudel, Fernand. *The Mediterranean and the Mediterranean World in the Age of Philip II.* Translated by Siân Reynolds. 2 vols. London, 1972–73.

Brunke, José de la Puente. *Encomiendas y encomenderos en el Perú.* Seville, 1992.

Burckhardt, Jacob. *The Civilisation of the Renaissance in Italy.* London, 1950.

———. *Reflections on History.* London, 1943.

Busto Duthurburu, J. A. del. *Diccionário histórico biográfico de los conquistadores del Perú,* 2 vols. Lima, 1973.

———. *Pizarro.* 2 vols. Lima, 2000.

———. *La tierra y la sangre de Francisco Pizarro.* Lima, 1993.

———. *Los trece de las fama.* Lima, 1989.

Cabeza de Vaca, Álvar Núñez. *Naufragios y comentarios.* Edited by Robert Fernando. Madrid, 1984.

Cadenas y Vicent, Vicente de. *Caminos y derroteros que recorrió el emperador Carlos V.* Madrid, 1999.

———. *Carlos I de Castilla, señor de las Indias.* Madrid, 1988.

Campbell, L. *Renaissance Faces: Van Eyck to Titian.* London, 2008.

Carande, Ramón. *Carlos V y sus banqueros.* 3 vols. 3d ed. Barcelona, 1987.

Carmack, Robert M. *Historia general de Centro América.* 2 vols. Madrid, 1993.

Carolus. Ghent, 1999, Toledo, 2001. Exhibition catalog.

Carolus V. Barcelona, 1999. Exhibition catalog.

Carreño, Alberto María. "La primera biblioteca del continente Americano," in *Divulgación histórica,* Mexico, vol. 4, 1943.

Carvajal. See Medina, José Toribio.

Castañeda, Pedro de. *Spanish Explorers of the Southern United States.* New York, 1907.

Castelló Yturbide, Teresa. *El arte plumaria en México.* Mexico, 1993.

Cervantes de Salazar, Francisco. *México en 1554 y túmulo imperial.* Mexico, 1964.

Chabod, Federico. *Carlos V y su imperio (Carlos V e il suo imperio).* Translated by Rodrigo Riza. Madrid, 1992.

Chamberlain, Robert S. *The Conquest and Colonization of Yucatan, 1517–1550.* Washington, D.C., 1948.

———. "La controversía entre Cortés y Velázquez." *Anales de la sociedad geográfica de Guatemala* 19 (September 1943).

———. "The Lineage of the Adelantado Francisco Montejo and His Last Will and Testament." *Revista de historia de America,* no. 8 (April 1940).

Chaunu, Pierre, and Huguette. *Séville et l'Atlantique.* 7 vols. Paris, 1956 onward.

Chevalier, François. *La formation des grandes domaines au Mexique.* Paris, 1952.

Chipman, Donald E. *Moctezuma's Children.* Austin, Tex., 2005.

———. *Nuño de Guzmán and the Province of Pánuco in New Spain, 1518–1533.* Glendale, 1967.

Cieza de León, Pedro. *Descubrimiento y conquista del Perú.* Edited by Carmelo Sáenz de Santa María. Madrid, 1986.

Clendinnen, Inga. *Ambivalent Conquests.* Cambridge, U.K., 1987.

Colección de documentos inéditos para la historia de Chile desde el viaje de Magallenes hasta la batalla de Maipo. Edited by José Toribio Medina. 30 vols. Santiago de Chile, 1888–1902.

Colección de documentos inéditos para la historia de España. Edited by M. de Navarette, 113 vol., 1842 onward. This collection is referred to in the notes as CDIHE.

Colección de documentos inéditos relativos al descubrimiento, conquista y colonización de las antiguas posesiones Españoles en Ultramar. 2nd selection. 25 vols. Madrid, 1884–1932. This collection is referred to in the notes as CDIU.

Colección de documentos inéditos relativos al descubrimiento, conquista y organización de las posesiones Españoles en América y Oceania. Edited by Joaquín Pacheco and Francisco Cárdenas. 42 vols. Madrid, 1864–89. This collection is referred to in the notes as CDI.

Constant, G. "Le mariage de Marie Tudor et Philippe II." *Revue de l'histoire diplomatique* 26 (1912).

Conway, G.L.R. "Hernando Alonso." Publications of the American Jewish Historical Society. 1928.

Cooper, Edward. *Castillos señoriales en la corona de Castilla.* 3 vols. Salamanca, 1991.

Coronado, Francisco Vázquez de. *An Account of His Voyage to Cibolla.* In Hakluyt Society. Vol. 9. London, 1888.

Cortés, Hernán. *Cartas de relación.* Edited by Angel Delgado Gómez. Madrid, 1993. The best English translation is that of Anthony Pagden, *Letters from Mexico,* with an introduction by Sir John Elliott, New Haven, 1986.

Covarrubias, M. *Mexico South: The Isthmus of Tehuantepec.* New York, 1946.

Crane, Nicholas. *Mercator: The Man Who Mapped the Planet.* London, 2002.

Cuesta, Luisa. "Una documentación interesante sobre la familia del conquistador del Perú." *Revista de Indias,* no. 8 (1946–47).

Cuevas, Mariano, S.J., ed. *Documentos inéditos del siglo XVI para la historia de México.* Mexico, 1914.

D'Altroy, Terence. *The Incas.* Oxford, 2002.

Defourneaux, Marcel. *La vie quotidienne en Espagne au siècle d'or.* Paris, 1964.

Deive, Carlos Esteban. *La Española y la esclavitud del Indio.* Santo Domingo, Dom. Rep. 1995.

Delmarcel, Guy. *Los Honores: Flemish Tapestries for the emperor Charles V.* Mechlin, Belg., 2000.

Díaz del Castillo, Bernal. *Historia verdadera de la Nueva España.* 2 vols. Madrid, 1982. Translated by P. P. Maudslay, *The True History of the Conquest of New Spain.* 5 vols. London, 1908–16.

Díaz y Mesa, Guillermo. *Leyendas y episodios chilenos.* Santiago de Chile, 1930.

Dios, Salustiano de. *El consejo real de Castilla.* Madrid, 1982.

Dorantes de Carranza, Baltasar. *Sumario de relación de las cosas de la Nueva España.* Revised edition. Mexico, 1970.

Duncan, David Ewing. *Hernando de Soto.* New York, 1995.

Duran, Fray Diego. *Historia de las Indias de Nueva-España.* 2 vols. Mexico, 1867.

Dworski, R. J. "The Council of the Indies in Spain." Thesis, Columbia University, 1979.

Eichberger, Dagmar, ed. *Women of Distinction.* Leuven, Belg., 2005.

Elliott, Sir John. *Empires of the Atlantic World: Britain and Spain in America 1492–1830.* New Haven, 2006.

Elvas, A Gentleman of. *True Relation of the Vicissitudes Which Attended Governor Hernando de Soto and Some Nobles of Portugal in the Discovery of the Province of Florida.* In *Narratives of de Soto in the Conquest of Florida.* Translated by Buckingham Smith. Gainesville, Fla., 1968.

Enríquez de Guzmán, Alonso. *Libro de la Vida de.* Edited by Howard Keniston. Madrid, 1960.

Erasmus, Desiderio. *Collected Works.* Edited and translated by Robert D. Siler and Jane E. Phillips. 48 vols. Toronto, 2008.

Estete, Miguel de. "Descubrimiento y la conquista del Perú." Edited by Carlos María

Larrea. *Boletín de la sociedad ecuatoriana de estudios americanos* 1, no. 3 (Quito, 1918).

Ezquerra, Ramón. "Los compañeros de Cortés." *Revista de Indias* 1 (1948).

Fabié, Antonio María. *Vida y escritos de Bartolomé de las Casas.* Madrid, 1879.

Federmann, Nikolaus. *Indianische Historia: eine schöne kurtz-weilige Historia, Nicolaus Federmann des Jungers von Ulm.* Hagenau, 1557. Translated by Juan Friede. In Joaquín Gabaldón Márquez. *Descubrimiento y conquista de Venezuela,* 155–250. Caracas, 1962.

Fernández Álvarez, Manuel. *Carlos V, el césar y el hombre.* Madrid, 1999.

———, ed. *El corpus documental de Carlos V.* 7 vols. Salamanca, 1973–82.

———. *Sombras y luces en la España imperial.* Madrid, 2004.

Fernández de Enciso, Martín. *Suma de geografía.* Seville, 1519.

Fernández de Navarrete, Martín. *Colección de viajes y descubrimientos que hicieron por mar los Españoles.* Edited by Carlos Seco Serrano. 3 vols. Madrid, 1959.

Fernández de Oviedo, Gonzalo. *Batallas y quinquagenas: batalla prima.* 4 vols. Madrid, 1983–2002.

———. *Historia general y natural de las Indias.* Edited by Juan Pérez de Tudela. 5 vols. Madrid, 1959. Referred in the text as Oviedo.

Fernández Martín, Luis. *Hernando Pizarro en el Castillo de la Mota.* Valladolid, 1991.

Fita, Fidel, S.J. "Los judaizantes Españoles en los primeros cinco años del reinado de Carlos V." *Boletín de la real academia de historia* 33 (Madrid, 1898).

Fontán, Antonio, and Jerzy Axer, eds. *Españoles y polacos en la corte de Carlos V.* Madrid, 1994.

Foronda, Manuel de. *Estancias y viajes de Carlos V.* Madrid, 1895.

Friede, Juan. *Documentos inéditos para la historia de Colombia.* 3 vols. I, 1509–28, Bogotá, 1955.

———. *Gonzalo Jiménez de Quesada a través de documentos históricos, estudio biográfico, 1509–1550.* Bogotá, 1960.

———. *Vida y viajes de Nicolás Federmann.* Bogotá, 1964.

———. *Los Welser.* Bogotá, 1965.

Gachard, Louis-Prosper. *Correspondance de Charles V et d'Adrien VI.* Brussels, 1859.

———. *Relations des ambassadeurs vénitiens sur Charles Quint et Philippe II.* Brussels, 1855.

———. *Retraite et mort de Charles Quint.* Brussels, 1854.

Galíndez de Carvajal, Lorenzo. *Crónicas de Castilla desde de Don Alfonso el sabio hasta los Católicos don Fernando y doña Isabel.* Madrid, 1875–78.

García-Baquero González, Antonio. *La Carrera de Indias.* Seville, 1992.

García Bernal, Manuela Cristina. *Población y encomienda en Yucatán bajo los Austrias.* Seville, 1978.

García Bravo, Alonso. *Información de méritos y servicios de.* Edited by Manuel Toussaint. Mexico, 1956.

García Icazbalceta, Joaquín, ed. *Colección de documentos para la historia de México.* 2 vols. Mexico, 1980.

García Mercadal, J., ed. *Viajes de extranjeros por España y Portugal.* 2 vols. Madrid, 1952.

Garcilaso de la Vega, El Inca. *Royal Commentaries of the Incas.* Translated by Harold Livermore. 2 vols. Austin, Tex., 1966.

Gasca, Pedro de la. *Descripción del Peru.* 1553. Edited by Josep M. Barnadas. Caracas, 1976.

Gerhard, Peter. *La frontera sureste de la Nueva España.* Translated by Stella Maestrangelo. Mexico, 1991.

———. *Geografía histórica de la Nueva España 1519–1821.* Translated by Stella Maestrangelo. Mexico, 1986.

Getino, Luis G. A. *Domínicos españoles confesores de reyes.* Madrid, 1917.

Gil, Juan. *Los conversos y la inquisición.* 8 vols. Seville, 2000–2.

Giménez Fernández, Manuel. *Bartolomé de las Casas.* 2 vols. Seville, 1953, 1960.

———. *Bartolomé de las Casas, Bibliografía crítica.* Santiago de Chile, 1954.

———. *Breve biografía de Fray Bartolomé de las Casas.* Seville, 1966.

Ginés de Sepúlveda, Juan. *Obras completas.* Pozoblanco, 1995–2008.

Glave, Luis Miguel. *Trajinantes.* Lima, 1989.

Gómez Pérez, María del Carmen. *Pedro de Heredia y Cartagena de Indias.* Seville, 1984.

Góngora, Mario. *Los grupos de conquistadores en Tierre Firme, 1509–1530.* Santiago de Chile, 1962.

González Palencia, A., and E. Mele. *Vida y obras de Don Diego Hurtado de Mendoza.* 3 vols. Madrid, 1941.

Goulding, Michael et al. *The Smithsonian Atlas of the Amazon.* Washington, D.C., 2003.

Granvelle, Cardinal. *Papiers d'état du.* Edited by C. Weiss. Paris, 1841–52.

Graziani, Antoine-Marie. *Un prince de la renaissance.* Paris, 2008.

Griffin, Clive. *Los Cromberger: La historia de una imprenta del siglo XVI en Sevilla y México.* Madrid, 1991.

Grunberg, Bertrand. *L'univers des conquistadors.* Paris, 1993.

Guicciardini, Francesco. *The History of Italy.* Translated by Sidney Alexander. New York, 1969.

Guillén, Edmundo. *Versión Inca de la conquista.* Lima, 1974.

Gussaert, Ernst. *Espagnols et Flamands.* Brussels, 1910.

Hamilton, Earl J. *American Treasure and the Price Revolution in Spain 1501–1650.* Cambridge, Mass., 1934.

Hampe Martínez, Teodoro. *Don Pedro de la Gasca, 1493–1567.* Lima, 1989.

Hanke, Lewis. *All Mankind Is One.* DeKalb, 1974.

———. *Aristotle and the American Indians.* London, 1959.

———. "Pope Paul III and the American Indians." *Harvard Theological Review* 30 (1937).

———. *The Spanish Struggle for Conquest of America.* Philadelphia, 1949.

Haring, C. H. *The Spanish Empire in America.* New York, 1947.

———. *Trade and Navigation Between Spain and the Indies in the Time of the Habsburgs.* Cambridge, Mass., 1918.

Harth-Terré, Emilio. "Esclavas blancas en Lima." 1537. *El Comercio,* Lima, June 3, 1963.

Harvey, L. P. *Islamic Spain 1250 to 1500.* Chicago, 1990.

———. *Muslims in Spain 1500–1614.* Chicago, 2005.

Headley, J. M. *The Emperor and His Chancellor.* Cambridge, U.K., 1983.

Helps, Sir Arthur. *The Conquerors of the New World and Their Bondsmen.* London, 1848–52.

Hemming, John. *The Amazon.* London, 2009.

———. *The Conquest of the Incas.* London, 1970.

———. *Monuments of the Incas.* New illustrated edition. London, 2010.

———. *The Search for El Dorado.* London, 1978.

Henig, Stanley. *Numbers Never Lie.* Unpublished manuscript. Madison, Wisc.

Heredia, Beltrán de Vicente. *Cartulario de la Universidad de Salamanca.* Salamanca, 1960.

Herrera, Antonio de. *Historia General del mundo, del tiempo del señor rey don Felipe II el prudente.* 3 vols. Madrid, 1601.

Huizinga, J. *The Waning of the Middle Ages.* Translated by F. Hopman. London, 1924. A more recent translation by Rodney J. Payton and Ulrich Mammitzsch, *The Autumn of the Middle Ages* (Chicago, 1996), seems less inspired.

Iglesias Ortega, Luis. *Bartolomé de las Casas: Cuarenta y cuatro años infinitos.* Seville, 2007.

Jaquit, J. *Les fêtes de la Renaissance.* Paris, 1960.

Jerez, Francisco de. See López de Jerez.

Jones, R. O. *The Golden Age: Prose and Poetry.* London, 1971.

Kamen, Henry. *Philip of Spain.* New Haven, 1997.

Kellenbenz, Hermann. *Los Fugger en España y Portugal hasta 1560.* Salamanca, 2000.

Keniston, Ralph Hayward. *Francisco de los Cobos.* Pittsburgh, 1958.

———. *Garcilaso de la Vega.* New York, 1922.

Kubler, George, and Martin Soria. *Art and Architecture in Spain and Portugal and Their American Dominions 1500–1800.* Harmondsworth, U.K., 1959.

Láinez Alcalá, Rafael. *Pedro Berruguete: Pintor de Castilla.* Madrid, 1935.

Landa, Fray Diego de. *Relación de las cosas de Yucatán.* Edited by Miguel Rivera. Madrid, 1985.

Las Casas, Fray Bartolomé de. *Apologética historia sumaria.* Edited by Juan Pérez de Tudela. 2 vols. Madrid, 1957.

———. *Brevísima relación de la destrucción de las Indias.* Edited by Consuelo Varela. Madrid, 1999.

———. *Obras escogidas.* Edited by Juan Pérez de Tudela. Madrid, 1958.

———. *Los tesoros de Perú.* Edited by Angel Losada. Madrid, 1958.

———. *Tratado de las doce dudas.* Madrid, 1958.

———. "Tratado sobre los hombres que han sido hechos esclavos." In *Opúsculos, cartas y memoriales.* Biblioteca de Autores Españoles. Madrid, 1958.

Laso de la Vega, M. *Doña Mencía de Mendoza, Marquesa de Cenete 1508–1554.* Madrid, 1942.

Lavallé, Bernard. *Bartolomé de las Casas.* Paris, 2007.

Lawley, Althea. *Vittoria Colonna.* London, 1888.

Lockhart, James. *The Men of Cajamarca.* Austin, Tex., 1972.

———. *Spanish Peru 1532–1560.* Madison, Wisc., 1968.

Lohmann Villena, Guillermo. *Los americanos en las ordenes militares.* 2 vols. Madrid, 1975.

———. *Les Espinosa.* Paris, 1968.

———. *Las ideas jurídico-políticas en la rebelión de Gonzalo Pizarro*. Valladolid, 1977.

López, A. "Confesores de la familia real de Castilla." *Archivo ibero-americano* 31 (1929).

López de Gómara, Francisco. *La conquista de México*. Edited by José Luis Rojas. Madrid, 1987. English translation by L. B. Simpson. Berkeley, 1964. First published in Saragossa, Spain, 1552.

———. *Hispania Victrix, historia general de las Indias*. Madrid, 1846. First published in Saragossa, Spain, 1552.

López de Jerez, Francisco. *Verdadera relación de la conquista del Perú, o provincia del Cuzco, llamada Nueva España*. Seville, 1534.

López de Mendoza, Íñigo, Count of Tendilla. *Correspondencia del conde de Tendilla*. Madrid, 1974.

López Rayón, Ignacio. *Documentos para la historia de México*. 2 vols. Mexico, 1852–53.

Losada, Angel. *Un cronista olvidado de la España imperial, Juan Ginés de Sepúlveda*. Madrid, 1998.

Loyola, Ignatius de. *Powers of Imagining*. Collected works. Edited by Antonio de T. de Nicholas. Albany, N.Y., 1986.

Lucía Megías, José Manuel. *Antología de libros de caballerías castellanos*. Alcalá de Henares, 2001.

Ludeña, Hugo. "Versiones temporanas sobre la muerte de Don Francisco Pizarro." *Boletín de Lima* 37 (January 1985).

McDonald, Mark, ed. *The Print Collection of Ferdinand Columbus*. 2 vols. London, 2004.

Machiavelli, Niccolò. *Literary Works of Machiavelli: With Selections from the Private Correspondence*. Edited by J. R. Hale. London, 1961.

———. *The Prince*. Oxford, 1913.

Magalhães-Godinho, V. *Os descobrimentos e a economia mundial*. Lisbon, 1963.

Malfatti, Cesare V. *The Accession, Coronation and Marriage of Mary Tudor as Related in Four Manuscripts in the Escorial*. Barcelona, 1956.

Marías, Fernando. *El hospital Tavera de Toledo*. Seville, 2007.

Marineo Siculo, Lucio. "Don Hernando Cortés." Edited by Miguel León-Portilla. *Historia* 16 (April 1985). First published in *De rebus hispaniae memorabilibus libri*. Vol. 25. Alcalá de Henares, 1530.

Marmolejo, Alonso de Góngora. *Crónicas del reino de Chile*. Madrid, 1960.

Martín González, J. J. "El palacio de Carlos v en Yuste." *Archivo Español del arte*, nos. 23–24 (1950–51).

Martínez, José Luis. *Hernán Cortés*. Mexico, 1990. With four volumes of documents (*Documentos cortesianos*) 1990–92.

Martínez Millán, José, and J. Esquerra Revilla. *Carlos V y la quiebra del humanismo, eds. político en Europa, 1530–1558*. 4 vols. Madrid, 2001.

——— et al., eds. *La corte de Carlos V*. 5 vols. Madrid, 2000.

Martyr, Peter (Pedro Mártir (de anglería)). *Cartas sobre el Nuevo Mundo*. Madrid, 1990.

———. *De Orbe Novo*. Translated by Francis MacNutt. 2 vols. New York, 1912. Spanish edition by Ramón Alba. *Décadas del Nuevo Mundo*. Madrid, 1989.

———. *Epistolario*. Vols. 9–11. In *Documentos inéditos para la historia de España*. Madrid, 1953.

Medina, José Toribio. *Cartas de Pedro de Valdivia.* Seville, 1929.

———. *Descubrimiento del Río de las Amazonas.* 1894. An English edition with invaluable appendices was published as *The Discovery of the Amazon* by the American Geographical Society in New York, 1934. It includes an English translation of the account of Fray Gaspar de Carvajal.

Mena, Cristóbal de. "La Conquista del Perú." In *Relaciones primitivas de la conquista del Perú.* edited by Raúl Porras Barrenechea. Paris, 1937.

Mena García, María del Carmen. *Un linaje de conversos en tierra americanas.* Salamanca, 2004.

———. *Pedrarias Avila.* Seville, 1992.

———. *Sevilla y las flotas de Indias.* Seville, 1998. Based on the accounts of the flota of Pedrarias, which Professor Mena García found in AGI, *Contratación* 3253.

———. "El traslado de la ciudad de Nombre de Dios a Portobelo." *Anuario de estudios americanos* 40 (1982): 71–102.

Menéndez Pidal, Ramón. *La idea imperial de Carlos V.* Buenos Aires, 1955.

———. *La lengua de Cristóbal Colón, el estilo de Santa Teresa y otros estudios sobre el siglo XVI.* Madrid, 1958.

Mexico: Splendours of Thirty Centuries. Catalog introduction by Octavio Paz. London, 1991.

Mier, Lucía, and Terán Rocha. *La primera traza de la ciudad de México.* 2 vols. Mexico, 2005.

Molina Martínez, Miguel. "El soldado cronista." *Anuario de estudios americanos* 40 (1984).

Montell, Jaime. *México: El inicio.* Mexico, 2005.

Morales Padrón, Francisco, ed. *Primeras cartas sobre América (1493–1503).* Seville, 1990.

Morán y Checa, F. *El coleccionismo en España.* Madrid, 1990.

Morel-Fatio, Alfred. *Historiographie de Charles Quint.* Paris, 1913. Includes a French translation of the autobiography of Charles (as well as the 1620 edition in Portuguese).

Morison, Samuel Eliot. *The European Discovery of America.* New York, 1974.

Mörner, Magnus. *La mezcla de razas en la historia de América Latina.* Buenos Aires, 1969.

Morrison, K. F. "History *malgré lui*: A Neglected Account of Charles V's Coronation in Aachen." *Studia Gratiana Postscripta* 15 (Rome, 1962).

Motolinía, Fray Toribio de. *Epistolario, 1526–1555.* Mexico, 1986.

———. *Memoriales; o, libro de las cosas de la Nueva España y de los naturales de ella.* Edited by Edmund O'Gorman. Mexico, 1971.

Munda, Salvatore. *El asesinato de Francisco Pizarro.* Lima, 1985.

Muñoz, Andrés. *El viaje de Felipe Segundo a Inglaterra.* Madrid, 1877.

Muñoz de San Pedro, Miguel. *Tres testigos de la conquista de Perú.* Madrid, 1964.

Muriel, Josefina. *Hospitales de la Nueva España.* Mexico, 1956.

Murúa, Martín de. *Historia general del Perú, origen y descendencia de los Incas 1590–1611.* Edited by Manuel Ballesteros-Gabrois. 2 vols. Madrid, 1962, 1964.

Navarrete. See Fernández de Navarrete.

Ondegardo, Polo de. *El mundo de los Incas.* Madrid, 1990.

Otte, Enrique. "Aspiraciones y actividades heterogéneros de Gonzalo Fernández de Oviedo, cronista." *Revista de Indias,* no. 18 (1958).

———. "Cartas de Diego de Ordaz." *Historia Mexicana,* July–Sept. 1964.

———. *Cartas privadas de emigrantes a Indias.* Seville, 1988.

———. *Las perlas del Caribe.* Caracas, 1977.

———. *Sevilla y sus mercaderes a fines de la Edad Media.* Seville, 1996.

Oviedo. See Fernández de Oviedo.

Pagden, Anthony. See Cortés.

Palmer, Colin. *Slaves of the White God: Blacks in Mexico 1570–1650.* Cambridge, Mass., 1976.

Paso y Troncoso, Francisco de. *Cartas de Nueva España.* 18 vols. Madrid, 1922.

Pastor, Ludwig von. *History of the Popes, from the Close of the Middle Ages.* Translated by Mgr. Ralph Kerr. Vols. 5 to 20. London, 1898–1930.

Pérez, Joseph. *Carlos V.* Madrid, 1999.

———. *Los comuneros.* Madrid, 2001.

———. "Moines frondeurs et sermons subversifs." *Bulletin hispanique* 67 (January–June 1965).

Pérez de Tudela, Juan. *Crónicas del Perú,* 5 vols., Madrid, 1963–65.

———. *Documentos relativos a don Pedro de la Gasca y a Gonzalo Pizarro.* 2 vols. Madrid, 1964.

Pérez-Mallaína, Pablo. *Spain's Men of the Sea.* Translated by Carla Rahn Phillips. Baltimore, 1998.

Pérez Villanueva, J., and B. Escandell. *Historia de la inquisición en España y América.* Madrid, 1984.

Pietschmann, Horst. *El estado y su evolución al principio de la colonización española de América.* Mexico, 1989.

Pike, Ruth. *Linajudos and Conversos in Seville.* New York, 2000.

Pizarro, Pedro. "Relación del descubrimiento y conquista de los reinos del Perú." In *Colección de documentos para la historia de España,* edited by Martin Fernández de Navarrete. Vol. 5, 201–388. Madrid, 1844. English translation by Philip Ainsworth Means, Cortés Society. New York, 1921.

Polavieja, General Camilo. *Hernán Cortés; copias de documentos existentes en el Archivo de Indias . . . sobre la conquista de México.* Seville, 1889.

Popol Vuh: The Maya Book of the Dawn of Life. Translated by Dennis Tedlock. New York, 1996.

Porrás Barrenechea, Raúl. *Cartas del Perú 1524–1543.* Lima, 1959.

———. *Cedulario del Perú.* 2 vols., Lima, 1944–48.

———. "Dos documentos esenciales sobre Francisco Pizarro." *Revista Histórica* 17 (Lima, 1948).

———. "El Nombre del Perú." *Mar del sur* 6, no. 18 (1951).

———. *Pizarro.* Lima, 1978.

———. *Las relaciones primitivas de la conquista del Perú.* Lima, 1967.

Puga, V. de. *Provisiones, cédulas, instrucciones para el gobierno de la Nueva España.* Facsimile edition. Madrid, 1945. First published Mexico, 1563.

Quiroga, Vasco de. *Utopia en América.* Edited by Paz Serrano Gassent. Madrid, 1992.

Ramos, Demetrio. *El consejo de las Indias en el siglo XVI.* Valladolid, 1970.

———. "El negocio negrero de los Welser." *Revista de historia de América* 1, no. 8 (Mexico, Jan.–June 1976).

————. *Ximénez de Quesada en su relación con los cronistas y el epítome de la conquista del Nuevo Reino de Granadá.* Seville, 1972.

Rayón. See López Rayón.

Recinos, Adrián, and D. Goetz. *The Annals of the Cakchiquels.* Norman, Okla. 1953.

Resplendence of the Spanish Monarchy. Metropolitan Museum of Art catalog, New York, 1991.

Ricard, Robert. *La conquête spirituel du Mexique.* Paris, 1933. Translated by L. B. Simpson as *The Spiritual Conquest of Mexico 1523–72.* Berkeley, 1966.

Rivet, P., and H. Arsandaux. "La metallurgie en Amérique pré-colombienne." *Travaux et mem. institut d'ethnologie* 39 (Paris, 1946).

Rodríguez de Montalvo, Garcí. *Amadís de Gaula.* Edited by Juan Bautista Avalle-Arce. 2 vols. Madrid, 1991. English translation by Anthony Munday. Aldershot, U.K., 2004.

Rodríguez Villa, Antonio. *El emperador Carlos V y su corte, según las cartas de don Martín de Salinas.* Madrid, 1903.

Ryder, A.J.C. *Benin and the Europeans, 1485–1897.* London, 1969.

Sahagún, Fray Bernardino de. *Florentine Codex: The General History of the Things of New Spain.* Translated by Charles Dibble and Arthur J. Anderson. 12 vols. New Mexico, 1952 onward. Spanish edition translated by Fray Angel Garibay. 4 vols. Mexico, 1956.

Salinas. See Rodríguez Villa.

Sampaio García, Rozendo. *Aprovisionamiento de escravos negros na América.* São Paulo, 1962.

Sancho de la Hoz, Pedro. *Relación de la conquista del Perú.* Edited by Joaquín García Icazbalceta. Madrid, 1962.

Sandoval, Fray Prudencio de. *Historia de la vida y hechos del emperador Carlos V.* 3 vols. Madrid, 1956. First published in Valladolid, 1604–6.

Santa Cruz, Alonso de. *Crónica del emperador.* 5 vols. Madrid, 1920–25.

Sanuto, Marino. *Diarii.* 58 vols. Venice, 1887.

Sanz, Eufemio Lorenzo. *Comercio de España con América en la época de Felipe II.* 2 vols. Valladolid, 1986.

Sarabia Viejo, María Justina. *Don Luis de Velasco: Virrey de Nueva España, 1550–1564.* Seville, 1978.

Sauer, Carl Ortwin. *The Early Spanish Main.* Cambridge, U.K., 1966.

Saunders, A. C. de C. M. *A Social History of Black Slaves and Freedmen in Portugal.* Cambridge, U.K., 1982.

Scelle, Georges. *La traite négrière aux Indes de Castile.* 2 vols. Paris, 1906.

Schäfer, Ernst. *El consejo real y supremo de las Indias.* 2 vols. Seville, 1936. New edition by Antonio-Miguel Bernal. Madrid, 2003.

Schick, Léon. *Un grand homme d'affaires au début du xvième siècle: Jacob Fugger.* Paris, 1957.

Schmidt, Ulrich. *Historia y descubrimiento del río de la Plata y Paraguay.* Tübingen, Germany, 1567. London, 1891.

Schmitt, E., and F. K. von Hutten. *Das Galt der Neuen Welt: Die Papiere des Welser-Konquistadors und General-kapitans von Venezuela Phillipp von Hutten 1534–1541.* Hilburghausen, 1996.

Scholes, France V., and Dave Warren. "The Olmec Region at Spanish Contact." In Steward, J., ed., *Handbook of the Middle American Indian* 3, Austin, 1965.

Schwaller, John. "Tres familas mexicanas del siglo XVI." *Historia mexicana* 31, no. 2 (Oct.–Dec. 1981).

Segovia, Bartolomé de. *Relación de muchas cosas acaecidas en el Perú.* Vol. 209. Madrid, BAE.

Serrano, Luciano. "Primeras negociaciones de Carlos V con la Santa Sede 1516–18." *Cuadernos de trabajo de la escuela española y historia en Roma* 2 (1914).

Serrano y Sanz, Manuel. *Historiadores de Indias,* 2 vols. Madrid, 1909.

Service, Elman. *Spanish-Guarani Relations in Early Colonial Paraguay.* Westport, Conn., 1954.

Simpson, L. B. *The Encomienda in New Spain 1492–1550.* Berkeley, 1966.

Skinner, Quentin. *The Foundations of Modern Political Thought.* 2 vols. Cambridge, U.K., 1978.

Sobaler, María A. *Los colegiales mayores de Santa Cruz: una élite de poder, 1484–1670.* Valladolid, 1988.

Soisson, Jean-Pierre. *Marguerite, Princesse de Bourgogne.* Paris, 2002.

Solano, Francisco de, ed., *Proceso histórico al conquistador.* Madrid, 1988.

Solorzano, Juan de. *Política Indiana.* 3 vols. Madrid, 1996.

Spivakivsky, Erica. *Son of the Alhambra.* Austin, Tex., 1970.

Squier, E. G. *Peru: Incidents of Travel and Exploration in the Land of the Incas.* New York, 1877.

Steward, J. *Handbook of the Middle American Indians.* Several vols. New York, 1973.

Stirling, Stuart. *The Last Conquistador.* Stroud, 1999.

———. *Pizarro, Conquistador of the Inca.* Stroud, 2005.

Stirling-Maxwell, William. *The Cloister Life of the Emperor Charles V.* London, 1853.

Studnicki Gizbert, Daviken. *A Nation Upon the Ocean Sea.* Oxford, 2007.

Suárez de Peralta, Juan. *Tratado del descubrimiento de las Yndias y su conquista.* Mexico, 1949.

Tena Fernández, Juan. *Trujillo histórico y monumental.* Trujillo, 1967.

Thayer Ojeda, Tomás. *Formación de la sociedad chilena y censo de la población de Chile en los años de 1540 a 1565.* 3 vols. Santiago de Chile, 1939–41.

———. *Valdivia y sus compañeros.* Santiago de Chile, 1950.

Thomas, Hugh. *The Conquest of Mexico.* London, 1993.

———. *Quién es quién de los conquistadores.* Madrid, 2000.

———. *Rivers of Gold.* London, 2003.

Toussaint, Manuel. "El criterio artístico de Hernán Cortés." *Estudios americanos* 1, no. 62.

Tovar de Teresa, Guillermo et al. *La utopia mexicana del siglo xvi.* Mexico, 1992.

Tremayne, Eleanor E. *The First Governess of the Netherlands, Margaret of Austria.* London, 1908.

Trujillo, Diego de. *Relación del descubrimiento del reyno del Perú.* Seville, 1948.

Valdés, Alfonso. *Diálogo de las cosas ocurridas en Roma.* Madrid, 1956.

———. *Obras completas.* Madrid, 1960.

Valdivia, Pedro de. For letters of, see Medina.

Van den Wyngaerde, Anton. *Ciudades del siglo de oro: Las vistas españoles de Anton van den Wyngaerde.* Edited by Richard Kagan. Madrid, 1986.

Varón Gabai, Rafael. *Francisco Pizarro and His Brothers.* Norman, Okla., 1997.

———. *La ilusion del poder: apogeo y decadencia de los Pizarro en la conquista del Perú.* Lima, 1996.

———, and Auke Pieter Jacobs. "Peruvian Wealth and Spanish Investments." *Hispanic American Historical Review* 67 (1987).

Varón Velasco, Balbino. "El conquistador de Nicaragua, Gabriel de Rojas." *Anuario de Estudios Americanos,* 1985.

Vassberg, David. "Concerning Pigs, the Pizarros and the Agropastoral Backgrounds of the Conquerors of Peru." *Latin American Research Review* 13, no. 3 (1978).

Vázquez, A., and R. S. Rose. *Algunas cartas de Don Diego Hurtado de Mendoza, escritas en 1538–1552.* New Haven, 1935.

Vega, Juan José. *Manco Inca, el gran rebelde.* Lima, 1995.

Vergara, Alejandro. *Patinir.* Madrid, 2007.

Vernon, Ida Stevenson Weldon. *Pedro de Valdivia, Conquistador of Chile.* Austin, Tex., 1946.

Vila Vilar, Enriqueta, with Guillermo Lohmann Villena. *Familia, linajes y negocios entre Sevilla y las Indias.* Seville, 2003.

Vilar Sánchez, J. A. *1526: Boda y luna de miel de Carlos V.* Granada, 2000.

Vives, Juan Luis. *Obras políticas y pacifistas.* Edited by F. Calero et al. Madrid, 1999.

Walser, Fritz. *Die spanischen Zentralbehörden und der Straatsrat Karls V; Grundlagen und Aufbau bis aum Tode Gattinares.* Göttingen, 1959.

Warren, J. Benedict. *The Conquest of Michoacán.* Norman, Okla., 1985.

Watts, David. *The West Indies: Patterns of Development.* Cambridge, U.K., 1987.

Weber, David J. *The Spanish Frontier in North America.* New Haven, 1992.

Whitelock, Anna. *Mary Tudor.* London, 2009.

Winship, G. P. "The Coronado Expedition." *XIVth Annual Report of the [US] Bureau of Ethnology.* Washington, D.C., 1896.

Wright, I. A. *The Early History of Cuba, 1492–1586.* New York, 1916.

Yupangui, Diego. *An Inca Account of the Conquest of Peru.* Translated by Ralph Bauer. Boulder, Colo., 2005.

Zavala, Silvio. "Debate with Benno Biermann." In *Historia Mexicana.* Vols. 17–18 (1968–69).

———. *Ideario de Vasco de Quiroga.* Mexico, 1941.

———. *Las instituciones jurídicas en la conquista de América.* Madrid, 1935.

———. *Recuerdo de Vasco de Quiroga.* Mexico, 1987.

Zorita, Alonso de. *Historia de la Nueva España.* Madrid, 1909.

Notes

The first time a work is named, the full title is given; afterward an abbreviation is used.

ABBREVIATIONS

  AGI: Archivo General de Indias, Seville
  APS: Archivo de Protocolos de Sevilla
 BRAH: Boletín de la Real Academia de la Historia
  CDI: Colección de Documentos Inéditos, see full title page 562.
CDIHE: Colección de Documentos Inéditos, second series, see full title page 562.
 HAHR: Hispanic American Historical Review.

CHAPTER 1. CORTÉS AND THE REBUILDING OF MEXICO-TENOCHTITLAN, 1521–1524

1. See my *Conquest* (New York, 1993), chapters 1–4.
2. Peter Martyr, *De orbe novo,* translated by Francis MacNutt, 2 vols. (New York, 1912); Spanish edition by Ramón Alba, *Décadas del Nuevo Mundo* (Madrid, 1989), 358.
3. See Renate Pieper, "Cartas, avisos e impresos," in José Martínez Millán and J. Esquerra Revilla, eds., *Carlos V y la quiebra del humanismo político en Europa, 1530–1558* (Madrid, 2001), 4: 434.
4. See p. 568ff. of *Conquest.*
5. See Anthony Pagden, *Letters from Mexico* (New Haven, 1986), 482, n. 119,
6. CDI, 26: 59. The *Cédula* of October 15, 1522, speaks of "*las tierras y provincias de Aculuacán e San Xoan de Olua llamada La Nueva España.*" Cortés wrote five letters to Charles V. The first, either lost or not yet found, was written in July 1519 in Veracruz; the second in "Segura de la Frontera" on October 30, 1520. The third, the longest, was completed in Coyoacán on October 15, 1522; the fourth and the fifth were written in Mexico-Tenochtitlan on October 15, 1524, and September 3, 1526, respectively.
7. See AGI Justicia, leg. 220, p. 2, f. 128.
8. CDI, 26: 65–70.

9. Ibid., 66.

10. CDI, 27: 65–70. Text also in CDIHE, 1: 97.

11. Martyr, *De orbe novo,* 406. The four men were to be paid: Estrada, 510,000 maravedís; Albornoz, 500,000; Almíndez de Chirino, 500,000; Salazar, 170,000 maravedís.

12. I wonder if this house has any connection with the old mansion shown nowadays to tourists as "the house of Cortés."

13. *Información de méritos y servicios de Alonso García Bravo,* (Mexico 1956), 57.

14. Lucía Mier and Terán Rocha, *La primera traza de la ciudad de México* (Mexico, 1993), 1: 13ff.

15. Instruction of June 26, 1523, in José Luis Martínez, *Documentos cortesianos,* 1: 270.

16. Cited in Manuel Toussaint, "El criterio artístico de Hernán Cortés," *Estudios Americanos,* no. 1, 62.

17. A *vara* was a measure of 835 millimeters and 9 *décimas.*

18. Motolinía, in Joaquín García Icazbalceta, *Colección de documentos para la historia de México* (Mexico, 1980), 1: 18.

19. Ibid., 19.

20. George Kubler and Martin Soria, *Art and Architecture in Spain and Portugal and Their American Dominions* (Harmondsworth, U.K., 1959), 70.

21. Martyr, *De orbe novo,* 418.

22. Ibid., 193, 358.

23. Josefina Muriel, *Hospitales de la Nueva España* (Mexico, 1956), 36.

24. Pagden, 280.

25. The wife of Amerigo Vespucci, María Cerezo, may have been a relation. For the family's converso connections, see Juan Gil, *Los conversos y la Inquisición Sevillana* (Seville, 2000), 3: 500ff.

26. See Peter Gerhard's splendid *Geografía histórica de la Nueva España 1519–1821* (Mexico, 1986), 252, 254.

27. These understandings would be reflected in laws of July 12, 1530, cited in V. de Puga, *Provisiones, cédulas, instrucciones para el gobierno de la Nueva España* (Mexico, 1563); facsimile ed. (Madrid, 1945), fol. 45.

28. See Nicholas Crane's *Mercator: The Man who Mapped the Planet* (London, 2002), 63.

CHAPTER 2. VALLADOLID, 1522

1. Eleanor Tremayne, *The First Governess of the Netherlands* (London, 1908), 217.

2. *Memorias,* Spanish Academy of History, vol. 6, inventory of plate and jewels presented to Margaret, April 3, 1497.

3. The site is now occupied by the Teatro Calderón. From a home of nobility to the stage would seem an agreeable translation for any building. On the main gate of the old house of the Enríquez there is the rhyme:

Viva el Rey con tal Victoria
Esta casa y su vecino
Queda es ella por memoria
La fama renombre y gloria,
Que por él a España vino
Año MDXXII Carlos

It is signed *Almirante Don Fadrique, segundo de este nombre.*

4. These designs have been admirably reproduced, with an introduction and essays on the places concerned, by Richard Kagan, ed., *Ciudades del siglo de oro: Las vistas españolas de Anton van den Wyngaerde* (Madrid, 1986).

5. Marquess originally meant someone who was a lord of some territory within the territory of the kingdom.

6. José García Mercadal, ed., *Viajes de extranjeros por España y Portugal* (Madrid, 1952), 455, tells us that there were thirty-nine religious houses in 1820 on the eve of dissolution. San Felipe Neri himself (1515–95) was in 1522 still a child in Florence!

7. See Joseph Pérez, "Moines frondeurs et sermons subversifs," in *Bulletin hispanique* 67 (Jan.–June 1965).

8. Later used by the Banco Castellano.

9. Uncle of the inquisitor Fray Tomás. The cardinal was the greatest Spanish theologian of the century.

10. The counts of Oropesa were hereditary protectors of the Jeronymite monastery of Yuste, where Charles V went in 1556 to retire and die.

11. *Huelga* in the sixteenth century indicated not a strike, as it now does, but a fertile stretch of land.

12. On Berruguete, see Diego Angulo, *Pedro Berruguete en Paredes de Nava* (Barcelona, 1946) and Rafael Láinez Alcalá, *Pedro Berruguete: Pintor de Castilla* (Madrid, 1935).

13. On Navagero, see the Nota Preliminar in J. García Mercadal, 835. On Vital, see the same, 706.

14. Marcel Defourneaux, *La vie quotidienne en Espagne au siècle d'or* (Paris, 1964), 148.

15. These wonderful occasions are beautifully described in Bennassar's admirable history, *Valladolid au siècle d'or* (Paris, 1967), especially 534.

16. See Inmaculada Arias de Saavedra, "Las universidades hispánicas durante el reinado de Carlos V," in Martínez Millán, *Carlos V y la quiebra*, 3: 396.

17. "We don't seek and we should not seek only the purity of Latin but the knowledge of many other things." In M. Andrés, *La teología española en el siglo* (Madrid, 1977), 2: 48.

18. Letter of February 26, 1517, Erasmus to Wolfgang Fabricius Capite, quoted in J. Huizinga, *The Waning of the Middle Ages* (London, 1924), 31.

19. Marcel Bataillon, *Erasmo y España* (Mexico, 1950), 302.

20. Ibid., 484.

21. Bennassar, 116–19.

22. L. P. Harvey, *Muslims in Spain 1500–1614* (Chicago, 2005), 112.
23. Kubler and Soria, 351.
24. Vigarny was supposed to have come from Burgos, but he may have originated in Burgundy.
25. For Carranza, see chapter 46–47.
26. María A. Sobaler, *Los colegiales mayores de Santa Cruz: una élite de poder* (Valladolid, 1988).
27. On Glapion, see Millán and Esquerra, *La corte de Carlos V.*

CHAPTER 3. CHARLES, KING AND EMPEROR

1. The only known men named Carlos in Spain in the sixteenth century, apart from the King, were Carlos de Viana, prince of Aragon; and Carlos de Valera, a captain in the Spanish-Portuguese war of the 1470s and the son of a converso historian, Diego de Valera.
2. The day of Saint Matthew was changed by the Council of Trent in the late sixteenth century.
3. As a child, she had been for a few years the first wife of King Charles VIII of France, till he announced that he preferred to marry, for dynastic reasons, the last duchess of Brittany. This crude rejection was the source of her dislike of France.
4. On Margaret, see Tremayne, *The First Governess;* Jean-Pierre Soisson, *Marguerite Princesse de Bourgogne* (Paris, 2002); and Dagmar Eichberger, ed., *Women of Distinction* (Leuven, 2005).
5. Tremayne, 154.
6. The founder was Geert Groote.
7. See Crane, 29.
8. See my *Rivers of Gold* (New York, 2003), 48.
9. Francesco Guicciardini, *The History of Italy,* Sidney Alexander (trans.) (New York, 1969), 330–31.
10. Quoted by Ludwig von Pastor in *History of the Popes,* Monsignor Ralph Kerr (trans.) (London, 1898), 9: 115.
11. Ibid., 128.
12. See Adrian's letter to Charles from Saragossa, May 3, 1552, quoted in Tremayne, 193.
13. Pastor, 9: 226.
14. On Charles and Chièvres, see Karl Brandi, *The emperor Charles V,* C. V. Wedgwood (trans.) (London, 1949), 99.
15. Contarini, in García Mercadal, 393.
16. On Chièvres, see Manuel Giménez Fernandez, *Bartolomé de las Casas* (Seville, 1960), 2: passim.
17. Huizinga, *Waning,* 77.
18. On the family history, see P. Gargantilla Madera, "Historia clínica del Emperador," in Martínez Millán, *Carlos V y la quiebra,* 4: 33ff.
19. Contarini, in Eugenio Alberi, *Relazione degli ambasciatore veneti a Senato,* series 1 (Florence, 1840), 2: 60ff.

20. Alonso de Santa Cruz, *Crónica del emperador* (Madrid, 1920), 1: 123.
21. A description by Lorenzo Pasqualingo, in Marino Sanuto, *Diarii* xx, 422; xxx, 324.
22. Santa Cruz, 2: 374.
23. In preface to the edition in Barcelona, 1987.
24. Brandi, 504. However, this affected him in 1541.
25. This paragraph is based on Brandi, 394.
26. Maximilian, quoted in Tremayne, 117.
27. Granvelle Papers (1534) 2: 124. The same in 1548, quoted in Federico Chabod, *Carlos V y su imperio*, Rodrigo Riza (trans.) (Madrid, 1992), 46. Like so much of old France, the chartreuse was ruined in the revolution, to no good end.
28. Monsignor Anglés, cited in Fernández Álvarez, *Carlos V*, 182. The clavichord had established itself in the fifteenth century as a small instrument for use in the home.
29. On Lannoy, see Martínez Millán, *La corte*, 3: 225ff. Lannoy was born in Valenciennes in 1482. He followed his father into working for the imperial family. He was with the archduke Philip before he worked with Charles as "supreme master of the horse." He married Françoise de Montbel in 1510. He accompanied Charles to Spain in 1517 as chamberlain and member of Charles's council. Lannoy, Hugo de Moncada, and Pescara were in favor of an agreement with France as opposed to a more belligerent line taken up by Gorrevod and Gattinara.
30. Alfred Morel-Fatio, *Historiografie de Charles Quint* (Paris, 1913), 154.
31. Santa Cruz, 2: 37–40.
32. Quentin Skinner, *The Foundations of Modern Political Thought* (Cambridge, U.K., 1978), 1: 24, 220, 221.
33. Philip was affected by this parental opinion.
34. On Gattinara, there is a fine study by J. M. Headley, *The Emperor and His Chancellor* (Cambridge, U.K., 1983). See also Martínez Millán, *La corte*, 3: 167ff.
35. Headley, 33. Manuel Rivero Rodríguez has a study of Gattinara's autobiography written in the third person in his "Memoria, escritura y estado, la autobiografía de Mercurino Arborio de Gattinara," in Martínez Millán, *Carlos V y la quiebra*, 1: 199ff.
36. Claretta, quoted in Headley, 41. Keniston thought the letter was not written until 1526. There are some stories in the memoirs of the Venetians Navagero and Contarini about angry exchanges between the Emperor and Gattinara in 1525.
37. R. Accacioli, in Desjardins 2: 861, quoted in Pastor, 10: 30–34.
38. Ibid., 46.
39. Manuel Fernández Álvarez, *Carlos V*, 287, 288.
40. The grant was for 154,000,000 maravedís, or 411,000 ducats. Valladolid in 1518 had granted 204,000,000 maravedís, or 545,000 ducats. Juan M. Carretero Zamora, "Liquidez, deuda y obtención de recursos extraordinarios," in Martínez Millán, *Carlos V y la quiebra*, 4: 448.
41. See Joseph Pérez, *Los comuneros* (Madrid, 2001).
42. As "a Catholic King" of Spain. See Fernández Álvarez, *Carlos V*, 209.
43. Cited in Headley, Martínez Millán, *Carlos V y la quiebra*, 1: 8.

44. Oviedo, quoted in David Brading, *The First America* (Cambridge, U.K., 1991), 34.

45. In the second letter of *relación* of Cortés to Charles V, in Cortés. 159.

46. Letter of October 1524, in Pagden, *Letters,* 412.

47. *"Se junten con V. sacra majestad en amistad y paz verdadera como monarca y señor del mundo para que sean en exterminar y perseguir los páganos y infieles."* Perhaps Cortés derived this notion from his own captain, Jerónimo Ruiz de la Mota, of Burgos, who was a cousin of that episcopal tutor of Charles's who had talked of the matter in a speech at Corunna in 1520. His titles reflected this idea in their first line: *"por la divina clemencia, emperador semper augusto."* Fernández Álvarez, *Corpus documental de Carlos V* (Salamanca, 1973–82), 1: 120 and 3: 304.

48. Question 2 of *pequeño interrogatorio* of Cortés's *residencia,* in AGI, Justicia 221.

49. Guicciardini, 305.

50. Fernández Álvarez, *Carlos V,* 165.

51. Patinir began to paint about 1515 and would die in 1524. He painted Charon in 1520. See the catalog *Patinir,* Alejandro Vergara (Madrid, 2007), 161.

52. Fernández Álvarez, *Carlos V,* 374. See, too, the same author's fascinating *Sombras y luces en la España Imperial* (Madrid, 2004), 185.

53. Pastor, 16: 355.

54. Brandi, 631. This was his fifth will, it appears.

55. Bucer, quoted in Brandi, 504. This was in 1541.

56. See Luciano Serrano, "Primeras negociaciones de Carlos V con la Santa Sede 1516–18," in *Cuadernos de trabajo,* Spanish School of Archaeology and History in Rome (1914).

57. See Juan Gil, 1: 304.

58. See biography in Martínez Millán, *La corte,* 2: 225. Manrique de Lara lost much influence by defending Dr. Juan de Vergara of Toledo. He died in 1538, leaving four bastard sons, one of whom, Jerónimo, became *inquisidor general* at the end of the century.

59. See Lorenzo Vital, *Relación del primer viaje de Carlos V a España,* in J. García Mercadal, *Viajes de extranjers por España y Portugal.* 2: 711 (Madrid, 1952). See Fernández Álvarez, *Carlos V,* 97–99.

60. Fernández Álvarez, 264–69.

61. Ibid., 591.

CHAPTER 4. CHRISTIANITY AND THE NEW WORLD

1. Bernal Díaz del Castillo, *Historia verdadera de la Nueva España* (Madrid, 1982), 2: 141.

2. See *Rivers of Gold,* 129.

3. Ibid., chapter 4.

4. See Francisco de Solano, "El conquistador hispánico: señas de identidad" in *Proceso histórico al conquistador* (Madrid, 1988), 31.

5. The letter from Las Casas is in *"Memorial de remedios para las Indias,"* in *Obras escogidas* by Pérez de Tudela (Madrid, 1958), 5: 15. The text reads: "Thus I beg

your most Reverend Lordship . . . that you send to these isles of the Indies the Holy Inquisition, of which I believe there is a great need, because wherever we have newly to plant the faith, as in those lands, to ensure that there is nobody who sows any seed of heresy since there such people have been found and two people have burned as heretics and there remain more than fourteen; and these Indians who are simple people and then believe what may be said by some malign and diabolic person who brings there their damnable doctrine and heretical iniquity. Because it could be that many heretics have fled there from these realms [Spain] thinking thus to save themselves."

6. Bull of May 9, 1522, *Exponi nobis fecisti.*
7. *Artes de México* 19, no. 150 (Mexico, 1972).
8. Leopoldo de Austria, bishop of Córdoba, and Jorge de Austria, bishop of Liège. Both were born about 1505.
9. CDI, 13: 156.
10. I. A. Wright, *The Early History of Cuba, 1492–1586* (New York, 1916), 155.
11. Marcel Bataillon, "Novo mundo e fim do mundo," in *Revista de historia* 18 (São Paulo, 1954).
12. Fray Toribio de Motolinía, *Memoriales o libro de las cosas de Nueva España* (Mexico, 1971), 178.
13. Robert Ricard, *La conquête spirituel du Mexique* (Paris, 1933), 361.
14. Ibid., 365.
15. His evidence in AGI *Justicia* leg. 224 p. 1, f. 462–64, was on January 21, 1535. See R. E. Greenleaf, *The Inquisition in New Spain* (Oxford and London, 1969), who argued that the Inquisition was used against Cortés and his affiliates.
16. Ricard, *Conquête spirituel,* 136.
17. The history, written in 1541, was published as *Historia de las Indias de Nueva España* by García Iczabalceta, *Colección de documentos.*
18. Mexico would for the time being control Toluca, Michoacán, Jilotepec, and Tula; Texcoco would have authority over Otumba, Tepeapulco, Tulancingo; Tlaxcala would control Zacatlán, Jalapa, and Veracruz; and Huejotzingo would exercise authority over Cholula, Tepeaca, Tecamachalco, Tehuacan, Huaquechula, and Chietla. The last named is now the oldest monastery in the Americas.
19. *Colloquios,* quoted in my *Conquest.*
20. Ricard, *Conquête spirituel,* 49, 50.
21. Fray Tomás de Ortiz, quoted in Lewis Hanke, *All Mankind Is One* (DeKalb, 1974), 13.
22. See Horst Pietschmann, *El estado y su evolución al principio de la colonización Española de América* (Mexico, 1989), 108–109.
23. Peter Martyr, *De orbe novo,* 2: 275.
24. Pastor, 9: 92–93.
25. Ibid., 9: 175–76.
26. Ibid., 9: 135.
27. Ibid., 10: 253.

CHAPTER 5. CHARLES AT VALLADOLID, 1522–1523

1. This was the view of Fritz Walser, *Die spanischen Zentralbehörden* (Göttingen, 1959), 199–228, but opposed by Martínez Millán, in *La corte*, 1: 219. For this remarkable individual, see *Rivers of Gold*, 416ff.

2. Gonzalo Fernández de Oviedo, *Batallas y quincangenas: batalla prima* (Madrid, 1983–2002), 1: 141. See, too, M. Laso de la Vega, *Doña Mencía de Mendoza, Marquesa de Cenete 1508–1554* (Madrid, 1942).

3. See my *Conquest*, 341.

4. See Martínez Millán, *La corte*, 3: 350.

5. Martínez Millán, *La corte*, 3: 377. For the Ruiz de la Mota family, see John Schwaller, "Tres familias mexicanas del siglo XVI," in *Historia Mexicana* (1981), 122, 178.

6. J. Zurita, *Historia del rey don Hernando el Católico*, p. 12 verso; quoted in Martínez Millán, *La corte*, 3: 264.

7. Hannart continued in the national service since, between 1531 and 1536, he was ambassador in France.

8. See Salustiano de Dios, *El consejo real de Castilla* (Madrid, 1982).

9. See for Rojas, Martínez Millán, *La corte*, 3: 369ff.

10. See Demetrio Ramos, *El consejo de las Indias* (Valladolid, 1970); and R. J. Dworski, "The Council of the Indies in Spain," thesis, Columbia University, New York, 1979, 1433.

11. See *Rivers of Gold*, 120.

12. Ernst Schäfer, *El consejo real y supremo de las Indias* (Seville, 1935), 1: 47.

13. Perhaps because the papers of the Dominicans in San Esteban in Salamanca are not yet in the public domain.

14. Headley, 37.

15. See Luis G. A. Getino, *Dominicos españoles confesores de reyes* (Madrid, 1917), and A. López, "Confesores de la familia real de Castilla," *Archivo Ibero-Americano* 31 (1929): 5–75.

16. See J. Pérez Villanueva and B. Escandell, *Historia de la inquisición en España y América* (Madrid, 1984), 1: 447.

17. Fernández Álvarez, *Carlos V,* 208.

18. Joseph Pérez, *Charles V* (Madrid, 1999), 68.

19. Brandi, 395.

20. Ibid., 294.

21. Ibid., 492. There is a good biographical essay in Martínez Millán, *La corte*, 3: 228–38.

22. See letter from Dantiscus to Alfonso Valdés, in Pérez Villanueva, 1: 458, fn. 76.

23. See also Juan de Areizaga's account of the journey of one of the ships, the *Santiago*, to Cortés in Mexico.

24. See Martyr, *De orbe novo*, 2: 239.

25. Carlos Javier de Carlos Morales, in *Carlos V y la quiebra*, 4: 411–13.

26. Martyr, *De orbe novo*, 1: 254.

27. Peter Martyr, *Epistolario* in *Documentos inéditos para la historia de España* (Madrid, 1953), 83–84.

28. Among them were the dukes of Cardona and Villahermosa; Juan Carrillo; García de Toledo, the heir of the duke of Alba; Pedro Hernández de Córdoba; Alfonso de Silva, heir of the Conde de Cifuentes; Pedro Fajardo, Marquess de los Vélez; Luis Hurtado de Mendoza, Marquess de Mondéjar (future president of the Council of the Indies); Pedro Girón; Pedro de Aguilar; Pedro de Mendoza; and Álvar Gómez de Villareal.

29. Martyr, *De orbe novo* 2: 345–46. "My feelings for Jamaica are certainly sincere," he said elsewhere, "but perhaps exaggerated." 2: 348.

30. Ibid., 1: 338, 348.

31. *Epistolario familarum,* lib. 17. See Martínez Millán, *La corte,* 3: 46f.

32. Manuel Giménez Fernández, *Bartolomé de las Casas* (Seville, 1953, 1960) 1: 283.

33. García de Loaisa, in Keniston, 31.

34. Keniston, 33.

35. Bartolomé de las Casas, *Historia de las Indias* (Mexico, 1963), 3: 170.

36. Keniston, 117.

37. Fernández Álvarez, *Carlos V,* 391–92.

38. Las Casas, *Historia de las Indias,* 3: 259.

39. Keniston, 120.

40. His Renaissance hospital was founded by Tavera as a general hospital but also as a sepulchre for himself. It is an echo of Cardinal González de Mendoza's hospital of Santa Cruz. The chief architect was Alonso de Covarrubias, assisted by Tavera's secretary, Bartolomé de Bustamante. See Fernando Marías, *El hospital Tavera de Toledo* (Seville, 2007). Later architects included Nicolás de Vergara, father and son.

41. Pérez Villanueva, 1: 523.

42. Giménez Fernandez, *Las Casas* 2: 16; R. J. Dworski, 206. See, too, Fidel Fita, S.J., "Los judaizantes Españoles en los primeros cinco años del reinado de Carlos I," in *Boletín de la Real Academia de Historia,* 33 (Madrid, 1898): 307–48.

43. Salinas, in a letter to the treasurer Salamanca, 100, in Schäfer, 1: 61.

44. Martyr, *Epistolario,* 170. This was in 1521.

45. CDI, 12: 328. Galíndez de Carvajal came from an Extremeño family, the Carvajals, but his father was archpriest of Trujillo. Lorenzo was the offspring of his liaison with a Galíndez girl from Cáceres.

46. Beltrán also received money from Almagro and Pizarro. The investigation is to be seen in AGI Patronato leg. 185, no. 34 of 1542.

47. Giménez Fernández, *Las Casas* 2: 264, 953.

48. Enrique Otte, *Sevilla en el siglo XVI,* 39.

49. Carande Ramón, *Carlos V y sus banqueros* (Barcelona, 1987), 2: 378.

50. Ibid., 2: 85ff, 58ff.

51. Manuel Fernández Álvarez (ed.), *El corpus documental de Carlos V* (Salamanca, 1973–1982), 1: 189.

52. Giménez Fernández, *Las Casas,* 2: 953.

53. Hermann Kellenbenz, *Fugger en España y Portugal hasta 1560* (Salamanca, 2000), 356.

54. Salinas, 109.

CHAPTER 6. CORTÉS IN POWER, 1521–1524

1.   Díaz del Castillo, 2: 208.

2.   See *Rivers of Gold*, 489; also his *Información de servicios y méritos*, in AGI Patronato leg. 54, no. 7 of August 11, 1530.

3.   M. Covarrubias, in *Mexico South: The Isthmus of Tehuantepec* (New York, 1947), 38.

4.   France V. Scholes and Dave Warren, "The Olmec Region at Spanish Contact," in *Handbook of the Middle American Indians* (Austin, 1969), 7: 784.

5.   Díaz del Castillo, 2: 229.

6.   The father of Bernal Díaz del Castillo was a *regidor,* a council member of Medina, as was Montalvo also. What a wonderful coincidence!

7.   Bernal Díaz claimed to have been with Grijalva, but there are a few indications that that was not so.

8.   See Gerhard, *Geografía,* 141.

9.   Others with Sandoval included Rodrigo de Nao of Ávila, Francisco Martín of Vizcaya, and Francisco Ximénez of Extremadura.

10. Scholes and Warren, 784.

11. "*Mas pendenciero que luchador.*"

12. Rosin was a resin produced by distilling oil of turpentine.

13. Díaz del Castillo, 2: 512; Gerhard, *La frontera sureste de la Nueva España,* (Mexico, 1991), 124.

14. J. Benedict Warren, ed., *The Conquest of Michoacán* (Norman, Okla., 1985).

15. Fray Diego Durán, *Historia de las Indias de Nueva-España* (1867), 2: 284.

16. An *Información* was published in the Archivo General de la Nación XII (Mexico, 1927), 232. Cortés gave evidence, among others. Martín de Gamboa had sailed to New Spain with Grijalva and had been among those who had urged him to establish a settlement near Veracruz. He fought all the way up with Cortés in the conquest of Mexico and had been the first to reach the edge of the lake after the attack of the Noche Triste on the causeway to Tacuba. Afterwards, he had returned and, by brilliant horsemanship, saved several of his comrades— Sandoval, Antonio de Quiñones, and even the great Alvarado, whom he carried for a while on his horse after his famous "leap."

17. Warren, 295.

18. Cortés, third letter, in Pagden, 277.

19. Ignacio Bernal, in *Handbook,* III, II, 809.

20. Florentine Codex (1952 onward), 3: 113.

21. As was suggested by Alfonso Caso in a splendid essay in *Handbook,* vol. 3, part 2, 915.

22. As argued by P. Rivet and H. Arsandaux, "La metallurgie en Amérique pré-colombienne," *Travaux et mem. instit. d'ethnologie* 39 (Paris, 1946).

23. Díaz del Castillo, 2: 246.

24. CDI, 26, 71–76.
25. Dr. Ojeda and Dr. Pedro López, neither of them friends of Cortés, both said that they believed this to be a natural death. See Martyr, *Cartas sobre el Nuevo Mundo* (Madrid, 1990) 279ff., and Ignacio López Rayón, *Documentos para la historia de México* (Mexico, 1852–53), 1: 284.
26. Díaz del Castillo, 2: 278.
27. See Donald Chipman, *Nuño de Guzmán* (Glendale, 1967), 66.
28. Fourth letter of *relación*, Pagden, 327.
29. Of course Cortés had no idea of the geography of the area concerned.
30. Pagden, fourth letter, 392.
31. Martyr, *De orbe novo*, 534.
32. Díaz del Castillo, 2: 368.
33. Cortés's relation with this Las Casas family was through his mother.
34. The Dávilas seem to have come directly from Ciudad Real, but ultimately from Montalván in Ávila. The brothers were the sons of Alonso Dávila, a *comendador* of the Order of Calatrava, and of Elena Villalobos.
35. Cortés so reports. Díaz del Castillo thought that Cortés had 130 horsemen and 120 foot (4: 364).
36. See Jerome Montell, *México: el inicio.* (Mexico, 2005), 165ff.
37. Fifth letter of *relación*, Pagden, 431.
38. Ignacio Bejarano, *Actas del Cabildo* (Mexico, 1889), 25.
39. Lucia Mier and Rocha Terán, *La primera traza de la ciudad de México, 1524–1535.* (Mexico, 2005), 168.
40. Martyr, *Décadas,* 46; letter in Icazbalceta, *Colección de documentos* 1: 484ff.
41. Mier, 195.
42. Fifth letter to Charles, Pagden, 433.
43. Mier, 196. Grado would die in 1528. Cortés then gave Techuipo to Pedro Gallego, before which Cortés himself gave Techuipo a child, who would become Leonor Cortés Moctezuma. When Gallego died, Techuipo was married yet again, to Juan Cano of Cáceres.
44. Martyr, *Décadas,* 417.
45. Oviedo, 5: 238.
46. Francisco Paso Troncoso, *Cartas de Nueva España* (Madrid, 1922), 1: 97.
47. Account by Bartolomé de Zarate in 1542, in Paso, 4: 132ff.
48. By 1570, the European population of Spanish America was said to be about 150,000.

CHAPTER 7. CHARLES V: FROM VALLADOLID TO THE FALL OF ROME, 1527

1. Charles V, quoted in Federico Chabod, *Carlos V y su imperio* (Madrid, 1992), 154–58.
2. Denia was related via the Enríquez family, of which Admiral Fadrique was the head, and of which the mother of King Fernando had been a member.
3. Fernández Álvarez, *Corpus documental,* 1: 83.

4. Qu. García Mercadal, 793.

5. Martyr, *De orbe novo,* 409. He died in 1524.

6. *Información,* in AGI Mexico, leg. 203, no. 13.

7. García Mercadal, 795.

8. Bayard was Pierre Terrail, seigneur de Bayard, "*sans peur et sans reproche,*" who had been in Charles VIII's expedition. He was mortally wounded near Milan.

9. His blood relationship to Cortés is a rumor.

10. These were plays and poems published in 1517 in Naples, "the first things of Pallas."

11. Alethea Lawley, *Vittoria Colonna* (London, 1889), 20.

12. Chancellor of Francesco Sforza, Duke of Milano. He was a learned theologian and later cardinal and papal nuncio to the empire in Germany.

13. Fernández Álvarez, *Corpus documental,* 1: 98, n. 21.

14. See Guicciardini, 350, for his argument for "a loving and brotherly liberation."

15. Brandi, 127.

16. Vives to King Henry VIII, in J. L. Vives, *Obras políticas y pacifistas,* ed. F. Calero et al. (Madrid, 1999), 77.

17. Headley, 151ff.

18. Headley, 6. See also Ernst Gussaert, *Espagnols et Flamands* (Brussels, 1910), 250ff.

19. See Fray Prudencio Sandoval, *Historia de la vida y hechos del emperador Carlos V* (Madrid, 1956), 2: 209.

20. Harvey, *Muslims in Spain,* 15.

21. Fernández Álvarez, *Corpus documental,* 1: 104.

22. Martínez Millán, *La corte,* 1: 236.

23. Dantiscus, in García Mercadal, 801.

24. Fernández Álvarez rightly wonders why Seville was chosen, why the King traveled there via Extremadura, and why the future queen was asked to wait.

25. Martínez Millán, *La corte,* 2: 351.

26. He was born May 21, 1527. See J. A. Vilar Sánchez, *1526: Boda y luna de miel de Carlos V* (Granada, 2000).

27. See Guicciardini, 221, on the exchange of prisoners at Fuenterrabía, on the border of France and Spain.

28. Bataillon, *Erasmo,* 321.

29. Alonso Valdés, *Obras completas* (Madrid, 1964), 250. On Charles and Manrique M. Avilés, see "El Santo Oficio en la primera etapa Carolina," in Villanueva and Escandell, *Historia de la Inquisición.* 1: 443–72.

30. Brandi, 251.

31. Francisco Vettori to Machiavelli in Niccolò Machiavelli, *Literary Works of Machiavelli: With Selections from the Private Correspondence* (London, 1961), 346.

32. Headley, *The Emperor and His Chancellor.*

33. Fernández Álvarez, *Corpus documental,* 1: 121.

34. Pastor, 10: 352ff.

35. Vicente de Cadenas, *Caminos y derroteros* (Madrid, 1999), 68.

36. Fernández Álvarez, *Corpus documental,* 1: 120.

37. L. P. Harvey, *Muslims in Spain,* 58.

38. Ibid., 97.

39. Pastor, 14: 332.

40. Abbot of Nájera to the Emperor, after May 6, 1527, cited in Rodríguez Villa, *El emperador Carlos V y su corte* (Madrid, 1903), 134–41.

41. Bataillon, *Erasmo,* 407.

42. Charles to Bourbon, June 6, 1527, quoted in Rodríguez Villa, *El emperador,* 202–203. See comment by Martínez Millán in *Carlos V,* 142.

43. See Fernández Álvarez, *Carlos V,* 371–72; Alfonso Valdés, *Diálogo de las cosas ocurridas en Roma* (Madrid, 1956), 14.

44. These had been commissioned by Charles's aunt Margaret and designed by Bernard van Orley and Jan Gossaert. The tapestries are a visual mirror of princes and depict all the things needed by a good one: fortune, prudence, virtue, faithfulness, fame, justice, nobility, and honor itself. Charles bought this series from the Fuggers, each tapestry being sixteen feet five inches high and eight feet wide. The series was taken to Seville in 1526 and is now in Segovia.

45. Francisco Paso, *Epistolario de la Nueva España* (Mexico, 1939), 1: 104.

46. Álvar Núñez Cabeza de Vaca, *Castaways* (Berkeley, Calif., 1993), xv.

47. Bataillon, *Erasmo,* 257; Brandi, 49–60, 64.

48. Pérez Villanueva and Escandell, 1: 668.

49. Ibid., 1: 252–56.

CHAPTER 8. FOUR BROTHERS IN A CONQUEST: THE ALVARADOS AND GUATEMALA

1. Alvarado led an expedition there with two hundred foot, including twenty crossbowmen headed by Francisco de Orozco, and forty horse. The venture was characterized by Alvarado's swift execution of two Spaniards who apparently planned to kill their leader.

2. Cortés, fourth letter, 301.

3. *Persona de lo más estimada entre todos los capitanes que el dicho marqués tenía en su ejército.* AGI Patronato, leg. 69, r. 1. Interrogation of Leonor de Alvarado.

4. Díaz del Castillo, 2: 410.

5. Ibid., 1: 295.

6. A game played with quoits.

7. Among Alvarado's men in Guatemala there were several who had fought with him throughout the campaigns in Mexico: Juan León Cardona, for example, and Antonio de Salazar. Others were: his secretary, Antonio de Morales; Gonzalo Carrasco, who had been the lookout for Narváez at Cempoallan; Alonso de Loarca; Pedro González de Nájera and Francisco de Tarifa, both of whom had been with Cortés; and Francisco de Andrada.

8. Alonso de Loarca said that Alvarado "*traya trezientos y treynta hombres poco mas o menos y este testigo fue uno de ellos.*" AGI, Patronato 69, r. 1. But Pedro González de Nájera testified that there were more than five hundred men with Alvarado.

9. Ramón Ezquerra, "Los compañeros de Cortés," in *Revista de Indias,* 1: 45.

10. AGI Patronato, leg. 35, no. 3, r. 1.

11. Jorge de Alvarado had always fought alongside his famous brother and married a sister of Luisa, the Tlaxcalan mistress of Pedro. See Gerhard, *La frontera,* 130.

12. Stephan de Borheygui, in Steward, *Handbook of the Middle American Indians,* 2: 282.

13. Ibid.

14. "There is no question," says Stephan de Borheygui, in *Handbook,* 2: 56, "that by the end of the sixteenth century, these competing nations, weakened as they were by internal and external conflicts, would have fallen victim to the rapidly expanding and military confederation [of the Mexica]."

15. *Residencia of Pedro de Alvarado* (Mexico, 1847), 86.

16. "One of those marine landscapes not very uncommon on the coast of South America. You behold a range of exhausted volcanoes. Not a flame flickers on a single pallid crest. But the situation is still dangerous. There are occasional earthquakes and, ever and anon, the dark rumbling of the sea." Robert Blake, *Disraeli* (London, 1966). After Keats's inaccurate description of Cortés, this was the most famous declaration made about Latin America in the English language before 1914.

17. Adrián Recinos and D. Goetz, *The Annals of the Cakchiquels* (Norman, Okla., 1953).

18. See *Handbook,* 2: 284.

19. Adrián Recinos and D. Goetz, *Crónicas indígenas* (Norman, Okla., 1952), 141–54.

20. Recinos, *Crónicas,* 62.

21. *Residencia,* 246.

22. Ibid., 25, 28. Francisco Flores, Bernadino Vázquez de Tapia, Rodrigo de Castañeda, and Alonso Morzillo also testified to Alvarado's rough methods.

23. Recinos, *Crónicas,* 63.

24. General Camilo Polavieja, *Hernán Cortés, copias de documentos* (Seville, 1889), 75.

25. Alvarado's attachment to Guatemala is thus reported by López de Gómara, *Hispania victrix,* 12.

26. *Popol Vuh: The Maya Book of the Dawn of Life,* translated by Dennis Tedlock (New York, 1996), 18.

CHAPTER 9. CHARLES AND HIS EMPIRE

1. The Spanish empire in America is scarcely mentioned in *The World of Charles V* (New York, 2000), the admirable work of Wim Blockmans and Nicolette Mout.

2. Juan Friede, *Los Welser* (Bogotá, 1965), 123.

3. See *Rivers of Gold,* chapter 36.

4. These *juros* played a key part in Spanish royal undertakings for the rest of the century.

5. See Earl J. Hamilton, *American Treasure and the Price Revolution in Spain* (Cambridge, Mass.), 361.

6. See my *Conquest,* chapter 23.

7. Luis Arranz, *Repartimientos y encomiendas en la isla Española* (Madrid, 1991), 418. Mosquera, a controversial figure in La Española, had a large *encomienda* of 257 Indians in Santo Domingo.

8. Wright, *Early History,* 104.

9. A letter of lic. Zuazo to Croÿ says *"quien dice que es converso,"* CDI, 1: 308.

10. Two hundred forty Indians, according to Arranz, *Repartimientos y encomiendas,* 532.

11. Carlos Deive, *La Española y la esclavitud del Indio* (Santo Domingo, 1995), 141; Enrique Otte, *Las perlas del Caribe* (Caracas, 1977), 113.

12. Quoted in Hanke, *The Spanish Struggle for Justice in the Conquest of America* (Philadelphia, 1949), 44.

13. See my *Conquest,* 353.

14. See the *Información de servicios y méritos of Vázquez de Ayllón,* in AGI Patronato leg. 63, r. 24.

15. AGI Patronato, leg. 170, r. 39.

16. AGI Indif. Gen., leg. 421, lib. 2.

17. Vicente de Cadenas, *Carlos I de Castilla, señor de las Indias* (Madrid, 1988), 212.

18. See the coat of arms of Cortés, which can be seen in the *Revista de Indias,* 1948, with its heads of dead monarchs.

19. José Manuel Lucía Megías, *Antología de libros de caballerías castellanos* (Alcalá de Henares, 2001), 134, 275.

20. The first council was composed of García de Loaisa, Dr. Beltrán, and bishops Maldonado and Cabeza de Vaca, with Cobos and Samano as secretaries and Gattinara as an occasional visitor.

21. Giménez Fernández, *Las Casas,* 1: 59.

22. Antonio-Miguel Bernal, *La financiación de la carrera de Indias* (Seville, 1992), 164. The Basque merchants were probably Nicolás Sánchez de Aramburu and Domingo de Alzola.

23. Schäfer, 1: 95. Alejo Fernández had been born in Spain of Flemish origin. Perhaps he studied in Italy. In Seville, he is known for four large panels in the cathedral now in the Chapel of the Cálices (chalices): Saint Joaquín and Saint Anne embracing; the Birth of the Virgin; the Adoration of the Magi; and the Presentation of Christ in the Temple in the same great building; and the depiction of Christ bound to a pillar in a chapel of piety.

24. Cadenas, *Carlos I,* 225.

25. For the text of this document, see ibid., 28–33.

26. Deive, *La Española,* 221.

27. Friede, *Welser,* 113.

28. Wright, *Early History,* 145.

29. Ibid., 122. Ubite was bishop of Cuba from February 17, 1517, till April 4, 1525. Was he the first bishop of Cuba, or was Hernando de Mesa before him (see ibid., 121)? See Giménez Fernández, *Las Casas,* 96, fn. 297, for this prelate. He had been preacher at the service of Queen Leonor of Portugal.

30. Pastor, 10: 365.
31. See biographical article in Martínez Millán, *La quiebra,* 3: 369.
32. He was of a Muslim family of Aragon. See Giménez Fernández, *Las Casas,* 1: 29.
33. Díaz del Castillo, *Historia,* 2: 342.
34. See the biographical essay in Martínez Millán, *La corte,* 3: 353ff.
35. Mariano Cuevas, *Documentos inéditos del siglo XVI* (Mexico, 1914), 230.
36. CDI, 1: 39.
37. Otte, *Perlas,* passim. The main Spanish pearl fishermen in these days were Gonzalo Hernández de Rojas; Pedro de Barrionuevo; Pedro Ortiz de Matienzo; Juan López de Archuleta, who became inspector (*veedor*) and a town councillor in Santo Domingo; and Juan de la Barrera. These each had two pearl-fishing canoes.
38. Otte, *Perlas,* 221.
39. Oviedo, *Historia,* 1: 109.

CHAPTER 10. PEDRARIAS, PANAMA, AND PERU; GUZMÁN IN NEW SPAIN

1. The *Residencia* is in AGI, Justicia, leg. 230.
2. Las Casas, *Historia de las Indias,* 3: 357.
3. Oviedo, *Historia,* 5: 15.
4. Pascual de Andagoya, *Relación y documentos* (Madrid, 1986), 29.
5. See Juan Tena Fernández, *Trujillo histórico y monumental* (Trujillo, 1967).
6. David Vassberg, "Concerning Pigs, the Pizarros and the Agropastoral Backgrounds of the Conquerors of Peru," *Latin American Research Review* 13, no. 3 (1978): 48.
7. J. A. Busto Duthurburu, *La tierra y sangre de Francisco Pizarro* (Lima, 1993), passim.
8. The "dogs of the conquest" deserve a study.
9. Martyr, *Décadas,* 341.
10. Carmen Mena, *Sevilla y las flotas de Indias* (Seville, 1998), 160.
11. Carl Ortwin Sauer, *The Early Spanish Main* (Cambridge, U.K., 1966), 252.
12. Deive, *La Española,* 139.
13. Mena, *Pedrarias,* 148–50.
14. Las Casas, 3: 357; Pizarro to de los Rios, June 2, 1527, in Raúl Porrás Barrenechea, *Pizarro* (Lima, 1978), 5.
15. Letters in Porrás Barrenechea, *Pizarro,* 6–18.
16. Pedro Cieza de León, *Descubrimiento y conquista del Perú* (Madrid, 1986), 74–76.
17. The Andalusians were Cristóbal de Peralta, Nicolás de Ribera, Pedro de Halcón, Alonso de Molina, and García de Jerez; the Castilians were Francisco de Cuéllar and Antonio de Carrión; the Extremeños were Juan de la Torre, Rodríguez de Villafuerte, and Gonzalo Martín de Trujillo; the Cretan was Pedro de Candía; the Basque was Domingo de Soraluce; and the unknown was called Paez or Paz.
18. Oviedo, 5: 41.

19. Busto Duthurburu, 1: 57. See also Dario Vassberg, "Pigs," *Latin American Research Review* 13, no. 3 (1978): 47–62.

20. See James Lockhart, *The Men of Cajamarca* (Austin, Tex., 1972), 140–41.

21. Raúl Porras Barrenenecha, *Cedulario del Perú* (Lima, 1959), 393.

22. Alonso Enríquez de Guzmán, *Libro de la vida* (Madrid, 1960), 498.

23. El Inca Garcilaso de la Vega, *Royal Commentaries of the Incas* (Austin, Tex., 1966), 95.

24. Ibid., 892.

25. Ibid., 893.

26. Pedro Pizarro, *Relación del descubrimiento y conquista de los reinos del Perú* (Madrid, 1844), 134.

27. Enríquez de Guzmán, *Vida,* 341.

28. Garcilaso, 2: 891.

29. Enríquez de Guzmán, *Vida,* 350.

30. Motolinía, *Memoriales,* 146, describes this ceremony.

31. Techuipo is the heroine of a famous poem of the Mexica published in *La visión de los vencidos,* 170 n.

32. *Res. vs Guzmán,* AGI Justicia, leg. 234.

33. Díaz del Castillo, 1: 136.

34. Gerhard, *Geografía,* 224.

35. Ibid., 219.

36. CDI, 12: 245.

37. CDI, 40: 260.

38. CDI, 14: 316.

39. CDI, 27: 130*ff.*

40. G.L.R. Conway, "Hernando Alonso," *Publications of the American Jewish Historical Society,* 331, 1928. The details of this tragic case were only revealed in 1574.

41. Ibid., 350.

42. The treasure included 1,500 marcos of silver, 20,000 pesos of superior gold, 10,000 of inferior gold, fine emeralds, cloaks of plumage and skin, obsidian mirrors, and fans, as well as two jaguars and barrels of balsam.

43. CDI, 3: 419.

44. See *Rivers of Gold,* 353.

45. On Vázquez de Ayllón, see AGI Patronato 63, R. 24.

CHAPTER 11. GIANTS OF THEIR TIME: CHARLES, CORTÉS, PIZARRO

1. Text in Santa Cruz, 2: 454ff. Menéndez Pidal thought that the speech was written by Antonio de Guevara; Brandi thought that it was by Gattinara. See Chabod, *Carlos V,* 117.

2. Brandi, 282.

3. The Medina Sidonias' palace was on the site of the modern Corte Inglés.

4. This jewel vanished in the nineteenth century.

5. Díaz del Castillo, 2: 367–68.

6. Memorandum of Cortés of July 25, 1528, summarizing the position, in *Documentos cortesianos,* 3: 21.

7. Texcoco, Chalco, Otumba, Huejotzingo, Coyoacan, Tascuba, Cuernavaca, four townships in Oaxaca including Cuilapan, the isthmus of Tehuantepec, Tuxotla, Coataxla (Veracruz), Charo-Matalcingo in Michoacán, and Toluco. To these were subsequently added the *peñoles* of Xico and Tepeapulco on the Lake of Mexico, large sections of the city of Mexico-Tenochtitlan between the causeways of Chapultepec and Tacuba, and the two large palaces of Montezuma next to the Zócalo, where Cortés first lived.

8. Díaz del Castillo, 2: 503.

9. CDI, 12: 381.

10. Fernández Álvarez, *Corpus documental,* 3: 37.

11. The children were Martín Cortés, a son whom he had had with Marina; Luis de Altamirano, a son whom he had had with Antonia Hermosilla; and Catalina Pizarro, whom he had had with the half-Indian Leonor Pizarro in Cuba.

12. Martínez, *Hernán Cortés,* 516.

13. Enrique Otte, "Nueve cartas de Diego de Ordaz," *Historia Mexicana* 14, no. 53 (July–Sept. 1964): 105–12.

14. Antonio Fontán and Jerzy Axer, *Españoles y polacos en la corte de Carlos V* (Madrid, 1994), 324.

15. See my *Quién es quién de los conquistadores,* 77.

16. I am grateful to Julie Pastore for pointing this out to me. This picture I have included in my illustrations, but now think it is a seventeenth-century product.

17. Fernández de Enciso was author of *La suma de geografía.*

18. He was the son of Pedro Manrique, count of Osorno, and Teresa de Toledo, daughter of the duke of Alba and María Enríquez, and so was a cousin of Fernando the Catholic.

19. Alonso Enríquez, in Giménez Fernández, *Las Casas,* 2: 975, fn. 3282.

20. See Martínez Millán, *La corte,* 3: 125–30.

21. CDI, 19: 19.

22. Cieza de Léon, 136–38.

23. Lucía Megía, *Antología,* 46.

24. The *capitulación* between Pizarro and the empress Isabel was dated July 26 but signed only on August 17.

25. Varón Gabai, *Francisco Pizarro and His Brothers,* 40.

26. AGI, Escribanía 496 A ff. 685–86 v, April 24, 1566.

27. Oviedo, part III, lib. VIII, chap. 1, p. 265.

28. Other Extremeños recruited in 1529 included Diego de Aguero de Deleitosa, Hernando de Aldama, Juan Herrera, Francisco Peces (actually from Toledo), Lucas Martínez, Francisco de Almendras, Sancho de Villegas, Diego de Trujillo, Hernando de Toro, Alonso de Toro, the trumpeter Alconchel, the *pregonero* Juan García, Francisco de Solares, and Francisco González. See Lockhart, *The Men.* There were probably a number of European (white) slaves taken to Lima at this

time, as there had been such people taken to New Spain. See Emilio Harth-Terré, "Esclavas Blancas in Lima 1537," in *El Comercio,* Lima, June 3, 1963.

29. Carande, 1: 300.
30. J. A. Busto Duthurburu, *Pizarro* (Lima, 2000), 250.
31. Cadenas, *Carlos I,* 206.
32. Fernández Álvarez, *Carlos V,* 201.
33. See letter of Giovanni Bautista de Grimaldi to Ansaldo de Grimaldi, a cousin, in Genoa, cited in J. M. Headley, *The Emperor and His Chancellor,* 36.
34. Pastor, 10: 68.
35. All kinds of interesting conversations occurred in the exchanges of power: For example, the humanist Juan Ginés de Sepúlveda found that the young aristocrats from Spain who had come with Charles to Bologna were unable to reconcile the idea of piety with military efficiency and strength. This conversation was one that led Sepúlveda to write his dialogue *Demócrates* in 1535. Sepúlveda at that time was at the university in Bologna.
36. Cited in K. F. Morrison, "History *Malgré Lui:* A Neglected Bolognese Account of Charles V's Coronation in Aachen," in *Studia gratiana, postscripta 15* (Rome, 1972), 684.
37. See José Martínez Millán and Manuel Rivero Rodríguez, "La coronación imperial de Bolonia y el final de la vía flamenca," in Martínez Millán, *Carlos V y la quiebra,* 1: 131–50.
38. As discovered by Valdés. See Manuel Rivero Rodríguez, "Memoria, escritura y estado," in *Carlos V y la Quiebra,* 1: 223.
39. In Tremayne, 327.
40. The list of her possessions in her will included paintings by Roger van der Weyden, Michel Coxcie, Van Eyck, and Memling. There was also a treasure from the Indies, given to her by her nephew through Charles, lord of La Chaulx (Poupet), then a councillor: "*Accoustremens de plumes, venuz des Indes, présentées de par de l'Empereur à Madame à Bruxelles, le XXè jour d'Aoust, XVCXXIII et aussi de par Mgr. de La Chaulx le tout estant en ladite librairie.*" Soon the collections of the Habsburgs would be enhanced by new treasures sent back by such conquistador families as the Welsers.

CHAPTER 12. THE GERMANS AT THE BANQUET: THE WELSERS

1. See *Rivers of Gold,* chapter 28.
2. Otte, *Perlas,* 74–75.
3. CDI, 8: 21.
4. This was a wonderful era for the lending of money. For example, in 1527, not just Charles but Pope Clement borrowed 195,000 golden scudi from the Genoese Miguel Girolamo Sánchez of Barcelona and Ansaldo Grimaldi—the first being of the famous converso family, the second being the richest of the well-known bankers' family of Genoa (he later became a creditor of Charles also).
5. Oviedo, 3: 77: "*le faltaba dinero pero no palabras.*"

6. Muñoz, 78f, 247, cited in Georges Scelle, *La traite négrière aux Indes de Castile* (Paris, 1906), 1: 174.

7. D. Ramos, "El negocio negrero de los Welser," *Revista de historia de América*, no. 8, Mexico.

8. Rozendo Sampaio García, *Aprovisionamiento de escravos negros na America* (São Paulo, 1962), 8.

9. Friede, *Welser,* 121.

10. Otte, *Perlas,* 283.

11. Friede, *Welser,* 118. The Maestro Pedro Márquez saw these poor miners arrive in Seville and then set off for Santo Domingo. Most had been recruited in Silesia. Juan Ehinger, Juan Reiss, and Jorge Neusesser went to Leipzig to arrange their passage, going down the Elbe to Hamburg and to Antwerp and then Seville. The miners were eight months in Santo Domingo before, exhausted, they applied to go home. They reached Antwerp and thence walked home to Silesia. Only eleven of them got back. They began a lawsuit against the Welsers.

12. Ibid., 149.

13. Ibid., 186.

14. Antonio García-Baquero, *La carrera de Indias* (Seville 1992), 121.

15. Scelle, 1: 150.

16. Ibid., 178.

17. APS, 6: 1547. See *Rivers of Gold,* 379.

18. APS, 6: 762.

19. Ibid., 1104.

20. Eufemio Lorenzo Sanz, *Comercio de España con América en la época de Felipe II* (Valladolid, 1986), 1: 316.

21. Characteristic of this slave traffic was a long lawsuit. Espiñola found himself being sued by Esteban Justiniani, the representative of the Genoese, and Agustín de Ribaldo, one of the purchasers of Gorrevod's license of 1518, who took the affair to the Council of the Indies. AGI Justicia leg. 7, no. 3. The lawsuit is in no. 4 of this *legajo.*

22. A. C. de M. Saunders, *A Social History of Black Slaves in Portugal* (Cambridge, U.K., 1982), 23.

23. V. Maghalhaes Godinho, *Os descubrimientos e a economia mundial* (Lisbon, 1963), 550.

24. A.J.C. Ryder, *Benin and the Europeans* (London, 1969), 66.

25. CDIHE, 9: 239–42.

CHAPTER 13. NARVÁEZ AND CABEZA DE VACA

1. The *capitulación* (contract) is in CDI, 12: 86ff, dated March 8, 1528. We learn from CDI, 35: 514 that María de Valenzuela was owed 300 *pesos de oro* by Diego Velázquez at his death in 1524.

2. Núñez, *Castaways,* 5.

3. Friede, *Welser,* 156.

4. Núñez, *Castaways,* XV.
5. CDI, 28: 391.
6. Samuel Eliot Morison, *The European Discovery of America* (New York, 1974), 513, 515.
7. A cubit was the length of a forearm.
8. Almost all the references here derive from Núñez's *Castaways.*

CHAPTER 14: ORDAZ ON THE ORINOCO; HEREDIA AT CARTAGENA

1. Polavieja, 272.
2. In one of the letters published by Otte, in *Historia mexicana,* July–September 1964.
3. See his evidence in a *probanza* in Santo Domingo, 1521, in CDI, 150: 74.
4. Díaz del Castillo, *Historia,* 2: 254; 1: 82.
5. Ordaz to Verdugo, in Otte, *Historia mexicana,* July–September 1964.
6. Paso, 1: 152.
7. CDI, 4: 466.
8. Figure is from para. 5 of a *probanza* of July 1532. See my *Quien es quien de los conquistadores.* Oviedo, 2: 384 suggests 450.
9. At that time, the Orinoco was often known as the Marañón.
10. Question 6 of the Ordaz *probanza,* in CDI, 40: 74ss.
11. The cloth was so called because it was sent to Holland to be bleached.
12. See AGI Patrimonio, leg. 74, no. 1, r. 10 of 1575. John Hemming has a fine account of Ordaz's courageous journey in *The Search for El Dorado* (London, 1978), 9ff.
13. He actually was born in Sotodosos, Guadalajara.
14. María del Carmen Gómez Pérez, *Pedro de Heredia y Cartagena de Indias* (Seville, 1984), 307.
15. CDI, 1: 586.
16. On landing, the expedition was led by twenty Indians inland to near Turbaco, where Juan de la Cosa had suffered his disastrous defeat twenty years before. There were skirmishes, and several Spaniards were killed. Heredia returned to his landing place and founded there the city of Cartagena de las Indias, on what had been the site of an indigenous town. Immediately, as usual on this kind of occasion, magistrates and councillors were named. They had surnames that are to be found in all lists of this kind: Gabriel de Barrionuevo and Juan de Sandoval were the magistrates; the councillors were Juan de Peñalosa, Alonso de Saavedra, and Luis de Soria. The official notary was Miguel Sanz Negrete (*escribano de número*), and Juan Velázquez was inspector. Carmen Gómez Pérez has published an analysis of conquistadors who were with Heredia. Most (48 percent) were in their twenties, a few (22 percent) were under twenty. None had been in Cortés's expedition to New Spain. Of the 204 Spaniards who arrived in Cartagena, 26 came from Old Castile, 21 from Extremadura, 19 from Seville, and 18 from Toledo.

17. Gómez Pérez, *Cartagena,* 108.
18. Ibid., 289.
19. Ibid., 319ff., for list of witnesses.

CHAPTER 15. CORTÉS AND THE *AUDIENCIA* IN NEW SPAIN

1. Lewis Hanke, *Aristotle and the American Indians* (London, 1959), 100.
2. Silvio Zavala, *Recuerdo de Vasco de Quiroga* (Mexico, 1987), 53–55.
3. Tension was not reduced by the arrival in early 1529 of another expedition of twenty Franciscans under Fray Antonio de Ciudad Rodrigo. The expedition included the remarkable Fray Bernardino de Sahagún, who became the chronicler par excellence of old Mexico through his famous *General History of the Things of New Spain* (the Florentine Codex). The ship included several of the Indians taken to Spain by Cortés; some have thought that Sahagún's learning of Nahuatl and study of ancient Mexican ways began on this vessel. García Icazbalceta so thought, but the contrary opinion was held by Antonio Toro, Wigberto Jiménez Moreno, and Luis Nicolau d'Olwer. See *Quarterly Journal of the Library of Congress,* April 1969.
4. That is, Psalm 51, from the words with which it begins.
5. Guzmán's agents at Veracruz, Juan Pérez de Gijón and Juan Camino, interfered with the letters of at least three friars, Antonio de Aveñado, Juan de Angayo, and Juan de Montemayor. Juan González, *alcalde* of Veracruz, testified in 1531 that Guzmán had ordered him to do this.
6. The count of Osorno was the acting chairman, and the other members were now Dr. Beltrán, Bishop Maldonado, Bishop Cabeza de Vaca, Gaspar de Montoya, Rodrigo de la Corte, Álvaro Núñez de Loaisa, and Juan Suárez de Carvajal.
7. Chipman, *Nuño de Guzmán,* 228.
8. Schäfer, *El consejo real,* 1: 75.
9. Arthur Aiton, *Antonio de Mendoza* (Durham, N.C., 1927), 36.
10. Ricard, *Spiritual Conquest,* 260. See also CDI, 41: 5–6.
11. Magnus Mörner, *La mezcla de razas en la historia de América Latina* (Buenos Aires, 1969), 55.
12. See CDI, 23: 423–26.

CHAPTER 16. MONTEJO IN YUCATÁN

1. A *caballería* was a measure of land that in Spain was equivalent to 60 *fanegas* or 3,863 acres. In Cuba, it meant 1,343 acres; in Puerto Rico, 7,858. I assume that the Yucatán measure was close to the Cuban one.
2. CDI, 12: 201ff; CDI, 22: 201ff.
3. Díaz del Castillo, 2: 253.
4. See Gil, *Los conversos,* 2: 321.
5. I don't, however, find him in Carmen Mena's brilliant study of the expedition of Pedrarias.
6. Díaz del Castillo, 1: 136.

7. Polavieja, 156–57.

8. Robert Chamberlain, "La controversía entre Cortés y Velázquez," *Anales de la Sociedad Geográfica de Guatemala* 19 (September 1943).

9. Paso, 1: 57.

10. Fifth letter from Cortés, in *Letters from Mexico,* Pagden, ed., 440.

11. Paso, 1: 78.

12. Ruiz de la Mota, evidence in his *Información de servicios,* Patronato 54, leg. 54, no. 7, r. 6. A copy is in my possession.

13. See his *Información.* In AGI, Patronato, leg. 54, no. 7, r. 6 of August 1531.

14. Among them the great jade mosaic mask of Palenque, or the Leyden Plaque.

15. Fray Diego de Landa, *Relación de las cosas de Yucatán* (Madrid, 1985), 29.

16. Ibid., 66.

17. Oviedo, 3: 398.

18. *Probanza* of Ibiacabal in AGI, Indiferente General 1204, quoted in Chamberlain.

19. Landa, *Relación,* 110.

20. Oviedo, 3: 399.

21. Letter of Montejo to Charles the Emperor, April 13, 1529, in CDI, 13: 87; Oviedo, 3: 399.

22. Robert S. Chamberlain, *The Conquest and Colonization of the Yucatán* (Washington, D.C., 1948), 49.

23. Landa describes, 51.

24. Oviedo, 3: 402.

25. Chamberlain, 54.

26. See my *Conquest of Mexico,* 96.

27. Landa, 57.

28. Enrique Otte, ed., *Cartas privadas de emigrantes a Indias* (Seville, 1988), 70–82.

29. Inga Clendinnen, *Ambivalent Conquests* (Cambridge, U.K., 1987), 26.

30. *Handbook,* vol. 3, part 2, 675.

31. Landa, *Relación,* 57.

32. Ibid., 72.

33. See *Handbook,* vol. 3, part 2, 661. An estimate of Ralph Roys.

34. Landa, *Relación,* 330.

35. Bernal Díaz, *Historia,* 1: 136; also my *Conquest,* 60.

36. Oviedo, 3: 404–405.

37. Ibid., 404.

38. Chamberlain, *The Conquest,* 73–74.

39. CDI, 13: 87–91.

40. Chamberlain, *The Conquest,* 36.

41. AGI Patronato, leg. 68, no. 1, r. 2.

42. Oviedo, 3: 411. There is an interesting illustration in the first edition of Oviedo of a horse in these circumstances.

43. Chamberlain, *The Conquest,* 88.

44. See my *Conquest of Mexico,* 324.

45. Chamberlain, *The Conquest,* 92.

46. *Probanza* of Lerma in AGI, Santo Domingo, leg. 9, r. 3.

47. *Relación* of Alonso de Ávila in CDI, 14: 100: *"que las gallinas nos darían en las lancas y el maíz en las flechas."*
48. CDI, 14: 105: *"falsa y con mal proposito."*
49. Oviedo, 3: 420–21.
50. CDI, 14: 111: *"el señor Adelantado nos tenía por muertos."*
51. Oviedo, 3: 420.
52. Pagden, *Letters,* 414.
53. Chamberlain, *The Conquest,* 127.
54. Blas González, *Probanza* in AGI, Patronato, leg. 68, no. 1, r. 2.
55. Pedro Álvarez, in AGI, Mexico, leg. 916, no. 1, r. 1.
56. Clendinnen, *Ambivalent,*153.
57. *Probanza* of Francisco de Montejo in AGI, Patronato, leg. 65, no. 2, r. 1.
58. CDI, 2: 312.
59. Perhaps, says Pagden, there was a little gold mixed in, too.
60. Landa, *Relación,* 81–83.

CHAPTER 17. TO PASS THE SANDBAR

1. Pablo Pérez-Mallaína, *Spain's Men of the Sea* (Baltimore, 1998), 64.
2. James Boswell, *The Life of Samuel Johnson LLD* (London, 1912), 1: 253, March 16, 1759.
3. Carande, 3: 123; C. H. Haring, *Trade and Navigation Between Spain and the Indies* (Cambridge, Mass., 1918), 198.
4. Antonio García-Baquero, *La carrera.*
5. Carmen Mena, *Sevilla,* 241.
6. Bernal, *Financiación,* 132.
7. Carande, 1: 368.
8. Bernal, *Financiación,* 133.
9. Carmen Mena, *Sevilla,* 251.
10. See APS, cited in my *Conquest,* 632.
11. Carmen Mena, *Sevilla,* 212.
12. Pierre and Huguette Chaunu, *Séville et l'Atlantique* (Paris, 1956), 6: 178–231.
13. Pérez-Maillaína, 102.
14. Gil, 1: 239–43. See, too, Enriqueta Vila Vilar and Guillermo Lohmann, *Familia, linajes y negocios entre Sevilla y las Indias* (Seville, 2003).
15. James Lockhart, *Spanish Perú* (Madison, Wisc., 1968), 119.
16. Pérez-Mallaína, 231.
17. Ibid., 192.
18. Ibid., 15.
19. C. H. Haring, *The Spanish Empire in America* (New York, 1947), 7.
20. C. H. Haring, *Trade and Navigation* (Cambridge, Mass., 1918), 120.
21. This is to run ahead of the narrative, but the supreme calculator Earl Hamilton estimated that from 1560 to 1650, precious metals counted for 82 percent of all the exports. Precious metals, remarked Pierre Chaunu, carried alone the weight of the Spanish empire.

NOTES 597

22. This was the diet on Pedro Menéndez de Avilés's ships in 1568.
23. Pérez-Mallaína, 143.
24. Haring, *Trade*, 288ff.
25. From 1569, a fine of 100,000 maravedís would have to be paid by anyone who traveled without a permit. The arrangement was made final in 1604, when anyone traveling without a permit would also be punished by four years in the galleys or, if the person was someone of quality, ten years in Oran. From 1614, ships leaving Seville could complete their cargoes at Cádiz. Seville maintained only the bureaucracy rather than the vigor of the real trade, and from 1664, ships could start off from Sanlúcar.

CHAPTER 18. BIRÚ

1. Terence D'Altroy, *The Incas* (Oxford, U.K., 2002), 291.
2. There have been found 470 varieties of potato (D'Altroy, 31).
3. A good account is in D'Altroy, 15ff.
4. Pedro Pizarro, *Relación*, 155.
5. Marx was interested in Peru but knew nothing of it.
6. See an interview with Jerónimo López, in *Rivers of Gold*, 515.
7. D'Altroy, 192.
8. "Oh! Can anything similar be claimed for Alexander or any of the powerful kings who ruled the world?" Cieza de León, 213–14. See, too, D'Altroy, 243ff.
9. D'Altroy, 233.
10. Hemming, 124–26.
11. D'Altroy, 172–74.
12. Pedro Pizarro, *Relación*, 89–90.
13. On the indigenous nature of this disease, see *Rivers of Gold*, 151–52.
14. D'Altroy, 44, suggests that the word *Quechua* was imposed by the Spaniards. It meant "valley speech": *qheswa simi*.

CHAPTER 19. PIZARRO'S PREPARATIONS

1. Francisco de Jerez, *Verdadera relación*, vol. II; Cieza de Léon, 146. But Diego de Trujillo and Cristóbal de Mena wrote that there were 250 men (*Relación*, 45; *Conquista del Perú*, 70), and Pedro Pizarro said that there were 200 (*Relación* V, 171).
2. Raúl Porrás exposed the idea that he was a partner on the same level as the others. Raúl Porrás, "El Nombre de Perú," *Mar del Sur* 6, no. 18 (1951): 26.
3. See also Guillermo Lohmann, *Les Espinosa* (Paris, 1968), 206ff. This conquistador, said to have converso origins, is the only one whose family still possesses their home in Peru, which they obtained in 1535.
4. See Lockhart, *Cajamarca*, 75.
5. The notion of the small company perhaps with two or three members in search of commerce is considered well in Carande, 1: 289.
6. Oviedo, 5: 33.

7. Pedro Pizarro, 341.
8. Garcilaso, 2: 636. See, too, Carande 1: 289.
9. Enríquez de Guzmán, *Libro*, 106.
10. See Luisa Cuesta, "Una documentación interesante sobre la familia del conquistador del Perú," *Revista de Indias* 8 (1946), 866ff.
11. Hernando Pizarro, *Carta a oidores de Santo Domingo*, Panama. It is published in Oviedo, 5: 84–90.
12. Pedro Pizarro, 341.
13. Cieza de León, 370.
14. Garcilaso, 2: 916, 972, 1076.
15. Pedro Pizarro, 146.
16. Garcilaso, 2: 601.
17. Pedro Pizarro, 148–49.
18. Ibid.
19. Pedro Pizarro, 150.
20. Cieza de Léon, 150.
21. Ibid., 152.
22. See Edmundo Guillén, *Versión Inca de la conquista* (Lima, 1974), 78.
23. Cieza de Léon, 154.
24. Garcilaso, 2: 662.
25. Pedro Pizarro, 151.
26. Others included Jerónimo de Aliaga, Gonzalo Farfán, Melchor Verdugo, and Pedro Díaz.
27. Cieza de Léon, 159.
28. For Ruiz de Arce's account, see Miguel Muñoz de San Pedro, *Tres testigos de la conquista de Perú* (Madrid, 1964), 72–119.
29. Guillermo Lohmann, *Les Espinosa*.
30. Pedro Pizarro, 158.
31. See David Ewing Duncan, *Hernando de Soto* (New York, 1995), passim; also Busto Duthurburu, *Pizarro*, 1: 320.
32. The word is Hemming's, *The Conquest*, 27.
33. Pedro Pizarro, 166.
34. See Garcilaso, 2: 820; and Hemming, *The Conquest* 302–304, pays much attention to him.
35. Garcilaso, 2: 663.
36. Miguel de Estete, "*Descubrimiento y la conquista del Perú*" (Quito, 1918), 20.
37. Cieza de Léon, 176.
38. Pedro Pizarro, 167.
39. Busto Duthurburu, *Pizzaro*, 1: 340.
40. Pedro Pizarro, 163.
41. Ibid., 162.
42. Ibid., 165, 88.
43. Estete, 21; Cieza de Léon, 181. Pizarro gave the name of San Miguel either because the archangel Michael had appeared in the sky during the recent battle or to recall his own baptism, at San Miguel in Trujillo.

44. Oviedo V, 2: 29.

45. Busto Duthurburu, 1: 369.

46. Lockhart, *The Men*, 352–53.

47. Busto Duthurburu, *La Tierra*, 385.

48. Pedro Pizarro, 173.

49. Ibid., 172.

50. Garcilaso, 2: 665.

51. Jerez, 326.

52. Oviedo, 3: 80.

53. CDHI, 18: 59.

CHAPTER 20. CAJAMARCA

1. Ruiz de Arce, cited in Lockhart, *The Men*, 346.

2. Oviedo, 84: "*El camino era tan malo que de verdad si así fuera que allí nos esperaran . . . muy ligeramente nos llevaran.*"

3. Ruiz de Arce, cited in Hemming, *The Conquest*, 32; Lockhart, *The Men*, 346.

4. Martín de Murúa, *Historia general del Perú* (Madrid, 1962), 206; Pedro Pizarro, 185.

5. Hemming, *The Conquest*, 34.

6. Ibid., 35, 549.

7. Pedro Pizarro, 176; Carmen Mena, *Sevilla*, 326.

8. Hemming, *The Conquest*, 37, 200.

9. Lockhart, *The Men*, passim.

10. Lockhart says one had been in Mexico but in a "marginal capacity." Having made a special study of the men who accompanied Cortés, I see no sign of anyone of his band being important in Peru.

11. See Lockhart, *The Men*, 35–36.

12. Pedro Pizarro, 36.

13. Estete, 28–29.

14. Hemming, *The Conquest*, 37.

15. Diego de Trujillo, *Relación del descubrimiento del reyno del Perú* (Seville, 1948), 58.

16. Some chroniclers thought that there were three units of twenty horse each, the third being led by Benalcázar.

17. Pedro Pizarro, 86.

18. Hemming, *The Conquest*, 39–41.

19. Garcilaso, 2: 687.

20. Murúa, 269.

21. Garcilaso, 2: 691. See Hemming, *The Conquest*, 42–44, 442–43, 551.

22. Lockhart, *The Men*, 320.

CHAPTER 21. THE END OF ATAHUALPA

1. "Every schoolboy knows who imprisoned Montezuma, and who strangled Atahualpa." Macaulay, *Essay on Lord Clive*.

2. Garcilaso, 2: 693.
3. Murúa, 210.
4. Hemming, *The Conquest,* 48, makes good sense of these figures.
5. Pedro Pizarro, 187.
6. Cristóbal de Mena, in "La conquista del Perú," in *Relaciones primitivas de la conquista del Perú,* Raúl Porrás Barrenechea, ed. (Paris, 1937), 250.
7. Ibid., 248; Hemming, *The Conquest,* 47.
8. Lockhart, *The Men,* 196, looks on the expedition of Soto and del Berco as a myth.
9. Mena, 36–37. A palmo was the distance from the thumb to the little finger, the hand extended. "Hand" is a good translation.
10. Ibid., 263; Hemming, *The Conquest,* 64–65.
11. Guillén, *Versión Inca,* 58–59.
12. Hemming, *The Conquest,* 56.
13. Ibid., 65–67.
14. These two journeys need to be distinguished. See Lockhart, 285.
15. Murúa, 213.
16. *"La persona del cacique es la más entendida e de más capacidad que se a visto e muy amigo de saber e entender nuestras cosas; es tanta que xuega el ajedrez harto bien."* Gaspar de Espinosa to Cobos, Panama, August 1, 1533, in CDI, 13: 70.
17. Hemming, *The Conquest,* 49.
18. Pedro Pizarro, 352.
19. Hemming, *The Conquest,* 55.
20. Murúa, 210.
21. Hemming, *The Conquest,* 52.
22. Ibid., 72–73, 408.
23. Duncan, 156.
24. Harkness Collection in the Library of Congress (Washington, D.C., 1932), 1: 7; see Lockhart, *The Men,* 299.
25. Lockhart, *The Men,* 96–102.
26. Actually of Cazalegas, five miles east of Talavera de la Reina; Lockhart, *The Men,* 189.
27. Oviedo, 5: 122.
28. Pedro Pizarro, 247; Hemming, *The Conquest,* 78.
29. Pedro Pizarro, 247.
30. Pedro Sancho de la Hoz, *Relación de la conquista del Perú* (Madrid, 1962), 127.
31. Pedro Pizarro, 220, 226.
32. CDI, 1: 523; Hemming, *The Conquest,* 80–81.
33. Cartas de Perú, *Colección de documentos inéditos para la historia de Perú* (Lima, 1959), 3: 64; Hemming, *The Conquest,* 89.

CHAPTER 22. NEWS OF PERU

1. CDI, 12: 46. Here "Dortal" is rendered "de Hortal."
2. Jerez, *Verdadera relación,* 346. The actual figures were 708,580 and 49,008.

3. Hemming, *The Conquest,* 89.
4. Garcilaso, 2: 709.
5. Keniston, *Cobos,* 161.
6. Enríquez de Guzmán, *Libro,* 78.
7. Crane, *Mercator,* 66.
8. See Rafael Varón Gabai and Auke Pieter Jacobs, "Peruvian Wealth and Spanish Investments," *Hispanic American Historical Review* 67 (1987).
9. Hemming, *The Conquest,* 144–45.
10. Not the Juan Fernández after whom Robinson Crusoe's island was named.
11. Garcilaso, 2: 741.
12. Pedro Pizarro, 230.
13. See Hemming, *The Conquest,* 95–102, his source here being especially Sancho de Hoz.
14. Pedro Pizarro, 236.
15. These were Hernando de Toro, Miguel Ruiz, Gaspar de Marquina, Francisco Martín, and a certain Hernández.
16. Pedro Pizarro, 245.
17. Hemming, *The Conquest,* 118–19.
18. Sancho, *Relación,* 169.
19. Pedro Pizarro, 273.
20. Sancho, *Relación,* 88.
21. Cieza de León, 236–37.
22. *"No aconteció cosa notable en el camino, ni tuvo cual dificultad ni contraste alguno."* Murúa, 224.
23. Ibid.
24. Hemming, *The Conquest,* 132.
25. Lockhart, *The Men,* 80–81.
26. Sancho, *Relación,* 164.
27. Estete, *El descubrimiento,* 54.
28. Ibid., quoted in Hemming, *The Conquest,* 127–28.
29. Pedro Pizarro, 273.
30. See Muñoz de San Pedro, *Tres testigos,* 54; Diego de Trujillo, *Relación,* 26.
31. Hemming, *The Conquest,* 136, thought that much of the treasure was probably stolen by Manco Capac's servants (*yanaconas*).
32. See José de la Puente Brunke, *Encomienda y encomenderos en el Perú* (Sevilla, 1992), especially his extraordinary Appendix 1.
33. Hemming, *The Conquest,* 152.
34. The best account is in Oviedo, 5: 204.
35. Hemming, *The Conquest,* 158.
36. Garcilaso, 2: 741.
37. *Colección de documentos inédita para la historia de Chile desde el viaje de Magallenes hasta la batalla de Maipo,* Jose Toribio Medina, ed. 30 vols. (Santiago de Chile, 1888–1902) II, 244, cited in Hemming, *The Conquest,* 162.
38. Hemming, *The Conquest,* 143.

39. Juan Ruiz de Arce, *Advertencias de Juan Ruiz de Arce a sus succesores,* in Muñoz de San Pedro, *Tres testigos,* quoted in Lockhart, *The Men,* 55.
40. Francisco López de Gomara, *Hispania victrix* (Madrid, 1846), 1: 231.
41. Juan Ruiz de Arce, *Servicios en Indias,* Antonio de Solar and José de Rújula, eds., quoted in Lockhart, 56.
42. Ruiz de Arce, *Advertencias,* 435–36.
43. Hemming, *The Conquest,* gives a wonderful account, 142.

CHAPTER 23. THE BATTLE FOR CUZCO

1. Cadenas, *Carlos I,* has the text, 76–81.
2. CDI, 16: 390.
3. Hemming, *The Conquest,* 174–75.
4. José Luis Martínez, *Documentos cortesanos,* 3: 40–41.
5. The document is in Cadenas, *Carlos I,* 1: 81.
6. CDI, 20: 217–485, gives the case for Almagro in great detail.
7. The first *cabildo* of Lima consisted of the treasurer Riquelme, the inspector (*veedor*) García de Salcedo, and the following Pizarrists: Rodrigo de Mazuelas, Alonso Palomino, Nicolás de Ribera el Mozo, Cristóbal de Peralta, Diego de Aguero, Diego Gavilán, and the mayor, Nicolás de Ribera. Mazuelas had represented Pizarro before the court, and he and Ribera became lifetime *regidors.* They were soon joined by Diego de Aguero and Nicolás de Ribera el Mozo. Antonio Picado, who was now Pizarro's secretary, Crisóstomo de Hontiveros, and Pizarro's half brother Francisco Martín de Alcántara also became members, as did Martín de Ampuero. Other officials appointed in those days included Pedro de Añasco as chief constable of Quito, Martín de Estete as lieutenant-governor in Trujillo, and Antonio de la Gama as the same, in Cuzco.
8. Antonio Bonet Correa, *Monasterios Iberoamericanos* (Madrid, 2001), 159.
9. CDI, 10: 237–332. An interesting report.
10. Lohmann, *Espinosa,* 233–34.
11. See Juan José Vega, *Manco Inca, el gran rebelde* (Lima, 1995).
12. She married later and lived in Cuzco. Hemming, *The Conquest,* 181.
13. Pedro Pizarro, 341.
14. Garcilaso, 2: 916.
15. Ibid., 1076.
16. Bartolomé de Segovia, *Relación de muchas cosas acaecidas en el Perú,* BAE, 209: 82.
17. Hemming, *The Conquest,* 183–88.
18. CDI, 24: 224.
19. Murúa, 233.
20. Pedro Pizarro, 300–301.
21. Garcilaso, 2: 799.
22. Pedro Pizarro, 304.
23. Ibid., 302. Others killed at this time included Juan Becerril and Martín Dominguez.

24. Murúa, 235–36.
25. The Spanish captains in this attack included Pedro del Barco, Diego Méndez, and Francisco de Villacastín. The first named, from Lobón, Medellín, had come to the Indies with Gil González Dávila, and went to Peru with Soto. Méndez was an Almagrist who was a half brother of Rodrigo de Orgóñez.
26. D'Altroy, 137.
27. Hemming, *The Conquest*, 215.
28. Enríquez de Guzmán, *Libro*, 127.
29. Busto Duthurburu, *Pizarro*, 2: 287.
30. See "Hernán Cortés y el Perú," in *Revista de Indias*, 1948, 339.
31. Garcilaso, 839.

CHAPTER 24. ALMAGRO

1. Miguel Martínez Molina, "El soldado cronista," *Anuario de estudios americanos*, no. 40 (1984): 167.
2. CDI, 22, 338.
3. CDI, 9: 526 and 20: 401.
4. Pedro Pizarro, 349.
5. D'Altroy, 147.
6. Garcilaso, 2: 823.
7. Alvarado in Oviedo, *Historia*, 5: 167.
8. Murúa, 248.
9. Valdivia was from either Castuesa or Campanario in the Serena in Extremadura. Others were: Antonio de Villalba, as sergeant major; Ansínez Diego de Rojas and Alonso de Mercadillo, being captains of horse; Diego de Urbina, being captain of pikemen; and Pedro de Vergara and Nuño de Castro, being captains of arquebusiers.
10. Enríquez de Guzmán, *Libro*, 133.
11. Garcilaso, 2: 855.
12. Ibid., 860. For commentary, see Busto Duthurburu, 2: 325.
13. Lockhart, *The Men*, 359.

CHAPTER 25. PIZARRO'S TRIUMPH AND TRAGEDY

1. Instruction of July 1536, published in Porrás Barrenechea, *Cedulario*, 177–95.
2. CDI, 3: 92–137.
3. The two brothers were sons of Pedro Suárez de Talavera and Catalina Carvajal. Juan's fortunes surely had something to do with the fact that he had married Ana, a niece of García de Loaisa. When his wife died, he became a churchman and eventually bishop of Lugo.
4. Hemming, *The Conquest*, 239–41.
5. Valdivia, in a letter to Charles V, in José Toribio Medina, *Cartas de Pedro de Valdivia* (Seville, 1929), 215.

6. Pedro Pizarro, 389.

7. "Mire vuestra Señoría que yo me voy á España y que el remedio de todos nosotros está despues de Dios en la vida de vuestra Señoría. Digo esto porque estos de Chile andan muy desvergonzados, y si yo no me fuera no habia de que temer. Y decía la verdad Hernando Pizarro porque temblaban dél. Vuestra Señoría haga dellos amigos dándoles en que coman los que lo quisieren, y á los que no lo quisieren no consienta vuestra Señoría que se junten diez juntos en cincuenta leguas alrededor de adonde vuestra Señoría estuviere, porque si los deja juntar le han de matar. Si á vuestra Señoría matan, yo negociaré mal, y de vuestra Señoría no quedara memoria. Estas palabras dijo Hernando Pizarro, altas que todos le oimos." *Colección de documentos inéditos para la historia de España,* 5: 1844.

8. Varón Gabaí and Jacobs, 672. Hernando was arrested at Coatzacoalcos but released by the viceroy.

9. Pedro Pizarro, 404; Hemming, *The Conquest,* 254.

10. CDI, 3: 138.

11. But as we have seen, Medina del Campo was also the city where such great experts in fantastical journeys as Garcia de Montalvo, the reviver of *Amadís de Gaula,* and Bernal Díaz del Castillo, had been born and lived. See Luis Fernández Martín, *Hernando Pizarro en el Castillo de la Mota* (Valladolid, 1991).

12. Garcilaso, 2: 886; Hemming, *The Conquest,* 285.

13. Pedro Pizarro, 418.

14. On Pizarro's house, see Busto Duthurburu, 2: 352. It had a *ranchería* and a corral, for Indian servants and black slaves.

15. See Salvatore Munda, *El asesinato de Francisco Pizarro* (Lima, 1985); also Hugo Ludeña, "Versiones temprana sobre la muerte de Don Francisco Pizarro," *Boletín de Lima* 37, January 1985.

16. Varón Gabai and Jacobs, 661.

17. Well discussed in ibid., 82, 206ff.

18. AGI Patronato, leg. 192, no. 1, r. 12, cited in Varón Gabai and Jacobs, 110.

CHAPTER 26. VACA DE CASTRO IN PERU

1. James Lockhart, *Spanish Peru* (Madison, Wisc., 1968), 134.

2. Otte, *Las Perlas,* 89. See also Schäfer, 2: 177.

3. See Bonet Correa, "Santo Domingo de Lima," in *Monasterios Iberoamericanos,* 227.

4. Pedro Pizarro, 429.

5. Garcilaso, 2: 902.

6. Ibid., 912.

7. Ibid., 921.

8. Ibid., 922.

9. Pedro Pizarro, 234.

10. Garcilaso, 2: 931.

CHAPTER 27. GONZALO PIZARRO AND ORELLANA SEEK CINNAMON AND FIND THE AMAZON

1. José Toribio Medina, *The Discovery of the Amazon* (New York, 1934), 13.
2. Michael Goulding et al., *The Smithsonian Atlas of the Amazon* (Washington, D.C., 2003), 206.
3. See Genealogy III in my *Conquest of Mexico*.
4. See Medina, *Descubrimiento*, 238, fn. 4; and Antonio de Herrera, *Historia general del mundo, del tiempo del señor rey don Felipe II el prudente* (Madrid, 1601), Dec. 5, Bk. 10, ch. 14.
5. Medina, *Descubrimiento*, 42, fn. 68.
6. Gonzalo Pizarro in ibid., 249.
7. Gonzalo letter quoted in ibid., 56.
8. Fifty-three names can be found in Oviedo, 5: 237–38, but see Carvajal, 42, who speaks of fifty-seven men.
9. Medina, *Descubrimiento*, 71.
10. Ibid., 74.
11. Carvajal, in ibid., 227.
12. Ibid., 53.
13. Ibid., 55.
14. Carvajal, in ibid., 58.
15. Ibid., 69.
16. Ibid., 71.
17. John Hemming, *The Amazon* (London, 2009), 31.
18. Carvajal, in Medina, *Descubrimiento*, 73.
19. Ibid., 88.
20. Oviedo, 5: 394.
21. Carvajal, in Medina, *Descubrimiento*, 96.
22. Gonzalo Pizarro, quoted in ibid., 79.
23. Oviedo, 5: 373ff.
24. Medina, *Descubrimiento*, 250.

CHAPTER 28. ORELLANA AND NEW ANDALUSIA

1. Carvajal, in Medina, *Descubrimiento*, 97.
2. Oviedo, 5: 373–402.
3. AHN, Simancas, Estado, leg. 61, f. 19, quoted in Medina, *Descubrimiento*, 320.
4. Ibid., 128, fn. 180.
5. Ibid., 328.
6. Cadenas, *Carlos I*, 65.
7. Officials were named: Juan García de Samaniego, inspector; Juan de la Cuadra, keeper of accounts; Francisco de Ulloa, treasurer; Cristóbal Maldonado, chief constable; Vicente del Monte, revenue collector; while Fray Pablo de Torres would be inspector-general and have with him a secret package naming a succesor to Orellana if he were to die.

8. Medina, *Descubrimiento,* 326.
9. Ibid., 355–56.
10. Ibid., 336.
11. CDI, 42: 269.

CHAPTER 29. THE DEFEAT OF THE VICEROY

1. Garcilaso, 2: 951–52.
2. Ibid., 963.
3. Pedro Pizarro, 235.
4. Garcilaso, 2: 992; and commentary by Hemming, *The Conquest,* 268.
5. Garcilaso, 2: 970.
6. He apparently gave his wife the pearl known as La Peregrina, which eventually, via Mary Tudor, Philip II, Joseph Bonaparte, Napoleon III, and the duke of Abercon, would be given by the actor Richard Burton to his wife, the actress Elizabeth Taylor.
7. Garcilaso, 2: 996–1000.
8. Ibid., 1011.
9. Ibid.,1056, 1058.
10. José Puente Brunke, *Encomiendas and encomenderos en el Perú* (Seville, 1992), 141.
11. Lockhart, *Spanish Peru,* 185.
12. Bartolomé Martínez y Vela, cited in Stuart Stirling, *The Last Conquistador* (Stroud, 1999), 130.

CHAPTER 30. GONZALO AND LA GASCA

1. J. A. del Busto Duthurburu, *Diccionário histórico biográfico* (Lima, 1973), 1: 323.
2. Garcilaso, 2: 1008.
3. Ibid., 1073. See also G. Lohmann Villena, *Las ideas jurídico-políticas en la rebelión de Gonzalo Pizarro* (Valladolid, 1977).
4. Garcilaso, 2: 1083.
5. Lohmann, *Las ideas,* 11.
6. Fernández Álvarez, *Corpus documental,* 2: 399.
7. Gasca in Valencia is discussed in Teresa Canet Aparisi, "La justicia del emperador," in *Carlos V y la Quiebra,* 2: 175ff.
8. Garcilaso, 2: 1084.
9. Instructions dated February 10, 1546, are in CDI, 23: 506–515. See also Schäfer, 2: 26.
10. Andagoya, *Relación,* 29.
11. Teodoro Hampe Martínez, *Don Pedro de la Gasca, 1493–1567* (Lima, 1989), 106.
12. Garcilaso, 2: 1091.
13. Ibid., 1092.
14. Letter in ibid.,1094.
15. Garcilaso, 2: 1094–96.

16. Cited in Hampe, 125.
17. Garcilaso, 2: 1160.
18. AGI Justicia, leg. 451, no. 2, r. 10.
19. Cited in Hampe, 92.
20. Juan Pérez de Tudela, *Documentos relativos a don Pedro de la Gasca y a Gonzalo Pizarro* (Madrid, 1964), vol. 1, 368.
21. Ibid., 1: 375ff.
22. Ibid., 1: 119.
23. Garcilaso, 2: 1196–97.
24. Ibid., 1197.
25. See Marcel Bataillon, "La rébellion pizarriste, enfantement de l'Amérique espagnole," *Diogène* 43, July–Sept. 1963; and "Les colons du Pérou contre Charles Quint 1544–1548," *Annales,* May–June 1967, 479–94. Also Lohmann Villena, *Las ideas,* passim.
26. Varón Gabai, *Francisco Pizarro and His Brothers,* 149.
27. See CDI, 20: 487–537, for a list of about four hundred condemned supporters of Gonzalo, with their birthplaces mentioned. Most of those were punished by being sent to the galleys—many for life—and some were whipped. Almost all were exiled from Peru.
28. Polo de Ondegardo, *El mundo de los Incas* (Madrid, 1990), 46. See, too, Brian S. Bauer, *The Sacred Landscape of the Inca: The Cusco Ceque System* (Austin, Tex., 1998), 16–19, cit. D'Altroy, 156, who discusses the implications with rigor and intelligence.
29. Cited in Sir John Elliott, *Empires of the Atlantic World* (New Haven, Conn., 2006), 89.

CHAPTER 31. VALDIVIA AND CHILE

1. Letter from Pedro de Valdivia to Charles V, quoted in Medina, *Cartas,* 56.
2. Medina, *Cartas,* 39–40.
3. See his *Relación de la conquista del Perú* (Madrid, 1962).
4. CDI, 23: 7. The key phrase was *"sin que entreis en los límites y paraje de las islas y tierra que estan dadas en governación a otras personas."*
5. Medina, *Cartas,* 66.
6. CDI, 1, 3.
7. CDI, 2, 167.
8. Medina, *Documentos inéditos,* 8: 32; 11: 541.
9. Ibid., 22: 566.
10. Ida Vernon, *Pedro de Valdivia, Conquistador of Chile* (Austin, Tex., 1946), 71.
11. Tomás Thayer Ojeda, *Valdivia y sus compañeros* (Santiago de Chile, 1950), 31.
12. Vernon, *Pedro de Valdivia,* 73.
13. Letter of Valdivia to Charles V, September, 4, 1541.
14. Letter of Valdivia to Charles V, June 1, 1541.
15. *Actas de historiadores de Chile,* 1: 89–90.

16. "Actas del Cabildo," in *Actas de historiadores de Chile,* 1: 89–90.
17. Medina, *Cartas,* 21.
18. Letter of Valdivia to Charles V, September 4, 1545.

CHAPTER 32. VALDIVIA'S CONSUMMATION

1. Medina, *Cartas,* 17.
2. Ibid., 28–29. There was a similar report of Cortés's behavior in New Spain.
3. Ibid., 29.
4. Guillermo Pérez de Arce, "Santiago comienza una nueva vida," in Guillermo Díaz y Mesa, *Leyendas y episodios chilenos* (Santiago de Chile, 1930), 300.
5. Medina, *Documentos inéditos,* 160.
6. Medina, *Cartas,* 33.
7. Ibid., 35.
8. CDHI, 25, 60.
9. Medina, *Cartas,* 49.
10. Ibid., 42–43.
11. Vernon, *Pedro de Valdivia,* 115.
12. Ibid., 116.
13. Medina, *Cartas,* 160.
14. Garcilaso, 2: 1092.
15. Díaz y Mesa, *Leyendas y episodios,* 92ff.
16. "Actas del Cabildo de Santiago," in *Historiadores de Chile,* 1: 129.
17. Errazuriz, 2: 188.
18. "Actas del Cabildo," in *Historiadores de Chile,* 1: 154.
19. Vernon, *Pedro de Valdivia,* 127.
20. Medina, *Documentos inéditos,* 8: 258–311.
21. Vernon, *Pedro de Valdivia,* 150; Medina, *Cartas,* 244.
22. Ibid., 159.
23. Letter to Charles V, October 15, 1550.
24. Medina, *Cartas,* 199, 147.
25. Ibid., 225.
26. Letter from Valdivia to Charles V, September 25, 1551, in *Cartas,* 223.
27. Medina, *Cartas,* 245.
28. Alonso Góngora de Marmolejo, *Crónicas del reino de Chile* (Madrid, 1960), 35.
29. Vernon, *Pedro de Valdivia,* 214.

CHAPTER 33. CAROLUS AFRICANUS

1. Erasmus, *Consultatio de bello Turcis inferendo,* 1530, in Desiderio Erasmus, *Collected Works* (Toronto, 2008).
2. Letter of May 6, 1543, in Fontán and Axer, 372.
3. CDHI, 10: 38–41.
4. Fernández Álvarez, *Corpus documental,* 4: 35.

5. Carande, 3: 69.

6. See Antoine-Marie Graziani, *Un prince de la Renaissance* (Paris, 2008).

7. Participating in the battles was the Dutch painter Jan Vermeyen, from whose sketches the famous tapestries in the Kunsthistorisches Museum of Vienna were later made.

8. Possibly this codex is that now known as the Codex Borgia. It became named as such in the eighteenth century when Cardinal Stefano Borgia owned it, though he did not really prize it. It is now in the Vatican library. Coming originally from Tlaxcala, it depicts the gods in control of the ritual calendar.

9. Wright, *Early History of Cuba,* 200.

10. Fernández Álvarez, *Corpus documental,* 4: 483.

11. Pastor, 11: 242.

12. Ibid., 11: 76.

13. *"Yo mismo con mis manos tomé en la Goleta estas cartas que tengo en la mano que las enviaba a Barbarroja en una fragata el rey de Francia en las cuales hay palabras de tan familiar amistad cuanto en ellas podra bien ver quien quisiere."*

14. Pérez, *Carlos V* (Madrid, 1999), 90.

15. Granvelle (Nicolas de Perrenot) became one of Charles's most important advisers in the 1530s, with the title of *consejero de estado* after 1528.

16. Quoted in Ramón Menéndez Pidal, *La lengua de Cristóbal Colón* (Madrid, 1958), 66.

17. Ramón Menéndez Pidal, *La idea imperial de Carlos V* (Madrid, 1958), 31.

18. "Everything is well in Spain and we are awaiting the marvelous gold from the Indies." Letter from Granvelle to Asti, May 30, 1536, quoted in Fernández Álvarez, *Corpus documental,* 1: 515.

19. Anne de Montmorency became constable of France in 1538. He had been brought up with King Francis I. The Montmorencys had had for centuries the title of "first barons of France."

20. Charles to Nassau, Roeulx, and Praet, November 14, 1536, quoted in Fernández Álvarez, *Corpus documental,* 1: 515.

21. See Clive Griffin, *Los Cromberger* (Madrid, 1991), 117.

22. The *cédula* is dated May 21, 1534, and was reproduced by Alberto María Carreño in "La primera biblioteca del continente Americano" in *Divulgación histórica,* Mexico 4 (1943), 428.

23. Contract between Cromberger and Pablos signed June 12, 1539. See Griffin, *Cromberger,* 121.

24. Esteban Martín, who was in New Spain in 1538, also has a claim to be the first printer of the country, and he, too, seems to have been a protégé of Cromberger.

25. Griffin, *Cromberger,* 132.

26. Keniston, *Cobos,* 202. Nájera was the second duke of that title.

27. Pastor, 13: 298.

28. CDHI, 10: 448.

CHAPTER 34. THE INDIES FINANCE EUROPE

1. Ricard, *Spiritual Conquest,* 56. It was now that to avoid confusion between the Indian word *papa,* used constantly for priests, and the pope, Bishop Zumárraga ordered that the Latin *papa* should never be employed, only "pontifex."
2. Pérez, *Carlos V,* 125: "*Marchese, no necesitamos aquí secretario alguno.*"
3. *De rebus gestis,* quoted in Alfred Morel-Fatio, *Historiographie de Charles Quint* (Paris, 1913), 61.
4. Brandi, 393.
5. Ibid., 414–15.
6. Schäfer, 1: 100.
7. Pérez, *Carlos V,* 84.
8. Schäfer, 1: 78.
9. Keniston, *Cobos,* 250.
10. See my *Rivers of Gold,* chapter 27.
11. Consuelo Varela, introduction to Las Casas, *Brevísima relación de la destrucción de las Indias* (Madrid, 1999).
12. Other items were: ordinary subsidies, 268,000 ducats; extraordinary subsidies, 125,867; *maestrazgos,* 152,000; clerical subsidies, 166,667; and *Cruzada* 125,900. See James D. Tracy, in Blockmans and Mont, *The World of Charles V,* 73.
13. Brandi, 465.
14. Keniston, *Cobos,* 272.
15. AGI, *Escribanía de Cámara,* leg. 1007, no. 19.
16. Schäfer, 1: 82.
17. CDI, 16: 397.
18. Wright, *Early History of Cuba,* 226; Bernal, *Financiación,* 12.
19. Keniston, *Cobos,* 264.
20. Brandi, 521.
21. Ibid., 523.
22. A summary of the discussion in the *consejo de estado* between the archbishop of Seville, Tavera, Alba, Valdés, Osorno, and Dr. Guevara, can be seen in Chabod, *Carlos V y su imperio,* 244–51.
23. Keniston, *Cobos,* 270.
24. Ibid., 300–301.
25. All these quotations derive from Brandi.
26. Ibid., 548.

CHAPTER 35. FEDERMANN AND JIMÉNEZ DE QUESADA

1. AGI Justicia, leg. 56.
2. Juan Friede, *Vida y viajes de Nicolás Federmann* (Bogotá, Colombia, 1964), 150.
3. Ibid., 58.
4. Oviedo, 3: 55.
5. See Kohler in British Museum, Additional Manuscripts, 217.

6. Letter of November 1, 1537, in AGI, Santo Domingo leg. 218, quoted in Friede, *Federmann,* 132.

7. Friede, *Federmann,* 159.

8. See ibid., 19. There is, however, no explicit mention of the family in Juan Gil's great work on the conversos.

9. He had been *adelantado* in the Canaries. He was a nephew of the conqueror and first governor of La Palma and Tenerife, Alonso Fernández de Lugo. See Gil, *Los Conversos,* 4: 369, 371.

10. Céspedes was a converso and related to the onetime judge *de las gradas* in Seville of his name.

11. AGI, Justicia, leg. 599, no. 2, published in Friede, *Federmann,* 136ff.

12. See question 6 of Questionnaire in AGI, *Escribanía de Cámara,* leg. 1006-A Cuaderno 1, in Juan Friede, *Gonzalo Jiménez de Quesada* (Bogotá, 1960), 168. Evidence about the death of Sagipa was given by six Spaniards, including two who "were there."

13. Friede, *Jiménez de Quesada,* 323.

14. The text of the agreement of Federmann with Jiménez de Quesada is in AGI Justicia, leg. 1096, in Friede, *Jiménez de Quesada,* 128.

15. Friede, *Jiménez de Quesada,* 68–69.

16. Ibid., 304.

17. For Raizer, see Hermann Kellenbenz, *Los Fugger,* 115.

CHAPTER 36. THE RETURN OF CABEZA DE VACA

1. Nuñez, *Castaways,* 107.
2. Ibid., 117.

CHAPTER 37. SOTO IN NORTH AMERICA

1. A Gentleman of Elvas, *True Relation of the Vicissitudes Which Attended Governor Hernando de Soto and Some Nobles of Portugal in the Discovery of the Province of Florida,* trans. Buckingham Smith, *Narratives of de Soto in the conquest of Florida* (Gainesville, Fla., 1968), 136.

2. Garcilaso, 2: 1,110.

3. Wright, *Early History,* 234.

4. Las Casas, 2: 510. No sign remains of old Havana on the south coast.

5. Elvas, *True Relation,* 56; CDI, 3: 417.

6. Wright, *Early History,* 220–22.

7. See Duncan, *Hernando de Soto,* 243, for a discussion, and references to the work of Charles Hudson on the matter.

8. Oviedo, 2: 163; Wright, *Early History,* 170–71.

9. Duncan, 307.

10. Ibid., 355.

11. Ibid., 316.

12. Ibid., 318.
13. Oviedo, 2: 168.
14. Elvas, *True Relation*, 58.
15. See a fascinating discussion in Duncan, 352ff., as to where Coosa might be.
16. Elvas, *True Relation*, 229.
17. Ibid., 244.
18. Ibid., 246.
19. Ibid., 228.
20. Ibid., 167.

CHAPTER 38. THE MAGIC LURE OF THE NEW WORLD

1. Otte, *Las Perlas*, 209.
2. Friede, *Welser*, 376.
3. Ibid., 378.
4. Ibid., 380.
5. See E. Schmitt and F. K. von Hutten, eds., *Das Gelt der Neuen Welt: Die Papiere des Welser-Konquistadors und General-Kapitans von Venezuela Philipp von Hutten 1534–1541* (Hildburghausen, 1996).
6. Aguado, *History of Venezuela*, 1: 262.
7. Otte, *Las Perlas*, 394.
8. Friede, *Welser*, 392–400.
9. Ibid., 405.
10. Ibid., 407.
11. Ibid., 406.

CHAPTER 39. BUENOS AIRES AND ASUNCIÓN: PEDRO DE MENDOZA AND CABEZA DE VACA

1. See my *Rivers of Gold*, 496, or for the scene on the river, see Casas, 3: 105.
2. The date usually given for his birth, 1487, cannot be correct since at that time Guadix was still part of the Muslim kingdom of Granada. Guadix fell to the Christians in 1489.
3. CDI, 23: 350ff. The *capitulación* is dated May 21, 1531.
4. Oviedo, 2: 364.
5. See Richard Hakluyt, *The Principal Navigations, Voyages, Traffiques and Discoveries of the English Nation* (London, 1599–1603), 3 vols., vol. 2.
6. CDI, 23: 8.
7. Nuñez, *Castaways*, 33.
8. *Commentaries*, 120.
9. Ibid., 115.
10. Nuñez, *Castaways*, 23.
11. Elman Service, *Spanish-Guarani Relations in Early Colonial Paraguay* (Westport, Conn., 1971), 19–20. The admirable Stanley Henig has a fine chapter on the size of the Guarani population "at contact" in his *Numbers Never Lie*.

CHAPTER 40. NEW SPAIN WITH ANTONIO DE MENDOZA

1. CDI, 23: 423ff.
2. Ibid., 554.
3. A mint antedated Mendoza's arrival, because one was established for silver and copper coin in May 1535, under the direction of a formidable gathering of officials.
4. See A. González Palencia and E. Mele, *Vida y obras de Don Diego Hurtado de Mendoza* (3 vols. 1941; Madrid), also E. Spivakivsky, *Son of the Alhambra* (Austin, Tex., 1970). There is also A. Vazquez and R. S. Rose, *Algunas cartas de don Diego Hurtado de Mendoza, escritas en 1538–1552* (New Haven, Conn., 1935).
5. Chipman, 237.
6. CDHI, 10: 38–43.
7. See my *Conquest of Mexico,* chapters 26 and 29.
8. Gerhard, *Geografía,* 303.
9. Bertrand Grunberg, *L'univers des conquistadors* (Paris, 1993), 121. The Franciscan mission in New Spain, hitherto part of the "province" of San Gabriel de Extremadura, became its own autonomous province of "the holy Evangelist."
10. Salmerón had been much involved in the foundation of Puebla.
11. CDHI, 10: 10. See, too, L. B. Simpson, *The Encomienda in New Spain* (Berkeley, Calif., 1966), 125.
12. See the essays in Zavala, *Recuerdo.*
13. Like many *letrados,* Díaz de Luco was son of a curate, Cristóbal Díaz of Seville. He was provisor of Tavera at Toledo; he became known for his *Doctrinae magistrales* and *Avisa de curas.* He later became a Jesuit and was at the Council of Trent.
14. See the French translation of Guevara's essay on Marcus Aurelius.
15. CDI, 13: 420–29.
16. CDI, 10: 363. "*Con mucha causa y razón este de aca se llama Nuevo-Mundo y es lo 'Nuevo-Mundo' no porque se halló de nuevo, sinó porque es en gentes y cuasi en todo como fué aquel de la edad primera y de oro,*" 1535.
17. See Gerhard, *Geografía,* 354.
18. See letter of Quiroga of August 14, 1531, to the Council of the Indies, in CDI, 13: 420.
19. CDI, 13: 428.
20. Ibid., 10: 376.
21. Zavala, *Recuerdo,* 90.
22. Schäfer, 2: 21. "Governors" of these subordinate territories were appointed by the Viceroy subject to approval of the Council of the Indies.
23. Haring, *The Spanish Empire,* 85.
24. CDIU, 10: 29ff. See François Chevalier, *La formation des grands domaines du Méxique* (Paris, 1952), 28.
25. Juan de Solorzano, *Política Indiana* (Madrid, 1996), Lib. 5, chapter 2.
26. Zavala, *Recuerdo,* 92.
27. Aiton, *Antonio de Mendoza,* 113.
28. Ricard, *Spiritual Conquest,* 37.

29. Pastor, 12: 297.
30. See my *Quién es quién de los conquistadores,* 259.
31. Ricard, *Spiritual Conquest,* 173.
32. "*Destros son los Gilofos* [Wolofs] *y muy guerreros con vana presunción de caballeros.*" Castellanos was a Sevillano, who went to live in Santiago de Tunja, Colombia, and whose best-known poem was his *Elegías de varones ilustres de Indias,* written in one hundred thousand verses, in 1589.
33. Baltasar Dorantes de Carranza, *Sumario de relación de las cosas de la Nueva España* (Mexico, 1970), 280; Gerhard, *Geografía,* 390.
34. Memorial of June 25, *Documentos inéditos para la historia de España,* 1: iv, 210.
35. Aiton, *Mendoza,* 139–41.
36. Fray Toribio de Motolinía, *Historia de los Indios de la Nueva España,* 179.
37. Ricard, *Spiritual Conquest,* 272.
38. Fray Antonio de Segovia, Fray Martín de Vera Cruz, Fray Martín de la Coruña, and Fray Pedro de la Concepción.
39. Ricard, *Spiritual Conquest,* 388.
40. Ibid., 388.
41. Arthur Aiton, *The Secret Visita Against Viceroy Mendoza in New Spain and the American West* 20, quoted in Hanke, *The Spanish Struggle,* 89.
42. Discussed in Martínez, *Hernán Cortés.*
43. Fernández Alvarez, *Corpus documental,* 3: 256.
44. CDI, 3: 510–11.
45. CDI, 14: 165–91. This is not much more than a log. But the name *California* is freely used, for example, "*Domingo á 2 dias de julio, tuvieron visita en la California, tardaron en atravesar, por amor de los tiempos que no fueron muy favorables, casi cuatro días.*"
46. Zavala, *Recuerdo,* 36.

CHAPTER 41. CORONADO AND THE SEVEN MAGIC CITIES OF CIBOLA

1. His instructions are in CDI, 3: 325ff.
2. Quoted in G. P. Winship, "The Coronado Expedition," 24th annual report of the U.S. Bureau of Ethnology, 362, quoted in Aiton, *Mendoza,* 121.
3. Pedro de Castañeda, *Spanish Explorers of the Southern United States* (New York, 1907).
4. Coronado to Mendoza in Hakluyt's voyages, 1st series, vol. 9, 145–69.
5. See Fray Marcos de Niza's voyages as described in a letter by Viceroy Mendoza to the Emperor, April 17, 1540, in CDI, 2: 356.
6. CDI, 3: 511.
7. Castañeda, in Winship, 539.
8. Further testimony in CDI, 14: 304 (Jaramillo's testimony), 373; and letter from Coronado to the Emperor in CDIHE, 3: 363.
9. Juan Suárez de Peralta, *Tratado del descubrimiento de las Yndias y su conquista* (Mexico, 1949), 159.

CHAPTER 42. MONTEJO AND ALVARADO IN YUCATÁN AND GUATEMALA

1. Álvaro de Paz, *Información*, in AGI Patronato, leg. 69, r. 1.
2. AGI Patronato, leg. 69, r. 1. *"E oyo decir a el dicho adelantado que yba a China en cumplimiento de cierta capitulación que avia hecho en España con su majestad."*
3. Peralmíndez to Juan de Samano in Spain, July 28, 1541, in Paso, *Cartas*, 4: 25.
4. Aiton, *Mendoza*, 101.
5. Ricard, *Spiritual Conquest*, 193.
6. *Probanza* of Andrea del Castillo, AGI, Mexico, leg. 974.
7. AGI, Mexico, leg. 299.
8. Clendinnen, *Ambivalent Conquests*, 29.
9. Chamberlain, 206.
10. Clendinnen, *Ambivalent Conquests*, 204.
11. Diego Sánchez, *probanza* in AGI, Patronato, leg. 69, no. 8.
12. Cogulludo, *Historia de Yucatán*, 3–7, cited in Chamberlain, 216.
13. AGI, Mexico, leg. 900.
14. The Nahuatl for *vasallo* merely seems to signify *"gente plebeya."* See Fray Alonso de Molina, *Vocabulario en lengua castellana y mexicana, y mexicana y castellana*, new ed. (Mexico, 1992), 116.
15. *Relación de Valladolid*, cited in Chamberlain, 231.
16. Clendinnen, *Ambivalent Conquests*, 43.
17. Ibid., 44.
18. Where he had been lodged by the Virreina María de Toledo, taking the ashes of her father-in-law, Christopher Columbus, to the cathedral there.
19. Paso, 4: 223.
20. See AGI, Mexico, leg. 68.
21. *Probanza* of Juana de Azamar in AGI, Mexico, leg. 983.
22. Ibid., leg. 923.
23. Letter of February 13, 1547, by Montejo to Charles V, quoted in Chamberlain, 252.
24. *Residencia* of Montejo in AGI, Justicia, leg. 244, r. 3.
25. Chamberlain, 126.
26. See *méritos y servicios del gobernador y capitán general, don Francisco de Montejo*, in AGI, Patronato leg. 63, r. 24, testimony of Andrea del Castillo: *"Porque no menos conquistadora puedo decir que soy los conquistadores . . . muchas veces las mugeres principales y de mi calidiad quando se hallan presentes en las conquistas y guerras, los caballeros y soldados con su bista se esfuerzan y animan a senarse y bien obrar y a servir a sus Reyess y señores con más ánimo y valor."*

CHAPTER 43. LAS CASAS, POPE PAUL, AND THE INDIAN SOUL

1. Luis Iglesias Ortega, *Bartolomé de Las Casas: Cuarenta y cuatro años infinitos* (Seville, 2007), 362.
2. Antonio María Fabié, *Vida y escritos de Bartolomé de las Casas* (Madrid, 1879), 2: 60–82.

3. Oviedo, 1: 138. *"No estuvo muy en gracia de todos en la estimativa . . . a causa de cierta regociación que emprendió."*

4. Carreño, "La imprenta y la inquisición en el siglo XVI," in *Estudios eruditos en memoriam de Adolfo Bonilla, y San Martín* (Madrid, 1924), 1: 91.

5. Erasmus, *Ecclesiastes,* quoted in Bataillon, appendix to *Erasmo,* "Erasmus and the New World," 807ff.

6. Getino, *Dominicos españoles confesores de reyes,* 28.

7. Bernard Lavallé, *Bartolomé de las Casas* (Paris, 2007), 128.

8. Guicciardini, 442.

9. Bataillon, *Erasmo,* 535.

10. Cuevas, 84. See Hanke's "Pope Paul III and the American Indians," in *Harvard Theological Review* XXX, 1937, 65–102; and Alberto de la Hera, "El derecho de los indios a la libertad y a la fe: La bula 'Sublimis Deus' y los problemas indianos que la motivaron," *Anuario de la historia del derecho español* 26 (Madrid, 1956).

11. A ceremony in which the celebrant pronouncing the word *ephphatha* ("be opened") (Mark 7:34), touches the mouths and ears of the candidate for baptism.

12. Ricard, *Spiritual Conquest,* 3: 93.

13. See Martínez Millán, *La corte,* 3: 477.

14. The meeting was also attended by Licenciado Pedro Mercado de Peñalosa, Dr. Hernando de Guevara, Dr. Juan de Figueroa, Licenciado Gregorio López, and Jacobo González de Arteaga of the Consejo de Órdenes. Perhaps there was also Licenciado Juan de Salmerón, fiscal of Castile.

15. Sahagún, quoted in Ricard, *Spiritual Conquest,* Sp ed., 226.

16. See AGI, Patronato, leg. 184, no. 27, cited in Jesús Bustamante Garcia, *Carlos V y la Quiebra,* 4: 15.

17. See AGI Patronato, leg. 184, r. 27, cited in Bustamante García in *Carlos V,* 4: 15.

18. Ibid., 19.

19. Ricard, *Spiritual Conquest,* 285.

20. This is the year that the historian of Colombia Juan Friede believed marked a change in Las Casas's attitudes to the world from idealism to realism.

21. See Consuelo Varela's introduction to the work of Las Casas, 23.

22. Cieza de León, quoted in Hanke, *The Spanish Struggle,* 90.

23. Cadenas, *Carlos I,* 131.

24. *". . . instruendi sint in mysteriis theologicis et artibus liberalibus."*

25. Cited in Hanke, *All Mankind,* 24.

26. Cited ibid., 58.

27. See my *Rivers of Gold,* 430.

28. See commentary of Consuelo Varela. He became Bishop of Chiapas in March 1544.

29. CDI, 16: 376ff. See Haring's commentary in *The Spanish Empire,* 565ff.

30. CDI, quoted in Schäfer, 2: 245.

31. The expression is that of Schäfer.

32. Hanke, *All Mankind,* 60.

CHAPTER 44. CONTROVERSY AT VALLADOLID

1. See debate between Silvio Zavala and Benno Biermann in *Historia mexicana.* vols. 17–18, 1968–69.
2. This was the suggestion of Hanke in *The Struggle,* 46.
3. Found by Marcel Bataillon, in AGI, quoted in Hanke, *All Mankind,* 64–65.
4. CDI, 6: 484–515.
5. Quoted in Hanke, *The Struggle,* 116–17.
6. Díaz del Castillo, 2: 473.
7. That is, Cuba, Jamaica, La Española, Puerto Rico, Cubagua, and the coast of Venezuela as far as Santa Marta.
8. Letter of Gonzalo de Aranda to the King, May 30, 1544, in Aiton, *Mendoza,* 98.
9. Letter of Aranda, quoted in Aiton, *Mendoza,* 98.
10. CDI, 7: 532–42.
11. Letter to Charles V, February 19, 1545, in CDIU, 6: 241–46. The letter was signed by Vázquez de Tapia, Antonio de Carvajal, Jerónimo López. and even Gonzalo de Salazar, one of the officials sent in 1522 by the emperor Charles.
12. AGI, Indif. Gen., leg. 153ff, 783–85.
13. Letter from the *audiencia,* March 17, 1545, quoted in Aiton, *Mendoza,* 99.
14. Henry Kamen, *Philip of Spain* (New Haven, Conn., 1997), 29.
15. Martínez Millán, *La corte,* 3: 379.
16. AGI, Indif. Gen., leg. 1530.
17. Martínez Millán, *La corte,* 3: 238–40.
18. Fernández Álvarez, *Corpus documental,* 2: 398. This was when Gasca was chosen.
19. Ibid., 399.
20. Wagner, 123, quoted in Hanke, *All Mankind,* 27.
21. CDI, 7: 436–37.
22. Ibid., 254–62. Letter of Motolinía to the King, January 2, 1555.
23. Aiton, *Mendoza,* 167.
24. On Cortés's death, see my *Conquest of Mexico,* 600.

CHAPTER 45. LAS CASAS AND SEPÚLVEDA

1. It was four hundred years before the text of the disputation was published. Only in the 1950s did Stafford Poole transcribe the Latin text and translate it into English.
2. Did he say this? The text that Las Casas had when preparing his reply included this reference to monkeys. But the most complete version published omits it.
3. Quoted in Hanke, *All Mankind,* 85.
4. Burckhardt, *Reflections,* 38.
5. The original is in the Bibliothèque Nationale in Paris.
6. Text prepared and translated into English by Stafford Poole as "Defence Against the Persecutors and Slanderers of the People of New World Discovered Across the Seas."

7. Hanke, *All Mankind*, 82.
8. Ibid., 94.
9. Ibid., 95.
10. Printed at Seville in 1552 and widely distributed in the Indies, even soon in Manila.
11. Schäfer summarizes, 2: 268–69.
12. Pastor, 20: 12.
13. Hanke, *Aristotle*, 40.
14. Consuelo Varela, *Introducción*, 26.

CHAPTER 46. THE KNIGHT OF THE BLACK EAGLE

1. The queen Empress Isabel had died after a miscarriage in May 1539.
2. Salinas, summer 1536, quoted in Rodriguez Villa, *El emperador Carlos V y su corte*.
3. See Woodrow Borah, *The Cortés Codex of Vienna*, vol. 2, *The Americas*, 1962.
4. Fernández Álvarez, *Corpus documental*, 3: 225.
5. On his tragic end, see José Nieto, "Herejía en la capilla imperial," in *Carlos V y la quiebra*, 4: 213ff.
6. See Antonio Álvarez-Ossorio, "Conocer el viaje del Príncipe Felipe 1548–1549," in *Carlos V y la quiebra*, 2: 53ff.
7. Coxcie was a Flemish painter born in the archduchess Margaret's city of Malines.
8. Vicente Álvarez, *Relation du beau voyage que fait aux Pays-Bas en 1548 le prince Philippe*, M-T Dovillé, ed. (Brussels, 1964), 119.
9. Fernández Álvarez, *Corpus documental*, 3: 222.
10. Ibid., 3: 225ff.
11. Ibid., 3: 252–53.
12. Hamilton, *American Treasure*, table 19: 3,628,506 pesos for the Crown, 6,237,024 pesos for private people.
13. Fernández Álvarez, *Corpus documental*, 3: 259.
14. Kamen, *Philip of Spain*, 49.
15. Fernández Álvarez, *Corpus documental*, 3: 381.
16. Ibid., 3: 393.
17. Hampe, 206.
18. Ibid., 207.
19. That monarch had been the last king of both France and Germany, and it was his division of the realms into three at the Treaty of Verdun in 843 that provided the agenda for modern European history.
20. Fernández Álvarez, *Corpus documental*, 3: 429.
21. Ibid., 3: 445.
22. The escudos could be converted as 66,718,841 maravedís or 1,482,508 pesos. Hampe, 198.
23. R. O. Jones, *The Golden Age* (London, 1971), 54.
24. Fernández Álvarez, *Corpus documental*, 3: 505–506.

25. Ibid., 3: 548.
26. Ibid., 3: 626–27.
27. See Fernández Martín, *Hernando Pizarro.*
28. For the Pizarros' holdings in Spain, see Rafael Varón Gabai and Auke Pieter Jacobs, "Peruvian Wealth and Spanish Investments," HAHR 67 (1987): 657–95. For their holdings in Peru, see Varón's *Francisco Pizarro and His Brothers* (Norman, Okla., 1997), passim.
29. Varón, *Francisco Pizarro,* 285.

CHAPTER 47. THE EMPEROR AT BAY

1. *Memorial que embió Francisco Duarte de lo que le dixó Nicolás Nicolai,* in AGS E leg. 98, f. 274, quoted in Kamen, 55.
2. For Diocletian's withdrawal to Salona, see Edward Gibbon, *The Decline and Fall of the Roman Empire,* chapter 13.
3. Simón Renard was French, born in Vesoul, and had been persuaded by Granvelle to work for him and for Spain.
4. G. Constant, "Le mariage de Marie Tudor et de Philippe II," *Revue de l'histoire diplomatique* 26 (1912): 36.
5. See David Loades, "Charles V and the English," in *Carlos V y la quiebra,* 1: 263; Anna Whitelock, *Mary Tudor* (London, 2009), 136.
6. (English) Calendar state papers, Spain, 11: 290, 4045.
7. With his commoner wife, the beautiful Philippina von Welser, he would establish a collection or *Kunstkammer* in Ambras near Innsbruck, the Ferdinandeum, which would house many interesting Mexican objects, some from his great-aunt Margaret's collection.
8. William Howard, first Lord Howard of Effingham, was a great survivor, being lord high admiral under Queen Mary, 1553–57, and lord chamberlain, 1558–72, under Queen Elizabeth. He was a son of the second duke of Norfolk and had studied and been a protégé of Gardiner at Trinity Hall, Cambridge.
9. Kamen, 57.
10. Andrés Muñoz, *El viaje de Felipe segundo a Inglaterra,* Gayangos, ed. (Madrid, 1877), 97, 113.
11. Sandoval, *Historia de la vida,* 3: 127.
12. English state papers, Spain, 13: 138–39.
13. Skinner, 2: 94.
14. For a study of Charles's journeys, see Cadenas, *Caminos,* 147ff.
15. CDI, 4: 390ff.
16. He added: "*Acordándome de ruestra fidelidad y lealtad, y del amor y oficción especial que entre rostros he conocido, mandaría mirar por lo que general y particularmente os tocare, haciéndo os merced al favor en lo que justo sea, como lo merceis.*" CDI, 4: 392ff.
17. Carande, 3: 210.
18. On the Emperor in Yuste, there is W. Stirling-Maxwell, *The Cloister Life of the*

Emperor Charles V (London, 1853), especially 8–15; and G. Gachard, *Retraite et mort de Charles-Quint* (Brussels, 1854–55). There is also J. J. Martín González, *El palacio de Carlos V en Yuste,* Archivo Español del Arte, 1950–51).

19. Citing F. Morán y Checa, *El coleccionismo en España* (Madrid, 1990).
20. The list includes what is described as "a portrait on wood by Thomas More of the Queen of England," which would seem improbable.
21. Dávila had been with the Emperor on nearly all his campaigns, about some of which, notably those in Germany, he had written a book. He became Marquess of Mirabel.
22. David Watts, *The West Indies. Patterns of Development, Culture and Environmental Changes Since 1492* (Cambridge, U.K., 1987), 125.
23. Damián de la Bandera, cited in Luis Miguel Glave, *Trajinantes* (Lima, 1989), 84.
24. Colin Palmer, *Slaves of the White God* (Cambridge, Mass., 1981), 67.
25. Grunberg, *L'univers,* 151.
26. See Zavala, *Ideario de Vasco de Quiroga.*
27. Zavala, *La utopía,* 13, in *Recuerdo de Vasco de Quiroga.* It would be a mistake to overlook Quiroga's magnificent *ordenanzas* for the two hospitals called Santa Fe that appear in his will of 1565.
28. The Castillos were illegitimate descendants of Enrique IV's wild queen Juana.
29. Burckhardt, *Reflections on History,* 39.
30. See Francisco Cervantes de Salazar, *Túmulo imperial* (Mexico, 1564). There were also funeral services in Lucca, Bologna, Naples, Mainz, Rome, Florence, Valladolid, and Augsburg, as well, of course, as Brussels.

Index

ABOUT THE AUTHOR

HUGH THOMAS studied history at Cambridge and Paris. His career has encompassed both America and Europe, and history and politics, as a professor at New York and Boston Universities and as chairman of the Centre for Policy Studies in London. He was awarded a peerage in 1981. Hugh Thomas is the author of *The Spanish Civil War,* which won the Somerset Maugham Prize; *Cuba: The Pursuit of Freedom; An Unfinished History of the World,* which won the National Book Award for History; *Armed Truce: The Beginnings of the Cold War; The Conquest of Mexico;* and *The Slave Trade.* He won the Nonino prize and the Boccaccio prize in Italy in 2009, the Gabarrón prize and the Calvo Serer prize in Spain in 2006 and 2009, and the PEN prize in Mexico in 2011. He has the Grand Cross of the Order of Isabel the Catholic in Spain, the Order of the Aztec Eagle in Mexico, and is a Commander of the Order of Arts and Letters in France.

ABOUT THE TYPE

This book was set in Minion, a 1990 Adobe Originals type-
face by Robert Slimbach. Minion is inspired by classical
old-style typefaces of the late Renaissance, a period of elegant, beautiful, and highly readable type designs. Created
primarily for text setting, Minion combines the aesthetic
and functional qualities that make text type highly readable
with the versatility of digital technology.